A HISTORY OF EURO

From 911–1198

A History of Europe

FROM 911 TO 1198

—

Z. N. BROOKE

LITT.D., F.B.A.

*Late Professor of Medieval History
in the University of Cambridge
Fellow of Gonville and
Caius College*

LONDON : METHUEN & CO LTD
11, New Fetter Lane, E C 4

First published November 1938
Second edition July 1947
Third edition 1951
Reprinted with minor corrections 1956
Reprinted 1960, 1962 and 1969
3.5
SBN 416 43510 6

First published as a University Paperback 1969
1.1
SBN 416 29640 8

Printed in Great Britain by
Butler & Tanner Ltd, Frome and London

10037016XT

Distributed in the USA by
Barnes & Noble Inc.

PREFACE

THE arrangement of this volume needs, perhaps, some explanation. It is no easy matter to describe the history of numerous European States (for only the internal history of the British Isles is omitted from the scheme of the series), and at the same time to preserve some unity in the telling. I have attempted this by developing three main themes—the Empire (later, Empire and Papacy), Christianity and Islam (or, alternatively, East and West), and France, which if subsidiary at first develops into a main theme later on. Each of these I have traced in four stages : up to the middle of the eleventh century, in the second half of that century, and in the two halves of the twelfth century. In the first two periods the other topics have been dealt with as subordinate parts of the greater themes, but they have been given a more detailed and individual description in general chapters inserted in the middle of the twelfth century.

The question of nomenclature raises a further problem. I have adhered, with a few exceptions, to the system adopted in the *Cambridge Medieval History*, though with some misgivings. In a book written for English readers it is obviously right to speak of Rome, Venice, Milan, and even Cologne, but I am not very happy about writing Mayence for Mainz and Trèves for Trier. A difficulty arises for the reader, to distinguish the numerous Conrads, Henrys, Ottos, &c., from each other. Here I hope that the guidance given in the Index, supplemented by the genealogical tables, will be sufficient.

In one respect this volume differs from its predecessors in the series, in the absence (apart from an introductory outline of Europe) of sketch maps. This was found necessary, owing to the recent heavy rise in the costs of book-production, in order to avoid the greater evil of an increase in the price of the book. Though I had prepared other maps, I was only too glad to jettison them. I have never found small-scale uncoloured maps to be of any value ; an historical student must equip himself with an historical atlas containing coloured maps. My attitude to the bibliographies, which may invite some criticism, I have explained in a preliminary note.

This book has occupied my spare time during the past seven years, and I can only hope that it does not betray too many signs of having been written thus, unavoidably, piecemeal. I have certain, most grateful, acknowledgements to make. Firstly, to my wife, who undertook the typing of the whole manuscript. Secondly, to my colleague, Mr. Philip Grierson, who read through the typed manuscript and enabled me to make a number of important and necessary corrections before the book was in proof. Lastly, to my wife again, and also to my three sons, who rendered me invaluable assistance throughout the reading of the proofs and in the laborious task of compiling the Index.

Z. N. B.

September, 1938

PUBLISHER'S NOTE TO REPRINTS

No changes have been made in the text ; but the bibliographies were revised for the 1951 edition by Dr. Janet Matthews (Mrs. Sondheimer), and for the 1956 and 1969 impressions by the author's son, Professor Christopher Brooke.

CONTENTS

PART I

TO THE MIDDLE OF THE ELEVENTH CENTURY

vii

PART II

THE SECOND HALF OF THE ELEVENTH CENTURY

PART III

THE TWELFTH CENTURY

MAP

BIBLIOGRAPHICAL NOTE

THE purpose of the suggestions for reading appended to the various chapters is to enable the reader who is interested in any subject to know where he can obtain fuller information about it. The lists have been designed so as to mention books in English or in English translations as far as possible, supplemented by French works and to a lesser extent by German. It is not likely that many readers will wish to read the original authorities in Latin, and to make a short list of such authorities is always unsatisfactory. In a few cases it has been thought worth while to mention important authorities of which there is an English or a French translation. A useful selection of documents translated into English will be found in Laffan, R. G. D., *Select Documents of European History*, Vol. I, 800–1492 (London, 1930), [and B. Pullan, *Sources for the History of Medieval Europe from the mid-eighth to the mid-thirteenth century* (Oxford, 1966)].

Anyone who wishes to research more deeply into any period should consult some of the following bibliographical works. A valuable general account is given by Paetow, L. J., *Guide to the Study of Medieval History*. On a larger scale, with fuller critical accounts, is *A Guide to Historical Literature*, edited by W. H. Allison and others and published in New York in 1931. *The Annual Bulletin of Historical Literature*, published by the Historical Association, is extremely helpful. For Germany and Italy, there is the large work of Dahlmann-Waitz, *Quellenkunde der deutschen Geschichte*, supplemented by an annual critical survey, *Jahresberichte für deutsche Geschichte*. [Also, on a smaller scale, H. Quirin, *Einführung in das Studium der mittelalterlichen Geschichte* (Braunschweig, 1961)]. For France, there is Molinier, L., *Sources de l'histoire de France*, and for the Low Countries, Pirenne, H., *Bibliographie de l'histoire de Belgique*. Besides this, most of the large general works, especially the *Cambridge Medieval History*, contain full bibliographies.

For some of the following chapters, especially XVIII and

xix

XIX, in which a number of topics have been touched upon which could not be treated at length, a considerable list of books has been given. But it is not easy to find satisfactory modern works dealing with the subjects of many of the political chapters. The deficiency can be supplied by reference to some of the following general works. The *Cambridge Medieval History* is one of the largest of them. [One volume of this work, Vol. IV, *The Byzantine Empire*, has been entirely rewritten; 2 Parts, ed. J. Hussey, 1966–7]. A smaller work, Hill, D. J., *A History of European Diplomacy* (Vol. I, London, 1905) is interestingly written ; perhaps the best modern work on this scale is Hampe, K., *Das Hochmittelalter. Geschichte des Abendlandes von 900 bis 1250* (Berlin, 1953). For France, Lavisse, E., *Histoire de France* is very complete and useful. For Germany, Giesebrecht, W. von., *Geschichte der deutschen Kaiserzeit,* if a little old, is still one of the best to read ; on the constitutional side, Waitz, G., *Deutsche Verfassungsgeschichte,* brought up to date by later editors, is the most complete. Of still greater value to the medieval student is Hauck, A., *Kirchengeschichte Deutschlands,* which is admirable alike for Church history and for the whole story of Empire and Papacy. Pirenne, H., *Histoire de Belgique* is the standard work for the Low Countries, while for Rome and the Papacy, Gregorovius, F., *History of the City of Rome in the Middle Ages* (translated by Mrs. Hamilton) is a mine of information. *Studies in Medieval History* (ed. G. Barraclough) will be found useful, especially Vol. IV, Kern, *Kingship and Law.*

The best historical atlases are : Spruner-Menke, *Hand-Atlas für die Geschichte des Mittelalters und der neueren Zeit,* and Poole, R. L. (ed.), *Historical Atlas of Modern Europe.* For historical geography, Freeman, E. A., *Historical Geography of Europe* should be consulted in the edition of J. B. Bury : a more modern work, East, W. G., *An historical Geography of Europe,* will be found exceedingly stimulating to interest in the subject.

Addendum. Among recent general works, the following are particularly useful: C. W. Previté-Orton, *The Shorter Cambridge Medieval History* (ed. P. Grierson, 2 vols., Cambridge, 1952); G. Glotz (ed.), *Histoire générale: Histoire du Moyen Âge* ; A. Fliche and V. Martin (ed.), *Histoire de l'Église* (in progress).

INTRODUCTION

EUROPE IN THE NINTH CENTURY

WHEN Charlemagne was crowned in Rome on Christmas Day 800, the old Roman Empire seemed to have been recreated in the West. All Christian Europe, save only Britain and Spain and the south of Italy, acknowledged his sway and was included in his Empire. The great advantage of Empire was the elimination of a diversity of governments and therefore of occasions for war ; the more extensive the Empire, the greater the area of internal peace. One of the chief blessings which Rome had given to the world was the *pax Romana*, which made possible a widespread development of civilisation. In the same way, the restoration of peace to the West had as its first result the renewing of civilised life. Encouraged and inspired by the Emperor himself, men looked back to the past with an eager desire to renew and to re-create : to build up trade and enrich the material side of life, to pay heed to the inner and more spiritual life, and, as a beginning to learn and to advance knowledge.

This valuable period of reconstruction was, unfortunately, very brief. The Carolingian Empire experienced the same disaster that had befallen the Roman four centuries previously, and as before the most fatal effects were seen in the overthrow of civilised life. The peace of the Empire depended on a strong ruler, but after Charlemagne the sceptre passed into the feeble hands of Louis the Pious, and from him to successors equally incompetent. It depended also on unity of government, and a fatal weakness lay in the Frankish custom of division between the sons. Louis the Pious was sole ruler because he was the sole surviving son, but in his lifetime the process of division had already begun. In theory, indeed, the Empire, like the *regnum Francorum* before it, was indivisible ; subordinate kingdoms were created within

1

it for the younger sons. In practice this system of a federation of kings under an Emperor broke down at once owing to the ambition of these feeble rulers. They fought with one another, each to increase his own kingdom; no one of them was strong enough to be master of his own territory, much less of the whole Empire of which one or other of them was for a time the titular head. A triple division was soon apparent—the kingdoms of the West Franks and the East Franks north of the Alps, and in the south the kingdom of Italy. The two former were to crystallise into France and Germany, and though the dividing line between them was never to be exactly determined, the cleavage of race and language was already marked. Italy, on the other hand, was never to achieve unity until modern times; but it was always an object of ambition, an acquisition necessary for the ruler who aspired to the title of Emperor.

The ninth-century invasions

For a time the process of division seemed likely to be continued indefinitely. There were forces, both within and without, that accelerated the tendency to disruption. As the barbarians in the fifth century had coveted the lands of the Empire and had seized the opportunity which the weakness of its rulers afforded, so did the barbarians in the ninth century. This time they came mainly to plunder and to destroy, and only when the ease of their conquest was revealed did they attempt to make a settlement. Of the greatest importance were the Northmen, who showed the ferocity and destructiveness of which Northmen were always capable until they acquired territory of their own, when they diverted the violence of their energy most effectively to the work of organisation and government. The Moslems from the south, and later the Magyars from the east, were equally destructive, and Italy, France, and Germany all suffered from their ravages. The Moslems established themselves in Sicily and South Italy, and for a time retained a hold on the Campagna and even on the southern coasts of France. The Magyars, or Hungarians, settled in Pannonia, the former home of the Avars whom Charlemagne had so decisively crushed. The work of destruction had gone far, and raiding still continued. The peaceful habitations of monks and scholars suffered especially. Education was again at a standstill; public law was useless where there was no one to enforce it; industry

and trade were impossible with no one to protect the merchant
and make safe the roads.

As far as the kings were concerned, the internal danger Feebleness of
was equally important. They were unable not only to repel royal
authority
the invaders, but even to maintain order within their kingdoms. They could enforce neither the obedience of their
subjects nor even the duties of their officials. The essential
link in the structure, provided by the *missi dominici*, had
disappeared. Margraves and counts, who had been royal
officials under Charlemagne, became independent masters of
the territory they were supposed to govern for the king, and
took advantage of his weakness to disregard their duties and
to destroy his sovereignty. In the initiative they displayed
against the invaders lay the justification of their disobedience.
Robert the Strong, count of Paris, and his son Odo, had fought
the Northmen while the kings, Charles the Bald and Charles
the Fat, had weakly yielded to them. The house of Liudolf
had defended Saxony against Slavs and Northmen, the
margrave Liutpold had organised the defence of Bavaria
against the Magyars. These had won great prestige, and
their families a position of independent greatness, as a result.
And lesser men looked to them, and to such as them, for the
protection which it was the king's duty to give. The weak
man could only preserve his land from the invader if he put
himself and it under the protection of a stronger. Hence
the system of *commendation*, by which the small man gave
up his land to the great man, and received it back, with the
lord's protection, in return for definite services that he had
to render. As the lord's domain increased, he became more
important and more exclusive. The small freeholder became
a tenant, and lost his status thereby. The extent of the land
he surrendered determined his position ; the less he had to
give, the lower his place in the social scale. Commendation
and class distinctions were not novelties, but in the past they
had been mainly due to economic causes ; in the ninth
century the causes were mainly political, and so the principal
effect was to introduce a radical change into the political
structure of society.

Thus began that organisation of society to which we give The begin-
the name feudal. It was not a system, thought-out and nings of
feudalism
clearly defined ; it developed naturally from conditions

already existing, which had to be adapted empirically to meet the disorder and confusion of the times. It depended on land (the fief, *feudum*, *beneficium*), and in this there was nothing new. Land was already the source of livelihood and of wealth ; grants of land had long been, and long remained, the method of rewarding the king's faithful subjects, or of paying his officials. But the holding of land is now the first condition ; services are due from the holder to his lord, instead of land being the payment of service. It is a system depending on the relations of lord and tenants rather than of king and subjects. There is a twofold bargain, a contract, in which each gives and each receives, the one giving protection, the other service. Service may take many forms—it may be service in kind, in labour, in war, even in prayer——and its nature will definitely be stipulated. The ordinary peasant will be forced to work, because on him the whole system depends ; without his labour no one could live. His labour makes it possible for those above him to perform more dignified services to their lords ; he alone is so placed that he has no one from whom to demand service. The more important tenant will increasingly become bound by military service, and this is an important breach with the past. It was formerly the duty of all freemen to obey the king's summons to the host, and the officials, counts and margraves, had to see that they or a certain number of them came. Now these counts have, in virtue of their fiefs, to provide so many men to the king's army ; the military obligation falls on the nobles.

As we have seen, the nobles were assuming the function of protection, formerly the prerogative of the king alone. So they too claim the same services in return, and receive homage and an oath of fealty from their vassals. Within their own territories they aim at an independent authority. The king has sovereign rights, of justice, coinage, tolls, and the like ; but often the importance of these has been seriously diminished by grants, exemptions, and immunities. All the tenants-in-chief owe him direct service, but he is often unable to enforce its execution. Though in theory ruler of the whole kingdom, he will mainly, and sometimes entirely, have to depend on the territory of which he is the direct landlord—the royal demesne. This reduces him to the level of the nobles ; he like them has to live of his own, and to look to the demesne for food, soldiers, and officials. The extent, and also the compactness, of the royal estates will frequently be the best means of gauging the royal authority. If he needs to win support, he will have to alienate more of his estates, and by becoming poorer will become weaker in power. The longer this process continues, the more, through failure of his own resources, will he be at the mercy of his subjects.

It is customary to speak of feudalism as a pyramidal structure with the king at the head and the peasant at the foot. This is, indeed, the logical conclusion derived from the ideas inherent in feudal society, where everyone was supposed to have a lord and the king to be the supreme overlord ; but the picture it gives is too precise. The whole was never in exact equipoise ; the various parts never remained in stable relations with one another. Men will not act like mathematical formulae, and there is a considerable difference between the letter and the spirit of contracts. Everyone, where possible, exaggerated the rights due to him from his overlord or from his vassals, and minimised the duties due from himself in return. So there was a constant struggle between king and tenants-in-chief, between greater and lesser nobles, and sometimes one prevailed and sometimes the other. It must not be assumed that feudalism necessarily implies the ascendancy of the nobles, though in the ninth century this was the form it took ; William the Conqueror and Philip Augustus were both kings of the feudal type. Again, there is the essentially human question of inheritance. The nobles soon established the right of passing on their estates to their heirs, and the more ambitious were anxious to create a dynasty and bequeath an undivided dominion, which made them still more independent of the king. He in his turn sought to pass on his kingdom undivided to his eldest son. The fatal custom of a division of the kingdom was soon abandoned ; but the issue between hereditary right and election by the nobles was long contested, and with very different results in the various kingdoms.

Contrast of theory and practice

The great difficulty, then, in describing feudalism is to avoid generalisations that make it appear too conscious or too uniform a system. Moreover, the change from the old to the new was nowhere completed by the tenth century, and in some places had hardly begun. It had come into being confusedly and empirically, and it depended on conditions and customs which varied from country to country and from place to place. Not all lands were held as fiefs; much was still allodial (freehold). The relations of lord and tenant varied enormously, in accordance with local custom. Even the English manorial system, so commonly described as typical, was not universal in England, much less elsewhere; we have to be careful to refer it to certain parts of the country only, and similarly to limit it in point of time. In France the normal development to feudalism took place most rapidly, for there the power of the king was weakest. The feudal baron, his castle, hereditary fiefs, soon became the

Germany much less feudalised than France

rule. In Germany, on the other hand, where the last Carolingians proved themselves not ineffective, the Carolingian machinery in outward appearance persisted. The nobles, as a rule, retained their official status. The land went with the office, and it was as officials not as tenants-in-chief that they held from the king. The summons to the host, therefore, was still the method of raising an army, though the nobles, as officials, were responsible; tenure by military service was a late development in Germany. The nobles were as eager as the French to hand on their possessions to their sons, but it was the office in Germany that became hereditary.

The division into kingdoms after 887

The rapidity of the change in France was due to the early process of disintegration. When Charles the Fat was deposed owing to his incompetence in 887, the Empire broke up into a number of kingdoms. In Italy, Berengar of Friuli was proclaimed king, but was dispossessed for a time by his rival, Guido of Spoleto, and by Guido's son Lambert, both of whom were crowned Emperor; their early deaths left him master of Italy in 898. The West Frankish throne was occupied by Odo, the son of Robert the Strong. In the south of France, however, two independent kingdoms were created, Burgundy under Rudolf and Provence under Louis. In Germany alone, the king, Arnulf, a Carolingian though illegitimate, was without a rival; and he not only received imperial coronation at Rome, but was also recognised as

The disintegration of France

overlord by the other four kings. On the death of Odo in 898, the Carolingian line was reinstated in France, but with no recovery of unity. Besides Burgundy and Provence, the duchy of Aquitaine in the south-west was practically independent, as also the petty states of Gascony, Toulouse, and Barcelona. In the north, Brittany, Flanders, and Normandy (which was created a duchy under Rollo in 911) were in almost the same state of independence. And most important of all was the family of Robert and Odo, counts of Paris and overlords of Anjou, Maine, and Blois; they were practically masters of the kings, who retained their hold upon the throne because they were descended from Charlemagne, but otherwise were left almost without resources.

In Germany, even after the Carolingian line came to an end with the death of Arnulf's son, Lewis the Child, in 119, the disintegration was nothing like so complete. The opposite might have been expected, for in France there was an old tradition of unity, first under the Romans, and then under the Franks. In Germany the only unity had been that imposed by Frankish conquest, which naturally broke down when there was no one to maintain the succession from Charlemagne. But Germany was occupied, in the main, by four great tribes—Franks, Saxons, Alemanni (or Suabians), and Bavarians—and this fact for a long time dominated its history. It broke up into four parts, but the disintegration went no farther. Tribal feeling was strong and kept the tribe united. Tribal laws, or rather customs, had persisted under Charlemagne, who had even encouraged their survival by causing them to be written down. In the break-up of the Empire and the danger arising from the barbarian invasions, the tribe rallied round the family which took the lead in repelling the invaders. So in Saxony the house of Liudolf, in Bavaria the house of Liutpold, attained to the headship of the tribe, and the head of the family took to himself the title of duke.[1] This was a return to the old tribal dukedoms abolished by Charlemagne, under whom the functions of a duke were solely military. These new dukes are once again heads of the tribe, and the territory of the tribe becomes a duchy. The same thing happened, without the same justification, somewhat later in the other tribes. Burchard (in the tenth century) was the first to hold ducal authority in Suabia, and the Conradin family achieved the headship in Franconia,

Greater cohesion in Germany

The tribal duchies

---

[1] In 907, when Liutpold of Bavaria was killed in battle against the Magyars, his son Arnulf succeeded him and styled himself " Dei providentia dux."

the duchy of the Franks east of the Rhine. West of the Rhine another Frankish duchy came into being—Lorraine—which was for some time an object of keen rivalry between the Eastern and Western Frankish Kings. Its name recalled the old kingdom of Lothar II, and it contained the old family domain of the Carolingians including Charlemagne's favourite town of Aix. The ruler to whose kingdom it was attached could feel that he had entered into the inheritance of Charlemagne. Though derived from the same tribe as Franconia, it was entirely distinct as a duchy. The German kingdom, to which it soon adhered, was thus a federation of four tribes or of five tribal duchies. In each duchy the dukes owed their position to the tribe and not to the king. They held high office, but not of his creation. They took an oath of fealty to him as king, not as feudal overlord; and they would brook no interference within their duchies, where they governed supreme. And so they interposed themselves between the king and his officials; margraves and counts remained, but tended to become ducal officials rather than royal.

The Church
in France
and
Germany

There is another important distinction between France and Germany. The Church was a pre-barbarian institution in France. The bishops were numerous and individually not very powerful. But they had shown their independence as a united body, and the Church in France had played an important part, claiming a say in the government, especially under Louis the Pious. In Germany, the Church was of comparatively recent formation. Bishoprics were created as the work of conversion proceeded, but they were few and the dioceses were consequently of considerable extent. The authority of the German bishops was therefore much greater than that of the French, but at the same time they had no tradition of ancient independence to recall. They had always been subject to lay control, and when the tribal duchies came into being, the dukes sought to exercise over the bishops in their duchies the control formerly exercised by the kings. This happened in France also, and in both countries the united episcopate was royalist in sympathy, from conviction and from self-interest. But in France the individual bishops were of less importance, and the Papacy under Nicholas I by subordinating them to itself had reduced their corporate efficiency. In Germany their authority, both individual and corporate, made them a permanent asset to the royal power. Beneath the episcopate, the Church in both countries was definitely subordinate to lay control, and here even in Germany the nobles were masters in their own territories. The monasteries had, as other freeholders, to seek noble protection in the times of invasion, and the secular clergy were, apart from the cathedral churches, for the most part appointed to their benefices (the term itself is significant) by the lord on whose land their churches had been built. Lay patronage becomes more and more a definite feature of the ecclesiastical system.

The remaining third of Charlemagne's Empire—the Italian kingdom—presents peculiarities of its own. It was, and it remained, linked continually with the imperial title, since it contained Rome, the capital of the Empire. This title passed at first by direct descent to the eldest son, then it fell by election to the rulers of the West or East Frankish kingdoms, to which the Italian kingdom became a mere adjunct. The failure of the Carolingian line in Germany brought this connection temporarily to an end, and opportunity was given for the formation of a third independent kingdom. But Italy broke up into a number of petty states, the rulers of which contested the kingdom and the imperial title as well, while from Provence and Burgundy came other competitors for power. There was no really dominant house, like the Saxon in Germany or the Capetian in France, to whom the other nobles would submit. The kingship had to be won by force and held by force. So, whereas in the other two kingdoms the passing of the Carolingians gave the prospect of better order and more centralised government under a stronger ruler, it resulted in Italy in nothing but anarchy and brigandage—feudalism in its ugliest form. *The Italian kingdom*

But Rome was not only the capital of the Empire; it was also the seat of the Papacy. Now the Papacy had had a considerable share in the creation of the Empire, quite apart from the actual coronation of Charlemagne by Pope Leo III in 800. Gregory the Great had taken the first step when he sent Benedictine monks to convert England. The English Church was peculiarly under Roman direction, and the monks who later came from England to convert the *The Papacy its rise and decline* heathen in Germany acted as servants of the Papacy. They performed a double service, to the Franks by assisting the work of conquest, and to the Papacy by extending the area of Papal authority. They thus forged a link between the Franks and the Papacy, and this link was made firmer, firstly when the greatest of them, Boniface, was given the task of reorganising the Frankish Church, and secondly when Pepin received papal sanction for deposing the last Merovingian king and, together with his two sons, was anointed king by Boniface. There followed the appeal of the Papacy for help against the Lombards, and the consequent acquisition by the Franks of the Italian kingdom. The imperial title was a natural result, and the Papacy, now at feud with the Eastern Emperor, readily transferred its allegiance to the ruler of the West. To a strong Emperor, such as Charlemagne, the Papacy was naturally subordinate ; but it profited by the weakness of his successors to become independent, and even something more. For a short time it claimed authority over the power to which it had formerly been subject, and the relative positions of the temporal and spiritual authorities were reversed. But it was helpless in the presence of temporal violence, and the potentialities of the office made its control an object of greedy ambition. Weakened by the Moslem invasions, which also led to the building of the Leonine city to guard St. Peter's and the virtual division of Rome into two fortified towns, it became the prey of the local nobles who contested among themselves the mastery of Rome. While they kept the Papacy in their possession, the Pope from being a universal authority sank to the position of a merely local potentate.

Potentialities in the papal office However, the brief period of the greatness of the Papacy was of much more significance than the long period of its degradation. It created a number of precedents in the ninth century, which were to be recalled when it rose from its obscurity in the eleventh. Its headship of the Church was under Nicholas I a reality, and received from the Forged Decretals a definitely legal basis. It was now accepted that the imperial title could only be given by papal coronation, and moreover the Papacy had taken a leading part in the elections of Charles the Bald and Charles the Fat. It had taken over, as a matter of course, the claims of its subjects, the bishops of France, to dictate to kings on moral issues. The Papal States, the donation of Pepin and Charlemagne, were the basis of its temporal rule, which had even greater potentialities in the Donation of Constantine. All these powers lay dormant when the Pope was a puppet in the hands of the local nobility, but they merely lay dormant; they did not die.

When the tenth century opened, the outlook of Western Christendom was indeed gloomy. The Empire had broken up into a number of parts, and the process of disintegration seemed likely to be carried farther ; the prospect had appeared brighter in Germany, but the death of Arnulf in 899 and the accession of his feeble son, Lewis the Child, produced a critical situation there too. Moreover, on all sides the former Empire of Charlemagne was encircled by a ring of foes, whose attacks, if they had been simultaneous and concerted, might well have compassed its destruction. This hostile encirclement has been already alluded to, but needs to be more particularly described. *Map of Europe at the beginning of the tenth century* *Perilous condition of Western Christendom*

In the north, there was the constant menace of the Vikings from Scandinavia. The flood of surplus population that poured thence in the ninth century is a fact of great historical importance, and, like the later dwindling of that flood, difficult of explanation. Until the eleventh century it is not possible to speak of three definite kingdoms, though the three races— Danes, Norwegians, and Swedes—can already be distinguished. They all shared in the great Western expeditions, which were prompted by the need for new homes, the love of adventure, the desire for booty and, in a lesser degree, trade ; but it was principally Norsemen who settled in the Orkneys and Shetlands and established kingdoms in Ireland, at Dublin and elsewhere, and it was mainly Danes who settled in the east of England and the north of France. Meanwhile, the Danes by land and the Swedes by sea had been ravaging Frisia and north Germany along the Baltic coast. The Swedes played the chief part in these eastern expeditions, and their interest was more definitely in trade. A band of them, the Rus, penetrated into Russia (to which they gave their name) in the ninth century, and under Rurik they captured Novgorod. His successor Oleg won Kiev also; **in** *The Vikings*

907 he actually attacked Constantinople, and forced the Eastern Emperor to pay tribute and to grant important trading privileges. Though the Swedish element soon disappeared, the Varangians (as the Byzantines called them) were responsible for the beginnings of the Russian kingdom and the early importance of its trade.

The Slavs On the East, Germany was bounded mainly by Slav peoples. The Baltic Slavs, or Wends, comprised a number of scattered tribes extending from the Wagri and Obotrites in Mecklenburg and Holstein to the Pomeranians east of the Oder [1]; farther south, between the Elbe and the Oder, were the Liutizii (or Wilzi) and others. They were as inimical as the earlier Vikings to Christianity, but they lacked unity and were not usually aggressive. East and south-east of them were already in process of formation the States of Poland, Bohemia, and Moravia. The two latter were peculiar in that they had already been brought into a subject relation to the German kingdom, and that Christianity had been introduced into them by the labours of the apostles to the Slavs, Cyril and Methodius, in the ninth century; the Slav alphabet, based on the Greek writing of the period, was invented, and the Bible and the liturgy translated into Slavonic. In the latter part of the century the Moravian kingdom had increased in size and importance under Zwentibold, only to dwindle again after his death. Bohemia became the dominant partner, and on the death of Arnulf even renounced its subordination to Germany. One of the causes of the collapse had been the rise of the Magyar kingdom of Hungary in the south-east; this now emerged into history and began to exercise its devastating influence upon Western civilisation.

The sphere of the Eastern Empire South of the Danube, we enter the sphere of the Eastern Empire. Greece and the northern coasts of the Aegean were definitely part of it, but to the north, from ancient Macedon to the Black Sea, stretched the great kingdom of the Bulgars, a people akin to the Magyars, and north-west of them came Slav peoples, Serbs and Croats, from whom the west protected itself by the Marks of Istria, Carniola, and Styria. The Western Empire was thus cut off from contact at this point with the Eastern, which might otherwise have provided a

[1] Farther east still were non-Slav peoples, Letts and Finns, as yet unknown to the Germans.

powerful bulwark.   The two did, however, come into contact
in Italy, where the Byzantines since the time of Justinian had
retained a hold on the south and on Sicily.   During the eighth
and ninth centuries they had been engaged in continual
conflict with the Moslems, here as in Asia Minor.   The first
two Emperors of the Macedonian dynasty, Basil I and
Leo VI, great as were their achievements in administration
and legislation, were uniformly unsuccessful in the west.
Syracuse was lost in 878, and with the capture of the last
fortified post, Taormina, in 907 the island of Sicily fell into
Moslem hands.

This further advance of the Moslems was the more serious The Moslems
because it synchronised with a consolidation of Moslem power in Spain
in Spain.   The emirs of Cordova had long been independent
of the Caliphate, but in the ninth century their authority was
undermined by constant civil war and later by the hostility
of the Fatimites in North Africa.   The Christian States in
the north were able to profit by Moslem dissensions, and to
begin tentatively the work of reconquest.   The lead was
taken by the kingdom of Asturias (or Leon, as it became
early in the tenth century); Castile was as yet only a
county, and the other kingdom, Navarre, was interested in
combating Franks as well as Moslems.   But this temporary
advance was immediately checked on the accession of
Abd-ar-Rahman III to the emirate in 912.   He not only
united Moslem Spain under his sway but added the neighbouring coasts of North Africa, and in 929 assumed the
title of Caliph.   The Caliphate of Cordova was to last for a
hundred years, and during that time the hopes of a Christian
reconquest were definitely frustrated.

A feature of this period is the importance of sea-power. Importance
It was one of the disastrous results of the weakness and division of sea-power
of authority that the naval provisions of Charlemagne were
allowed to lapse.   The Vikings, ranging at will over their
native element, had an easy task in raiding peoples who could
not retaliate.   So far afield did they travel that even the
coasts of Spain and Portugal experienced their ravages.   But
here at last they came into contact with the Moslems, and had
to retire.   The Moslems had always recognised the importance of naval strength, and had become masters of the
Mediterranean.   This made possible the conquest of Sicily,

2

and their settlement in Italy and even on the southern coasts
of France. The imperial fleet of Charlemagne and Louis the
Pious no longer existed, and the Italian cities had not perfected
their navies ; Venice was unable to keep the Moslems out
of the northern Adriatic. Temporarily, too, the Byzantine
fleet was eclipsed, and suffered successive defeats. Crete
found a base for Moslem " corsairs " to dominate the Aegean.

Dawn of a brighter outlook   But, though the tenth century opened in this ominous
fashion, there were almost immediately signs of a brighter
outlook for Christendom, except in Spain. The year 911 was
marked by great happenings. Charles the Simple, by the
treaty of St-Clair-sur Epte, ceded to Rollo the nucleus of
what was to become the duchy of Normandy ; the energy
of the Northmen, turned constructive, established a strong
frontier-State, which protected France from the danger of
further raids. In the same year, the English won a victory
over the Danes which began the reconquest of the Danelaw,
and led ultimately to the uniting of England under a single
king in 954. And, again in 911, the last Carolingian king
of Germany, Lewis the Child, died ; the way was prepared
for a stronger régime, which was realised when the first of
the powerful Saxon dynasty ascended the throne eight years
later. In Italy, in 915, the Moslems were decisively defeated
on the Garigliano, and lost their permanent footing on the
Italian mainland. Moreover, they suffered from their internal
dissensions, and only in the Caliphate of Cordova was their
strength unimpaired. Slowly the Eastern Empire recovered,
and was able in the second half of the century to regain the
command of the Aegean. So, while the history of Western
Christendom in the ninth century is mainly concerned with
destruction and disintegration, in the tenth century there is
a cessation of destruction and a revival of order : the construction of a new framework of government, especially in
Germany and Italy, and a renewal of civilisation, which was
not to be followed again by reaction. The year 911 marks
the beginning of the change ; and already in the previous
year an event had occurred of great moment for the future—
the foundation of the monastery of Cluny.

Of all these happenings in or about the year 911, each
of which was a factor in the creation of a new age, the most
important was the foundation of a powerful dynasty in

Germany. It supplied the essential need—a strong monarchy, with the will to unite Christendom and to repel the invader, and thus to restore order and organisation and the conditions in which the old civilisation might be pieced together again and men pursue their ordinary vocations. Nor was there to be another reaction into chaos. It was the Saxon kings that conferred this boon on Western Europe. They entered into the heritage of Charlemagne, and thanks to them Germany for long dominated the European stage.

PART I

TO THE MIDDLE OF THE ELEVENTH CENTURY

CHAPTER I

THE NEW MONARCHY IN GERMANY

WITH the death of Lewis the Child in 911 the Carol- ingian line came to an end in Germany. The centrifugal forces were strong; it would not have been surprising had they caused the tribal duchies to separate from one another and four independent States to be created. But the kingdom of the East Franks survived. Already there was a sense of German unity, and the kingdom had become an accepted tradition which nobody desired to disturb. Moreover, it was in the general interest to preserve unity and co-operative action in view of the dangers that threatened from outside. So it seemed both obvious and necessary that there should be a king. There was no longer a legitimate heir, and no inclination to accept the rule of the Western Carolingians. It was left, therefore, to the nobles to select whom they pleased, and the election of their ruler remained with them always as a fundamental right. The elective principle, which in Germany never yielded to heredi- tary right as it did in France (though the hereditary principle constituted a strong claim to election), was for long a source of strength to the monarchy. The king was in a surer position when he owed his throne to the general choice, and until the thirteenth century the electors recognised that the interests of the kingdom demanded a capable ruler. In the act of election all the nobles of a certain rank participated; these were technically known as the princes (*principes*) of the kingdom, and the archbishops and bishops were included in this category besides the dukes, margraves, and counts. In practice, of course, a few individuals were usually able to exercise a controlling influence upon the result; from the beginning the dukes were especially important, and so were the three great Rhenish archbishops of Mayence, Cologne, and Trèves.

The character of royal government

In any case a complicated task was imposed upon the ruler of the German kingdom. It was not a State in the modern sense of the term. There was no capital city, no fixed centre of government; where the king was, there was the government, the Council Chamber, the seat of judgment. The king was constantly on the move. He had to travel from manor to manor in order to obtain the necessaries of life for himself and his court (a prolonged stay elsewhere would be too burdensome for his host); and, though his family territories were probably concentrated, there were royal manors in various parts of his kingdom. The machinery of local government organised by Charlemagne had ceased to function. There were no longer any royal *missi*, and the counts were officials only in name; the king did not even appoint them, unless a count had died without an heir or had been deprived of his county by the judgment of his peers.

The policy of the dukes

The king's greatest difficulty, however, was in dealing with the dukes. In 911 they held an outstanding position of authority in the tribes, which made it certain that one of their number would be elected as king. No lesser man would be allowed to rank above them, nor could anyone else provide the necessary cohesion or be adequate to undertake the defence of the kingdom. But, while they acted in the interests of the kingdom in electing one who had the resources of a duchy behind him, their altruism went no further. Each of them was determined to remain the independent master of his own duchy, and in this he could count on the loyalty of his tribe. Something like a federation of tribes was visualised by them, with a king as suzerain who would allow complete local autonomy within each duchy. Naturally the king could not acquiesce in this. He wished to make his authority effective everywhere, and not merely the king's personal ambition but also the welfare of the kingdom required that its ruler should be able to enforce internal order and to defend it from external attack. A contest was therefore inevitable, and this question of the duchies proved so difficult of solution that it remained one of the most harassing problems of the monarchy until the final break-up of the old tribal duchies in the second half of the twelfth century. A man of strong personality, with large domains of his own, could make himself master of the kingdom ; but the position would always be precarious, for the order he had maintained might vanish at his death, sometimes even during his absence from the country.

The most obvious choice would have been the duke of Saxony, who held an unquestioned authority over the strongest and most homogeneous of the tribes, but the duke, Otto, was too old to undertake such a burden. The choice, therefore, of the nobles who assembled at Forchheim fell upon duke Conrad of Franconia ; and perhaps as the leader of the East Franks he was regarded as the most suitable ruler of the kingdom of the East Franks (for so the German kingdom was still usually styled). To Conrad I, then, was given the task of governing and defending Germany, and he proved entirely unequal to it. The other dukes held aloof and maintained their local autonomy in spite of all his efforts. Otto of Saxony was friendly, and so for a time was Henry, who succeeded his father as duke in 912. But soon friction arose over Thuringia, in which both the king and the archbishop of Mayence had landed interests ; Henry was powerful enough to remain independent, and to keep Thuringia entirely under his control. In Suabia, Burchard, who now styled himself "Duke, by the providence of God," was equally independent. Arnulf of Bavaria suffered a reverse in 916, but recovered his position almost immediately. Lorraine under Reginar actually broke away from the East Frankish kingdom, preferring to accept the more legitimate headship of the weak Carolingian ruler of the West Franks, Charles the Simple ; and his son Gilbert, who succeeded to the duchy in 915, took the same line. Conrad, therefore, was little more than a nominal king, and he failed signally to perform his function of defender of the kingdom. Four times in his reign—911, 913, 915, and 917—did the Magyars invade Germany. Arnulf of Bavaria defeated them in 913 ; in 915 it was Saxony alone that suffered. On the other occasions they were free to spread their usual devastation and destruction, in which churches and monasteries suffered most severely, since they provided the best hopes of booty ; Conrad could do nothing to protect them.

Yet his reign was not wholly without significance. Monarchy had an ally which was to prove its strongest support

Election of Conrad I (911–18)

His incapacity

The Church as the ally of monarchy

in the future, and which came out into the open on Conrad's side. The Church had always preached the divine right of the ruler, who was now regularly crowned by ecclesiastical hands and anointed with the holy oil ; it brought to the king what he most required—a tradition of loyalty ; it championed the unification as opposed to the federation of Germany. Nor was the motive entirely altruistic. Instead of being directly dependent on the king, the bishops had become subordinate to the dukes ; there was no scriptural or other precedent for the divine right of dukes, and the bishops were anxious to recover their former position in the kingdom.

Missionary character of the German Church

From its inception, the Church in Germany had had a peculiar character. It had been, and to a considerable extent it still remained, a missionary Church. Hence the large size of the bishoprics, and the vast and increasing extent of the archbishoprics. Germany had been completely heathen when it was conquered by the Franks, and the ecclesiastical provinces to some extent reflect the process of conquest and of conversion ; it was still bounded on the north and east by heathen peoples—Northmen, Slavs, Hungarians—and any advance in these directions enlarged the spheres of the adjacent archbishoprics. For the whole kingdom there were at present only five ecclesiastical provinces. Greatest of all was Mayence (Mainz), of which St. Boniface, the apostle to the Germans, had been bishop. It covered the duchies of Franconia and Suabia, Thuringia and the eastern part of Saxony ; every extension eastwards of Saxony, every conversion in Bohemia, brought fresh territory and people under its ecclesiastical authority. Second to it in importance was Cologne (Köln), which covered Lower (i.e. northern) Lorraine, and also extended north to Frisia and north-east to Westphalia (the western part of Saxony). Third in order came Trèves (Trier), which occupied Upper Lorraine and so was entirely west of the Rhine and temporarily outside the German kingdom. The fourth was Salzburg, in the south-east, corresponding roughly to the duchy of Bavaria, and with Moravia and Hungary as possible spheres of expansion. Lastly, there was Bremen (formerly Hamburg), occupying the northern part of the duchy of Saxony and particularly concerned with the maintenance and expansion of missionary work among the Northmen. Ecclesiastically, then, the German kingdom

Its five provinces

was divided into five provinces, as it was politically into five duchies (for the defection of Lorraine was only temporary). The occupants of these great archbishoprics could not fail to take a leading part in events, and their support was invaluable to the Crown.

The first occasion of its public manifestation was at a great synod held in 916 at Hohenaltheim, the meeting-place of the three duchies of Franconia, Suabia, and Bavaria. It was well attended by the clergy of all these duchies, but the Saxon bishops, obedient to Duke Henry, held aloof. A papal legate was present, for Conrad had appealed to the Pope for his support, and the occasion was taken to express the authority of the spiritual power and of the Papacy; but John X, flushed with the victory over the Moslems on the Garigliano, was over-confident in his attempt to assert himself in Germany. Much more important were the decrees which declared unreservedly for the king and condemned as traitors those who refused obedience to him. Some result was obtained, for two of the most troublesome counts, troublesome especially to the Church, Erchanger and Berthold, were actually executed after condemnation by the synod. But the dukes could ignore the decrees with impunity, and even the Saxon bishops, safe under Henry's protection, could disregard the penalties for their non-appearance.

The synod of Hohenaltheim (916)

The value of this alliance of monarchy with the Church was to be demonstrated later on, but Conrad's position was not improved thereby. The dukes were too strong for him, and in 917 he was completely defeated both in Bavaria and Suabia. He confessed his helplessness at the end of 918, when on his death-bed he bequeathed his duchy of Franconia to his brother Eberhard, but recommended Henry of Saxony for the kingship. He showed himself at least superior to the selfishness of the time in that he preferred the interests of the kingdom to the advancement of his family.

In May 919, the Franconian nobles, obedient to Conrad's last wishes, met the Saxon nobles at Fritzlar in the north of Franconia, close to Saxony; Forchheim, which was central for all the duchies, was the usual place of election, but the other duchies took no part on this occasion. The two tribes concurred in the election of the duke of Saxony as King

The election of Henry I (919–36)

Henry I (known, in later times, as Henry the Fowler). Thus
began the line of Saxon kings, and for a hundred years Saxony
occupied a predominant place in Germany. The greatness
of Saxony, and therefore of the kingdom, was largely due
to the spade-work of Henry I. His power depended on
Saxony, and there his interest lay; the kingship seems to
have interested him only in its value to Saxony. He refused
to be crowned and anointed, as the custom was, by the
archbishop of Mayence, and to avoid giving offence professed
himself to be unworthy of the honour; but his true reason
was doubtless that he was unwilling to give an opening to
ecclesiastical claims, remembering the decrees of the Synod
at Hohenaltheim and his strife with the previous archbishop
of Mayence. Later, especially under the influence of his pious
wife Matilda, he proved himself a generous benefactor to the
Church; the Church owed much to him, but he did not wish
to be in its debt.

His mastery
of the dukes
Though his main interest was in his own duchy, it was
important to him to be recognised by the other dukes as their
master; he would not endure the humiliations of Conrad I,
and so far only Eberhard of Franconia had recognised him.
The upstart Burchard of Suabia was easily forced to submit
in 919 and to accept Henry's overlordship. Much more
important was the submission of Arnulf of Bavaria in 921.
Arnulf had an established position, and alliance with him
against the Magyars was necessary. Finally, Henry recognised the importance of Lorraine, and was determined to
recover it for the German kingdom and to obtain the remains
of the Carolingian domain for his own use. He had to
contend with the obstinate attempts of Charles the Simple
to keep it in the West Frankish kingdom and the ambitions
of king Rudolf I of Burgundy, as well as the tergiversations
of duke Gilbert. But eventually, in 925, he forced Gilbert to
submit, and bound him to himself more closely by giving his
daughter Gerberga to him as wife in 928. Having vindicated
his kingship, however, he was content to leave the dukes with
a large degree of autonomy, provided he himself dictated the
measure of their independence. Arnulf was allowed to retain
his authority over the episcopate in Bavaria, with the right
of appointment. This was not conceded in the other duchies,
but even Burchard of Suabia was allowed to wage war on

his own initiative, and was under no obligation to supply troops to the royal army.

Henry had shown, at any rate, that he could enforce obedience, and satisfied with that he devoted his great organising abilities to the strengthening and security of his own duchy. It was exposed to attacks from the Northmen, the Slavs, and, most dangerous of all, the Magyars. In 924 the Magyars invaded Saxony, and Henry was compelled to act strictly on the defensive. He received no assistance from any other duchy, nor did he render aid to the south when it was invaded in 926. But the lucky capture of a Hungarian prince enabled him to arrange a truce for 9 years, during which he agreed to pay an annual tribute. This gave him a breathing space in which to organise his defences, and the advantage he took of it prepared not only the defence of Saxony but also its internal development and its eastward expansion.

Truce with the Magyars

An obvious step was to extend the system of marks or border-counties, under margraves whose special duty was to maintain the defence of the frontiers against the Slavs ; this also gave prospect for offensive measures. Besides this, a number of fortresses were established, within the duchy as well as upon the frontiers, which made settlement possible in peaceful times, since their walls afforded a refuge to the local peasantry in case of attack, and these in turn helped to swell the garrisons and make invasion more difficult. In many places—such as Merseburg, Quedlinburg, Meissen, Goslar—active town life begins with their creation as fortresses for defence, a cause of town growth which can be paralleled elsewhere in Europe. But defensive measures were not enough. The freemen of Saxony assembled in the *heerban*, which closely resembled the Anglo-Saxon *fyrd*, fought on foot and were no match for the lightly-mounted Magyars, who invariably outmanœuvred their terrified opponents by the rapidity of their movements and the skill with which they could, often in pretended flight, discharge their arrows from horseback. Henry met the problem, in the same way that the Franks had met it when they encountered the Arabs. He instituted a mounted force among his own retainers and elsewhere whenever possible, so that the cavalry, in Saxony as in other parts of Germany, soon became

The military reorganisation of Saxony

the effective military arm. It was a change in national customs and characteristics which says much for the foresight and capacity of the king who brought it about.

Expeditions against the Slavs This new army was given the training for the more serious work it had to perform by being employed in expeditions against the Slavs. In 929, in company with duke Arnulf of Bavaria, Henry invaded Bohemia and forced duke Wenceslas (later the saint of the carol) to accept his over-lordship. In the same year had begun the advance of Saxony eastward against the northern Slavs, which was renewed in 932 and again in 934. The land between the Elbe and the Oder was eventually conquered; important places, such as Brandenburg and Meissen, became German towns; and together with conquest went conversion and colonisation to consolidate the territory that had been won. By the same methods that Charlemagne had used to subdue the heathen Saxons, the Saxons set out to subdue the heathen Slavs on their eastern borders; but while Charlemagne achieved his purpose in a few years, the Saxons were to take centuries. Revolts and reconquests alternated in bewildering succession, but the eastward expansion of Saxony slowly continued, and the East Saxons, trained by Henry I and hardened by this long border warfare, became the most redoubtable fighting men in Germany.

Defeat of the Magyars Accordingly, when the Magyars came again in 933, Henry was prepared, and inflicted on them a defeat which only the speed of their flight prevented from being decisive. The safety of Saxony was at any rate assured, and the need of paying tribute had disappeared. So secure was he that he Expedition against the Danes was able to take the aggressive against the Northmen, the third of the heathen foes of Saxony, and to invade Denmark in 934. The old Danish mark was re-formed, and from Bremen Christian missions went into Denmark to help again the work of conquest. The Church was much in Henry's mind in his last years. Foundations, especially in Saxony, and donations to churches show him in a different mood from that with which he had begun his reign. The old distrust of the Church had gone, because he was master and had nothing to fear and much to give; he is said even to have contemplated a pilgrimage to Rome.

His great work had been done for Saxony, and over all its

foes—Slavs, Danes, Magyars—he had been successful. The The achievement of Henry I
prestige he had won, especially by his victory over the
Magyars, and the perfecting of the military machine, were
assets for a wider sphere. And in that sphere he had shown
that he had to be obeyed. The dukes had been forced to
submit, and Lorraine had been reunited to the German
kingdom. Eberhard of Franconia had assisted in his election ; Arnulf of Bavaria was friendly and had co-operated
with him against Bohemia ; Gilbert of Lorraine was bound
to him by marriage-ties and self-interest ; finally, in Suabia,
on the death of Burchard, the duchy was given to a Franconian
count, Herman, who married Burchard's widow, and his
fidelity was to be a great asset to Otto I. The dukes were
left with a large measure of autonomy, but they were not
independent. Henry I was thus more than a Saxon king.
He differed from his predecessors, in that he made no attempt
to govern the whole kingdom. He concentrated on strengthening the part where were his domains and his real power,
and in this way he laid the political foundations of the
German kingdom.

As the eldest legitimate son of Henry I—for his half- Otto I
brother Thankmar had been born of a marriage which the (936–73)
Church refused to recognise—Otto was the unquestioned
heir to the duchy of Saxony. Further, his succession to the
throne had been ensured by his father, who, shortly before
his death, had obtained the assent of the magnates at a
council at Erfurt in 936. The principle of election had to
be accepted, but the king was usually allowed to designate
his successor. The only objection came from Otto's younger
brother Henry, who thought he had the better right since
he was born when his father was king, and he nursed a
grievance which led to much future trouble. Otto I was
in his twenty-fourth year when his father died. He had had
the normal training of his kind—in hunting, fighting, and
knightly exercises. Of other education he had received
nothing, save in the stories of the heroes of old, which were
calculated to fire the young warrior to emulation ; in later
years, with his sturdy frame, ruddy complexion, long beard,
and shaggy chest, he was a fit subject himself for a saga.
In letters he received no training, and, like Charlemagne, he

only learned to read in middle life. He married early, in 929, Edith, an Anglo-Saxon princess ; and their two children, Liudolf and Liutgarde, were both born before he came to the throne. Liudolf was brought up as his father had been, but the son of Otto's second marriage, Otto II, received an education of an altogether different nature, to fit him for his imperial inheritance.

His imperial ambition

Otto was of a very different temperament from his father ; but each of them possessed the qualities exactly required at the moment. In the condition of the kingdom at the time of Henry's accession, what was needed was a man of his cautious and constructive character, content with a limited authority as king. His patient building gave scope for the more brilliant talents of his son. Otto had the broader vision and the more exalted ambition, so that he was able to make the most of his inheritance. He had rarer qualities too ; he pursued his course, amid the usual intrigues and treacheries to which the primitive and selfish passions of the times gave rise, with an evenness of temper and an absence of vindictiveness that particularly distinguish him from his fellows. His objective was Empire, and his model was Charlemagne. Therefore he could not be content, like his father, to rule Saxony, and to leave local autonomy to the other dukes. He had to make himself their master, and to be a king in the old sense of the word. He had also to establish that the succession to Charlemagne was in the East Frankish, and not in the West Frankish, kingdom. The West Frankish rulers could point to their descent from Charlemagne, but they were too weak to assert themselves effectively. The chief issue between the two kingdoms was their rivalry over Lorraine, where lay the ancestral domains of the Carolingians. Otto owed this also to his father, that Lorraine was included in his kingdom. With it in his control he could hope to attain his ultimate goal—Italy.

Ecclesiastical coronation at Aix

With this imperial outlook, he naturally did not reject ecclesiastical coronation as Henry had done ; rather, he insisted on it, and that it should take place within the duchy of Lorraine, at Aix, the favourite residence of Charlemagne. There archbishop Hildebert of Mayence, taking the first voice in the election, a right his successors were always to retain, presented him to the princes as " the chosen of the

Lord "; after he had been acclaimed king by all present, Hildebert anointed him with the holy oil and bestowed upon him the crown and the other insignia of royalty. So had Pepin, the father of Charlemagne, been crowned by St. Boniface, bishop of Mayence. Another revival of the past was seen at the ceremonial banquet which followed, when the king was served at table by the four dukes. These formal services were always rendered by the highest officers of State—Chamberlain, Steward, Butler, Marshal—since the household servants of the king were originally his most trusted followers. It was a recognition that the dukes stood next to the king in rank ; but it was also a sign that they were his officials, not beside but beneath the king, to whom they accordingly rendered homage.

The general prospects for the reign seemed bright, for Henry I had created a position of apparent security. The appearance, however, was illusory. There was no constitution in the modern sense of the term ; there was no general desire for a closely-knit State, and no bond of union apart from the head. Everything, therefore, depended on the personality of the new ruler, and the accession of a king, especially one who was young and comparatively untried, always awakened hopes among those to whom a strong central authority was irksome. The enemies on the frontier were immediately active upon the death of their conqueror, and internal unrest soon raised its head, provoked moreover by the obviously masterful policy of the new ruler. There was already trouble in Bohemia. A reaction, partly national, partly heathen, had broken out in 929 against the duke, St. Wenceslas, who had imported clergy, books, and relics from Germany to assist him in the Christianisation of his duchy. He was murdered by his brother Boleslav I, who succeeded to the duchy and threw off the German yoke. He twice defeated troops sent against him from Saxony and Thuringia, and maintained his independence until 950 when Otto himself led an expedition into Bohemia and made it tributary to Germany once more.

There was a rising also of the Slavs on the Elbe. Herman Billung was given the command against them as general of the Saxon army. To his extensive domains west of the Elbe, within which were such important places as Lüneburg

The difficulties confronting the new king

Bohemia

The northern Slavs

and Bardowiek, was added the control of the most northerly mark, known later as the Mark of the Billungs. He acquired, too, the title of duke, and his descendants definitely became dukes of Saxony by hereditary right until the extinction of the male line in the twelfth century; but their authority seems to have been mainly confined to East Saxony, where the chief strength of the duchy was concentrated. Farther south, count Siegfried was in command between the Saale and the Elbe, and on his death in 937 Otto appointed count Gero to succeed him. Between them, Herman and Gero divided the responsibility for the eastern frontier of Saxony, and well repaid the confidence that Otto placed in them. Through all the ensuing troubles they remained loyal to the king and faithful to their trust; not only did they quell any aggressive action by the Slavs, but they actually advanced the sphere of German control from the Elbe to the Oder. Otto's wise choice, however, raised up enemies for him in his own duchy. Both his half-brother Thankmar and Herman's elder brother Wichman were offended at being passed over when these appointments were made, and they joined in revolt. The trouble came to a head in 938, but Wichman, alarmed at the increasing disorder, returned to his allegiance; while Thankmar, after conspiring with the duke of Franconia, was defeated and killed.

The Magyars   Meanwhile the Magyars had seized this favourable opportunity to make one of the most widespread and devastating of all their raids. In 937 they broke into Germany *en masse*, and though Otto was able to defend the frontiers of Saxony he could do nothing to help the rest of Germany. One band penetrated through Franconia into Lorraine and thence as far as Rheims and Sens; another went through the south of Germany into Burgundy; and a third penetrated to the south of Italy. In 938 they made another unsuccessful attempt against Saxony, the last from which that duchy had to suffer; and for a few years even South Germany was free from their raids.

The revolt of the dukes   The Saxon revolt and the Magyar invasions were the more serious because they came at a time when Otto had to face the ducal challenge to his authority. Fortunately for him Herman of Suabia remained loyal throughout, and the other three dukes did not take concerted action. Arnulf of

Bavaria died in 937, and his son Eberhard refused to do homage. At the same time Eberhard of Franconia was engaged in local warfare with a Westphalian count. In 938 Otto punished the duke of Franconia with a fine for his breach of the peace, and also overthrew the rebel duke of Bavaria, appointing in his place his uncle Berthold, brother to the late duke Arnulf. But the next year he was faced by a formidable coalition, engineered by Eberhard of Franconia, who won over to his side the king's brother Henry, duke Gilbert of Lorraine, and the new archbishop of Mayence, Frederick. All the Rhineland was aflame, and Otto's fate was in the balance. And then came a marvellous stroke of fortune, and the danger was over. The dukes of Lorraine and Franconia were returning from a successful raid across the Rhine when they were caught unawares by two Franconian counts and both of them were killed. The coalition immediately collapsed. Henry and the archbishop had to make their peace with the king, who forgave them and even entrusted the duchy of Lorraine to Henry. But Henry had not recovered from his disappointment at seeing the kingdom slip from his grasp ; he broke away again and for two years tried every means to raise a party against Otto. At last, in 941, he realised the hopelessness of his cause, made his final submission, and henceforward remained loyal to his brother.

The coalition against Otto had raised hopes in another quarter. The king of France, Louis IV, saw the opportunity it gave him to imitate his father's success in Lorraine. But his ambition was easily checkmated. Otto allied himself with his brother-in-law, the powerful count of Paris, Hugh the Great, who was only too ready to prevent Louis' attempt to escape from his leading-strings. Yet the collapse of the coalition had its aftermath in France also. For the widowed duchess of Lorraine, Gerberga, Otto's sister, married the king of France, and so Otto was connected by marriage with the two rival powers in France ; he was in a strong position as the arbitrator between the husbands of his two sisters. In general, he kept the balance even by supporting the weaker, Louis, and both in 946 and 948 he got papal assistance against Hugh. He had, at any rate, a free hand in dealing with Lorraine, which, as a duchy, was quite unlike the other four. It was not bound together by strong tribal

The king of
France and
Lorraine

feeling, but united quite loosely by the memory of its former existence as a kingdom ; the Church was exceptionally strong within it ; the local counts were powerful and divided in their sympathies ; and the king had an especial interest in its close attachment to the Crown. Therefore the ducal authority was not comparable with that in the other duchies, while the king's presence was frequently needed to settle its disputes and to maintain his own interests.

The mastery of Otto

In the first three years of his reign Otto I had been faced with a series of dangers from every side. Fortunately for him they had not been quite simultaneous, or he must have succumbed to their united weight ; and in the last and most pressing he had been saved by an almost miraculous accident, without even the issue of a battle. But he had proved himself in adversity, by the coolness and judgment with which he had confronted each crisis as it occurred. He had shown himself capable not only of retaining the position his father had won, but even of extending it considerably during these perilous years. And so he had earned the respect which his contemporaries would only give to one whom they acknowledged as their master, and he ensured himself thereby a period of comparative peace for some

His plan of government

twelve years. He employed it in consolidating the government of his kingdom, and especially in tackling the problem of the duchies ; the control of them had fallen into his hands, for three out of the four had become vacant by the treason of the dukes. His ultimate policy was to make them appanages of the royal family, but his brother Henry was not at first to be trusted, and his two children were not yet of age. It was only in 947 that his plan could be put fully into effect. Franconia was not properly reconstituted as a duchy ; Otto kept it in his own hands, and it was always to remain attached to the kingship. For Lorraine his first idea was his brother Henry, but as he continued to plot revolt, a loyal Lotharingian count, Otto by name, was appointed as duke. He died in 944 and then the duchy was given to the leading noble in Franconia, Conrad the Red, whom Otto married to his daughter Liutgarde in 947. The previous year, following on the death of his wife Edith, he had designated his son Liudolf as his successor and obtained the consent of the magnates to his election. In 947 Liudolf married Ida, daughter and heiress of duke Herman of Suabia, and on Herman's death in 949 succeeded to the duchy. Finally, again in 947, duke Berthold of Bavaria died, and Otto appointed his own brother Henry, whose loyalty could now be relied upon and who cemented his hold on the duchy by marrying Judith, the daughter of the former duke Arnulf.

This, then, was Otto's project for dealing with the great problem of the duchies. Franconia and Saxony were in his own hands, administered for him by subordinates. The other three dukes were his son, his son-in-law, and his brother. This did not ultimately prove a successful solution. But, at any rate, the old tribal autonomy had been broken down. Otto had established his right to appoint the dukes. They were thus royal officials, and they owed their position to him, not to the choice of the tribe. Moreover, the old attachment of the tribe to the duke was impaired ; in each case he was an alien from another tribe, and therefore there was not the old bond between duke and tribe which had made the tribal duchies so formidable an obstacle to royal authority.

With the duchies allotted among members of his family, Otto might well feel satisfied that his German kingdom was now securely organised. The one rebel to his authority, the duke of Bohemia, had to be attended to, and to Bohemia Otto went himself in 950 and forced Boleslav to recognise his overlordship and resume the payment of tribute. Bohemia was not yet a part of Germany, but as a buffer state on the eastern frontier it was essential that it should be subject to the German Crown. The time was now ripe for his Italian plans to be matured, and at this moment an appeal for help came to him from Italy which gave him a welcome excuse for intervention. But to explain this it is necessary to digress for a space, and to give some account of the tangled history of the kingdom of Italy and of Rome, and also of Burgundy, with which the fortunes of the Italian kingdom were inextricably linked.

In 911, Berengar I was still maintaining his seat upon The Italian the unsteady throne of Italy. He had successfully resisted kingdom the challenge of King Louis of Provence, whom he had driven back, blinded, to his own country in 905. There Louis lingered on for another twenty-two years, but the real ruler

of Provence was Hugh of Arles, who also coveted the Italian
kingdom, and who, like Louis, could justify his claim by
his descent from Charlemagne. His attempts were foiled
while Berengar was alive ; and even when Berengar died in
924, the most likely successor seemed to be the king of
Burgundy, Rudolf II. But in 926 the Italian nobles veered
round again, and Hugh achieved his ambition. By guile
and murder he disposed of his most likely rivals for power,
and managed to retain his throne for twenty years ; he was
also able to get his son Lothar crowned joint-ruler with
himself, and hoped to found a dynasty. The next object
of his ambition was the imperial crown.

During the first half of the tenth century Rome was
dominated by a noble family, the head of which, the Senator
Theophylact, had already obtained control in 911. The
Papacy, as well as the city, was in the hands of this family,
and thus subjected it lost altogether the great position won
for it by Nicholas I ; but it sunk to its deepest depth of
degradation during the career of Theophylact's infamous
daughter Marozia, mistress of one Pope and mother of
another. Only one Pope of note emerges into history,
John X (914–28), who took a leading part in effecting the
alliance of the Byzantines with the Latin States in the south
of Italy, and so brought about the defeat of the Moslems
on the Garigliano in 915 and their expulsion from Italy. He
it was, too, who sent a papal legate to the Synod at Hohenaltheim in 916, aiming doubtless at a recovery of papal authority
outside Italy. But after Theophylact's death he fell a victim
to the intrigues of Marozia, who for four years was supreme
in the Eternal City. Twice married, to the marquis of
Spoleto and the marquis of Tuscany, and twice widowed, she
aimed higher now in her search for a new husband to keep
her in power. She tempted the king of Italy with her hand
and also with the prospect of receiving the imperial crown
from her illegitimate son, now Pope John XI. Hugh came
to Rome in 932 and married Marozia, but, before he could
be crowned, another son of Marozia, Alberic, the child of her
first marriage, intervened. He drove out his stepfather,
caused his mother Marozia to disappear, and kept his papal
half-brother a prisoner. For twenty-two years he ruled
Rome and the Popes with a strong hand, and the Romans

even obeyed his dying behest in 954 and on the next vacancy
elected his son as Pope John XII.

Meanwhile, Hugh, though he had failed at Rome, was
for some time still the master of northern and central Italy.
He made more certain of the centre by creating his illegitimate son Hubert marquis of Tuscany in 937, and later of
Spoleto as well. In order to be freed from the rival who had Burgundy
so nearly been preferred to him as king, he had made a Provence
compact with King Rudolf II of Burgundy in 933, ceding united into
to him Provence in return for his non-intervention in Italy. one kingdom
This cession, which meant the uniting of Burgundy and
Provence into a single kingdom, does not seem to have become
effective until Hugh's death in 948, for in 937, when
Rudolf died and his son Conrad III became king, Hugh
showed that he had not given up his pretensions in Burgundy.
He attached himself by a double tie to the new king; he
himself married Conrad's mother Bertha, and his son Lothar
married Conrad's sister Adelaide.

In Italy, Hugh's tyranny led to his eventual undoing. Hugh of
His most dangerous rival, Berengar of Ivrea, grandson expelled
through his mother of Berengar I, had to escape in 942 to from Italy
Germany, where he put himself under the protection of Otto
I. But when he returned to Italy a few years later, there
was a general rising in his favour, and Hugh had no alternative but to abdicate; he was fortunate to be able to retire
in 947 to his native Provence. Lothar remained as nominal
king until his death in 950. Then Berengar II was elected,
and with him his son Adalbert as joint ruler. The chief
danger to them was that the fickle wind of Italian favour
might veer round to Adelaide, Lothar's widow. So they
got her into their custody and kept her in confinement.
She proved to be more dangerous in prison than at liberty. The appeal
An appeal for help came to Germany, and this it was that to Otto I
brought Otto I into Italy.

Otto had already taken a close interest in Burgundy, Otto's
and in fact had established a sort of protectorate over the Burgundian
kingdom. The schemes of Hugh to establish himself there kingdom
after the death of Rudolf were checkmated by the sudden
action of Otto in getting possession of the young king Conrad
III. It is a mark of Otto's capacity that he achieved this
coup during the hazardous three years at the beginning of

his reign, and a sign of his policy and his sagacity that he realised the necessity of it. The wisdom of the step is made clear by the history of the past. Rudolf I had made a great effort in Lorraine, though Charles the Simple had won the prize. Rudolf II had been a danger in the south-west of Germany and had annexed Suabian territory. It was, therefore, important for the sake of Germany that Burgundy should be a dependency, if possible, of the German Crown, a buffer State on the south-west like Bohemia on the east. But for Otto's ultimate purpose it was equally important to have control of the passes into Italy, and with Burgundy as well as Germany under his authority he controlled them all. Not only did he checkmate Hugh by thus getting possession of Conrad ; he also foiled the plan of the king of France who hoped for some recompense in Burgundy after his failure in Lorraine. Otto kept Conrad by his side until 942 when he felt sufficiently sure of his fidelity to allow him to return to his kingdom. Even after this we find Conrad III not infrequently in Otto's company.

When the appeal came to him on behalf of Adelaide, Otto had a double excuse for responding to it. It was only right that he should give the help asked for by his subject, the king of Burgundy, Adelaide's brother ; and he could justly consider that Berengar II, who had put himself under his protection in 942, was answerable to him for his actions. The moment exactly fitted in with his plans. He came not only to rescue, but also to marry Adelaide. The fame of her beauty might well attract one who, though a grandfather, was still only thirty-eight years of age. But Otto was no mere knight-errant. Adelaide had the added attractions that she was a descendant of Charlemagne, queen of Italy in her own right and sister of the king of Burgundy. She was a splendid bride to win, and his marriage with her would be a step to the ultimate goal of his ambition—Rome and the imperial crown.

Otto's first Italian expedition

So in 951 without opposition he entered, as of right, into Pavia, the capital of the Italian kingdom. He sent his brother Henry as escort for Adelaide, who had escaped from her prison, and the marriage was celebrated immediately. But his other object was not to be attained on this occasion. He sent an embassy to Pope Agapetus, who would himself

have been prepared to crown Otto Emperor.   But his master,
Alberic, would have none of it, and Agapetus was compelled
to send a refusal.   This unwelcome rebuff had to be endured,
for out of this Italian expedition had arisen serious domestic
discord, and Otto had to return to Germany early in 952
to deal with it.   Five months was the extent of his first stay
in Italy.

The discord which now broke out within the royal family
divided Germany into two camps, and the effect of it lasted
beyond the reign of Otto I.   On the one side was the duke
of Bavaria, whose ambition caused as much trouble when he
supported the royal authority as when previously he had
revolted against it.   Opposed to him was his nephew Liudolf,
duke of Suabia, with whom Conrad of Lorraine was soon to
be associated.   There were many causes of ill-feeling, of
which rivalry in Italy was the first.   The duchies of Suabia
and Bavaria were both adjacent to Italy, and their dukes
looked to aggrandise themselves in that direction.   Both of
them had made an expedition to Italy just before Otto's,
but while Henry had been successful at Aquileia, Liudolf
had failed miserably ; and he attributed his failure to Henry's
treachery in revealing his plans.   Also, while Henry had
won the friendship of Adelaide, Liudolf was resentful and
suspicious of the marriage and the possibility of a half-
brother supplanting him.   He hastily left Pavia, and retired
in sulky rage to Suabia.

Conrad of Lorraine was no more pleased than Liudolf at
the marked favour shown by both Otto and Adelaide to
Henry.   And he soon had a grievance of his own.   He was
left in Italy to reduce Berengar II to submission.   In this
he was successful, and he brought Berengar to Germany.
But he seems to have promised his captive more honourable
terms than Otto intended, and to have been coldly received
in consequence.   Berengar eventually did homage for his
kingdom, but the marks of Verona and Aquileia were taken
from him and attached to the duchy of Bavaria.   So, once
again, Henry was the chief gainer.   The offended dukes soon
got into touch, and they were joined by archbishop Frederick
of Mayence, who was also aggrieved by Otto's attitude to
him ; he had been the unsuccessful ambassador to Rome,

Feud of the dukes of Suabia and Lorraine with the duke of Bavaria and he had seen Bruno, Otto's brother, preferred to himself for the dignified post of arch-chancellor of Italy. In 953 Germany was once more in the throes of civil war.

Civil war in Germany

Of the ill-temper of the conspirators Otto must have been aware, but he obviously had no idea that it would provoke them to rebellion. He went to Mayence to bring them to reason, and found himself instead in their power; they showed the greatest animosity against Henry, and they forced humiliating conditions upon the king. These, extracted by force, he immediately repudiated on his return to Saxony. Certainly, the odds seemed to be with him. He was opposed by two dukes only. Henry of Bavaria was obviously on his side, and the duchies of Franconia and Saxony were in his own control. But he soon found himself faced with the most serious crisis of his life. For the old tribal particularism flared out once more, kindled by civil war, though it now took a new direction. It was no longer the sentiment supporting the dukes against the king; rather, it found expression in hostility to the strangers Otto had appointed as dukes. This is most evident in Bavaria, where Henry was as unpopular as elsewhere; under his brother-in-law, the count-palatine Arnulf, this duchy formed one of the chief centres of revolt. Lorraine was loyal to the king, in opposition to its duke Conrad; but Conrad was powerful in his native Franconia. As an exception to this, Liudolf had the allegiance of most of Suabia, partly, perhaps, on his wife's account. Even in Saxony there were some defections, and though Herman Billung was able to deal satisfactorily with these, the king's resources were thereby weakened. Otto could certainly count on support from the Church in general, especially in Lorraine; and elsewhere too, for Udalric, bishop of Augsburg in eastern Suabia on the borders of Bavaria, was largely instrumental in preventing the union of all South Germany against the king.

The course of events in 953 was most unfavourable for Otto. He failed to take the two chief centres of revolt, Mayence and Ratisbon, the capital of Bavaria, and retired at the end of the year to Saxony in something like despair. But in 954 fortune came to his aid, as it had done in 939, though in a different and quite unexpected manner. The Magyars, who had been twice defeated by Henry since he took over the duchy of Bavaria, seized the opportunity of civil war in Germany to make a new invasion, and the disunion in Bavaria left their path open into Franconia and Lorraine. Liudolf and Conrad welcomed the invaders, and supplied them with guides; they hoped with their aid to crush the royalist supporters in western Germany. But the event fell very differently from their expectation. Their allies contented themselves with their usual plundering, and this treacherous bargain with the national enemy proved the undoing of the two dukes. Their cause was everywhere discredited. Meanwhile, Otto was able to defeat the Bavarian rebels, who had been thrown into confusion by the Magyar invasion. Conrad and Frederick of Mayence came at once **Submission** to make submission; Liudolf later and more reluctantly, **of the rebels** when he found that he had no other recourse. They were all pardoned and restored to the king's favour, but the two dukes were not re-instated in their duchies. Suabia was given to a local count, Burchard, who by marrying Hedwig, daughter of Henry of Bavaria, was attached more closely to the royal house. Lorraine was entrusted to Otto's brother Bruno, now archbishop of Cologne, who divided it into two parts for the purpose of administration, a division which was later to become permanent.

Otto's victory was only just in time. For in 955 the **Defeat of the** Magyars, misled by their success of the previous year, put **Magyars on** their whole might into a new invasion on a greater scale. **the Lechfeld (955)** They had overrun Bavaria and arrived at Augsburg, which was stoutly defended by bishop Udalric, before Otto was able to assemble his forces against them. Strategically, he had them at a great disadvantage. With the river Lech at their backs they were unable to employ their favourite tactics; they could not use their rapidity of movement to avoid the hand-to-hand fighting in which they were outweighted. Moreover, for the first time Germany under its king was united to confront the Magyar peril. Lorraine could not send troops in time, and Saxony could spare only a few detachments, as the disturbances in Germany had encouraged the Slavs to revolt. But Bavaria and Suabia were well represented, and the Bohemians were present in force; while at the last moment Conrad arrived with a strong body of Franconians. His prowess played a large part in the great

victory that was won on the banks of the Lech, and by his
death in battle against the Magyars he made final atonement
for his former treachery. The enemy were defeated with
great slaughter, and those that escaped were killed or taken
captive in the pursuit that followed.

Effects of Otto's victory
The battle on the Lechfeld was one of the decisive events
in history, greater even in its results than the victory of
Charles Martel over the Moors, to which contemporaries
compared it. The consequences show that the Magyars had
expended all their strength in this, their last invasion. They
had now to live as best they could on their own, and they
were forced to settle down and abandon their marauding
practices; the career of Hungary as a civilised State begins
from this date. To the West the relief was enormous; the
hand of the destroyer was stayed, and the inhabitants of
Germany, France, Burgundy, and Italy could lift their heads
again and renew their material, mental, and spiritual well-
being. Population, wealth, culture, religion, all began to
expand. Security, as in the days of Charlemagne, meant
progress in civilised life. Otto had rendered a great service
to European civilisation, and from this victory dates his
title of " the Great." The embassies that came to him from
the Eastern Emperor, from the Moslems, from Russia and
elsewhere, show the extent of his fame and the universal
respect in which he was held.

His new scheme of government
And nowhere was this more true than in his own kingdom. The defeat of the Slavs followed the rout of the
Magyars, and in the remaining years of his reign—and one
half of it was still to run—he had no more trouble in Germany.
He had therefore the leisure to spend in the work of reorganisation. His former solution of the problem of local government—to make the duchies appanages of the royal house—
The duchies had not been successful, and there were no longer any
lay members of his house to utilise in this way. Conrad
was dead, and his wife Liutgarde had died in 953. Henry
of Bavaria, who had been too ill to take part in the battle
on the Lechfeld, died that same year. Liudolf was sent to
Italy in 956 to reduce the ever-rebellious Berengar II and
Adalbert to order, and accomplished his task with brilliant
success; but he succumbed to fever in 957 before he could
return home. The next generation were all children—

Otto II, born to Otto I and Adelaide in the year of victory
(955), after two previous sons had died in infancy ; Otto,
the son of Liudolf and Ida ; a third Otto, the son of Conrad
and Liutgarde ; and finally Henry, son of Henry of Bavaria.
So Otto had to revert to the old system in a modified form.
In Suabia he had appointed a local count, Burchard, and the
same thing was done under Bruno's administration in Upper
and Lower Lorraine.   It amounted almost to the same in
Bavaria too.   Henry was succeeded by his son Henry, who
was to prove as great a source of trouble to the kingdom as
his father, and well-earned his nickname of " the Wrangler."
But in 955 he was only four years old ; the government of
the duchy was in the hands of his mother Judith, and as the
daughter of duke Arnulf she could rely on the loyalty of the
local nobles who had been so hostile to her husband.   So
the dukes were chosen from the tribe once more, but they were
not, as before, chosen by the tribe.   Otto had at any rate
established the fact that their appointment rested with him
and that they were his officials.   This was only a limited
success, and did not solve the problem of the duchies.   The
office, like that of count, tended soon to become hereditary
(it always was so in Saxony), and the value of the king's right
of appointment was thereby discounted.

The centrifugal tendency had gone far, and some check _Check on_
on the independence of the local magnates was necessary. _ducal_
It has commonly been held that Otto I designed the counts- _authority_
palatine (_pfalzgrafen_) to act in this capacity.   Under Charle- _not provided_
magne they were the king's justices ; sometimes they were _by counts-_
appointed as _missi_, but essentially they were Court officials. _palatine_
From the late tenth century onwards they re-appear in
Germany as local officials, one in each of the duchies.   One of
them retains something of his former character—the count-
palatine of the Franks.   His sphere was not Franconia but
the other Frankish duchy, Lorraine, and his seat was at Aix,
the centre of Court life in Charlemagne's day.   Soon he came
to be known as count-palatine of Lorraine, and later as count-
palatine of the Rhine.   He was always one of the great
officials of the kingdom, supreme after the king in justice,
and frequently acting as regent during the royal absence in
Italy.   East of the Rhine, however—in Bavaria, Saxony,
Suabia, and (later) Carinthia—the counts-palatine were little

different from other counts, save in the precedence their title gave them. In theory they were the representatives of royal authority, possibly as judges, certainly as stewards for the royal manors ; as such, they might have been instituted as a useful check on ducal independence. All that Otto I actually did was to appoint Arnulf as count-palatine of Bavaria. But Arnulf was a member of the ducal house of Bavaria, with which his office was always to be associated, and he was actually the leader of the revolt of 953. From this one unsatisfactory appointment it is not safe to deduce that Otto was initiating a new policy, however wise such a policy might appear to be. Otto was, after all, a child of his age. His ambition was to revive the Empire of Charlemagne, but he made no attempt to restore the strong centralised Carolingian State. Obviously a radical reconstruction of the administration was needed. He was content to make himself as powerful as existing conditions and ideas allowed him to be ; and that he certainly achieved.

Otto's reliance on the bishops

But there was one method which he could employ in accordance with tradition, and this he was to use with very good effect. We have seen already that the German Church was naturally on the side of the king and against the dukes, and that it had come out into the open in 916 with a condemnation of the opponents of the king as traitors. This natural alliance, mistrusted by Henry I, was immediately resumed by Otto I at his coronation. The effect of the alliance, skilfully exploited by Otto, was to give the king definite spheres of influence within the duchies. Especially did it give him control over the urban centres. For every bishop, in accordance with canon law, had his seat in a town and there was a bishop in every important town in Germany. The royal authority in the town and its adjacent countryside was delegated to the bishop, who was given comital powers. So we find that in the earliest royal charters to towns in Germany the grant is actually made to the bishop as governor of the town ; not until the second half of the eleventh century is a commune recognised as self-governing. The bishops, then, are royal officials (as in a lesser degree they had already been under Charlemagne), and so can be used as a counterpoise to the dukes and counts. And as the king imposed secular duties upon them, he also enriched them with lands. The leading (royal) abbeys were similarly enriched. Grants to the Church were the usual feature of royal charters, and these were made as much from self-interest as from motives of piety. Moreover, an ecclesiastical office could not become hereditary ; during a vacancy the temporalities were resumed by the king, and re-granted by him to the new bishop or abbot.

Since the king put so much power into the hands of the bishops, it was essential for him to maintain his control over them, and especially over their appointment. Here again Otto was only following tradition, for the Frankish kings had always so controlled appointments. From the clerks of the royal chapel, as in Charlemagne's day, the episcopate was largely staffed. Trained under his eye, experienced often in the business of his chancery, the king could rely on their loyalty and capacity. The canonical rules for episcopal elections were easily circumvented, and the normal procedure illustrates how effectively the king's control was exercised. First of all, it was customary for the electing body (at present ill-defined as " the clergy and the people ") to obtain the king's consent to an election. At this point the king usually intimated whom he wished to be elected, but in any case it rested with him to ratify or to refuse consent to the canonical election which followed. The bishop-elect did homage and took the oath of fealty to the king, who invested him with the temporalities of the see (his lands, his secular office and other privileges) ; and only after the bishop had thus become the king's man did the ecclesiastical consecration take place. The bishops, therefore, were usually royal nominees, at any rate acceptable to him and bound to his person. In the highest posts Otto I eventually followed the same policy that he had adopted with the duchies, of filling them with members of his own family. In 953 his brother Bruno was made archbishop of Cologne ; in 954 his illegitimate son William succeeded the rebellious Frederick as archbishop of Mayence ; and in 956 his cousin Henry became archbishop of Trèves, in succession to Otto's uncle Robert.

His control of appointments

Being satisfied as to the personnel, Otto could safely add to the authority and domains of the bishops, and use them as a check on the power of the lay nobles. But what he thus

The ultimate ill-effects of the system

effected was a temporary expedient and not a remedy; instead of building the monarchy on a secure constitutional foundation, he buttressed it up with ecclesiastical support. It was, therefore, dependent upon the continuance of this support. The Church was also in a hazardous situation. Wealth and power were in themselves demoralising, and the ecclesiastical duties of the bishop ultimately became subordinate to his secular functions. Lay patronage extended to monasteries and to the lower clergy as well, and the Church suffered from an increasing secularisation. The evil effects of this were to lead to the great attack on lay control in the eleventh century. The king clung to it, because it was necessary to him as a means of government. But the attack succeeded, and as a result royal authority was fatally impaired.

Its immediate advantages

These were the ultimate results of Otto's policy, but in his own lifetime it was the advantages that predominated, for the Church as well as for the king. The Church was given the means to spread its influence and the opportunity to cure its own ailments. Aided by Otto himself, to whom the health of the Church was of obvious moment, the reform of the monasteries was undertaken, especially through the influence of his brother Bruno in Lorraine. Otto, too, had conferred by his victories the priceless boon of peace, which made possible the renewal of education and learning ; here again Bruno played a leading part. The advantages to Otto himself were not confined to the assistance given to him by the clergy in the central and local government of the kingdom. In the eastward expansion of Saxony the Church made a most important contribution. Conversion went hand in hand with colonisation as a means of settling the conquered country. The clergy were richly rewarded with lands and tithes in the newly-won territory, and a feature of the movement was the foundation of new bishoprics at Brandenburg, Merseburg, Meissen, and elsewhere. Above all, Otto had set his heart on the formation of a new ecclesiastical province to embrace the area which had thus been added to Germany, and in 967 he obtained the papal authorisation for the creation of the archbishopric of Magdeburg. The archbishop of Mayence, Otto's son William, stoutly resisted this curtailment of his own province, but on his death in 968 the plan

was carried into effect. The missionary character of the
German Church was enhanced by the formation of an essentially missionary archbishopric. Mayence had some compensation in the advance of Christianity among the southern
Slavs, which led to the foundation of the bishoprics of Prague
in Bohemia and Olmütz in Moravia. Both of these came
within the metropolitan jurisdiction of Mayence, and so
remained until the elevation of Prague into an archbishopric
in the fourteenth century.

CHAPTER II

THE EMPIRE OF THE OTTOS

Otto I's
second
expedition
to Italy

PEACE and reconstruction were the features of the second half of Otto's reign in Germany. The security of his position made it possible for him to turn his eyes to Italy again, and once more the violence of Berengar II and his son Adalbert provoked an appeal to him for aid. This time the appeal came from the Pope himself, John XII; the path to Rome was now open, and the goal of Otto's ambition—the imperial crown—awaited him there.

The appeal came in 960, and there could be no doubt as to his response. But first measures must be taken for the security of his kingdom. To ensure the succession, Otto II was elected and anointed king, and placed under the guardianship of the archbishops of Mayence and Cologne; the northeastern frontier remained under Herman's charge. Then in the latter part of 961 the journey to Rome began. On 2 February 962 Otto was crowned Emperor by the Pope and his wife, Adelaide, Empress. Before entering Rome Otto had sworn to protect the Pope's rights and to preserve the privileges of the city, and had confirmed and enlarged the donations of Pepin and Charlemagne. In return, the privilege of Pope Eugenius II to Lothar I—the right of the Emperor to confirm the election of a Pope—was revived in his favour.

His coronation as
Emperor
(962)

The Empire
of Otto the
Great compared with
that of
Charlemagne

Thus Otto had fulfilled his purpose. The coronation at Aix, the control of Lorraine, the suzerainty over Burgundy, the kingship of Italy, the victory won over the heathen enemies of Europe, had all been stages on the path he trod in the footsteps of Charlemagne which brought him, unchallenged, to the imperial throne. Otto may be regarded as the creator of the Empire which was known to the Middle Ages. For Charlemagne's had broken into fragments a century before, and Otto's was really a new creation, not a revival as he and his contemporaries conceived it. It was quite different

46

in character from the old, it was incomplete and incoherent ; the glamour of Empire remained, but much of the reality was gone.

Empire implied universality, and Charlemagne had been ruler of almost all of Christian Europe. This could not be said of Otto, for the important kingdom of the West Franks lay outside his control. Still less was it true of his successors a century later, when England became an important power and the Christian kingdoms of Spain were rapidly expanding. The Emperor was not ruler of the West but only the chief among Western rulers. His Empire was confined to the three kingdoms of Germany, Italy, and Burgundy.[1] There was some compensation in the expansion of Germany eastward beyond the limits of Charlemagne's Empire. This also made more evident, what had been true even in the time of Charlemagne, that the Empire was Germanic rather than Roman.

Empire also implied an autocratic Emperor, and this, with certain limitations, had been fulfilled in the person of Charlemagne. It was far otherwise with Otto and his successors. Feudal, centrifugal forces had upset the centralised system of Charlemagne. The difficulties of the king were the same in Italy as in Germany, and were met by Otto in much the same way. The greater nobles—marquises, who ruled over several counties—were placated by conciliatory methods, but again chief reliance was placed upon the bishops. In Italy the cities had always had a peculiar importance, and the bishop's authority over his city dated from Roman times. They were, therefore, more valuable allies even than the German bishops. As in Germany, Otto added to their territorial authority and possessions, and used them as a check on the lay nobles ; at the same time he kept a careful control over elections. He thus acquired powerful adherents, especially in Lombardy, and in this way ensured a measure of uniformity in the government of the two kingdoms. *The government of the Italian kingdom*

Fundamentally, however, the two kingdoms were distinct. The source of Otto's power lay in Germany ; in Italy he was a foreigner, and though the Italians were accustomed to foreign rule, they were never constant in allegiance to a *The immediate and the ultimate effects of the union of Italy and Germany*

[1] Otto exercised a suzerainty over Burgundy. It was not, however, part of the empire until the reign of Conrad II.

foreign ruler. There was also the supreme problem of Rome
and the Papacy. The Pope had been Charlemagne's subject,
and it never occurred to Otto that the relations between
himself and the Pope could be otherwise. His successors
could not abandon the precedent which he had followed, with
results ultimately fatal to their authority in both kingdoms.
The immediate effect of the union of the two kingdoms was,
indeed, advantageous to them both. Germany gained from
its contact with a higher civilisation, and the position of its
ruler was enhanced by the prestige of the imperial title.
Italy was freed from the anarchy of the preceding century,
and a period of peace and settled government made possible
the civic and industrial development which was to have so
brilliant a future. The Papacy was released from its subordination to the Roman nobles, and owed to its association
with the Emperor its restoration to its proper sphere. But
while the advantages to Italy and the Papacy were enduring
and became increasingly fruitful, the gain to Germany was
transitory. The constant preoccupation of the Emperors
with Italy, their long absences, the drain on the imperial
resources, the effect of the Italian climate, and, ultimately,
the struggle with the Papacy which ended in their complete
defeat and the triumph of the forces of disintegration in
their own country—this was the legacy of Otto to his successors. Had they concentrated on Germany, they could
have retained the position he had won, and Germany would
have prospered under a régime of strong government. As
it was, she suffered the disaster of a long period of civil war
and disorder, which more than counterbalanced the advantages that she had obtained from contact with Italian
civilisation.

Otto's
contest with
the Roman
nobles for
the control
of the
Papacy

The future was already foreshadowed in Otto I's reign,
during the last twelve years of which Italy commanded
almost all his attention. His presence was constantly needed
to maintain his hold over North Italy and over Rome.
Berengar II was captured at the end of 963 and died three
years later in exile in Germany, but his son Adalbert escaped
and entered into an alliance with the Pope and the Romans.
John XII could not endure to be a subject where his father
Alberic had reigned supreme, and the Roman nobles refused
to acquiesce in the loss of their control over the Papacy. The

struggle that ensued was to decide the rival claims of Emperor and Romans ; it was not a contest between the *imperium* and the *sacerdotium* as in the eleventh century, but the later struggle was essentially affected by the measures which Otto took to ensure his mastery. In November 963 he came to Rome and forced the Romans to swear that they would never elect a Pope without the consent and choice of himself and his son. John had escaped from Rome, and a synod was easily induced to declare him deposed in consequence of his recalcitrance and the notorious scandals of his Papacy. In his place Otto nominated a layman as Pope Leo VIII.

No sooner had Otto left Rome, early in 964, than John XII was reinstated and Leo VIII expelled. John died in May, and the Romans tried to improve their position by electing a man of learning and high character, Benedict V. Otto immediately returned, restored Leo, and sent Benedict into exile in Germany, whither he went himself at the end of 964. During his absence Leo VIII died, and the Romans, obedient to Otto's command, elected John XIII ; but they almost immediately rose against him, and only the news of Otto's third expedition to Italy in 966 caused them hastily to restore him again. Their tardy repentance did not avert the wrath of Otto, who this time meted out severe punishment to the ring-leaders of the revolt. His drastic action was effective, and when John XIII died in 972 there was no opposition to the imperial nominee, Benedict VI. Henceforward Otto was master, and his dominance over the Papacy was unconcealed ; it extended even to the Papal States, in spite of the Emperor's oath in 962.

Otto came into Italy in 966 partly to make a final settle- His policy in ment of the Roman question, partly to deal with Adalbert, South Italy who had allied himself with the Eastern Emperor, Nicephorus Phocas. Perhaps it was this that turned his attention to South Italy. At any rate his ambition was now extended to the conquest of the whole peninsula. In January 967 he gained the valuable allegiance of the ruler of Capua and Benevento, Pandulf Ironhead, whom he created marquis of Salerno, and so became suzerain of the old Lombard duchies which had formerly recognised the suzerainty of Charlemagne. This brought him into contact with the Byzantine power in Apulia and Calabria. At first he negotiated, like Charle-magne, for a Byzantine bride for his son Otto II, who was

Otto II
crowned co-
Emperor
(967)

crowned co-Emperor by the Pope at Christmas 967. The negotiations failed, and Otto then attempted the conquest of Apulia from the Eastern Emperor, who was embarrassed by Moslem raids and had recently had to submit to the surrender of the whole of Sicily. An early victory was followed by failure to capture Bari, and though Otto gained some further success he lost the aid of Pandulf, who was taken prisoner by the Byzantines. The murder of the Emperor Nicephorus in December 969 brought this indecisive warfare to an end. His successor, John Tzimisces, was wholly occupied in the East, and consented to come to terms. Otto retained his suzerainty over Capua and Benevento, but abandoned his attack on Byzantine territory. In return, he achieved what had been denied to Charlemagne when in April 972 his son, Otto II, was married at Rome to the Greek princess, Theophano, daughter of Romanus II. This completed his task in Italy, and in August he returned to Germany, from which he had been absent for six years. He had only a few months to live, but his work was done, and his fame was world-wide. From all lands, even from the Moslems in Africa, embassies came to Germany to do him honour. This universal recognition was a fitting ending to the great reign which closed on the 7 May 973. His chief associates had preceded him to the grave—his brother, Bruno, in 965, his son, William, in 968, and the faithful Saxons, Gero in 965 and Herman in the same year as his master. The destinies of the Empire lay in the hands of young men, as yet untried, ambitious but lacking in the statesmanship and the devotion of the generation that had passed away.

Marriage of
Otto II
with the
Byzantine
princess,
Theophano
(972)

Death of
Otto the
Great

Otto II
(973–83)

The new ruler was barely eighteen years of age. Small, sturdy, and of a ruddy complexion which caused him to be known as " the Red," he was filled with pride in his exalted position and self-confidence in his capacity to maintain it. He soon found that, as was usual, the accession of a new ruler gave the signal for the outbreak of disturbances; though not so serious as those with which his father had been faced when he came to the throne, they were sufficiently troublesome to keep him occupied with German affairs for seven years, and unable to turn his attention to his more attractive kingdom of Italy.

The chief danger came from his ambitious cousin, duke The diffi-
Henry II (the Wrangler) of Bavaria. Henry had a powerful culties of
Otto II's
friend in the king's mother, Adelaide, who continued to the early years
son the favour she had shown to the father, dating from her (1) The
marriage with Otto I and the rebellion of Liudolf and Conrad. revolt of
Otto II, for his part, showed a special tenderness for his two duke Henry
of Bavaria
namesakes, the sons of those two former enemies of his
mother. When duke Burchard of Suabia died in 973, he
gave to Liudolf's son the duchy which had once been Liudolf's.
This was doubly distasteful to Henry, for besides his dislike
of the new duke, the two duchies had previously been closely
united owing to the marriage of Burchard with Henry's
sister, Hedwig. To restore his influence in the kingdom, and
possibly with the ultimate object of winning the crown for
himself, he formed an alliance with his Slav neighbours, the
dukes of Bohemia and Poland. This was a serious matter for
the king, since Bohemia was a vassal state, and German
influence was spreading in both countries as the result of their
Christianisation by German missionaries ; it was about this
time that the bishopric of Prague was founded in Bohemia,
and also the bishopric of Posen in Poland. They were entering into the orbit of Western civilisation, and it was necessary
for the ruler of Germany that these border states should be
subordinate to himself. Otto took immediate action. He
summoned Henry to the royal court and kept him a prisoner
at Ingelheim.

At the same time there was a threat to Otto's authority (2) The
French king
on the western frontier. Lorraine, composed, as we have and
seen, of a number of ill-co-ordinated parts, and divided for Lorraine
the purposes of administration into two duchies, always
required a considerable amount of attention from the king
himself. A rising in Hainault of the sons of a rebellious
count Reginar, who had been dispossessed in 959, needed the
presence of Otto II to suppress it in 974. Also the death
in 969 of his aunt Gerberga, the mother of king Lothar of
France, had made a considerable difference to the security
of Lorraine. Lothar was seeking an opportunity to revive
the claims of his predecessors, and though he made no actual
move until 978 he was constantly giving secret encouragement to the disaffected elements in Lorraine.

More immediately dangerous was an invasion of Saxony (3) Denmark in 974 by the king of Denmark, Harold Bluetooth. Here again Otto had to take the field in person. He was completely successful in defeating Harold and in forcing him to become his tributary. To ensure the frontier, the Danish Mark was further protected by the building of castles.

Protracted contest with Henry of Bavaria and his allies The settlement of the south-east was a much more protracted business. Henry escaped from captivity in 976, and started a fresh revolt in Bavaria. The Church issued its ban against the rebel, local resistance was organised by the Babenberg brothers, Berthold of the Nordgau and Liutpold, and when Otto himself appeared with an army Henry was forced to take refuge in Bohemia. His duchy was declared forfeit, and was handed over to Otto, duke of Suabia. But it was first reduced in size and importance. Berthold was made independent of ducal authority in the Nordgau, and so was Liutpold, who was made margrave of the East Mark (later to be the duchy of Austria); thus was founded the future greatness of the Babenberg family. Finally, a new duchy of Carinthia was created out of the marks of Carinthia and Verona, and was assigned to Henry (known as " Henry the Younger "), the son of a former duke of Bavaria, Berthold.

The dispossessed duke, however, was back in Bavaria the following year. He was joined by his cousin, bishop Henry of Augsburg, and even by the new duke of Carinthia in what was termed " the war of the three Henries." Otto had little difficulty in crushing this fresh outbreak ; the three Henries surrendered at Easter 978 to the king at Magdeburg and were placed under close confinement. Henry of Carinthia also lost his duchy, which was given to Otto, the son of Conrad the Red. Thus the southern duchies were held for Otto by his two namesakes, and Otto I's family policy was in this way revived. Moreover, after several failures, Otto was at last able to reduce the duke of Bohemia, Boleslav II, to submission, and received his homage at the same time at Magdeburg ; the next year Duke Mesco of Poland also submitted. The settlement of the south-east was now completed, and peace was finally restored.

Invasion of Lorraine by the French king and counter-invasion of France by Otto Only in Lorraine was the situation still uncertain, and thither Otto hurried immediately after the surrenders at Magdeburg. He had in the previous year appointed Charles, the brother of king Lothar of France, as duke of Lower

Lorraine, which had the effect of dividing the French ranks
and also of reconciling those elements in the duchy that still
regarded a descendant of Charlemagne as their rightful ruler.
Lothar was naturally alarmed and irritated, and he decided
on a bold coup, which, if successful, would have put him
more on terms of equality with his own powerful vassal, Hugh
Capet. Making a skilful use of the element of surprise, he
suddenly invaded Lower Lorraine, and captured Aix-la-
Chapelle, from which Otto barely managed to escape. But
he had not the resources, nor did he gain the assistance,
necessary to make good this early success, and after sacking
the royal palace he returned to France. Otto retaliated as
soon as he could collect a large army, and swept through
France to the very gates of Paris. Here he met a more
formidable foe in Hugh Capet, before whom he had to retreat,
suffering severe losses on his march back into Germany.
Feeble as was his generalship, however, he gained his chief
purpose, for Lothar came to a meeting with him in 980 on
the frontier between the two kingdoms and solemnly renounced his claims to Lorraine. To ensure the permanence
of this renunciation, Otto entered into negotiations with Hugh
Capet ; but his early death prevented this from becoming a
regular alliance.

The year 980 marks the zenith of Otto II's power. Ger- The
situation in
Italy
many was secure on all its frontiers, and he had at last a
son to succeed him, for Otto III was born this same year.
It was at least desirable that he should display his authority
in Italy. Thither, too, he was drawn by his own inclinations,
and was further fired with the ambition of succeeding where
his father had failed, by uniting the whole of Italy under his
government. The condition of affairs in South Italy encouraged this expectation. After John Tzimisces' death in 976,
the Eastern Empire had been a prey to civil war and disorder, so that little attention could be paid to its Italian
territories, and its forces were insufficient to prevent the
Moslems from raiding and plundering both in Apulia and
Calabria. The weakness of the Greeks gave Otto the opportunity, and the danger from the Moslems gave him the
excuse, to intervene himself in South Italy.

Leaving archbishop Willigis of Mayence, duke Bernard Otto's
expedition
of Saxony (the son of Herman Billung), and duke Charles of to Italy

Lower Lorraine as regents of Germany in his absence, Otto
at the end of 980 commenced the journey to Italy from which
he was never to return. He first came to the old Lombard
capital of Pavia, and there was reconciled with his mother
Adelaide, who had been so much opposed to his Bavarian
policy that she had been living in retirement at the court of
her brother, Conrad of Burgundy. From Pavia he went to
Rome, and so far all was plain sailing. But he found Pandulf
dead and his territories divided among various usurpers. He
could not expel those who had seized control of the different
parts ; he recovered his suzerainty, but only at the price of
recognising the intruders.

This was a bad beginning for Otto, who expected the
Greeks also to accept his suzerainty and to join him in the
conquest of the Moslems. They despised him as a barbarian,
and were not impressed by his display of authority. So he
wasted time and strength in trying to force them to submission, the only result of which was the capture of Taranto in
982. Then the arrival of the Moslems in force engaged his
whole attention. Allied with the Greeks he would probably
have been successful, for they could have supplied the
military science in which he was so lamentably deficient, as
he had already shown in his French campaign. As it was,
he trusted to the weight of his cavalry, which was indeed
effective at the first onset ; but as he had neglected to discover
the enemy's dispositions, he was overwhelmed by a simultaneous attack on both flanks which involved his army in complete
disaster. Otto himself, after hairbreadth escapes from
capture first by the Moslems and then by the Greeks, managed
to draw off the remnant of his troops to the north, but he had
lost the best part of them, and his most important lieutenant,
duke Otto of Suabia and Bavaria, died during the retreat.
That his Italian kingdom remained secure was due to the
loyalty of the marquises and bishops to the imperial authority
—a testimony to the constructive work of his father.

Whatever his defects as a general, Otto was certainly not
lacking in courage and determination. He set to work at
once to prepare an expedition for the following year. At a
diet at Verona, at which he arranged for the raising of troops,
he also obtained the election of Otto III as king and settled
the succession to the duchies of Suabia and Bavaria left

**His defeat
by the
Moslems
(982)**

**His plan of
a second
expedition
frustrated by
his death**

vacant by duke Otto's death. Suabia was given to a Franconian count, Conrad, nephew of a former duke, Herman. To Bavaria Henry the Younger was appointed, and at the same time he recovered his old duchy of Carinthia ; the existing duke, Otto, was simply dispossessed. Probably the entire reversal of policy evinced in these appointments was due to the revived influence of Adelaide. At the same time Otto II was opening negotiations with the Venetians, whose fleet would have been invaluable to him against the Moslems ; but again he coveted suzerainty rather than alliance and had to try to subdue them by force. This and all his other schemes were brought to a sudden end by his death on 7 December 983. He was buried at Rome in St. Peter's, unique at any rate among the Emperors in this. Italy had already ruined the prestige which he had won in Germany, and now its climate, as so often, proved fatal to its foreign master and made an end of all prospect of uniting the whole peninsula under the imperial crown.

Nor was this all. The tidings of imperial disaster spread like wildfire among the heathen races subject to Germany and spurred them to throw off the yoke. First there was an invasion of the Danes under Svein Forkbeard, who over-ran the Danish Mark and destroyed the castles built by Otto in 974. Svein had deposed his father, Harold Bluetooth, whose zeal for Christianity had provoked a heathen reaction, and he now avenged his father's defeat and Denmark ceased to be tributary to Germany. But far more serious was the uprising of the Slavs between the Elbe and the Oder. The patient work of colonisation, the long missionary effort, were alike undone. Churches were burnt, the new episcopal towns of Brandenburg, Havelberg, and Zeitz were destroyed, even Hamburg was plundered ; all Otto I's ecclesiastical organisa-tion was ruined. Though we read in the chroniclers of striking victories won by Saxon nobles and bishops, and though the bishoprics were re-created, the province east of the Elbe was virtually lost to Germany for more than a century. Not until the twelfth century, when a duke of Saxony was again king of Germany, was this province finally re-won. The disaster must have reached Otto's ears, for it prevented duke Bernard of Saxony from being present at the diet of Verona. But Italy now had the first place in the

The revolt of the northern Slavs

imperial mind, and the local nobles were left to retrieve the situation as best they could.

Otto III (983–1002)

As the German nobles had already elected Otto III as king, there was no dispute as to the succession. But it was an added complication that in circumstances which required a strong ruler the king was an infant of three years old. A regent had to be provided for a long minority, and this gave additional opportunity for individual ambition. In other respects the situation was not unlike that at the accession of Otto II. The chief danger came from Bavaria, supported by the Slav peoples on the eastern frontiers, who had their recent success to encourage them; while on the western frontier French hopes for Lorraine were again excited. The villain of the piece was, as before, Henry the Wrangler. As the next of kin he could claim the right to protect the infant king and to rule in his name, and perhaps it was their loyalty to the dynasty and their desire for a strong central government that caused so many of the leading bishops to support him at the outset. When by a sudden coup he got possession of the person of the young king, who had just been crowned at Aix-la-Chapelle, the prospect seemed so bright that his ambition looked beyond the regency to the throne itself. He again had the support of Bohemia, and was allied with some of the northern Slavs as well. But this very fact united Saxony against him, and the leading nobles in Suabia, Franconia, and Lorraine soon showed themselves to be equally hostile. Their resistance was solidified under the lead of archbishop Willigis of Mayence. And when at their invitation Adelaide and Theophano returned from Italy, Henry realised that the opposition was too strong for him and came to terms at a diet at Rara in 984. The possession of Otto gave him the power to bargain, so that, while he surrendered Otto to his mother and with him the regency, he was himself reinstated in the duchy of Bavaria. Henry the Younger had perforce to be content again with Carinthia, which on his death in 989 was reunited to Bavaria. For the rest of his life Henry the Wrangler seems to have remained quiescent, if not a help, at any rate not a danger to the government. When he, too, died in 995, he was succeeded by his son Henry, who showed himself, in strong contrast to his father and

The attempt of Henry of Bavaria to gain control of the government

grandfather, to be of a peaceful disposition and a loyal subject.

Formally a regency was not created. Otto was officially regarded as the actual ruler, and public acts were signed as by the king himself. In practice, therefore, those who had the care of the king had the care of the kingdom also. At first the responsibility was shared by Adelaide and Theophano, but this only lasted for a year. Adelaide lost her influence, as she had in the preceding reign, and Theophano remained in sole charge until her death in 991, " consors imperii " as the diplomas describe her. From the diplomas, too, it is clear that she was assisted in the direction of affairs by archbishop Willigis of Mayence and bishop Hildibald of Worms, the German chancellor. But in Italy, which had a separate chancery, she acted on her own responsibility as Empress. Here she was exercising an imperial authority to which her Byzantine upbringing had accustomed her ; in Germany she was content to maintain herself by the traditional reliance on ecclesiastical support.

Theophano as guardian of the young king (983–91)

As ruler of Germany, she undoubtedly acquitted herself well. She kept the country free from internal strife, and was able to maintain both the eastern and the western frontiers of the kingdom. The more immediate danger was in the west, where king Lothar of France revived his claim to Lorraine and captured Verdun in 984. But the Lothringian nobles showed themselves hostile to his ambition, and Beatrice, the widow of duke Frederick of Upper Lorraine, obtained the co-operation of her brother, Hugh Capet, which made Lothar's retirement inevitable. He died in 986, and his young son, Louis V, a year later. The election of Hugh Capet as king in 987 altered the whole situation, and relieved the German government of any further fear of Carolingian claims to Lorraine.

Her able conduct of the government

On the eastern frontier, the reconciliation with Henry the Wrangler had not included his allies. There was constant fighting in the district recently re-won by the northern Slav tribes, who were assisted by the Bohemians. Duke Mesco of Poland, on the other hand, was faithful to the allegiance he had promised to Otto II and supported the German cause, doubtless owing to the persistent enmity between Poland and Bohemia. In later history, this enmity remained, but it was

Bohemia that was faithful to Germany and Poland that asserted its independence. The only result of this desultory warfare was the reconstitution of the mark of Meissen, so that on the whole the German government rather more than held its ground.

Adelaide as guardian (991-4)
When Theophano died in 991, Adelaide took her place as guardian of the king. She had not the vigour or the resolution of her daughter-in-law, and a weakness is apparent in the German government which encouraged the Danes to make an inroad in 991, and to repeat it on a larger scale in 994 when they took captive a number of Saxon nobles. Fighting continued incessantly with the Slavs between the Elbe and the Oder until Otto patched up a truce in 995, which enabled him to leave Germany in comparative security while he embarked on his first expedition to Italy.

The early training of Otto III
For in 994, having reached the age of fourteen, he had passed out of wardship and become the actual ruler of the kingdom. His eager mind chafed at the petty business of fighting barbarians on the frontier, and was impatient to be in Rome and to wear the imperial crown. His mother had rendered a great service to Germany by her skilful management of its government, but she had moulded the mind of her son in a direction quite contrary to its interests. The two men who had been entrusted with his early training had inspired him with his imperial mission—the German Bernward, bishop of Hildesheim, who was perhaps responsible for his hero-worship of Charlemagne, and the Greek John Philagathus, abbot of Nonantula, who taught him also a contempt for his native Saxony ; so that he regarded Italy, and especially the more cultured south of Italy, as his true home, and looked on the Italian kingdom rather than the German as the more important half of his Empire.

The situation in Italy
Italy, left to herself, had not broken away from Germany. The bishops saw the value of imperial authority and remained loyal to it ; so did the leading magnates, especially Hugh, marquis of Tuscany, who had become marquis of Spoleto as well and, like his father Hubert before him, dominated the centre of Italy. Rome, however, was exceptional in desiring independence. There the house of the Crescentii obtained a position like that of Theophylact and Alberic in the past. Pope John XIV, the Lombard whom Otto II had

The Crescentii in control of Rome and the Papacy

appointed in 982, was deposed in 984, and his successful rival, Boniface VII (who had already appeared as a rival to Benedict VI in 974), caused him to be murdered. Boniface died in 985, and his successor, John XV, was under the thumb of John Crescentius, who took to himself the title of " patricius," a title borne in olden days by the imperial governors of Italy and later by the Frankish rulers after they had delivered Rome from the Lombards. Theophano came to Rome in 989, and asserted her imperial authority, nor was her right to do so disputed ; but she was content to leave Crescentius as " patricius." After her death there was no one to gainsay him, until John XV at last roused himself to appeal to Otto III for help.

The appeal came as opportunely as that of John XII to Otto I in 960, and it gave the young king the excuse to prepare immediately for the journey on which he had set his heart. But hardly had he arrived in Italy at the beginning of 996 when he received the news of John XV's death, and the request that he would nominate a successor. The Romans were frightened by his imposing army and dared not risk another independent election. Otto's choice fell upon Bruno, son of his cousin Otto of Carinthia,[1] the first German to be Pope. The appointment was thus unique, and it was also dangerous. The Romans resented a foreign Pope even more than they did a foreign ruler, and Bruno, who took the name of Gregory V, had neither age nor discretion to recommend him. He was only 24 years old, which may indeed have seemed a ripe age to the sixteen-year-old king. At any rate, Otto, filled with the sense of his imperial mission, was blind to the realities of the position. He came to Rome, where his army was sufficient to force Crescentius to submission, and was crowned Emperor by the Pope. His immediate purpose attained, with an ease that fatally misled him, he returned to Germany to follow the dictates of his romantic imagination.

His objective was Aix-la-Chapelle, the favourite residence of Charlemagne and therefore the place which the new

Otto III's first expedition to Italy

Appointment of his cousin Bruno as Pope

---

[1] This Otto had apparently recovered in 995, on the death of Henry the Wrangler, the duchy of which he had been so unceremoniously dispossessed in 983. Though he was himself treated as a mere pawn in German politics, he has some claim to remembrance, for he was the father of a Pope and the grandfather of Conrad II, the first of the Salian line of German kings.

Emperor delighted to honour, enriching it with presents and endowing the cathedral and also new monasteries of his own foundation. From there he had to go to defend the frontiers of Saxony against the Slavs, with whom, after two short campaigns, he again came to terms. Once more an appeal came to him from Italy, and after another visit to Aix, which received further proofs of his favour, he started upon his second Italian expedition.

Already another influence had come into his life, which quickened his imperial ardour and reinforced the sentiments already implanted in him by his early education. This was Gerbert of Aurillac, whose mathematical knowledge acquired in Spain (and therefore indirectly from the Arabs) had caused him to be brought by Pope John XIII to the notice of Otto I. Later he studied philosophy and became *scholasticus* (master) of the cathedral school at Rheims. His fame as a teacher attracted the attention of Otto II, who made him abbot of Bobbio. Unhappy in his new environment, he returned to Rheims after Otto's death. But he had become an imperial subject, and remained in that allegiance. This he showed by the influence he exerted in Lorraine not only against Henry the Wrangler of Bavaria but also in opposition to the French king. In 987 he played a part in the election of Hugh Capet as king of France, and had his reward when he was appointed archbishop of Rheims in place of the deposed Arnulf. But here the Papacy interposed and insisted on Arnulf's restoration. After Hugh Capet's death Gerbert had to take refuge in Germany, and in 996 was invited to Otto III's court at Aix. He was a man exactly after the young Emperor's heart. He could supply the learning for which Otto craved, he was an ardent imperialist, and he had just that love of Roman antiquity which was working in Otto to transform the character of his imperial vision. The Emperor took Gerbert with him on his Slav expeditions in 997, relieving their tedium by obtaining instruction in philosophy from his new friend. He took him also to Italy, where in 998 he appointed him archbishop of Ravenna.

Otto himself went on to Rome, which had not long remained quiescent after his departure in 996. Crescentius took advantage of a temporary absence of Pope Gregory V from Rome to re-establish his authority over the city and

Side notes:

Otto's second Italian expedition

Gerbert of Aurillac

The revolt of the Crescentii and Otto's retaliation

to set up an anti-Pope, John XVI. This was no other than the Emperor's former tutor, John Philagathus, who was now occupying the see of Piacenza with the rank of archbishop. He had been employed in 994 as ambassador to Constantinople to obtain a Byzantine bride for his master.[1] He was won from his imperial allegiance by the bribe of the Papacy. Crescentius was gambling on the hopes of Byzantine assistance, and Otto's own ambassador was therefore a valuable ally. But Byzantine diplomacy was cautious and preferred to await the event of the contest, which might have been seriously affected by Byzantine intervention but without that intervention could only terminate in one way. Otto came to Rome in 998 and restored Gregory V; Crescentius was executed, John XVI treated with contumely and mutilated. The next year Gregory V died, and Otto appointed Gerbert as Pope. He took the name of Sylvester II, which recalled the traditional association of Sylvester I with Constantine the Great.

Appointment of Gerbert as Pope

It was, indeed, as a Constantine that Otto now viewed himself. In Germany, Charlemagne, who had renewed the Western Empire, was his model; but he wanted to make a more complete renewal—of the old Roman (though also Christian) Empire. " Renovatio imperii Romanorum " figured on his seals, and was the directing motive of the latter part of his reign. Like his father he styled himself *imperator Romanorum* (Otto I had been content with *imperator* alone), and he denied the Eastern Emperor's right to this title. Of such an empire Rome must be the capital. Here he had his palace, on the Aventine, and he lavished affection and honours on " Aurea Roma " and her citizens. The Crescentii he had overthrown, but others of the nobles he exalted with imperial offices, especially Gregory, count of Tusculum, and his son Alberic, who were directly descended from those former rulers of the city, Theophylact and Alberic. For these and others he revived old Roman offices and introduced Byzantine titles as well. He won the adhesion of the Romans while he flattered their pride. The diplomas that proceeded from his chancery reveal the new orientation that had been given to the government. Formerly they had

The " Renovatio imperii Romanorum "

---

[1] This ambition of Otto was eventually realised, but the chosen princess only landed in South Italy in 1002 in time to hear the news of Otto's death.

been issued with the co-operation of archbishop Willigis of Mayence and the German chancellor Hildibald. In place of these appear the Italian chancellor Heribert, Peter bishop of Como, Leo, who now became bishop of Vercelli, marquis Hugh of Tuscany, and, of course, Gerbert. The chancery, too, was no longer divided, for Heribert became German as well as Italian chancellor on Hildibald's death in 998 ; and its headquarters was at Rome, or at any rate in Italy, even though Heribert became archbishop of Cologne in 999.

Its religious aspect   There was another side to all this, for Otto was deeply imbued with the religious aspect of his imperial mission. The picture of the righteous ruler given by St. Augustine in his *City of God* had become a commonplace in men's minds ; Charlemagne himself had tried to live up to it, Like Charlemagne, Otto regarded himself as responsible for the renewal of the spiritual as well as the material well-being of the Empire, and Sylvester II seems to have been content to accept the subordinate position that this view implied. When, in a bull of 1001, Otto styles himself for the first time " servus apostolorum," the reference is obviously to St. Peter and St. Paul, with the implication that he is their representative. In that bull he makes a donation of eight counties in the Pentapolis to the Papacy, but insists that this is an act of imperial grace, not a restitution to the Popes of what had been their own ; he denounces the behaviour of former Popes in this matter, and, ignoring the confirmation of Otto I, condemns Charles the Bald's grant as invalid and denounces the Donation of Constantine as a forgery.

Mystical influences on the young Emperor   The " Renovatio imperii Romanorum," therefore, meant, as well as the Romanisation, the evangelisation of the Western world, and the programme was burdened and complicated by the various religious influences which worked upon the plastic mind of the young Emperor. From three fresh sources did he receive additional inspiration. On his first Italian expedition he had been powerfully attracted by St. Adalbert, who was so enthusiastic about missionary enterprises that he could not be kept in his duties as bishop of Prague ; in 997 he met a martyr's death in Prussia, and his body was taken to Gnesen in Poland for burial. From him Otto acquired a zeal for missionary work, to increase his Christian Empire by conversions. From the ascetic hermits

of South Italy, especially St. Nilus, he acquired a mystic
exaltation finding expression in devotions and penances. A
similar influence was exerted by St. Romuald of Ravenna,
who formed a link between the southern hermits and the
movement of monastic reform north of the Alps. Not only
did Otto deeply admire these zealots; he felt it to be part
of his duty to emulate them.

The fruit of all these enthusiasms, imperial and religious, The imperial pilgrimage in the year 1000
was seen in the long pilgrimage which he undertook in the
year 1000. It was preluded by a penitential journey in 999
to South Italy, where he visited hermitages and monasteries
and imitated the austerities he witnessed; at the same time
he attempted, though with only temporary success, to
establish a suzerainty over Lombard and Byzantine towns
in the south. Then in 1000 he started upon the first part of
the pilgrimage, a visit to the tomb of St. Adalbert at Gnesen.
It was essentially part of the " Renovatio," for he was
accompanied by Roman nobles and cardinals and by a
representative of the Pope, and his purpose was to increase
direct dependence on the Empire and to establish Christianity
everywhere within it. The attachment of the duchy of
Poland to the Empire was denoted by the visit of Otto; and
the Church in Poland was developed and brought into closer
contact with Rome by the formation of an archbishopric at
Gnesen, which made it independent of the German Church.
In Hungary, about the same time, the newly-founded Church
was similarly constituted with the creation of an archbishopric
at Gran; and the ruler of Hungary, Stephen, received a
crown from Rome. To Dalmatia, newly conquered by the
Venetians, was sent a Christian mission, and an embassy
went to Russia, which it was hoped might be won from the
Eastern to the Western Church. A further sign of Otto's
purpose appears in the title he bore in his diplomas throughout
this pilgrimage—" servus Jesu Christi." Thus had St. Paul
described himself in his Epistle to the Romans, and St. Peter
in his Second Epistle. Otto went to Poland as an apostle
as well as an Emperor.

Returning from Poland with relics from the tomb of St.
Adalbert, after a brief visit to Saxony he went on the second
stage of his pilgrimage, to the tomb of Charlemagne at Aix-
la-Chapelle. The tomb was opened that he might gaze on

the body of his hero, whom he then caused to be reverently entombed again. Aix, the second city of his Empire, was honoured by being given some of the relics of St. Adalbert; the remainder he took with him to Rome, which he reached in the autumn. In January 1001 he made the donation to the Papacy which has already been mentioned, styling himself " servus apostolorum." This completed the most glorious year of his reign, and the most tragic, the last, was immediately to follow. For, a fortnight later, his dream of a " Renovatio imperii Romanorum " was shattered, and he awoke to a grim reality.

Revolt of the Romans   The Romans had complacently accepted the proud position in which their city had been placed, but they were quite unworthy of the responsibility assigned to them by Otto. Local politics meant much more to them than imperial, and when he treated with leniency the revolt of Tivoli, which they wished to see utterly destroyed, their anger broke out uncontrollably against the foreigner who disregarded their wishes. The Tusculan nobles, on whom he had placed especial reliance, took the lead in the outbreak, and Otto had to take refuge in the Castle of Sant' Angelo. From there he addressed the crowd, reminding them of his love for them, for whose sake he had left country and kin and abandoned Germany, and how he had spread their name and fame to the ends of the earth. " And now you have cast out your father." His appeal met with an emotional response, but had no lasting result; and he soon left Rome, which his forces were inadequate to conquer, and retired to Ravenna. There he was torn between two conflicting impulses. St. Romuald urged him to become a monk, and in his disheartened state he thought of making his peace with God by taking the vows at Jerusalem, for he saw in his defeat the punishment of God. But the sense of his imperial mission prevailed and his desire for vengeance on the Romans. The appearance of reinforcements from Germany made this **Death of Otto III** possible, but hardly had they reached him when he was stricken with fever and died at Paterno, in the region of Mt. Soracte, on 24 January 1002.

The glamour of his short career   He was then only twenty-one years of age. Yet for seven years he had been the actual ruler of the Empire, and under his direction its character was largely remodelled.

His contemporaries were dazzled by his career, and among those who co-operated with him were some of the ablest men of the day. The memory of him that remained to posterity caused him to be known as the " Wonder of the World." He was a dreamer and a visionary, but an active one, eager with all the impatience of youth to put his visions into immediate practice. He dreamed noble dreams, and on the religious side they were not out of tune with contemporary ideas. But the revolt of the Romans showed how grievously he had misconceived the political situation. Even had they been faithful, the result would have been little different. He was trying to pivot his Empire upon Rome, whereas his power was based entirely on Germany. The neglect of Germany aroused the deep resentment of the nobles, especially in his native Saxony ; open revolt was threatened, and only the fidelity of his cousin Henry of Bavaria prevented it from breaking out. The German bishops, on whom so much depended, were equally estranged by the diminution of their importance ; and their leader, archbishop Willigis of Mayence, had a private grievance of his own, because Otto had upheld the rights of the bishop of Hildesheim over the convent of Gandersheim (where Otto's sister Sophia was a nun) against the claims of the metropolitan.[1]

The disastrous effects of his policy (a) in the German kingdom

At the same time, the Italian kingdom was in process of dissolution. Rome reverted to the state from which Otto I had rescued it. The Tusculan nobles and the Crescentii disputed the mastery of the city and of the Papacy, which lost its universal character on the death of Sylvester II sixteen months after that of Otto. In the centre, the faithful marquis Hugh of Tuscany was already dead. In the north, marquis Ardoin of Ivrea, who had twice revolted during Otto's lifetime and even arrogated to himself the title of king, was able at once to assume the crown of Italy. The German troops, taking with them the body of Otto for burial, as he had desired, at Aix, had to fight their way back through North Italy. The peace and unity which Otto I had given to the Italian kingdom was at an end.

(b) in the Italian kingdom

On the one hand, then, the reign of Otto III is a fascin-

---

[1] This issue was provocative of continual discord. With kings and Pope against them Willigis and his successors continued to raise it, until at last in 1125 Aribo renounced his claim and peace was restored.

CHAPTER III

THE EMPIRE, 1002–1046

THE imperial experiment of Otto III was only a brief episode, and was followed by a return to the normal; but the effect of it was seen in the difficulties that faced his successor. The nobles, especially in Saxony, had been alienated by Otto's neglect of Germany, and left to themselves had recovered their taste for independence. The bishops had similar grievances, but they were at any rate interested in the persistence of royal government, in which they had an important share, and in the suppression of the independence of the nobles, which was so prejudicial to their own position. This was equally the case in the kingdom of Italy, where Ardoin championed the lesser nobility and the middle-class interests, in part against the marquises, but much more against the bishops who had been the mainstay of the German king's authority. A further difficulty had arisen with regard to the tributary states to the east and south-east of Germany. Otto III's policy of attaching them directly to the imperial rather than to the German crown had encouraged in them the idea of independence; Poland and Hungary had also become ecclesiastically separate from Germany. Finally, at Rome, the Tusculan house, while it returned to friendship with the German king, used that friendship to defeat the Crescentii and gain control especially over appointments to the Papacy; they were allies rather than subjects of the Emperor.

The whole structure, then, was showing ominous cracks, to which the kings had to pay constant attention; they had to be continually on the alert to apply the hammer of force or the cement of diplomacy wherever there were signs of a rift; they eventually mended the framework, and kept it in repair. This is, in the main, the story of the years 1002–1046, and by a steady application along the lines laid down by Otto I the end was achieved.　The patient, plodding work of Henry II restored the internal organisation of Germany, and Conrad II was able to consolidate this more firmly and to establish his suzerainty east and south, making possible the still fuller realisation of imperial authority under his son Henry III.　The culmination was reached in 1046 when Henry III at last arrived at the final objective, which his two predecessors had avoided, of bringing Rome and the Papacy once more under imperial control.　By so doing, he not only revived the position of Otto I, but he also raised the Papacy to the position of a world-power once more, and thereby opened a new chapter in the ecclesiastical and political history of Europe.

The election
of Henry II
(1002–24)
　　　The death of Otto III created a vacancy that could only be filled by election.　There were two obvious candidates— duke Henry of Bavaria, the only descendant in the direct male line from Henry I, and duke Otto of Carinthia, the son of Otto I's daughter Liutgarde.[1]　The latter continued his self-effacing career by refusing to be a candidate, so that the way seemed clear for Henry.　But Germany had lost its unity during the long absence of its king, and each part of it had to be separately won over.　To complicate the situation other competitors for the throne appeared.　First of all, Eckhard, margrave of Meissen, a distinguished soldier ; but his ambition was checkmated by the hostility of his fellow-nobles in eastern Saxony, and his sudden assassination by private enemies removed him from Henry's path.　Several of the magnates inclined to the duke of Suabia, Herman II, son of the Conrad whom Otto II had appointed duke ; his mild nature made him acceptable to those who had already enjoyed a measure of independence.　What decided the issue for Henry was the adhesion of Willigis, archbishop of Mayence, who played the part that his predecessor had played at Otto I's coronation.　Even then the Saxons had to be conciliated by the promise to respect their peculiar customs, the bishops in Lorraine, especially archbishop Heribert of Cologne, were

---

[1] No one seems to have considered the claims of the son of Otto III's youngest sister, Matilda (his other sisters, Adelaide and Sophia, took the veil and became abbesses of Quedlinburg and Gandersheim).　Matilda, in marrying the son of the count-palatine of Lorraine, was considered to have made an unequal marriage ; and her son was only an infant.

very slow in giving their adhesion, and it was not until nine months after Otto's death that the resignation of Herman removed the last opposition to the recognition of Henry. A kingdom won in the face of so much reluctance would obviously not be an easy one to govern.

Henry II was exactly the type of ruler required at a time when practical common sense and persistent effort were needed in the work of restoration. He was upright and pious, intensely aware of his high dignity and its duties, but free from imaginative dreams and idealistic aims. The Italian kingdom had to be re-won, but he was not to be lured away by its fascination into idle adventure; the Empire once more depended upon Germany as its base. Patiently he set to work to retrieve the situation there, travelling continually throughout his dominions to enforce obedience upon the nobles and to check them, especially in Saxony and Lorraine, in their favourite pursuit of private warfare. On the whole, he had less trouble than might have been expected within the borders of Germany proper. The only overt acts of rebellion came from his own duchy of Bavaria and from his wife's family in Lorraine. *His character and policy*

In Bavaria, the Babenberg family had obtained an important position when Otto II made the brothers Berthold of the Nordgau and Liutpold of the East Mark directly dependent upon the Crown. The son of Berthold, Henry, now margrave of the Nordgau, disappointed in his hopes of succeeding the king as duke of Bavaria, entered into a treacherous alliance with duke Boleslav of Poland, and gained the assistance of his cousin Ernest, a son of Liutpold, and also of the king's brother Bruno. The revolt broke out in 1003, and was brought to an end the following year by the submission of the three rebels. They were pardoned, and the king secured their future loyalty by the favours he heaped upon them. Bruno took orders and was appointed chancellor of the German kingdom and later bishop of Augsburg; Ernest was given the duchy of Suabia when it became void in 1012, and on his death in 1015 his son Ernest succeeded him. Meanwhile, in 1004, the duchy of Bavaria had been filled by the appointment of Henry of Luxemburg, the eldest brother of the Queen. This, however, was not sufficient for the ambition of the Luxemburg house. A second brother, Dietrich, *Disturbances in Bavaria and Lorraine*

obtained the bishopric of Metz in 1005 against the wishes of
Henry II, and a third, Adalbero, seized upon the archbishopric
of Trèves in 1008, and defied the royal and papal nominee,
Megingaud, and his successor Poppo. Their elder brother
took up arms in their defence, and was deprived of his duchy
by the king, who kept it in his own hands. This family feud
went on until 1017, when the king was at last reconciled with
his brother-in-law; Henry of Luxemburg was reinstated as
duke of Bavaria, Dietrich (who had made his peace earlier)
retained Metz, but Adalbero had to yield Trèves to Poppo.

In Upper Lorraine the Luxemburgers had defied the
king himself. In Lower Lorraine there was similar disorder,
but in opposition to ducal rather than to royal authority.
In 1012 Henry, on the death of Otto, son of the Carolingian
Charles, appointed count Godfrey of the Ardennes as duke.
He had great difficulty in preserving order, even when the
king intervened in his assistance; the counts of Hainault,
Louvain, Holland, and Alsace, among others, were frequent
disturbers of the peace. Equally troublesome was the
powerful count of Flanders, Baldwin IV, nominally a vassal
of the French king, until he became a vassal of the German
king also in return for the grant of Walcheren and Valen-
ciennes in 1012. In East Saxony, it was not resistance to
authority so much as private feuds that caused disorder.
Henry's intervention sometimes led to defiance of his
authority here too, but on the whole this was neither serious
nor lasting.

Henry's
limitations
The sum total of these disturbances in the different parts
of the kingdom is considerable, though separately they were
not particularly significant. There was no suggestion of a
combined rising against the king, such as had twice menaced
the position of Otto I. On the other hand, Henry never
attained the mastery that Otto had achieved. He was always
eventually successful in restoring order wherever breaches of
the peace occurred, but he could not prevent them from
occurring. He inspired respect for his authority, but not
awe. That was a tribute which the age would only pay to
a great soldier, and he won no striking military success; in
fact he was notably unsuccessful in his numerous campaigns
against the duke of Poland, in which, as well as in Italy, a
considerable amount of his time had to be employed.

It had been the chief asset of the Saxon kings that they The position of the duchies had the full strength of Saxony, the most powerful duchy in Germany, behind them, which enabled them to overcome the spirit of particularism, of local independence, elsewhere. Saxony was now the duchy where this spirit was most manifest; cherishing its own conservative customs, which stood in the way of a centralised government of Germany, it maintained the hereditary succession of its dukes without interference from the king. Henry II, indeed, did not interfere with hereditary succession elsewhere, save in Carinthia, where on the death of Conrad (son of the self-effacing Otto) he passed over Conrad's son and appointed a local count, Adalbero of Eppenstein, as duke. But he was fortunate in that the failure of some ducal houses gave him, as we have seen, the opportunity of creating dukes favourable to himself. On the other hand, the dukes he created were so little able to control the unruly nobles beneath them that his presence was continually needed to maintain order; the manifest weakness of ducal authority was perhaps due to the frequent change of personnel. In his own duchy of Bavaria the duke's authority had already been diminished, because of the rebellious spirit of his father, so that he did not bring to the service of the Crown, as Henry I and Otto I had done, the resources of a united duchy. He did not even retain the duchy in his own hands, except temporarily owing to the defection of his brother-in-law.

In other respects he was able to command the same Royal resources resources as his predecessors. He was in possession of an extensive royal domain. In this was included the remnants of the Carolingian domain in Lorraine, but much more important was the private domain of the Liudolfing house in East Saxony, which fell to him both as king and as heir. To this he added his patrimonial estates in Bavaria, and though royal and personal domain were reckoned as distinct, there was little or no distinction in fact in the king's employment of them. They supplied him with food for himself and his household, with soldiers, and sometimes with officials; and their geographical distribution is one reason for his frequent journeys, and especially for his long periods of residence in Saxony.

Besides this, he relied, as his predecessors had done, on

the support of the Church. He was lavish in adding to the possessions of the bishops, he increased their territorial administration and jurisdiction, and in return he reaped the full advantages of the alliance. Its political importance has already been described. The military importance must also be taken into account ; there is an illustration of this in a document of Otto II in 981 summoning reinforcements from Germany, in which the contribution required from the bishops was greater than that required from the lay nobles.[1] Henry II seems to have been responsible for making the Church important from the economic point of view as well. The royal abbeys furnished services in kind. From this the bishops were exempt, but, unlike lay nobles, they apparently had to provide *hospitalitas* for the king and his servants during his residence in an episcopal town. Whereas the itineraries of the Ottos show them residing for the most part in royal manors, it was at episcopal towns that Henry II (and his successors after him) principally stayed. Similar to this treatment of episcopal resources as available for his own needs was his arbitrary redistribution, in two instances, of episcopal territory. The re-foundation of the bishopric of Merseburg was, indeed, only the undoing of a wrong committed by the archbishop of Magdeburg, who had quashed the bishopric in order to extend his own diocese. But the foundation of the see of Bamberg in Eastern Franconia in 1007 was another matter. Bamberg was Henry's favourite residence, and he was anxious to exalt it ; there was the further excuse that it was adjacent to a colony of heathen Wends, and it was to justify its existence by the missionary work which it successfully propagated. But it could only be created at the expense of the neighbouring sees of Würzburg and Eichstädt, whose bishops were naturally hostile to the scheme. Henry overrode their opposition by means of a compliant synod and a papal bull. With the same outward observance of ecclesiastical forms, he respected canonical elections to bishoprics and abbeys but forced the electors to appoint the candidates of his choice. Ecclesiastical, and especially monastic, reform was carried out under his direction, and the decrees of synods,

---

[1] As there were reinforcements, it is of course possible that the original quota from the lay nobles had exceeded that from the bishops.

in which he himself took part, were published by his authority.

So, while in his government of the German kingdom he was hampered by severe limitations of custom and the circumstances of the time, he ruled the German Church almost as an autocrat. The ecclesiastical sphere was the one most congenial to him; he was distinguished for his piety, which was to result in his canonisation. Like Charlemagne he felt that as " Vicar of God " he was in authority over the Church, and that it was his task to direct the Church for its good and to enforce on his subjects their duty to God. In his own time he was opposed only by those who had been intimately associated with Otto III, especially by archbishop Heribert of Cologne, Otto's chancellor, who survived until 1021; his successor, both as archbishop and as Italian chancellor, was Pilgrim, a Bavarian and a close friend of Henry. In later days, the more extreme advocates of Church reform severely criticised the actions of Henry II, especially his arbitrary interference with diocesan organisation and property on the occasion of the foundation of Bamberg. *Henry's autocracy in ecclesiastical matters*

In domestic affairs, then, he followed the policy inaugurated by Otto I, and since his hold over the secular nobles was much weaker, he endeavoured to redress the balance by a still greater reliance on the episcopate. But the insufficiency of his resources, especially from a military point of view, was evidenced by his lack of success on the eastern frontiers and in Burgundy; and this was only partially retrieved by a certain measure of success in Italy.

The policy of Otto III had tended to release the newly-Christianised States of Bohemia, Poland, and Hungary from their dependence, both political and ecclesiastical, upon Germany, and to attach them directly to the imperial Crown and to the Roman Church. Hungary, however, remained quiescent, and Bohemia was in a state of internal disorder owing to the family strife of Duke Boleslav and his two stepbrothers, Jaromir and Udalrich.[1] But Poland had suddenly *The eastern frontier-states* *Poland under Boleslav the Mighty*

---

[1] The house of the Premyslids was in undisputed possession of the duchy of Bohemia, but there was no definite law of succession, and violent contests between members of the family, marked by the savagery of the participants, were a feature of its history at this time.

become, for the first time in its history, a formidable State under the rule of its great duke, Boleslav the Mighty (992–1025). Taking advantage of the unsettled condition of Germany at the time of Otto III's death, Boleslav proceeded to expand his duchy westwards and to conquer the territory lying between Poland and Germany proper, including Lausitz, the East Mark as far as the Elbe, and even the Mark of Meissen, which was vacant owing to the murder of Eckhard. He then went himself to Merseburg to obtain Henry's consent to the retention of these conquests. Henry indignantly refused and invested Eckhard's brother Gunzelin with the Mark of Meissen. Boleslav promptly turned south and, taking advantage of the civil war in Bohemia, first of all restored the expelled duke Boleslav, and then displaced this namesake of his and had himself proclaimed duke. Once more Henry refused his recognition without avail, and he was further embarrassed in 1003 by the revolt of the Babenberg family and their alliance with Boleslav. In the next year, however, he did succeed in expelling Boleslav from Bohemia, over which he restored his own suzerainty and appointed Jaromir as duke. But this was the limit of his achievement against the Polish duke. Repeated campaigns—in 1005, 1007, 1010–12, 1015–18—all resulted in failure. He had the support of Bohemia, and even of the Wendish tribes, an alliance with pagans against a Christian duke which gave great offence in Saxony; but all to no purpose. He was forced at last to make peace with Boleslav at Bautzen in 1018, ceding to him Lausitz (whether as a fief or in full possession is uncertain). Boleslav, too, was anxious for peace; his ambition was now turned eastward towards Russia, and he proceeded successfully to attack the principality of Kiev. At the end of Henry's reign he displayed his independence, with some justification, by assuming the title of king.

Henry's failure in Burgundy

While he was thus unable to maintain his suzerainty over an eastern State, Henry II was also unsuccessful in his attempt to convert a protectorate over a western State into actual possession. Burgundy was important to the German king because of its connexion with Italy, and Otto I had assumed authority over its king before undertaking his first Italian expedition. Rudolf III, who was now on the throne, was the last male of his line, and various claimants were eagerly asserting their rights to the succession. Henry II, as the son of Rudolf's sister Gisela, was among these, and in 1006 he obtained a foothold in Burgundy by getting possession of Basle. Rudolf was a feeble ruler, quite unable to enforce obedience upon the Burgundian nobles. He was anxious for powerful support, and selected Henry as his heir. But Henry was unable to make good his claims. He intervened unsuccessfully in 1016 and an expedition he sent in 1018 was also a failure ; in the same year that he made peace with Boleslav he was compelled also to renounce his ambitions in Burgundy. Moreover, as he died before Rudolf, the actual vacancy did not occur during his lifetime.

In North Italy there was still a German party, composed of the bishops, with Otto III's friend, Leo of Vercelli, at their head, and of the greater nobles ; it was directly at their expense that Ardoin had gained and was maintaining his authority. A German army under Otto of Carinthia in 1002 proved inadequate to defeat him. Henry's presence was obviously essential. Henry was a practical man, with his main interest where his strength lay, in Germany, and the experience of his predecessor was sufficient warning against Italian adventure. All the same, the kingdom of Italy had become a recognised appendage of the German Crown and therefore must not be abandoned. His expedition to Italy in 1004, at a time when Bohemia was still in the hands of the Polish duke, shows the importance he attached to its recovery. Ardoin effaced himself before the German army, and Henry was crowned king of Italy at Pavia. But friction soon arose there between his soldiers and the inhabitants, which resulted in the destruction of the Lombard capital. Lombardy was terrified into submission, and Henry was content with this and with his royal title and hastened home to set about the recovery of Bohemia also. But he had aroused deep resentment by the burning of Pavia, and his adherents found it a difficult task to maintain themselves against the constant attacks of Ardoin. The revival of disorder in North Italy showed that Henry's power there was only nominal.

Henry's first expedition to Italy

It was nearly ten years before he came again, and it was an appeal from Rome that brought him, as it had brought Otto I, to achieve the imperial crown. John Crescentius II had been ruling Rome as patricius, but on his death in 1012

His second expedition

the Tusculan candidate for the Papacy, Benedict VIII, prevailed over his Crescentian rival, Gregory, and the latter appealed in person to Henry II for help. Henry, however, was determined to maintain his friendship with the Tusculan house, and he came to Italy at the end of 1013 to uphold Benedict VIII. His appearance produced order and submission in North Italy once more, and he was even received with enthusiasm at Rome, where on 14 February 1014 he and his wife Kunigunda were crowned Emperor and Empress by the Pope. Yet almost at once the accustomed tumult broke out in Rome against the Germans, and Henry had to retire north again. He stayed for a time in Tuscany, and appointed as its marquis Rainier, who was already marquis of Spoleto and thus held the centre of Italy firmly for Henry II, as marquis Hugh had done for Otto III. Then, after a month in Pavia spent in administrative measures designed to make his authority more directly effective, he returned to Germany. At once Ardoin and his confederates were in arms, and disorder was again rife throughout Lombardy. This time the German party was eventually successful and Ardoin withdrew to a monastery ; with his death in the following year (1015) the nationalist party in North Italy lost their only effective leader, and the bishops recovered their former predominance.

At his imperial coronation Henry had promised to defend the Roman Church and to adhere to the Pope and his successors. This pledge had been formally given by his predecessors, but he adhered to it in spirit also, and left the Papacy untrammelled by his dictation. Benedict VIII was an effective Pope, though his interests were more martial than spiritual. He succeeded in crushing the Crescentii, made headway against Moslem raids, and was largely responsible for the attack by Pisa and Genoa on the Moslems' recent conquest, Sardinia ; these two cities, already naval powers, won a great sea-victory and a foothold in Sardinia in 1016. Benedict had also formed a league with the Lombards in the South and their Norman associates against the Byzantine power. To further this ambitious project, Benedict with his chief confederates went in person to Germany to win the assistance of the Emperor. It was a diplomatic act for, as the first Pope to visit Germany since the ninth century, his presence made a great stir. Pope and Emperor met at

Margin notes:

Imperial coronation (1014)

Relations with the Pope ; Henry's third Italian expedition

Bamberg, where the Pope took the new see under his special protection and Henry promised his co-operation in South Italy. The campaign of 1021-2 opened with a striking success in the taking of Capua; it closed, in the usual way, with fever in the German army, and Henry returned north to Pavia, accompanied by the Pope. The Emperor had assisted the military designs of the Pope; the Pope now furthered the Emperor's schemes for the reform of the Church. Together they took part in the Synod of Pavia in August 1022, where decrees, especially against clerical marriage, were issued, with papal authority and promulgated by imperial decree.

The last two years of his reign were spent in Germany. They were years of political peace and ecclesiastical friction. Henry had time to devote to the congenial task of Church reform. He was in advance, however, of contemporary opinion; he aroused opposition, especially from the archbishop of Mayence, Aribo, both by upholding the claims of the bishop of Hildesheim in the interminable dispute over Gandersheim, and by the weight he gave to papal authority. An appeal to the Pope against a synodal decision of Aribo was supported by Henry, but a provincial synod at Seligenstadt in 1023 prohibited appeals to Rome without episcopal permission. A crisis was brewing when Benedict VIII died in June 1024. His brother, a layman, who was appointed to succeed him as John XIX, had no interest in upholding the ecclesiastical authority of the Papacy, so the dispute went no farther. Benedict had been led by Henry to regain something of its old prestige for the Papacy, but Benedict's death was followed by that of Henry himself. Possibly, had he lived, he might have intervened to prevent the degradation of the Papacy under John XIX and his successor. But he was himself partly responsible for it. His predecessors had rescued the Papacy from dependence on the Roman nobles, and though themselves its masters had restored its universal authority. Henry II tried to guide it, not as his servant but as his ally, along its right path as head of the Church; but he did not give it a position independent of the Roman nobles, and while they controlled papal elections its relapse was inevitable.

Henry died on July 13, 1024, and his body was taken

Ecclesiastical difficulties in Germany

4

for burial, where in life it had been happiest, to Bamberg.
It had been a busy reign with little relaxation except at the
very close, and the achievement had been considerable. He
had restored order and a respect for royal authority in Germany, and had renewed the attachment of the Italian kingdom to the German Crown. By patient reconstruction he
provided a firm basis for his successors to build a more solid
structure. He was handicapped by constant ill-health and
by lack of military genius, and he was singularly unfortunate
in having to contend on his eastern frontier with Boleslav
the Mighty. On the other hand, by his high character, his
practical common sense, and his devotion to duty he rendered
a considerable service to German monarchy. In ecclesiastical affairs he showed himself more at home than in political,
and was able to take a stronger line. Here he was perhaps
too dictatorial, but in his work for reform and his respect
for papal authority he was correctly foreshadowing the
developments of the future.

Henry II, like Otto III, left no heir, so that it rested
with the German princes once more to decide who should
be their king. There had been some disposition after Otto
III's death to exercise the electoral power in their own
interests, but the claims of the next of kin had finally been
recognised. No such disposition was shown after Henry
II's death. The two grandsons of Otto of Carinthia, who
had himself refused to be a candidate in 1002, were alone
considered in the election of 1024. They were first
cousins, and both of them were named Conrad. Their
rivalry was of brief duration, for the younger cousin effaced
himself as his grandfather had done previously, and the
princes who assembled for the election followed the lead of
archbishop Aribo of Mayence and unanimously elected the
elder Conrad as king. His priority in descent gave him a
strong claim, while the fact that, unlike his cousin, he was
not in sympathy with the ecclesiastical reforms of Henry II
decided not only the lay nobles but also the archbishop
himself in his favour. Lorraine, therefore, under the lead of
Pilgrim of Cologne, held aloof from the election, but its
recognition was soon obtained. The Saxon nobles were also
absent from the election; once more they made their

adhesion to the king dependent on his recognition of their ancient and peculiar customs.

Conrad II succeeded as king to the domains, both royal and personal, which Henry II had possessed. He himself added little, for the family estates in Franconia [1] had passed to the younger branch, owing to the early death of Conrad's father Henry; so had the duchy of Carinthia, though, as we have seen, it remained there for one lifetime only. But, though his personal possessions were small, he brought with him to the throne one great asset—a strong and vigorous personality. A rough-hewn man, lacking altogether the pious devotion of his predecessor, he excelled him in forcefulness of character. From the ecclesiastically-minded Henry to the purely secular Conrad was a great change, but there was much also of similarity. Conrad was noted for his personal integrity and keen sense of justice, and he was as fully convinced as was Henry of the greatness of the position to which he had attained, and equally determined to vindicate it in every quarter. He owed much to the patient plodding of his predecessor, he used the same resources and adopted the same methods; but, while he favoured the episcopate and gained the same advantages, political and economic, from his control of it, he showed a complete disregard of ecclesiastical interests in the appointments that he made, so that the Church became more and more secularised and the evils of lay control more manifest. In another direction he made a special contribution of his own to the royal resources. He was responsible for the reliance placed by the monarchy on the class of *ministeriales*, the unfree tenants on the royal domain, who were equipped as soldiers and often employed by the king as officials. The German nobles, who followed the practice to some extent with their own tenants, viewed with jealousy the rise in the king's service of men of humble birth, who often attained not merely to a free status but even to noble rank. It was, however, a great asset to the king to have at his disposal a body of men who were completely dependent on his favour,

His character; the contrast with Henry II

Use of royal ministeriales

---

[1] These estates derived from Otto of Carinthia's father Conrad the Red, the husband of Otto I's daughter Liutgarde. Conrad II, because of his Franconian origin, was later known as the "Salic," and the dynasty he founded is usually spoken of as the Salian dynasty.

and the employment of *ministeriales* becomes henceforward a regular practice. This use by the king of his unfree vassals is peculiar to the German kingdom.

His relations with the nobles

Apart from his stepson, Ernest of Suabia, Conrad had little difficulty with the greater nobles. In accordance with his pledge, he did not meddle with the internal affairs of Saxony, and so had no opposition from that quarter. Elsewhere, he made no attempt to interfere with the normal order of succession, for like Henry II he respected the hereditary principle. To this he was particularly attached, as it had always been a grievance with him that the possessions of his family had descended to the junior branch. He even rectified Henry's one deviation from it, when in 1036 he caused Adalbero of Carinthia to be dispossessed of his duchy on a charge of treason, and gave it to the rightful heir, his own cousin Conrad. But, like Henry II again, he was fortunate in the vacancies that gave him the opportunity of making appointments, and he used the opportunity to strengthen his control. Both Bavaria (in 1026) and Suabia (in 1038) fell vacant, and he gave them both to his son Henry, whom he had caused to be crowned king in 1028. When Upper Lorraine fell vacant by the death of duke Frederick in 1033, he gave it to the duke of Lower Lorraine, Gozelo, thereby obtaining a powerful adherent who was able to keep better order than had obtained heretofore. With the other nobles he was usually on the best of terms. A man after their own heart, a strong ruler and a keen soldier, he respected in their case too the natural desire to hand on their inheritance to their sons, giving them in this way a certain independence from ducal control. He had his reward when the nobles of Suabia refused to follow duke Ernest in his revolt; but as the duchies gradually came into his own hands, the direct adhesion to himself of the lesser nobles was no longer of the same importance.

Dispute over the Burgundian inheritance

Duke Ernest of Suabia was practically the only important German noble to rebel against Conrad. He seems to have been offended at his mother's marriage with Conrad and at being under his stepfather's tutelage during his minority. The actual occasion of his revolt was the dispute over the Burgundian succession. Conrad II, shortly after his election, asserted his claim, both as the successor to Henry II and as the husband of Gisela, Rudolf III's niece.   Ernest as Gisela's son considered himself to have the better claim, and there was another rival to Conrad in count Odo of Blois, Rudolf's nephew.   Ernest gained support from the still disaffected nobles in Lorraine, Odo had the backing of the king of France, and the two claimants joined forces to defeat the ambition of the king of Germany.

At the same time, revolt had broken out again in Italy. The people of Pavia had never forgiven the burning of their city; they took the opportunity of Henry II's death to revenge themselves by destroying the royal palace, believed to have been built by the great Theodoric and formerly their pride, but now the hated symbol of German domination. The news of this had a profound effect especially in the towns, where imperial control was most disliked, and simultaneously there was a rising of the marquises of North Italy, in which even Rainier of Tuscany took part, animated especially by their jealousy at the authority given to the bishops. They invited duke William V of Aquitaine to be their king; he accepted the position for his son, and by allying himself with Ernest and Odo he formed a coalition which threatened grave danger to the newly elected king of Germany. *Revolt in Italy*

Yet in a few months the danger had disappeared.   The king of France and Odo found themselves too much occupied at home to risk adventure in Burgundy.   The Lorraine nobles quickly made their peace with Conrad, and Ernest had perforce to follow suit.   And William of Aquitaine, finding the situation in North Italy to be much less favourable than he had anticipated, renounced his ambition for his son.   So when Conrad came into Lombardy in 1026, he had no more difficulty than his predecessor had had in restoring his authority.   Pavia was duly punished, a rising at Ravenna repressed, and the marquises were reduced to submission.   In 1027 he proceeded to Rome, and on Easter Day he and his wife were crowned Emperor and Empress by Pope John XIX.   As far as South Italy was concerned, he was content with homage from the princes of Capua, Salerno, and Benevento, who had recognised the overlordship of Henry II.   In fact, on this first visit to Italy, he was concerned merely with vindicating for himself the position acquired by his predecessor.   He showed no disposition to *Conrad's first Italian expedition*   *Imperial coronation (1027)* control the actions of the Pope, though he regarded him as his subordinate. He did, indeed, induce John XIX to summon a synod at the Lateran, but solely with the aim of settling disputes which might lead to disorder : the precedence of Milan over Ravenna was proclaimed, and also the subjection of the see of Grado (and therefore of Venice) to the patriarchate of Aquileia. He was naturally not inclined to encourage the Pope, as Henry II had done, to take the lead in Church reform. He was not moved by the degradation into which the Papacy was gradually sinking, and he made no attempt to interfere in the election after John XIX's death in 1033, when John's worthless nephew Benedict IX became Pope.

Acquisition of the Burgundian kingdom

The imperial coronation had been attended by Rudolf III of Burgundy, who had been induced by Gisela to recognise Conrad as his heir. Ernest of Suabia after two more revolts was killed in battle in 1030, and his duchy passed to his brother Herman, who was continuously loyal. When Rudolf himself died in 1032, Odo of Blois was Conrad's only rival for the succession ; and as Conrad was engaged with Polish affairs at the time, Odo managed to effect a temporary occupation of Burgundy. Within two years, however, his resistance was overcome. Conrad was crowned king, received the adhesion of the Burgundian nobles, and thus Burgundy was at last definitely attached to the German Crown. It brought prestige to the king of Germany, and it ensured his control of all the passes into Italy ; but it was a kingdom in name only, geographical and political conditions alike preventing any real unity. The king's authority over it was often merely nominal ; because of Italy, not for its own sake, it was important to him.

Recovery of German authority in Poland

A far more valuable success was won in south-eastern Europe, where Henry II had experienced his chief failure. During the interval between his two visits to Italy, Conrad's attention was mainly occupied in this quarter, and at the outset he was greatly favoured by fortune. For in 1025 Boleslav the Mighty died, and in Poland, as its chronicler says, " the golden age was converted into one of lead." His second son, Mesco, who assumed the power and the title of king at the expense of his elder brother, had the ambition of his father without the talent. Disregarding the treaty of Bautzen, he savagely devastated the German frontier-lands and even eastern Saxony. Conrad's campaign against him in 1029 was as great a failure as those of Henry II against Boleslav. He was defeated by the terrain, swampy and thickly wooded, which prevented him from coming to grips with the enemy and wore out his troops. Two years later he organised a more successful campaign, in conjunction with Yaroslav of Kiev, who attacked from the east, so that Mesco was unable to pursue his tactics of avoiding battle and was forced to come to terms. The territory won by his father was ceded, and Poland became once more a duchy under German overlordship, reduced in size to what it was before the reign of Boleslav the Mighty. Moreover, after Mesco's death in 1034 his widow Richeza, a niece of Otto III, had to take refuge with her son Casimir in Germany; and Poland fell back into a primitive state of civil war and anarchy. There was one less fortunate result of the defeat of Poland. The pagan Slavs in the north-east, especially the Liutizii, had made common cause with the Germans against the Poles. Now that this danger was removed, their old feud with the Saxons broke out again, and Conrad had to undertake two expeditions against them, in 1035 and 1036, before they were reduced to obedience.

Between the defeat of Conrad in Poland and his final victory, he had had to turn his attention to Hungary. St. Stephen, who was responsible for the Christianisation of his country in 1000 and had received a crown from Rome, had continued in friendly relations with Otto III's successor, whose sister Gisela he had married. Friction, however, had arisen in Conrad's reign, probably out of border disputes with Bavaria, and in 1030 Conrad led an expedition into Hungary which was as unsuccessful as his Polish expedition of 1029. A counter-expedition of the Hungarians into the East Mark succeeded in capturing Vienna.[1] Peace was made the following year, when Vienna was restored and Hungary gained a slight addition of territory at the expense of Bavaria. *Unsuccessful conflict with Hungary*

Of the three south-eastern States, Bohemia had always been the most submissive to German authority. It took sides with Germany against Poland in 1029, when Bratislav, *Bohemian revolt overcome*

[1] The Roman Vindobona thus re-appears in history, and for the first time under its modern name.

the son of duke Udalrich, won renown by recovering Moravia, and against Hungary in 1030, when once again Bratislav was victorious. The failure of the royal army on both occasions and the success of the Bohemian may have caused Udalrich to entertain the idea of independence. At any rate, he paid no heed to the summons to the Polish campaign in 1031, or to a further summons to answer before a diet for his neglect. An expedition in 1033 under the young king Henry, now sixteen years of age, sufficed to force him to submission. He was temporarily deposed in favour of his brother Jaromir, but later was restored, and on his death in 1034 his son Bratislav was allowed to succeed him. Bohemia, after this brief show of independence, reverted again to its position as a vassal State.

Alliance with Canute the Great

In the north of Germany, Conrad was relieved from anxiety by his friendly relations with Canute the Great, king of England and Denmark. Conditions had considerably changed in Scandinavia since the tenth century, when Viking invasions were always to be feared and the only true kingdom was that of Denmark. By the beginning of the eleventh century it was still the chief power, but the other two Scandinavian kingdoms, Sweden and Norway, had become properly established. Norway, conquered by Denmark in 1000, regained its independence under St. Olaf in 1016, only to lose it again when Olaf, allied with Sweden against Canute, was killed in battle in 1030. The wisdom of Conrad's policy in turning this troublesome neighbour into a friend was amply justified by the security it gave to his northern frontiers. He had cultivated Canute's friendship at the beginning of his reign, and Canute had been present at the imperial coronation in 1027. In 1035 the friendship was cemented by a marriage alliance between the young Henry, who had already won his spurs in Bohemia, with Canute's daughter Gunnhild ; while Canute received from Conrad the mark of Schleswig. Unfortunately, Canute died the same year at the early age of forty ; his dominions were divided, and Norway recovered its independence.

Conrad's policy of linking Italy with Germany

There was at any rate nothing to be feared from that quarter. Germany was now secure on all its frontiers and untroubled by domestic disorder. The only task outstanding for Conrad was to establish in the Italian kingdom a régime by means of which order could be maintained and obedience to imperial authority even in the absence of the Emperor. One part of his plan consisted in the closer union of the two countries by the appointment of Germans to Italian bishoprics, and the arrangement of marriage alliances between German and Italian noble families. Two of these marriages deserve mention because of their later importance ; that of Boniface of Canossa (who had been made marquis of Tuscany on Rainier's death in 1030) with Beatrice of Lorraine, and that of marquis Azzo of Este with Kunigunda, heiress to the Welf estates in Suabia and ancestress of all the Welfs to come.

The particular conditions in Italy at the time of his second visit gave him an opportunity of which he was quick to make use. The noble families in Italy (apart from the marquises and counts), who dominated in the towns as well as in the countryside, had become divided into two classes— the greater vassals or *capitanei* and the lesser vassals or *valvassores*.[1] The former had full disposal of their possessions, which was denied to the latter, who began to form associations to obtain their independence ; a regular civil war developed, especially in the Milanese province, where the *valvassores* by force of numbers succeeded in defeating the archbishop and the *capitanei*. This civil war was the principal cause of Conrad's expedition at the end of 1036. His inclinations were naturally on the side of the *valvassores*, partly owing to his support of the hereditary principle even for the lesser nobility, which he had already displayed in Germany, and partly because of the opportunity given to him to reconcile to himself a numerous military class which had formerly been antagonistic to the German occupation. By the famous edict of 1037 he gave them what they wanted —security of tenure and the hereditary succession of their fiefs.

Conrad thus changed the character of imperial government in Italy. By introducing Teutonic blood into the bishoprics and marquisates and by ensuring the fidelity of

Civil war between the capitanei and the valvassores

Conrad's settlement in favour of the valvassores

[1] The distinction between tenants-in-chief and mesne tenants, between barons and knights, in England will give some idea of the distinction between these two classes, about whom see Dr. C. W. Previté-Orton in *Cambridge Medieval History*, vol. V, p. 217.

the large class of *valvassores*, he broadened the basis of his authority and secured its stability ; to the non-noble classes he paid no heed, but they were as yet of little account.   His

Revolt of the
archbishop
of Milan
policy provoked violent opposition from the leading ecclesiastic in Italy, archbishop Aribert of Milan, who expected the imperial control in North Italy to be exercised through the bishops, and was offended by the Teutonic infiltration as well as by the weakening of episcopal authority.   Immediately on Conrad's appearance he displayed his hostility.   He was imprisoned, but escaped ; and the enthusiastic welcome he received from the Milanese provides an early instance of the solidarity of town patriotism in Italy.   Conrad characteristically decreed his deposition without recourse to the ecclesiastical authorities ; later he somewhat regularised the position by obtaining a papal bull of excommunication against Aribert.   But he was unable to capture Milan, and he had to leave Italy in 1038 with the defiant archbishop still unsubdued.

Conrad in
South Italy
For this affairs in South Italy in 1038 were largely responsible.   Conrad showed no disposition to extend his kingdom by conquests in the south, but he had to answer an appeal for help from his subjects against the tyrannous Paldolf III, who had possession of Capua.   Paldolf was expelled, and Capua bestowed on the Prince of Salerno, Guaimar ; at the same time recognition was given to the Norman colony at Aversa, as a fief of Guaimar.   But this all took time, and it was mid-June before he came north again.   In the previous year, and also on his first visit to Italy, he had avoided the summer heat by retiring to the mountains.   Now, immediately on his return to North Italy, it proved, as usual, the most deadly enemy of the Germans.   Fever attacked them, and many died ; among the most illustrious victims were his daughter-in-law Gunnhild and his step-son Herman of Suabia.   A sick man, himself, he had to return with the remnant of his army to Germany, there to make what proved to be his final dispositions.   Suabia was given to the bereaved Henry, who was also crowned king of Burgundy the same year.   Conrad was now following the policy of Otto I of keeping the chief posts in his own family.   He had only one son, so all was given to him.   There were disagreements between father and son, for their characters were widely

different, but they were united by mutual affection and respect, and Henry well deserved his father's confidence. Their joint rule was a short one, however. Conrad never really recovered from his illness in Italy. He died on June 4, 1039. His death

The most convincing proof of Conrad's achievement (for Henry III which Henry II too deserves his share of the credit) is to (1039–56) be found in the strength of Henry III's position on his accession. No other medieval German sovereign had so few difficulties to combat or found such ready acceptance of his authority. There was no rival to be overcome, for he had already been elected and crowned as king. Apart from Saxony, which retained its special privileges and the hereditary succession of its dukes, and Lorraine, where Gozelo's loyalty could be depended upon, the duchies were all in the king's own hands. For Henry was already duke of Bavaria and Suabia, and Carinthia came to him both as king and heir in 1039 when his cousin Conrad died and also the ex-duke Adalbero. Though only twenty-two years of age, he had already had practical experience in government and as the leader of an army. He had the advantage of a careful education, which his father had lacked, and while Conrad's was the more forceful personality, there was some compensation in the gentler and more attractive disposition of the son. Nowhere was the difference between them more marked than in the realm of ecclesiastical politics. Henry III was distinguished for his piety and his deep interest in the spiritual welfare of the Church, and this characteristic was accentuated after his second marriage with the devout Agnes, daughter of duke William V of Aquitaine, in 1043 ; in his keen sense of his duty to God [1] and in his absorption in matters ecclesiastical, he seems to be the son of Henry II rather than of Conrad II. So, while Conrad and Aribert of Milan were irreconcilable, less than a year after Henry's accession the archbishop came to Germany and made his peace with the king. In the Italian as well as in the German kingdom the reign opened under the happiest auspices.

---

[1] It was typical of him that in 1043, in order to prevent private warfare, instead of issuing a *landfriede* (i.e. decreeing peace as a duty to the king), he held a " Day of Indulgence " at Constance at which he publicly announced his forgiveness of all who had wronged him and exhorted his subjects to follow this Christian example.

Bohemian
revolt
overcome

But disturbances had arisen again in the south-east. Bratislav of Bohemia had taken advantage of the anarchy in Poland to invade it with fire and sword; even Cracow itself was plundered and burnt. From Gnesen he took the bones of St. Adalbert to Prague, the bishopric of which he tried to induce the Pope to erect into an archbishopric, in order that his country, like Poland and Hungary, might be ecclesiastically independent of Germany. Whatever view Henry might take of this, it was certain that he would be gravely offended by the devastation of one vassal State by another, and Bratislav attempted to placate him. The king would be content with nothing less than Bratislav's appearance in person to do homage and make reparation, and as Bratislav failed to appear he led a punitive expedition against him in 1040. He fell into an ambush and had to beat a humiliating retreat. However, in the next year he took more precautions. Advancing with a large army on Prague, and supported by a simultaneous Bavarian attack in the south, he forced Bratislav to a complete surrender. The Bohemian duke had to abase himself before the king at Ratisbon, and after doing homage was reinstated in his duchy; he had learnt his lesson, and henceforward remained a faithful vassal. At the same time Casimir regained the duchy of Poland, also as a vassal of the king of Germany.

Hungary
recognises
German
overlordship

Hungary was by this time a centre of disturbance also. St. Stephen, left without a son, had passed over his brother's children and bequeathed the throne to Peter, the son of his sister Gisela and the Venetian doge Otto Orseolo. Stephen himself had married a sister of the Emperor Henry II, and valued the German and Italian connexion; his kinsfolk, he knew, were hostile to German influences and probably also to Christianity. Peter, who succeeded to the throne in 1039, showed no sense of the danger that threatened him, and even alienated German sympathies by allying with Bratislav. Then what Stephen had feared came to pass. A revolt broke out, and Peter had to fly for refuge to Henry III. The Hungarian nobles set up one of their number, Obo, as king, and he took the aggressive at once by raiding Bavaria with the ferocity of the Magyars of old. Henry after two expeditions forced Obo in 1043 to surrender the territory ceded by Conrad II, and in 1044 he restored Peter to the throne of

Hungary. Hungary, like Bohemia and Poland, now recognised his suzerainty, and its king did homage.

Everything so far had gone extremely well for him, but he was labouring under one disadvantage, the lack of a family to assist him in the work of government; he had no brother, and his eldest son was not born until 1050. He was himself the duke in three duchies, and it soon became evident that some delegation of authority was necessary. The danger from Hungary in 1042 decided him to appoint a duke of Bavaria; he chose Henry of Luxemburg, nephew of the duke whom he himself had succeeded. Then, in the year 1044, which witnessed his final triumph in Hungary, the serenity of the German sky was broken by what seemed a small cloud in the west, but proved to be the prelude to disaster for the monarchy. Duke Gozelo of Lorraine died, and his eldest son Godfrey, expecting to succeed his father in the whole duchy found himself confined to Upper Lorraine, while Lower Lorraine was given to his brother Gozelo. He never forgave this blow to his pride and ambition. He obtained allies in Lorraine and Burgundy, and soon broke into open revolt. Defeated, he was forced to submission in 1045 and was imprisoned. He was reconciled with the king in 1046 and received back his duchy; but, though his brother had died, Lower Lorraine was kept apart, and was given to Frederick of Luxemburg, the brother of duke Henry of Bavaria. Lorraine was not united again, and royal authority was never so strong there as it had been under the loyal government of Gozelo; more and more it tended to disintegrate into smaller sections, which often were only nominally subordinate to the king. A more immediate effect of the revolt of Godfrey and his allies was that it determined Henry in 1045 to appoint a duke to control the neighbouring Suabia in his interest; he chose Otto, count-palatine of the Rhine, a nephew of Otto III and uncle of duke Casimir of Poland.

By 1046 Henry III seemed to have reached a position of greater strength than any ruler since the time of Otto I. The weaknesses were to be revealed later—the unreality of his hold on Hungary, and the danger from Godfrey, who was implacable in his resentment. For the moment the prospect appeared completely bright, and it was now that he turned

Henry III and the duchies

Revolt of Godfrey of Upper Lorraine

The prospect in 1046

his attention to Italy and particularly to Rome, where the conditions were such as to shock all earnest Christians, chief among whom was the king himself.

Henry II had not interfered in papal elections except to support the nominee of the Tusculan house. Conrad had paid no heed at all to Roman politics; he had used the Pope as an instrument, and was not concerned as to his character. The dissolute life of Benedict IX was notorious, and in 1044 there was the further scandal of a schism, since the rival family of the Crescentii set up an anti-Pope, Sylvester III. Benedict was victorious, but he tired of his office and, it is said, was anxious to marry; and John Gratian, a man of high character, bought the Papacy he was anxious to reform, and became Pope Gregory VI. Soon Benedict repented of the bargain and sought to resume office; and Sylvester was still at large. It was a tangle that needed an overriding authority to unravel, and in 1046 Henry III came to Italy to undertake the task.

The situation at Rome

His first action on entering Italy preluded what was to come. He summoned a synod at Pavia which passed decrees especially against simony. On his way south he was met by Gregory VI, whom he treated as the rightful Pope. But Gregory had bought the Papacy and so was guilty of simony, and a second synod, summoned at Sutri, decreed his deposition; he passed into exile in the Rhine district and died the following year. Sylvester was disregarded as an intruder, and Benedict IX, who had little claim after his resignation, was probably deposed by a synod at Rome. At any rate, the papal throne was now held to be vacant, and on Christmas Day 1046, at Henry's instigation, bishop Suidger of Bamberg was elected as Pope Clement II. His first act was to crown Henry and Agnes as Emperor and Empress. At the same time the Romans gave Henry the title of " patricius," and thus recognised both his authority in Rome and his right to play a leading part in papal elections.

Henry comes to Rome

The reform of the Papacy

So Henry stood at the summit of his career. After half a century of aloofness, the king of Germany had again intervened in a papal election, and rescued the Papacy from the control of the Roman nobles; and, as before, the effect was to restore the prestige of the Papacy. There was an essential difference, however. For Henry III's purpose was not so much to make the Papacy subordinate to himself as to render it fitting to undertake the headship of the Church in the work of ecclesiastical reform. He was so successful that it did not now lose the prestige he had given it or fall again under the domination of the Roman nobles. Its advance was continuous from this moment, until at last it overthrew the power that had raised it up. The events of Christmas Day 1046 really brought the old régime to an end; from this date commences a new epoch in European history.

Before he returned to Germany, Henry paid a visit to South Italy; he renewed Conrad II's grant of Aversa to the Normans, but he reduced the power of their overlord Guaimar by taking Capua from him and restoring it to Paldolf. Superficially the political situation in South Italy had altered little during the eleventh century; the Moslems in Sicily hardly troubled the mainland any longer, and it was divided in allegiance between the Eastern and Western Empires. The old Lombard principalities—Salerno, Capua, Benevento, Naples—acknowledged the overlordship of the Western Emperor but enjoyed practical independence, except on the rare occasion of an imperial visit. The remainder was directly governed by Byzantine officials; Calabria they held securely, Apulia with more difficulty, since their Lombard subjects were alienated by imperial taxation and repression. In 1009 a certain Melo headed a revolt at Bari, and again with more effect in 1016. This revolt was responsible for the coming of the Normans into South Italy. *South Italy and its divisions*

In 1016 a body of Norman pilgrims landed in Apulia on their way back from the Holy Land. Melo tried to enlist them in his service; they refused, but they took back to Normandy with them his envoys to obtain recruits for him against the Greeks. There was at once a ready response, increasing in volume from 1017 onwards. The prolific families of the Norman nobility led to overcrowding in the restricted territory; there was a powerful inducement to seek a career abroad, while the love of adventure or the desire to escape the consequence of crimes committed at home brought a further and a less desirable reinforcement. For some time they served only as mercenaries, first of all under Melo, and then, when he was defeated by the Greeks *The coming of the Normans* and fled for refuge to Germany, under Guaimar of Salerno and Paldolf of Capua. They were rewarded ultimately with grants of land, the most important being that to Rainulf at Aversa, which he held from Guaimar, and which was confirmed to him by Conrad II and to his successor by Henry III.

The family of Tancred de Hauteville

A typical Norman family was that of Tancred de Hauteville, who had a modest patrimony and a numerous progeny to support upon it; of sons alone, he had five by his first wife and seven by his second. The three eldest, William, Drogo, and Humphrey, came to seek their fortunes in South Italy shortly before Conrad II's visit in 1038, and they soon took a leading position among their compatriots. They joined in a successful invasion of Sicily by the Greeks in 1038, and then in the revolt of the Lombard subjects of the Greeks which followed it. By this time the Normans were becoming so important that they were beginning to play a leading rather than a subordinate part. This was the position when the eldest son of Tancred de Hauteville's second marriage, Robert Guiscard, the future master of South Italy (who was to be followed later by his youngest brother Roger, the future master of Sicily) arrived in 1046. His step-brothers gave him a cold reception and a meagre portion of land; he had to fight his own way to success. This he did with typical Norman brutality, plundering and destroying, without mercy for individuals or respect for churches or monasteries. In Italy as elsewhere, the Normans before they acquired the land for their own were terrible in destruction, and South Italy still bears scars from the wounds they inflicted. When they became the masters of the land they showed a still greater genius in construction, but that time had not yet arrived. In 1046 the change was only just taking place. They had been helping others in return for pay; they were now beginning to help themselves.

SUGGESTIONS FOR READING ON CHAPTER III

Cambridge Medieval History, Vol. III, chapters 10, 11, 12.

Hampe, K.: *Deutsche Kaisergeschichte im Zeitalter der Salier und Staufer.* 7th ed. by F. Baethgen, Leipzig, 1937; 10th ed., Heidelberg, 1959.

Gay, J.: *L'Italie méridionale et l'Empire byzantin* (867–1071). Paris, 1904.

CHAPTER IV

FRANCE, 911–1050

THE French kingdom in the tenth and eleventh Weakness of the monarchy in France centuries presents a striking contrast with that of Germany. For the main current of European history we have to look to Germany, which under the Saxon kings became a powerful and a unified State. The kings of France, though recognised as such from the Channel to the Mediterranean and the Pyrenees, were far too weak to make their kingdom a reality ; when they attempted to play a part on a larger stage, they were brushed aside by the German kings, who excluded them from Lorraine and deprived them of contact with the kingdoms of Burgundy and Italy. France having no unity had no voice ; its interests were local and it was out of the main stream. The rapid growth of feudalism in France was both a sign and a cause of weakness of royal authority ; the great nobles, who had taken the place of the king in defending the country from invasion, ceased to be royal functionaries and used the power they obtained for their own and not for the kingdom's advancement. The kings themselves, in order to provide for the military defence of the country, united adjacent counties into a march or a duchy ; and the marquises and dukes were soon stronger than the power which created them and were unwilling to submit to its control. So France became divided into many sections, and the confusion is the greater because these sections, thus arbitrarily formed, had in themselves little unity or permanence. There is rarely a racial bond to hold a duchy together ; the counties of which it was composed struggled to separate themselves from ducal overlordship and were often successful. The only thing permanent was the vague recognition of royal authority in every section and sub-section ; this was the great asset monarchy possessed and ultimately its salvation.

The separ-
ateness of
the South

There was, in the first place, a radical line of cleavage between North and South. South of the Loire the king was rarely able to penetrate, and when he came there he found himself among a people of different manners and different dialect; the northerner and the southerner had difficulty in understanding one another, and each was contemptuous of the ways of the other. In a sense, the North and the South formed two separate kingdoms, though each recognised the same king; the later Carolingians styled themselves " kings of the Franks and the Aquitanians." The old kingdom of

Aquitaine

Aquitaine had been reconstituted by Charlemagne for his son Louis the Pious, and it was only as recently as 877 that it had been converted into a duchy by Louis II. In 911 the duke was William the Pious, count of Auvergne, who the previous year had founded the abbey of Cluny. His line came to an end in 928, and the duchy was contested between the counts of Poitiers and Toulouse. By the middle of the century the former had established themselves in definite possession, and a long succession of Williams, who styled themselves equally as duke of Aquitaine or count of Poitiers, followed one another by hereditary right. Occasionally they entered into general history, both indirectly, owing to their constant association with Cluny, and directly. William V had the ambition of the crown of Lombardy for his son, but the coalition he formed against Conrad II was a failure; however, the marriage of his daughter Agnes with Henry III was an important and a disastrous event in German history. But in general they kept to themselves and were singularly successful in maintaining their duchy and in extending its borders. In spite of spasmodic attempts of the French kings to intervene, they retained both their independence and their isolation, until at last the male line came to an end with the death of William X in 1137. His daughter and heiress Eleanor married first the king of France and then the king of England and took with her in each case the duchy of Aquitaine as her dowry.

Gascony,
Toulouse,
Barcelona

The duchy of Aquitaine was not commensurate with the former kingdom. The rest of the South, however, remained equally aloof from the king. The Gascons in the south-west had never been properly subjugated; their local independence came to an end shortly before the middle of the eleventh century, when the duchy of Gascony was incorporated with that of Aquitaine. East of Gascony the counts of Toulouse compensated themselves for their failure in Aquitaine by extending south and acquiring the march of Gothia—formerly Septimania, the last of the Visigothic possessions in Gaul—which brought them to the Mediterranean.[1] Finally, beyond the Pyrenees, lay the Spanish March, now dominated by the counts of Barcelona, who recognised French suzerainty to the extent of obtaining charters from the French king and requiring his aid against the Moors; as part of Catalonia, however, this district was associated rather with Spanish history than with French.

The South, then, was practically left to work out its own salvation both under the later Carolingian and under the early Capetian kings. The history of the kingdom proper is almost entirely concerned with the northern half. Here the creation of great marches, designed for the defence of the kingdom, had reduced the king not merely to impotence but even to dependence on his leading subjects. The duchy of Brittany in the north-west was peculiar in that it was inhabited by a people of strange speech and in French eyes semi-barbarous; through all this period it was as much aloof as Gascony in the south-west. East of Brittany came Normandy, also united by racial ties, but more truly part of the kingdom. The north-east was occupied by the march of Flanders, whose counts were easily able to ignore the claims of their royal suzerain; their importance increased with the growing wealth of their subjects owing to the revival of the woollen industry in the eleventh century; and they added to their possessions by acquiring territory which made them vassals of the king of Germany, though in no way subject to his authority. Another march had been formed in the south-eastern portion of this northern half of the kingdom, where by successive acquisitions the count of Autun, Richard known as the Justiciar, had become master of the whole of French Burgundy [2] with the title of duke. On his death in 921 the duchy of Burgundy passed intact to his son Raoul.

> The northern half of the kingdom. Brittany, Normandy, Flanders, Burgundy

---

[1] The county of Toulouse and the march of Gothia together came to be known as Languedoc.

[2] This must be carefully distinguished from (a) the kingdom of Burgundy, soon to be attached to the German Crown, and (b) the county of Burgundy (later Franche-Comté), which was part of the kingdom of Burgundy.

The march of
Neustria

But the greatest march of all was that of Neustria, created for Robert the Strong, who besides being count of Paris also dominated the counties of Maine, Anjou, and Blois. The ambition of the Robertine house dictated the fortunes of the French kingdom in the tenth century. Sometimes it grasped at the throne itself, at others it was content to govern without the title, until at last in the person of Hugh Capet it dispossessed the Carolingians for good and all. Robert the Strong's son Odo had been king of France, and though on his death in 898 the Carolingian Charles the Simple succeeded to the throne, the new marquis of Neustria, Odo's brother Robert, had no fears as to his capacity to bend the king to his own will. Besides his great principality in the centre, he was supported by his two sons-in-law, duke Raoul of Burgundy and count Herbert II of Vermandois. Hemmed in by Vermandois on the north, Burgundy on the south, and Neustria on the west, the Carolingian king, whose only important possession was Laon, was indeed in wretched state.

Charles the
Simple and
Lorraine

Yet Charles the Simple showed a capacity which belied his name and surprised his masters. Whether or no he visualised all the consequences, he must at least be given some credit for the treaty of St. Clair-sur-Epte, which created the duchy of Normandy for Rollo in 911. Though it did not immediately put an end to Norman aggression, it proved to be the correct solution of the problem. His own most urgent need was to extricate himself from the strangle-hold of Robert and Robert's sons-in-law ; he saw the one possibility, and he acted upon it with a vigour that deserved success. His only outlet was to the east, and though this meant an intrusion upon the German kingdom, the prospects both in place and time were propitious. The Carolingian line had come to an end in Germany, the new ruler was helpless against the dukes, and Charles could justly lay claim to the family domains in Lorraine. The Lothringian nobles were of the same view, and transferred their allegiance to the French king. There seemed to be the opportunity of building up the power of Austrasia again, and of restoring the family fortunes in the same way that they had been created, by a victory over Neustria. Charles showed less wisdom in his selection of Hagano, a humble-born Lorrainer, as his chief adviser and the principal recipient of his bounty ; he could not make of such a man a counterpart to the powerful nobles of France. But he was so far successful that he held Lorraine against Conrad I and even against Henry I, who in 921 recognised his possession of the duchy.

By this time, Robert of Neustria and his allies had realised the danger and accepted the challenge. In June 922 Robert was crowned king by archbishop Walter of Sens, who had crowned his brother; at the same time Charles lost his most important adherent in France by the death of the archbishop of Rheims. In a pitched battle at Soissons in 923, though Robert lost his life, Charles and the Lorrainers were decisively defeated. As Robert's son Hugh was too young, Raoul of Burgundy took his father-in-law's place and was immediately crowned king, again by the archbishop of Sens. This was not to the liking of Robert's other son-in-law, Herbert of Vermandois, who, himself a descendant of Charlemagne, was not content any longer to be a subordinate. The dissensions of his enemies, however, did not assist Charles. With a simplicity which he had not shown before, he trusted to the assurances of Herbert and put himself in his power; till his death in 929 he remained a prisoner, and the count of Vermandois found him a valuable pawn in his rivalry with king Raoul. The history of the French kingdom degenerates for a time into the story of a local family feud.

There were other factors contributing to the confusion of these years. The grant to Rollo had not satisfied his ambition, or induced him to cease from his destructive raids, while it encouraged the Normans invading by the Loire to further efforts in hopes of gaining a settlement for themselves. Rollo was bought off by the addition of the district of Bayeux to his duchy, but did not remain quiet for long. Equally terrible were the raids of the Magyars which had begun in the reign of Charles the Simple; in 926 after ravaging South Germany they penetrated almost to the gates of Rheims. Raoul made no more attempt than his predecessors had done to undertake the defence of the country as a whole. Each noble was left to defend his territory as best he could; the king was concerned only with his own domains, and so little sense was there of the common weal that it was normal practice to try to divert the invaders into the territory of a neighbour. In these circumstances, it was no wonder that

Robert of Neustria rival king

The reign of Raoul of Burgundy

Condition of the kingdom

Lorraine returned to its German allegiance in 925 ; Raoul had no better claim to it than Henry I, and he was helpless against German arms.

Improvement during Raoul's reign

But in the second half of his reign affairs took a different turn. After the death of Charles the Simple, Herbert of Vermandois could no longer pretend to be upholding the legitimate ruler, and Raoul was able to defeat him with the valuable assistance of his other brother-in-law, marquis Hugh of Neustria. Moreover, in a chance encounter with the Normans on the Loire in 930 he won so striking a success that the raids in this quarter seem to have come to an end. In Normandy, when Rollo died in 933, his son William Longsword did homage to Raoul, and was rewarded with the districts of Avranches and Coutances, the final stage in the formation of Normandy ; it now began to settle down and to become an integral part of the French kingdom. Raoul was also successful in defeating a Hungarian raid into Burgundy in 933. He even received recognition from the southern nobles. So, when he died in 936 he had done much to restore the prestige of the monarchy. Unfortunately he left no son to continue his work. His brother Hugh succeeded him as duke of Burgundy, but it was once again the marquis of Neustria who was master of the destinies of the kingdom.

Hugh the Great of Neustria and king Louis IV

This powerful noble, known as Hugh the Great, had succeeded to all his father's possessions and received in addition the title of " Duke of the Franks," an honorific designation rather than an office, and one that ranked him as the second person in the realm. The crown was in his grasp if he cared to take it. But the sentiment for a Carolingian ruler was still strong, especially among the clergy, and Hugh was satisfied to be second in rank to a king of whom he would be in fact the master. He took a leading part in the election of the son of Charles the Simple, Louis IV, known as " d'Outremer," since he had taken refuge with his mother " over the sea " in England when Charles was made a prisoner. Hugh treated the new king as the instrument of his own ambition, took him to Burgundy and there used royal authority to establish his own suzerainty over the duchy, a suzerainty which he converted shortly before his death into actual possession. But Louis was not content to remain passive. With hardly anything he could call his own, he saw like his father that his one hope was to build up a great principality in Lorraine. Again the moment seemed propitious, for Henry I was dead and Otto I was faced with revolt on every side. Yet the only result was to bring Otto and Hugh into alliance against him, and when the duke of Lorraine was killed in 939 Louis' cause was hopeless. His chief partisan in France, archbishop Artaud of Rheims, who had crowned him king, was driven from his see and Hugh, son of Herbert of Vermandois, was installed in his place.

Otto I was now in a position to hold the balance between his two brothers-in-law,[1] and he had no desire to see the duke of the Franks exalted further at the expense of the king. So Louis was able to make his peace in 942, renouncing his claim to Lorraine but gaining in return a powerful protector. Even this did not save him from further humiliation. In 945 he was unlucky enough to fall into Hugh's hands, and was not released until he had ceded his last possession, Laon. This outrage on the person of a king roused Otto to immediate action. He helped Louis to recapture Rheims in 946 and restore Artaud, and in 948 the two kings were present at a synod at Ingelheim where sentence of excommunication was pronounced on Hugh; and papal excommunication followed shortly afterwards. It brought Hugh to submission in 950, and for the last four years of his reign Louis, who had recovered Laon, was at least his own master. When he died in 954 there was no opposition to the election of his eldest son Lothar as king.

The intervention of Otto I

But Lothar was only fourteen years of age, and Otto I, embarrassed by the revolt of Liudolf and Conrad and by the invasion of the Magyars which followed, was not in a position to assist his nephew. Hugh the Great accordingly took charge of the young king, and used him to further his ambition, which now extended to the southern half of the kingdom. He obtained the title of duke of Aquitaine, and took Lothar with him on two ineffectual campaigns against Poitiers. Then in 956 he died, and his elder son Hugh Capet succeeded to the family possessions and the title of duke of the Franks, while his newly acquired duchy of Burgundy passed to his second son, Otto, and later to a third son Odo Henry. Thus

The reign of Lothar

[1] See above, p. 31.

Lothar was freed from tutelage, since Hugh Capet was too young to play the dictator. Moreover, Otto I had restored peace in his kingdom and had just won resounding fame by his great victory over the Magyars. France profited enormously by the cessation of the Magyar raids, the last and one of the most devastating of which had taken place in 954, and Lothar could look to the German king for protection against his domestic enemies; both Otto I and his brother Bruno, his regent in Lorraine, kept a watchful and a not disinterested eye on the security of the French king. Hugh Capet had to satisfy his ambition in other quarters, and attempted, with slight success, to extend his influence southward into Aquitaine and westward into Brittany; he was also not so strong in Neustria as his father had been. In these circumstances twenty years passed in peace such as the king of France had not known since the time of Charlemagne. These years are in consequence almost without incident, and the only event of importance reveals the improvement in the king's position. In 965, when count Arnulf of Flanders died, Lothar entered the county with an army, and not only forced the new count to do him homage but also acquired the towns of Arras and Douai. That the monarchy failed to maintain these possessions was due to the rash ventures of his later years.

His ambition in Lorraine   Not unnaturally he chafed at the need for protection, and lapse of time made him forget how great that need was. So when Otto I died and the youthful Otto II was immersed in domestic troubles, Lothar was tempted to make another bid for the Carolingian inheritance so long usurped by the German kings. He encouraged the plots that were being fomented against Otto II's authority in Lorraine, and in 978 came his own invasion and the counter-invasion of Otto which have been already described. He entirely missed his objective and he lost the friendship of the German king, who forthwith entered into an alliance with Hugh Capet; this would have been fatal to Lothar but for Otto's defeat in Italy and his death in 983. Meanwhile Lothar tried to win success in another quarter. In 979 he caused his son Louis V to be elected and crowned as his successor, and further revived in his favour the old title of king of Aquitaine; but he could not maintain him there, and soon had to go south again to extricate his son from an untenable position. Foiled in Aquitaine, he took advantage of the minority of Otto III to make one last attempt to win Lorraine. He even captured Verdun in 984, but it was only a flash in the pan. Not only did he retire discomfited, but by his Lothringian adventure he sealed the fate of his dynasty.

The one asset which the Carolingian house had retained in France when it lost its material possessions was the support of a section of the French clergy headed by the greatest of them, the archbishop of Rheims. The present archbishop, Adalbero, came from a family in Lorraine which was loyal to imperial authority; he had been alienated by Lothar's policy, and still more by the capture of Verdun where his brother was count. He was ably backed by the pro-imperial Gerbert, who had returned to Rheims after Otto II's death, and they allied themselves with Hugh Capet to frustrate the aims of Lothar. The Carolingian house was indeed in a desperate plight, for it had no friends left in France and had alienated the sympathies of Germany. Mercifully its end was swift, for Lothar died in 986 and his son Louis V the following year. The only surviving member of the royal family was Lothar's brother Charles, duke of Lower Lorraine, and as he was a subject of the king of Germany his claims were immediately dismissed. In the assembly held to decide the new election, the archbishop of Rheims, taking the lead as the archbishop of Mayence did in Germany, had no difficulty in persuading the nobles to choose Hugh Capet to be king of France.

The end of the Carolingian line in France

The accession of Hugh Capet has often been described as the victory of the feudal principle over the monarchical, of the idea of suzerainty over the idea of sovereignty; in the words of Montesquieu, "the title of king was united to the greatest fief." This is a mistaken view, for the Capetian kings had the same universal recognition and the same attributes of sovereignty as their predecessors. Though, in spite of the Teutonic practice of election, hereditary succession had become the practice, a crisis might demand a different choice; and when the royal line failed, election was obviously necessary. The king so elected had as good a title as the king by hereditary right. Nor was the election of Hugh Capet in any

Accession of Hugh Capet (987)

way surprising, for the only rulers other than Carolingian had been members of his family ; his great-uncle Odo, his grandfather Robert, and his uncle Raoul had all been kings before him.

The Capetian dynasty and hereditary succession

But what has made his election appear to future generations so different from that of his ancestors is the fact that, while their reigns were episodes interspersed in the history of the Carolingian dynasty, he founded a new line of kings which lasted for over three hundred years. It was at the time only the election of a new king ; it turned out to be the beginning of a new dynasty. As there were no rivals of the old legitimate line, it was easy for the early Capetians to obtain in their lifetimes the election of their sons, and they were fortunate in that there was always a son to succeed his father. Thus Robert II was already king when Hugh Capet died, and he caused his own eldest son Hugh to be crowned ; as Hugh died before him, the second son Henry I was elected and, in spite of his mother's partiality for her third son Robert, succeeded in due course. The age of the heir made no difference ; Philip I was only seven years old when he succeeded Henry. From being the custom, hereditary succession to the throne became the law in France, the rights of the eldest son being paramount ; when at last the male line failed in the fourteenth century, the only question was, who was the next heir.

Advantages of the Capetians over their Carolingian predecessors

Besides the fact that there was no rival house competing with them for the mastery, the early Capetian kings were obviously much more favourably placed than the later Carolingians. Hugh Capet had an extensive domain with Paris as its centre, and numerous adjacent counties under his lordship. The fragmentary remnants of Carolingian domain, too, naturally passed to the king, while adjacent to them were the territories of the faithful archbishop of Rheims, and farther south his brother's duchy of Burgundy. He had nothing to fear from the invasions which had exposed and perpetuated the weakness of the Carolingians. The Magyars had made their last raid, and Normandy had become an integral part of the French kingdom ; its duke, Richard I, was married to the king's sister. There was no conflict with Germany, for the Capetians had no claim to Lorraine, and there was no excuse for a German protectorate.

Nor were there any advantages that their predecessors had possessed which were denied to them. They were regarded as the legitimate sovereigns throughout the kingdom, even where they could exercise no actual authority; and there were many advantages and potentialities in kingship. They had the support of the Church, which had been largely instrumental in bringing Hugh Capet to the throne. This gave them material as well as moral backing, for in the previous half-century some of the leading bishops had been endowed with counties; for instance, the archbishop of Rheims and the bishops of Langres and Châlons. Like the kings of Germany, though on a much smaller scale, the Capetians could look to episcopal help and thus find supporters even outside the royal domain.

Yet, in spite of all these advantages, it is the weakness rather than the strength of the early Capetian kings that is evident in the somewhat meagre records of their reigns that we possess. The narrow limitations of royal authority are already manifest in the time of Hugh Capet, and from his reign onwards there was a progressive decline which was not arrested until the twelfth century. A new process of disintegration had begun by which the king and his family were principally affected. Whereas the grouping together of a number of counties had created the marches and duchies into which France was divided, a movement in the opposite direction was now in progress; the counties were striving to throw off the ducal yoke and regain their separate identity. The dukes of Aquitaine were singularly successful in maintaining their authority during the eleventh century, and in the north the dukes of Normandy and the counts of Flanders preserved their States intact; Brittany was, of course, peculiar in its racial aloofness. But in the territories that had been united under the single control of Hugh the Great the new movement was most effective. Blois was the first to take an independent line, Maine followed suit, and finally Anjou, which under the early Fulks and Geoffreys was extending its possessions in Touraine and south of the Loire was eating into Aquitaine as well; the formidable Fulk Nerra, the real founder of the Angevin fortunes, with his extravagant brutalities and his equally extravagant penances, became count in the same year that Hugh Capet became king.

Causes of continued weakness of the monarchy

The fact is that the march of Neustria had disintegrated, and that except in the county of Paris and some important towns, such as Orleans and Soissons, the authority of the duke of the Franks had become merely nominal. The situation would have been entirely different had Hugh the Great become king, but it is clear that Hugh Capet, before he ascended the throne, was already much weaker than his father had been. In his brother's duchy the same thing had happened. Burgundy was crumbling into fragments, as counties such as Troyes and Meaux became detached, while important bishops such as those of Autun and Langres ignored the duke and looked to the king as their overlord ; the duke, in fact, had little but the title left of his former greatness.

And, finally, the very fact of their sovereignty was a further cause of the weakness of the early Capetians. Instead of concentrating on the territories where their strength lay, they dissipated their energies in attempts to make their kingship more of a reality. Also the pressure of circumstances led them to grant out portions of their domains, as the Carolingians had done, as fiefs to their adherents (whose obedience they afterwards had difficulty in retaining) or as gifts to the Church ; hence their increasing impoverishment. Never did they sink so low as their predecessors had sunk, nor were they humiliated as their ancestors had humiliated the Carolingians ; but it was not until the twelfth century that they learnt to concentrate on what was really theirs, and so to give scope later for the potentialities of their royal office.

Alliance of Hugh Capet with Normandy   Since they were not powerful enough to command the obedience of the great feudatories, the king's best chance was to secure the assistance of some of them against the others. Hugh Capet was not unfortunately placed, for the duchy of Normandy to the north of his domain was consistently loyal to the Crown, and it remained so until the middle of the eleventh century. To the west of him, Fulk Nerra of Anjou and Odo I of Blois were so busy trying to enlarge their possessions at one another's expense that they gave him little anxiety ; and by judiciously throwing his influence into the scale against Odo, he secured the loyalty of Anjou.

On the other hand, he was involved almost at once in a conflict for his eastern possessions, developing into an ecclesiastical crisis which overshadowed in its importance everything else in the reign. It all began with the determination of duke Charles of Lower Lorraine, excluded from the French throne, to make good his rights as heir to the Carolingian domain. In 988 he seized Laon, and Hugh was unable to eject him. He even threatened Rheims, and the death of archbishop Adalbero in 989 greatly improved his prospects. Hugh then made what seemed to be a clever move. He secured the election as archbishop of Arnulf, a bastard son of king Lothar, thereby, as he hoped, dividing the Carolingian party. In the event, he only strengthened it, for Arnulf, elected in March, turned traitor in September and handed over Rheims to Charles. For two years Hugh was helpless and then he turned their own weapon against them; by the treachery of bishop Adalbero of Laon he got them both into his own hands. Charles he kept a prisoner till his death a year or two later, but he could not treat the archbishop so arbitrarily. He summoned a council of bishops, which declared Arnulf deposed and elected Gerbert to succeed him. By canon law the deposition of an archbishop needed papal assent, and Pope John XV, who had not been consulted, indignantly refused his sanction. His authority, however, commanded no respect, since he was notoriously under the thumb of the patricius Crescentius. The French bishops defied the Papacy and maintained their own view of Church law and government against the Pope. Papal legates presided over synods in France, but were unable to arrive at an accommodation. This was still the situation when Hugh Capet died in 996.

Conflict with surviving Carolingians leads to quarrel with Papacy

The new king, Robert II, who is generally known as "Robert the Pious," owes this appellation to the laudatory biography of him by his chaplain Helgaud; it is mainly a collection of anecdotes designed to depict Robert as a pattern of all the Christian virtues. He was, indeed, well-instructed in the learning of the day, so that he was interested in matters theological, but he was also a man of action, and often roused himself to uphold, and even to extend, the interests of the monarchy. He was gentle in a rough age, and lacking in the ferocious determination which marked so many of his

Robert II (996–1031)

contemporaries; this gives him an appearance of ineffectiveness which is perhaps not wholly deserved.

Conflict with
the Papacy
over his
marriage

At any rate, there was nothing of the saint about him in the early years of his reign. Inheriting a dangerous ecclesiastical conflict from his father, he proceeded to make it more acute by marrying Bertha, the widow of Odo I of Blois, though he was her cousin and had also stood godfather to one of her children. The marriage was doubly a breach of the law of the Church. It was unfortunate for him that the Papacy was at this very time released from its thraldom to the Roman nobles and had the imperial authority behind it to enforce its aims. Gregory V demanded both the restoration of Arnulf to Rheims and the repudiation of Bertha. The king sacrificed Gerbert, expecting in return to be granted a dispensation for his marriage with Bertha. It was a shabby bargain, and of no avail; the Papacy naturally pressed for a complete surrender. At last, when Gerbert had become Pope Sylvester II, Robert gave way and dismissed Bertha. In her place he married Constance, daughter of William of Arles. It was some compensation that Constance bore him children whereas Bertha had been childless; but they were an ill-assorted pair and domestic discord was added to the difficulties of his reign.

Weakness
of his
government

His infatuation for Bertha had other unfortunate consequences besides his humiliating surrender to the Papacy. It brought him into alliance with Blois and broke the tie with Anjou. When he repudiated Bertha, he estranged her son Odo II without recovering the friendship of Fulk Nerra. Odo was severely defeated by Fulk in 1016, but he gained an important success at the king's expense in 1023 when he vindicated his claim against the king's to the county of Champagne on the death of Stephen of Troyes; and as count of Blois and Champagne he menaced the royal domain on both sides. It was little wonder that Robert was so ineffective against Odo, for he was unable to preserve order even in the royal domain. He had spells of activity against the turbulent vassals who molested peaceful travellers and plundered monasteries, but it needed a greater and a more continuous effort than he was capable of; he could not obtain in his own domain the obedience that the great feudatories commanded in theirs.

Partly this was because he dissipated his energies. In Vindicates his claim to the duchy of Burgundy the earlier part of his reign he achieved one important success. When his uncle Odo Henry died in 1002, leaving only an adopted son Odo-William, count of Mâcon, Robert pressed his own claim to the vacant duchy of Burgundy with a persistence he rarely showed elsewhere, and though it took him thirteen years finally to defeat Odo-William, he did in 1015 achieve his purpose. Besides his own determination, it was Norman assistance that made his victory possible; with his own resources alone he certainly could not have achieved it. Odo-William was no mean foe, as he showed when he at last retired from the duchy and turned his attention to the kingdom of Burgundy. He ruled the " county " of Burgundy and he was one of the aspirants to the succession to Rudolf III. It was he, in fact, that frustrated the efforts of the Emperor Henry II in 1016 and 1018.

On this occasion Robert did not ally with Henry II Relations with Germany against their common enemy, but they did act elsewhere together where they had interests in common. They joined in an expedition in 1006 against Baldwin IV of Flanders, who was a source of danger to them both, and in 1023 they united against Odo II of Blois who after his acquisition of Champagne was beginning to make inroads into Lorraine. But when Henry II died in 1024, this valuable alliance came to an end. In 1026 Robert allowed himself to be drawn into the coalition against Conrad II which aimed at placing Odo of Blois on the throne of Burgundy and the son of William V of Aquitaine on the throne of Italy. Robert's share was to be the acquisition of territory in Lorraine. As we have seen, it came to nothing. It was a foolish scheme, recalling the follies of the Carolingians in the tenth century, this attempt at aggrandisement at German expense on the part of a French king who could not keep the vassals on his own domain in order. He could not even keep order in his domestic circle. The death of his eldest son Hugh in this very year, 1026, was followed by the attempt of Constance to obtain the succession for the youngest son Robert, and the king had great difficulty in effecting the election of Henry. Domestic feuds form the principal feature of the last five years of the reign; both his marriages may be ranked among his greater misfortunes.

Henry I
(1031–60)

Henry I started his reign in 1031 with the same domestic crisis. His mother and his brother broke into immediate revolt against him, and were joined by Odo of Blois ; the king, as usual, had the assistance of Normandy and to some extent of Anjou. He was successful in 1032, but in order to maintain peace found it necessary to hand over the duchy of Burgundy to his brother. So he surrendered his father's one important acquisition ; but perhaps it was not so important an acquisition after all, for the ducal authority of Robert and his descendants, who retained the title for over 300 years, was little more than nominal.[1] In the same year Rudolf III of Burgundy died, and this diverted the attention of the count of Blois.[2] With more wisdom than his father, Henry allied with Conrad II against him, and Odo was eventually forced to relinquish his attempt. He started at once on another adventure in Lorraine, where he met his death in battle in 1037. His territories, divided between his two sons, Theobald III receiving Blois and Stephen Champagne, were reunited again on Stephen's death in 1047. But Blois, though independent, was no longer the chief source of danger to the king. Its place was now taken by Anjou.

Cedes
Burgundy
to his
brother

The growing
power of
Anjou

The counts of Anjou, Fulk Nerra and his son Geoffrey Martel who succeeded him in 1040, showed a steady persistence in adding to their domains at the expense of their neighbours—Maine, Blois, Aquitaine [3]—and they avoided the reckless adventures in which Odo II of Blois wasted his resources, while they were at least his equals in audacity and brutality. Yet Fulk had his own distractions, for he went on no less than four pilgrimages to the Holy Land, the last at the age of 76 just before his death. Fulk had defeated Odo in 1016, Geoffrey defeated Theobald even more decisively in 1044 and forced him to cede Touraine, which definitely turned the balance in favour of Anjou.

The king was alarmed by the growth of this dangerous

---

[1] Robert was succeeded as duke of Burgundy by two grandsons in turn, the sons of his son Henry who predeceased him ; a third brother, Henry, went to seek his fortunes in the Spanish peninsula, and founded the first royal house of Portugal.

[2] Odo-William had died in 1026, so Odo of Blois was now Conrad II's only rival.

[3] Geoffrey Martel, even before he became count, had defeated the duke of Aquitaine in 1033 and held him prisoner for five years.

neighbour, and again he turned for assistance to Normandy. Alliance of
It had been the Norman duke, Robert I, who had made it Henry with
Normandy
possible for him to maintain himself at the beginning of his against
reign.   In return Henry had ceded to him the Vexin and had Anjou
promised to recognise Robert's illegitimate son William as
the next duke.   When Robert died in the Holy Land in
1035, he kept his promise, and later when a rebellion broke
out against the young William (then twenty years of age)
in 1047, Henry fought in person against the rebels and assisted
in their rout at the battle of Val-es-Dunes.   William accordingly joined him in an attack on Anjou, which was proceeding
successfully when the king suddenly changed sides.   He was Henry's
apparently satisfied with the check that had been given to volte face;
its conse-
Angevin aggression, and felt that more danger was to be quences
apprehended from the growing power of Normandy.   Perhaps
he hoped by playing them against one another to advance
his own position.   If so he was taking a gambler's risk, for
his resources were inadequate, and the loss was not commensurate with the gain.   The end of the Norman alliance,
which had meant so much to the monarchy, was an event of
the first magnitude in the history of France.   It occurred
just at the middle of the century, and coincided with the
regeneration of the Papacy by Henry III, the event which
radically altered the history of the German and Italian
kingdoms.

SUGGESTIONS FOR READING ON CHAPTER IV

Cambridge Medieval History, Vol. III, chapters 4, 5.
Lavisse, E. : *Histoire de France*, Vol. II.
Luchaire, A. : *Histoire des institutions monarchiques de la France sous les
    premiers Capétiens*, 2 vols.   Paris, 1891.
Petit-Dutaillis, C. : *The Feudal Monarchy in France and England from the
    10th to the 13th Centuries* (Eng. trans.).   London, 1936.
Fawtier, R. : *The Capetian Kings of France* (Eng. trans.).   London,
    1960.
Lot, F. and Fawtier, R. (eds.), *Histoire des institutions françaises au moyen
    âge*, 3 vols.   Paris, 1957–62.

CHAPTER V

THE REVIVAL OF CHRISTIANITY

Effects on the Church of the political disasters of the ninth and tenth centuries

THE Church was a principal sufferer from the evils which afflicted Europe in the ninth and tenth centuries. It suffered directly because it provided the main target for the savage attacks of the pagan Northmen and Magyars as well as of the Moslem Arabs. The hostility of the invaders to Christianity was vented on its churches and monasteries, its priests and monks. Being unarmed and unprotected as a rule, they were also an easy prey ; and finally their treasures were a magnet to the invaders, whose principal object was booty. The monks lost their homes and their possessions, and there was little encouragement for them to start their life again. It was equally hard for the bishops to train the clerks in their households and to provide the religious education required of them. The result, then, of the invasions of the ninth and tenth centuries was to cause not merely destruction of the material property of the Church, but also a collapse of its spiritual life. To this the internal discord and constant civil strife also contributed ; if less destructive it was at any rate more widespread and more continuous than the raiding of the enemies of Christianity.

Indirectly, too, the Church suffered a more permanent injury during this period. The royal power, which had as its principal duty the defence of the Church, was too weak to fulfil the task ; and both seculars and regulars were compelled, like the laity who were in a similar predicament, to put themselves under the protection of powerful nobles, who took over the charge of their property and often of appointments to ecclesiastical offices. The feudal system began to be extended to the Church, and the lay protection produced a steady growth of secularisation. Churches were treated as a form of property, and the rapid extension of lay patronage gravely interfered with the lawful functions of the bishops, who themselves were becoming, especially in Germany, engrossed in secular rather than in ecclesiastical employments.

The effects of this might have been only of a temporary character if the Church had been united under a centralised government. But the collapse of the Empire had been followed in a very short time by the collapse of the Papacy, and the same process of decentralisation that worked within the Empire worked within the Church also. Its grouping was determined by the political grouping, the boundaries of each portion of it coinciding with the political boundaries, as had been the case before, when the Roman Empire in the West was partitioned into barbarian kingdoms. As there had been a Frankish Church, a Visigothic Church, a Lombard Church, so now there was a German Church, a French Church, an Anglo-Saxon Church. Further subdivision came about, as the disintegration in the French kingdom proceeded. Though royal authority over the Church extended beyond the borders of the royal domain, there were some duchies from which it was excluded, and it would be almost correct to speak of a Breton Church, a Norman Church, or an Aquitanian Church as distinct entities. Further, the various parts into which the body of the Church was divided were almost separate from the head. When Otto I revived the Empire, a revival of the Papacy followed, but its competency was practically confined to the limited area which the Empire now embraced. It was possible for the French Church in the time of Hugh Capet to defy the Papacy, and to adopt what later was to be known as a Gallican attitude; and, but for the surrender of Robert II on personal grounds, it might have continued to maintain that position.

By the middle of the eleventh century a great deal of progress towards recovery had been made. First of all, Christianity was no longer on the defensive; it had taken the aggressive against paganism. Secondly, it was proceeding with its own internal regeneration, beginning with a great and widespread movement of monastic reform, which was followed by a movement for the reform of the secular clergy. And though little had actually been done towards the centralisation of Church government, there were various tendencies working in that direction; there was a sense of co-ordination of effort, which created a feeling of Church unity and so prepared the

The progress towards recovery

way for the centralisation which is the particular feature of
the succeeding period.

Advance of Christianity against paganism   The advance of Christianity against paganism has already
frequently been mentioned. Not only the Northmen who
settled in Normandy and England had become Christians,
but so too had the Scandinavians in all three kingdoms. The
final introduction of Christianity, against which there had
been several reactions, coincided with the formation of these
national kingdoms, in Denmark in the tenth century, and
in Sweden and Norway at the beginning of the eleventh.
They were all, ecclesiastically, within the province of Bremen,
but they maintained a national aloofness, and some of the
most popular saints, such as King Olaf of Norway who died
in battle against Canute, were really national rather than
Christian heroes. At the middle of the eleventh century the
archbishop of Bremen, Adalbert, was engaged in a strenuous
campaign to make his metropolitan authority more effective.
We have seen that the conquest of the Northern Slavs was
accompanied by missionary work for their conversion, and
that Otto I effected the creation of a new province of Magdeburg for that area. Bohemia and Poland had been Christianised also, and though Bohemia remained ecclesiastically
within the province of Mayence, Poland had its own archbishop. Finally, Hungary under St. Stephen had become a
Christian country, and it too had its own archbishop.

The expulsion of the Moslems from France and Italy   The victory over paganism was, therefore, almost complete, and the offensive against the Moslems had already
begun. They had been expelled from central Italy and the
south of France in the tenth century, though they still held
Sicily and were not completely dislodged from South Italy.
The Eastern Empire had been engaged in four centuries of
warfare with them, both in the east and in the west ; since
the great victory of Leo the Isaurian at the beginning of the
eighth century it had been mainly a question of border
skirmishes with varying results. The recovery of their naval
pre-eminence had improved the Byzantine position, but in
the west the hostility of Latins and Greeks, of Western
and Eastern Christians, delayed the advance. In the first
half of the eleventh century, however, the Moslems were
confined to Sicily, and even there the Byzantines, with

Norman and Lombard assistance, had made temporary conquests.

But in Spain the Moslems still retained the upper hand. The Caliphate of Cordova, founded by Abd-ar-Rahman III in 929, had united them and checked for a century the advance of the Christian States. Both Abd-ar-Rahman himself until his death in 961 and Almanzor (" the Victorious "), vizier of Hisham II during the last quarter of the tenth century, inflicted frequent defeats on the Christians. Their armies were recruited, not only from the Berber tribes of North Africa, but also from the native population, some of them " Renegades " who had embraced the Moslem faith, others " Mozarabs " who remained Christians though they usually adopted Arab speech and customs. Under Abd-ar-Rahman a fleet was necessary against the Fatimites in North Africa, and it became the most powerful in the Western Mediterranean; after his death, with the decline of the Fatimite power in North Africa the necessity disappeared and the fleet was neglected. But it had played its part in promoting the commercial prosperity of the Caliphate. During the tenth century Moslem civilisation attained to its height in Spain; in industry, commerce, agriculture, and finally in learning, Spain under the Caliphate was the foremost country in Western Europe, and Cordova with its great buildings and its royal library the most brilliant city. All this prosperity had been made possible by political unity, and it began rapidly to decline with the outbreak of civil strife that followed the death of Almanzor in 1002. The Caliphs were becoming mere figure-heads. Almanzor, though only vizier, was the real ruler of the State; but after his death the power of his family aroused jealousy and caused numerous revolts, and a Council of State eventually took over the government. By this Council the last Caliph, Hisham III, was deposed in 1031, the Caliphate was declared to be at an end, and independent kingdoms took its place. The Moslem State had lost its unity; it accordingly lost its predominance in Spain.

The Caliphate of Cordova (929–1031)

It says something for the tenacity of the independent Christians that they were in a position to take immediate advantage of the divisions of their enemies. At the time of the Moslem conquest of Spain in the eighth century they had

Beginnings of the Reconquest

been driven into the Cantabrian mountains in the north-west, where the little kingdom of Asturias was formed, with its capital at Oviedo, under a king Pelayo, whose semi-mythical career is the beginning of the great epic of the Reconquest. Slowly they advanced from the hills and had reached Leon by 866. Profiting by the Moslem divisions they actually attained the line of the Douro by the beginning of the tenth century ; King Ordono II moved his court from Oviedo to Leon, and changed his title from king of Asturias to king of Leon. Then again the Moslems were united under Abd-ar-Rahman III, and the Christian advance came to an end ; but, in spite of his frequent victories and those of Almanzor at the end of the century, the Moslems made no permanent occupation of the territory they overran. The kings of Leon were able gradually to consolidate their position. Leon and the surrounding countryside were repeopled by " Mozarabs," who immigrated from the south and put the land into cultivation once more. The eastern part of the kingdom, Castile, still only a county, was repeopled by inhabitants of the mountain regions who had never been subject to Moslem rule. East of Castile, the kingdom of Navarre emerges into history in the ninth century and begins to take a part in the task of reconquest. Farther east still was the Spanish March of the Franks, comprising the northern half of Catalonia ; it was dominated by the counts of Barcelona, who throughout the tenth century recognised the overlordship of the French king but were beginning also to join in the southern advance. The weakness of the Christians lay especially in their divided authority. There were three main States, which became four when in the middle of the tenth century Castile established its independence of Leon.

The Christian kingdoms in Spain

The death of Almanzor in 1002, and the internal dissensions of the Moslems culminating in the end of the Caliphate in 1031 gave the Christians their opportunity. In this period the lead was taken by Navarre under its king Sancho Garzia III (1000–35), who not only extended his kingdom north and east but also acquired Castile by inheritance. There was a prospect of unity under his authority, but when he died he divided his kingdom into three—Castile in the west, Navarre in the centre, and Aragon to the east—so that there were now four kingdoms besides Catalonia. The most important was Castile under Ferdinand I; in 1037 he achieved the conquest of Leon, which became permanently attached to the Castilian crown. So by the middle of the eleventh century the three kingdoms of Castile, Navarre, and Aragon were in existence, and the real Reconquest was about to commence under the lead of Castile, which almost always played the principal part in it. From this date the initiative in the Spanish peninsula begins to pass from the Moslems to the Christians.

The zeal for the expansion of Christianity and the mis- Church Reform
sionary endeavour could not have been possible if the Church
had remained stagnant and unregenerate. The same missionary zeal was at work within the Church itself, to drag
it from the slough into which it had sunk and to revive
its spiritual life once more. This began naturally with the The monasteries
monasteries, for more could be expected of those who were
supposed to be living the higher life, apart from the world.
In actual fact, many of them were living openly in the world,
for the prohibition to leave the monastery, like most of the
provisions of the Rule of Benedict, had become a dead letter;
and this was hardly to be wondered at when laymen, often
married, were abbots, and the vows of chastity, poverty,
and obedience were completely ignored. It was a symptom
of the better conditions that were to prevail in Europe in
the tenth century that at its very inception there began two
movements for monastic reform : the one, famous, at Cluny ;
the other, less known but equally important, with its centre
in Lorraine.

In 910 the abbey of Cluny, situated in the south of the Cluny in the tenth century
duchy of Burgundy, was founded by duke William the Pious
of Aquitaine, who appointed as its abbot a certain Berno,
already abbot of a monastery founded by himself at Gigny
in the same neighbourhood. Berno set to work at once to
establish in his new monastery the strict observance of the
Benedictine Rule, to which were added customs peculiar to
Cluny though not at first conflicting with the essentials of
the Rule. Silence was enforced in the cloister, the eating
of meat was forbidden, but no encouragement was given to
the excessive asceticism so common in monastic revivals,
which though it attracted the zealot at the moment was

extremely difficult to maintain over a long period. Here again the spirit of the Rule was followed ; it was to be one that the ordinary man who felt that he had a vocation could reasonably be expected to observe. Cluny had been founded by a great noble, and it drew the attention of the great, especially those who wished to see elsewhere enforced the principles Berno had established at Cluny. But it already departed in one important point from the Benedictine Rule. It was exempt from any authority save that of the Pope alone, and in the existing condition of the Papacy this meant practically complete independence. What mattered most of all was that it was free from lay control, and that by its charter of foundation it had free choice of its own abbot. It was fortunate, too, in its tenth-century abbots—Berno, Odo, Aymer, and Mayeul. Berno from the beginning—and his successors after him—was called upon to reform older monasteries elsewhere, in France and Italy, even in Rome. This was a personal undertaking, and not done on behalf of their abbey ; for the monasteries, when the work was done, did not remain subject to Cluny. Cluny had, in fact, very few dependent houses in the tenth century. Its fame was due to the example it set and to the reputation of its abbots.

Lorraine in the tenth century

Almost simultaneously with the foundation of Cluny, and quite independently, a monastic revival was begun by Gerard of Brogne in Lower, and the monks of Gorze in Upper, Lorraine. Here too the principal feature of the movement was the strict enforcement of the Benedictine Rule, which was interpreted even more conservatively than at Cluny. There was no single abbey to serve as a model, but it was rather a general movement and was especially directed by the bishops in Lorraine. From there it spread into Flanders and into Germany, where it received the support of Otto I, his brother Bruno of Cologne, and his son William of Mayence. The foundation of new monasteries as well as the reform of older ones was a feature of the movement. But these monasteries did not enjoy the freedom of Cluny. They were not exempted from diocesan authority. The greater ones especially were under royal control, and the policy of Otto I, which applied to abbeys as well as to bishoprics, caused the abbots usually to be royal nominees and imposed secular duties upon them which made true Benedictine observance almost impossible. There was, therefore, in Germany at any rate, a reaction after the first revival.

A very considerable effort towards monastic reform had been made during the tenth century. It was in the eleventh century, however, that the really important development took place. This is the golden age of Cluny under its two greatest abbots, Odilo and Hugh, who divided the century between them; Odilo (994–1048) was the originator, Hugh (1049–1109) the perfector. It was through them that the Cluniac system proper was developed, and that Cluny from being only a single Benedictine monastery became the head of an Order. It was soon the mother of a huge family; numerous daughter-houses were founded in Italy, Spain, and England as well as in France and Burgundy. In the Benedictine system each monastery was an independent unit. In the Cluniac they were all directly dependent on Cluny. There was only the one abbey; its dependencies were all priories. The work of reforming older monasteries was increasingly added to the labours of the abbot, but these monasteries were now made directly subject to Cluny; a few regained their independence, but most of them remained Cluniac, and some were reduced to priories. A vast organisation was created, for Cluny had some hundreds of houses dependent upon her; and to these dependent houses was extended the immunity granted to Cluny, exemption from diocesan authority. Wealthy, for kings and nobles vied with one another in giving him money and lands, and powerful owing to the wide range of his authority, the abbot of Cluny was one of the great princes of the Church. He was the head of a monastic order, and in this his time and his interests were fully engrossed. *The Cluniac movement in the eleventh century*

In Germany, and especially in Lorraine, there was also an important development of monastic reform at the beginning of the eleventh century. Henry II especially favoured it, and so did his friend Pilgrim, archbishop of Cologne. The influence of Cluny now began to be distinctly felt. Monasteries were temporarily made subject to others for the purpose of reform, and the Customs of Cluny formed the basis for the constitutions of several monasteries. But, though much of the spirit of Cluny was introduced, its particular feature, a centralised organisation, was lacking. The monasteries *The movement in Lorraine in the eleventh century* remained Benedictine monasteries of the old type, being with few exceptions independent of one another and at the same time subject to diocesan authority. In fact, besides the king, it was the bishops who played the leading part in directing the movement. Cluny and its dependent houses were isolated, a separate organisation. In Lorraine there was equal fervour for reform but no isolation; the monasteries were closely associated with the bishops and so with the general organisation of the Church.

Its influence elsewhere

This movement in Lorraine influenced other parts of the Church as well. Both in the tenth and in the eleventh centuries it spread not only east into Germany, but also north into Flanders and west into Normandy. The dukes of Normandy were ardent promoters of Church reform and especially of monasticism; they built monasteries, and gave monks, as they were to do in England later, a leading part in the life of their Church. Here, too, influences from Cluny mingled with the original impulse from Lorraine; when Lanfranc gave new constitutions to his cathedral monastery at Canterbury it was on the Customs of Cluny that he based them. In England, Dunstan had already in the tenth century led the way in monastic reform, and here again the continental examples were doubtless his model.[1] Monasticism played a special part in England, since some of its cathedrals were served by Benedictine monks and not by secular canons, a peculiarity which was even extended after the Conquest. So monasticism had come to take a great part in the life of the Church, but now two types must be distinguished : the one, Cluniac, a separate branch of the Church, as it were ; the other, reformed Benedictine, a part of the normal organisation of the Church.

Reform of the secular clergy

The reform of the rest of the Church lagged behind that of the monasteries, though ultimately it was more important and more permanent. In the tenth century little progress was made, though in some areas there was improvement, especially where the lay power favoured it. A ruler like Otto I was naturally anxious to see order and decency prevail in the Church, though his policy otherwise handicapped the

---

[1] When in exile, he had stayed at St. Peter's, Ghent, one of the Flemish abbeys reformed by the Lothringian Gerard of Brogne.

spiritual activities of the ecclesiastical officials. But at the beginning of the eleventh century the movement for reform began in earnest and had several centres.

The monasteries had set the example, and they gave their assistance, but they did not take the lead. The credit for the reform, especially in its later and more advanced stage, has commonly been attributed to Cluny. Perhaps this was because the great figure in that later stage, Pope Gregory VII, was believed, quite erroneously, to have come from Cluny. Individual Cluniac monks were called in to assist, and were sometimes, as in Normandy and England, given bishoprics. The Pope might beg for a monk from Cluny, and one such, the prior Odo, was made cardinal by Gregory VII and later became Pope as Urban II.[1] The advice of the abbot of Cluny was naturally sought, and his co-operation at councils was sometimes obtained. But to describe Cluny as the source and inspiration of the movement is quite contrary to fact. The Cluniac programme was a monastic programme. Its abbot, who had absolute control, was fully occupied with his task of governing a great monastic Order. He did not, like St. Bernard afterwards, feel it his business to dictate upon the general management of the Church. *Its direction not due to Cluny*

The direction of the movement, and the character it took, depended at first upon those who controlled the Church in each locality—that is to say, primarily on the lay rulers, and secondarily on the ecclesiastical officials ; it was the former who initiated it wherever it came into being. There was no unity in the movement, because the head of the Church, who alone could give it unity, was not interested. However, the Emperor Henry II was keenly interested, and it was largely his zeal which gave the movement so much initial vigour. From some of the bishops, especially his friend Pilgrim of Cologne and others in Lorraine, he received enthusiastic support ; he forced concurrence from others who were lukewarm if not secretly hostile ; he even in 1022 obtained the co-operation of Pope Benedict VIII. The kings of France did not imitate him, but some of the leading nobles took a part ; the dukes of Aquitaine seem to have been fairly *But to lay rulers and bishops*

---

[1] He is the only Pope at this time who came from Cluny. His successor, Paschal II, is often said to have been a Cluniac monk, but this has recently been disproved.

active in the south, while in the north the dukes of Normandy were energetic reformers. In fact, the very people who were responsible for the development of monastic reform (apart from Cluny) in the eleventh century were the people who were promoting reform among the secular clergy. The two movements were closely associated where the monasteries were part of the normal organisation of the Church and subject to the bishops. Monks were constantly employed to fill the highest offices in the Church. In Germany the king, in Normandy the duke, watched over the whole and kept it under his direction. In Lorraine, where ecclesiastical authority was strong and lay power was becoming gradually weaker, the reformers were able to develop along their own lines ; and it was from this region rather than from Cluny that the more advanced reformers were to come.

Simony

In this early stage there were two evils against which the reformers directed their main attack—Simony and Clerical Marriage. Simony, the sin of Simon Magus, the buying or selling of ecclesiastical office or preferment, was widespread. Many bishops had bought their sees, and recouped themselves by selling the offices within their gift and even charging for ordination to the various grades in the ministry. It was a difficult problem for it touched all, high and low, and moreover it touched the lay power as well, since ecclesiastical preferment depended to so large an extent on lay nomination. Henry II, though he was financially the loser, strove to stamp it out. Conrad II had no interest in reform, and to him the payment of a sum from a bishop who succeeded to lands derived from the Crown was only the natural counterpart of the fine a lay vassal would pay on inheriting an estate on the king's domain. Henry III, on the other hand, was as strongly opposed to it as Henry II. They were acting in their best interests, as events proved. In the case of rulers who were keen reformers, like themselves or like William the Conqueror, the fact of their control of the Church was hardly criticised. But when a ruler allowed or encouraged the practice of simony, he drew the fire of the reformers on to the lay control which made the practice possible.

Clerical marriage

While simony affected all ranks of the clergy, clerical marriage concerned the lesser clergy only, since the celibacy of bishops was unquestioned. There were a number of reasons why the question of clerical celibacy was felt to be so important. It had regularly been prescribed by the law of the Western Church (unlike the Eastern Church, where married priests, though not married bishops, were the rule), and it was enforced not only on priests but on deacons and subdeacons as well ; only the lowest orders—acolyte, exorcist, lector—were exempt. The law had the force of religious sentiment behind it, since chastity was felt to be so essentially a part of the higher life. In accordance with the views on the Eucharistic Sacrifice formulated in the ninth century, it was felt that those privileged to " make " (*conficere*) the Body of Christ must keep their bodies wholly pure. So, at a council at Augsburg in 952, in which Otto I himself participated, marriage was forbidden to priests, deacons, and subdeacons, because they handled the divine mysteries. There was another reason of an entirely different nature. In spite of the regulations, probably a considerable majority of parish priests were married. They wished to make provision for their families, and especially to pass on their benefices to their sons. The lay patrons made little objection, as the benefice was to them like any other property, so that benefices were becoming hereditary and Church property was being alienated. Though priests' sons were declared illegitimate and therefore disqualified for ordination, the practice went on. Even in the twelfth century, we can see from papal decretals how difficult it was to prevent benefices being handed down from father to son.

Decrees against simony and clerical marriage were multiplied at synods, but little advance was made against practices that were of long standing and well-nigh universal. The object of the reformers was to ensure that spiritual offices should be held by spiritually-minded persons. The root of the whole matter lay in getting the right people appointed, and this did not rest with the Church but with laymen. The higher offices were filled by royal nomination, or even sometimes, as in France, by ducal ; canonical election was a mere formality. The parish churches were regarded as the property of the lords on whose lands they stood, and these lords therefore asserted the right to nominate the incumbents. In both cases the Church claimed the final say, but the archbishop who had to examine the qualifications of the bishop elect, the bishops who had to examine the priest presented by the lay patron, were often negligent in performing their duties ; very rarely had they the inclination or the capacity to stand up for their rights.   The lay control of appointments was so customary that it was not at first realised that it was in fact the chief obstacle to reform. Bishop Wazo of Liége, who made a clear distinction between the spiritual and secular functions and obedience of the bishops, and who reproached Henry III for his interference with papal elections, was adopting a standpoint soon to be common, but at that time quite exceptional.

Against some of the more violent interferences of laymen the Church did make a stand.   The holding of Church property, especially of tithes, by the laity was prohibited, if *The Truce* *and the* *Peace of God* not prevented.   And the Church had taken important action to protect itself from the effects of the warfare that was the chief pursuit of the baronage by the proclamation of the *Truce of God* ; this was initiated in the South of France at the end of the tenth century, and forbade under pain of ecclesiastical penalties any violence to be done to the persons or property of non-combatants.   Fifty years later, a further advance was made in the *Peace of God* (*c.* 1040), which forbade any fighting to take place between Thursday night and Monday morning in each week so that there might be perpetual peace on the days which commemorated the Passion and Resurrection of Our Lord.   It had only a temporary success, but at the time it did something to curb violence, and it set an example.   Henry III's " Day of Indulgence " in 1043 was only an enlargement of the Church's idea.

Lack of central organisation The Church was suffering under a handicap, for it was practically divided into sections, and it lacked the central authority which alone could give it unity.   It had become, as it were, a loose federation under the nominal headship of the Papacy.   Reform depended on the local authority, and it would have been useless to look to the Pope to take the lead, for the Roman Church was perhaps the one that most of all needed reform.   Obviously the reform of the Papacy was a necessary precedent to a true reform of the Church, and this could only be brought about, in accordance with precedent, by the Emperor.   Till that was

done there could be no question of unity or of a central
authority.

It was just such a situation as was now existing in the Papal
government of the Church that the author of the pseudo- authority
Isidorian Decretals had set out to combat in the ninth precedent
century.   In order to destroy the local autocracy of metropolitans and lay rulers, and to restore what he believed was
the old state of affairs—unity under papal headship—he had
compiled his famous forgeries.   Under Nicholas I papal
headship became a reality, and this was an important precedent.   The False Decretals were still more of a reality,
since they remained in existence and no one knew them to be
other than genuine.   They were not very widely known before
the middle of the eleventh century.   Older collections of
Church law, especially the genuine collection to which the
forger had attached his spurious documents, were more
common.   But they were known to a few ; for instance,
bishop Wazo of Liége bases upon them his views on the
exalted position of the Papacy and the distinction between
spiritual and secular functions.

The state of the law of the Church is important in this The
connexion.   It had never been codified like Roman Law, character of
and it was not quite certain of what it was composed, since Church law
there was no single authoritative collection.   The decrees of
Councils (local as well as general), the decretals (judgments)
of Popes, the writings of the Fathers, even chapters of Roman
Law—these were the materials out of which individuals made
collections, which were usually not widely published, so that
the books of law differed from place to place ; especially
since each individual naturally chose the material which
fitted in best with his own view of what the government and
constitution of the Church ought to be.   But at the beginning
of the eleventh century a noted canonist, bishop Burchard
of Worms, drew up a large collection, which had an unusually
wide currency, in Germany, France, and North Italy.   He
used many of the earlier collections, among them the False
Decretals, but he selected according to his own view, which
was that the normal government was by provinces, under
the metropolitan and his suffragans ; and though he clearly
recognised the headship of the Papacy, the authority of its
court in important cases, and its competence as the source

and interpreter of the law, he certainly did not envisage its interference with provincial self-government. On the other hand, though in practice he worked quite happily under Henry II, he included several decretals against lay interference with the Church; and therefore the book of law most widely used did make clear that much of the prevailing practice was contrary to the law. Moreover, anyone who made use of the False Decretals, without coming to it with a preconceived idea as Burchard did, would be faced with the constant reiteration of the supreme authority of the Papacy in every department of Church government.

The influence of the Cluniac movement There was, therefore, both precedent and law to be adduced on behalf of a centralisation of the Church under papal authority. And there was one great fact in this period which must not be left out of account. Cluny was not directly concerned with the reform movement, except in monastic reform, but it was itself independent of lay control and it was dependent directly on the Papacy. This great organisation, then, was one part of the Church which did recognise the direct authority of the Papacy over it, and many other monasteries were anxious to be in a similar position. Here indirectly Cluny does contribute to the future, not by any interference with lay authority elsewhere, for the abbot of Cluny never took the lead in this; but by the example it set of independence and of direct subjugation to the Papacy.

The reform of the Papacy Papal authority in the first half of the eleventh century was feeble and local, but this was because the Papacy was in the hands of the Roman nobles. There were potentialities in the law and in its past history which it only needed release from its thraldom to reveal. Henry III gave it that release in 1046; he gave, besides, reforming Popes to the Roman Church. Naturally they took the lead in the reform movement, and in this way resumed again the headship of the Church. And then they found themselves faced by the lay control which made the headship so ineffective and the reform so difficult, and which also threatened their own independence. Between a determined Pope and a determined king conflict was inevitable.

SUGGESTIONS FOR READING ON CHAPTER V

For Spain see books suggested in Chapter XVI.
For Church reform :
  Cambridge Medieval History, Vol. V, chapters 1, 2.
  Hauck, A. : *Kirchengeschichte Deutschlands*, Vol. III.
  Lea, H. C. : *History of Sacerdotal Celibacy*, 3 ed. 2 vols. London, 1907.
  Stutz, U. : *Die Eigenkirche als Element des mittelalterlich-germanischen Kirchenrechts*. Berlin, 1895 (trs. Barraclough, G., in *Medieval Germany*, Vol. II. Oxford, 1939).
  Schmitz, P. : *Histoire de l'Ordre de Saint Benoît*. 5 vols. Maredsous, 1942–9.
  de Moreau, E. : *Histoire de l'église en Belgique*, Vols. II (2 ed.) and III. Brussels, 1945.
  Knowles, D. : *The Monastic Order in England, 940–1216*. 2nd edn., Cambridge, 1963.

CHAPTER VI

THE EASTERN EMPIRE, 912–1056

The place
of the
Eastern
Empire in
European
history

IN modern times the terms European and Western have become almost synonymous. All European nations have been attracted into the orbit of Western ideas and civilisation, so that in spite of their diversity there is a certain coherence in European history. So, when we speak of medieval Europe, we naturally think first of those States which were then Western in civilisation ; in a general history of Europe there is justification for this, because it is from those States that modern European civilisation has been derived. In the Middle Ages, however, and particularly in the tenth century, European and Western were not synonymous. Bohemia, Poland, and Hungary had thrown in their lot with the West, but not yet Russia, the Balkans, or Greece. The nucleus of the West was that half of the Roman Empire which the Germanic peoples had over-run. The other half, which, after the Empire of Charlemagne had come into being, may properly be styled the Eastern Empire, had a distinctive and a higher civilisation of its own ; it derived its chief strength from its Asiatic provinces, and, though its capital, Constantinople, impregnable and magnificent, was actually in Europe, it may in a certain sense be described as non-European. This is still true at the end of the eleventh century, when it had lost so much of Asia Minor and geographically was more European than Asiatic. Its civilisation is Eastern and Greek, in striking contrast with the Western and Latin civilisation that dominated most of Europe.

Its influence
on western
civilisation

But, though the Western world has the chief claim to consideration in the history of Europe in the Middle Ages, the Eastern Empire cannot be left out of account, for it exercised both directly and indirectly a considerable influence on the history of the West. It was in direct contact owing to its retention of South Italy, until the conquest by the

Normans in the second half of the eleventh century. Its presence there gave various advantages to Italy. The constant struggle in which it was engaged with the Moslems, in the west as well as in the east, protected Italy from their raids. In this connexion the naval strength of the Eastern Empire is important; there was no other Christian naval power in the Mediterranean in the tenth century save Venice, and Venice recognised the nominal suzerainty of Constantinople. Roman Law was kept alive by its use in the Byzantine provinces of South Italy, whence the higher culture of the East, its art and architecture, assisted the revival of Western culture; this came in, too, in the north, via Venice and Ravenna, and at second hand through the Moslems into Spain. In constant conflict with barbarian hordes to the north and Bulgarians to the west of Constantinople, the Eastern Empire acted as a bulwark to Western Europe. Yet its relations with the Westerners were never friendly. It regarded them as barbarians who had stolen its inheritance; they regarded it as an interloper in their domain. There was continual friction, too, between the Popes and the Patriarchs of Constantinople over the question of papal authority. The ill-feeling which is so clearly evinced during the Crusades was already deeply rooted long before the eleventh century.

For practically 200 years the Macedonian dynasty was in possession of the Imperial throne of the East; it had been reigning in Constantinople for 45 years when the new German monarchy began in 911, and it did not become extinct until 1056, the year that the Emperor Henry III died in Germany. There were some striking military successes, which did much to maintain the prestige of the Empire and to preserve its integrity; there was a tradition of learning, of literary and legal attainment, fostered principally by the Emperors themselves. On two occasions a long minority occurred, but this did not make for weakness, since the power was seized by successful generals whose capacity was of service to the Empire. Rather it was the legitimate Emperors who, with few exceptions, proved themselves to be unfitted for their difficult task; especially were they unable to maintain the internal order necessary to a State with so many dangerous enemies on its frontiers. The tale of domestic discord, of palace intrigues, of ecclesiastical quarrels, is monotonously

The Macedonian dynasty

reiterated. There were frequent periods of degeneracy and decline; the worst and most fatal of all set in during the last thirty years, leading almost to a collapse of government, just at the very time that the Empire needed all its resources to stay the gathering momentum of the great empire of the Seljuk Turks.

Basil I and Leo VI

The first two Emperors of the Macedonian house—Basil I and Leo VI—had done valuable work in financial, judicial, and legal reorganisation; they had shown as well a keen interest in culture and art. Basil, besides, was an able general. Leo had no military capacity, though he wrote a famous treatise, *Tactics*, on the art of war, but he has left a name for himself as one of the greatest of imperial legislators; his famous work, the *Basilics*, in 60 books, re-codified in one collection the code of Justinian, and brought it up to date with the Novels (i.e. new law) of later Emperors. He died in 912, and was succeeded by his son Constantine VII (known as Porphyrogenitus, " born in the purple "), who was officially Emperor until 959, though he only actually ruled during the last fifteen years. There was a long minority, since he was only seven when he came to the throne : for a year his worthless uncle Alexander was regent; then for six years there was a Council of Regency, which by its internal dissensions produced hopeless disorder; finally, in 919, the general Romanus Lecapenus seized the power, at first as regent, soon with the title of Emperor, and held it until 944, when his ambition to secure the throne for his family and exclude Constantine brought about his downfall.

The minority of Constantine VII

Reign of Romanus Lecapenus

Actually, the reign of this usurper was of considerable advantage to the Empire. Constantine, as he showed when he obtained the power, was not a man of action, and the Empire at this time needed a general and a statesman at its head. Apart from the petty warfare that was ceaselessly being waged with the Moslems in the south-east, in the Aegean, and in South Italy, there were numerous and more dangerous enemies to Constantinople in the north and north-west. There were the Slav tribes in Russia, especially the rising principality of Kiev, whose prince Igor actually led an expedition to the gates of Constantinople in 941. In between, and dominating the earlier Slav invaders, there were various hordes of peoples akin to the Huns and the

Turks, who had migrated from the Far East. At the opening
of the tenth century, the most important of these were the
Patzinaks to the north of the Black Sea ; the Magyars, who
by 911 had been forced to leave their earlier settlement and
had migrated to Pannonia, where they formed an alien
wedge interposed between Slav peoples to the north and
south of them ; and above all the Bulgars, whose first settlement had been made in the seventh century, and whose
empire now extended, with the Danube as far as Belgrade as
its northern frontier, from the Black Sea through Thrace
and Macedon almost, though not quite, to the Adriatic. In
dealing with these and other similar hordes the Emperor was
sometimes reduced to the expedient of buying them off.
Often he could use one against the other ; the Patzinaks were
on the whole friendly to the Empire and especially hostile to
Kiev ; the Magyars, once in Pannonia, were dangerous only
to Bulgaria. And he gained a certain advantage by the
Christianisation of the Slavs in the ninth century. Though
Bohemia and Moravia joined the Western Church, Russia
became attached to the Eastern ; and Bulgaria, which had
adopted the Slav language, was similarly Christianised and
joined the Eastern Church. Through the Patriarch of
Constantinople, whose master he was, the Emperor gained a
measure of control within the newly converted countries.

Bulgaria was by now the most constant source of danger The
to the Empire. When Constantine VII succeeded Leo VI Bulgarian
in 912, the ruler of Bulgaria was Simeon, whose father, the under
famous Boris, had abdicated many years before his death in Simeon
907 and had retired to a monastery. Simeon's ambition was
to create a rival Empire to that of Constantinople and to
extend it by conquests, and he soon broke off the friendly
relations his father had maintained with the Eastern
Emperors. Leo VI called in the Magyars against him ;
Simeon allied himself with the Patzinaks, and their joint
victories over the Magyars caused the latter to migrate
definitely to Pannonia. In 917, when the Council of Regency
was in office, he annihilated a Byzantine army at Anchialus,
and in 923 captured Hadrianople and laid siege to Constantinople. Here, after a curious interview with the
Emperor Romanus Lecapenus and the Patriarch Nicholas, he
asserted two of his aims, taking to himself the title of Tsar,

which made of him an Emperor, and giving a unity and an importance to the Bulgarian Church by the creation of a Bulgarian Patriarchate. He had already, by translation of Greek works, tried to foster an intellectual movement with the view to forming a national culture. But his thirst for conquest was insatiable. He turned now against his Slav neighbours on the north-west, and though successful against **Its decline after his death (927)** the Serbs he was severely defeated by the Croatians. When he died in 927, his Empire was undiminished in extent, but exhausted and incapable of further military effort. His son Peter wisely made peace and a marriage alliance with Romanus, who recognised his title of Tsar and the Bulgarian Patriarchate, now definitely attached to the Eastern Church. The peace was maintained for forty years. Peter was fully occupied at home, where he had to face family strife and civil war within, and invasions from Magyars and Patzinaks without; while the introduction of the Bogomile heresy [1] divided Bulgaria into two factions and added to the general disorder.

Romanus Lecapenus was therefore freed from any further anxiety on the score of Bulgaria. His diplomatic skill, which had been evinced in his dealings with Tsar Peter, assured a breathing-space to the Empire and added allies to it in the Far East. But his ambition to found a dynasty proved fatal to him. He had installed three of his sons as co-Emperors, and a fourth, Theophylact, as Patriarch of Constantinople, when the three eldest turned against him, and Constantine, hitherto ignored, was able to rally the **Overthrow of Romanus; Constantine VII recovers power** supporters of legitimism and to send the sons to share their father's exile. But twenty-three years of obscurity had not fitted him for imperial government. As Emperor, he continued to live, as before, mainly as a student and a patron of art and letters. It is to his lasting credit that he promoted a great intellectual movement, and was no inconsiderable author himself. The history of his time and the details of imperial administration are largely known to us from his own works. But while he studied and wrote, gave his

[1] This was akin to, and probably largely responsible for, the heresy of the Cathari in South France two centuries later. The Bogomiles believed in a dualism of supernatural powers, good and evil, God and the Devil. Holding matter to be the creation of the Devil, they went far beyond the Church in their hostility to marriage and advocacy of general celibacy.

attention to ceremonial and etiquette, and especially to the sending of embassies to the Western powers as well as to the east, the business of government was sadly neglected. It fell into the hands of his wife Helena, his son Romanus, and Theophylact, who remained Patriarch till his death in 956. Their sole interest was in licence and extravagance, in which they were imitated by the officials, and this state of affairs continued after Constantine's death for the four years of Romanus II's own reign.

But then, in 963, a great revival took place. Basil II, Romanus's elder son, was only five years of age, and so another long minority began. The power and the imperial title were usurped by two great generals in turn, Nicephorus Phocas and John Tzimisces. The military organisation had not been impaired in the demoralisation of the civil government, and while licence reigned in official quarters at Constantinople, Nicephorus had been winning victories for the Empire against the Moslems in the east. His greatest achievement was the capture of Crete in 961, which freed the Eastern Mediterranean from the pirates. In the following year he engaged the Moslems on the mainland in a successful campaign of sieges, thus inaugurating an aggressive movement quite different from the desultory frontier fighting of the past. On the death of Romanus II his troops proclaimed him Emperor (Nicephorus II). He returned to Constantinople and, to give himself a more legitimate authority, married the late Emperor's widow, Theophano, who had been acting as regent for her sons. *The minority of Basil II*

Reign of Nicephorus Phocas

His reign of six years was memorable for his military triumphs, especially in Asia Minor. In 965 he achieved the conquest of Cilicia, and in the same year the island of Cyprus was captured. By land and sea he was now able to threaten Syria, and in 969 he finally reached his main objective with the capture of Antioch and Aleppo. His success might have been more speedily won had not the cares of the central government at Constantinople frequently demanded his presence. External events, too, engaged his attention. In 967, Tsar Peter of Bulgaria, after 40 years of quiescence, suddenly sent a demand for the resumption of the payments that had been made to his father. Nicephorus's indignant reply led to war, and the Emperor, unwilling to detach troops *His military achievements* for this new front, hired the Russian prince Svyastoslav, the son of Igor, to invade Bulgaria. So successful was Svyasto-slav that Nicephorus was seriously embarrassed, and decided to ally with the Bulgarians to expel him. The alliance came to nothing, for Svyastoslav had to return to Kiev in 969 to deal with an invasion of the Patzinaks, and both Nicephorus and Peter died the same year.

In 968, a year after his insult from Peter, Nicephorus received an embassy from Otto I, asking for the hand of a Byzantine princess for his son, which equally offended the imperial pride. The indignation of Nicephorus, his ill-treat-ment of the ambassador, bishop Liudprand of Cremona, and Liudprand's revenge in the account [1] he has left to posterity of the Emperor and his court, illustrate vividly the mutual contempt and dislike of East and West. After this episode Nicephorus went off on his last and most successful expedition to Syria, and returned from there to meet his death by

His unpopularity and murder

assassination. He had never been popular in Constantinople, in spite of the glory he brought it by his military exploits. He alienated a very powerful section of the community, the monks, by forbidding the foundation of new monasteries or the making of donations to old ones, and by his exactions from the Church to pay the expenses of his wars. He alienated the landed aristocracy by his attempts to check their acquisition of territory, and by the allotments he secured for his soldiers. The opportunity for revolt came when his wife Theophano fell in love with a rival general, John Tzimisces, who had been disgraced by Nicephorus. Together they plotted his murder, with no lack of con-federates, and so brought to an end in December 969 what promised to be one of the most glorious reigns in Byzantine history.

Reign of John Tzimisces

The reign of John I (John Tzimisces) was not unlike that of Nicephorus II. It lasted for six years and it was dis-tinguished by the military triumphs of the Emperor. First of all, however, he had to overcome the hostility aroused by his usurpation and the murder of Nicephorus. The Church he quickly pacified by exiling the partner of his guilt, Theo-phano, and by reversing the anti-clerical policy of his pre-

[1] In his *Relatio de legatione Constantinopolitana* addressed to Otto I and his son.

decessor. By his marriage with a daughter of Constantine VII, Theodora, he further consolidated his position. It was challenged by the Phocas family, but their revolt, led by Nicephorus's nephew Bardas, was easily crushed by the Emperor's brother-in-law Bardas Sclerus. Then John I had leisure to turn to the two fields of war where his presence was most necessary, Bulgaria and Syria. In South Italy he had less interest ; he preferred to make peace with Otto I, granting what Nicephorus had refused, a Byzantine princess as bride for Otto II.

Bulgaria first claimed his attention. Svyastoslav had invaded it again, this time on his own account, and had taken prisoner the new Tsar Boris II, the son of Peter ; he then turned his arms against the adjacent Greek provinces. In 971 John himself led an expedition against him, drove him out of Bulgaria, and set free the Tsar. But he did not restore him to his throne. Instead, he annexed eastern Bulgaria to the Empire, while western Bulgaria remained independent under the rule of the four sons of an ambitious noble, Sishman, and eventually of the youngest of them, Samuel, alone. Meanwhile in the east, in Mesopotamia as well as in Syria, the Byzantine arms had been progressing. John went to both regions himself in 974–5, and advanced almost to Jerusalem, boasting that all Phoenicia, Palestine, and Syria were freed from Moslem rule. This was his last exploit, as after his return to Constantinople he died suddenly, in January 976.

Basil II was now of age, and his reign proper begins from this date. Officially he was co-Emperor with his younger brother, Constantine VIII, but Constantine, idle and pleasure-seeking like his father, was quite content to leave the cares of State to his brother. Basil succeeded to a legacy of military glory and he proved himself worthy of it. But for the first thirteen years of his reign he was mainly occupied with another legacy of a very different kind, the discord arising from the jealous rivalry of the heirs of his two predecessors, each of whom aimed at the imperial throne. In John I's reign it had been Bardas Phocas who had revolted and Bardas Sclerus who had defeated him. Now that John was dead, it was Sclerus who revolted and who, after defeating Basil's generals on three occasions and capturing Nicaea in

Basil II in power. Civil wars

978, was himself defeated by Bardas Phocas in 979. He sought protection with the Caliph but was kept by him in custody for seven years. While he was out of the way, Bardas Phocas felt that his chance had come, and he engineered a conspiracy in 985 with the Emperor's great-uncle, and hitherto his chief adviser, the eunuch Basil. Basil II showed his capacity by the energy and the rapidity with which he crushed this dangerous plot. But Phocas was still at large, and in 986 Sclerus escaped from his confinement at Bagdad. Each of them had himself proclaimed Emperor, and they then joined forces to dethrone Basil and divide the Empire between them. Such a division of the spoils was not really to the taste of either, and Bardas Phocas, who could count on the allegiance of most of Asia Minor, took his rival prisoner and at the head of a large army marched on Constantinople. Once again Basil proved himself at a crisis. He won the powerful support of the Church by repealing the anti-clerical legislation of Nicephorus, and he called in to his aid the prince of Kiev, Vladimir the Great, who had abandoned the policy of his father Svyastoslav and had kept on friendly terms with the Emperor. He lent 6,000 soldiers [1] to Basil, who with their aid defeated Bardas Phocas in 988, and again decisively in 989, when Bardas fell on the field of battle. Bardas Sclerus, released from captivity, made his peace with the Emperor, and at last the long period of civil wars was at an end.

During these years, especially as so large a part of his army looked to Bardas Phocas as its natural leader, the Emperor had little opportunity to engage in any enterprise of his own. He could not go in person to the east, in spite of appeals for help from Aleppo, which the Moslems from Egypt were attacking. A nearer and a more critical peril confronted him in Bulgaria, where Samuel had seized the opportunity of John I's death to revive the former greatness of the Bulgarian Empire. He overran Thrace and invaded southern Greece, even threatening the Peloponnese. Not until the first revolt of Bardas Sclerus had been successfully crushed could Basil take any steps to deal with him. In 981 he

Danger from Bulgaria

---

[1] They remained at Constantinople as the bodyguard of the Emperor, the famous " Varangian " bodyguard, which for some time to come continued to be recruited from Russia.

himself led an expedition into Bulgaria, but he met with defeat and was forced to accept the status quo.   Samuel then proceeded to make conquests on his western frontiers; he obtained temporary possession of Durazzo, and so for a short time his empire extended from the Black Sea actually to the Adriatic.

But when once domestic peace had been restored to the Empire, Basil was able, after a necessary pause for reorganisation, to pay heed to the more pressing dangers that threatened outlying parts of the Empire.   Though fighting of a desultory nature seems to have recommenced in Bulgaria in 990, it was first of all to the east that Basil gave most attention. In 994–5, he relieved Aleppo, but failed both then and in a later campaign in 999 to take Tripolis.   In 1001 he made peace with the Egyptian Moslems, which lasted for the rest of his reign and assured to the Empire all its recent conquests. Just previously he had visited Armenia to secure his north-eastern frontier.   Armenia, which at this time was enjoying a period of unwonted prosperity, was important to the Empire as a guardian of the passes over the Caucasus as well as a buffer state against the Arabs.   Proud of its newly-won independence, and of its national Church, it was able to resist imperial suzerainty until at the end of Basil's reign the pressure from the Seljuk Turks caused it to yield, and Basil was able to extend his Empire to the Caucasus.

The eastern campaigns were only incidental, for the purpose of security, to the main task to which he had set himself, the crushing of Bulgaria.   In 996 the contest began in earnest, and though it opened with a victory of Samuel over a Byzantine general, his power was soon on the decline. Basil could not give his whole attention to it until his return from the east in 1001, but from that time annual invasions led to the piecemeal conquest of western Bulgaria.   At last a pitched battle in 1014 resulted in the decisive defeat of Samuel and his death a few days later.   Disorganised and rent by internal factions, the Bulgarians struggled for four years longer to maintain their independence, but in 1018 came the final surrender, and for a century and a half Bulgaria remained a Byzantine province.   Only its language and its ecclesiastical organisation were left intact; but its Patriarch was reduced to the rank of archbishop, and as his successors

Basil in the east

Armenia

The conquest of Bulgaria

were all Greeks, the Bulgarian Church lost in fact its former autonomy.

Last years of Basil II

The name of " Bulgar-slayer " (Bulgaroctonos), by which Basil II came to be known, perpetuates the great achievement of his reign.   In the north, he had promised his sister Anna in marriage to Vladimir the Great of Kiev in return for Vladimir's assistance to him in 988.   As the promised bride did not come, Vladimir invaded the Crimea ;   peace was resumed in 989, when the marriage took place.   In that year, too, Vladimir was baptised.[1]   His example led to the general Christianisation of Russia, and to its close contact, ecclesiastically, with Constantinople ;   this was intensified when Vladimir's territories were invaded by Boleslav the Mighty of Poland, who adhered to the Roman obedience. With the Western Empire Basil was on friendly terms, especially during the regency of Theophano, and a marriage alliance arranged with Otto III was only prevented by Otto's sudden death.   Venice was particularly friendly, and got what she wanted, commercial privileges, in return.   There remained only South Italy, where the contest with the Sicilian Moslems continued.   Basil was contemplating an expedition for the reconquest of Sicily when he died in 1025.

The Empire at its zenith

He left the Empire at the zenith of its power.   Thanks to himself and to the two other great soldiers who had ruled the Empire during his minority, its borders had been increased so that it extended along the north continuously from the Adriatic Sea to the Caucasus Mountains, and in the south penetrated as far as Palestine ;   the Abbasid Caliphate was in rapid decline.   Not since the first Arab invasions had the Empire covered so wide a range or seemed so secure, and never again was it to recover the greatness of the days of Basil II.

Weaknesses in the imperial organisation

Basil was a soldier and a statesman, devoting himself whole-heartedly to his task, and denying himself distractions. He had no love of art or letters, for which his dynasty had previously been distinguished.   But with all his practical efficiency he could not remove from the State those elements of weakness that impaired its unity and its order.   Chief

---

[1] He had previously depended largely on his Varangian Guards, who were attached to their pagan idols.   After dispatching the greater part of them to Constantinople, he was no longer tied to heathenism.

among them was the power of the great aristocratic families, derived from the possession of great estates, to which they were constantly adding at the expense of the small landowner, until the land came to be exclusively in the hands of the few—a process familiar in Roman history from republican times onwards. The Emperors were alive to the danger and often legislated against it, as Romanus Lecapenus had done, mainly in the interests of his veterans. Basil II issued a famous Novel in 996 forbidding any further encroachments upon the lands of others, and restoring to its original owner any property acquired since the Novel of Romanus. He also was careful that the burden of taxation should fall upon the rich. Besides the danger from the power of these great families, there was also the danger from the ambition of a successful general. The aristocratic and the military classes tended to unite in opposition. Together they had threatened the unity of the Empire in the first thirteen years of Basil's reign, and there was a minor recurrence of the same discord in 1022, when a conspiracy was launched by Nicephorus Xiphias, the general responsible for the final defeat of Tsar Samuel, and Nicephorus Phocas, the son of Bardas. However, as before, the conspirators quarrelled. Xiphias murdered Phocas, and was himself easily overcome. With the death of Nicephorus the Phocas family disappears from history. But there were others to take its place, and they played an important part in the increasing confusion of the next fifty years.

There was another weakness yet more fatal to the Empire, the dependence of an autocratic government on the personality of the autocrat. Basil left no direct heir, and the Crown passed to his brother Constantine VIII, who, after having been nominally co-Emperor for sixty-two years, was at last actual ruler for three. A lifetime of dissipation was not a good prelude to the government of an Empire, and Constantine's only idea was to exalt his former associates at the expense of the trusted servants of his brother. The succession to him was a problem, as he had no son. Of his daughters the eldest, Eudocia, was a nun and therefore ineligible. There remained two others, Zoe and Theodora, and the only solution was to find them fitting husbands to rule in their name ; but Zoe was approaching the age of fifty and Theodora

The successors of Basil Constantine VIII and his daughters

was only a year or two younger, so there was little hope of perpetuating the dynasty. The sisters, kept in virgin seclusion for so long, enjoyed their unwonted freedom but created factions by their mutual dislike. Zoe, as the elder and through her three husbands the ruler, had the upper hand over Theodora who obstinately refused to marry. Theodora, however, had the last word, as she survived her sister and had the melancholy distinction of being the last sovereign of the Macedonian house.

Zoe and her husbands

Zoe's first husband, Romanus III, who had been compelled much against his will to dismiss his first wife and become Emperor, reigned from 1028 to 1034. He was a dull mediocrity, financially incompetent though full of generous impulses, and intent mainly on architectural triumphs. Zoe soon tired of him and fell in love with a young Paphlagonian. So Romanus was murdered and Zoe married her lover, who thereupon became Emperor as Michael IV (1034-41). He showed unexpected capacity, but he was handicapped by epilepsy and finally by dropsy, which carried him off at an early age. Zoe was firmly kept in the background, while the chief offices of State were filled by the various members of Michael's family; corrupt and self-seeking as they all were, the eldest brother, John Orphanotrophos, was an able administrator and did much to restore the finances. He and Michael planned to keep the succession in their family, and Zoe was induced to adopt their nephew, who on Michael IV's death duly succeeded to the throne as Michael V. He proved to be entirely worthless, and when he tried to banish Zoe, the populace, always devoted to her, rose and expelled him. Zoe was restored, but this time Theodora was associated with her as joint ruler. Yet Zoe triumphed once again, by taking a third husband, Constantine IX (1042-55), an elderly debauchee, of some capacity but little energy, save for his own amusements. He had cultivated tastes, however, and surrounded himself with men of learning. In the decline of imperial authority there was a regular literary renaissance, in which the revival of philosophy and jurisprudence also played a part.[1] Zoe and Theodora were once again relegated

---

[1] Psellus, the historian of the period, who taught philosophy, was the most distinguished figure ; other famous names were Xiphilin, head of the law school, and Michael Cerularius.

to the women's quarters, where Zoe died in 1050. But
Theodora outlived Constantine IX, and in 1055, at the age
of 75, she was at last the real head of the State—for eighteen
months. She was still unmarried, and so, when she died in
1056, the Macedonian house came to an end.

During this period, in which the only ruler at all worthy
of the name was Michael IV, the civil functionaries of the
Court were mainly in charge of the government. The powerful aristocratic families remained quiescent; for this the
surprising popularity of Zoe, combined with the sentiment
of loyalty to the legitimate line, seems to have been responsible. The influence of the Church, too, was on the side of
the reigning sovereigns. Both Romanus III and Michael IV
heaped favours upon it, while in the reign of Constantine IX
the Patriarch, Michael Cerularius, became the most influential
person at Constantinople. Easily dominating the indolent
Emperor, he was able to achieve his ambition of ecclesiastical
autonomy by engineering a formal breach with Rome in
1054. The Schism between the Eastern and Western
Churches which resulted was ultimately to prove fatal to
the Eastern Empire. Its immediate effect was also disastrous.
It prevented the meditated alliance with the Pope and the
Lombard princes in South Italy against the Normans, who
were soon to expel the Byzantines from South Italy and
then to take the offensive against them in Greece.

The Schism was due to the Patriarch and was against the
wish of the Emperor. But the Emperors themselves were
responsible for the policy in the north-east which was equally
disastrous to the Empire. Armenia had admitted the
suzerainty of Basil II, but had soon re-won her independence.
The Emperors not unnaturally sought to regain their authority, but the deliberate overthrow of Armenian power was a
grave blunder; it was only achieved after a long struggle,
exhausting to both, which ended when Constantine IX gained
by guile what he and his predecessors had failed to win by
force of arms alone. But by the complete subjection of
Armenia he paved the way for disaster to the Empire. The
value of Armenia as a buffer state was gone. Already the
Seljuk Turks were beginning to invade it from the east, and
it had lost the power of resistance.

Corruption at the centre had not yet spread to the ex-

The strife between the civil and military authorities

tremities. The military machine was still effective, and was able to maintain to its full extent the Empire over which Basil II had ruled. A dangerous rising in Bulgaria was suppressed by Michael IV. In Syria, though Romanus III suffered a severe defeat near Aleppo in 1030, this was offset by the signal success of George Maniaces, the most brilliant general of the period, who captured Edessa in 1031. He too, in command in South Italy in 1038, inaugurated a successful invasion of Sicily, capturing the chief harbours on its eastern coast. But his success frightened the government and led to his recall, after which the Moslems recovered the whole of the island. Sent back to Italy by Michael V, he was again recalled by Constantine IX, and the intrigues against him drove him to a revolt in 1043 in which he met his death. There were other revolts of military leaders, especially that of Leo Tornicius in 1047, which for a time threatened grave danger, but was eventually easily suppressed owing to the ineptitude of its leader. The hostility between the civil government and the army was now beginning to become more pronounced.

Since the death of Basil II the Empire had lacked a strong man at its head, capable of directing its government and leading it in war ; the discordant elements within it were soon to prove fatal to its unity. The end of the Macedonian house left the crown a prize for successful ambition, and gave the opportunity to the aristocratic and military caste, without, however, producing anyone worthy of the occasion.

The coming of the Seljuks

The struggle for power diverted attention from the pressing need to concentrate upon defence, especially on the eastern frontiers where the Seljuk Turks were just commencing their great career of conquest. In 1055 their leader, Tughril Beg, entered Bagdad as the ally and protector of the Caliph, who gratefully named him Sultan ; a new power had now arisen in the east which was to take the place of the Arabs as the great enemy of the Empire and of Christendom.

SUGGESTIONS FOR READING ON CHAPTER VI

Cambridge Medieval History, Vol. IV, new edn. (see p. xx).
Baynes, N. H. : *The Byzantine Empire*. London, 1925.
Diehl, C. : *Byzance : grandeur et décadence*. Paris, 1919.
Runciman, S. : *Byzantine Civilisation*. London, 1933.
Bréhier, L. : *Le Monde Byzantin*, 3 vols. Paris, 1947–50.
Ostrogorsky, G. : *History of the Byzantine State* (Eng. trans.). Oxford, 1956.
Baynes, N. H. : *Byzantine Studies and other Essays*. London, 1955.

PART II

THE SECOND HALF OF THE ELEVENTH CENTURY

CHAPTER VII

THE EMPIRE, 1046–1075

IN the year 1046 the newly-crowned Emperor was at the height of his power. With peace in Germany, the Eastern States all recognising his suzerainty, Italy obedient, even Rome submissive, the Pope his nominee, Henry III was in a position attained by none of his predecessors since Otto I, and not to be reached by any of his successors in the future. The decline began, indeed, immediately after his greatest triumph, and the peace he had established throughout the Empire he was no longer able to maintain. Italy was not, on this occasion, responsible for wasting imperial resources or decimating the German forces; and Rome remained entirely pacific. It was in the German kingdom that he was troubled, and the difficulties which he had mastered so easily in the first half of his reign proved far less easy of solution in the second half.

The summit of Henry III's power

Decline in his later years

Immediately on his return in 1047 he found himself confronted with a fresh revolt of Godfrey of Upper Lorraine, allied with counts Baldwin V of Flanders and Dirk IV of West Frisia (Holland). They concentrated especially against the bishops, on whom the king principally depended for the maintenance of his authority in Lorraine. Henry declared Godfrey's duchy forfeit and assigned it first to a Lotharingian, Adalbert, whom Godfrey defeated and killed, and then to Gerard, a kinsman of Adalbert; but it was not until 1049 that Godfrey and his allies were forced to come to terms with the king. Godfrey was again made a prisoner, though later the king, following his usual conciliatory policy, restored him to some portion of his possessions. Half-measures were no use against Godfrey; the only way to have peace with him was to give him all he wanted or to crush him completely. He bided his time, and then in 1054 made his most daring *coup.* He went to Italy and married Beatrice, daughter of

The revolts of Godfrey of Lorraine

a former duke of Upper Lorraine, and widow of marquis Boniface of Tuscany ; she was ruling Tuscany in the name of her young son Boniface, who died shortly afterwards. Such a marriage, celebrated without his consent, was an affront to their overlord ; and Henry could not leave Godfrey in a position which gave him the command of central Italy. He had, therefore, to go himself to Italy in 1055. Godfrey escaped to Lorraine, leaving Beatrice to bear the brunt of Henry's anger ; together with her famous daughter, the future countess Matilda, she was taken captive to Germany. Henry had again the task of defeating Godfrey and his ally Baldwin in the field ; in 1056 Godfrey made his submission for the third time. The sudden and fatal illness of the Emperor prevented a final settlement of this grave issue. Just before his death, Henry tried, by releasing Beatrice and Matilda, to create an atmosphere of peace ; but with Godfrey quite unreconciled, he left a legacy of trouble for his son.

The loss of Hungary

The western portion of his kingdom was thus a continual source of anxiety during the last half of his reign.   There were frequent breaches of the peace both in Lower and Upper Lorraine, and the attitude of the king of France was anything but satisfactory.   At the same time the south-eastern frontier demanded urgent attention.   Already, while on his way to Rome in 1046, Henry had been checked by the news that Peter, whom he had restored to the throne of Hungary, had been expelled by his cousin Andrew, and that an anti-German and anti-Christian reaction had set in. He continued his journey, however, intending to deal with Hungary immediately on his return to Germany.   But the revolt of Godfrey kept him employed on the western side of the kingdom until 1049.   Then in 1050 he led an expedition into Hungary, without being able to come to grips with the enemy. He was more successful in 1052, when he captured Pressburg, but he could not subdue Andrew, who retaliated in 1054 by invading Carinthia.   Hungary, in fact, ceased to be a vassal-state of Germany.

Henry's disposition of the duchies

Henry was still handicapped by the lack of any near relative with whom he could share the responsibility of government.   He placed most reliance on the family (descended like himself from Otto I) of Otto III's sister Matilda, wife of Ezzo count-palatine of the Rhine.   One son, archbishop Herman of Cologne, was his most trusted friend and adviser; another son, Otto, he had made duke of Suabia in 1045; and a grandson, Conrad, he appointed duke of Bavaria in 1049. When Suabia again fell vacant, he appointed in 1048 another Otto, of the Babenberg family. The last duchy he had retained in his own hands, Carinthia, he gave in 1047 to the Suabian count Welf. The principle behind these appointments seems to have been to put at the head of the duchies not only men whom he could expect to be loyal, but who at the same time had no possessions within their duchies and therefore could not become over-powerful. Often, however, they were not powerful enough to preserve order, and sometimes they were not even loyal. Conrad of Bavaria started a violent quarrel with the bishop of Ratisbon, and refusing to keep the peace was deposed in 1053. Till his death in 1055 he remained a rebel, intriguing with king Andrew of Hungary and drawing other nobles in south-eastern Germany into the conspiracy. Henry gave the duchy of Bavaria to his infant son, Henry IV, so that in effect he resumed authority himself. Nor did he fill up the vacancy which occurred in Carinthia in the last year of his reign; Welf dying childless, his Suabian estates passed to his nephew of the same name, the son of marquis Azzo of Este.

In the north, the security of the frontier was guaranteed by a renewal of the alliance with Denmark. In this region, Henry relied especially on the friendship and loyalty of the powerful archbishop of Bremen, Adalbert (1043-72), who by his missionary work in Scandinavia and among the Baltic Slavs was rapidly extending German influence and prestige. He attained eventually his ambition to be recognised by the rulers of all three Scandinavian Kingdoms as primate over their Churches, for which he had obtained a papal bull. He might even have been Pope, for Henry III wished to nominate him, but he preferred his northern province. His influence over the Baltic Slavs, however, aroused the jealousy of the East Saxon nobles, especially Duke Bernard II. They considered that their own sphere was being invaded, and they suspected that it was part of a deliberate royal policy to encroach upon their isolation, which Henry and his two predecessors had hitherto been forced to respect. They felt

Adalbert of Bremen and the Saxons

it the more since Henry himself so frequently visited the extensive royal domain in East Saxony. This was only natural, since it supplied so much to the maintenance of the royal household, and Henry also found his chief relaxation in hunting expeditions in the neighbourhood of Goslar, which under his favour grew rapidly in size and industrial importance. But out of the suspicions of the Saxons developed the civil wars which afflicted the reign of his successor.

Henry's illness and death

The loss of Hungary, so recently acquired, was not a matter of great importance. The danger from Godfrey and from Saxon discontent was much more serious. Probably a solution of both these difficulties would have been reached, had Henry III's life been of normal length. His weak health had always been a serious handicap to him, and on more than one occasion he had apparently been on the point of death and there had been grave anxiety about the succession. The birth of Henry IV in 1050, therefore, came as a great relief; in 1053 he was elected king by the princes, who swore to accept him as Henry III's successor; and he was crowned the following year. But in 1056 sickness again attacked the Emperor, this time fatally. He was still under forty when he died on October 5, and his heir was a child of only six years of age.

The minority of Henry IV; his mother's weak rule

So, once more, as in the case of Otto III, a child was on the throne of Germany, and his mother, in whose charge he was, had to rule the kingdom in his name. But Agnes was not a Theophano. Pious and dutiful, she attempted to follow in her husband's footsteps. She looked for help especially to the bishops, but here she was unfortunate. Henry III's friend, archbishop Herman of Cologne, had died, and his successor Anno was a self-seeking *parvenu*; Adalbert of Bremen was engrossed in the extension of his metropolitan authority; Siegfried, whom she nominated to Mayence in 1060, was a weak man, always at the mercy of a stronger will, and unable to take the leading position which was his by right of his see. In her choice of laymen to assist her she was equally unfortunate. The duchy of Bavaria was in her own hands, Carinthia had recently become vacant, and Suabia also fell vacant in 1057. She could not manage them herself, and while looking for faithful supporters she was

careful to follow her husband's principle of not giving a
duchy to anyone who had possessions within it. For Suabia
she chose Rudolf of Rheinfelden, a Burgundian count, and
she bestowed on him the hand of her eldest daughter Matilda [1]
as well; Carinthia she gave to a Suabian count, Berthold of
Zähringen. Finally, in 1061 she appointed one of the leading
nobles of East Saxony, Otto of Nordheim, to the duchy of
Bavaria. None of them had much authority in his own
duchy, but they were all important nobles; and they used
their new position to further their own interests. Agnes, in
trying to create powerful adherents for her son, raised to
power three of his most dangerous enemies. With Saxony
of course she did not interfere, and when duke Bernard died
in 1059 his son Ordulf succeeded him by hereditary right.

So, during the first six years of Henry IV's reign, the
government was in the hands of a harassed and incompetent
woman; the leading nobles took advantage of her weakness
to secure their own positions, and for the interests of the
kingdom there was a very general disregard. Here was a
situation of which the rebellious Godfrey of Upper Lorraine
was able to make the best advantage. Joining his wife in
Tuscany, he dominated central Italy, acting as if he were
the representative of royal authority, which in fact he prevented from functioning. So far as the Italian kingdom was
concerned, Agnes could depend only upon the Lombard
bishops, whose hostility to the advance of papal power
caused them especially to value their attachment to the
German Crown.

Godfrey of Lorraine in Italy

In these circumstances, it was not to be expected that
the queen-mother would be able to recover the suzerainty
over Hungary. Yet for a time this seemed almost possible.
King Andrew was in difficulties owing to his brother Béla's
revolt against him, and was anxious for German support.
He made his peace in 1058, and his son Salomo was betrothed
to Henry's sister Judith. Probably this cost him his throne,
for the anti-German feeling, on which he had depended before,
was now on his brother's side. In spite of German assistance
he was defeated and killed in 1060. Béla became king of
Hungary, and Salomo had to take refuge at the German

Hungary, Poland, and Bohemia

---

[1] Matilda died the following year. Rudolf later married Henry IV's
sister-in-law.

Court; German resources were wasted in attempts to restore him, ultimately to no purpose. Poland, too, under Boleslav II, who succeeded his father Casimir in 1058, broke away from German suzerainty. A strong ruler, Boleslav restored Poland to something of its former greatness; he took the offensive against Bohemia and Hungary and even against Russia, but he showed no disposition to aggrandisement at German expense. Of the three Eastern States, Bohemia alone remained loyal; its constant hostility to Poland prevented it from severing its connexion with Germany.

Archbishop
Anno of
Cologne
usurps the
governmentMeanwhile archbishop Anno of Cologne had been working for his own ends. His province included western Saxony, where he came into touch with Adalbert's province of Bremen. In Adalbert he probably recognised his chief rival, and he formed an alliance with Adalbert's enemies, the nobles of East Saxony, thereby fomenting a quarrel which in the interests of the kingdom it was urgently necessary to compose. Probably it was his influence that obtained the appointment of Otto of Nordheim to the duchy of Bavaria. In 1062 his intrigues came to a head. With his Saxon confederates, the new duke of Bavaria and count Egbert of Brunswick, he decoyed the young king onto a boat at Kaiserwerth on the Rhine, hurried him to Cologne, and there assumed the government as tutor (magister) of the king. Agnes retired from the world and devoted herself to the religious life. For two years Anno was supreme. He set to work to consolidate his position, especially by lavish grants from the royal domains. In East Saxony, where lay the most important domain, he had allies, and he secured further partisans as well. He had already obtained the appointment of his nephew Burchard as bishop of Halberstadt, and in 1063 secured the archbishopric of Magdeburg for his brother Werner; these two prelates were always in the forefront of rebellion in Saxony against Henry IV. Then in 1064, full of his own importance, he went to Italy and, in league with the king's most dangerous enemy, Godfrey, took upon himself to settle the papal schism in favour of Alexander II. Here his pride had its due reward, for the Pope was indignant at the presumption of the archbishop in sitting in judgment upon him, even though the verdict was favourable, and later humiliated him on more than one occasion by calling him to account for simony. His absence, too, gave Adalbert Superseded by archbishop Adalbert the opportunity to get the chief power into his hands, and so to make head against his Saxon enemies. The defeat of Anno and his allies was in the best interests of the kingdom, but Adalbert was led astray by his success and his ambition became as personal as Anno's. In 1065 the king was declared of age and girt with the sword of manhood, though Adalbert remained in control until another conspiracy of Anno and the Saxons in 1066 caused his downfall. They even captured Bremen, and for three years Adalbert was banished from his metropolis. Anno, however, was foiled in his attempt to recover power, and so at last the king, free from the control End of the minority of these ambitious prelates, was his own master. His reign proper may be said to begin in 1067.

The misfortunes of Henry IV in Germany during his long Upbringing and character of Henry IV reign of 50 years had their origin in this decade of misgovernment. The East Saxon nobles had become hostile and aggressive ; they were encroaching, too, on the royal domain. Elsewhere, the greater nobles had been pursuing their own ends, independent of royal authority, and with no care for the general interest. In Italy, the king had not as yet put in an appearance. Godfrey blocked the centre, and even prevented Henry from going to Rome for the imperial crown ; meanwhile the Papacy had become quite independent. Henry's upbringing had been of the wretchedest kind. His mother was unfitted to train him for his task as king, and after his abduction in 1062 he had had to follow where Anno, and then where Adalbert, led, the unwilling instrument of their unworthy ambitions. It was a frequent charge against him in later times that his youth had been spent in dissipation, and that he preferred to consort with men of low birth, from whom he chose his counsellors afterwards. It is hardly to be wondered at, considering the circumstances of his early life ; and if the friends of his choice were not the best of counsellors, they were at least faithful friends, and among the greater nobles he could find none such.

Here was a grave situation for a youth of seventeen to handle. After Henry III's death, as after Otto III's, it seemed as if fifty years of careful building had gone for nothing. The German kingdom was so little of an organised State in the modern sense that everything depended on the personality of its ruler. Henry IV was young, and suffered from lack of experience and training. He was intelligent and quick to learn, but too hasty in judgment and temper. Though he sometimes exhibited the gentler traits of Henry III he was more like his grandfather Conrad II, whom he resembled in his outbursts of passion and his opposition to Church reform. But it was dangerous for him to do what was safe for Conrad. He had to build up again, and for this he lacked the patience that Henry II had exhibited. He was also lacking in his judgment of men, though indeed he could hardly have anticipated the treachery which it was so continually his fate to meet. His reign exhibits a series of alternating ups and downs ; only in the exhaustion of his later years was there any stability.

His prospects as ruler   However, it made all the difference that the minority was at an end, and that the king himself was ruling. The power and prestige of a century of German monarchy did not go for nothing, and there were many who looked to the king for order and security, especially the bishops ; though no reliance could be placed as yet on the great metropolitans others were faithful, and future appointments depended now on Henry's own choice. Even the lay nobles, self-interested as they were, had not as yet conceived the idea of creating independent principalities for themselves, as their successors were to do in the fourteenth century, and as some dukes in France were already doing. Agnes had been unfortunate in her choice of dukes, but she had been wise in one respect. They had not the necessary foundations—in personal domain —within their duchies on which to build up a centralised ducal authority. If it came to a conflict with a duke, Henry could always be sure of support from within the duchy. Saxony, at any rate East Saxony, was an exception. Here there was a separatist tendency, not due to the central authority of the duke but to the common interests which bound the nobles together in their constant warfare with the heathen Slav tribes and in the pride of their ancient customs. They were willing to acknowledge the king as their overlord, provided he did not interfere with them, but they regarded themselves as apart from and superior to the

rest of Germany; their exclusiveness and their pride gave
rise to bitter resentment elsewhere. In Henry IV's reign,
Saxony and the rest of Germany seem almost like two separate
kingdoms, and against Saxony Henry could usually depend
on assistance from southern Germany, at first even from the
dukes. But in their case the assistance was only given to
humiliate the Saxons; his mistake was in regarding it as a
proof of their acquiescence in royal authority over themselves.

Henry was, like his predecessors, filled with a deep sense His policy
of his high office. He was determined to recover all that
they had held, much of which had been lost during his
minority, so that he naturally considered he was recovering
what was his by right. The summit, therefore, of his ambition was the imperial crown, with the Pope as his subject;
in fact, to stand again as his father had stood in 1046. Wisely
he put that aside for the time and concentrated on Germany,
with the recovery of the full possession of the royal domain
as his first objective. The most important part of this was
in East Saxony, and here it had been particularly encroached
upon. His plan was to build castles to protect it from
further encroachment and to ensure that the due services
were rendered from it. It was a bold move for the young
king to do what must appear to the neighbouring nobles as
a threat to their independence. Possibly this was not unin-
tentional; he had not forgotten the part some of them had
played in his abduction by Anno in 1062. At any rate, the
downfall of one of the chief participants in that outrage is
the event from which the subsequent development to civil
war may logically be traced.

In 1070 a charge of treason (whether with Henry's con- Revolt of
Otto of
nivance or not is unknown) was brought against Otto of Bavaria and
Nordheim, duke of Bavaria. Otto disdained to meet his Magnus
low-born accuser in trial by battle and was condemned by Billung
his Saxon peers to the loss of his possessions; obviously
Saxony as a whole was not yet awake to the possibility of
danger from the king. The duchy of Bavaria was given to
Welf (IV), who had succeeded to the Suabian estates of his
uncle and was heir too to the Italian estates of his father,
the marquis of Este. The appointment, a most unfortunate
one for the king, was made at the instigation of duke Rudolf

of Suabia, who gained a valuable ally for the future ; Rudolf, Welf, and Berthold of Carinthia acted in concert henceforward, and by their united action decided the varying fortunes of the king in his conflict first with the Saxons and later with the Papacy.　Meanwhile, Otto had fled to Saxony and with Magnus Billung, son of duke Ordulf, raised the standard of revolt.　The rising was easily suppressed, and the two rebels placed in confinement.　Otto was released in 1072 and allowed to retain his county of Nordheim.　Magnus was kept a prisoner ; he was too valuable a hostage to be surrendered, especially when in 1072 he became duke by the death of his father.

Henry's strong position in 1072　　Henry had begun with a great success, and proceeded to exploit it by strengthening and garrisoning the castles on the royal domain, which could be used as a centre for his own power and also as a means for curbing Saxon independence. The revolt had given him an excuse especially for precautionary measures against the Billung family, and he took possession of their chief town, Lüneburg.　He had so far had the co-operation of the other dukes, and his position in Germany seemed assured.　He planned the recovery of his suzerainty over Poland.　He even believed himself strong enough to interfere in Italy, and, as will be seen later, his conflict with the Papacy really started at this point.　But he soon had to withdraw from that contest, for rapid as had been his rise in Germany his downfall was almost more sudden.

Revolt of the Saxons in 1073　　What he had done was to excite the alarm of all the East Saxon nobles, and at the same time to arouse fears among the southern dukes for their own independence. Secretly concerted by the margraves of the north-eastern frontier, especially Egbert of Meissen (the son of the Egbert of Brunswick who had taken part in Henry's abduction in 1062), by the acting head of the Billung family, Herman, the uncle of the captive duke Magnus, by Otto of Nordheim, and by the archbishop of Magdeburg and the bishop of Halberstadt, revolt spread through all East Saxony and suddenly flared out in August 1073.　Lüneburg was recaptured, Henry was forced to flee, and duke Magnus was released. The king had still a chance.　He had issued a summons for a Polish expedition, and the army was assembling.　But the leading nobles refused to fight against the Saxons; they had the upper hand and were determined to maintain it, and they opened negotiations with the Saxons in their own name. The king found himself almost helpless. Yet in his distress there was revealed to him the prospect of assistance from an unexpected quarter. Coming in January 1074 to Worms, where the bishop was hostile to him, he was received with great pomp by the citizens, and in return granted them a charter. This was the beginning of a direct alliance with the trading classes in the Rhine towns, who were to prove valuable supporters of the monarchy, since a strong central government was in their best interests. A similar rising in Cologne against the archbishop occurred the same year, but Anno was strong enough to suppress it. The towns wanted self-government, and this meant in almost every case exemption from the control of a bishop. The king was hampered by his dependence on episcopal support, so that he could only deal directly with the townsmen when the bishop was disloyal. So for the present he could not exploit this new alliance to the full. *Humiliation of the king*

The incident at Worms was only a glimmer of light in a situation of deep gloom. The king had to come to terms with the Saxons in February and cede their full demands, including the withdrawal of his garrisons and the demolition of his castles. It seemed a complete and most humiliating surrender. But, not for the last time, Henry showed his statesmanship by surrendering to one enemy and dividing the forces against him. The Saxons in making terms had ignored the southern dukes, who were furious at this ingratitude and at being deprived of the conduct of affairs. Ill-feeling arose again between Saxony and the rest of Germany, and the king by skilful propaganda made known the excesses and the sacrilege committed by the Saxons while destroying the castles, and aroused further indignation against them. So, when he summoned an expedition against Saxony in the spring of 1075, he was able to raise a strong army, keen to take vengeance on the Saxons. With Rudolf and the Suabians in the van it won a decisive victory in June on the river Unstrut, and Saxony was invaded in force. The dukes of Suabia, Bavaria, and Carinthia were satisfied, and returned home. But the king's vengeance was not complete. The *The royal recovery and defeat of the Saxons* troops that remained to him proved sufficient to reduce East Saxony to complete submission. The leading nobles surrendered in the autumn and were kept in confinement, and the rebuilding of the castles was at once taken in hand. This was the height of Henry's achievement in Saxony; it was the last time that he was able to enter it as master.

Henry's misjudgment of the situation

The completeness of the king's victory, achieved in its final stage without their aid, was more than the dukes had counted upon. The king was becoming too strong for their liking, and they held sullenly aloof from him. Henry had won a triumph beyond his expectation, and was too much elated by his success to give a thought to those who had already once played him false. He turned naturally now to his Italian kingdom, where an opening for intervention offered itself; and he was eager to come to grips with that other power which had been encroaching upon his authority —the Papacy. So far the German kingdom has had a history of its own; now it becomes fatally merged in the great struggle of Empire and Papacy.

CHAPTER VIII

THE BUILDING-UP OF THE PAPAL MONARCHY

HENRY III in 1046 had rescued the Papacy once **The** again from the Roman nobility, and during his life- **reformed** time its independence was assured. The Romans **Papacy** had named him *patricius*; they therefore recognised his authority and showed no signs of revolting from it. On each vacancy they asked him to nominate the new Pope, and elected his nominee without question, though in each case it was a German bishop whom Henry chose. Henry had done more than merely rescue the Pope. With his zeal for reform he had been careful to choose men on whom he could rely as keen reformers. This meant that the Reform Movement had a centre, and looked for its inspiration and its direction to its natural leader, the Head of the Church. It meant even more than that. For, by taking the lead in this way, papal headship of the Church became a reality; the potentialities of the office, deriving from law and from precedent, enabled the Popes at once to undertake the direction of the whole Church, not merely of the Roman Church. It was a necessary step, too; for unless they could exert this authority their work for reform would be nullified. So from this moment began, in close connexion with the movement for reform, the building-up of the centralised authority, the monarchical authority, of the Papacy.

Henry III did not interfere with this. He had in a sense **Henry III's** an over-riding authority, for the appointment of Popes was **position** in his hands, and in this way he ensured his control of ecclesiastical policy. But he recognised that ecclesiastical affairs, especially the direction of reform, was in their department, and he left them complete freedom of action. He was there to assist and to encourage; when Pope Leo IX held a council at Mayence in 1049 he was present, and he gave imperial authority to the enforcement of the decrees. He

acted, as before, as master over the Church in Germany, but
the Pope when present took the lead in the direction of affairs.
The harmony between the temporal and spiritual departments, so essential for the fulfilment of the medieval ideal
but so rarely achieved, was for the time being complete.

Of the four Popes nominated by Henry III, the first two
—Clement II and Damasus II—died so soon after their
elections that they had no opportunity to do anything of note ;
their sudden deaths aroused suspicion of poisoning, but the
usual effect of the Roman climate upon Germans is a sufficient
explanation. The third—Leo IX—reigned for five years
(1049–54), and in that time he managed to achieve so much
that he may almost be termed the re-founder of the papal
power. He had been bishop of Toul in Upper Lorraine, and
therefore came from a district which was one of the chief
centres of reform. He was careful to surround himself with
reformers, particularly from that region. The archbishop of
Trèves, the bishops of Metz and Verdun, accompanied him
to Rome and were in his company afterwards in Lorraine ;
the Burgundian archbishops, Halinard of Lyons and Hugh
of Besançon, were constantly by his side, assisting in the
work of ecclesiastical legislation ; there were abbots too,
Hugh of Cluny among them. But what mattered most was
the permanent element, those whom Leo attached to his
service by making them cardinals of the Roman Church.
Thus, Humbert, a monk of Moyenmoutier in Leo's own
diocese of Toul, became cardinal bishop of Silva Candida ;
he was the most advanced reformer of all, and later wrote a
treatise against simony in which lay investiture was for the
first time attacked. Frederick of Upper Lorraine, brother
of duke Godfrey, became cardinal deacon ; he was made
abbot of Monte Cassino by the next Pope, and then himself
became Pope as Stephen IX. And there was a young monk,
who had gone from Rome as companion to Gregory VI in
exile in the Rhine district, and whom Leo IX took with him
to Rome in 1048 and made cardinal subdeacon, thus laying
the foundations of a great career—Hildebrand, the future
Pope Gregory VII. These were the kind of men that Leo
was gathering round him ; as clergy of the Roman Church
they formed the Pope's permanent staff for his reforming
crusade. The existence of such a staff ensured the continuity

Pope Leo IX

His cardinals

of the work in the future, and their enrolment from different parts of the Church emphasised the universal character of the authority wielded by the bishop of the Roman Church.

The method he employed, which was to become a regular feature of Church government, was the holding of annual councils at Rome in Lent, at which the reforming decrees were promulgated; these decrees were repeated at local councils in the various countries, so that they might be known everywhere and the local episcopate be made responsible for their enforcement. In future this task was delegated by the Pope to his representatives, whether the archbishops on the spot or legates sent *a latere* for the purpose. But Leo IX did it all himself. With his imposing retinue of assistants he spent the first four of the five years of his Papacy in a kind of royal progress through North and South Italy, France, and Western Germany, holding councils wherever he went. In this way, not only were all the various reforming movements gathered into one under his guidance, but the various countries were made accustomed to the idea of the government of the Church under papal direction. Popular enthusiasm greeted him everywhere, though the bishops as a whole were far less enthusiastic; for many of them were punished, some even deposed, for simony, and apart from the punishment the manifestation of papal authority over them was new and most distasteful. The most important year was 1049, when he held four great councils—at Rome, at Pavia, the capital of Lombardy, and at Rheims and Mayence, the chief metropolitan sees of France and Germany. In France, the king absented himself and prevented the attendance of many bishops as well; it made little difference, and the Pope indeed had a freer hand in his absence. The decrees of the council covered a wider range than usual, and Leo was not afraid to deal with lay princes as well; for instance, he issued his prohibition of William of Normandy's proposed marriage with Matilda.[1] In Germany he had the full support of the Emperor, who journeyed with him through Lorraine and took part in the council at Mayence. North Italy was

---

[1] The marriage took place later, when Leo was a prisoner of the Normans in South Italy, but William was called to account by Leo's successors and forced to do penance.

more difficult, and at Mantua in 1053 we hear of a riot against
the decree enforcing clerical celibacy.

The effect of
his work
These four years put the Papacy on an entirely new footing.   It had re-established itself in the eyes of Europe and
made a very considerable advance towards the centralisation
of its authority.   But the last year of Leo's life was signalised
by two disasters, both of which left their mark on future
His
disastrous
campaign
against the
Normans
history.   The first came to him at the hands of the Normans,
who in the immediately preceding years had been rapidly
mastering the Lombard principalities in the south.   Their
devastations and their brutality caused them to be universally
detested, and the cries of the oppressed came to the Pope,
who on his visits to South Italy received many appeals for
aid.   This was one cause of his intervention, but he had a
more personal interest when the town of Benevento put
itself under papal protection in 1051, and passed with the
Emperor's permission to the Pope in exchange for the
bishopric of Bamberg, which had nominally been under papal
protection since the time of Henry II.   Papal appeals to the
Normans were in vain, and when Drogo, the eldest of the
surviving sons of Tancred, was assassinated, the temporary
lack of leadership among the Normans seemed to give the
Pope an opportunity.   With an army of volunteers, including
many Germans (though the Emperor withdrew the support
he first promised), and allied with most of the Lombard
princes in the south, Leo himself took the field in 1053.
Against this motley array the Normans, under Richard of
Aversa and the two remaining sons of Tancred, Humphrey
and Robert Guiscard, were completely successful at the battle
of Civitate.   The Pope was taken prisoner, Benevento fell
into the hands of the Normans, and Leo had to endure for
nearly a year the indignity of living under surveillance in
the town of which he claimed to be the lord.   Released in
March 1054 he came back to Rome to die a month later.
The Normans continued their work of depredation, no one
among them being strong enough as yet to unite the others
under him and form a settled State.   But a new situation
had arisen from Leo's attempt and its failure.   The claim to
papal overlordship in South Italy had now been advanced,
and it was clear that the Papacy could not make good its
claim unless it either defeated the Normans or allied itself

with them. The link of Norman and papal history was there-fore definitely established.

The danger from the Normans had also alarmed the Eastern Emperor, Constantine IX, and an alliance between him and the Pope was negotiated. Hitherto, papal relations with the Eastern Emperor had been anything but friendly. Furthermore, the gap between the Eastern and Western Churches had considerably widened. In ritual and in law there were obvious differences between them, but the vital question was one of authority. Theoretically, there was only one Church, and over it the Popes claimed the headship; this was constantly resisted by the Patriarchs of Constantinople, usually by the Emperors as well. In the long degradation of the papal office, this could hardly be a live issue; but it awoke to life again when the Papacy was reformed and Leo was making the headship a reality in the West. The Patriarch, Michael Cerularius, who was a man of much greater force of character than the Emperor, was determined to maintain his independence. Accordingly he opposed the alliance with the Papacy, realising that the result would be the extension of papal authority in South Italy, even over the Church in Apulia and Calabria at present subject to himself. He not only prevented the alliance; he also managed to bring the controversy on the question of authority to a head, in spite of the fact that Constantine for reasons of policy was favourable to the papal claims, just at the time that Leo was in the hands of the Normans. A papal embassy, headed by cardinal Humbert, a man as rigid and obstinate as the patriarch with whom he had to treat, only made matters worse. The legates reached Constantinople in the month that Leo died, and after an acrimonious controversy failed in their mission in spite of the Emperor's friendliness to them, and departed leaving behind them a bull anathematising the patriarch. This enabled the latter to force the Emperor's hand. With popular acclamation the bull was publicly burned on 20 July 1054, and, as the patriarch designed, the schism between the two Churches was made a definite fact. In spite of many attempts, it was never healed, for the same reason that had brought it into being—the refusal of Constantinople to recognise papal authority over it. Not only did this schism prevent union against the common enemy in

The schism between the Eastern and Western Churches (1054)

South Italy. It embittered the relations between Eastern and Western Christians during the period of the crusades, and its fatal influence extended down to the fall of Constantinople in 1453.

Pope Victor II

To succeed Leo IX, Henry nominated his friend bishop Gebhard of Eichstädt, who took the name of Victor II. He did not arrive in Rome until 1055, and he only survived the Emperor by one year, dying in 1057. Just for a few months his experience was invaluable to the helpless Agnes. Had he survived, she would have had a powerful and loyal friend to strengthen her in the work of government. As it was, the co-operation of Emperor and Pope that had worked so happily during the last ten years of Henry III's reign was now at an end, and a new era of separation and hostility was to begin.

The changed situation after Henry III's death

Pope Stephen IX

Imperial nomination ceased at once, for there was no Emperor and, more important, no *patricius*. All the same, it was again a German, Frederick of Lorraine, cardinal and abbot of Monte Cassino, who in August 1057 was elected Pope with the name of Stephen IX. This does not mean, however, that the influence of the German court was responsible, but rather that the reformers at Rome were strong enough to obtain the election of one of their number. It was certainly significant that they should choose the brother of that Godfrey who had defied imperial authority and was usurping its place in Central Italy. They gained thereby an ally, and this may have determined their choice, for the Papacy was politically in a weak position, especially in the face of Norman aggression. For the same reason, it was necessary to keep on good terms with the German government, and Stephen dispatched an embassy, with Hildebrand at its head, to obtain the assent of Agnes, on her son's behalf, to the election. This it secured, but before its return to Rome the Pope was dead, another German victim to the Italian climate, after a reign of little more than six months.

His chief contribution to the work of reform was to add a notable figure to the Curia by making Peter Damian cardinal bishop of Ostia. This hermit-monk, an ardent zealot, was a valuable champion of reform, especially because of his unworldliness and single-mindedness. In spite of the forceful phrases in which he excelled and which have often been quoted as a proof of fanaticism in him, he was by no means in sympathy with the more intransigent party headed by cardinal Humbert, nor would he associate himself with those like Hildebrand (though he felt the attraction of his personality, and once called him his " holy Satan ") who were especially concerned with the monarchical authority of the Papacy. He devoted himself entirely to the spiritual side of the Church's work and its independence ; as legate, at Milan and elsewhere, he did yeoman service in the cause of reform.

Stephen IX was the last of the succession of German Popes, of whom there had been five in the space of twelve years. And now, with the German government too weak to intervene, it seemed as if the old story was to be repeated and the Papacy to be recaptured by the Roman nobles. The Tusculan and Crescentii families laid aside their former rivalry and united to raise Mincius, cardinal bishop of Velletri, to the papal throne ; significantly he took the name of Benedict X. The leading reformers were many of them away from Rome at the time, but they met in Tuscany and chose Gerard, bishop of Florence, a Burgundian by origin, as Pope Nicholas II. They were not strong enough to stand alone, and they requested and obtained the assent of Agnes to the election. But it was again the assistance on the spot of duke Godfrey that was the more effective, and with his aid Nicholas was enthroned at Rome in January 1059 and his rival deposed. This was an amazing victory, since it was achieved by the initiative of a few reforming cardinals. It was not merely the reform of the Papacy by Henry III but equally the reform of the Curia by Leo IX which had made possible this first step towards complete papal independence.

Nicholas II and Benedict X Victory of the reformers

Nicholas II was not a man of striking personality in himself, and he was Pope for less than three years, but he was surrounded by men of determined and forceful character, and the events of his short Papacy were of outstanding importance. First came the famous Election Decree of 1059. The experience of the previous year made it essential to prevent the Roman nobles from recovering their control over the election ; so the first step was to make this illegal. In accordance with Church law, election to the Roman as to other sees was made by the clergy and people, but the parts taken by each were not clearly defined. It was now laid down

The Papal Election Decree (1059)

that the election of the Pope was to be a matter for the cardinals alone. The cardinal bishops were to have charge of the election, taking the place that a metropolitan would occupy in his province and also having the first voice; then in concert with the other cardinals they were to proceed to election; if possible, they were to hold the election at Rome and were to choose one of their own number. The rest of the clergy and the laity were left with no share other than that of giving their assent. Finally, there was a clause which ran: " saving the due honour and reverence due to our beloved son Henry, king now and Emperor, it is hoped, to be, which we have granted to him personally, and to such of his successors as shall obtain the same grant from the apostolic see." The vagueness of this was doubtless intentional, but the other clauses made it clear that the king was not to interfere with the election; his formal confirmation of it was doubtless the favour implied, and it was not contemplated that he could refuse assent.

This was the great charter of papal independence. Directed primarily against the Roman nobles, it freed the election from all lay interference, even that of the Emperor. It has a further effect in establishing the position, and magnifying the importance, of the College of Cardinals,[1] who in the new organisation became princes of the Church, like the German princes who were the electing body in the German kingdom. The cardinals were more than that, because they formed a permanent council of advisers, they provided a continuity of government sadly lacking in Germany, there was no hereditary tendency to limit their choice, and each of them was a possible future Pope. Such were the consequences ultimately reached when the acceptance of the decree became general. The imposing attendance of 113 bishops, as well as abbots and other clergy, gave a special sanction to the Council, but it was not likely that either the German king or the Roman nobles would meekly acquiesce in the decree. It had to be successfully enforced before it would be universally accepted. It also contained a defect, in that no provision was made to meet the case of the cardinals failing

[1] The College of Cardinals at this time consisted normally of 7 cardinal bishops attached to the sees collateral to Rome; 28 cardinal priests attached to the great basilicas as well as the abbots of San Paolo and San Lorenzo; 12 cardinal deacons and 6 Palatine deacons.

to agree on a candidate.   In this way there was still the danger
of schism and the opportunity for lay interference.

The Election Decree was the Council's greatest work, but Other
even apart from that it would have been important.   It decrees of
the Council
passed decrees to establish the independence not only of the
Papacy but of all the clergy from lay control.   No one was
to receive a church from a layman, even as a free gift.   Clergy
were not to be judged, or evicted from their churches, by
laymen, who were to surrender tithes or other Church dues
in their possession.   The old decrees against simony and
clerical marriage were again repeated, and additional measures
were taken to enforce them.   In future no one was to receive
ordination from a simoniacal bishop, and the laity were
forbidden to attend the mass of an " unchaste " (no longer
do they use the term " married ") priest.   The object was to
obtain obedience to the decrees by isolating and ostracising
the offenders.

These papal manifestoes of its own and the Church's Peace with
the Normans
independence were a courageous defiance of existing conditions.   The reformed Papacy was, and knew itself to be,
in a precarious position.   The death of Henry III had really
been a disaster for it as for the Empire ; his co-operation
would have given it the necessary temporal backing.
Deprived of that assistance—and duke Godfrey proved a
feeble substitute—the Pope was forced to compromise with
the most formidable of his enemies, the Normans, to gain
the temporal support that was so necessary.   After the great
Council of 1059 he went south, and in August met the Norman
leaders, Richard of Capua and Robert Guiscard, at Melfi.
Richard was invested with the principality of Capua, Robert
with the duchies of Apulia, Calabria, and even Sicily.   In
return they took an oath of fealty to the Pope, promising
their assistance to the Papacy, especially for the enforcement
of the Election Decree.   Norman troops accompanied the
Pope back to Rome, and secured him from danger from the
Roman nobles.

The treaty of Melfi was one of the most important events The
in European history.   The alliance with the Normans gave significance
of the treaty
the Papacy the temporal assistance necessary to ensure its of Melfi
independence, and at the same time the recognition of its
suzerainty over South Italy and Sicily.   This was perhaps

the most surprising feature in the whole transaction. The Papacy granted to Richard territory which had previously recognised the overlordship of the Western Emperor, and to Robert Guiscard territory which was actually in the possession of the Eastern Emperor and of the Moslems. The assumption of suzerainty over South Italy and Sicily, which was to play so large a part in papal policy for the next two centuries, is here for the first time expressed. It can only be inferred that the donation of Charlemagne was taken to include all South Italy, while Sicily was included by virtue of the forged Donation of Constantine.[1] The recognition of papal overlordship by the Normans turned this theoretical claim into actual fact. For their part, the Normans got what they wanted—a legal title from a suzerain—and from their destructive brigandage they pass to the building-up of an ordered State. But first of all Robert Guiscard had to conquer the territories with which he had been invested. Sicily and the Moslems had to be postponed until the Greeks had been overcome. A long struggle ensued with the Eastern Empire, which was fatally handicapped by the dangerous advance of the Seljuk Turks. In 1071 the Emperor Romanus Diogenes suffered the disastrous defeat of Manzikert in the east, and in the same year Robert Guiscard captured Bari and the Byzantine authority in Italy was at an end. So came into being the Norman State under papal suzerainty. Its existence profoundly affected the course of papal and imperial history. The Normans in the last resort could always be relied upon to defend the Pope against the Emperor, in order to preserve their own independence of the Empire. But their ambition was insatiable. Once settled in South Italy, they aimed at expansion in every direction, not only southwards into Sicily and eastwards into Greece, but also northwards into papal territory. The Papacy had often cause to regret that it had lost its natural defender, the Emperor.

After the great events of 1059 the remainder of Nicholas's Papacy was less stirring. There was a Council at Rome in 1060, and legates were sent to enforce the Roman decrees

---

[1] In the new canon law which was being evolved at Rome, the pseudo-Isidorian Decretals played a leading part, and included in them the Donation of Constantine. Gregory VII (who had a considerable share in the treaty of Melfi) certainly made use himself of the Donation of Constantine, and Urban II definitely based his claim to Sicily upon it.

elsewhere, especially in France. Hildebrand, who had played an important part in the treaty with the Normans, was rewarded for his administrative ability by being made arch-deacon of the Roman Church. When Nicholas II died in July 1061 there seemed to be little besides local opposition to interfere with the steady development of the reform programme. But the treaty of Melfi and the Election Decree *The opposition created by the papal programme* together had definitely alienated the German government; even Agnes had been bitterly offended by the entire disregard of imperial rights displayed in both these events. The Lombard bishops were hostile to the policy of the reformers ; the Roman nobles were chafing under their recent defeat. The common aim was to make the Election Decree of no effect ; so they bided their time until there was a vacancy on the papal throne.

The death of Nicholas II gave the opportunity. The *Its attempt to establish Cadalus of Parma as Pope* Romans sent an embassy to Henry IV, and by creating him *patricius* recognised his right of appointment ; the Lombard bishops, for their part, had a satisfactory candidate ready at hand. Altogether the prospects for the recovery of royal authority seemed to be most favourable when in October the young king, arrayed as *patricius*, met the Roman and Lombard representatives at Basle and nominated Cadalus, bishop of Parma, who took the name of Honorius II. But the assembling of these scattered allies had taken time, and they had lost the tactical advantage of priority. The *The cardinals elect Alexander II* cardinals, fully aware of the danger, had met outside Rome and in September had elected Anselm, bishop of Lucca, a sincere reformer who had done good service as legate, especi-ally at Milan, and had the support of duke Godfrey. He took the name of Alexander II. The treaty of Melfi now came to the assistance of the Election Decree. Norman soldiers brought the new Pope to be enthroned at Rome in October, before his rival had even been elected.

Cadalus was therefore at a disadvantage, which could only *His victory over his rival* be overcome by resort to arms. With a Lombard army he forced his way through Tuscany and in March 1062 arrived at Rome, where local support enabled him to gain a temporary victory. Duke Godfrey intervened to bring about a truce in the fighting, and at this very time (April 1062) occurred the abduction of the young king of Germany by Anno and his Saxon confederates, which altered the whole situation. The new German government withdrew its support from Cadalus; Anno, anxious to assert himself as imperial vicar, presided in 1064 at a Council at Mantua, at which Alexander II was adjudged to be the lawful Pope. His rival lived on, recalcitrant, with a few supporters for nine more years, but the schism was definitely at an end. The Election Decree had won its first success, helped, it is true, by the political situation in Germany. But this was soon forgotten. Anno by his absence in Italy had lost control in Germany, and in the Church the Pope speedily taught him who was the real master by calling him to account on the charge of simony. The charge was probably justified, but it was in part a punishment for his arrogance. Papal independence and papal headship of the Church were linked together, and it was derogatory to both that an archbishop should sit in judgment upon a Pope.

Alexander II's papacy a period of comparative inaction

The triumph of the reforming party in the Curia was followed not, as might have been expected, by a further advance especially in the extension of papal authority, but by a period of comparative inaction. Alexander was Pope for twelve years. Compared with the twelve preceding years —from the accession of Leo IX to the death of Nicholas II— crowded with events of the highest importance, or again with the twelve years of Gregory VII's Papacy which followed, Alexander's reign was a period of stagnation. The work of reform went on steadily, at any rate in France, where owing to the weakness of royal authority the papal authority could most easily be exerted. Even in Germany a notorious simonist, the bishop of Constance, was deposed by a provincial synod. But Alexander himself contributed nothing new. He apparently held few councils, and at the only important one—at Rome in 1063—the decrees were only repetitions of those of Nicholas II in 1059. He seems to have been content merely to maintain the *status quo*. His caution was not unnatural, for the reformed Papacy was still too weak to stand upon its own feet, and had had to lean on the very dubious support of the Normans. Moreover, the coming of age of Henry IV introduced a new and an unknown factor, while in 1069 the death of duke Godfrey removed the barrier which had previously kept Henry from contact with Italy and Rome.

Though a great victory had been won for papal independence, a period of peace was necessary to consolidate the position, and a forward policy would have been certain to stir up strife. The most advanced member of the Curia, especially in his utterances against the lay power, cardinal Humbert of Silva Candida, had died in 1061, and the more moderate policy advocated by Peter Damian was in the ascendant. Clearly Hildebrand was not " the power behind the throne," as he is usually depicted, for he must often have chafed at the papal inaction ; it certainly disappeared at once when he became Pope.

Yet in these years of comparative idleness there were some solid gains. A new temper seems to have prevailed at Rome, where the Pope no longer needed Norman weapons to protect him. Possibly Hildebrand had something to do with this. The wealthy family of the Pierleoni, with which he was probably connected, became staunch papal adherents, and his own personal popularity was evinced by the clamour for his election after Alexander's death. It was certainly his advocacy that decided the Pope to give his blessing to William of Normandy's conquest of England in 1066, from which the Papacy rightly anticipated an extension of the movement of reform. It hoped, though vainly, for something more, for we possess a fragment of a letter from Alexander II to William in which he suggested papal overlordship of England, a claim repeated in a more precise form by Hildebrand after he became Pope. The authority of the Papacy in the moral sphere was vindicated by Peter Damian, when as papal legate in 1069 he compelled Henry IV to abandon his intention of separating from his wife. But the most important event of these years was the definite establishment of papal control over the Milanese church. Here Alexander was stirred into action on his own initiative, on behalf both of reform and of papal authority, but as it led to conflict with the royal power it will be described in the next chapter. Alexander's papacy, for the most part quiet and peaceful, began in conflict and ended with the threat of a still more dangerous conflict to come.

Some solid gains

Alexander II died on April 21, 1073, and there could have been little doubt as to who would be his successor ; for

Pope Gregory VII (1073–85)

Peter Damian had died the previous year, and of the out-standing figures in the Curia during the last twenty-five years only the archdeacon Hildebrand was left. The choice of the cardinals, indeed, was anticipated by the populace, who hardly allowed the body of Alexander to be laid to rest before they began to clamour vehemently for Hildebrand as Pope. The formal election followed, but it was not prejudiced by the popular disturbance. The Pope-elect was not the nominee of Roman nobles or of German king, and so for the second time the real purpose of the Election Decree was fulfilled and papal independence vindicated. And on this occasion the choice had been made from the Roman Church, as the Decree prescribed. For, except for his three years in the Rhine district, Hildebrand had spent his life in the service of the Roman Church. He took the name of Gregory VII in memory of the Gregory VI in whose service he had left Rome to go into exile in 1046.

His personality   Thus began one of the greatest pontificates in history. Contemporary writers picture him to us as small and strikingly ugly, but with flashing eyes which mirrored his ardent soul, and they attest his power of fascination, of which his influence over the Romans is a proof. He falls far short of many Popes in learning, theological or legal, but in zeal, in deter-mination, and in practical knowledge and ability he was second to none. When we observe the sudden change from the easy-going practice of his predecessor to the vigorous and violent activity of his reign, when we consider the vast range of his vision and the permanence of his achievement, whether we approve or condemn, we cannot fail to be impressed by his personality. He is one of the great men who have left their imprint upon the history of the world, and the enthusiasm and the hatred that he aroused among his contemporaries have been kindled again in every succeeding generation. Round such a figure legends inevitably gather. He has been made responsible not only for his own acts as Pope but also for all the stirring events of the preceding quarter of a century, when he was only a subordinate agent of the policy inaugurated by others. The youth whom Leo IX brought with him to Rome in 1049 has been depicted as the master of the Church from that time onwards. So, whereas the original names of other Popes are hardly remembered, the name Hildebrand is as familiar as Gregory VII.[1] Yet the events themselves point to the moment when he really became master.

Gregory VII is chiefly remembered as the great protagonist of the spiritual power in its conflict with the temporal, but apart from that tremendous issue, which will be described in the next chapter, his Papacy was of outstanding importance, both for the establishment of the principles of the reform movement and for the general recognition of an effective papal headship of the Church. The two are intimately connected, since the enforcement of reform had been the chief object of the exercise of papal authority and the cause of its development. At the time of Gregory's accession, there was almost as much opposition as acquiescence to both of these points. The vigorous campaign inaugurated by Leo IX had not been sustained.

His first step was to restore the machinery into proper order again, and to keep it working at high tension. He revived Leo's practice of holding regular synods at Rome,[2] and he began by repeating in them the decrees of Nicholas II against simony and clerical marriage. Leo's other practice of presiding over local synods himself involved lengthy absences from Rome which were now inadvisable. Gregory therefore sent instructions to the archbishops to publish the decrees at provincial synods, and made them responsible for their local enforcement. At the same time he dispatched legates to act with full authority in his name, wherever the local officials were idle or recalcitrant. *The policy and methods of his early years*

In Germany and North Italy there had been a definite reaction since the days of Henry III. The lower clergy resisted the enforcement of celibacy and there were violent outbreaks against it. The bishops were often lukewarm in *His relations with Germany*

---

[1] Thus the whole movement of advanced reform and centralised government is commonly known as the Hildebrandine movement. It is also known, still more unsuitably, as the Cluniac movement, since Cluny initiated the monastic reform which preluded the later movement. The legend that Hildebrand was a monk, even prior, at Cluny has helped to harmonise these two conceptions and to confirm the double mistake. While his friends spoke of him as Hildebrand in glorification of his past, his enemies also called him Hildebrand, as they disputed his right to be Pope.

[2] From 1074 to 1081 he held a synod each Lent, except in 1077, the year of Canossa; in 1078 there was a second synod in November, and apparently in 1074 also.

the cause of reform, and many of them were personally affected by the decrees against simony; while, with few exceptions, they were bitterly opposed to the interference of papal authority within their jurisdictions. The legates sent at the beginning of 1074 found the greatest difficulty in carrying out their orders. Siegfried of Mayence, who lacked the courage either to defy the Pope or to deal firmly with offenders, tried to wriggle out of his obligations. Liemar of Bremen, who had succeeded Adalbert in 1072, though a reformer was antagonised by the peremptory tone of the legates. Gregory then took personal action. He summoned Liemar and Siegfried, as well as a number of German and Italian bishops who were accused of simony, to attend the Lenten synod of 1075. Liemar disdained the summons and was suspended from his office; three German and three Lombard bishops were also suspended for non-attendance. Siegfried's plea of ill-health was accepted, but the decrees of the synod were sent to him and he was ordered to publish them forthwith at a provincial synod. He did his best to find excuses, but Gregory insisted, and eventually a synod was held at Mayence in October, only to be broken up by the turbulence of the married clergy. The cause of reform was making slow progress, but the battle for papal supremacy was more than half won.

With France

Legates were sent to France also in 1074, and here, though the episcopate was no less hostile to papal interference, it was less united and less capable of resistance, while the reform movement was more firmly grounded. So successful were the legates—bishops Hugh of Die and Amatus of Oloron— that they were established as permanent legates, Hugh for the north and centre, Amatus for the south. They united in holding synods, in spite of opposition which sometimes took a violent form, they published the reform decrees, they even deposed recalcitrant bishops. Through their agency, not only did the reform movement progress but papal authority over the French Church became firmly established.

With England

No legates were sent to England, for there was no need of them. William I, following his practice in Normandy, was an ardent supporter of the reform movement. His assistance and the energy of archbishop Lanfranc of Canterbury, who had in his possession a copy of the decrees of the

Roman Council of 1059 at which he had been present, made it unnecessary for Gregory to interfere. He wrote to the king in terms of warm affection, for he welcomed lay co-operation and claimed that it ought always to be given to the work of the Church. But, as he said, William was alone among kings in opposing the abuses within the Church. Henry IV, humiliated by the Saxons, was careful not to offend the Pope, but he also avoided putting pressure on the archbishops to obey the papal legates. Philip I of France was more openly hostile, though he was too weak to make his opposition effective. Apart from England, where the work was done for him, Gregory had to depend entirely on his own resources.

It was becoming increasingly evident that the lay control of the Church was, in fact, the chief obstacle to the success of the papal programme, and Gregory began to take more direct action. Simony, especially in the appointments to bishoprics, had become widespread in Germany. This was laid to the account of Henry IV's counsellors,[1] five of whom were threatened with excommunication at the Lenten synod of 1075. At the same time, Philip I of France, who apart from other offences had gone so far as to despoil merchants and pilgrims on their way to Italy, was similarly threatened. Finally, passing from individuals to general principles, the Pope at the same synod promulgated the first decree against Lay Investiture. *The issue of lay control*

The practise of investiture was of long standing, but in process of time it had changed in character. The king now, in investing the bishop-elect, handed to him the episcopal ring and staff, with the words " Receive the Church " (*Accipe ecclesiam*). This ceremony seemed to the Pope to signify a lay control over spiritual offices which was a usurpation of his own functions as head of the Church, as well as a principal cause of the persistence of abuses within the Church. So in the words of the only writer (Arnulf of Milan) who actually describes the decree, " he removed all lay persons from the investiture of churches." Or, to quote the text of the decree *The decree against lay investiture (1075)*

---

[1] Probably rightly. Payments to acquire bishoprics were certainly made, notoriously in the case of Herman, who became bishop of Bamberg. It would seem that this was often made to those who had influence with the king, rather than to the king himself.

when it was promulgated for the second time, in November 1078, " no cleric was to accept investiture of bishopric, abbey, or church from the hand of Emperor, king, or any lay person, male or female " ; such investiture was declared null and void, and the penalty was excommunication of the recipient. The wording is quite clear. Only investiture with the spiritual office was condemned ; nothing was said about the temporalities, territorial and jurisdictional, which the king conferred upon the bishop. It is a mistake to conclude, as, for instance, Bryce does in his *Holy Roman Empire*, that " Gregory declared that it was sin for the ecclesiastic to receive his benefice under conditions from a layman, and so condemned the whole system of feudal investitures of land to the clergy." All the same, the decree was of outstanding importance. If obeyed, it left the Pope supreme in the ecclesiastical sphere, and it made disobedience to him more difficult to maintain. At the same time, it represented a breach with the traditional practice which the lay rulers would naturally resist. Gregory, though claiming that he was doing nothing new but only returning to the better ways of the Early Church, knew that the matter needed most delicate handling. He even avoided publishing the decree while he negotiated with Henry IV for its acceptance. In France, his legates had no hesitation in publishing it openly at the synods they summoned. England it never reached, but there the chief reason for its enforcement was absent.

The
" Dictatus
Papae "

In the first two years of Gregory's papacy, the establishment of papal authority over all ecclesiastical officials and the consequent removal of lay control over things purely ecclesiastical were the means employed to the end of Church reform. But these means were already primary objectives in themselves. The magnitude of his responsibility as the successor, and therefore the representative, of St. Peter weighed heavily upon Gregory, and he felt it his manifest duty to uphold the greatness of his office. He had been obsessed with this even before he became Pope, and we know that he had urged Peter Damian to compile a collection of all the canons bearing on papal authority. Though Damian refused, Gregory found someone willing to do this, since in 1075 about the same time as the Lenten synod appeared the famous *Dictatus Papae* containing a series of dicta, twenty-seven in number, derived from the False Decretals and other collections, on the powers and privileges of the Roman Church, which " has never erred and on the testimony of Scripture will never err." Here the supremacy of the Pope in government, jurisdiction, and legislation was emphatically stated ; it could be exercised, too, intermediately through legates, who have the power of deposing even their superiors in rank. The Pope can judge all, but be judged by none ; he is an absolute monarch.

The *Dictatus Papae* was included in the official register of Gregory's letters, but was not published to the world. It shows us what was in the Pope's mind rather than what he felt it immediately possible to achieve ; up to this time he had not allowed his zeal to override the practical experience and diplomatic ability he had acquired in his long years as cardinal. He looked back regretfully to the days of Leo IX and Henry III, when Pope and Emperor co-operated in the work of reform and archbishops had perforce to be submissive. He was anxious to renew this harmony with Henry IV, and to arrange an amicable settlement on the question of Lay Investiture. But within a few months this question had faded into the background and his plans were all upset ; he had to face a challenge to the independence of the Papacy itself. Henry IV, victorious over the Saxons, in the autumn of 1075 threw off the mask of friendliness he had been obliged to adopt, and for over a year the contest between Empire and Papacy completely occupied the mind and the energies of Gregory VII.

With the resumption of peace in 1077 he was able to resume his normal programme, and it is noticeable that he attacked the problem of reform with renewed vigour born of the confidence he had gained from his victory over the temporal power. The decrees, especially in the November synod of 1078, became sharper in tone. Besides the repetition of the decree against Lay Investiture, now openly published, it was enacted that bishops who permitted clerical immorality in their dioceses were to be deposed ; that bishops who accepted money for ecclesiastical offices were likewise to be deposed ; while ordinations obtained by simoniacal or other uncanonical means were declared invalid. *His legislation in the years 1078-9*

Little could be done in Germany owing to the state of civil war, but the German episcopate as a whole had been

7

forced to recognise the Pope as its master, the Saxon bishops were friendly for political reasons, and centres of reform, at Constance, Hirschau, and elsewhere, were being created in **Papal authority in France** South Germany. In France, papal authority was vigorously advanced by the zeal of the legates, especially bishop Hugh of Die, and episcopal resistance was overcome by ecclesiastical sentences. The leading prelate in France, Manasse, archbishop of Rheims, was actually deposed in 1080, and Gregory confirmed the deposition. His success in France led him to a further step in the direction of centralisation, by which certain archbishops were given a closer connexion with Rome and a wider sphere of influence with the rank of primate. In 1079, for instance, the archbishop of Lyons was made primate of the four provinces of Lyons, Rouen, Sens, and Tours, and the practical purpose of the Pope was made evident when he authorised the translation of Hugh of Die to Lyons in 1082. Philip I was naturally opposed to this policy, especially since Lyons lay outside the French kingdom, but his resistance to this, as to Manasse's deposition, was of little avail.

Friction with William the Conqueror However, this new move aroused the opposition of a much more important person, William I of England, since Rouen, the metropolitan see of Normandy, was included in the primacy of Lyons. There were, moreover, other causes of offence in 1079, for the disciplinary action of the Pope and his legates had been extended to Normandy. The harmony due to a common zeal for reform was endangered by the assertion within William's dominions of papal authority. The two issues, identical in the Pope's view, were by William kept sharply distinct; and though the differences in Normandy were accommodated, William allowed no interference with his and Lanfranc's government of the English Church. To this the Pope, albeit with a bad grace, had to submit, acknowledging William's exemplary attitude in the matter of reform. He made one further attempt to attain his end by a different means, when in 1080 he renewed Alexander II's claim that England was subordinate to the Pope, demanding fealty from William and at the same time the more regular payment of Peter's Pence.[1] To the latter demand William

---

[1] For the connexion between these two demands, see my *English Church and the Papacy*, pp. 140 foll.

assented, as the payment had become traditional; but to the demand for fealty he returned a brusque refusal, since it had neither precedent nor promise from himself to justify it.

This attempt by Gregory was in the nature of a forlorn hope; it was not, however, an isolated incident. The respon- sibility he felt as the representative of St. Peter obliged him to vindicate all the claims of his see to temporal as well as to ecclesiastical authority. He declared that Spain had formerly been among the possessions of the Holy See until it was conquered by the Moslems, and that the new Christian kingdoms ought to recognise the Pope as their overlord. A similar claim was advanced to Corsica, and in both cases the Donation of Constantine would seem to be the basis of the claim. The kingdom of Hungary, he asserted, was subject to the Roman Church because St. Stephen had received his crown from Rome. He welcomed the proposal of the Russian prince Isyaslav to place his kingdom under papal overlordship, but the downfall of Isyaslav disappointed his hopes; and he failed to induce Svein Estrithson to seek papal protection for his kingdom of Denmark as he had contemplated doing in Alexander II's Papacy.

Only in the papal States and in South Italy was his suzerainty definitely acknowledged, but the maintenance of his authority caused him from the beginning the greatest anxiety. At the northern extremity of the papal States, archbishop Guibert of Ravenna was constantly striving to reassert the independence of his see; he had already been excommunicated in 1078 before he committed the final sin of arrogating to himself the papal title in 1080. In the south, papal suzerainty extended not only over the Normans in Apulia, Calabria, and Capua, but also over the intervening Lombard principalities, of which Benevento and Salerno were the most important; they had put themselves under papal protection as a means of defence against Norman encroachment. In vain the Pope strove to prevent his Nor- man from conquering his Lombard vassals. His only recourse was to divide the Norman forces, and he was successful in gaining over to his side Richard of Capua. Robert Guiscard, however, showed no signs of yielding and was excommuni- cated at the Lenten synods of 1074 and 1075. In 1076 the Normans seized the opportunity of Gregory's conflict with

Gregory's claims to temporal authority

Insecurity of papal suzerainty

Ravenna

The Normans

Henry IV to reunite; Robert and Richard took Salerno in 1077 and laid siege to Benevento. Once more, in Lent 1078, the papal ban of excommunication was issued against them; and though Richard of Capua died and his son Jordan made his peace with the Pope, Robert Guiscard was still defiant. He had to overcome a serious revolt of his vassals in 1079, but in 1080, when the conflict between Gregory VII and Henry IV was resumed, he was at the height of his power and determined not to yield any of the conquests he had made by his encroachments on papal territory.

Gregory's success in the ecclesiastical sphere

The temporal sovereignty of the Papacy Gregory found, therefore, both difficult to maintain and impossible to extend. His success was entirely in the ecclesiastical sphere, and here it was both decisive and permanent. Not only did he make papal authority effective in the parts of Europe (England alone excepted) where Christianity had long been established, he extended it also to countries such as Norway, Sweden, and Poland where Christianity was still fighting its way, and missionary work was promoted under papal direction. Further, as Gregory I had been able to welcome and organise the victory of Orthodoxy over Arianism in Spain, so Gregory VII was able to welcome and organise the advance there of Christianity against Islam. It was no small gain that the new Christian kingdoms abandoned the Spanish and adopted the Roman liturgy. Uniformity in ritual was a phase of the new unity of the Church under papal direction, and marks another stage in the steady progress towards a complete papal headship of the Church. Finally, to realise the full extent of Gregory's achievements as described in this chapter, it must be remembered that they were all compassed within the brief space of six years. During half of the twelve years of his Papacy he was almost entirely absorbed by the bitter contest he had to wage with the ruler of the Empire, the temporal head of Christendom.

CHAPTER IX

THE FIRST CONTEST OF EMPIRE AND PAPACY,
1076–1106

IN his famous letter to the Emperor Anastasius I Pope **The Gelasian theory**
Gelasius I at the end of the fifth century had expressed
what was to become a medieval commonplace : " There
are two powers by which this world is governed in chief, the
consecrated authority of priests and the royal power."
Priests must be subject to royal laws in matters pertaining
to the State ; kings must be obedient to priests in matters
affecting salvation. At the same time, it was axiomatic
that the Christian community was a single body, the Church,[1]
of which the Head was Christ. The difficulty was to reconcile the unity of the Church with the duality of its earthly
government, and to define the frontiers between the two
authorities. Gelasius himself insisted on the greater burden
imposed upon priests, " since they will have to render account
at the judgment-seat of God for all men, even kings." The
authority of the spiritual department was over the soul, that
of the temporal department only over the body. Already
the greater importance of the ecclesiastical authority is
posited.

There could be no doubt in the medieval mind that **Interpreta-**
authority in both departments was derived from God. That **tion of this by the**
alone gave it its justification, and there was ample proof in **Papacy**
the Bible of the divine origin of both powers. Kingship
had been created for the chosen people, the Jews, by God,
and Our Lord had recognised imperial authority. At the
same time, He had founded His Church on the rock, Peter,

---

[1] The Church (*ecclesia*) is the comprehensive term including both spheres
of government ; but it is also used to denote the ecclesiastical department
alone (the *sacerdotium* as opposed to the *regnum*). It is not always easy
to keep the two senses distinct, and this identity of name gave a distinct
advantage to the ecclesiastical claims.

and had given him the power of binding and of loosing in heaven and on earth. On this the Popes, as the successors of St. Peter in the see of Rome, laid their claim to the head-ship of the Church (the ecclesiastical department). They recognised, indeed, the divine origin of temporal power. But the ruler must be a righteous man (*justus*). This had been laid down by St. Augustine in his *City of God*, and, repeated by Gregory the Great, the ideas of St. Augustine had become a commonplace of medieval thought. The ideal of the Christian commonwealth is *pax*, the ordered sub-mission of mankind to the will of God. It must be governed by *justitia*, which St. Augustine defined as obedience to the commandments of God. *Justitia*, therefore, should be trans-lated " righteousness," not " justice," which might imply obedience to the laws of man.

The supposition that the king must be a *justus homo* at once raises an obvious question, to which St. Augustine supplied no answer. Who is to decide whether a king is morally fit to govern, and if he is not, what steps can be taken ? The Gelasian theory afforded a solution. The matter obviously came within the priestly domain. Holding this view, the bishops of France in the ninth century had asserted their right to deal with an unrighteous ruler, and in concert with the Pope had declared Louis the Pious deposed. Later, Nicholas I had assumed this as the special right of the Pope, and had manifested his authority by excom-municating Lothar II for his offence against the moral code.

The stand-point of Pope Gregory VII Gregory VII, though in practice he went far beyond his predecessors, could rightly claim that he was no innovator. The word *justitia* in its exact Augustinian sense was con-stantly in his mouth ; he used it regularly as the test of fitness to rule, and he clearly considered it his duty to inter-pret God's will to man, to reprove the wicked, and if necessary to depose the unrighteous ruler. Quoting the words of Gelasius he told William the Conqueror in 1080 that " the apostolic and pontifical dignity would have to render account at the Last Judgment for the sins of all men, even of kings." He felt himself to be in the position of a Samuel, whose rebuke to the disobedient Saul he was fond of quoting. In his famous *Dictatus Papae* it was stated that the Pope can depose

Emperors, and that he can absolve from their allegiance the subjects of unrighteous men. And when he declared Henry IV deposed (for his pride, falsehood, and disobedience—the marks of the unrighteous ruler, according to St. Augustine), he adduced as a precedent the deposition (by the Pope, he declared) of the last of the Merovingians and the elevation of Pepin to the kingship; he quoted the instance of St. Ambrose excluding Theodosius the Great from his church until he had done penance for his sin in the massacre at Thessalonica; and finally he produced his conclusive argument for the superiority of the sacerdotal over the royal authority, for, he asked, what lay ruler can vie with the humblest priest, who " can make with his own mouth the Body and Blood of Our Lord " ? So was built up the claim of the ecclesiastical department, and especially of the Pope its head, to interfere within the temporal department whenever the moral law was in question. Kings are liable to papal judgment, while the Pope can be judged by no man. The Gelasian doctrine of the two powers was still maintained, but the extension of the ecclesiastical sphere left little scope for secular independence.

The papal case, worked out in accordance with medieval ideas, was certainly a strong one. But so, too, was the imperial. It started from the same premises and arrived at the opposite conclusion. The king was willing to admit the divine origin of papal authority, though he considered his own to be overriding. He could not deny his duty of obedience to God's commandments, but he could claim that he was following Augustine more truly than the Pope.[1] For Augustine had clearly contemplated a secular head of the Church upon earth, taking Constantine as his model. Charlemagne followed implicitly the teaching of his favourite book, Augustine's *City of God*, and believed it to be his first duty to enforce obedience to God; later Emperors, such as Otto III, Henry II, and Henry III, acted in the same spirit. All of them treated the ecclesiastical department as subordinate to them. The Papacy could produce precedents for its claim

The imperial point of view

---

[1] It may be noted that one of the sturdiest champions of Henry IV against Gregory VII, the anonymous writer of the treatise significantly entitled *Liber de unitate ecclesiae*, quoted at length from the *City of God*, especially Book XIX.

to punish and to depose kings. These were exceptional, however, and the general tradition of the past centuries supported the royal claim. Numerous Popes had been created or deposed on the initiative of Emperors. Nor was it enough to reply that this control of the Church had been a usurpation. The king was something more than a mere layman. He was anointed with the holy oil at his consecration, and could claim as " the Lord's anointed " to be above human judgment. " There's such divinity doth hedge a king " was essentially a medieval idea.

The clash between the two theories Here, then, were two opposing theories, both of them based on Old Testament history, on passages in the New Testament, on St. Augustine and other Fathers, and finally on precedents from the more recent past. As each side was firmly convinced of the rights of its case, a clash was bound to come. It had not come before, because the Emperors had usually been strong enough to enforce their will upon a dependent Papacy. The Papacy under Gregory VII was at last in an established and an independent position. Concrete issues were not lacking to put the rival theories to the test. The king, offended by the loss of the control his predecessors had exercised, and particularly by the Election Decree and the papal assumption of overlordship in South Italy, was waiting his opportunity to reduce the Papacy to its traditional subordination. The Pope was faced with the particular obstacle of lay control, which prevented the realisation of his main objectives. He was powerless unless he could obtain the full obedience of his ecclesiastical subordinates. On the other hand, the government of the Empire had been so designed that the king depended on the bishops as his local officials, and therefore on his control of appointments to ecclesiastical offices. The vital thing was the spirit in which he made the appointments. When he allowed simony to flourish, and considered only the secular duties of the episcopate, he put himself completely in the wrong. The Pope was able to emphasise the unrighteousness of his actions, and the whole weight of the reform movement, to which Henry III had so largely contributed, was thrown into the balance against Henry IV. Each side, then, was indignant at what it regarded as the usurpations of the other. It only needed a particular instance to create a conflagration out of this inflammable material, and it was events at Milan that provided the necessary spark.

In the disturbances at Milan in Conrad II's reign, the Events at Milan archbishop Aribert and the *capitanei* had been opposed by the *valvassores*. The non-noble element (the *popolani*) had been ignored by both parties. It, too, was composed of two classes—the merchants (*negotiatores*) and the mass of the populace, mainly artisans; the one had wealth, the other numbers to make them formidable; and they had a common grievance in being excluded from political rights, while the commerce and industry on which both depended for their livelihood were gravely handicapped by the violence and tyranny of the feudal nobility. What they needed was a leader. So, in 1042, when a *capitaneus* Lanzo espoused their cause, they were actually able to expel the nobles. Peace was restored in 1044, but the *popolani* had now become a definite party which could no longer be ignored. The new archbishop, Guido, appointed by Henry III in 1044, was a *valvassor* and was meant to hold the scales between nobles and people, but he lacked the personality of his predecessor and proved quite unequal to the crisis.

In 1056, the year of Henry III's death, another and a The revolt of the Pataria much more serious rising began, known as the revolt of the Pataria, from the contemptuous nickname of " rag-pickers " (Patarini) given by the nobles to their opponents. Again the *popolani* were led by nobles, Landulf and Ariald, a deacon; but on this occasion the attack was primarily directed against the clergy, who provided an easy target, since reform had made no progress in the Milanese Church. The clergy were regularly married, and simony was a normal practice; there was, in fact, an accepted tariff of payments for promotion to every grade in the ecclesiastical hierarchy. The Patarini, therefore, were able to pose as champions of reform, and appealed to the Pope for his assistance. A new issue was thereby introduced, to add to the bitterness of the opposing factions; for the Milanese Church, proud of its tradition as the see of St. Ambrose, had always maintained its autonomy and its difference from Rome in the matter of ritual. The Papacy was quick to seize the double opportunity of extending its authority and of enforcing reform.

Anselm, bishop of Lucca (a former cleric of Milan and later to be Pope as Alexander II), and Hildebrand were sent as legates by Stephen IX, but it was in Nicholas II's Papacy, when Anselm was accompanied by Peter Damian in 1059, that decisive steps were taken. The clergy were compelled to dismiss their wives and to abjure their simoniacal practices, while the archbishop was summoned to Rome and forced to recognise his dependence on the papal see.

The various interests concerned   The rising of the Pataria was only partly religious in character. The Milanese clergy were recruited from noble families, and the attack upon them was part of a general attack upon the political and social position of the feudal nobility. This soon became evident when Landulf died and was succeeded by his brother Erlembald, who made himself the real master of the city and was the originator of communal government. The lay nobles saw the danger and allied with the clergy, but in vain. The murder of the deacon Ariald in 1066 only inflamed the populace still further and strengthened the alliance of Erlembald with the Papacy. Guido was now thoroughly frightened, and contemplated retirement in favour of a younger and bolder champion of Milanese independence, but Pope Alexander II intervened to prevent this. At last, in August 1071, Guido died, and the question of his successor provoked a fresh crisis. For when contemplating retirement he had designated one Godfrey to succeed him, and Godfrey had already obtained investiture with ring and staff from Henry IV ; in 1072 the suffragan bishops of Milan consecrated him archbishop. On the other hand, Erlembald had his own candidate, by name Atto, and Alexander II at a Roman synod declared him to be the lawful archbishop. So, out of the revolt of the Pataria had developed a struggle for the mastery in Milan, in which the rival interests of king and Pope had now become deeply involved.

The attitude of Henry IV   It was, indeed, a matter of the highest importance for the king of Germany, who in the government of Lombardy depended primarily upon the bishops, and particularly on the greatest among them, the archbishop of Milan. His authority was gravely impaired when the government at Milan was usurped by a commune not recognising his overlordship, and again when the archbishop was made dependent on the papal see. Unfortunately for him the revolt of the Pataria occurred during his minority, when no intervention from Germany was possible. Even when he became his own master, Germany, especially Saxony, claimed his attention, and he still had to leave Italy to itself. He dared not risk an encounter with the Pope, and though he certainly looked forward to the time when he would be able to assert himself as his predecessors had done, he was compelled to leave that to the future and meanwhile to give no cause for offence. To the advance of reform in South Germany, though not sympathetic to it, he raised no impediment. And in 1069, when he was seeking to repudiate his wife, Bertha of Turin, to whom he had been married in 1066, he abandoned his purpose when the Pope, through the mouth of Peter Damian, sternly prohibited it.

But by 1071 he had crushed revolt in Saxony and was master of Germany. No longer did he feel it necessary to defer to the Pope, and the chance had come to assert himself at last in his Italian kingdom. Readily he espoused the cause of Godfrey and the nobles at Milan against Pope and commune, and paid no heed to the appeals of Alexander II. Then, in 1073, at the Lenten synod at Rome just before his death, the Pope declared five of Henry's counsellors excommunicate for the ill counsel they had given Henry in this matter. The king would not dismiss them, and so he too came under the ban. There was thus actually a schism between king and Pope at the moment when Gregory VII ascended the papal throne, and the first efforts of the new Pope were directed towards a reconciliation; his mind was centred on the work of reform, and peace with the ruler of Germany and Italy was the first essential for its progress. *His first breach with the Papacy*

It was not, however, the papal endeavours but a reversal of political conditions in Germany that caused Henry to change his mind. The disasters of 1073 made it essential for him once more to placate the Pope; he decided to throw over Godfrey, and in August he wrote the Pope a humble letter, acknowledging his offences especially with regard to Milan, and promising the obedience in ecclesiastical and moral affairs which Gregory claimed. The Pope was completely satisfied, and readily granted his absolution. For two years relations between them remained perfectly amicable, and Gregory was able to proceed with his task of reform and *The reconciliation of 1073* centralisation, if not with royal co-operation at any rate without any fear of royal opposition. His confidence in the king's sincerity was shown by his statement in 1074 that he hoped to lead an expedition to the help of the Eastern Christians, and in that case would leave the care of the Church to Henry during his absence. The king, for his part, was careful to give no cause for offence ; even against the sentences and decrees of the Lenten synod of 1075 he raised no protest.

Henry's challenge in 1075

Meanwhile, however, the king's position in Germany was improving, and at last in June 1075 he won his great victory over the Saxons. At the same time events in Milan took a new turn ; Erlembald was killed in a riot and the nobles were once more in the ascendancy. They sent to Henry asking him to appoint a new archbishop, Tedald, as rival to Atto. But Henry was still engaged in conquering Saxony, and his desire for imperial coronation made him hesitate to offend the Pope. At last, in September, his triumph in Saxony was complete, and he felt strong enough to throw off the mask and seize the opportunity in Italy again. An embassy came from him to grant investiture to Tedald, who was forthwith consecrated archbishop of Milan, and to make appointments to the sees of Fermo and Spoleto which lay actually within the Roman province. It was given the further task of forming an alliance with Robert Guiscard, who being under papal excommunication might be expected to join forces against the Pope ; Henry was naturally anxious to recover the overlordship in South Italy usurped by the Papacy in 1059, and the alliance would have deprived the Papacy of its chief temporal support in the contest on which Henry had now decided. However, Robert Guiscard refused the alliance ; papal excommunication was less irksome to him than the possibility of royal overlordship in South Italy.

The Pope's reply

The news of this embassy brought bitter disillusionment to Gregory. He recognised now that the king's repentance had been entirely conditioned by the political situation in Germany, and never could he again feel confidence in his sincerity. Moreover, the king's purpose was manifestly directed at the very independence of the Papacy. Gregory was not content merely to take measures for its defence ; he replied to the threat by a forcible counter-threat. He wrote immediately to reproach the king for his breach of faith, to rebuke him for his disobedience and his manifold offences, and with the letter he sent a private message threatening that if the king continued in the same path he would issue the ban of excommunication against him and separate him from the communion of the Church.

This letter reached Henry early in January 1076. In the full flush of his recovered authority, the papal threat came as an outrage on his sovereignty and stung him into a violent passion. Hastily he took steps to punish the Pope's presumption and to ensure his own domination for the future. He summoned a council of bishops to meet at Worms on January 24. He could count on their ready support, for they were only too anxious to be rid of the authority that Gregory was exercising over them. In spite of the shortness of the notice, two archbishops and twenty-four bishops assembled at Worms and renounced their allegiance to the Pope, a step which was followed shortly afterwards by the North Italian bishops in council at Piacenza. From Worms two letters were addressed to the Pope, one by the king the other by the bishops, ordering him to descend from the papal throne. It was not easy for the bishops to justify their action, and there was little beyond the commonplace of medieval controversy in the violent abuse of the personal character and motives of Gregory VII contained in both letters. But in Henry's letter, in the indignation with which he denounced the papal threat, in his insistence on his divine right, that he had received his kingdom from God, that he could be judged by no man but by God alone and could not be deposed save for apostasy from the faith, there was the ring of real conviction. It was a sincere statement of the imperial point of view.

And the papal reply to it was equally emphatic and equally sincere. When the letters of Henry and the bishops arrived the Lenten synod was in session, and was roused to a tumult of rage. The Pope intervened to protect the bearer of the letters from the angry synod, and then in measured tones delivered his sentence. He first decreed the deposition of the German and Lombard bishops who had taken part against him, and then pronounced judgment on the king. To give a special solemnity to his words, they were shaped

Outbreak of the first contest of Empire and Papacy (1076)

as an address to St. Peter, who could witness to the truth
of what he said; he quoted the authority given to him to
bind and to loose, he recited the king's offences, he declared
him to be deprived of his German and Italian thrones and
his subjects absolved from their oaths of allegiance; finally,
he pronounced a solemn excommunication. The more
detailed justification of his actions he wrote in letters to the
German princes, and of his power to excommunicate and
depose the king in a letter to bishop Herman of Metz. The
papal point of view thus received clear expression, and it was
echoed in numerous pamphlets by his supporters.

The coalition against Henry

So began the great contest between Pope and Emperor,
each proclaiming his power to judge and to condemn the
other, while declaring himself to be above all earthly judgment. Beside this great issue, subsidiary questions such as
lay investiture faded into the background. Each power had
pronounced sentence on the other, and the validity of these
sentences was now to be put to the proof. It was soon made
evident that Henry's hasty action had not power to justify
it; he had fatally over-estimated his strength. As in 1073,
he had reckoned without the dukes of Suabia, Bavaria, and
Carinthia, who were alarmed by the completeness of his
victory over the Saxons and feared that he had become
independent of their assistance. They took advantage of his
breach with the Pope to assert themselves again, and this
time they were determined that the control of affairs should
not escape from their direction. They were no longer content to hold the balance between king and Saxons; they
actually joined forces with the Saxon leaders, who had managed to escape the guards Henry had set over them, and
accepting the papal excommunication gained ecclesiastical
sanction for their rebellion. They rapidly perfected their
plans and began to close in upon the king.

His humiliation

Henry was quite unprepared for this powerful and unexpected coalition; the forces he was able to collect were
inadequate, and they rapidly began to dwindle. For, while
lesser men were perplexed as to their duty to an excommunicated king, the bishops who had sat with him in judgment on the Pope deserted the losing cause and hastened to
Italy to seek papal absolution. At last, in October, Henry
and his enemies faced one another at Oppenheim and Tribur,

on opposite sides of the Rhine. The king was powerless to resist and had to submit to the humiliating terms they imposed : he had to promise and to publish abroad that he would be obedient to the Pope and give satisfaction for his offences. But that was not all. Having vindicated the papal sentence on the king, the diet of nobles at Tribur proceeded to decree that Henry would be deprived of his kingdom if he failed to obtain absolution within a year of his excommunication (i.e. by February 22, 1077), and they invited the Pope to come to a council at Augsburg on February 2, where the question of the king's fitness to reign was to be debated. While determined to keep the upper hand over the king, they were fully alive to the value of papal co-operation. Their invitation gave the Pope immense satisfaction. It opened up a prospect that, with the government of the Empire itself made subject to papal dictation, his ideal of the rule of righteousness might be fulfilled. He set out on his journey to Germany in the highest hopes ; but in Lombardy he heard that Henry was approaching, and expecting an armed attack he took refuge in Countess Matilda's fortress at Canossa.

Gregory need have had no fear of violence, for nothing was further from Henry's mind. He saw how fatal to his power would be the conjunction of the Pope with his German enemies, and that this must be prevented at all costs. It could only be done by making his peace with Gregory before the Pope came into Germany, and with that object he eluded the vigilance of the dukes and accompanied by his wife and infant son and a few attendants made a memorable journey over the Alps in one of the severest winters on record. He could have raised an army in Lombardy, but reconciliation with the Pope was his purpose ; and so he appeared at the gates of Canossa, " for three days continuously," as Gregory himself testified, " laying aside all royal pomp, in wretched guise, barefooted and clad in humble woollens "—in fact, the penitent sinner pleading for absolution. His abnegation of royal dignity was the strongest card he could play. It roused the compassion even of Gregory's stoutest supporters, such as Countess Matilda of Tuscany. She, and abbot Hugh of Cluny, godfather to Henry and Gregory's personal friend, earnestly interceded with the Pope on the king's behalf.

Canossa (Jan. 1077)

During those three days Gregory was in a serious quandary, for after his disillusionment in 1075 he could put no faith in the king's sincerity; and he was naturally reluctant to abandon the prospect of a council in Germany under his own presidency. So he kept the king waiting for three days before he could make up his mind to accept Henry's penitence as genuine; then he admitted him, gave him absolution, and received him back into communion with the Church. At the same time, Henry had to promise on oath to obey the Pope's advice in respect to the charges brought by the nobles against him, and also to put no hindrance in the way of the Pope's coming into Germany. For he still, as he wrote to the German princes, was as anxious as ever to go there; but though he lingered for a time in Lombardy, it was soon evident that the situation had entirely changed, and he made his way back by slow stages, only arriving in Rome in September.

The election of the anti-king Rudolf

Henry, indeed, had achieved his purpose, though at a great cost. He had been compelled to recognise the Pope's power to excommunicate him (which he had so indignantly denied at Worms), and accordingly to lay aside his royal dignity in order to obtain absolution. But he was now able to rally his adherents again, and to checkmate his enemies in Germany. They were confounded by the news of the absolution, and went as far as they dared in hinting that the Pope had not kept faith with them. Like Gregory, they recognised that the situation had entirely altered but tried to pretend that it had not; and by spreading a false version of Henry's oath at Canossa, they made it appear that he had broken his word and that the excommunication still held good. Employing this fiction they declared that the year had elapsed and the kingdom was forfeit; and they summoned a diet to meet at Forchheim in Franconia on March 13 for a new election. It was not a representative assembly, but the presidency of the archbishop of Mayence gave it an appearance of legality. Duke Rudolf of Suabia was elected king, and was crowned by Siegfried at Mayence; but the townspeople rose on behalf of Henry, and Rudolf had to retire to Saxony where he took up his headquarters.

Civil war in Germany (1077–80)

For three years the throne of Germany was disputed between Henry and Rudolf. Pitched battles were rare and indecisive in result; there was one at Melrichstadt in Franconia in August 1078, another at Flarchheim in Thuringia at the beginning of 1080. Rudolf had an advantage in the fighting qualities of the Saxon army, but this was balanced by Henry's superiority in numbers. He was able, too, to prevent Rudolf from establishing contact with his supporters in South Germany. Here the chief fighting, mainly of a desultory character, occurred in Suabia, where Berthold and Welf owing to their ancestral domains had greater resources than in their own duchies. In fact, the Carinthian and most of the Bavarian nobility supported Henry, and he could also count on regular military assistance from the duke of Bohemia, Vratislav II, whose loyalty he ultimately rewarded with the title of king; the towns, especially in the Rhine district, also supplied their quota. Moreover, though he could gain no decisive military success, he took politic steps to consolidate his position. The three rebel dukes had been declared deposed, and, while keeping Bavaria in his own hands, he made new appointments to Carinthia and Suabia; but, as he needed powerful dukes to assist him, he had to depart from the old principle and give the duchies to local counts. Carinthia he gave to Liutold of Eppenstein, Suabia to Frederick of Staufen, to whom he married his daughter Agnes, and thus founded the fortunes of the Hohenstaufen family. Finally, in Saxony too he won a great diplomatic success, just after the battle of Flarchheim, by detaching the two leading nobles of East Saxony, duke Magnus and margrave Egbert of Meissen, from their allegiance to Rudolf. So the end was already in sight when the great crisis of the year 1080 occurred.

During these three years both sides had looked to the Pope for recognition, Henry claiming it as the legitimate ruler, Rudolf as a consequence of the agreement made in 1076. Though neither suggested that the decision between them lay with the Pope, this was now the claim that Gregory advanced. Ever since the invitation to him to come to Germany in 1076, there had floated before his eyes the vision of himself as arbiter in the government of Germany; it had become an obsession with him and was ultimately to lead him to disaster. In the original idea he was to judge as to Henry's fitness to rule, then between the rival claims of *Attitude of the Pope*

Henry and Rudolf; his decision was to be given at a council in Germany, and though he had abandoned the idea of going to Germany himself, his legates were to preside in his place. Again and again he repeated that his decision would be given in favour of the king who was proved to be a righteous man, that is to say obedient, and obedient to the Pope. For the council was to provide the test; whichever of the kings hindered the coming of the legates or the holding of the council would be declared unrighteous and therefore unfit to rule. At the three synods held at Rome in the years 1078–9, at each of which the representatives of Henry and Rudolf pressed their claims, he gave them this same reply.

But he was deluding himself with vain hopes. Neither side was in a position to defy the Pope, but neither was prepared to abide by the papal judgment unless it was in his favour. Henry had everything to lose by the holding of a council. Rudolf, on the other hand, might justly expect a favourable decision, especially since two papal legates had been present at Forchheim and had confirmed his election; while one of them, the cardinal deacon Bernard, in the following November at Goslar had joined with Siegfried of Mayence in publishing Henry's excommunication. Gregory repudiated the action of his legates, which had been taken without his authority, and insisted on his own impartiality. But he could not really be impartial with the knowledge he had of the mind of Henry; he had full confidence in Rudolf's repeated promises of obedience, and this begins to appear in the tone of his letters to Rudolf in 1079. When he wrote to encourage him to persist in the way that he had begun and to rely on papal support, it was evident that his mind was already made up.

His final decision against Henry in 1080

It was, therefore, not surprising that at the Lenten synod of 1080 he at last gave his decision in favour of Rudolf, and that he adduced as the reason that Henry by impeding the holding of the council had been proved disobedient. He gave no evidence in support of this assertion. Henry, it would seem, was beginning to turn from appeals to threats, and attempting to force a decision in his favour. The Pope did not mention this; he apparently based his decision on his view of Henry's character derived from the past. His sentence in its finality is even more solemn than was that of

1076. Henry, convicted of unrighteousness, is not only excommunicated; he is deprived of his kingdom for good and all. Rudolf, who bore all the marks of the righteous ruler, is declared to be the true king, and absolution from their sins is granted to him and to his adherents. Again the sentence is made more impressive by being framed in the form of an address, this time to both St. Peter and St. Paul, who can bear witness to the truth of his assertions, and to whom he appeals to vindicate upon Henry the justice of the papal sentence. Finally, a year later, he sent to bishop Herman of Metz a famous letter in which he again justified his power to excommunicate and depose the king, and asserted with emphasis the superiority of the ecclesiastical over the temporal department.

His action was fully in accordance with the principles enunciated in the *Dictatus Papae* of 1075, but he had now lost his sense of the practical. He had chosen both his time and his ground ill. Henry's party was gaining the upper hand in Germany, and the papal sentence, so far from causing consternation in its ranks as in 1076, tended to stiffen it in defiance to the Pope. For Gregory was no longer acting in righteous retaliation for an outrage upon himself; he was interfering in the government of Germany and outraging the royal dignity. Henry acted as rapidly, but more effectively than in 1076. At Easter the German nobles and bishops met with the king in council at Bamberg in eastern Franconia, at Whitsun at Mayence in the west, and on June 25 in the south at Brixen, whither came the North Italian bishops in large numbers. On each occasion they decreed the deposition of Gregory VII, and their sentence, too, was intended to be final. For at Brixen they proceeded to elect a successor, Henry IV, perhaps by virtue of the title of *patricius* conferred on him in 1061, nominating archbishop Guibert of Ravenna, who was already under the ban for his defiance of papal authority.

Once more the great issue was joined and the validity of the rival sentences was to be put to the test. Gregory entered upon the contest with the confidence of one who felt that his cause was righteous; he even prophesied that the proof of this would be given by the death or the deposition of Henry within a few months. But it happened quite

Henry sets up an anti-Pope

Death of the anti-king Rudolf

otherwise, for in October Rudolf, whom he had declared the rightful king, was mortally wounded at the battle of Hohen-Mölsen ; to many this seemed the judgment of God upon him. The Pope, however, was not discouraged ; he scornfully rejected the suggestion that he should now come to terms with Henry, and at the Lenten synod of 1081 renewed the excommunication. He was still determined that the final say in the government of Germany must rest with him, and he wrote that the successor to Rudolf must be a person approved by himself and must take an oath of obedience to the Pope. But his orders fell on deaf ears, since the question of the German kingship was virtually settled. For some months Henry was without a rival, owing to the divisions and jealousies among his enemies ; and when in 1081 they made their choice, it was a petty Lothringian count, Herman of Salm, who was elected king.[1] He made an attempt to assert himself in Suabia in 1082, after which he retired into insignificance again, and some years later met his death while besieging a castle in his native Lorraine. Henry could safely disregard this puny rival and proceed with his purpose of carrying his sentence into effect.

The Pope comes to terms with the Normans

Gregory, meanwhile, had not neglected measures of self-defence. At the very beginning, even before the election of the anti-Pope at Brixen had revealed the full extent of the danger that threatened him, he had taken stock of the situation in Italy and made his preparations. He could rely on the constant support of Countess Matilda of Tuscany to counteract the hostility of Lombardy. He had every reason, too, to believe in the fidelity of the Romans.[2] But in South Italy the Normans were continually encroaching, and at the Lenten synod of 1080 he had once again issued his ban against them. They could be reconciled with the Papacy and used as its allies if they were paid the price—the territory they had unjustly seized. Against his principles he decided to do this, for everything was now subordinate to the contest

---

[1] Perhaps they hoped to gain support in Lorraine, where a brother of Herman was count of Luxemburg and an uncle count-palatine of the Rhine. But neither of these showed the least favour to their relative.

[2] His popularity at Rome had been strikingly evinced at Christmas 1075, when a noble, Cencius, had seized on the person of the Pope ; Gregory had been immediately rescued by the populace, and Cencius barely escaped with his life.

with Henry. So in June 1080 he went south to Ceprano and there made peace with Robert Guiscard ; he released him from the ban and enfeoffed him not only with his former duchy, but also with the territory the seizure of which had been the cause of his excommunication. Guiscard was willing enough, for he wanted peace in order to turn his arms against the Eastern Empire and invade Greece. Regardless of papal appeals he started in 1081 and won a brilliant success ; he was even on the point of marching on Constantinople when he was recalled by revolt in South Italy. Not until 1084 did Gregory get any assistance from the Normans, for whose alliance he had sacrificed so much.

He needed their help in the intervening years, for his allies in Germany were now helpless, and Henry was able, for the first time in his reign, to lead a military expedition into Italy. He came to execute the sentence of Brixen and to establish his nominee on the papal throne, and he preluded his coming by letters to the Romans, expecting to renew with them the alliance of 1061 against an independent Papacy. In this he was disappointed, for when he appeared before the city in 1081 he found no response from within, and the small forces at his disposal were inadequate to attempt a direct assault. Nor was he any more successful in the following year. But the strain of successive sieges began to have their effect. In 1083 he made a more prolonged effort, and at last in June he succeeded in capturing St. Peter's and the Leonine City. Then the fortitude of the Romans gave way. They tried to persuade Gregory to come to terms, and his firm refusal gave them an excuse for deserting him. In March 1084 Henry was admitted into the city proper on the other side of the Tiber. Gregory with a small following (for even some of the cardinals had gone into the other camp) remained entrenched in the Castle of Sant' Angelo. The course of events now followed, designedly no doubt, the precedent of 1046. A synod declared Gregory VII deposed, and Henry IV's nominee, Guibert, was enthroned in St. Peter's, taking significantly the name of Clement III in memory of the Clement II whom Henry III had nominated to succeed the deposed Gregory VI. By him Henry and his wife Bertha were crowned Emperor and Empress ; the victory of the temporal power seemed now to have been achieved, and

The sieges and capture of Rome by Henry

Imperial coronation

Henry IV to have arrived at the summit his father had attained.

The
Normans
rescue the
Pope

And then at last Robert Guiscard moved to the help of his overlord; and he came in such strength that Henry found it prudent to abandon Rome. So Gregory was rescued. But he had conjured up a force which he was powerless to control. The savagery of the Normans wreaked a terrible revenge for the infidelity of the Romans to the Pope; by fire and sword they created a desolation which was visible for many years to come, unique in the manifold experiences of the Eternal City. The Pope could not be left behind at the mercy of the embittered populace; he had to go south with his rescuer, and to pass the last year of his life in exile in the very territory which had been the price of this unfortunate alliance. In the agony of defeat his spirit failed him at last, and it seemed to him that the day of anti-Christ was at hand. In the last utterance attributed to him there is the familiar insistence on *justitia* and the conviction that he had himself pursued it. " I have loved righteousness and hated iniquity " ; so far he is quoting from the Psalms, but

His death
in exile

his conclusion is quite different—" therefore I die in exile." In this mood of despair, in the belief that the rule of unrighteousness had begun upon earth, the great Pope passed away at Salerno on May 25, 1085.

Pope
Victor III
(1086-7)

For three years this atmosphere of defeat and despair persisted. The anti-Pope, who had returned to Rome on the withdrawal of the Normans, was in almost undisputed possession of the city and was recognised in most of Germany and North Italy. The papal Curia in South Italy, deprived of its head, seemed incapable of initiative. For a year the place of Gregory VII was left unfilled, and when in 1086 Desiderius was elected as Pope Victor III, the choice seems to have been determined solely by Norman predilections. Desiderius was abbot of Monte Cassino, the original home of Benedictinism, situated half-way between Rome and Naples. Exposed as he was to Norman attack, he had always advocated peace and acted as mediator between Pope and Normans. The more ardent disciples of Gregory VII, especially archbishop Hugh of Lyons, distrusted his moderation, and a division in the party was threatened. To the Normans he was naturally acceptable, but their support had become much less effective. For Robert Guiscard died two months after Gregory VII, and his son Roger, who succeeded him as duke of Apulia, was unable to control his unruly vassals including his brother Bohemond, while Guiscard's brother Roger was engrossed in the conquest of Sicily. With Norman aid the new Pope was indeed able to obtain consecration in St. Peter's, but he could not maintain himself in Rome. He retired to Monte Cassino, where he died in September 1087, and there was another vacancy which lasted for six months.

Then, in March 1088, Otto, cardinal-bishop of Ostia, was elected as Pope Urban II. A Frenchman of high birth, educated at the cathedral school at Rheims, afterwards a monk and eventually prior at Cluny, he was released by his abbot to enter the service of Pope Gregory VII, by whom he was created cardinal ; at the time of Gregory's death he was on an important mission organising support for the Papacy in Germany. Urban II was learned, especially in the Canon law, and his legal training, while it gave him confidence in the rectitude of his own policy, enabled him also to do valuable work in the construction of the ecclesiastical organisation. Ardent in his adherence to the principles of Gregory VII, he was acceptable to those reformers whom Victor III's election had alienated. Such a man, and he was personally attractive besides, was well qualified to lead the papal party out of the slough of despond in which for three years it had laboured, and to win back the ground that had been lost.

Pope Urban II (1088–99)

Luck was on his side, for in North Italy the tide began to turn at the very beginning of his Papacy. First of all, he received in 1088 the noteworthy adhesion of the archbishop of Milan, Tedald's successor, who had been invested by Henry IV and had been imperial in his allegiance hitherto. The communal movement brought about this change, and the same thing was beginning to happen elsewhere in Italy. The bishops, yielding perforce to the communes the authority in government which they themselves had exercised as imperial representatives, had less reason and less power to resist papal authority over them. This was a striking change in the Lombardy which had been hitherto so strongly imperial. Secondly, duke Welf of Bavaria, who had Italian as well as German interests owing to the domains he had inherited from

Papal advance in North Italy

his father, formed a close alliance with countess Matilda of Tuscany. This was cemented by the marriage in 1089 of Matilda with Welf, the young son of the duke. The situation in North Italy was indeed so serious for Henry IV that he found it necessary to come himself to deal with it.

Henry makes peace with the Saxons

Until this moment everything had seemed to be going well for Henry. The Saxons themselves had grown war-weary, and even the efforts of cardinal Otto, who in 1085 held a synod at Quedlinburg and excommunicated Henry and his supporters afresh, could not prevent them from coming to terms with the king. Henry at first mistook the situation, and thought he could act again as master in Saxony; and he tried to replace the bishops who would not recognise his anti-Pope by supporters of his own. So there was a renewal of civil war, and Saxon troops under the banner of the archbishop of Magdeburg, managing to effect a junction with the troops of Welf, inflicted a severe defeat on the king at Pleichfeld and captured the neighbouring town of Würz-burg. The defeat taught Henry a lesson, and when over-tures were renewed in 1088 he was content to accept the conditions demanded by the Saxons, and to leave to them the local independence guaranteed by his predecessors. Only margrave Egbert of Meissen remained recalcitrant, but after two years of revolt he fell a victim to assassination, and all opposition in Saxony was at an end. Even the martial archbishop of Magdeburg and his suffragans recognised Henry as king, but they would not recognise Clement III as Pope. The anti-Pope, whose election seemed a sign of Henry's strength, was beginning to prove a source of weakness. As king, however, Henry had no rival, and in 1087 he had obtained the election and coronation of his eldest son, Conrad, so that his dynasty seemed assured. The same year his wife Bertha died, and this made possible his marriage in 1089 with the Russian princess Praxedis, an event which preluded a new series of troubles for the unfortunate king.

Defeat of Henry in Italy

The campaign in Italy opened auspiciously for him with the capture of Mantua, followed, in 1091, by a signal victory over the troops of Countess Matilda at Tricontai. But the intrigues of his enemies proved effective when their arms had failed. His son Conrad and his wife Praxedis were seduced into joining Welf and Matilda, and they came into Italy, where they created a strong prejudice against the king, spreading gross slanders about him as a pretext for their own infidelity. A league of Lombard cities was formed, and Conrad was crowned with the iron crown of Lombardy. Henry, overwhelmed by the treachery of his wife and son, could make no headway against the new coalition. He remained until 1097 in isolation at Verona, unable, since Welf held the neighbouring passes, even to escape into Germany.

Meanwhile, Urban II had emancipated himself from Norman tutelage and had brought the Curia back to Rome. Content at first to live there in humble circumstances, as he was unwilling to use force to gain his objective, he had at least the satisfaction of seeing his rival expelled from the city in 1089. But it took him six years of constant effort before he could weaken the resistance of the Romans, who had still before their eyes the devastation wrought by his Norman allies. In 1094 the castle of Sant' Angelo, formerly the refuge of Gregory VII, remained as the last stronghold of the supporters of the anti-Pope. The time was ripe for a reassertion of papal authority elsewhere, and, like Leo IX, Urban decided to effect this by a personal progress ; though Germany was inaccessible, he could anticipate a warm welcome in northern Italy and in France. *The Papacy restored to Rome*

In March 1095 he arrived at Piacenza, where he presided over a largely-attended synod ; the most important of its decrees laid down the conditions under which schismatics (i.e. those who had adhered to the anti-Pope) could be restored to communion with the Church. The need for this betokened the change that had come about. Urban was now in close touch with the coalition which had been so successful against Henry IV. At Piacenza, Praxedis told her tale, and was readily believed. At Cremona, where Urban made his next halt, he met Conrad, who actually did fealty to him. The marriage of the " king of Italy " with a daughter of count Roger of Sicily united the vassals of the Pope in North and South Italy. The result was not up to his expectations, for the alliance of Welf and Matilda soon broke up, and the two instruments that they had used to bring discredit upon Henry were consequently discarded ; Praxedis disappears from history, and though Conrad lived on for another *Urban II's progress through North Italy and France* six years, we hear no more of him as king of Italy. To Urban perhaps it made little difference, as he was concerned with the ecclesiastical rather than with the temporal sovereignty of the Papacy; and from this point of view the situation in North Italy was more satisfactory than it had ever been.

It was equally so in France, to which Urban passed in July and in which he spent over a year, travelling from place to place, dealing with ecclesiastical matters of all kinds great and small, and received with the deference and the enthusiasm due to the undisputed head of the Church. The greatest moment of all was the Council of Clermont in November 1095. Here a number of important ecclesiastical canons were promulgated, the excommunication pronounced by the papal legate on the king of France for his adulterous marriage with the wife of the count of Anjou was confirmed, and finally the First Crusade was initiated. During the rest of his sojourn in France he continued to hold synods and to preach the Crusade, and he met with an enthusiastic welcome on his return to Italy and to Rome in the autumn of 1096. There was no doubt now that the Papacy had fully recovered its position, when Urban could ignore the excommunicated Emperor, the excommunicated king of France, and the unfriendly king of England who had only just grudgingly recognised him as Pope, and call on Western Christendom to rally under his banner for the rescue of the Holy Places from Islam. His serene self-confidence was justified and it was amply rewarded; for, as the initiator and the director of the great crusading movement, he gave the papal headship of the Church a fuller meaning and a wider basis of universal consent.

Urban's government of the Church

In the government of the Church he abated none of the claims advanced by Gregory VII, whose decrees he repeated and whose programme he faithfully continued. The centralisation of Church government was materially advanced; the system of giving certain archbishops the rank of primate was extended, while at the same time the local independence of archbishops was limited by the direct contact of the Papacy with their suffragans, and the authority of bishops by the exemptions from episcopal control granted to numerous monasteries, which were made like Cluny directly dependent upon the Pope. Uniformity was furthered by decrees enjoining local churches to adhere to Roman customs and ritual. Lay interference was, as before, the principal hindrance to the papal idea of ecclesiastical independence, and the decrees against lay investiture were repeated and amplified by Urban. The contest with the Emperor continued, and outlasted his reign, though it was more a matter of formal schism than of direct conflict. In one respect Urban differed from his great predecessor. He did not renew Gregory's widespread claims to papal overlordship over secular rulers ; for instance, he did not expect from England any more than the payment of Peter's Pence. There was one exception : when king Peter of Aragon in 1095 asked for papal protection in return for the payment of tribute and the recognition of papal overlordship, Urban naturally did not refuse the request. The Normans in South Italy and Sicily continued to admit that they held their territory as vassals of the Pope, but on the whole they continued to get more than they gave, and Urban was forced to allow to them considerable authority in matters ecclesiastical.

His last three years were spent mainly in Rome ; there His last was still some unrest there, but the castle of Sant' Angelo years fell into his hands in 1098, so that the last supporters of the anti-Pope were driven out. He received with great honour archbishop Anselm of Canterbury, in exile from England, and employed him as the champion of Western doctrine against the Greeks at Bari in 1098. Anselm, too, was present when Urban, shortly before his death in 1099, held his last synod at Rome, and, by repeating the chief decrees that he had promulgated at Clermont and elsewhere, provided an epitome of the ecclesiastical programme of his Papacy.

By this time Henry IV was back in Germany, to which Henry IV peace had at last been restored after twenty years of civil in Germany war. Naturally his authority had been impaired by his long absence in Italy. In place of the old alliance of dukes Welf, Rudolf, and Berthold there was now an alliance of Welf with Berthold's son, Berthold of Zähringen, who had succeeded to his father's estates and also to those of Rudolf,[1] his father-in-law. He aspired also to Rudolf's duchy of Suabia, and was a formidable competitor to duke Frederick,

[1] In 1091, when Rudolf's son Berthold died.

the king's son-in-law.   Berthold and Welf allied themselves
with the papal party now reviving in South Germany under
the energetic leadership of bishop Gebhard of Constance,
Berthold's brother.

End of the civil war

But this alliance of south Germans with the Papacy was
shattered owing to the rift in Italy between Welf and countess
Matilda.   Welf had married his son to Matilda with the
object of acquiring a position in Italy like that held by the
Godfrey of Lorraine who had married Matilda's mother,
Beatrice.   He found he had been deluded, since Matilda's
object was solely to gain support for the Papacy, to which
she had already in Gregory VII's time surrendered her
domains, receiving them back as a fief from the Papacy.
Accordingly Welf broke off his alliance with Matilda and the
Papacy, opened the passes to Henry, who returned to Germany in 1097, and together with Berthold made his peace
with the king.   He formally received back his duchy, to
which no rival duke had been appointed ;   soon afterwards
he departed on crusade to the Holy Land, where he died in
1101, and Welf V, the husband of countess Matilda, succeeded him as duke.   Berthold was compensated for the
resignation of his claims to Suabia by the title of duke (of
Zähringen) and the grant, as a fief from the Empire, of the
town of Zurich.   So there was an end to lay opposition to
Henry in Germany, and the succession was secured by the
promise of the nobles in 1099 to recognise his second son,
Henry, as the heir to the throne.   Yet the restoration of
peace did not imply the real recovery of royal authority,
but rather a return to the conditions at the beginning of
Henry's reign ;   he was obliged, in fact, to allow local autonomy within the southern duchies as well as in Saxony.
His reign, thanks to the long schism with the Papacy, had
from the monarchical point of view been a failure.

Pope Paschal II

And the schism still remained, nor could any concessions
avail to bring about peace with the Papacy.   On Urban II's
death in 1099, Rainer, cardinal priest of San Clemente, was
elected and took the name of Paschal II.   The new Pope,
Tuscan by birth, was like his three immediate predecessors
a monk,[1] who had been made abbot of San Lorenzo fuore
le mura by Gregory VII and later cardinal.   Pious and

[1] Of some South Italian monastery, not, as used to be thought, of Cluny.

unworldly, he was most unwilling to occupy the high position
for which he was indeed unfitted by temperament. He was
an excellent subordinate, who could be relied on to execute
orders implicitly, but he had not the practical experience or
the personality to take the lead. So he was rigid in his
obedience to the decrees of Gregory VII and Urban II and
in enforcing them on his subordinates such as Anselm, but
he had not the strength of character to maintain his position
when he met a determined opponent face to face. In the
early years of his Papacy it was his rigidity rather than his
weakness that was evident. He had to face Henry IV, who
was worn out by conflict and domestic calamity and willing
to make any concession to obtain peace. When the anti-
Pope Clement III died in 1100, the chief obstacle seemed
to have been removed. But Paschal was adamant. He
renewed the sentence of excommunication and deposition,
would not hear of reconciliation, and thus achieved the one
victory of his reign, a victory over a beaten man.

Henry was in an unhappy position, separated from com- Revolt of
munion with the Church, having lost his Italian kingdom, Henry V
and depending in Germany on the good-will of the princes. father
His son, the young Henry, soon took cognisance of the
increasing weakness of the monarchical authority to which
he was to succeed. He determined to prevent any further
decline by getting the power into his own hands as soon as
possible, and the opportunity came to him at the end of
1104. He found allies easily among the lesser nobles, who
had soon tired of the inaction of peace, and he made himself
the champion of the papal party against his excommunicated
father. He was quite devoid of scruples : he broke without
compunction the oath that he had taken in 1099 that he
would never act with independent authority during his
father's lifetime ; he seduced from their allegiance the leading supporters of his father, such as the duke of Bohemia
and the margrave of Austria ; and in 1105, when his hopes
were foiled by the resistance of the Rhine towns, he persuaded
his father to an interview and treacherously held him as a
prisoner. The new duke of Bavaria remained neutral, and
Frederick of Suabia, whose loyalty to his father-in-law
might have turned the scale, had died earlier in the year.
Henry IV managed to escape in 1106, and his son was twice

Death of
Henry IV
(1106)

severely defeated by the nobles of Lorraine and the citizens of the Rhine towns. But on August 7 the reign of the unhappy Henry IV at last came to an end. He died at Liége, and the citizens there, and in other towns through which the body was taken to its last resting-place in the royal town of Spires, publicly manifested their loyalty and their grief, disregarding the papal excommunication ; he had been their friend, and by their enemies, the feudal nobles, he had been dragged down. But the Church had the last say, and for five years the body of the excommunicated king lay in an unconsecrated chapel, denied Christian burial.

End of the
schism
between
Empire and
Papacy

The death of Henry, after his tragic reign of fifty years, commencing with the misgovernment during his minority, which was responsible for most of his subsequent troubles, and closing with the vile treachery of his son, brought to an end the first conflict of Empire and Papacy. For Henry V, born during the schism, had been formally received into communion with the Church in 1105, and so the long schism was at last healed. In one sense the conflict was indecisive, for both sides had tacitly given up the claim to supremacy over the other. But in fact the whole situation had altered materially. The king, engaged in two conflicts, had been beaten in both. He had failed signally to re-establish royal control over the Papacy, and he had failed to overcome local autonomy in Germany, being dependent on the consent of the nobles ; from this dependence the monarchy was never wholly to emerge, and it was a principal cause of its humiliation in the fourteenth century. The Papacy, on the other hand, was stronger at the end than at the beginning. It had not merely vindicated its independence ; its effective headship of the Church, for which Gregory VII was largely responsible, was still disputed in 1076 ; in 1106 it was established on a firm basis, to remain unchallenged until the end of the Middle Ages.

SUGGESTIONS FOR READING ON CHAPTERS VII, VIII, IX
(AND XII)

In general :
   Cambridge Medieval History, Vol. V, chapters 1, 2, 3.
   Fliche, A. : *Études sur la polémique religieuse à l'époque de Grégoire VII.*
      Les Prégrégoriens. Paris, 1916.
   Hampe, K. : *Deutsche Kaisergeschichte* (as in Chapter III).

Scharnagl, A. : *Der Begriff der Investitur in den Quellen und der Litteratur des Investiturstreites.* Stuttgart, 1908.
Whitney, J. P. : *Hildebrandine Essays.* Cambridge, 1932.
Fliche, A. : *La querelle des Investitures.* Paris, 1946.
Ullmann, W. : *The Growth of Papal Government in the Middle Ages.* London, 1955.

Many of the letters of Gregory VII are translated in :
Emerton, E. : *The Correspondence of Pope Gregory VII.* New York, 1932.
Cf. also, relevant documents in Henderson and Laffan (see Bibliographical Note).

Political Theory :
Cambridge Medieval History, Vol. VI, chapter 18.
Bryce, J. : *The Holy Roman Empire.* New ed. London, 1906.
Folz, R. : *L'idée d'Empire en Occident du Ve au XIVe siècle.* Paris, 1953.
Carlyle, A. J. : *A History of Medieval Political Theory in the West,* Vol. IV.
Gierke, O. : *Political Theories of the Middle Age* (Eng. trans.). Cambridge, 1900.
McIlwain, C. H. : *The Growth of Political Thought in the West.* New York, 1932.
Arquillière, H. X. : *L'augustinisme politique.* Paris, 1934.
Tellenbach, G. : *Church, State and Christian Society at the Time of the Investiture Contest* (Eng. trans.). Oxford, 1940.

For the Normans in South Italy and Sicily, see Chapter XIII, below.

CRITICAL TITLE PALACE, BORTON 204

CHAPTER X

FRANCE IN THE SECOND HALF OF THE ELEVENTH CENTURY

Ill effects of Henry I's enmity with Normandy

THE monarchy in France had been temporarily re-invigorated by the transference of kingship from the Carolingians to the Capetians, but it had soon begun to show signs of renewed weakness. Lacking sufficient domain to be able to enforce obedience, the kings had had to depend on the consent of their vassals and on the support of some of them; it was the loyal assistance of the dukes of Normandy that had made them seem stronger than they really were. When Henry I renounced the alliance with Normandy, and united with the turbulent and entirely self-seeking counts of Anjou to attack that duchy, he may have hoped to improve his own position by playing off these two powerful vassals against one another; but in fact he lost one of the chief buttresses of his throne and gained nothing to replace it. In company with Geoffrey Martel of Anjou he twice invaded the duchy of Normandy, in 1054 and 1058, and on both occasions was decisively defeated. The permanent hostility of Normandy was as damaging to the French king as its former friendship had been beneficial. And then, in 1066, when the duke of Normandy became king of England, he was a still more dangerous enemy. From this time the destinies of England and France, usually at enmity with each other, become inextricably linked.

Philip I (1060–1108)

The alienation of Normandy was one cause for the weakness of the French monarchy in the second half of the eleventh century. Another lay in the personality of the ruler. For 48 years, from 1060 to 1108, Philip I, the son of Henry I, was king of France, so that his reign coincides almost exactly with that of Henry IV of Germany. Otherwise there is little except of superficial resemblance between them. Compared with the tragic drama, the swift reversals of fortune, the great crises of Henry IV's reign, Philip's is almost barren of important events, owing to the incapacity of the king to achieve them.   He had ability, as he showed at the beginning, but very little staying power ; he was self-indulgent, greedy and sensual, and the corpulence which soon began to impede his bodily activity increased the natural indolence of his character.   For most of his reign he was content to let things drift, and so the French kingdom remained in a backwater, and in the main current of events it played an inconspicuous and an ignoble part.

He has this in common with his great neighbour that the more important incidents in his reign were concerned with his relations with the Papacy.   The rise of the Papacy and its increasing control over the episcopate provide a third reason for the weakness of royal authority.   Already in Henry I's reign, Pope Leo IX had held a council in France, and in spite of the king's attempts to checkmate him had made an example of those bishops who were disobedient to the papal decrees.   In subsequent years papal legates were frequently engaged in the task of imposing the principles of reform upon the French Church.   Finally came the appointment of permanent legates by Gregory VII, and, as has already been described, the definite establishment of papal authority.   The effect of this was considerable.   The royal authority, where alone it could be exercised outside the domain, was seriously impaired.   For while the dismemberment of the territories that had once been in the possession of Hugh Capet and his family (including the duchy of Burgundy as well as the duchy of Neustria) had reduced to meagre proportions the extent of the royal domains, the king had retained his authority over the bishops whose sees lay within the extensive territories once subject to him. The Church in most of the south of France, and in the north also in Brittany and Normandy, was not under his control, but his authority extended over four archbishops—Rheims, Sens, Tours, and Bourges—and some twenty bishops.   From them as from the domain he could obtain men for his army and money for his treasury ; they supplied him also with officials for his government.   It was, therefore, a serious matter for him when papal authority was made effective. He had to endure one humiliation after another from Pope

The authority of the Papacy in France

8

and legates. The campaign against simony robbed him of
the financial advantages which he derived from appointments,
since he had made a practice of receiving payments from his
nominees. In 1075 he was himself threatened with excommunication by Gregory VII, and the decree against lay
investiture, which was enforced by the legates in France,
deprived him of another of his rights. In 1079 the primacy
given to the archbishop of Lyons over the provinces of Rouen,
Tours, and Sens placed two of the four archbishops whom
the king controlled under the authority of one whose cathedral
city lay outside the borders of the kingdom. But perhaps
the gravest blow to which he had to submit was the deposition
in 1080 of the leading archbishop in France, on whose support
he could always rely, Manasse of Rheims.

**The early
years of
Philip I**

The operation of these various causes led to a progressive
decline in the royal power, already enfeebled by the ill-success
of his predecessors, until it reached its lowest depths in the
last years of the century. But the early years of the reign
were not devoid of promise. Philip was only eight years old
when his father died in 1060, but he had been consecrated
king in the previous year, so that there was no difficulty
about the succession. The government, however, had to be
provided for during his minority. The queen-mother Anne
was not, like Agnes in Germany, left as guardian of her son ;
indeed she soon lost all influence at court by contracting a
second marriage with Raoul of Crépy, count of Valois.
Henry before his death had chosen a much more capable
person to be regent, his brother-in-law Baldwin V, count of
Flanders. The counts of Flanders had displayed a sagacity,
unusual at the time, in the management of their territories,
and Baldwin seems to have employed his experience to the
king's advantage. He took him with him on frequent tours
through the royal domain ; nor did he neglect his own
interests, for he took the king also on a tour through Flanders,
and used his presence to obtain royal sanction for the acts
of lordship which he performed. There was, however, one
event during his regency in which his personal inclinations
overrode the interests of the kingdom. His daughter Matilda
was the wife of duke William of Normandy, and so he looked
on with a benevolent eye while William achieved his conquest
of England in 1066. Philip was always aware of the danger

from Normandy, and had he been his own master, he would assuredly have done what he could to prevent William from obtaining this great acquisition of strength.

Philip's coming-of-age in 1067 coincided with the death of Baldwin, so that he was left entirely to his own devices. The importance of preserving the royal possessions intact seems to have been impressed upon him by his guardian, for he avoided the mistake of his predecessors and was careful not to parcel them out any further. Indeed, he exerted himself at first to add to them. In 1068 he took the opportunity of civil war in Anjou to obtain the county of Gâtinais as the price of his neutrality; similarly in 1071 he profited by the disputed succession in Flanders to regain Corbie, which his aunt Adela had received as her dowry when she married count Baldwin; and when his stepfather Raoul of Crépy died in 1074, he attacked the heir, Simon, and eventually forced him to surrender the county of Vexin. His only other acquisition was towards the end of his reign, in 1101, when he purchased Bourges from its viscount who needed the money to go on crusade. It is noticeable that he could only take direct action, when circumstances were peculiarly favourable. He could command no army of any size, being dependent entirely on the vassals within his domains and the ecclesiastical territories subject to his control. The greater vassals had dissociated themselves from the interests of the kingdom; they had established their own local independence, so that, apart again from certain ecclesiastical territories, the king's government was confined to the royal domain. *The royal domain*

Hence a great change gradually came about as the reign proceeded. Very rarely was there anything like a general assembly of notables, such as had met for the election and anointing of the young king in 1059. There were assemblies, fairly numerously attended, to which the king summoned the nobles of the immediate vicinity; but, as the king's usual places of residence were Paris, Orleans, or Senlis, and as the business generally concerned the royal domain only, it was mostly vassals on the domain that were summoned. In the second half of the reign he rarely summoned even these. It was the officials who resided at court and accompanied him wherever he went, the permanent element in the *Curia*, known as *palatini* or *curiales*, who by this time formed the *The great feudatories take no part in royal government* council of the king and assisted him in justice. That this happened was largely due to the weakness and the limitations of royal authority. At the same time, it had its advantages. The king was released from dependence on his greater vassals, and an official class was created which was wholly dependent on the king. There was the nucleus of administrative machinery ready for the time when the monarchy should re-establish itself in France. It proved, at any rate, an asset in the future.

The household officials

At the time there was a still further development, which proved to be anything but satisfactory. The household officials, familiar in Merovingian and Carolingian times, had come into notice again. There were four great officers—the chamberlain or treasurer, the seneschal (who was usually at the head of the king's troops), the butler, and the constable. A fifth, the chancellor, who drafted the acts of State, the royal charters, was at present inferior in dignity, since the charters dealt with matters relatively so unimportant. The four great officers played the leading part among the *palatini*, and came to have a controlling influence upon affairs, to be, as it were, royal ministers of State. So these positions were coveted by the greater vassals of the domain, and soon it came about that certain families, especially the Garlandes and Rocheforts, had almost a monopoly of office. Philip, partly through weakness, partly through indolence, allowed this natural feudal tendency to develop; the great offices in this way were no longer completely at his disposal. As far as justice was concerned, the royal writ did not extend usually beyond the domain, where alone he could control the local government. His chief officials here were provosts, who represented him in justice and were responsible for collecting the royal dues. They were to increase in importance later, when the domain increased in extent; but at present, since the central government was concerned mainly with the domain alone, the local officials held a very subordinate position.

The brigand-nobles of the domain

Now though Philip was careful not to alienate the domain by grants of land and managed even to make some additions, and though it was geographically something of a compact whole, it was lacking in political cohesion. A number of petty nobles had got seignorial rights and had secured themselves by building strong castles. Greedy and ferocious, they lived like robbers and brigands; they waylaid merchants and pilgrims on the highways,[1] and pillaged the lands of bishoprics and abbeys in their vicinity. Such were, to the north of Paris, the counts of Dammartin and Beaumont and the lords of Montmorency, who pillaged the estates of the abbey of St. Denis; to the north-east, the lords of Roucy, who similarly troubled the archbishop of Rheims; to the south and south-west, the lords of Rochefort, who interrupted communications between Paris and Chartres, and the lords of Montlhéry and Le Puiset who came similarly between Paris and Orleans. Until they could be reduced to obedience and their castles destroyed, there was no hope for peace and order in the royal domain. Philip was powerless against them, and his one serious effort came to an ignominious end. In 1079 there was a regular rising south of Paris headed by Hugh of Le Puiset. The king managed to get considerable help from the duchy of Burgundy, including the duke, the count of Nevers, and the bishop of Auxerre, and he laid siege to the castle of Puiset. But a sudden sortie threw the king's troops into such panic that they fled in confusion to Orleans; the count of Nevers, the bishop of Auxerre, and several knights were taken prisoners. The victor, naturally emboldened by his easy success, renewed his former practices and continued for years his depredations on the lands of the bishop of Orleans. Philip made no further attempt himself to reduce the robber-barons to order. It was to be left to Louis VI, when he took over the direction of the government, seriously to undertake this task.

Philip might truly have described himself as " rex Franciae," for the term *Francia* was used to describe, not the whole kingdom, but a small part of it—an ill-defined area, roughly commensurate with the royal domain. He chose, however, to maintain the old style, " rex Francorum," and he was justified in that over the area covered by the kingdom he was recognised as king even though no services were rendered to him. The great vassals had no interest in over-

South France

---

[1] Philip in his earlier and more energetic days was not above imitating them in order to make a little money. Gregory VII threatened him with excommunication in 1075 on the ground that he was waylaying and plundering Italian and other merchants.

throwing him ; they were concerned solely with maintaining their own independent principalities completely under their own control. The situation in the south and south-west remained unaltered. The dukes of Aquitaine continued their work of centralisation. William VIII (1058–86) acquired Gascony and also took the opportunity of civil war in Anjou to recover possession of Saintonge ; at the end of the century his son William IX, a cultured libertine, came into prominence by his spoliation of ecclesiastical property, which brought him into conflict with the Pope until he went on crusade in 1100. The counts of Toulouse retained possession of Languedoc, but their power had dwindled and they were only masters in name. In the eastern portion of the kingdom, the political insignificance of the dukes of Burgundy continued, and the county of Champagne, still united with Blois until count Theobald's death in 1089,[1] had a similarly obscure and uneventful history.

Normandy In the north and north-west, the situation was entirely different. Great changes took place in the relative positions of the leading powers ; in particular, the duke of Normandy by his conquest of England held a dominating position, and was far more powerful than his suzerain. In his duchy alone William was stronger than Philip was in the royal domain. His barons were obliged to render their fixed quota of military service, and they were not allowed to build castles without the duke's permission. Over the archbishop of Rouen and his six suffragans the ducal control was absolute ; they were his nominees (the archbishop of Rouen had often been a member of the ducal family), and they were supervised by the *vicomtes*, who represented ducal authority in the local government. In spite of this, his perfectly sincere zeal for Church reform brought him into high repute at the papal court, which at the same time was inflicting constant humiliations upon Philip. His marriage with Matilda, daughter of Baldwin V of Flanders, assured him of the friendly attitude of his powerful eastern neighbour during his conquest of England. Anjou, his hereditary enemy, was weakened by internal discord, and he took advantage of it to seize the

---

[1] Champagne went to his eldest son, Odo, who was succeeded a few years later by the second son, Hugh ; Blois went to the third son, Stephen, who married William the Conqueror's daughter, Adela.

county of Maine in 1063.   Here he somewhat overreached himself, for his rule in Maine was unpopular and gave rise to frequent revolts.   In Brittany, too, where the lack of unity in the duchy tempted him to establish his suzerainty, he met with constant opposition, and got more trouble than advantage from his interference.

The count of Anjou, Geoffrey Martel, had died in the same **Anjou** year as Henry I of France, 1060, and until 1068 there was continual civil war between his two nephews, Geoffrey the Bearded, whom he had designated as his heir, and Fulk Rechin.   Fulk was eventually victorious, but the county had been desolated by the long war, and for the rest of his life, which lasted until 1109, he had to deal with the revolts of his barons, a sequel of the discord to which his struggle with his brother had given rise.   His neighbours took the opportunity to enrich themselves at his expense, Philip acquiring the Gâtinais, William VIII of Aquitaine recovering Saintonge, and William of Normandy seizing Maine.   The last was far the most serious loss, and Fulk gave considerable trouble to William by his constant attempts to recover it.   On this account his hostility to Normandy could be relied upon to keep him on friendly terms with the French king.

Next to Normandy, Flanders was the most highly central- **Flanders** ised State in the north of France.   Count Baldwin V had extended it eastwards at the expense of Lower Lorraine, joining with Godfrey of Upper Lorraine in his revolt against the Emperor Henry III.   His son Baldwin VI survived him only a short time, and then another son, Robert the Frisian,[1] ejected his nephew Arnulf and seized the power.   Philip I summoned an expedition in the defence of Arnulf, but the royal army was decisively defeated at Cassel in 1071 and Arnulf was slain.   Robert made his peace with the king, and for twenty-two years was undisputed master of Flanders. His rule was marked by the extension of the count's authority ; the numerous castles were placed under castellans appointed by himself, and the local nobles, forbidden to build castles, were kept in subjection ; especial protection was given to the highways, so essential to the merchants, for Robert was careful to cherish, and to profit by, the growing commercial

---

[1] So called, because he had married Gertrude, widow of count Florence I of West Frisia (Holland), and ruled Frisia as her son's guardian.

importance of Flanders. He sought to extend his authority also over the Church and over ecclesiastical property, and though he came in this way into conflict with the Papacy he met with no humiliation such as his suzerain had to endure. Robert II who succeeded him reversed his father's ecclesiastical policy, and imitated Baldwin V in advancing the frontiers of Flanders on the north and east. But whether the policy was internal organisation or acquisition of territory at the expense of Germany, the result as far as Philip was concerned was the same. The count (or marquis, as he often justifiably styled himself) acted almost as an independent sovereign ; he recognised the suzerainty of the king of France, and also for some of his territories of the king of Germany, but felt himself under no obligation to either. Robert the Frisian on one occasion, in conjunction with his son-in-law king Canute of Denmark, formed a scheme for the invasion of England ; but he did no more than threaten, and he was scheming in his own interests, not in those of the king of France.

France and England

So against Normandy Philip I was left to do what he could by himself ; it was something, at any rate, that he could count on the goodwill of both Anjou and Flanders. But it was no use for him to summon a general expedition, and he did not attempt it. Instead he relied on his wits. Philip had considerable ability, though the weakness of the monarchy and his natural indolence tended to obscure it. He had displayed it in the shrewdness with which he seized opportunities for adding to his domain ; he displayed it again by the skill with which he used every opportunity to harass William I. For instance, in 1076, he came to the aid of the Bretons and assisted them to raise the siege of Dol. In particular, he made every use of the constant factions within the English royal family ; for over a century this was to be the chief way in which the French kings were able to make head against their dangerous neighbour. So in 1077, when William's eldest son Robert revolted against his father, Philip joined forces with Robert and assisted him to get possession of the stronghold of Gerberoy ; William was wounded in an unsuccessful attempt to recover it in 1079. This seems to have led to peace between the two kings, and Robert was also reconciled with his father. But in 1083

Robert was once again at Philip's court, and in 1087 William
retaliated by an invasion of the Vexin which was cut short by
his death. The division of the Anglo-Norman State which
followed—Robert becoming duke of Normandy, and William
II king of England—was all to Philip's advantage. But in
the subsequent discord between the two brothers, which only
ended when Robert, in order to go on crusade, mortgaged
his duchy to William, so that England and Normandy were
once more reunited, Philip played a feeble and an ignominious
part. His cupidity prevailed over the interests of the kingdom, and he allowed himself to be bought off by William II.
He ceased from this time to join in any military enterprise,
and he took no personal part in the successful defence of the
Vexin (in which his son Louis won his spurs) when it was
invaded by William in 1097. Lethargy and self-indulgence
had now gained the upper hand with him, and he did not
attempt to intervene in the struggle between Henry I and
Robert which followed the death of William II in 1099.

In this last period of his reign Philip allowed everything *The results*
to drift. He was entirely obsessed by his passion for Ber- *of Philip's*
trada, wife of count Fulk of Anjou. In 1092 he repudiated *second marriage*
his own wife, Bertha of Holland, and ran off with Bertrada ;
and he even found a complaisant bishop to celebrate their
marriage. This was a political as well as a moral crime ;
he risked the enmity of both Flanders and Anjou, for Robert
the Frisian was the stepfather of queen Bertha. Actually,
Robert died in 1093, and his son made only a brief show of
hostility ; while Fulk, after playing the part of the outraged
husband for a time, was won over by Bertrada and came
quite amicably to the king's court. That the fiery Angevin
should so tamely swallow such an insult is perhaps the most
curious feature of the whole story.

Philip was lucky to escape from political disaster, but he
could not avoid the penalty for his flagrant breach of the
moral code. He was pursued by the righteous indignation of
the Church. The papal legate, archbishop Hugh of Lyons,
pronounced excommunication on him in 1094, and this was
repeated in 1095 by Pope Urban II himself at the council of
Clermont. The majestic progress of Urban through the
French kingdom shows up in glaring contrast the papal
monarchy beside the puny kingship of Philip. Philip, how-

ever, was obstinate in adhering to Bertrada, and the papal excommunication was renewed by Paschal II. It was not until 1104 that Philip was at last induced to separate from Bertrada, and the ban was raised. That he kept his promise not to associate with her again seems very doubtful, but at any rate there was no further conflict with the Pope, whose attention was fully occupied with the question of investiture first in England and then in Germany.

The position
of bishop
Ivo of
Chartres
In the whole of this conflict Philip had been aided, and the Pope hindered, by the subservience of so many French bishops to the king's wishes. There was a notable exception —Ivo, bishop of Chartres, one of the outstanding figures of the time. He was particularly famous as a canonist, and before the appearance of Gratian's *Decretum* the collections of canon law made by Ivo were in general use north of the Alps. He recognised to the full the papal authority, he was a keen advocate of the principles of reform, but he was no stickler for the letter of the law. Like Peter Damian, he took a moderate and a sensible view of the leading questions of the day ; loyalty to the Pope did not with him preclude loyalty to the king. He was opposed to lay investiture, but viewed it in its right perspective, and was impatient with those extremists who wished to brand it as a heresy. He disliked, too, the autocratic methods of the papal legates, and reminded them of a decretal of Pope Leo I, that a papal legate had not the plenitude of power but only a share in the general work of the Church, a decretal which was to be turned to a different use later by St. Bernard and then by the Popes themselves. Ivo, though a moderate man, was no trimmer ; he tried to point the practical and reasonable path between the extremes of prejudice on either side. Fearlessly he combated the immorality of the king, and exposed the false-hoods by which Philip was trying to delude the Pope. At the same time, his moderating influence prevented an outbreak against the royal authority, and was responsible for the peace which was eventually made in 1104.

Philip's
son Louis
begins to
take control
While Philip was thus absorbed in the question of his second marriage, the direction of affairs was gradually passing into the hands of his son. Louis, born in 1081, had received in 1092 an appanage of his own—the county of Vexin with the towns of Mantes and Pontoise. He had proved his

courage in the defence of the Vexin against William II, and at the end of the century was dubbed knight and was elected by the nobles as the successor of Philip. Owing to his father's excommunication, the ceremony of crowning and anointing the new king could not take place, but already in 1100, when he paid a visit to Henry I of England, he appears with the title of king-elect. He was as energetic as his father was lethargic, but for some time he had to face the jealous opposition of Bertrada, now with a young family of her own. In 1103 the king seems at last to have reconciled his wife with her stepson, and at the same time practically to have resigned to him the reins of power. The close of the eleventh century saw the French monarchy at its weakest. A revival began with the opening years of the twelfth century, before Philip was dead. It is not to Philip, but to Louis, that the credit must be given ; at 1100, rather than at 1108, the reign of Philip I may be taken as ended.

SUGGESTIONS FOR READING ON CHAPTER X

As for Chapter IV.

Fliche, A. : *Le règne de Philippe I, roi de France,* 1060–1108. Paris, 1912.

CHAPTER XI

CHRISTIANITY AND ISLAM

The nature of the conflicts between Christianity and Islam

THE mutual hostility of Christians and Moslems forms one of the leading themes of medieval history. It would be an exaggeration, however, to speak of them as two great communities waging a constant war of religion. In the first place, Christendom was not a united body, either politically or ecclesiastically, and the divisions in the Moslem world were equally distinct. Moreover, while Christians and Moslems disputed large areas of Europe, of Asia, and of North Africa, it was the desire for territorial conquest or reconquest that motived the struggle. Religious animosity, indeed, added to the bitterness of the contest; and the sense of a common religion gave a feeling of unity to Christendom on the one hand and to Islam on the other which would otherwise have been lacking. But the idea of a united Christendom was never transformed into a political reality; it remained a sentiment, like the idea of a united Hellas in the days of the Greek city-states, and for similar reasons.

In the second half of the eleventh century, the various conflicts that were in progress may be grouped under three heads. In the west, Islam was on the defensive, fighting a losing battle in Spain, in Sicily, and on the Mediterranean. Only in Spain could the religious motive be said to have played a part; and even there it was not strong enough to unite the Christians in a common war against Islam, or to overcome racial distinctions and the ambition of each kingdom for its own territorial aggrandisement. The desire for military adventure attracted numerous recruits from other countries, especially from the south of France, and after the preaching of the First Crusade a certain crusading zeal added to the attractiveness of the adventure. But it was primarily, as it is styled in Spanish history, a war of Reconquest. In the east, though the roles were reversed,

216

the situation was much the same.   There the Eastern Empire
had to meet as best it could the victorious onrush of the
Seljuk Turks ; the Seljuks had embraced the Moslem creed,
but their purpose was conquest and empire.   So, while the
Western Christians were on the offensive, the Eastern Christians were on the defensive.   Then came a third development
with the proclamation of the First Crusade, which was in its
inception a holy war, and to which the Moslems soon replied
in the same spirit.   It cut right across the division of East
and West, for it was the Western Christians who now took
the offensive against the Eastern Moslems.   The Western
Moslems were disinterested in the struggle, the Eastern
Christians, though at first they gained distinct advantages,
were soon seriously embarrassed.   In fact, East and West
resumed their former contact, and in the result Christian
rivalries tended to eclipse the mutual hostility to Islam.

I.   THE ADVANCE OF CHRISTIANITY IN THE WEST

The struggle was already an ancient one in the Spanish *Spain*
peninsula, where the break-up of the Caliphate had now made The end
it possible for the Reconquest to be undertaken in earnest. Caliphate
The Caliphate had been glorious, though only with a reflected of Cordova
glory.   For the Moslems, bringing with them the civilisation
which they had acquired mainly from the Empire, had
entered into the inheritance of the Roman civilisation that
had remained or had been restored in Visigothic Spain.   There
was little Arab blood among the conquerors, who were mainly
of African stock, and they continued to recruit their armies
from the Berber tribes of North Africa.   Adapting themselves to the civilisation into which they entered, it exerted
a deteriorating effect upon them ; they were lax in their
observance of the rules of the Koran, and in intellectual circles
freedom of thought and scepticism became rife.   But they
vindicated their devotion to Islam at any rate by the savagery
with which they treated their Christian enemies.   Abd-ar-
Rahman III and Almanzor raided the north again and again,
inflicting grave damage and carrying off plunder and slaves.
In the booty they won they had a reason for not wholly
destroying so valuable a source of profit ; and it might have
been beyond their power to maintain the government of
the whole peninsula.   For the glittering edifice was insecurely

based.   If Africa supplied soldiers it was also likely to supply competitors, and the ports had to be anxiously watched. The Moslem population was not large and depended to a considerable extent on the labour of slaves, who were obtained by conquest or in the ordinary course of commerce from north-eastern Europe.   The Moslem supremacy could only be maintained by a strong ruler able to enforce unity, and after the death of Almanzor the Caliphate broke up into a number of parts, known as *taifas*, governed by kings but little more than city-states, of which Seville, Toledo, Granada in the south, Saragossa in the north, were the most important. The rulers of these *taifas* were more intent on culture or debauchery than on military glory, and were incapable of self-defence.

Christian advance under Ferdinand I of Castile

So, by the middle of the eleventh century, the situation had been completely changed, and the military ascendancy in the Peninsula had passed from the Moslems to the Christians.   Ferdinand I of Castile captured a large area in what was to be later the kingdom of Portugal, advancing his frontier from the Douro to the Tagus.   He even threatened Seville, and the kings of both Seville and Toledo in terror submitted to him as tributaries.   His rapid advance seemed to open the prospect of a speedy Reconquest of the Peninsula. But in fact there were many causes which prevented this. The Moslems had occupied all the most fertile regions, and had driven the Christians into the hilly country in the north. There they had impoverished them both in men and material by their constant raids.   The Christian kingdoms were consequently poor and thinly populated ; they were organised, too, on a feudal basis, which militated against long campaigns. It was difficult for them to people the territories they conquered ; they took the easier course of replenishing their resources with the plunder they obtained by their raids and the tribute supplied by the vassal kings.   In fact, they treated the Moslems much as the Moslems had treated them before, though with less ferocity.

Lack of unity in Christian Spain

But there was another factor which retarded the progress of the Christians.   They never attained to the unity which the Moslems had enjoyed for a century.   Already there were three Christian kingdoms in existence, and unity was not to be achieved until the end of the Middle Ages.   The kings were concerned with possessions and with territorial conquest rather than with a crusade against Islam. One thing tends to emphasise this fact—the treatment of the numerous Jews in the Peninsula. The Jews, engaged in industry and commerce, were a wealth-producing asset, and as such had been well-treated by the Moslems. The Christian kings imitated them in this. In other Western countries the launching of the First Crusade to the Holy Places was a signal for the persecution of the Jews. In Spain alone they were tolerated, until the fifteenth century, when Ferdinand and Isabella began a holy war to drive out Islam from the Peninsula ; then the Jews were expelled as well.

Of the three kingdoms, Aragon began, in conjunction with the counts of Barcelona, a tentative advance from the north-east which was to lead early in the twelfth century to the capture of Saragossa. Navarre was of little account and for some time recognised the suzerainty of Aragon. The main burden was shouldered by Castile, which had suffered the most severely in the previous century, and in which more than elsewhere there was the tendency to combine conquest with crusade. In Galicia, in the extreme north-west of the kingdom, was the famous shrine of St. James (Santiago) of Compostella, to which pilgrims came from all parts of Western Europe. This had been sacked by Almanzor in the most devastating of all his raids, though he had actually spared the shrine itself ; but the horror caused by his sacrilege remained to add recruits from outside to the Castilian armies. Yet even in Castile the need for a single head against the enemy could not overcome the principle of division of possessions. When Ferdinand I died in 1065 he divided his territories—Castile, Leon, Galicia—among his three sons, and the Reconquest was delayed while they fought out the mastery. At last Alfonso VI was successful in reuniting his father's possessions in 1072 and the advance began again, culminating in the conquest of the kingdom of Toledo in 1085.

This achievement was notable for many reasons. It was a united Christian effort, for Alfonso's army received contingents from the other Spanish kingdoms (that from Aragon being led by its king) and numerous auxiliaries from elsewhere. Yet in the measures Alfonso took to consolidate his conquests

Alfonso VI of Castile captures Toledo (1085)

he showed little of the spirit of a crusader. While he attracted numerous Christian settlers by free grants of lands and houses, he also allowed the Moslem population to remain under its own magistrates and laws and to enjoy free exercise of its religion, and afforded similar privileges to the Jews. The population of Toledo was divided into four communities —Castilians, alien immigrants (known as *francos*, since they were mainly Frenchmen), Moslems, and Jews—each self-governing and living under its own customs. The occupation of Toledo made possible also the re-peopling of the towns, Salamanca, Segovia, and the like, in the southern area of the Castile to which Alfonso succeeded. He was able to push southwards, too, and to capture towns which formed a screen for his new frontiers. In one of his raids he arrived even at the southern coast, and exulted that he had reached the limits of Spain. Seated in their ancient capital, Toledo, he felt himself now the true heir of the Visigothic kings.

Relations
with the
Papacy

But Alfonso was fully alive to the value of the crusading spirit behind him, and of being a champion of Christendom against the infidel. He received the blessing of the Head of the Church upon his enterprise, and Spain now entered into the papal orbit. In Alfonso's reign the Spanish Church renounced its own peculiar rite and adopted the Roman liturgy, an action which naturally won the warm approbation of Pope Gregory VII. He hoped for more, and claimed that Spain was a dependency of the Roman see. This Alfonso was not prepared to concede ; but the weaker State of Aragon was willing to pay the higher price, and its king Peter I in 1095 sought papal protection from Urban II and rendered an annual tribute to the Pope in return. Alfonso reaped a further reward for his victory over Islam. Toledo under the Visigothic kings had been the scene of numerous ecclesiastical councils, the canons of which were universally accepted as part of the law of the Church. Its archbishopric was now reconstituted, and its former ecclesiastical predominance was renewed when Urban II conferred on the archbishop of Toledo the primacy of the Spanish Church. By this act the Spanish Church was still more closely linked with Rome, and at the same time its official head was a subject of the king of Castile.

The capture of Toledo proved to be the culmination of

this period of the Reconquest. Alfonso had changed his father's policy by adding to his dominions what Ferdinand had been content to leave a vassal-state. His raids threatened the same fate to Seville, though meanwhile his first design was the conquest of Saragossa, the most northerly of the Moslem principalities. The king of Seville turned for help to Africa, where the sect of the Almoravides were in the ascendancy. The head of the sect, Yusuf ibn Tashfin, Sultan of Morocco, answered the appeal with a large army. He was joined by the Moslem kings in the south, while Alfonso, hastily abandoning the siege of Saragossa, united an army, as representative of united Christendom as that which had conquered Toledo, to meet the invader. Yusuf was victorious in the battle of Zalaca near Badajoz in October 1086, but was satisfied with his success and returned to Africa. He came again in 1090, this time to make subject to himself the kings of the *taifas*. Once more Moslem Spain was united under a single ruler. The story of the Caliphate was not to be repeated. The Christians were strong enough to retain what they had won. But the Christian advance was checked. The conquest of the whole of Spain by the king of Castile, which had seemed an imminent possibility, was definitely prevented by the appearance of the Almoravides.

The leading figures in this period of the Reconquest were the kings of Castile—Ferdinand I and Alfonso VI. But romance has selected as its hero a Castilian noble, Rodrigo Diaz, better known as The Cid. He won great military distinction in the reign of Ferdinand I, but as he was afterwards in the service of Sancho whom Alfonso displaced, he was out of favour with the latter, and his independence of action gave Alfonso the excuse to exile him. He took refuge with the Moslem king of Saragossa, and fought with him against the king of Lerida, though the king of Aragon and the count of Barcelona were on the other side. His chivalrous treatment of the count of Barcelona, whom he took prisoner, added to his fame, which was not affected by the fact that he was fighting on the side of Moslems and against Christians; indeed, this was not uncommon at the time. His final exploit was the conquest of the kingdom of Valencia, which he ruled till his death, though recognising himself as a vassal of the king of Castile. Strategically it was an important conquest, as it barred the way to the Almoravides who were then seeking to extend their rule to Saragossa. But after his death in 1099 it soon had to be abandoned. His career depicts the blend of motives that characterised the Reconquest —zeal for Christianity, loyalty to the feudal code, military adventure, personal ambition. Like Richard I of England, though he cared little for the interests of his native country, he has been invested with the glamour of romance by his fellow-countrymen because of those qualities which his generation admired : he was a chivalrous knight, a great soldier, and a terror to the Moslems.

Sicily
The Norman conquest of South Italy

Very different both in its character and its result was the struggle that was simultaneously being waged by the Normans in the island of Sicily. This was not in the nature of a holy war, nor was it a Reconquest, since the Normans themselves were newcomers. They were, however, able to claim that they were recovering papal territory and at the same time vindicating their own rights, for in the treaty of Melfi in 1059 Robert Guiscard had been invested with Sicily as well as with Apulia and Calabria.[1] He set out at once to make his title good, associating with himself his younger brother Roger, assigning him a share both in Calabria and Sicily in the future conquests. So successful were they against the Byzantines that in 1060 they reached Reggio. Sicily, fertile and prosperous, lay before their eyes, and they determined on its immediate invasion.

Capture of Messina in Sicily (1061)

They were assisted at the outset by the weakness of the enemy. The Moslem emirs of the island, who had emancipated themselves from the authority of the Zairid rulers of North Africa (Barbary), were engaged in civil strife. One of them, Ibn-ath-Thimnah, welcomed the invaders and by his assistance made it possible for the Normans to obtain a foothold on the island. Even so, the transport of their troops across the straits in the face of the Moslem fleet was a hazardous undertaking. It was skilfully effected, and in 1061 the capture of Messina, followed soon afterwards by that of Troina, gave the Normans a base for future operations. For some years progress was slow, as Guiscard had to confine his attention almost exclusively to South Italy. He always

[1] See above, p. 163.

laboured under a serious disadvantage. He could never overcome the sturdy independence of his own fellow-country-men, who felt themselves his equals though they had to admit his suzerainty, and he was recalled from Sicily by a serious rising, which encouraged the Byzantines to renew their resistance. Until the conquest of the latter was complete, his presence in South Italy was essential. To Roger, therefore, was left the direction of the Sicilian expedi-tion. But he had only a few hundred knights at his disposal against the much larger forces of the Moslems, and for some time he could do little beyond raiding the enemy whenever he could catch them off their guard. His presence in South Italy, too, was often required; his brother's success there was equally important to himself. In 1062 he lost a useful ally when Ibn-ath-Thimnah died, and in the same year the Norman cause was jeopardised by a quarrel between Roger and Guiscard over the division of the spoils; this was only ended when Guiscard agreed to ratify the former arrangement, and to hold in joint ownership certain strongholds in Calabria as well as their conquest in Sicily. The following years were critical, as the Moslems sought the aid of their former masters in North Africa, and Ayyub, the son of the Zairid emir, came over with an army and assumed command. But the Zairids were not to emulate in Sicily the success of the Almoravides in Spain. In 1068 Ayyub suffered defeat and returned at once to his own country. The Sicilian Moslems were left to fight their battles by themselves.

In 1071 Guiscard completed his task in South Italy with the capture of Bari, and operations on a larger scale could now be undertaken in Sicily. His former experience showed him the importance of sea power, and he was able to turn the seamanship of his new Greek subjects to good account and to equip a fleet. By a skilful tactical use of the combined arms the Normans achieved a striking success in the capture of Palermo in January 1072. The whole of the north coast together with the adjacent hinterland passed under their control, and though the Moslems still held the major portion of the island, the Normans were now firmly established. Moreover, Robert and Roger were in undisputed authority. There were no barons as in Italy powerful enough to raise the standard of revolt, and they were careful only to create

Capture of Palermo (1072)

small fiefs so that the danger should not arise in the future.

Robert Guiscard's interests elsewhere

The successful campaign of 1072 was followed, like that of 1061, by a long period of comparative inactivity, and for the same reason, that Robert Guiscard's chief interests were elsewhere. He was engaged in rivalry with Richard of Capua, in his attacks on the Lombard vassals of the Pope, in his expeditions to Greece, and he was constantly troubled by the revolts of his barons. So Roger was once more in sole command, with the title of count, though nominally under the overlordship of his brother. When Guiscard died in 1085, he was succeeded as duke by his son Roger Borsa (1085–1111), who was so weak that his barons defied his authority. The most turbulent of all was his brother Bohemond, until he went off on the First Crusade to win a principality in the east. Roger Borsa could exercise no authority over his uncle in Sicily ; he had, in fact, to look to him for protection, and in return to give him full possession of the Calabrian strongholds which had formerly been shared with Guiscard.

Count Roger gradually conquers the whole of Sicily

Left to himself, count Roger could achieve little at first. His own forces were small, and his assistance was often needed in South Italy, especially on the occasion of revolts. Any large undertaking was impossible, but he showed his military genius by the skill with which he organised successful raids, and he consolidated his gains by building castles to maintain them. Meanwhile he built up his resources. He repaired the deficiency in the Christian population by encouraging immigration from the Lombard principalities in South Italy. He recruited soldiers from his Moslem subjects, treating them with great favour and allowing them full exercise of their religion. He was also careful to create an effective naval force. It was not sufficient to cope with the African fleet, which was again being sent to the aid of the Sicilian Moslems. So, probably in 1076, he made peace with the Zairid emir, which was faithfully observed by both sides. By this diplomatic move he avoided the danger of an invasion from Africa, which in the case of Spain effectively brought the Christian advance to an end.

The result of his organising and diplomatic ability was seen in the capture of Trapani in 1077 and of Taormina in

1079. Then there came another pause while events in Italy called for his frequent absence. At last in 1084 he was able to plan a campaign on a much larger scale, designed finally to overcome Moslem resistance. He organised it as a crusade against the unbelievers, to gain the backing of the Church and to attract reinforcements; it was purely a politic move, for he continued to show toleration to his Moslem subjects and to recruit soldiers from among them. The objective was Syracuse, and the success was complete. Syracuse was captured in 1085, and though the Moslems continued to hold out in isolated places, the end was in sight. With the capture of Noto in 1091 the conquest of Sicily was finally completed. In the same year Roger's fleet sailed to Malta and forced its Moslem rulers to recognise his overlordship. That concluded his conquests from Islam, for he adhered to the peace he had made with the Moslems of North Africa.

Roger now occupied the position formerly held by Robert Guiscard. He was the dominant figure among the Normans. His alliance was sought by other rulers, and the Papacy looked to him for the aid it so often needed from the Normans. His nephew the duke held higher rank, but Roger was the real master. He possessed strongholds in Calabria, and he alone could keep the turbulent baronage in order. Over Italy, then, he exercised a protectorate; in Sicily he ruled a centralised State, with the title of count yet with more complete control than a feudal monarch could usually wield. His policy was as skilful in government as it had been in conquest. He ruled a population still largely Moslem; they were subject to taxation, but he did not interfere with their customs or their religion. The old Moslem divisions of the island remained, and Moslem titles were retained for some of the higher offices, though these were held by Normans. On the other hand, he encouraged Christian settlers from the mainland to make good the deficiency in the population, and he reorganised the ecclesiastical sees in Sicily, replacing the Greek rite by the Latin. The provision of new bishoprics created a dispute with the Pope, who claimed this as his function. But Roger's assistance was so necessary to the Papacy that he was able to have his own way, and he obtained peculiar concessions from the Pope, who left him in control of appointments and free from the hampering presence of papal

The power and policy of Roger I

legates in the island.   It was a well-governed and a prosperous
State that he bequeathed to his son when he died in 1101.

Roger I was one of the leading figures of the second half
of the eleventh century.   As brilliant a soldier as his brother
Robert Guiscard, he surpassed him by his mental qualities.
Guiscard never overcame the innate brutality of his race and
the thirst for conquest.   Roger showed himself the equal of
William the Conqueror as a statesman.   In him the Norman
genius for organisation and adaptability found full expression.
He was the first of a brilliant line, and his descendants, from
his son Roger II to his great-grandson the Emperor Frederick
II, owed much of their greatness to the foundation which
he so truly laid.

*The Western
Mediter-
ranean.
Venice*

While the Moslems were thus losing their hold of the
mainland, they were at the same time being forced to yield
the command of the Western Mediterranean to the naval
powers of Italy.   Religious sentiment had no part in the
struggle.   The victors were actuated solely by commercial
considerations.   In the tenth century the Venetians had
carried on a brisk trade with the Moslems of Africa, supplying
them with iron and wood, as well as with slaves, until the
Eastern Emperors intervened to prevent the materials for
weapons and ships from reaching their enemies.   Venice by
its situation on the lagoons was bound to be especially concerned with the sea, and already in the tenth century its fleet
had been successful in overcoming the Slav pirates from
Dalmatia.   Consequently, its allegiance was a matter of
rivalry between Eastern and Western Emperors.   To preserve
its independence and to secure commercial advantages,
Venice had thrown in its lot with the Eastern Empire, and in
992 Basil II confirmed by a Golden Bull its trading privileges
with Byzantine ports.   In return, it lent its fleet against
the Sicilian Moslems and won a great victory over them off
Bari in 1002.   The right of free passage in the Adriatic was
essential to it, and this necessitated a constant struggle with
the towns on the Dalmatian coast.   In the latter half of the
eleventh century, Venice was already on the way to becoming
the queen of the Adriatic, especially as the Norman conquest
of South Italy reduced the importance of Amalfi, the most
serious rival of Venice on the east coast of Italy·   When the

Normans built a fleet, however, and particularly when Robert Guiscard began his offensive against Greece, the supremacy of the Venetians was endangered and also their trading routes to Constantinople. They allied with the Emperor Alexius Comnenus, and assisted him to repel the Norman invaders; in return they received peculiar privileges in freedom from tolls and a special quarter at Constantinople.

It was not until the eleventh century that the coastal towns of western Italy began their naval and commercial careers. The constant raiding of their coasts by the Moslems in the tenth century had caused Pisa and Genoa to build ships in self-defence. Pisa, sacked in 1004, had retaliated and won a naval victory in 1005. In 1016 Pisa and Genoa had united in an expedition which resulted in the conquest of Sardinia, and had gradually obtained the mastery of the Tyrrhenian Sea, continuing their counter-offensive so far as to threaten the Barbary coast of North Africa. In 1063 a Pisan fleet appeared off Palermo, but the Normans were unwilling to enter into a partnership which, though it would have accelerated their conquest, would also have given the Pisans a share in the spoils. Finally, in 1087 Pisa and Genoa, once more acting in concert, captured Mahdiyah, the principal harbour of the Zairid emirs, burnt the Moslem fleet, and imposed a humiliating peace. *Pisa and Genoa*

This was the culminating triumph. The command of the sea had definitely passed to the Italian powers—Venice, Genoa, Pisa, and the Normans—and of all the disasters suffered by Islam in the West this was perhaps the most important. Islam was almost excluded from the West; only the Almoravides of Morocco remained unaffected, a serious handicap to the Christian kingdoms of Spain. As by their conquests from the seventh century onwards the communication by sea between East and West had been broken, so by their defeat the old intercourse was restored. The object of the victors was commerce, the acquisition of wealth by contact with Eastern trade. The result was the enrichment of the West and the heightening of its civilisation. Venice was concerned with the Adriatic and the overland routes to Constantinople, which it supplied with food-stuffs, bringing back spices and luxury articles to the West in return. Genoa and Pisa were concerned with the sea route to the south- *Results of the capture of Mahdiyah (1087)*

eastern Mediterranean, and they too brought back articles
of luxury which raised the standard of living in the West and
helped to advance its trade.

II. THE EASTERN EMPIRE AND THE SELJUKS

The weakness of the Eastern Empire

Between the extinction of the Macedonian house and the
accession of Alexius Comnenus, who founded a new dynasty,
the Empire passed through a disastrous quarter of a century.
No longer was there the attachment to the legitimate house
to counteract the hostility of the landed aristocracy and the
military leaders to the palace officials who controlled the civil
administration.   Michael VI, who had been nominated as her
successor by Theodora in 1056, was unfortunate also in that he
alienated the Patriarch Michael Cerularius.   This ambitious
prelate, after his successful schism with Rome, aimed at controlling the imperial government, and with the aid of the
military leaders he was successful in deposing Michael in 1057.

Isaac Comnenus

His choice as Emperor was the general, Isaac Comnenus, who
thus began the imperial career of his family.   For two years
he tried to drill Constantinople into order.   He instituted a
reform of the official class, and straightened the finances by
imposing heavy taxation, and even confiscated ecclesiastical
property.   Naturally he was unpopular, and the patriarch
was the first to take umbrage.   Foiled in his attempt to
control the government by deputy, he aimed now at the
throne for himself, and intrigued this time with the official
class against the Emperor and his military adherents.   But
it was he himself that was overthrown and driven into
retirement in 1057, and he only survived his downfall for a
year.   Isaac was now free to attend to the dangers that
threatened the Empire from outside.   In 1059 he repelled
invasions of the frontiers by Hungarians and Patzinaks.   But
the real danger was in Armenia, now overrun by the Seljuks.
To this he paid no heed.   A serious illness intervened and
seems to have left him a changed man.   He abdicated the
throne and retired to a monastery.

Constantine X

Before abdicating Isaac had named as his successor a
member of another great family, who might therefore have
been expected to continue his policy—Constantine Ducas.
But Constantine X preferred the popular course of reversing
the military régime of his predecessor, and restored the

former government by palace officials; he even went so far as to reduce the numbers of the fighting forces and to destroy the prestige of a military career. Through all the confusion and bad government of the years following the death of Basil II, the military efficiency of the Empire had been maintained. It was now fatally impaired, just when it was most required. Constantine died in 1067 leaving a young son, Michael VII, with his mother Eudocia as regent. She, *Romanus Diogenes* following precedent, married a general, Romanus Diogenes, and raised him to the throne as Emperor in 1068. But history was not to repeat itself any further. Romanus saw the danger and did what he could to reorganise the army. Yet it was his own incapacity as general that made definitive the collapse which the policy of Constantine X had prepared. In 1071 the Empire, so long victorious, suffered a crushing defeat at the hands of the Moslems.

To understand the circumstances that led to this disaster, *The Abbasid Caliphate* it is necessary to review the situation in the Moslem world. Just as Christendom had once been united under the rule of a single Emperor, so had the Moslems under the rule of a single Caliph. Since the Caliph, the successor of the Prophet, had to be a member of the Prophet's own tribe, Arab headship was perpetuated. But when, in 750, the Abbasid dynasty replaced the Ummayad, it owed its promotion to Persian and not to Arab influence. The seat of the Caliphate was removed from Damascus to Bagdad, where, isolated among people of another race, the Caliphs soon became mere figure-heads. Seeking to regain their independence, they surrounded themselves with Turkish mercenaries, only to become subject to them in turn; and finally the Persian Buwaihids supplanted the Turks. The Caliphate remained in an Arab family, but the government was in other hands. Moreover, whoever was in authority, the government at Bagdad could not keep in touch with the distant western provinces, which soon acted quite independently of it. In 909 a rival Caliphate was set up in North Africa under the Fatimite dynasty, which claimed descent from Fatima the daughter of the Prophet; and in 929 the Ummayad Caliphate of Cordova was founded in Spain. This lasted for a century, but only concerned Spain and the *The Fatimite Caliphate in Egypt* coast of Morocco. The Fatimites, on the other hand, achieved the conquest of Egypt in 969, established Cairo as

their capital, and for two centuries challenged the title of the
Abbasids to the headship of Islam in the East as well as the
West. The challenge was partly a religious one, for Islam,
like Christianity, had its religious schisms. The chief
cleavage was between the orthodox Sunnis and the dissident
Shiites ; the latter particularly maintained that the true line
of Caliphs descended from Ali, the husband of Fatima. The
Buwaihids were Shiites, and therefore had little respect for
the orthodox Abbasid Caliph. But the Seljuks who rescued
him from them had become Sunnis when they embraced
Islam ; they not only showed great regard for the Caliph,
they advanced westward as the champions of orthodoxy.
The Fatimites, on the other hand, were naturally Shiites,
and so between them and the Abbasids there was a religious
as well as a political schism.

It was over the Abbasid emirs of Syria and Palestine that
Nicephorus II had won his great victories in 969, when Aleppo
became a Byzantine dependency. This was the same year
that the Fatimites established themselves in Egypt, and they
too immediately turned their attention to Palestine and
Syria. John Tzimisces in his victorious expedition in 975
easily defeated their first attempts, but in the troublous years
of the beginning of Basil II's reign they had their opportunity
and gained a firm hold on Palestine. Basil and his successors
were engaged in a continual struggle with them, interrupted
by temporary peaces, for the possession of Syria, until in the
second half of the eleventh century a third competitor
appeared, the Seljuk Turks.

Rise of the   The genius of Tughril Beg and the title he received from
Seljuk Turks the Caliph enabled him to unify the marauding tribes of
Turks into a formidable army, and to create a Seljuk Empire.
The enfeebled condition of Armenia made it an obvious mark
for invasion, and its conquest was completed by his nephew
and successor, Alp Arslan (1063–72). This was a serious
matter for the Eastern Empire. The Taurus and Anti-
Taurus ranges, which hitherto had kept the Moslems out of
Asia Minor, were now passed by bands of adventurous Turks
moving west, and also south into Syria. Constantinople
was thoroughly alarmed, and the new Emperor, Romanus
Diogenes, hastily organised an army. He was successful in
driving back the invaders from Asia Minor and Syria, and

he then took the offensive himself.   At the head of a large but motley force he invaded Armenia in 1071, pressing on recklessly until at Manzikert he came face to face with the disciplined array of the Seljuks under their Sultan, Alp Arslan. Ignorant of the foe with whom he had to deal, he staked his whole resources on the issue of a single battle, and was completely defeated and himself taken prisoner.

Their victory at Manzikert (1071)

The main fighting force of the Eastern Empire was annihilated, and its defences lay exposed to the invader. Alp Arslan advanced into Syria in 1071 to ensure the conquest of Aleppo.   The next year he was murdered in Turkestan, and was succeeded by his son Malik Shah (1072–94), who was content to leave the western advance in the hands of his subordinates.   Atsiz, in command in Syria and Palestine, captured Jerusalem in 1071 and Damascus in 1075 ; in 1079 he was superseded by Malik Shah's brother Tutush.   The issue lay between Seljuks and Fatimites, and the latter were almost expelled from Palestine.   So the position remained until the death of Malik Shah in 1094.   For some years after this there was civil war in Mesopotamia, various claimants, among them Tutush, disputing the succession ; the Seljuk leaders in Syria and Asia Minor were left to their own devices. Tutush met his death in Mesopotamia, and the Egyptian Moslems took the opportunity to regain Jerusalem.   So, at the opening of the First Crusade, Syria and North Palestine were occupied by Seljuk emirs, acknowledging the Caliph of Bagdad and the authority of their Sultan but acting on their own and receiving no assistance from him, while South Palestine and, later, Jerusalem were occupied by Egyptian Moslems, acknowledging the Caliph of Cairo.   These two groups were as hostile to one another as they were to the crusading Christians.   It was actually during the course of the First Crusade that the Fatimites recovered Jerusalem.

Advance of the Seljuks and their divisions

With all this Constantinople was not concerned.   Its recent acquisitions in Cilicia and Syria had to be abandoned, for the frontiers were overrun and Asia Minor was being penetrated by Seljuk bands.   A powerful Seljuk principality under an independent Sultan was formed in Asia Minor, to which was given the name of Rūm, a fitting title [1] for a State

The Sultanate of Rūm

[1] For Rūm (i.e. Rome) was the name by which the Eastern Empire was known by its eastern neighbours.

founded within the Empire and aiming at replacing it. The
Sultan of Rūm, ultimately established his capital at Nicaea,
only 120 miles from Constantinople. The Empire held only
the coast line and a small area of the mainland east of Constantinople. It had lost provinces from which some of its
best fighting men were recruited, and in consequence it never
again was more than a shadow of what it had been in the
great days of Basil II. Its European provinces were fast
dwindling, too. In the same year as Manzikert, the Normans
took Bari, and the Empire was deprived of its last foothold
in Italy. In the Balkans, Croats, Serbs, and Bulgars rose to
gain independence, and there were raids of Hungarians,
Patzinaks, and others over the northern frontiers. The
vultures seemed to be swooping down upon the dying body.

For dissolution seemed to be the fate of the Empire. At
Constantinople all was confusion, and even the crisis did not
put an end to the intrigues that had so long prevailed.
Michael VII became actual ruler on the downfall of his
stepfather in 1071 and reigned miserably for seven years,
after which he was deposed in favour of a military leader,
Nicephorus Botaniates, who was no better able to cope with
the situation. During these years the family of the Comneni
had been steadily pushing to the front, thanks to the ambition
of Anna Dalassena, sister-in-law to the Emperor Isaac
Comnenus. She played a normal part in the intrigues of the
time, seeking to rival the position of the house of Ducas.
But her third son, Alexius, had a cooler head and wisdom that
was to make him the saviour of the tottering Empire. He
allied himself with the Ducas family and married Irene, great
niece of the Emperor Constantine X. The union of the two
imperial houses proved irresistible against the usurper
Nicephorus. In 1081 he was deposed and Alexius Comnenus
proclaimed Emperor in his place.

Alexius I, who is represented to us as a model of all the
kingly virtues in the *Alexiad* written by his daughter Anna
Comnena, was through his achievements not unworthy of an
epic biography. There was in him something of the pious
Aeneas, more of the wily Odysseus ; at any rate he possessed
the two qualities most necessary for the crisis—military
capacity and diplomatic astuteness. At first he had to rely
on the latter, for the military organisation was in a shocking

*Condition
of the
Eastern
Empire*

*Alexius I
Comnenus
becomes
Emperor
(1081)*

condition, thanks to the neglect of the army by Constantine X. The Emperors had had to enlist auxiliaries, principally from the West, attracted by pay or by the desire for military adventure ; but such a combination of heterogeneous elements could not be welded into a disciplined force. This was one of the causes of the disaster of Manzikert, and the loss of the greater part of Asia Minor had further deprived the Empire of its chief recruiting grounds. Alexius therefore had still to rely on auxiliaries, and in the first half of his reign he was rarely successful in the field. Gradually, however, he managed to reconstitute a true Byzantine army, disciplined on the old model, and once more a powerful weapon. It was the same with the navy. For some time he had to depend entirely on Venetian assistance ; later he was able to act with a fleet of his own.

However, many years elapsed before he could rely on his own strength. Till then he had to depend on his wits, and he showed consummate skill in dividing the enemies he could not face in the field, allying himself with Moslems against Moslems, with barbarians against barbarians, with Normans against Normans ; his accurate appreciation of the political situation in every case displayed his statesmanship. Thus by diplomacy and astuteness he maintained Byzantium as a great power. The same qualities were of service to him in dealing with the rival leaders of the First Crusade, though here he somewhat overreached himself and his success was only temporary. For what to him was dictated by the natural instinct of self-preservation appeared to them as unscrupulous trickery, and the mutual mistrust that was created led ultimately to disaster.

His foreign and domestic policy

Alexius's qualities were particularly adapted to dealing with the external enemies of the Empire. At home, he had for many years to face constant disaffection, a legacy from the civil disorders of the past ; there were frequent threats of revolt and at times he narrowly escaped assassination. He overcame these domestic enemies, but his mastery of them was never complete. In some respects his internal administration was unfortunate. Finance was a constant source of anxiety, for his frequent campaigns and his subsidies to his allies were expensive. Taxation, which did not spare ecclesiastical property, was naturally heavy and provoked much

discontent ; less unpopular but far more serious in its consequences was his debasement of the coinage. The Byzantine
gold coin (*bezant*) had provided a standard which attracted
trade to Constantinople and made it the financial centre of
the civilised world. This position was gravely prejudiced
by the debasing of the coinage, which continued after his
death.

Conflict with the Normans

The first years of the reign were critical indeed. The
outlook was already sufficiently grave when from a new
quarter there came a formidable addition to the Empire's
assailants. The Norman duke Robert Guiscard, who had
completed his conquest of South Italy from the Byzantines in
1071, saw a prospect of following up his success by an offensive
in Greece. He had a pretext when Michael VII, betrothed
to one of his daughters, was deposed in 1078, and the peace
he made with Gregory VII in 1080 gave him the opportunity.
In 1081 he and his son Bohemond crossed the Adriatic,
captured Corfù, and gained a foothold on the mainland of
Greece. Alexius's military resources were inadequate, but
he could fight the Normans with other weapons. In return
for trading privileges at Constantinople he gained the alliance
of Venice, who moreover was jealous of Norman interference
in the Adriatic. The Venetian fleet completely defeated the
Norman off Durazzo, but on land the Greeks were worsted
by the Normans, who captured Durazzo. However, Alexius's
diplomacy had been gaining other allies. As Gregory VII
was pledged to the support of Guiscard, Alexius allied with
Henry IV, and his money played a part in weakening the
resistance of the Romans. He also succeeded in promoting
disaffection among Guiscard's vassals in South Italy, and this
forced the Norman duke to return in 1082 ; Bohemond
remained in Greece for a year longer, until lack of pay for his
troops caused him also to return. In 1084, after the rescue
of Gregory VII and the sack of Rome, Robert Guiscard was
able to return to Greece ; and he won a naval victory over
the Venetians. But his death in 1085 brought the Norman
invasion to an end ; the Venetians recovered their mastery
of the Adriatic, and the new duke, Roger Borsa, was too weak
in South Italy to attempt a fresh offensive.

His other difficulties

The year of Guiscard's death brought relief to Alexius in
Asia as well as in Europe. Sulaiman, the Sultan of Rūm,

died in that year and Asia Minor was divided among a number of Seljuk emirs.   Alexius was able to make use of their mutual hostility to establish a balance of power which relieved him from any fear of a Moslem coalition against Constantinople. This was a fortunate chance, for in 1086 he had to meet a serious invasion of the Patzinaks across the Danube into Bulgaria.   Not until 1091, and then only with the aid of the Cumans, was he able to inflict a decisive defeat upon them. Three years later the Cumans made an incursion on their own and had to be repelled from the walls of Hadrianople.

For fourteen years Alexius had been struggling against external foes and domestic discord, and he appeared at last to have gained the upper hand.   The repulse of the Cumans coincided with the exposure of a dangerous plot against the Emperor's life, and the punishment of the chief conspirators seemed to offer the prospect of peace at home and a necessary breathing-space for reorganisation.   At this moment the launching of the First Crusade altered the whole situation, and necessitated a complete reconstruction of ideas and policy.

III.   THE FIRST CRUSADE

In the year 1095, when Pope Urban II was making his great progress through North Italy and France, he halted at Clermont in the Auvergne, and there presided at an important Church Council.   On 27 November, before a large multitude of ecclesiastics and laymen, he delivered a famous oration. He began by dwelling on the horror of the invasion of Christian lands in the East by " the people of the kingdom of the Persians," the destruction of churches, the dismemberment of the kingdom of the Greeks, and, most horrible of all, the defilement of the Holy Sepulchre at Jerusalem by " peoples unclean."   He exhorted his hearers to recall the valour of the Franks of old, to lay aside their petty feuds, and to take the road to the Holy Sepulchre.   He emphasised the hardness of life in the mountainous country of the Auvergne, and drew a glowing picture of Jerusalem, " the centre of the earth," " a land fruitful above others," " flowing with milk and honey."   Finally he urged them to undertake the journey for the remission of their sins, " assured of the imperishable glory of the kingdom of Heaven."   A Frenchman himself,

Urban II inaugurates the First Crusade (1095)

speaking to his fellow-countrymen, his eloquence was calculated to rouse them to the height of emotional enthusiasm.
The assembly responded with a great shout of *Deus vult* (" It
is God's Will "), and the first act in the great drama of the
Crusades had begun.

Its antecedents

Urban's speech was an admirable summary of Western
feeling, which had been profoundly shocked by the victorious
onset of the Seljuks. It needed papal initiative, however, to
galvanise this into action. After the battle of Manzikert and
the collapse of the defence of the Eastern Empire, Michael
VII had appealed to the Pope for assistance. Gregory VII
had responded to the appeal with enthusiasm, and in 1074
announced his intention of leading a large expedition to rescue
the Eastern Christians, expressing the hope that he might
even attain to the Holy Sepulchre itself. His anticipation of
support was too sanguine and his other tasks too manifold,
so that the scheme did not materialise; later, the conflict
with Henry IV engrossed his whole attention, and subsequently his alliance with Robert Guiscard led to an actual
breach with the Eastern Empire. Urban II was in a very
different position when he issued his appeal, and he showed
a more correct appreciation than had Gregory VII as to where
the stress should be laid. The West was ready to pity the
Eastern Christians; but there was no friendliness for the
Eastern Empire, and no altruistic desire to recover for it its
lost territories. What did matter was that Jerusalem was
in the hands of the Turks.

The Western point of view

The contact of the West with Jerusalem had been constant
throughout the centuries of Moslem occupation. Charlemagne had been on friendly terms with the Caliph, and whether
or no it is correct to speak of a Frankish protectorate of the
the Holy Places, access to them was certainly made easy.
Pilgrimages from the West were common; the usual route
was via the Rhine and Danube, through Hungary, and thence
to Asia Minor; there were regular travellers' halts and a
recognised system of tolls. Frenchmen were particularly
familiar with the journey; in the eleventh century we hear of
numerous pilgrimages, especially of Angevins and Normans.
The appearance of the Fatimites in Palestine did not at first
alter the situation, but in 1009 the Fatimite Caliph Hakim,
in a fit of fanatic frenzy, destroyed the church of the Holy

Sepulchre. The West was profoundly shocked but was not stirred to action ; and the damage was soon made good by the Moslems themselves. The chief consequence of the outrage was that the Eastern Emperors now, by treaty with the Fatimites, became the protectors of the Holy Places. The ill feeling between East and West, especially after the Schism of 1054, affected the security of the pilgrim routes. Pilgrimages continued but were more hazardous and had to be undertaken in large armed bands ; we read of one such host, led by bishop Gunther of Bamberg and including the archbishop of Mayence and other prelates, which was stated to have numbered 12,000.[1] At any rate, with the Fatimites in possession, the Holy Places were under Christian care and access to them was possible. When the Seljuks captured Jerusalem in 1071, the Christian protectorate came to an end and the roads to Jerusalem were barred to pilgrims. Pilgrims had been armed as a defensive measure. The Crusade was a pilgrimage but with an offensive purpose ; it was launched to reopen the way to Jerusalem and to restore the Holy Places to Western Christians.

But for the Seljuk conquests, then, the Crusade would not have come into being. Yet there would anyhow have been a movement eastward of those powers who had driven the Moslems from western soil and western seas. Genoa and Pisa, after the capture of Mahdiyah in 1087, were eager to establish trading posts on the shores of the eastern Mediterranean and, though acting no longer in concert but in bitter rivalry, welcomed the conquest of Palestine and Syria.[2] The Normans, who had expelled Greeks as well as Moslems, had already attempted an offensive against the Greeks and were only too ready to join an offensive against the Moslems. Their leader was Bohemond, who had played a large part in the invasion of Greece, and he and his nephew Tancred were both eager to carve out principalities for themselves in the East. This was a feature of the First Crusade that went

Material interests

---

[1] Medieval writers, when they wished to express a large number, invariably spoke in tens of thousands, just as children to-day talk in millions. This particularly applies to the Crusades. The figures given of the crusaders and the enemies they encountered are merely fanciful, and always hopelessly exaggerated ; no attempt at exact figures is ever possible.

[2] Venice, whose trade lay through Constantinople, was later in entering into this competition, and played only a minor part in the First Crusade.

counter to its high purpose.   Most of the military leaders were men of high rank but of little authority in their own country and therefore anxious to acquire territorial sovereignty in the East—for instance, Godfrey of Bouillon, duke (in name only) of Lower Lorraine, and his brother Baldwin ; Hugh of Vermandois, brother of the French king ; Robert of Normandy, most insecure in his own duchy and ready now to pawn it to William II ; Raymond of St. Gilles, count of Toulouse, a man of wealth but little consequence.   An exceptional case was the powerful count of Flanders, Robert II ; his father had already come into touch with Alexius when on pilgrimage, and he himself was probably actuated by genuine crusading motives.

Religious zeal the primary motive

So the acquisition of territory and trade, which had motived the advance against the Moslems in the West, were to have a part in the eastern offensive also.   But it still remained true that the Crusade in its inception was not actuated by these selfish aims.   It was a Holy War, proclaimed by the Head of the Church and conducted under his guidance through his legate, bishop Ademar of Puy ; the participants wore the badge of the Cross (they were *cruce-signati*) ; the Church took their possessions under its protection, whoever their temporal lords might be ; and it promised to those who died on crusade the spiritual reward of absolution from their sins.   The great majority of the crusaders were actuated by deep religious fervour, which fortified them to attain to their ultimate goal.   When misdirected it led to unfortunate results.   Before the expedition proper assembled at its rendezvous, undisciplined bodies led by fanatics such as Peter the Hermit (one of those commissioned by Urban to preach the crusade, but whose zeal outran his wisdom) rushed blindly to destruction.   They provoked attack from the Hungarians and others through whose lands they passed, and the remnant which reached Asia Minor fell an easy prey to the swords of the Seljuks.   Again, especially among those who did not take the cross, the zeal for the Holy Places took the form of frenzy against the Jews.   Particularly in the Rhine towns there was rioting and massacre ; to the crusading movement is mainly attributable the barbarous persecutions of the Jews in the Middle Ages.

The Crusade was initiated in an assembly of Frenchmen,

and of Frenchmen it was mainly composed. Apart from the Norman vassals of the Pope, all the leading crusaders except Godfrey of Bouillon were vassals of the French king. Papal authority was certainly more fully assured in France than elsewhere, but the fervour excited by Urban II and the preachers he commissioned was of a more general character, and it was not long before Germans and English also began to flock to Palestine. The Pope who appealed for volunteers for his army could promise them eternal rewards; this was not new, for Gregory VII had made the same promises to those who fought against the enemies of the Church; and there was to be a great development of these indulgences in the future, with a corresponding heightening of papal influence. But his claim to safeguard the possessions of crusaders, which overrode the rights of their temporal sovereigns, was a new departure; and since no one contested the claim, the universal sovereignty of the Pope was clearly demonstrated. Moreover, while he was launching this great expedition, to which the vassals of the excommunicated king of France were flocking, the nominal head of the temporal department, the king of Germany, also under papal excommunication, was isolated at Verona, unable even to get back to Germany. Beside the papal authority, the one universal authority in the West, the imperial authority presented a wretched contrast. One of the most abiding results of the crusading movement was its effect upon the papal position. The papal monarchy, built up by Leo IX and Gregory VII, was now securely established. *Enhancement of the papal power*

While the Crusade thus contributed to the stabilisation and enhancement of papal authority, it exercised a determining influence too upon the destiny of the Eastern Empire. It has long been debated whether Alexius I actually appealed to Urban II for help and so put the idea into his head. He had certainly sought Western assistance before (against the Patzinaks as much as against the Turks) and he had been accustomed to employ Western auxiliaries. But it seems unlikely that he contemplated a general advance against the Moslems in Asia Minor; his policy of allying himself with one emir against another had proved successful, and if he required assistance it was probably to make this *The attitude and policy of the Eastern Emperor*

policy more effective.   Certainly ambassadors from him were
present at the Council which Urban II held at Piacenza in
1095 before he proceeded to France.   They were there to
settle points at dispute as much as to appeal for aid, but
they seem to have depicted the unhappy state of Eastern
Christendom.   So Urban may have received his inspiration
from them.   If so, the original idea was entirely transformed
when he promoted a general offensive with Jerusalem as the
objective.

Alexius had certainly contemplated nothing of this kind ;
the launching of the Crusade necessitated an entire reconstruction of his whole policy, and the way in which he adapted
himself to the new situation displayed most clearly his
political genius.   He was confronted with the prospect of
grave danger, for the Westerners might be tempted to turn
their arms against Constantinople, especially as his former
enemy Bohemond was one of the most prominent leaders.
There was the further likelihood that they would retain in
their own hands the territories they won from the Seljuks,
and the Empire would be in a worse plight than before.   On
the other hand, if he could deal separately with each of the
leaders (and their numbers and disunion were as much an
advantage to him as they were a handicap to the Crusade),
he might be able to reap the fruits of their victories, at any
rate in Asia Minor and Syria.   It was a hazardous game to
play, but he had been facing similar risks throughout his
reign, and he matured his plans to avert the dangers and
to reap the gains.

The assem-
bling of the
Crusaders at
Constanti-
nople

The papal legate timed his departure for August 1096 ;
and it had been agreed that the various bodies of crusaders
should find their own way to Constantinople, a fitting point
of assembly from which to cross to Asia Minor and begin the
task of clearing the road to Jerusalem.   They entered Byzantine territory from three directions—by the pilgrim route
through Hungary, by a second route via North Italy and
Dalmatia, or by a third by sea from South Italy to the coast
of Greece.   Fortunately for Alexius they did not arrive simultaneously.   Hugh of Vermandois was the first, travelling via
South Italy and Greece and reaching Constantinople in
October 1096 ; he was followed in December by Godfrey of

Bouillon and Baldwin who came through Hungary. In the spring of 1097 Bohemond and Tancred arrived, followed at short intervals by Robert of Flanders, Raymond of Toulouse, and lastly Robert of Normandy, who was accompanied by Stephen of Blois. All of these, with the exception of Raymond who went overland via Dalmatia, took the sea passage from South Italy to Greece. Alexius's preparations were admirable. He had been able to obtain exact information as to the various expeditions, so that he had not anywhere been taken by surprise. At every point where the crusaders entered his territories he had guides to conduct them, and *en route* he provided them with supplies of food, at the same time posting troops to check any attempts at pillage. He was successful in shepherding them on their way, but when he tried to convoy them across to Asia Minor they resisted, and he had to submit to the rendezvous at Constantinople.

Still, as they came separately, he was able to deal with each in turn before they had an opportunity of concerting their plans. He showed his sagacity by demanding from each an oath of fealty to himself, thus assuring that the territories recovered by the crusaders would be restored to imperial suzerainty. Raymond of Toulouse alone refused to take the oath ; Godfrey of Bouillon hesitated for some time ; the others, even Bohemond, assented at once. To feudal barons, accustomed to an overlord, such an oath was natural and not humiliating ; but Alexius probably did not realise how lightly the obligation sat upon them. He did more to reconcile them to his service by the favours and the gold he showered on them when they had taken the oath. It was arranged that conquests in Asia Minor and Syria should be restored to the Empire, some of them in full possession some to be held as fiefs by the Latins ; Alexius promised military assistance, especially for the capture of Antioch, on which he set great store. Palestine, it was understood, was to be at the disposal of the Latins. Thus the difficulties and dangers attending the assembling of the crusaders at Constantinople were overcome, and Alexius reaped the first-fruits of his successful diplomacy when the crusading army captured for him the town of Nicaea in June 1097.

Their agreement with Alexius

The capture of Nicaea was important also for the crusaders, since an enemy in possession of it would have

The march through Asia Minor

threatened their rear. The march south could now begin. The route to be cleared ran diagonally through Asia Minor to the Taurus mountains, the passes over which gave access to Cilicia; thence it turned directly south to Syria with Antioch as the first main objective. The Sultan of Rūm, Kilij Arslan, seeking to avenge his loss of Nicaea, made a determined attack on them near Dorylaeum on July 1, but he was decisively defeated. Henceforward they had nothing to fear from the Moslems in Asia Minor, but the heat of the summer, the lack of provisions, and especially the shortage of water exacted a heavy toll of men and horses, and their ranks were much depleted by the time they reached the mountain passes. Here conditions were much more favourable. When the Seljuks conquered Armenia, a number of its inhabitants had withdrawn to the Taurus mountains and established a small principality in Cilicia, known as Lesser Armenia. They welcomed the crusaders, who received supplies from them and in return expelled the Turkish garrisons. At this point the selfish ambition of the leaders began to display itself. Baldwin, brother of Godfrey of Bouillon, and Tancred, Bohemond's nephew, were rivals for the conquest and acquisition of Cilicia. Baldwin with the larger army was successful, and he extended his conquests beyond the Euphrates to Edessa; with it as his capital he founded the first Latin State in the East—the county of Edessa.

The county of Edessa

The capture of Antioch

The rest of the crusaders marched on to Antioch, which was reached in October 1097. Yet it was not until the following July that the city was at last surrendered to them. Dearth of provisions enfeebled the besieging army until reinforcements arrived from Europe in the spring; through lack of siege engines it could not attempt a direct assault; the division of command weakened its effectiveness, and it was further embarrassed by Moslem forces coming to the relief of the city. Bohemond had proved himself to be the most effective of the leaders, and it was he who by the treachery of a defender was able to make the first breach on June 3, 1098. But two days later the besiegers were in deadly peril. Karbogha, emir of Mosul, arrived with a force far outnumbering theirs, and they were themselves besieged. In their danger they sunk their differences and gave to Bohemond the supreme command. On June 28 he won a decisive victory; the relieving force took to flight, and a few days later the garrison of Antioch capitulated.

Once more the territorial ambition of the leaders was aroused. Bohemond claimed possession of the city since he had been the first to enter it, and after months of wrangling he prevailed against the counterclaim of Raymond of Toulouse; the papal legate, who might have acted as mediator, died of plague, and only the general desire to press on to Jerusalem at last forced Raymond grudgingly to leave Bohemond in possession. The delay was serious, for, Seljuk resistance having been overcome, the road to Jerusalem was open; but the Fatimites took advantage of the delay themselves to make the easy capture. The crusaders' task was now more difficult, as they had a fresh enemy to encounter, with whom they had been negotiating on friendly terms before. But the dispute over the possession of Antioch had other and more serious results. By treaty Antioch should have been handed over to Alexius, but he had not kept his part of the bargain. He had been recovering towns in Asia Minor while the crusaders were in difficulties, and was on his way to join them when he was met by a number of panic-stricken fugitives, including Stephen of Blois, who had taken to flight on the approach of Karbogha. Believing their tale that the crusading army was annihilated, Alexius retraced his steps; and his non-arrival gave the crusaders justification for refusing to hand over Antioch to him. Raymond, who alone had refused to take the oath of fealty, was now alone in defending the rights of Alexius; but he was also actuated solely by self-interest. From this time friendly co-operation between Emperor and crusaders ceased. The grievances on both sides gave rise to a bitterness of feeling, which was deliberately made more intense by Bohemond,[1] to justify his refusal to hand over Antioch to Alexius. In the West a general belief was created of the duplicity of the Eastern Emperor and his hostility to the Crusade. By his failure to assist in the siege of Antioch, Alexius lost not only Antioch; he lost the goodwill of the Western Christians and prepared disaster for his Empire.

Leaving Bohemond at Antioch and Baldwin at Edessa, the crusaders resumed their march in January 1099. There

Marginal notes: Beginning of friction between crusaders and Eastern Emperor

The capture of Jerusalem

---

[1] In Anna Comnena's account in the *Alexiad*, Bohemond rightly appears as the villain of the piece.

was a delay of some months in a vain attempt to capture a fortified post near Tripolis, so that the advantage of the cooler weather was lost and it was not until June 7 that they at last arrived within sight of Jerusalem. Gazing at the Holy City the leaders themselves forgot their selfish differences, and were animated like the mass of their followers by religious enthusiasm alone. Their endurance was sorely tried, for the steep and rocky country around Jerusalem was in striking contrast to the glowing description given of it by Urban II. Once more there was a dearth of provisions, and with only the pool of Siloam from which to obtain water men and animals suffered tortures from thirst. But the welcome arrival of Genoese vessels, which had already rendered invaluable assistance at Antioch, supplied them with food and also with engineers for the assault. On July 15 the great object was attained and Jerusalem was captured. Then all the pent-up religious emotion burst forth. Men wept tears of joy at beholding the Holy Places, and in the excitement of religious zeal proceeded, like the Chosen People in the Old Testament, to exterminate the unbelievers. Only Raymond held aloof from this work of massacre. But he was peculiar in other ways, and was unpopular already for championing the rights of Alexius at Antioch. For his own disappointment

The county of Tripolis

there, however, he did receive compensation. He was granted a strip of coastal territory immediately south of the principality of Antioch—the county of Tripolis—most of which, including the town of Tripolis, still remained to be conquered.

Godfrey of Bouillon the first ruler of Jerusalem

For the possession of Jerusalem there was no contest. The instinct for secular dominion was quelled by its sacred associations. But a ruler was necessary; and the choice of the crusaders fell on Godfrey of Bouillon, who had distinguished himself in the siege. The territory he governed extended north as far as Beyrout, the southern boundary of the county of Tripolis, and was known as the kingdom of Jerusalem, though Godfrey refused the title of king and styled himself Defender [1] of the Holy Sepulchre. He justified

---

[1] *Advocatus.* This was the term regularly applied to the lay noble who protected property belonging to the Church, e.g. monastic property. The term was therefore particularly applicable at Jerusalem, ecclesiastical territory *par excellence.*

their choice of him when, a month later, he met and decisively defeated near Ascalon a large force of Egyptians marching to the relief of Jerusalem. This completed the triumph of the First Crusade. In spite of the selfishness and dissension of its leaders, their ignorance of the country and the inadequacy of their preparations, the objective had at last been attained. Antioch and Jerusalem had been captured, and both Seljuks and Fatimites had been routed in pitched battle and forced to leave the victors in possession. Four Latin States had been founded in Syria and Palestine, and it now remained to be seen whether these could be established in perpetuity, and a solid front be maintained against the efforts of the Moslems to recover what they had lost. At any rate, when the twelfth century opened, the Western Christians seemed to have triumphed over Islam in the East as definitely as they had previously in the West.

SUGGESTIONS FOR READING ON CHAPTER XI

Advance of Christianity in the West :
    For Spain see Chapter XVI, below.
    For Normans in South Italy and Sicily see Chapter XIII, below.

Advance of Islam in the East :
    Cambridge Medieval History, Vol. IV, chapters 10, 11 ; Vol. V, chapter 6.
    And books suggested in Chapter VI above.

The First Crusade :
    Cambridge Medieval History, Vol. IV, new edn. (see p. xx) ; Vol. V, chapters 6, 7.
    Bréhier, L. : *L'Église et l'Orient au moyen âge. Les Croisades.* 5 ed. Paris, 1928.
    Grousset, R. : *Histoire des Croisades et du royaume franc de Jérusalem.* 3 vols. Paris, 1934–6.
    Runciman, S. : *History of the Crusades.* 3 vols. Cambridge, 1951–4.
    Setton, K. M. (ed.) : *History of the Crusades.* Vol. I–. Philadelphia, 1955–.
    Erdmann, C. : *Die Entstehung des Kreuzzugsgedankens.* Stuttgart, 1935.
    Smail, R. C. : *Crusading Warfare, 1097–1193.* Cambridge, 1956.
    Gesta Francorum et aliorum Hierosolimitanorum. Ed. and trans. R. Hill. Nelson's Medieval Texts, 1962 (a valuable original source).
    Daniel, N. : *Islam and the West.* Edinburgh, 1960.

CHAPTER XII

HENRY V AND THE INVESTITURE CONTEST

THE first great conflict between Empire and Papacy ended with the death of the excommunicated Henry IV in 1106, and the schism was healed by the reconciliation of his son Henry V with the Church. The main issue between the *sacerdotium* and the *regnum* was not raised again for half a century, but the interval of peace between the king of Germany and the Pope was a short one. A new contest arose, out of the conditions of the preceding schism, but otherwise unconnected with it. The controversial literature, which had raged furiously over the rival claims to authority of the ecclesiastical and temporal powers, broke out afresh; but it was now solely concerned with a minor issue, one that had been little debated before—the question of Lay Investiture. So, when peace was finally reached in 1122, this was the question that was settled. To modern writers it has appeared that Henry V resumed immediately the contest his father had failed to decide, and they therefore speak of a conflict lasting for half a century—the Investiture Struggle, begun by the investiture decree of Gregory VII in 1075 and ended by the Concordat of Worms in 1122. Gregory's decree preceded the conflict with Henry IV, but did not provoke it; it was, however, the ultimate cause of the conflict of the Papacy with Henry V. There were, in fact, two contests: in the last quarter of the eleventh century, over the general issue between the *sacerdotium* and the *regnum*; in the first quarter of the twelfth century, over a particular issue, on which the king of Germany (as also the king of England) was determined to maintain his traditional rights.

Henry V began his reign in an ambiguous position. To gain the throne, he had entered into league with the two powers which, united, had defeated his father—the German nobles and the Papacy; and so he had to walk warily at first, to govern in concert with the nobles and to avoid, if possible, offending the susceptibilities of the ecclesiastical reformers. Yet his ultimate purpose, at any rate in Germany, was not different from that of his father. With an equal sense of the rights attaching to the throne, and unscrupulous in attaining his ends, as he had shown in his treatment of his father, he was able to force his way through many obstacles at first. But in the long run his ruthlessness defeated its purpose; it roused rather than intimidated opposition, and the dual conflict with an outraged Papacy and rebellious nobles proved at last too much for his strength also.

He started with two advantages which his father had not possessed. He was already twenty-five years of age, and for eight years he had been associated in the government of the kingdom. Secondly, in the first years of his reign there was a period of peace, of unwonted harmony, between king and nobles in Germany. Partly this was due to the sense of co-operation between them, partly to Henry's wisdom in not arousing their suspicions by any manifest encroachment on their local independence. The harmony was enhanced by the determination of both to resist interference from their common ally, the Pope. For almost at once relations between Pope and king had become strained. The question of lay investiture was now the cause of discord.

The ecclesiastical situation

A natural concomitant of the revival of papal authority under Urban II had been the regular holding of papal synods, in North Italy, in France, and at Rome, where canons for the good order and government of the Church were officially promulgated. Particular emphasis was laid on the renewal of Gregory VII's decrees against lay investiture. In France, thanks to the energy of the papal legates, especially Hugh, now archbishop of Lyons, these had been re-published at local synods; the bishops had perforce to obey, and the king, while still exercising considerable influence over appointments, had to give up the practice of investing with ring and staff. So in France there was no investiture conflict, and therefore no formal concordat on the subject as in England and Germany. Outside the French kingdom little attention had hitherto been paid to the decree; no attempt had been made to enforce it in England, and in Germany during the schism papal decrees were naturally disregarded.

Urban II was not content merely to prohibit lay investiture. At the Council of Clermont in 1095, he also forbade
ecclesiastics to do homage to laymen, and the decrees against
investiture and homage were repeated at his Roman council
of 1099.   This was a further, and from the point of the lay
ruler a much more serious, loosening of the tie which linked
the bishop in subordination to the king.   Archbishop Anselm
of Canterbury was present at the Roman council, and so for
the first time an English archbishop was brought face to face
with the decree against lay investiture, coupled now with the
decree against homage.   It would have been difficult for any
archbishop to refuse obedience to a decree he had heard
pronounced by the Pope ; it was unthinkable for Anselm.
When he was recalled from exile by the new king, Henry I,
in 1100, he felt himself obliged to refuse consecration to those
bishops who had been invested by the king or done homage
to him.   So the investiture contest began in England, for
Henry I was obstinate in maintaining both practices.   The
accession of Paschal II did not improve matters.   He followed
unquestioningly in his predecessor's footsteps, and he was
very firm in his orders to Anselm, who had to bear the brunt
of the conflict.   At last Henry I yielded on the question of
investiture, and in 1107 a compromise was arranged, Paschal
allowing Anselm to consecrate bishops though they had done
homage to the king.   He meant it to be only a temporary
concession, but Henry treated it as permanent and acted
accordingly ; he retained full control of appointments and
insisted on homage preceding consecration, but he abandoned
the practice of investing with ring and staff.

When Henry V was reconciled with the Church in 1105,
Paschal expected from him immediate compliance with the
papal decrees which had been passed during the schism.
Henry, however, indignantly protested against papal interference with royal rights, and in this he was supported by
the ecclesiastical as well as the lay nobles of Germany.   So,
just as he was on the point of settlement with England, the
Pope entered into a conflict over lay investiture with
Germany.   In 1107 Paschal was in the friendly country of
France, and much bolder accordingly ; he put under the
ban the leaders of the German Church who had disobeyed
his summons to a council in the previous year.   In 1108,

when he was again among friends in South Italy, he reissued most stringently the decree against lay investiture. Distance lent him courage, but he was soon to lose that safeguard. For Henry, who was anxious to obtain imperial coronation, saw the necessity of placating the Pope, and reopened negotiations in a milder tone. Paschal, while still refusing to compromise on the question of investiture, consented to crown him. This gave Henry his opportunity. In 1110 he issued his summons to an expedition to Italy for the imperial coronation.

His march
to Rome for
the imperial
crown

Henry could count on obedience to the summons, for the obligation to accompany the king with a full contingent when he went to Rome to receive the imperial crown was acknowledged to be peculiarly binding. So it was at the head of a large army that he entered Italy in August 1110, and was able to restore to the German Crown authority over the Italian kingdom. He received a welcome even from countess Matilda of Tuscany, and owing to the constant friendship she maintained with him the Pope lost a valuable ally. The Normans in South Italy made no move, being fearful themselves of being attacked by the formidable imperial army. So Paschal was left to his own resources. Henry was approaching, and had made it clear that he would not yield on the matter of investiture. The Pope suddenly brought forward a proposal which was at once a testimony to the sincere piety of his nature and to his inexperience of practical politics.

The proposal
of Paschal II

The crux of the whole matter was the lay control over the Church, and he had already attempted to cut the Gordian knot when in 1102 he had decreed that ecclesiastics were not to receive even their temporalities from lay hands. This was a position too extreme for him to maintain, but at any rate there was one point on which he could agree with the king ; for Henry repeatedly affirmed that though he invested with ring and staff it was only the temporalities of the see that he conferred. Paschal now proposed that the clergy should give up all the temporalities, including offices and jurisdictions as well as domains, which they held from the king, and that Henry should then renounce the ceremony of investiture, which would indeed be meaningless. " Let the clergy be content with tithes and offerings," said Paschal ; and again :

" the bishops must be exempt from secular cares." Reasonable and obvious as this solution may appear to modern
minds, it meant little less than a complete revolution at the
time, since it upset the whole social and political fabric. The
nobility saw in it the loss of their own influence over local
churches, and the closing of a career for many members of
their families. The ecclesiastics themselves were threatened
with the loss of position and wealth, and therefore (apart
from merely selfish considerations) of the means of protecting
themselves and doing their spiritual work amid the violence
of their lay neighbours. The king would have had to recon-
struct completely the bases of his political power. Yet he
was content to acquiesce, because he knew that it could not
be carried into effect. He threw on Paschal the onus of
enforcing it, and the unworldly Pope readily accepted the
responsibility.

The pact was made at Sutri on February 9, 1111, and on
the 12th it was to be promulgated in St. Peter's before the
imperial coronation. The stage was set, and Henry had
planned the dénouement. When the imperial renunciation
of investiture and the papal renunciation of temporalities
were read out, there ensued a violent clamour of protest,
perhaps spontaneous, possibly engineered ; the Pope and
cardinals were surrounded by armed men of Henry's bodyguard, ostensibly to protect them ; but it soon became
clear that they were captives, and they were hurried outside
the city and kept under guard until Paschal at last submitted
to the king's demands. On 13 April, again at St. Peter's,
Paschal conceded to the king the right of investiture, which
was in all cases to precede consecration, and then crowned
Henry as Emperor. The king had achieved his object ; and
as he was continually being harassed by the attacks of the
Romans, he was glad to return with all speed to Germany.

His triumph was short-lived. He had dealt in the same
violent and unscrupulous manner with his father, but then
he could plead that he was executing the will of the Church
upon an excommunicate ; now he had outraged the Church
in the person of its Head. Moreover, a settlement extorted
by force could only be maintained by force. It could not,
therefore, be permanent. And if he could intimidate Paschal,
so could others. There was no longer any peace for the un-

The scene in St. Peter's (Feb. 1111)

Paschal's surrender

happy Pope. He meant to keep his promise to Henry, just as he had meant to be firm against lay investiture, but when he was faced by zealous and determined reformers in Rome, in France, and elsewhere, he yielded; already in 1112 he revoked the privilege that had been extorted from him. Henry, though he had humiliated the Pope, had achieved nothing; the contest continued, but in a much more bitter form.

The situation in Germany

So far he had had Germany behind him, and his position there seemed to be secure. This gave him a confidence which proved to be unjustified. For, just as Henry IV had been tempted to challenge the Papacy when he had won a striking victory over revolt in Germany, so Henry V after demonstrating his mastery over the Pope felt that he could throw off the mask in Germany. In neither case was the initial victory as decisive as it first appeared to be, so that instead of dealing with each adversary in turn both kings found themselves faced with the double task. The task was too much for them, but their experiences were very different. Henry V did not rise so high, nor sink so low, as Henry IV. He had not all the old resources of monarchy. He made what use he could of the royal domains and the *ministeriales*, but he could no longer depend on the bishops, especially the greatest among them. And though he tried to win the favour of the Rhine towns by grants of charters, the loyalty which had been so strikingly evinced in their support of his father against himself was never transferred to him. On the other hand, his quarrel with the Papacy was not so serious and he had not to face an antagonist like Gregory VII; while the German nobility never united in revolt against him as it had against Henry IV in 1073 and 1076.

In fact, Germany was beginning to lose something of its political cohesion. In Bavaria, Suabia, and Saxony the old ducal authority was being revived, and the duchies were tending to become autonomous under their dukes. Almost

Bavaria

throughout the reign Bavaria held aloof, its duke maintaining a neutral attitude towards the political conflicts elsewhere; he was not unfriendly to the king, but he was disinterested

Suabia

in the affairs of the kingdom. Suabia was more intimately connected with the Crown, owing to the marriage of Henry V's sister Agnes with duke Frederick. But Frederick I had

died in 1105, and his heir Frederick II was at first too young
to be of much help, and later was engrossed in the task of
building castles and otherwise establishing his authority over
the lesser nobility ; [1] apart from the domains of the powerful house of Zähringen, he succeeded in his object, and
the centralised duchy of Suabia was the core from which
the future greatness of the Hohenstaufen derived.   For the
widowed duchess Agnes Henry speedily arranged a marriage
in 1106 with margrave Liutpold of Austria, and thus obtained
an ally on the eastern frontier of Bavaria, and a contact with
the duke of Bohemia who had always been faithful to his
father ; Bohemia remained loyal to him too, but, like Henry
IV, he had no authority in Poland or Hungary.

The chief problem, as usual, was Saxony, and especially Saxony
East Saxony, where local autonomy was traditional.   If
Henry's idea of kingship was to prevail, he must be assured
of large resources of his own, and the royal domain in East
Saxony was therefore all-important to him.   If not a dependent, at least a friendly, Saxony was essential.   Great changes
had been taking place in the personnel in East Saxony.   In
Henry IV's day, the Billung dukes and the counts of Nordheim and Brunswick, adjacent to the royal domain, had
been his most dangerous antagonists.   The two counts had
united with Anno of Cologne in abducting him from his
mother ; Otto of Nordheim and Magnus Billung had concerted the first Saxon revolt ; Egbert II of Brunswick, who
was also margrave of Meissen, had stood out when the rest
of Saxony made peace.   Now these three houses were all
extinct.   The first to fail had been Brunswick, on Egbert II's
death in 1090 ; his sister Gertrude's marriage with Henry
of Nordheim united the domains of the two houses.   But
Henry on his death in 1101 also left no male heir, and his
heiress Richenza was married to the petty count of Supplinburg, Lothar.   Finally, in 1106, just as Henry V began his
reign, duke Magnus died, and he too left no male heir.   His
domain west of the Elbe passed to his daughter Wulfhild,
who married Henry the Black, heir to the duchy of Bavaria
since his brother Welf was childless ; that east of the Elbe

[1] He is, however, often found in Henry's company, and his brother Conrad, afterwards king Conrad III, was given administrative control of Eastern
Franconia with the title of duke.

to his other daughter Eilica, whose marriage with Otto of Ballenstedt raised in importance a house soon to rival that of her sister. The Billung line, whose hereditary right to the duchy had been unchallenged, came to an end and the duchy was vacant; so at last the king of Germany had the power of appointing the duke of Saxony. Henry chose Lothar of Supplinburg, hoping perhaps to ensure the loyalty of one whose territories bordered so closely on the royal domain. But Lothar was determined to admit no royal interference with Saxon autonomy, and to make himself in fact the master of the duchy, which Magnus Billung had been in name only. Thanks to the dowry of his wife he was provided with the resources to make this possible.

The political situation, then, that gradually developed during the reign of Henry V, was almost a reaction to the days of the tribal duchies. There were now three great duchies in which the dukes were obtaining independent control; they passed on their office by hereditary right to their sons; and only from one of them could the king expect loyal co-operation.[1] Nevertheless, in 1111, when Henry returned victoriously from Italy with the additional prestige of the imperial title, he entered without misgiving on his other task,

Archbishop Adalbert

to make the kingship in Germany a reality. Almost immediately he was faced with opposition from an unexpected quarter. His right-hand man hitherto had been his chancellor Adalbert, whom he had nominated to the vacant archbishopric of Mayence before departing for Italy, but had kept him by his side during the expedition and only invested him with the temporalities after his return. The appointment of Adalbert seemed to ensure to the king the support of the leading ecclesiastic in Germany, but the event, as in the similar case of Henry II and Becket, proved exactly the opposite. Adalbert revealed an intense personal ambition, striving after lordship and dominion, not concerned with the ecclesiastical side of his office like Becket. Disputes between king and archbishop began almost at once over certain temporalities of the see which Henry had enjoyed during the vacancy. The rift was never healed; Adalbert proved to

---

It is noticeable that of the three only Frederick of Suabia came in person on the Italian expedition. Duke Henry of Carinthia was also there, but his duchy was relatively unimportant.

be the most dangerous of all Henry's enemies, irreconcilable, constantly intriguing in papal or Saxon circles to arouse ill-feeling against the king.

Meanwhile, Henry's exercise of his rights as sovereign had roused disaffection in two quarters, in Lorraine and in Saxony. Siegfried, count-palatine of the Rhine, united with the Saxon nobles in a rising against the king. Adalbert, on his way to Saxony to join them, was taken prisoner, and the rebels were decisively defeated in 1113 near Quedlinburg. Siegfried died of wounds, and his important office was conferred on count Godfrey of Calw; the other leaders made their submission, Adalbert alone refusing and remaining a prisoner. In January 1114, Henry, now at the height of his power, married Matilda, the daughter of Henry I of England, and the occasion was made more notable by the appearance of duke Lothar to be reconciled with the king. *Beginnings of revolt*

Like his father, Henry was rendered over-confident by the ease of his first success, and now by his arbitrary actions he went beyond the normal exercise of monarchical functions. In the Rhineland his imprisonment of Adalbert without the judgment of a diet gave offence to lay as well as to ecclesiastical prejudices, and he roused similar indignation in Saxony by imprisoning count Lewis of Thuringia, one of the leaders in the former rising, without bringing him to judgment by his peers. Starting at Cologne, revolt spread through Lorraine, and simultaneously broke out in Saxony under the determined leadership of duke Lothar; papal legates in Saxony, acting without the instructions of their master, gave their blessing to the movement by pronouncing excommunication on the Emperor. The rebels on this occasion had both a better cause and a more careful organisation, and Henry was decisively defeated, first in 1114 at Andernach in Westphalia and then in 1115 at Welfesholze in East Saxony. He was forced to retire to Mayence, where he had the mortification of being compelled by the citizens to release their archbishop and to become reconciled with him. Adalbert, for his part, had no intention of keeping the peace. He made use of his freedom to go to Cologne, where he joined with archbishop Frederick in issuing sentence of excommunication against the king. *Second outbreak* *Henry's defeat in Saxony*

Temporarily, then, Henry had lost control over the

Henry's
second
expedition to
Italy (1116)
northern half of his kingdom. The desultory fighting which
continued for some time was confined to this region and did
not spread to the southern half. So he decided, as he could
make no progress in Germany for the present, to leave the
direction of affairs in the capable hands of his nephew the
duke of Suabia, and to go himself in 1116 to Italy where a
new situation had arisen calling for his personal attention.
The immediate cause was the death of countess Matilda of
Tuscany in 1115. Though she had put her allodial domains
under papal overlordship, she now bequeathed them to her
" cousin " Henry V, thereby adding a new cause of discord
to the subsequent relations of Papacy and Empire. Henry
came to enter into possession of them, as well as of the fiefs
she held from the Empire, without heed to the rights of the
Pope as overlord. The increase of personal domain was a
valuable addition to his resources, and he took the occasion
to strengthen his position by numerous grants of charters
to cities, and so helped ultimately the cause of communal
independence.

Rome was his next objective ; he wished to repeat his
imperial coronation now that he had a wife to receive the
title of Empress, and he probably intended to get a clear
understanding on the question of investiture. So far there
had been no open breach ; the Emperor had simply ignored
Paschal's retractation of his concession, and the Pope had not
Flight and
death of
Pope Paschal
II
himself taken any action against the Emperor. But Paschal
could not endure to face Henry again, and on the news of
his coming he fled for refuge to the Normans in South Italy.
In his absence the archbishop of Braga took upon himself to
crown Henry and Matilda at Easter 1117, and for his presumption was excommunicated by the Pope. Henry stayed
in Rome till the end of the year ; in spite of the presence of
the Germans there was no disturbance, and the prefect of the
city governed in Henry's name. When he left, in January
1118, Paschal ventured to return, but he died before the
month was out. It must have been for him a merciful
release from his misery ; for the last seven out of the eighteen
years of his reign he had been practically a cypher, at the
mercy of men of sterner mould, and more than once he had
been obliged to act against his conscience.

His successor, John of Gaeta, had made a name for himself by his successful working of the papal chancery under his two predecessors, but as Pope Gelasius II he had an undistinguished reign of one year only. Yet his Papacy was fateful in that it saw a definite schism between Pope and Emperor break out once more. Henry came to Rome in March and again made use of the archbishop of Braga, this time to set him up as a rival Pope under the title of Gregory VIII. Gelasius in reply excommunicated both Emperor and anti-Pope, but he could do nothing to make the sentence effective. He took refuge first with the Normans, and then journeying by sea to Pisa made his way to the safer haven of France. He died in the abbey of Cluny in January 1119.

So far Henry, in his dealings with the Papacy, had had matters very much his own way, but he was now to meet his match. Immediately after Gelasius's death, the cardinals who had accompanied him to France elected Guy, archbishop of Vienne, as Pope Calixtus II. The new Pope, who was of exalted birth (he could speak of the Emperor as his kinsman), had already given proofs of his ecclesiastical statesmanship and proud bearing; and he had played a leading part in forcing Paschal II to retract his concession of investiture. He was anxious, indeed, for peace, but could not be intimidated by threats or force. At first the prospect of a settlement seemed hopeful; for in the negotiations that took place at Mouzon in October Henry promised to renounce " the investiture of churches," and Calixtus, who was holding a papal council at Rheims, set off for a personal meeting with the king. The papal party were nervous, expecting that Henry was meditating a coup similar to that of 1111; Henry tried to evade their precise formulas (designed to ensure that investiture with the temporalities was included in Henry's renunciation), and kept on postponing his final answer. In this atmosphere of mutual distrust the negotiations broke down. Calixtus returned to Rheims, where he pronounced a decree against investiture both of churches and of church property, and solemnly renewed the excommunication of Henry and the anti-Pope. In 1120 he made his way to Italy and to Rome, where he met with no opposition, and the next year took prisoner the anti-Pope, whom Henry had virtually discarded.

Matters seemed to have reached a deadlock. Neither

side took any active steps against the other, but there
appeared to be no possibility of settlement. Henry, when
he returned to Germany in 1118, had found the bishops for
the most part arrayed against him, headed of course by
Adalbert, whose prestige had been increased by his appointment as papal legate. The lay nobles, on the other hand,
showed no disposition to espouse the papal cause. Probably Henry had learned wisdom from experience and refrained
from offending their susceptibilities. At any rate, he was
able to recover his position in Lorraine, and even in 1120 to
visit his Saxon domain at Goslar ; moreover, duke Lothar
and other Saxon nobles appeared at his court. Adalbert was
obstinate in trying to stir up strife, but public opinion was
against him and in favour of peace. At last, in 1121, the
leading nobles [1] of Germany intervened and summoned a
diet at Würzburg to bring about an end of civil war and to
make peace between Emperor and Pope.

Probably this was the only way that a settlement could
have been arrived at, but that Henry was willing to consent
to the nobles taking the initiative was a sign of his own
failure. It was agreed at Würzburg that the *status quo*
should be maintained, so that existing rights and possessions
were respected and the bishops who had opposed the king
were left in lawful occupation of their sees. The nobles
further engaged themselves to effect a reconciliation with the
Papacy. In this way the suspicion of the papal party was
overcome, since the nobles were sureties for the good faith
of the king ; while Henry could rely on them not to sacrifice
the interests of the kingdom, as they had all along shown
their opposition to papal interference. The chief difficulties
in the way of a settlement were thus removed. The Pope,
for his part, sent three cardinals as his plenipotentiaries, at
their head Lambert, cardinal bishop of Ostia, who as Honorius
II was to succeed Calixtus on the papal throne. On 23 September 1122 a settlement was reached in the Concordat of
Worms, and the Emperor was received back into communion
with the Church.

---

[1] The duke of Saxony does not seem to have participated, but Henry
the Black, who became duke of Bavaria in 1120, now associated himself
with the work of making peace, and took a leading part, with the duke of
Suabia, in the ensuing negotiations.

The terms of the Concordat were by no means unfavour- able for the Emperor, and were not unlike those of Paschal's concordat with Henry I of England. The king renounced investiture with ring and staff, promised to allow canonical elections and free consecrations, and guaranteed restitution of papal territory and the security of the possessions of ecclesiastics. In return, elections of German bishops and abbots were to be made in the presence of the king, who was to exert his authority in the case of disputed elections; he was authorised to confer the temporalities by a touch of the sceptre, and the bishop or abbot elect had to do homage to him before consecration. In other words, the king gave up "investiture of churches," as he had promised at Mouzon, but continued to invest with the temporalities and to keep control over appointments. It was somewhat different in the rest of the Empire—in the Italian and Burgundian kingdoms, in which the German negotiators were much less interested. There free canonical election, followed immediately by consecration, was prescribed, and investiture with the sceptre and the performance of homage came later. In these two kingdoms, therefore, the control of appointments was not so easy, nor in the changed conditions in Italy (especially the decline of episcopal authority and the rise of communal government) was it anything like so important as in Germany.

This treaty of peace was not embodied in a single document but in two charters, imperial and papal, so that each side retained only the concessions made by the other. But there was a notable difference between them. The imperial charter [1] was a carefully-worded document, embodying a permanent grant to the Pope and his successors for ever, witnessed by some of the greatest magnates, lay and ecclesiastical, of Germany. The papal, on the other hand, was only in the form of an ordinary papal rescript, addressed to Henry and containing no mention of his successors; it was very different from the style of a Solemn Bull or Great Privilege employed for grants in perpetuity. Possibly this was intentional on the part of the papal legates; at any rate

---

[1] The original of this " Golden Bull " (i.e. one in which the imperial seal was cased in a gilded capsule) is still in the papal archives. The original of the papal document is not in existence.

it was not long before the Papacy was asserting that the concession held good for Henry's lifetime only. There was also considerable ambiguity in the phrasing of the clause relating to elections in the king's presence and his share in disputed elections, over which friction was later to arise. The Concordat did not, therefore, prove to be a final settlement of the questions in dispute.

The First
Lateran
Council
(1123)

It certainly seemed to be so at the time, and both parties to it adhered loyally to its conditions. Adalbert was alone in trying to stir up ill-feeling, but his letters to the Pope charging the Emperor with breaking the terms were ignored by Calixtus. It was confirmed in November at a diet at Bamberg by the leading princes (apart from Lothar) who had not been present at Worms, and was accepted as an imperial constitution ; in Germany its permanence was not questioned. Calixtus, too, solemnly confirmed it at the Council he held in the Lateran basilica at Rome in March 1123. This Council has a special place in Church history. There had been certain Councils in the early history of the Church which had been regarded as specially important, and their decrees had always been included in canon law. They were known as " ecumenical " or " universal " Councils ; they had all been held in the Eastern half of the Church, in the days when Rome was still subject to the Eastern Emperor. At a later date the Western Church, reviewing the papal councils held since the schism with the Eastern Church in 1054, ranked some of these as " ecumenical." The first to be given this distinction was the Council of Calixtus in 1123, which came to be known as the First Lateran Council. It ended the schism in the Church between Pope and Emperor, it was attended by representatives of the leading kingdoms in Western Christendom, which ensured the wide distribution of its decrees on various matters of Church order and government; it was, therefore, in a real sense " universal," and it was also a testimony to the reality of the papal headship of the Church.

Last years
of Henry V

After this there is little to record, for Calixtus died in December 1124 and Henry in the following May. At any rate, the peace which they had made endured for more than thirty years. At peace with the Pope, Henry was free to devote his whole time to his German kingdom. But he came no nearer to achieving his ambition. He had the mortification of another rebuff from Lothar of Saxony in 1123, when he tried to exercise the normal function of the monarch by filling up two vacant margravates on the eastern frontiers of Saxony. Lothar made his own appointments [1] and expelled Henry's nominees, and when summoned before a diet in 1124 he disdained to appear.   Henry did not attempt to punish this disobedience, as he was more concerned with recovering his ground in Lorraine.   Here he had some success, but he made the mistake of trying, at the instigation of his father-in-law Henry I of England, to add to it by conquest from France. This provoked a remarkable rally of the French nobles to the side of their king against a German invasion, and Henry had to beat a hasty retreat.   Shortly after this last failure he died, on May 23, 1125.   A son of his would doubtless have succeeded him, but his marriage with Matilda was childless. On his death-bed he tried to obtain the succession for his nephew, duke Frederick of Suabia, but Adalbert was still alive, and his rancour was unabated ;   as archbishop of Mayence he naturally played a leading part in the new election, and he was able to prevent Henry's wishes from being carried into effect.   With Henry's death the Salian house, which had reigned for exactly a century, came to an end.

SUGGESTIONS FOR READING ON CHAPTER XII

See books suggested in Chapter IX, above.

---

[1] They were both important for the future.   Conrad of Wettin, a grandson through his mother of Otto of Nordheim, became margrave of Meissen ; the house of Wettin now begins to take a leading position.   Albert the Bear, son of Otto of Ballenstedt who had married one of Magnus Billung's daughters, became margrave of the East Mark.

CHAPTER XIII

THE PERIOD OF PEACE BETWEEN EMPIRE AND PAPACY, 1125–1156

The period of peace

THE peace that was made at Worms in 1122 lasted for thirty-five years. It was a remarkable interlude, during which the former situation was completely reversed and the old antagonism was replaced by a friendly alliance. Empire and Papacy were united by common interests, ecclesiastical and political, as they had been in the later years of Henry III. There was a difference, however, for in ecclesiastical matters the Pope was now the predominant partner, and it was for political ends that he needed imperial assistance. At peace with the Empire, the Papacy was no longer dependent on the aid of the Normans and forced to pay the price they demanded; it could therefore adopt a consistent policy of resistance to their advance. The Emperor was naturally hostile to the Normans, and so, instead of the alliance of Pope and Normans against the Emperor, Pope and Emperor were allied against the Normans. In spite of this, the period was the most brilliant in Norman history. It coincided exactly with the reign of Roger II, who not only united South Italy and Sicily under his rule but also forced from an unwilling Papacy the recognition of his title as king. Only a continued effort on the part of the Emperor could have prevented this, but the rulers of Germany were for the most part occupied with the civil strife in their kingdom, which resulted in the bitter rivalry of Welfs and Hohenstaufen. In North Italy, the newly-formed communes pursued their independent careers, hardly interfered with by their overlord. They may be treated apart, but the affairs of Empire, Papacy, and Norman kingdom were so closely connected that they need to be told, as far as possible, in one story.

In Germany, the election which followed the death of

Henry V was a notable one in the history of the kingdom.
There was again no son to succeed, as had been the case
when Otto III, and also when Henry II, died. On both
those occasions the electors had eventually chosen from the
royal family that member of it who seemed to have the best
hereditary right.   Had they followed those precedents, they
would in 1125 have elected Frederick of Suabia, the nephew
and the chosen heir of Henry V.   What makes this election
remarkable is that in preference to Frederick they chose a
man with no royal blood in his veins—duke Lothar of Saxony ;
and by emancipating themselves from the influence of the
hereditary principle they took a step forward in the heightening of their own power.   The German princes who had elected
Rudolf at Forchheim in 1077 had taken the same attitude,
but theirs had been the act of rebels and it was ultimately
unsuccessful.   Left to themselves, the lay nobles on this
occasion might not have departed from precedent.   The
impulse came from archbishop Adalbert of Mayence, who at
last had the opportunity of avenging himself on Henry V
and was determined to prevent the succession of his heir.
His office gave him the right of initiative at the election of
a king, and he was supported in his policy by Frederick,
archbishop of Cologne, and other leading bishops.   He fixed
his choice on his former ally, Lothar, a friend of the Church
and the only noble in Germany who could compete on equal
terms with the Hohenstaufen.   Skilfully he displayed Frederick to the nobles as the opponent of their electoral rights,
and so was able to obtain their ready assent to the election
of his candidate.

      The issue was finally clinched by the adhesion to Lothar
of the duke of Bavaria, Henry the Black.   Though Bavaria
had held aloof from the civil war, its duke had not been
unfriendly to the late king and had assisted in the making
of peace in 1121 ;   moreover his daughter Judith was the
wife of Frederick of Suabia.   There was, however, in Bavaria
a strong supporter of the policy of Adalbert, archbishop
Conrad of Salzburg, whose ecclesiastical authority extended
over the whole duchy ;   his zeal for Church reform had made
him hostile to Henry V and his heir.   Probably it was
ecclesiastical influence that worked on Henry the Black and
led him not only to accept Lothar as king but even to abandon

his neutrality and enter into active co-operation with him.
In his decision more than Bavaria was involved, for Henry
by his marriage with Wulfhild had acquired the allodial territory of the Billungs west of the Elbe, with its centre in the
town of Lüneburg. For his part, Lothar had his wife's
dowry of Nordheim and Brunswick and now the rich royal
domain adjacent to it. If Lothar could gain Henry's friendship, the whole of East Saxony would be knit together, as
well as the support of Bavaria assured. Another consideration entered in : Lothar had only one child, a daughter Gertrude, and the choice of a husband for her implied the choice
of an heir to his power and possessions, possibly to the crown
as well. The betrothal of Gertrude to Henry the Proud, son
and heir of Henry the Black, decided the future course of the
duke of Bavaria. With his son as Lothar's prospective heir,
he was bound by self-interest to oppose the heir of Henry V.
So he threw in his lot with Lothar, and the alliance resulted
in the bitter rivalry of the Welfs and Hohenstaufen.[1]

The support
of the
Church

King Lothar III, who had thus risen from the obscurity
of a petty countship to the throne of Germany, was a typical
member of the Saxon nobility, a good soldier, conservative
in his ideas, especially as duke, to maintain the aloofness and
independence of his duchy. He was a solid man, who could
be relied on to uphold the dignity of the German kingdom,
now that the independence of Saxony was not in question ;
he was also a scrupulous man of whom the Church need have
no fear. The ecclesiastical hierarchy had been largely responsible for his election ; the Pope (Honorius II) through his
legates had given it his blessing. As duke of Saxony, too,
he had been allied with the Pope against the king, and he
justified the Church's confidence by making no attempt to
claim for himself the rights at episcopal elections granted in
the Concordat of Worms to his predecessor. Henry V had
also been largely helped in his rise to the throne by the support
of the Church, but Lothar, unlike Henry, did not attempt to
rid himself of the obligations he thereby incurred. He was
therefore constantly assured of the support of the Church
both in his German and in his Italian kingdom.

---

[1] The Hohenstaufen used the name of their ancestral castle of Weiblingen
as their battle cry. So the two parties were known as Welf and Weiblingen
in Germany, which south of the Alps became Guelph and Ghibelline.

The only enemy he had to fear was the family of the Hohenstaufen. Frederick of Suabia accepted his defeat and acknowledged Lothar as king. He was not himself ambitious for the crown, as was his brother Conrad. He had established ducal authority in Suabia on a strong centralised basis, and was satisfied with adding to his territorial possessions the inheritance he had received from Henry V. Part of this, especially the town of Spires, was the ancestral Salian domain, but Henry had in his latter years by escheat, by purchase, and by exchange been building up, especially in the Rhine lands, a new domain which Frederick also claimed as his own. Lothar equally laid claim to it, for lands acquired by the exercise of royal powers or in exchange for royal domain were obviously royal and not personal possessions ; and a diet at Ratisbon in November 1125 decided emphatically in his favour. Frederick and Conrad refused to submit to this decision and to surrender the lands in question. They were accordingly placed under the ban of the kingdom in January 1126, and once more Germany was afflicted with civil war.

Frederick in Suabia and Conrad in eastern Franconia were a formidable pair, and for some time Lothar took no steps to bring them to justice. At the beginning of 1126 he was occupied with an expedition into Bohemia to uphold the royal authority by deposing the new duke Sobieslav in favour of his rival Otto of Moravia. The plan miscarried, for the German army suffered a severe defeat, Otto was killed in battle, and Lothar had to extricate himself by recognising Sobieslav's title to the duchy. The losses among the Saxon troops had been heavy, so that no serious undertaking could be attempted in that year against the Hohenstaufen. In 1127, however, Lothar was in a stronger position. Duke Henry the Black died, leaving to his elder son, Henry the Proud, his duchy and estates in Bavaria and also the Saxon territory which had come to him by marriage.[1] Lothar now fulfilled his promise to the father, and the marriage between Gertrude and Henry the Proud took place in May. With his son-in-law's help and with the further assistance of a Bohemian contingent, he was able to take the offensive

[1] The younger son, Welf (VI), received the Suabian territories of the Welf house together with a small portion in Bavaria.

against the Hohenstaufen. His first objective was the town of Nuremberg, the most easterly of their possessions and an easy rendezvous for the various contingents. The town withstood a siege of two months, during which the Bohemians so exasperated the Bavarians by their widespread devastations that they had to be sent home. Then Conrad arrived with a relieving force and Lothar had to raise the siege and, constantly pursued by the enemy, to take refuge in Würzburg.

Conrad of Hohenstaufen's adventure in Italy

The Hohenstaufen in their triumph now conceived the idea of supplanting the defeated king. Frederick did not covet the honour, and it was Conrad who was proclaimed king by his supporters in December 1127. This was an impolitic move, for it was without a shadow of legality and it brought him no additional support; while he fell under the ban of the Church, which had every reason for wishing to maintain Lothar on the throne. Nor was Conrad content with one crown. Early in 1128 he crossed the Alps and found a ready ally in Milan, then at feud with the Pope; [1] its archbishop, Anselm, crowned him with the iron crown of Italy. To make his kingship a reality he needed an extensive domain, and he immediately laid claim, as the heir of Henry V, to the territories of countess Matilda. Over this the Pope claimed, and was exercising, overlordship. Conrad therefore came into conflict with the Pope in Italy on an issue similar to that which had brought him and his brother into conflict with Lothar in Germany. He was entirely unsuccessful in this project, and when in 1130 Milan and the Pope came to terms his cause was obviously lost and he returned to Germany. His Italian adventure had been fatal, for left to himself Frederick had been unable to resist the combined attack of Lothar and his son-in-law. Spires was taken and finally Nuremberg, and the Hohenstaufen fortunes were at a low ebb. That Lothar did not press home his advantage and force their submission was due to his preoccupation elsewhere, particularly with disturbances in Saxony. Moreover, he was now anxious to go himself to Italy, to which he was drawn both by the prospect of the imperial crown and by the urgent

---

[1] Milan claimed that its archbishop by traditional right should have his pallium sent him by the Pope. This Honorius II refused to do, insisting that like other archbishops he must come to Rome to receive it. On this occasion the whole city was united on the side of the archbishop in defending the ecclesiastical rights of Milan against the Pope.

appeals of the new Pope, Innocent II.   At any rate, Henry
the Proud was fully able to keep the Hohenstaufen in check
while he himself embarked on his Italian expedition in 1132.

In South Italy, meanwhile, a great change had taken *Roger II*
place.   The two Norman States of Apulia-Calabria and Sicily *of Sicily*
had been united into one under the strong hand of Roger II,
the son of Count Roger I the conqueror of Sicily.   An elder
brother, Simon, had succeeded his father as count in 1101
but had only survived for two years.   Roger II became count
in 1103 at the age of eight, his mother Adelaide having charge
of the government during his minority.   Their usual residence
was Messina, adjacent to the mainland, but when Roger came
of age in 1112 the ceremony took place at Palermo which
henceforward became his capital.   The next year his mother
sailed to Jerusalem to become the wife of king Baldwin I,
and Roger was left his own master.   At Palermo he was in
an environment rather Moorish and Greek than Norman and
Latin, and the culture and learning of the former appealed
to his imaginative curiosity just as their ways of government
and acquiescence in despotic rule appealed to his love of order
and sense of power.   The only disturbances came from his
Norman feudatories, but they were not formidable and could
easily be held in check ; he and his mother tended to rely on
Greeks as much as on Normans in government.   These early
years must have been mainly peaceful, for there are few
incidents for the chroniclers to record.   But his restless ambition is already manifest : first of all to be the successor to his
stepfather in Jerusalem, which was disappointed in 1117
when Baldwin repudiated Adelaide ; then to annex the
Barbary coast of North Africa, where, however, he suffered
defeat in 1123 ; and finally, and at last successfully, to be
master of South Italy.

The other Norman principality, the duchy of Apulia and *The Norman*
Calabria, was in very different shape.   Roger Borsa had *duchy of*
proved incapable of maintaining order, and his son William *Apulia*
(1111–27) was equally feeble.   The royal towns, such as
Salerno and Amalfi, established a communal independence.
The barons behaved much as the barons on the Capetian
domain whom at this time Louis VI was at last reducing to
order : they disregarded their suzerain, fought with one

another, and plundered the peaceful wayfarer. To protect himself from their direct insults, William from time to time appealed for help to Roger II, as his father had appealed to Roger I. Roger came to his aid, and in return William ceded his last rights in Sicily and more territory in Calabria. Bit by bit Roger was advancing, ready for the final spring when the childless William should die. The next of kin was Bohemond II of Antioch, son of Borsa's brother Bohemond and first cousin to William; but by 1126 he was too far away to be able to assert his rights.

Roger II acquires the duchy

In 1127 duke William died, and Roger immediately claimed the duchy. He acted with great promptitude, gained possession of Salerno by granting privileges to its citizens, and was there proclaimed as duke. His sudden stroke had taken everyone by surprise, but it was so generally unwelcome that resistance was not slow in appearing. Neither towns nor barons wanted a ruler who would be their master; to the Papacy, whose policy it had always been to encourage divisions among the Normans, the union of South Italy and Sicily was especially repugnant. Honorius II as overlord refused his consent to Roger's acquisition of the duchy and set to work to form a coalition against him. This was joined by most of the leading barons, among whom Robert the new prince of Capua had pride of place, though the most dangerous of Roger's enemies, in force of character and military genius, was Rainulf count of Alife, head of the line descended from the first Norman to be granted a fief in South Italy, Rainulf of Aversa. The Pope himself took part in the campaign which opened early in 1128. It was an ill-organised expedition, and when at last in July the allies came face to face with the army of Roger, they were in little mood for fighting and the feudal levies began to disband. The Pope, fearing the fate of Leo IX, thought it prudent to make terms with Roger and invested him with the duchy of Apulia and Calabria. This settlement did not include the Pope's former confederates, many of whom still refused to recognise Roger; but by the summer of 1129 he had reduced them all singly to submission.

His strong government

Roger had won the first encounter with surprising ease, and he showed his determination to be master when in September 1129 at Melfi, where his new tenants-in-chief appeared to

do him homage, he forbade private warfare, decreed the
security of the highways, and reserved all criminal jurisdiction
for the ducal court. The towns which had received privileges
before his position was assured now lost those privileges and
had to admit ducal garrisons. Good order and strong central
government was, as in Sicily, the programme. It was the
insatiable ambition of Roger II, in this more like Robert
Guiscard than his own father, that had made the Pope so
reluctant to invest him with the duchy. Yet the Church
had everything to gain from the establishment of peace and
order in South Italy ; eminent Churchmen such as the abbot
of Cluny depicted Roger's government of Sicily as a model
in this respect. And in time this advantage might have
reconciled the Pope to the situation. But time was not
given, for almost at once the Church was rent by a papal
schism, which tempted Roger to further aggrandisement and
led to the revival of civil war in South Italy, thus delaying
for some years the settlement of the duchy.

The schism arose out of the rivalry of two Roman families, The papal
the Frangipani and the Pierleoni, which owed their promin- schism of
ence to the support they had given to the reformed Papacy, 1130
and then became jealous each of the other's influence. When
Honorius II died in 1130, the cardinals were divided into two
camps and almost simultaneously there were two elections,
of Gregory Papareschi, favoured by the Frangipani, as Pope
Innocent II, and of Peter Pierleoni as Pope Anacletus II.
Both of them were cardinals and both were elected by cardinals. To this extent the Election Decree of Nicholas II
was complied with by both parties. Innocent had the advantage of priority of election (though only by three hours) and
the more weighty support, since all but one of the cardinal
bishops were on his side ; Anacletus, however, could claim
that the majority of the cardinals (27 to 16) voted for him.
The Election Decree had not contemplated a division among
the cardinals, and so there was no provision for dealing with
it. A schism of an unusual kind was therefore created, as
neither Pope would yield to the other. Both appealed to
Lothar, for his recognition would probably turn the scale ; but
he was not at present prepared to decide in favour of either.

At first it seemed that Anacletus would be successful.
He had Rome on his side. His rival had to leave the city

St. Bernard's championship of Innocent II

and take refuge first in Pisa and then beyond the Alps. But his exile turned to his ultimate advantage. For in France he met the famous abbot of Clairvaux, Bernard, and was able to convince him of the justice of his cause. The forceful personality of St. Bernard was already creating for him an authority in the Church far beyond that to which his rank entitled him, and any cause that he took up he pursued to the end. His championship won supporters for Innocent in every country and was the main cause of Innocent's ultimate success. He began by persuading the king of France to recognise Innocent; the king of England followed suit; finally, in 1131, assisted by Norbert, archbishop of Magdeburg, the founder of the Premonstratensian Order, he induced the king of Germany to give his recognition also. A meeting was arranged at Liége, where Lothar went so far as to hold the Pope's stirrup when he dismounted—a striking recognition of his subordination to the ecclesiastical authority—and promised to come in force to reinstate Innocent at Rome. On the other hand, he tried to recover the concessions granted to Henry V at Worms which he himself had renounced at his election. But the vehemence of St. Bernard would allow of no such bargain; he had to be content with doing his duty as a faithful son of the Church.

Anacletus II, supported by the Normans, confers title of king on Roger II

Meanwhile, Anacletus had also gained an important ally, though on very different terms. In September 1130 he met Roger II and in return for his assistance conferred on him the title of " king of Sicily and of the duchies of Apulia and Calabria "; on Christmas Day Roger was crowned king at Palermo. This was the height at which his ambition had been aiming, and the schism gave him his opportunity, for at last his assistance was necessary to the Pope at Rome. Innocent's fortunes were at a low ebb when the compact was made, and Roger might well believe that his support would be decisive for Anacletus. But the circumstances were altogether peculiar, and for once the Pope maintained by the king of Germany was to be victorious over the Pope to whom the Normans gave their support. Roger's title was as yet a barren one, and it gave great offence to his Italian vassals. Encouraged by the success of Innocent's cause north of the Alps, and especially by the prospect of Lothar's arrival in Italy, they broke out into revolt once more. The old confederation, headed by Robert of Capua and Rainulf of Alife, was re-formed, and a severe defeat was inflicted on Roger's army in 1132.   As Lothar was now on the point of starting, the hopes of the rebels ran high.

But Lothar disappointed their expectations. Since the Hohenstaufen were still at large, he could not bring from Germany the numerous troops that usually accompanied the king to his coronation as Emperor. He had to pick his way cautiously through a hostile Lombardy, for the communes, especially Milan, having tasted of independence resented the appearance among them of their German over-lord, and his army was not large enough to overawe them. As he approached Rome, which was strongly held by Anacletus, his difficulties increased.   Progress was very slow, and it was not until June 1133 that at last the imperial coronation took place in the Lateran church, St. Peter's being inaccessible. Though Emperor, he was still content, as at Liége, to take second place. He received the territory of countess Matilda as a fief from the Papacy, and on the same terms was allowed to hand it on to his son-in-law Henry the Proud. The general impression of the situation created by Lothar's acceptance of subordination was shown in a picture painted and hung in the Lateran : it portrayed Lothar kneeling before the Pope at his coronation, and an inscription in two hexameter lines described him as becoming " the Pope's man " before receiving the crown.   One concession he did get in return for his assistance, though it was only a portion of what had been conceded to Henry V in the Concordat of Worms : the German bishops and abbots were to receive the re-galia and to do homage to the king before their consecration.

Vis-à-vis the Emperor, the Pope had good reason for satisfaction.   But he had made no advance against his rival. Manifestly Lothar could do no more for the present.   His army too small, an expedition to South Italy in mid-summer would have been most imprudent, and he could not afford to be absent any longer from Germany until he had reached a final settlement with the Hohenstaufen.   He there-fore returned at once.   Innocent had to take refuge again in Pisa, and the Norman rebels were dispirited by their isolation.   Roger was able to gain the upper hand over them, and after Rainulf of Alife had come to terms in 1134 the

Lothar III crowned Emperor at Rome

revolt soon flickered out. For the second time Roger was master in South Italy.

The Hohen-
staufen
forced to
make peace

Back in Germany Lothar had little difficulty in over-coming the opposition. The year 1134 was spent in a piece-meal reduction of Suabia, and the Hohenstaufen brothers were forced to make their submission, Frederick in March 1135, Conrad the following September. They were restored to their ducal authority and their territorial possessions (the lands that had caused the dispute remained, of course, in Lothar's hands), and in return for this magnanimous treat-ment they had to promise to accompany the Emperor on the expedition he had planned for the following year against Anacletus and Roger. This could now be on a large scale, with a full quota from every territorial prince. Germany was at peace, the prestige of the king had risen high, and the frontiers were secure from aggression. In this same year, 1135, Lothar received the recognition of his overlordship from the new king of Denmark, Eric. His authority was similarly recognised beyond his eastern borders, where Poland and Bohemia were taking part, on opposite sides, in the disputed succession to the Hungarian throne. Lothar brought them to terms, and in 1135 the duke of Poland as well as the duke of Bohemia acknowledged himself as the vassal of the king of Germany.

Lothar again
in Italy
(1136)

The stage was now set for a trial of strength at Rome and in Italy. Innocent had not been idle during his enforced exile. He had persuaded Genoa and Pisa to lay aside their rivalry and make common cause against the Norman king, who was already becoming a formidable competitor for the trade of the Eastern Mediterranean. Milan had been won over (it was from Anacletus that its archbishop had received the pallium) by the fiery eloquence of St. Bernard. And in South Italy, the barons, excited by a false report of Roger's death, had once more broken into revolt. So when he crossed the Alps in August 1136 Lothar found the tide running strongly in his favour. As he was at the head of an imposing army, Lombardy offered no resistance to his passage ; he made no attempt to impose his authority on the communes, however, for the south was his objective. Dividing his forces, he took himself the coast route from Ancona to Bari. The other army was led by Henry the Proud, accompanied by the Pope, through Tuscany and the Papal States; the papal territory was thus secured for Innocent, but they avoided Rome, as the reckoning with Anacletus could come later, and marched on to meet Lothar at Bari. In May 1137 Bari was captured, and the fall of Salerno shortly afterwards completed the discomfiture of Roger, who retired to Sicily to wait until the storm had passed. In his place the duchy of Apulia was conferred on Rainulf of Alife, whose prowess had shown him to be the one man capable of holding it against the attacks of Roger. So far all had gone according to plan, but at this point a rift appeared. The Pope took it as a matter of course that he should invest Rainulf with the duchy. But the tradition of imperial overlordship had not been forgotten, nor had the papal claim ever been recognised by the rulers of the Empire; Lothar was stubborn on this point, and for the first time he refused to play second fiddle. It was a long time before the dispute could be settled; at last a compromise was arrived at, and Pope and Emperor jointly performed the ceremony of investiture. There were other causes of friction. In fact, the old harmony was broken; the Emperor and his German vassals were anxious to return, the Pope no longer wished to retain them. In September the march homeward began. On the way Lothar was taken seriously ill; a dying man, he was carried over the passes, and only just reached German soil before he died, in December 1137.

Lothar's second Italian expedition had, at any rate, added greatly to his prestige, and he died at the height of his fame. None of his predecessors had been able to play so masterful a part in South Italy. But the effects were transitory and barely survived his departure, while the fact that in Lombardy he had left the communes to themselves gave them a stronger sense of their independence and made it harder for his successors to assert their sovereignty. There was, however, one permanent advantage resulting from his expedition. It virtually brought the schism to an end. Isolated by the expulsion of Roger from South Italy, Anacletus was no longer able to maintain himself at Rome, and the Frangipani led back Innocent in triumph. When Anacletus died in January 1138, the few cardinals still adhering to him elected a successor (Victor IV); but, though he was assured of the support

Defeat of Roger II

Death of Lothar III

End of the papal schism

of Roger, he soon recognised that his cause was hopeless and abdicated after a few months. Innocent took the occasion to issue a general summons to a Council which was held in the Lateran in April 1139 ; it was attended by a large number of bishops from various countries and was therefore representative of Western Christianity, and later it was ranked as " ecumenical " and known as the Second Lateran Council. As the First Lateran had celebrated in 1123 the healing of the schism between Pope and Emperor, so the Second celebrated the end of the papal schism ; with his own hands Innocent stripped the bishops consecrated by his rival of their episcopal emblems.

The Second Lateran Council (1139)

But there his triumph ended, for his project of a final settlement with Roger, whom he had solemnly excommunicated at the Lateran Council, ended in disaster. Roger, after Lothar's departure, had taken the offensive again in South Italy, with little success at first ; in 1137 he suffered a severe defeat at the hands of Rainulf. But in 1139, only three weeks after the Lateran Council, Rainulf died and there was no one to replace him. In spite of this the Pope persisted, and took the field himself at the head of an army as ill-organised as that of Leo IX. He suffered the same fate as Leo. Defeated in battle, he was taken prisoner, and though his conqueror fell at his feet to ask his pardon, the Pope found that to gain his liberty he had to grant what Roger demanded. Accordingly he invested him with the kingdom of Sicily and Apulia, though to save the appearance of confirming what the anti-Pope had done he represented his action in a papal bull as a confirmation of the previous grant of Honorius II ; moreover, he invested Roger's sons, Roger and Alfonso, with the duchy of Apulia and the principality of Capua. In return the king and his sons did homage to the Pope and promised the payment of the regular annual tribute. So Roger had received his title from the legitimate Pope, and his kingship was now assured ; the last embers of revolt he left to his sons to extinguish.

Innocent II forced to recognise Roger as king

In 1140 he held a great Court at Ariano, where he promulgated a series of laws [1] confirming and amplifying the

The kingdom of Sicily

---

[1] Another edict promulgated at the same time created a new coinage for all his dominions, superseding all the local coins. The new coin was named " ducat " from the ducatus (duchy) of Apulia.

enactments at Melfi in 1129.   These new laws, based, often verbatim, on the Code of Justinian, and added to by later decrees, created a state on a Roman and autocratic model. There were feudal enactments among them, and the laws and customs of the various races under his sway were expressly retained ; but royal decree over-rode them all, and it was sacrilege to dispute the king's judgment.   The whole administration was a mosaic of Norman, Greek, and Arab titles and customs.   As in other European kingdoms, the Curia Regis was the supreme court of appeal, but the central government was in the hands of the great officers of State, who formed a privy council.   First of all came the Emir of emirs (*Ammiratus Ammiratorum*), supreme in justice after the king and in charge of the all-important department of naval affairs ; [1] a man such as George of Antioch when holding this office was the king's chief minister.   The Norman " Chancellor " took second place, and was largely entrusted with military duties.   The local officials present a medley of names—baillis, catapans, cadis, etc.—which show the preservation of the institutions of the different races ; in control of them all were the royal justiciars, whose duties were similar to those of itinerant justices in England.   At his court at Palermo there was the same mixture—Arab poets and geographers (such as Idrisi, who made a famous map of the world), Greek architects and theologians, Latin historians. In various forms of learning, especially scientific, Roger was keenly interested, and far in advance of his age.   In the patronage he gave to the arts and to learning he has been likened to the Italian despots of the Renaissance.   He was like them in his abandonment of medieval ideas, but he was unlike them too ; in his dress and in his mode of life at Palermo he followed Eastern rather than Western models. Towards despotism he was certainly inclining.   Feudal ideas stood in the way, but he was getting the measure of the barons.   The Church was also an obstacle, as it introduced a divided authority, but he was careful to keep control over his bishops, especially over their elections, in spite of constant opposition from the Pope.   Yet these two forces prevented him from being absolutely master.   The medieval still persisted in a State which was otherwise modern in character.

[1] Hence the modern title " Admiral."

It was his grandson, Frederick II, who resembled him in so many respects, that fulfilled the purpose of Roger II.

The election of Conrad III

It seems like going back into another age when we turn from the ordered and cultured life of the Sicilian kingdom to medieval Germany, once again distracted by civil war. The election that followed the death of Lothar was as significant as the one that had raised him to the throne. Once more the king had no son to succeed him but had designated his heir; once more the electors rejected the heir and led by a revengeful archbishop gave the crown to his chief rival; and though they chose on this occasion a man of royal blood, the election marked a further stage towards their ultimate control. Henry the Proud, the rejected heir, had recently been invested by Lothar with his own duchy of Saxony. Having already the allodial possessions that had come to him from his mother, with those that he now received as Lothar's heir, he occupied a territorial position in East Saxony unequalled since the days of the Liudolfing house. Henceforward Saxony is the centre of Welf power. And besides this he held the duchy of Bavaria and, in fief from the Pope, the lands of countess Matilda; his brother Welf had the family estates in Suabia and North Italy. Had the title of king been added, Henry would have easily mastered the Hohenstaufen, and he would have ruled Germany with a strong hand. By choosing his weaker rival, the electors perpetuated the dangerous feud of Welf and Hohenstaufen.

The German nobles were probably afraid of the masterful nature of Henry and disinclined to have him as their king. But again it was the Church that decided the election. Henry's pride had offended those who had been the stoutest champions of Lothar. The Pope in particular regarded him with suspicion (there had been considerable friction between them during the campaign in South Italy), and sent a legate to work for Conrad, with whom he had become reconciled. As there was no archbishop of Mayence and the archbishop of Cologne had barely been elected, the initiative in Germany lay with the third in rank of the ecclesiastical princes, the archbishop of Trèves, Albero. He had a long-standing grievance against Lothar and Henry, and like Adalbert of Mayence in 1125 had now the opportunity for revenge. At a hastily-summoned meeting at Coblenz in March 1138, at which neither Saxons nor Bavarians were present, he persuaded the assembled nobles to elect Conrad of Hohenstaufen, who was crowned by the papal legate at Aix-la-Chapelle a few days later. Conrad was personally popular. Martial and adventurous until the burden of kingship robbed him of his zest, he appealed to the German chivalry, and they came in large numbers to Bamberg to do him homage.

War with Henry the Proud was almost inevitable, and Conrad, after an unsuccessful interview which gave him the excuse for putting Henry under the ban, struck a double blow by declaring him dispossessed of both his duchies. Saxony he conferred on Henry's cousin Albert the Bear,[1] Bavaria on his own half-brother, margrave Leopold of Austria. Yet within a year Henry had recovered Saxony; a powerful royal army was collected to expel him, but the leaders were afraid of the issue and disbanded their troops after fruitless negotiations; and Henry was about to march to the recovery of Bavaria in 1139 when he suddenly died. His son and heir, Henry the Lion, was only ten years old, but his grandmother Richenza so ably conducted his cause that the Saxon princes decided to support him and expelled Albert, who had returned expecting to recover the duchy, even from the North Mark.

War with Henry the Proud of Saxony and Bavaria

Henry the Lion

In Bavaria, however, Conrad's nominee was successful. The Welf cause was here championed by the brother of Henry the Proud, Welf VI, who defeated Leopold in 1140. Conrad came to the rescue and invaded Welf's Suabian estates, laying siege to the castle of Weinsberg.[2] Welf gave battle outside the walls and was completely defeated; the fortress fell, and the rebellion in the south came to a speedy end. The struggle with Saxony went on rather perfunctorily for another year, but the death of Richenza in 1141 removed the most intransigent of Conrad's enemies, and negotiations conducted by archbishop Marculf of Mayence led to a settlement in May 1142. Henry the Lion was recog-

The Welfs lose Bavaria but retain Saxony

---

[1] Cf. above, p. 263, n. 1. Albert, a man of restless ambition, had been extending his possessions, largely at the expense of the heathen Slavs. His unruliness had caused Lothar to deprive him of the East Mark in 1131, but his subsequent loyalty was rewarded by the grant of the North Mark in 1134.

[2] A later tradition makes this the first occasion on which the battle-cries of " Welf " and " Weibling " were used.

nised as duke of Saxony, and Albert the Bear renounced his title and was restored to the North Mark. Leopold had died the previous October, and the duchy of Bavaria was given to his brother Henry Jasomirgott,[1] who married Gertrude, the mother of Henry the Lion. It was a compromise rather than a final settlement. Welf refused to agree to it and made one more unsuccessful attempt to get possession of Bavaria. It remained to be seen what Henry the Lion would say, when he came of age, to the loss of this duchy, to which his mother (who died in 1143) had consented in his name. It was an uneasy peace, but it lasted for some years. In 1143 Conrad even received a loyal welcome when he visited Saxony. There were the usual local feuds, especially in Lorraine, and their persistence showed that Conrad had not the personality required for the maintenance of order in Germany. There were expeditions, too, over the eastern frontiers. In 1142 Conrad intervened in Bohemia to ensure the succession of his brother-in-law Vladislav; in 1146 he failed to restore another Vladyslav, also a brother-in-law, to the duchy of Poland; and in the same year the new duke of Bavaria intriguing in Hungarian affairs was decisively defeated by the king of Hungary. But no major trouble disturbed the land until the proclamation of the Second Crusade in 1146.

Republican rising in Rome

During these years the Papacy had cause to repent that it had supported the weaker candidate to the German throne, and to realise that in a strong Empire lay its best security. For, shortly after his disastrous expedition to the south, Innocent II experienced even deeper humiliation in Rome itself. It had taken him seven years to get possession of Rome; two years' residence there and the glamour of the Lateran Council had made his position secure; but his prestige was gravely shaken by his surrender to Roger, and he was attempting to reinstate himself when a storm broke out which completely ruined his authority. It was a repetition of what had occurred when Otto III lost Rome. The smouldering feud of Rome with Tivoli had flamed up into war again. Tivoli after a long siege surrendered to the Pope, who while imposing conditions which ensured its complete depend-

---

[1] Doubtless a favourite phrase of his, " Ja so mir Gott—," which was used as a nickname for him.

ence on himself left it with its walls intact. This infuriated the Romans who were intent on its complete destruction, and their indignation with the Pope soon found vent in a direct revolt against his civil authority.

The revolt took an unusual form, for it was not the noble families who were on this occasion striving to get the power into their own hands. It was the middle class, the body of citizens, who, fired by the example of the northern towns, now aspired to self-government. Their movement was therefore directed against the great noble families as well as against the Pope, and it was joined by many of the lesser nobility, who had also previously had no share in the government of the city. It was natural for Rome to try to do what so many other towns had done, but conditions were entirely different. In commerce and industry it was insignificant; shopkeepers, innkeepers, moneychangers abounded, for Roman prosperity depended very much on the numerous visitors to the Holy City; and as it was the papal court that attracted the majority of the visitors, the citizens could never be wholly independent of the Pope. On the other hand, they had an organisation, in each of the fourteen regions of the city, both for formal ceremonial purposes and as a city militia. Thus they were accustomed to bearing arms and to collective action, and they had the Capitol and the Forum, the monuments of republican Rome, to stir their courage and stimulate them to self-government. It was to the Capitol that they went in 1143, and a Senate that they set up to undertake the government of the city. They did not, as many other towns did, appoint consuls, for in Rome this title had become associated with the oligarchic government of the nobles.

The death of Innocent II occurred shortly after the outbreak of revolt; it was a bitter end to a Papacy of thirteen years mainly spent in conflict. His successor, Celestine II, only survived for a few months and was helpless against the commune. Lucius II (1144–5) took a bolder course. He appealed for help to Conrad and, failing him, to Roger II, who was only too glad for a Pope to be in need of his assistance. Lucius, brought back to the city by Norman arms, was able to enlist most of the greater nobles on his side. The commune in response found a leader in Jordan, of the

Failure of successive Popes to suppress it

powerful family of the Pierleoni; for him the old title of *patricius* was revived, which gave him quasi-dictatorial power. The issue was soon joined. The Pope led an assault on the Capitol in person; he is said to have been mortally wounded in the attempt; at any rate, he died a few days later, in **Accession of** February 1145. In his place the cardinals elected a Cistercian **Eugenius III** abbot, a former pupil of St. Bernard, who wrote to them to express his surprise at the election of one so insignificant: " it was either a farce or a miracle," and he preferred to believe the latter. Eugenius III, however, showed himself to be possessed of considerable force of character and practical ability. As he could not be master in Rome, he betook himself to Viterbo, and from there issued his ban on the commune and its *patricius*. The citizens found that they suffered from his absence and desired his return; so a settlement was soon reached. They discarded their *patricius*, agreed to the appointment of a *praefectus Urbis* by the Pope, and that the Senate should receive investiture from the Pope. It was a not unsatisfactory compromise. The Senate was still appointed by the citizens, each region nominating four representatives to it; it retained legislative, executive, and judicial authority in civil affairs. The Pope's ultimate authority was recognised, and his prefect was nominally at least the official responsible for keeping order in the city.

Arnold of Yet the settlement did not bring peace, for the Pope had **Brescia** to leave Rome after only a month's stay and did not return **in Rome** again for three years. And during his absence a new influence was stiffening the hearts of the citizens against him—the doctrines of Arnold of Brescia. Like so many that have earned the name of heretic, it was the worldly lives and secular ambition of the clergy that drove Arnold into heterodoxy. Himself a priest and an Augustinian canon, he condemned the holding of worldly possessions and secular offices by the clergy and advocated a return to apostolic poverty. In 1139 his bishop denounced him before the Lateran Council and Innocent II punished him by expulsion from Italy. He went to France, where he warmly espoused the cause of Abelard, of whom, it is said, he had been in earlier days a pupil. This brought him at once under the notice of St. Bernard, who coupled Abelard and Arnold, dissimilar as they were in their views, under a joint accusation of heresy.

Abelard was condemned at Sens in 1140, Arnold was expelled from France by Louis VII. He went to Zurich, and again at the instance of St. Bernard he was expelled, but he found protection with a cardinal Guido and eventually was brought to Eugenius III at Viterbo. Eugenius gave him his pardon and sent him to do penance at the Holy Places of Rome. For a time he remained quiescent, obeying the papal injunction to silence, but amid the monuments of ancient Rome he was stirred to eloquence again. He had no political aspirations, nor did he waver from the essentials of the faith; his attack was directed against the structure of Church government with its basis of wealth and power, and his mission was to preach a return to the primitive simplicity of the early Church. He practised what he preached (even St. Bernard pays a reluctant tribute to the purity and austerity of his life), and his sincerity and earnestness made a great impression upon the inflammable Romans. His views, too, were eagerly assimilated by the republican party. If the Pope had no right to secular government, the commune was abundantly justified. Eugenius soon discovered that the most dangerous person in Rome was the sinner he had sent to do penance there.

But for three years the Pope could pay little attention to Rome. These were the years of the Second Crusade; urgent appeals for help had come from Syria after the fall of Edessa in 1144, and at Viterbo in 1145 Eugenius had already begun to plan a crusade. Unable to go north at this time to preach it himself as Urban II had done, he delegated this task to St. Bernard, whose passionate eloquence won a remarkable response; both the king of France and the king of Germany were persuaded to take the cross. This was more than the Pope had bargained for; Conrad's assistance was so necessary to him that he grudged his prolonged absence in the East. Early in 1147 he went himself to France, and even after Louis VII started for the East in June the Pope lingered on for another year; papal authority could be exercised far more effectively there than in Italy, and he needed military assistance before he could return to Rome. His last important act was the holding of a Council at Rheims, where a number of canons were passed; at this Council occurred the famous trial of Gilbert de la Porrée, when all St. Bernard's

The preaching of the Second Crusade

efforts failed to obtain a conviction for heresy. The rest of the year was spent in a leisurely progress through North Italy back to Viterbo again. By that time (the end of 1148) the crusade had run its disastrous course, and the crusaders were on their way home, so that Western politics could now resume their normal trend.

Intrigues of Roger II against the Eastern Emperor During these years, besides the changed situation in Rome resulting from the preaching of Arnold of Brescia, the restless activity of Roger II had added to the complexity of the general situation. The Normans in South Italy were obnoxious to all the great powers whose territory they had usurped. If the Papacy was often compelled to seek their alliance or to come to terms with them, the Western and the Eastern Emperors had always maintained a hostile attitude. The Eastern Emperor, John Comnenus, had been for some time in negotiation with Conrad for a joint expedition against Roger II, and these negotiations had borne fruit in 1146 when John's son and successor, Manuel Comnenus, married Conrad's sister-in-law, Bertha of Sulzbach. Roger seized the opportunity of the Second Crusade to attempt a counter-offensive against Manuel. He opened negotiations with Louis VII of France, proposed to join him on crusade, and offered provisions and transport for the French king's expedition; had Louis consented, the action of the Venetians in the Fourth Crusade might have been forestalled and the expedition diverted to Constantinople. But in this diplomatic contest Manuel was the victor; the French as well as the German king chose the land route to Constantinople, and Roger took no part in the crusade. However, Manuel was so seriously embarrassed by the presence of the crusaders that Roger saw his chance of profiting by the situation. He launched an expedition in 1147 which seized Corfù, and sailing up the Gulf of Corinth captured Corinth and Thebes. He had no more success than Robert Guiscard had had in the same quarter. With the aid once again of the Venetian fleet, the Eastern Emperor drove out the Normans in 1149 and recaptured Corfù. Roger had therefore effected nothing but the hardening of the resolution of his enemies against him. He gained some compensation in another quarter during these years; the capture of Tripoli in 1146 gave him a settlement in North Africa which he proceeded rapidly to extend.

In Germany, the absence of Conrad on crusade had not affected the situation. Before his departure he had provided for the succession by causing his ten-year-old son Henry to be elected and crowned king. The government of the kingdom was left in the capable hands of the archbishop of Mayence and abbot Wibald of Stablo. Moreover, the chief princes of Germany had all either taken the cross with Conrad, or had been engaged in a separate crusade against the heathen Slavs in the north. Both Henry the Lion and Albert the Bear had participated in this, and so had one of the principal Welf supporters in South Germany, duke Conrad of Zähringen, who had been created imperial rector of Burgundy by Lothar. Even the disastrous failure of the Second Crusade does not appear to have made any difference. In fact, when Conrad returned to Germany in 1149, he at first seemed to have increased in importance, for his support was eagerly sought from various quarters. On his way back he had met Manuel at Constantinople, and a definite alliance against Roger II had been concluded. Besides this, the Pope was petitioning for his aid, in the first instance against the Roman Senate ; while the Senate for its part sent frequent deputations urging him to assume authority over the city and to take the commune under his protection. It was a curious tangle. Conrad wanted imperial coronation, but was suspicious of the Pope's relations with Roger and was possibly not averse to the suggestion that he was the true master of Rome. The Pope looked to Conrad for help, and was very ready to join him against Roger, but disliked the intrusion of the Eastern Emperor in South Italy. It seemed that all the strings were in Conrad's hands if he could use his opportunity with discretion. He had therefore everything to gain by an expedition to Italy, for which he began eagerly to prepare.

But the diplomatic skill of Roger upset the scheme that threatened his destruction. His first idea had been to get together a Western coalition against the Eastern Emperor, who was declared to be responsible for the failure of the Second Crusade. He met Louis VII, who passed through Italy on his way home in 1149, and found him only too ready to acquiesce in any undertaking against the Eastern Emperor. But meanwhile Conrad and Manuel had come to terms, and

Roger had to take measures for his own defence. By instigating rebellion in the territories of both his enemies, he prevented either from taking the offensive against him. In the East he incited the Serbs and Hungarians to attack Manuel, and he paid Welf VI (also just returned from crusade) an annual subsidy to keep Conrad occupied by civil war in Germany. This proved to be easy, for Henry the Lion was only waiting for Conrad's return to press his claim, which he had raised before Conrad's departure, to the duchy of Bavaria; as might have been expected, he repudiated the surrender which his mother had made in his name. Conrad refused to admit the claim, and the war which resulted lasted for the rest of his reign. In the south, Welf was defeated by the young king Henry in Suabia in 1150 and Henry the Lion's expedition to Bavaria was a failure. But Conrad's counter-attempt to gain Saxony in 1151 was equally unsuccessful. All this time he had been continuing to prepare for the Italian expedition on which he had set his heart. But it was not to be; he fell ill, and died in February 1152.

Death of Conrad III, and its effects

During these years Eugenius was in an awkward position. He needed help against the Roman Senate, and it was from Conrad that he wished to receive it. He could easily obtain it from Roger, but he above all things wished to avoid paying the price that Roger demanded. Yet, since Conrad's coming was so doubtful, he was obliged to temporise with Roger, as he might have to fall back on him. Actually Roger sent him a contingent to aid him in his attack on Rome in 1149. In November he effected an entrance into the city, but the position was too difficult for him to maintain; especially he could not tolerate the presence of Arnold, whom the Senate refused to abandon. He went to a conference with Roger in 1150, but they could not come to terms; the Pope, still with his eye on Conrad, refused full recognition of Roger's sovereignty, even though Roger was willing to give way on the matter of episcopal elections. So he had nothing to do but wait for Conrad, who never came. Conrad's death brought relief to Roger and embarrassment to the Pope. The German king was most unlucky that the opportunity was denied him; he had, too, the melancholy distinction of being the only king of Germany, since Otto I had restored the Empire, who had so far failed to obtain the imperial title. " King of the Romans " he could call himself, but though he sometimes styled himself " Emperor," he had no right to the name.

Conrad's elder son, the young king Henry, had died in 1150. He had another son, Frederick ; but he was only six years old, and a regency in the conditions then prevailing could not be contemplated. Conrad himself had designated as his heir his nephew Frederick, known as Barbarossa (Red Beard). The situation, therefore, was not unlike that at the two previous vacancies. The king left an heir who was not his son, and his powerful rival survived him. But this time there was no great ecclesiastic with a wrong to avenge. Frederick, too, was friendly with the Welfs, and his mother Judith was the sister of Henry the Proud. Neither Henry the Lion nor Welf VI aimed at the throne. So, without a dissentient voice Frederick was speedily elected, and he was crowned at Aix-la-Chapelle less than two months after Conrad's death. *Election of Frederick I Barbarossa*

Frederick I at his accession was in his thirtieth year. He had been duke of Suabia for five years, succeeding his father Frederick (II) in 1147, and he had then immediately gone on crusade with Conrad. Apart from local feuds in Suabia this was his only experience. Like Otto I, he had received the ordinary knightly education of his time, as there had previously been no thought of him as king. Like Otto again, he wore the mantle of king as if he had been born in the purple. He was filled with the highest conception of the imperial office, its majesty and its rights, and at the same time its obligations. He had a rigid sense of justice, and dispensed it impartially. He could be merciful ; he could be severe, especially against the disorders that disturbed the peace of the kingdom. The German nobles soon feared his wrath and obeyed his edict of a land peace which forbade private feuds. He could be quite ruthless, too, in vindicating his rights, as the Lombard communes soon discovered. Withal he was a fine figure of a king, handsome and of powerful build, a genial companion, jovial and generous. His personality made a deep impression upon his contemporaries, and he is ranked among the greatest of medieval Emperors. But he had the defects of his upbringing and of his time. *His character and political outlook*

He had been trained in outdoor, martial pursuits; his mental education had mainly consisted in learning stories of the heroes and kings of old. He was nurtured on tradition, and all his instincts were conservative. The justice that he dispensed was feudal justice. If he made use of the leading experts in Roman Law as his judges in Italy, it was because they were the greatest lawyers of the day; the decisions they gave were in accordance with the principles of the customary Teutonic law. He never developed a sense of Roman imperialism; and so he had no thought of building up a centralised State as Roger II had done in Sicily. The permanence of the Empire depended on the creation of a stable structure of government; like his predecessors, his only idea of permanence rested on the continuance of his dynasty.

His attitude to the Papacy

With his masterful disposition and his sense of the exalted character of his office, there was much in the conduct of affairs during the last two reigns that was thoroughly distasteful to him. Not only could he not tolerate the continued independence of the Lombard communes; he also could not accept subordination to the Pope or allow the German Church to be independent of his authority. In fact, he assumed at once all the privileges granted to Henry V in the Concordat of Worms, and not merely the part that had been conceded to Lothar in 1133. But, though trouble was bound to arise, the alliance between the Pope and the king of Germany persisted for a few more years. A mediating influence was provided by abbot Wibald of Stablo, on whose counsel both continued to depend, as in the days of Conrad III. Moreover, the alliance was important to both. The Pope was in dire need of the help he had expected from Conrad, both against the Romans and against the Norman king. Frederick was anxious to be crowned Emperor, and he too was willing to come to conclusions with Roger. Co-operation with the Eastern Empire, however, was not to his liking; he had no intention of sharing with it the overlordship he claimed in South Italy.

Treaty of Constance (1153)

In 1153, two papal plenipotentiaries met him at Constance, and a treaty was signed by which the king promised to come in force to Italy, to make no truce or peace with the Romans or with Roger without the Pope's consent, and to reduce the

Romans to obedience; the Pope promised to crown him Emperor; and both agreed to concede no territory in Italy to " the king of the Greeks," and if he invaded the country to use all their resources to expel him. Unfortunately, Eugenius III died almost immediately afterwards, in July 1153; the Papacy lost its most effective champion when St. Bernard died the same year; and Eugenius's successor, Anastasius IV, a moderate and peace-loving man, was Pope for less than a year and a half. When he died, in December 1154, the cardinals chose an Englishman (the only English- Accession of Pope Hadrian IV man who ever became Pope), Nicholas Brakespear, who had distinguished himself by his recent mission to Norway, where he had given order and an organisation to the local Church, linking it directly to Rome and instituting, as in England, the payment of Peter's Pence. His election as Pope Hadrian IV followed hard on his return to Rome. He was a capable man, of strong and decisive character, a marked contrast to the gentler and more moderate Eugenius. Though well versed in the conduct of ecclesiastical affairs, he was not so intimate with local conditions or with the general political situation as his predecessor; his temperament led him to follow the counsel of the more advanced members of the Curia, particularly his chancellor, cardinal Roland. In the lofty conception he held of his exalted office, and in his determination to abate no jot of what he felt was its due, he was the papal counterpart of Barbarossa; it was hardly likely that, holding the views they did, the peace could long be kept between them. His first act was typical. In the increasing tension at Rome, there was an affray and a cardinal was severely wounded; this he felt to be a crime against the Church, and he used the Church's most powerful weapon to punish it. He laid Rome under an interdict, nor would he remove it until the city purged itself by expelling the heretic Arnold of Brescia. With one forceful stroke he achieved what Eugenius had attempted so long in vain.

Meanwhile, in February 1154, the great Roger had died. William I succeeds Roger as king of Sicily (1154) His sons Roger and Alfonso had both predeceased him, and it was his youngest son, William, who succeeded to the throne.[1] William I, known to posterity owing to the malice

[1] His youngest child, Constance, the future mother of Frederick II, was born after his death.

of a hostile chronicler as William the Bad, followed closely in his father's footsteps, and though lacking the energy of his father was no unworthy successor. He showed wisdom in his choice of ministers, especially Maio of Bari, who held the office of " Emir of emirs " until his fall in 1160, and steered the kingdom safely through its most dangerous crisis. William was faced at his accession with unrest among his barons, who were especially offended by the authority given to Maio, with the intrigues of those whom Roger had exiled in 1140, and with the prospect of a simultaneous attack from Constantinople and Germany. He tried to isolate the king of Germany by making overtures to the Eastern Emperor, to Venice, and to the Pope. His diplomacy won one important success when the Venetians consented to sign a treaty with him in 1154. Manuel, however, spurned his offer, and the Pope refused to recognise him as king. William retaliated by invading papal territory, but Hadrian felt secure in resisting him, for the German king was already on his way to Rome.

Frederick's expedition to Italy to receive the imperial crown

Frederick had begun his march south before the accession of Hadrian, but had been delayed for some time in Lombardy. His determination to enforce peace, as in Germany, and to prevent the feuds between cities was frustrated by the opposition of most of the communes, Milan at their head, to the exercise of imperial authority. If some, like Pavia, were friendly, it was only because of their rivalry with Milan. He made an example of Tortona, which he razed to the ground. The Lombard cities learnt his determination to be master and the ruthlessness with which he would suppress insubordination ; on the other hand, it had taken him some months, and considerable expenditure of his resources, to reduce this small town, and he for his part learnt the magnitude of the task before him. For the time he put it by, and hastened to Rome. On the way, at the Pope's request, he apprehended Arnold of Brescia and handed him over to the papal justice, by which he was sentenced to death and executed. The Pope was encouraged by Frederick's ready response to his first request, and went out in state to meet him. Then the inevitable friction began. The Pope waited for Frederick to act as his groom and hold his stirrup when he dismounted ; Frederick's pride revolted at the idea that he should play so humble a part. But as Lothar had done so and tradition was on the Pope's side, he had to give way. The meeting was re-staged and the ceremony was duly performed; it rankled with Frederick, however, and his temper was even more sorely tried when he saw in Rome the picture of Lothar doing homage to the Pope. So inauspiciously did Pope and king make each other's acquaintance.

But on the next stage they were certainly in agreement. The Senate had sent a deputation to meet the king, and the authoritative tone in which they addressed him disposed him more firmly in the Pope's interest. His coronation as Emperor took place in St. Peter's on 18 June, and the Romans, who had hoped to prevent it, rushed to attack the Leonine City. Desperate street-fighting took place, in which the citizens suffered heavy losses. But the city proper was not taken by the Germans. Frederick had to retire, and the Pope could not remain by himself. He proposed that, as any further attack on Rome was impracticable, the German army should now be employed against William I. Frederick refused: at the height of summer this would, indeed, have been folly, and his communication with Germany was not secure; even the return through North Italy was not accomplished without fighting. So ended Frederick's first expedition to Italy. He, at any rate, had been crowned Emperor. The Pope felt himself betrayed; he had not got possession of Rome, and he was left to the mercy of the Normans.

Frederick had a further reason for wishing to get back to Germany; the troublesome question of the duchy of Bavaria urgently needed settlement. The claimant, Henry the Lion, had proved his loyalty by accompanying Frederick on the Italian expedition and had played an important part in the defeat of the Romans. Henry Jasomirgott, the duke in possession, had defied the royal command and refused to appear at the diets summoned to settle the question; his recalcitrance justified his dispossession, which had been decided upon before Frederick left Germany. Yet Frederick was anxious not to take extreme measures against his uncle. Negotiations were resumed after his return, and at last, in September 1156, an agreed settlement was reached. Henry Jasomirgott surrendered the duchy of Bavaria to Henry the Lion, who like his father was now duke of both Saxony and *Settlement of the duchy of Bavaria*

Bavaria. In return, the Austrian march was separated from Bavaria in perpetuity and made into the duchy of Austria in favour of Henry Jasomirgott. This was not all, for the Emperor granted special privileges to the new duke of Austria. The duchy was to pass to his children, or, failing them, to whomever he should name as his heir; it was exempt from royal jurisdiction; and the duke was only liable to military service in Austria or its neighbourhood. It was therefore a semi-independent principality, such as had only been erected before in defiance of the king. It was the king himself who now created it, surrendering his own sovereign rights. Austria was of little importance, except for the defence of the frontier, and the surrender might seem to have been compensated by the peace it secured. But it was a dangerous precedent, which others would be anxious to follow, and it may be said to mark the first stage on the road which was ultimately to lead to the disintegration of the German kingdom.

The Byzantines at Ancona

On his way back to Germany, Frederick had been met at Ancona by a deputation from the Eastern Emperor, headed by Michael Palaeologus, offering money and men for a joint expedition against the Normans. He was tempted, but his troops were anxious to return home, and the offer was refused. The Greeks, however, decided to proceed on their own, and Palaeologus's diplomacy and his skilful use of the money entrusted to him won surprising results. First of all, Ancona agreed to put itself under the suzerainty of the Eastern Emperor, and some neighbouring towns followed suit; then he got into touch with the Norman exiles and also with the discontented barons in South Italy, and a concerted scheme was set on foot; finally the Pope, exiled from Rome and helpless against the Normans, consented to ally with the Eastern Emperor. This was a definite breach of the treaty of Constance, but he could justly urge that Frederick had already failed to keep its provisions. The alliance was at first remarkably successful. The chief towns in the south, especially Bari, were won over, and most of the former Byzantine territory was reconquered; Robert of Capua was also restored to his principality. In the last months of the year, William I was dangerously ill and his death was reported; even some of his Sicilian vassals revolted. and it

seemed as if the Norman king was at last doomed. The
Eastern Emperor was so elated by his success that he con-
ceived the idea of adding Italy to his dominions and reuniting
East and West in a single Empire under his authority.

But his occupation of Ancona and its neighbourhood had
given great offence, firstly to Barbarossa, as it was a usurpation of territory under his overlordship; and secondly to
the Venetians, who felt that their control of the northern
Adriatic, the guarantee of which had formed the chief clause
in their treaty with William I in 1154, was at stake. The
Venetian fleet was no longer available against the Normans,
and Manuel did not supply his generals with sufficient troops
to carry his ambitious schemes into effect. He was unfortunate, too, in that Michael Palaeologus had died, and John
Ducas, who succeeded to the command, did not show the
same capacity. At the beginning of 1156 William had
recovered from his illness, and the genius of Maio of Bari had
effected a thorough reorganisation of the royal resources.
In May the king's army met the Greeks and their allies in a
pitched battle outside Brindisi, and won a complete victory.
The towns were all quickly recovered; Bari was punished
by complete demolition, which frightened others into surrender; the Greeks were expelled from the south, and Robert
of Capua was again homeless. Manuel, however, still clung
to his great scheme of uniting the two Empires, in spite of
the fact that he had aroused the hostility of Venice and the
Western Emperor, and had intensified the Norman desire
for revenge. By his ill-fated attempt he sealed the destiny
of his Empire, and started the march of events which led to
the Fourth Crusade.

Bereft of all his allies, the Pope was in a desperate position
when William advanced to besiege him at Benevento. He
had to yield and to submit to the terms imposed by the
conqueror at the treaty of Benevento in June 1156. He
invested William with the kingdom of Sicily and Apulia,
which was defined to include the principalities of Capua and
Naples, Amalfi, Salerno, and the previously disputed territory
of the Marsi; William did homage to the Pope and agreed
to the payment of an annual tribute. The ecclesiastical
issues were also settled by making a distinction, which
corresponded with the political distinction, between South

*Victory of
the Normans*

*The Pope
makes the
treaty of
Benevento
with William
I (1156)*

CHAPTER XIV

FRANCE IN THE FIRST HALF OF THE TWELFTH CENTURY

A T the end of the eleventh century the monarchy in France had reached its lowest depths. The king, lethargic and sensual, hardly held the reins of government. Even in his own domain he had given up the attempt to maintain order; the barons with their castles dominated the highways, which were quite unsafe for the peaceful traveller, and plundered the Church lands in their vicinity. But the king's son was a man of very different mould and, fortunately for France, the reign of Louis VI, though he did not actually become king until 1108, really commenced with the beginning of the century when Philip surrendered to him the direction of affairs. He was possessed to a full degree of the energy in which his father was so strikingly lacking, and he employed it in military enterprises, for which there was abundant excuse in every part of the royal domain. His fearless courage won the admiration of his knightly contemporaries, and he had other qualities which were rarer in his time and which appealed to other classes : he was a lover of order and right, naturally kind of heart, and hated cruelty and oppression. His one physical failing, which he inherited from his father, has given him the name of Louis the Fat. His stoutness increased, until in 1126 he could no longer mount a horse. But the spirit was still willing, and it was in 1135, only two years before his death, that he took part in his last expedition.

Louis VI

A chronological list of the events of his reign would be mainly a catalogue of these expeditions, some of them against the king of England, one to Flanders, one even against the Emperor, but the vast majority of them directed to keep the peace and assert his authority in the royal domain. Of the numerous robber barons who infested the domain, some were

The suppression of the brigand-nobles on the royal domain

rebels against royal authority, such as Hugh of Crécy, son of Guy, lord of Rochefort; others were mere brigands, like Hugh of Le Puiset, who had humiliated Philip I in 1079. There were some still worse, who took a perverted delight in cruelty for its own sake, such as the infamous Thomas of Marle, son of the lord of Coucy, who tortured and murdered unoffending peasants, robbed and imprisoned merchants, and made his name a by-word for inhumanity. Against all of these Louis was unwearied in waging war, actuated partly by his desire for order, partly by a chivalrous impulse to help the oppressed, partly by a love of fighting for its own sake. Rarely was he unsuccessful in any of the expeditions he undertook, yet it took him most of his reign to complete the task; there were indeed numerous barons to be brought to book, but it was his own temperament that was largely responsible for the delay in accomplishment. It was almost as if he were engaging in tournaments rather than wars : the defeated knight must be treated chivalrously and pardoned ; and then he had to be defeated all over again. Thus in 1111 he captured Le Puiset, razed it to the ground, and kept Hugh prisoner. Released the next year, Hugh rebuilt his castle ; and once more it was attacked and demolished. This had to be done a third time in 1118, but not before Hugh had succeeded in killing with his own hand the seneschal Anseau of Garlande. After this there was no pardon for him ; he ended his life on pilgrimage in the Holy Land. Hugh of Crécy was personally more dangerous to the king; he engineered regular revolts, especially in 1112. He too was defeated more than once, though again it was not until 1118 that he was finally overcome ; he had treacherously murdered a fellow baron, which put him outside the pale, and he had to expiate his crime by entering a monastery. Thomas of Marle survived much longer. In 1112 he made common cause with the townsmen of Laon who had murdered their bishop, and thereby acquired strongholds from which to extend his depredations. The Church was roused : in 1114 a papal legate at Beauvais solemnly excommunicated him, and a regular crusade was preached against him. Louis captured his castles and forced him to yield unconditionally. But even Thomas of Marle was pardoned (it was only merchants and peasants that he had maltreated) and let loose on the countryside. He was still more formidable when he became lord of Coucy on his father's death in 1116, and it was not until 1130 that he was finally brought to bay. His end was in keeping with his life ; mortally wounded, he refused with his last breath to give the order for the release of the victims of his atrocities.

At any rate, owing to the king's persistence and in spite of his ill-timed clemency, the task was finally accomplished and all the robber barons on the domain were brought to book. By so doing Louis laid the foundations of a new monarchy, of which he may be said to have been the creator. He now had a strong centralised domain, providing him with resources and soldiers, the nucleus of the kingdom of the future. But he had done more than this. He had restored prestige to the monarchy, which had become once again the defender of law and order, the protector of the Church. So churches and towns outside the domain also began to appeal to him for aid, and the desire for royal protection resulted in the extension of royal authority. Quite rightly Louis VI had concentrated on the domain, and been little regardful of the general sovereignty claimed by his predecessors. Yet, because of what he achieved with his narrower aim, he was more truly king, and in a wider sphere, than they. Probably he did not realise the full consequence of his actions, but he had been guided by the right instincts towards the ultimate goal of monarchy.

Enhanced prestige of the monarchy

The barons of the domain were not all of the type described above, though most of them were guided solely by self-interest. Some of them aimed at a wider power by engrossing the high offices of State, and Louis VI, who was no statesman, did not realise that they in their way were equally dangerous to the monarchy. The rivalry for power of the Rochefort and Garlande families has already been mentioned. In the opening years of the century the Rocheforts held the upper hand, and Louis was betrothed to a daughter of Guy of Rochefort. His own inclinations were in favour of the Garlandes, and when in 1107 the Pope was persuaded to annul the contract of marriage on the ground of consanguinity, Louis openly threw in his lot with them. Doubtless it was this that caused the constant revolts of Guy's son, Hugh of Crécy. Once king, Louis showered favours on the Garlande

The Garlande family and the offices of State

family. Anseau, the eldest of four brothers, was made seneschal—the most important of the offices under so warlike a king. After his death at the hands of Hugh of Le Puiset in 1118, the second brother, William, became seneschal. Another brother, Gilbert, held the office of butler. The youngest, Stephen, who was in orders, was made chancellor, so that three of the five offices of State were in the hands of this family. Stephen was the ablest and the greediest of them all. He was a noted pluralist : a canonry, an archdeaconry, and three or four deaneries were among the ecclesiastical offices that he held at the same time. And when William died in 1120, he, though an ecclesiastic, actually became seneschal himself. There was a party opposed to him at Court, headed by the queen, Adelaide of Maurienne, to whom he had given great offence by his overbearing manner ; the king's favour enabled Stephen to ignore this danger, until his ambition mounted so high that he actually designated a nephew by marriage as the heir to his office. Then even Louis took offence, and in 1127 Stephen was degraded. Immediately he headed a revolt, and it took three years to subdue him. As usual, Louis pardoned him and even restored to him his former office of chancellor. The office of seneschal, left vacant for four years, was given by Louis to his cousin, Ralph of Vermandois,[1] a good soldier and a loyal servant of the king. But henceforward the great officers of State cease to engross the business of the kingdom. Ralph and his successors, great feudatories with estates of their own to manage, did not permanently reside at Court ; they were the agents rather than the chief ministers of the king. Moreover, Louis had set the example, which his successor was to follow, of leaving the chief office vacant for some years.

Abbot Suger It was at this time that Suger, abbot of St. Denis, first came into real prominence. While policy had been controlled by the royal favourites, Stephen of Garlande and his brothers, the administrative work (confined as yet almost entirely to the royal domain) had been carried on by obscure members of the household, clerks in the royal chapel for the most part. One of these, even before Louis came to the throne, was Suger.

[1] He was the son of Philip I's brother Hugh, who had married the heiress of Vermandois.

He represents, *par excellence*, the new type of royal servant
(civil servant, as we should say nowadays) that was coming
into existence in both France and England, and that was to
give a stability and continuity to the government, which was
so noticeably lacking in the German kingdom. It was not
until 1118 that he was entrusted with an important mission
(to welcome Pope Gelasius II on his arrival in France). In
1122 he was appointed abbot of St. Denis, and after the fall
of Stephen of Garlande in 1127 he began to take the first
place in the king's counsels. By years of diligent work he
had obtained a wide experience of men and affairs ; his whole
interests were bound up in the monarchy, his services dedicated to its well-being ; his personal devotion to his master
is attested in his *Life of Louis VI*, which is one of the chief
sources of our knowledge of the reign. It took Louis a long
time to realise the value of this " new man " of humble birth,
but, when he did, he gave him the confidence that he had
previously given to unworthy and greedy favourites. It
must be placed to his credit that he did recognise it at last
and so rendered a second service, little recking it himself,
to the French monarchy. He had conquered the royal
domain ; Suger and his staff of clerks saw to its wise administration. The one was a keen fighter with a strong hand to
repress disorder ; the other a man of peace, able to stabilise
and construct for the future. The effect was the more durable
since this happy partnership continued into the next reign.

Next to the king himself the chief gainer by the new
régime was the Church. In the conquest of the domain the
Church may almost be said to have taken the initiative. It
was usually in response to appeals from bishops and monasteries for the protection of their lands and tenants that Louis'
military expeditions were set on foot. The crusade against
Thomas of Marle is only the most notable instance of this.
Another, almost equally notable, is the expedition against
Hugh of Le Puiset in 1111, which was in response to a joint
appeal from the archbishop of Sens, the bishops of Chartres
and Orleans, and numerous abbots. Examples could be
multiplied, and outside the domain as well. For instance,
in 1122, and again in 1126, when the bishop of Clermont was
driven from his episcopal town by the count of Auvergne,
Louis went to his aid, expelled the count, and restored the

Louis VI and the Church

bishop. The Church had every reason to be grateful, and its consequent support was a great asset to the king. Indeed, it supplied him with considerable resources in men and money, which helped to make the expeditions possible ; he endowed it with lands, and got his profit from them. The advantages, in fact, were mutual. Suger, in his *Life* of his master, asserts that Louis had deserved the friendship of the Church by his generous defence of it, his protection of the poor and of orphans, his repression of tyranny ; in other words, he carried out what the Church always preached were the principal duties of a king. In return, the Church preached the duty of obedience to the divinely appointed king, and encouraged him to a wider exercise of his functions as sovereign. Moreover, the Head of the Church himself had cause for gratitude to the king of France. Gelasius II found a refuge in France, and a welcome from its king, in 1118 ; Calixtus II was elected in France and stayed there for over a year, for a time in Louis' company ; Innocent II, during his schism with Anacletus, also found a refuge there, and Louis was the first king to give him recognition.

But the Church had cause for dissatisfaction too. Neither the king nor his ministers were in sympathy with the views of the advanced reformers who had gained such a hold in France. Certainly he did not imitate his father : he did not revert to the practice of simony or to lay investiture ; he combated clerical marriage and was generous to monasteries, new and old. But he was careful to keep a control on episcopal elections and himself to bestow the temporalities ; this was important to him, since he gained so much from them. While he attended strictly to the material interests of the Church, however, he was much less careful about its spiritual well-being. His favourite, Stephen of Garlande, a notorious pluralist and a man of dissolute life, created a scandal which reflected on the king himself, who paid no heed to the reproaches of bishop Ivo of Chartres (he survived till 1115, but with steadily waning influence) or even of St. Bernard. The latter, in the full vigour of his reforming activities, gained the ear of the king on the occasion of the papal schism, but never attained the ascendancy that he did over his successor. Suger, too, though he was careful to introduce good order into his abbey, was not in sympathy with advanced

views ; he was king's servant first, ecclesiastic second.   The
Church suffered from the subordination of its interests to
political ends.   But Louis' merits outweighed his demerits,
and it was not to the Church's interest to quarrel with him.
When the archbishop of Lyons, supported by Calixtus II,
tried to make good his primacy over Sens, Louis wrote in
protest to the Pope and recited the services he had rendered
to the Church and in particular to the Papacy.   In effect he
won his case, as the primacy was not seriously pressed in the
future.   Possibly his reminder sank in.   At any rate, though
their ecclesiastical authority was greater in France than elsewhere, the Popes were coming to depend on that kingdom
in time of need ; and now that the kingship was beginning to
be a reality once more, it was especially on the king that they
had to depend.   He could not be treated as brusquely as
Gregory VII had treated Philip I, or ignored as Urban had
ignored Philip during his long stay in France.   By his services
both to the French Church and to the Papacy Louis created
another asset for his successors.

It is clear that in various ways changes were taking place The towns
which were of advantage to the monarchy.   For some of
them, especially the suppression of insubordination within
the domain, Louis was directly responsible ; but some seem
to have come about, almost despite him, by force of circumstances.   One such was the development of communal feeling
in the towns.   Though Louis in certain respects rose superior
in character to the majority of his contemporaries, especially
in his natural kindliness, he was essentially a man of his age
with all its prejudices.   So he saw eye to eye with the noble
classes, those who engaged, with him or against him, in martial
exploits ; and in dealing with them the customs of the feudal
code, the traditions of knightly behaviour, were his rules of
conduct.   Only when these were outraged was he relentless,
as he was at last with Hugh of Le Puiset and Hugh of Crécy.
It was natural to have men of noble birth as his chief counsellors and ministers.   That he could recognise efficiency even
among the humble clerks is shown by the rise of Suger ; but
he did not give Suger his complete confidence until after the
fall of Stephen of Garlande, and Suger had been in a sense
ennobled by being made abbot.   With his conservative outlook, Louis could not be expected to pay much regard to the

11

middle-class element in the towns, or to have any sympathy with their desire for self-government. He vaguely saw that they were creating wealth and could pay for what they wanted ; the few charters that he granted were with him only a means of raising money. He knew the value of a well-filled treasury, and the domain and the Church could not supply all his needs. But it was to be left to his grandson, Philip Augustus, to realise the advantages to be gained for the monarchy by an alliance with the bourgeoisie. Louis could not render it this service ; such an alliance would have been unthinkable to him.

The great feudatories

Now, though a great deal of Louis' energy was expended upon the barons within the domain, he like his predecessors could not ignore the great feudatories whose lands were adjacent to his. They, too, had been passing through a period of weakness ; this was true even of Normandy, previously so well governed, for owing to Robert's incapacity, and the discord first with his father and then with his brother, the barons had gained an almost independent position. Blois had been politically negligible for some time ; in Anjou, Fulk Rechin had never succeeded in reducing his barons to order ; and in Flanders, the absence of Robert II on crusade seems to have given the opportunity to the nobles to disturb the peace and to oppress the towns and the peasants. But in the early years of the twelfth century this was all changed, and in all these States, as in the royal domain, centralisation

Blois

became the rule. In Blois, Theobald (IV) succeeded his father Stephen in 1102, and soon began to display an activity which brought Blois again into political importance. He was on the one hand an ardent ecclesiastical reformer, on the other a constant rebel against royal authority. The count of Blois was count of Chartres as well, and so Theobald had been affected by the brigandage of Hugh of Le Puiset, and had joined in the general appeal to the king against Hugh in 1111. Yet the next year he was in league with this same Hugh, with Hugh of Crécy, and with the king of England against Louis, and as his territories lay immediately to the west of the royal domain he was a constant menace. On the

Anjou

other side of him, however, the count of Anjou, Fulk V, was loyal to his suzerain. He became count in 1109 and succeeded, where his father had failed, in centralising his

territories once more and instituting a régime of order and
strong government. His story is very like that of Louis.
He suppressed the barons and destroyed their castles, while
at the same time he checked any manifestation of urban
independence. He was content that his territories, which
included Touraine as well as Anjou, should be bounded on
the south by the Loire; he therefore made no attempt to
recover Saintonge from the duke of Aquitaine. His ambition
was to expand northwards again and recover Maine from
Normandy, and it was his hostility on this account to the
king of England that kept him loyal to the king of France.
He did actually obtain possession of Le Mans in 1110, but
the complete acquisition of Maine was never ceded to him
by the English king.

In Flanders, too, there had been a similar revival of order Flanders
and good government, first of all under Baldwin VII, who
succeeded his father Robert II in 1111, and then under his
cousin Charles the Good, son of the king of Denmark, who
became count in 1119. The nobles were brought to book
and justice was dispensed with a firm hand to all, regardless
of rank. So merchants, towns, peasants, and churches found
in the count a strong protector. Neither Baldwin nor Charles
was prejudiced like Louis in favour of dealing leniently with
men of noble birth, and they realised the advantages to be
gained from a close association with the wealth-producing
middle classes in the towns. They were friendly by tradition
with the king of France as they were antagonistic to England;
but their own territories engrossed their attention and their
friendship was of little practical value to Louis.

It was the changed situation in Normandy, and the Normandy
reunion of the duchy with the English kingdom, that most
seriously affected the king of France. William II died in
1100, and his youngest brother, Henry, was able to secure his
election as king before Robert returned from the Holy Land.
Robert with his glamour as a crusader had regained some
prestige, and he hoped to obtain recognition in England and
to displace his brother; but he won so little support that he
soon had to renounce the attempt. Even in Normandy he
could rally few supporters, and when Henry I took the
offensive there he was helpless. At the battle of Tinchebrai
in 1106 he was decisively defeated and taken prisoner, and

spent the last twenty-eight years of his life in captivity in England. Henry soon restored Normandy to the order it had enjoyed under his father, and this union of two well-governed States produced a very serious situation for Louis. He had missed his opportunity of intervening on Robert's behalf, and he now attempted to compensate for this by putting forward the claims of Robert's young son, William Clito, to the duchy. Henry was therefore treated as a usurper

War with Henry I of England

in Normandy by his suzerain, and he retaliated by taking possession of Gisors ; this fortress was within the Norman Vexin, but as it commanded the road to Paris it had previously been agreed that it should be held by a neutral castellan. This was an act of war, and hostilities opened in 1109. Louis, successful in 1112 against Theobald of Blois and the coalition of barons on the domain, could make no headway against Henry, and in 1113 had to sign a treaty recognising the English king's suzerainty in Maine and in Brittany. Hostilities were resumed in 1116, and culminated in a pitched battle at Brémule in 1119, where Louis suffered a severe defeat and had to fly for his life. He took the occasion of Calixtus II's presence at Rheims, where he was holding a council, to appeal in person to the Pope, reciting the outrages Henry had committed against his overlord, his ill-treatment of the rightful duke Robert, and his instigation of the revolt of Theobald of Blois and other vassals of Louis. Calixtus was in a difficult position, as he could not afford to offend the victorious king of England. He went to Gisors, and listened to Henry's defence, his denial of the charge of ill-treatment of Robert, and his counter-charges against Louis. He skilfully avoided taking sides and was able to bring about peace, which was agreed to in the following year. Yet neither side really kept the peace ; though there was no direct encounter, it was not until the death of William Clito in 1128 removed Louis' chief excuse for pressing the struggle that hostilities at last began to die out.

The repulse of the Emperor Henry V

If there were no pitched battles during these years, there were other events of at least equal importance. Henry I induced his son-in-law, the Emperor Henry V, to make an attack on France from Lorraine. The Emperor was tempted by the proposal, as it gave him the prospect of acquiring territory contiguous to the personal domain he was building up in Lorraine. The news of the threatened invasion in 1124 roused both the martial and the royal spirit in Louis ; he issued a general summons to the chief vassals of the kingdom, the first that had been issued for many years, and the remarkable response to the summons (even Theobald of Blois brought a contingent) was therefore the more impressive. It frightened the Emperor, so that he withdrew without risking a battle, and it greatly increased the prestige of Louis, who had revived with such success the sovereign powers of the king of France and inflicted an unprecedented humiliation on the ruler of Germany. The next year, however, was less fortunate for him. Hugh, who had been count of Champagne for thirty-five peaceful but quite inglorious years, in which the only incidents were his quarrels with his two wives and the three pilgrimages he made to the Holy Land, died during the last of these in 1125. His nephew, Theobald of Blois, succeeded him and so reunited Blois and Champagne once more. This turbulent vassal was now master of the territories to the east as well as to the west of the royal domain, and was therefore a greater danger than ever. *Champagne and Blois reunited*

A much more serious blow to Louis occurred in 1127 when the king of England and the count of Anjou renounced their enmity and formed a marriage alliance. Henry I had already, before the battle of Brémule, weaned Fulk from his French allegiance by the proposal of a marriage between his son William and Fulk's daughter. This came to nought when William was drowned in 1120 ; to add to Henry's difficulties, his second marriage failed to provide him with a male heir. He had a daughter, the empress Matilda, and, since Henry V died childless in 1125, he was able to recall her to England. First of all he persuaded his barons in 1127 to accept her as their future sovereign, and then he arranged her marriage with Geoffrey, son and heir of Fulk. The marriage took place in 1128, and in 1129 Fulk went on pilgrimage to the Holy Land [1] and resigned his county to Geoffrey. The effect of the marriage was not immediately felt, for both Henry and Matilda quarrelled with Geoffrey, and the English barons heartily disliked the idea of a feminine ruler. But the ultimate result was the union of Anjou, Maine, and Normandy *The Anglo-Angevin marriage alliance*

[1] Where he married the daughter of the king of Jerusalem, Baldwin II, and succeeded his father-in-law as king in 1131.

with England, which upset the old balance of power in the north and so retarded for many years the revival of monarchical authority in France.

These years, 1127–8, were two of the most important years of the reign. Besides the English-Angevin marriage, they are marked by the change in the king's counsels consequent on the fall of Stephen of Garlande and the confidence given to Suger, and finally by the eventful happenings in Flanders. There the stern justice of the count had roused deep resent-

Murder of the count of Flanders

ment among the nobility, and a conspiracy was hatched. On March 2, 1127, as Charles the Good knelt at prayer in the church of Saint-Donatien at Bruges, a band of them set upon him and stabbed him to death. The noble character and exalted position of the victim and the circumstances of the crime gave it a peculiar significance ; Charles the Good was invested with the halo of martyrdom and later became a

The struggle for the succession

national hero. The grief of his non-noble subjects was profound, and they had double cause to mourn him, since he left no son and there was at once a greedy scramble for the succession. Several candidates, of varying degrees of relationship to the dead count, were soon in the field ; among them, a bastard cousin, William of Ypres, who rapidly seized some of the chief fortresses in Flanders, and the future count, Thierry of Alsace, grandson, through his mother Gertrude of Holland, of Robert the Frisian. The king of France considered that as overlord it was his task to avenge the murder and restore the government ; the crime was such as to shock all his susceptibilities, and the opportunity of asserting his sovereignty in one of the great fiefs could not be missed. He had a candidate of his own, his protégé William Clito, whose only claim was that he was the grandson of William the Conqueror's Flemish wife. But such was the decision with which Louis acted that, three weeks after the murder, representatives from Flanders had agreed at Arras, where the king was assembling his forces, to accept William Clito as count. By May 6 Louis had marched on Bruges, hurled the murderers from the top of the tower in which they had taken refuge, captured William of Ypres and reduced all the castles he had seized. Once again, as in 1124, he had given a notable display of sovereignty, but he had considered his own interests and not those of Flanders, and he had served neither. For

William Clito proved to be as irresponsible as his father, nor would he in this situation have found a wise mentor in Louis VI; he made common cause with the nobles and left the towns to their mercy. Riots broke out in the towns, and the various claimants took advantage of the disorder to make their appearance again. Bruges and Ghent took the lead in promoting the candidature of Thierry of Alsace, and when Louis came again to restore order, the towns resisted him and he had ignominiously to retire. William Clito was killed in battle in July 1128, and on his death Louis' intervention in the affairs of Flanders as well as of Normandy was at an end. The only satisfaction he obtained was that Thierry came to do him homage and to receive investiture, desiring, owing to the continued antagonism with England, to maintain friendship with the king of France.

The remaining years of Louis' reign were mainly peaceful. His energy grew less as his corpulence increased, and the great strokes of fortune that befell him in his last years came too late for him to reap the profit. For in 1135 his great enemy, Henry I, died, and his most troublesome vassal, Theobald of Blois, made his peace with the king. The house of Blois now had a new outlet for its ambition. Theobald and his younger brother Stephen were, through their mother, grandsons of William the Conqueror. This gave them a claim, since Henry's heir was a woman. Theobald was a stranger to England, but Stephen had been a favourite with the late king and spent several years there; his brother Henry was bishop of Winchester; and his own popularity won him the crown of England. Theobald acquiesced in his brother's success and acted as his partner on the continent. Here, however, they met their match in Geoffrey of Anjou, who also had designs on Normandy; he was able to form a coalition of Norman nobles and to resist the attempts of the house of Blois to secure the duchy. England and Normandy were thus divided again, and Blois and Anjou were in bitter rivalry. The situation in the north was now more favourable to the king of France than it had been for a century. *The effect of Stephen's accession to England*

A still more surprising change was to come about two years later in the South of France, where for so long the

The marriage of Louis (VII) to the heiress of Aquitaine rulers of the great fiefs had pursued their own course regardless of their overlord. Duke William IX of Aquitaine had not only defied the king; he had even more directly defied the Pope, when ordered to take back the wife whom he had dismissed. He went on crusade, and on his return wrote ribald songs about it; he was one of the early troubadours. A man of parts, but without morals or scruples, he ruled his agglomeration of territories in a rough and ready manner, and from time to time made excursions against his neighbour of Toulouse; twice, indeed, he captured the town of Toulouse, and he held it for some years. This was no great undertaking, for the county was hopelessly divided, both nobles and towns arrogating to themselves self-government. Count Raymond went off in 1096 to seek better fortune on crusade, and eventually obtained the county of Tripolis. His elder son Bertrand preferred to remain there, and so did his son, Pons. But Raymond's younger son, Alphonse-Jourdain, returned, and during his long career as count he managed to tighten the reins and obtain some mastery over his principality. He recovered his capital from the duke of Aquitaine in 1120, and combated not unsuccessfully the independence of nobles and towns; his enterprises, too, extended into Spain. But it was the next duke of Aquitaine, William X (1127–37), who provided the greatest surprise. He resembled his father in character, though he was only a feeble reflexion of him; apart from his one singularity that he supported the anti-Pope Anacletus for four years, there is nothing to record of him until he came to die, when, having no son to succeed him, he announced his wish that to Louis VI should be entrusted the marrying of his daughter and heiress Eleanor and the care of his lands. That he turned to his sovereign when providing for the future of his principality showed that the monarchy had become a reality again in France, and was in itself a great tribute to Louis VI. The king accepted the trust and named his son Louis as Eleanor's husband, and he sent him at once to take charge of Aquitaine and celebrate the marriage. This was the last event of the reign, for Louis VI died the same year. It was a glorious ending: Aquitaine, formerly unapproachable, now to become an appanage of the crown; in the north, England and Normandy separated and hostile. The prospects for the monarchy were at

their brightest when Louis VI handed over the sceptre to
Louis VII.

The reign of Louis VII, therefore, which was to last for ^{Louis VII}
forty-three years, opened under most favourable auspices.
He had already been crowned king in 1131 directly after the
death of his elder brother Philip, so there was no question
of the succession. However, he was not equal to the good
fortune to which he succeeded, and by 1154 it had vanished :
Aquitaine was lost to him, and England and Normandy were
reunited and were joined with Anjou, Maine, and Touraine
under one ruler. For this the weakness of his character was
largely to blame. He was easily dominated by a stronger
will than his own ; though, when his wishes were thwarted,
he often exhibited the obstinacy of a weak man who refuses
to see that he is endangering his best interests. The immediate confidants of the king were, therefore, usually more
important than the king himself in the framing of policy.
First and foremost at the beginning was queen Eleanor, to
whom Louis was passionately devoted. With her was closely
associated by friendship and interest the seneschal Ralph of
Vermandois, whose aims were much more personal than they
had been in Louis VI's time ; this association only came to
an end in 1152, when Eleanor was divorced and Ralph died.
The king got rid of Stephen of Garlande from the chancellor-
ship, yet only to replace him by an equally unworthy and
self-seeking favourite, Cadurc. But there still remained the
invaluable Suger in his informal position at the head of the
administration, creating resources for the government but
disliked by Eleanor and Ralph because of his humble birth.
All might have gone well with Louis, if he had had the wisdom
to follow the cautious counsels of Suger ; he had at least the
sense to protect this faithful servant against the ill-will of
the queen and the count of Vermandois.

Only in this respect did he counter the wishes of the
queen. Eleanor was an imperious woman of strong passions,
in instincts and temperament a true daughter of the house
of Aquitaine. The interests of her duchy were put in the forefront when Louis wasted his resources in a vain attack on
Toulouse in 1141. The interests of the monarchy demanded
that Louis should keep a close watch on the north, and not

tamely suffer Geoffrey of Anjou to gather Normandy into his hands bit by bit. Yet he alienated his strongest supporter against Normandy, Theobald, count of Blois and Champagne, and engaged in a quarrel with the Papacy which occupied his whole attention and ended only in his humiliation. It started with an attempt to impose his chancellor, Cadurc, on Bourges as archbishop in opposition to the choice of the canons, Peter of La Châtre, who was supported by Pope Innocent II. Count Theobald, always on the side of reform, opposed the king and championed the cause of Peter, who was ultimately successful. Hard on this incident came another, when Ralph of Vermandois repudiated his wife and married the queen's sister. The Church immediately took action and excommunicated the guilty pair; once more Theobald was on the side of the Church, and he had a personal interest since the wife Ralph had discarded was his niece. Louis again sacrificed the interests of the kingdom to the wishes of Eleanor, who owing to her upbringing in Aquitaine paid little heed to ecclesiastical censure. Furious with Theobald, the king made a violent incursion into Champagne, and set fire to the town of Vitry-sur-Marne; hundreds of people who had taken refuge in the church were burned to death. At this point St. Bernard, a close friend of Theobald, intervened, and Suger, always anxious for peace, was on the same side. Louis was persuaded to evacuate Champagne, but did not get what he expected in return, the removal of the excommunication from Ralph and the queen's sister. He lost his temper and invaded Champagne again; but he was once more under the domination of a stronger will. His protests became feebler, and at last in 1144 he gave way completely, evacuated Champagne, recognised Peter as archbishop of Bourges, and left Ralph of Vermandois to fend for himself. While all this was happening, Geoffrey of Anjou, leaving Matilda to her own devices in England, was himself quietly proceeding with the conquest of Normandy, in the name of their son, Henry. In 1144 he crowned his success by the capture of Rouen, and the next year Louis accepted the *fait accompli* and invested Geoffrey with the duchy of Normandy.

The surrender of Louis in 1144 was largely due to the fact that Eleanor had begun to lose her power over him and he

Louis
under the
influence
of St.
Bernard

had fallen under a new influence—that of the Church in general and St. Bernard in particular. It seems to date from the burning of the church at Vitry—an act of sacrilege and horror, which, it would appear, left a deep impression on his mind, and weaned him from the wildness of his early years into a repentance which made him humbly submissive to the Church which he had previously defied. It was not a sudden conversion but a gradual change of mind, which was complete by 1145. In this new mood he listened to the exhortations of St. Bernard, and he was the first to take the cross when the Second Crusade was mooted. Here again he did not consider the interests of the kingdom ; it was obviously hazardous for the king to make a prolonged absence, but, though Suger tried to dissuade him, he insisted on going.[1] At any rate, Louis did one wise thing. Probably on the advice of his new mentor, St. Bernard, certainly " with the assent of the lord Pope," who was with him in France shortly before his departure, he left the care of the government in Suger's hands ; he associated with him Ralph of Vermandois and the archbishop of Rheims, but they were occupied as much with their own affairs as with public business. Suger proved to be more than equal to the trust. The royal government functioned in the royal absence, and possibly more efficiently than if the king had been there to disturb it by his caprices. The chief difficulty was finance. Louis had imposed a special levy for the crusade, especially on Church property. It was much resented, and it took nearly three years to collect. Suger managed, however, to raise enough money both for the needs of the home government and also for the king, who was continually writing and asking for more. It is a high testimony to Suger's ability that, without a suggestion against him of oppression, the finances of the kingdom were in a good state when Louis returned after two and a half years' absence.

Louis takes the Cross

Suger in charge of the government

Louis started in 1147 on the crusade which was to prove so disastrous. He could not act in harmony with the German king, nor could either of them with the Eastern Emperor ; neither of them, moreover, was sufficient of a general for such a campaign. In a year it was all over, and it was then

Louis in the Second Crusade

---

[1] He was not alone in this. The count of Toulouse, Alphonse-Jourdain, undid much of the valuable work he had done in making his territories into a unified State by going on the Second Crusade, during which he died (in 1148).

urgent that he should return, as Suger wrote to inform him.
Dangerous intrigues were going on in France, which Suger
had difficulty in overcoming. Louis' prestige had been
gravely affected by the failure of the crusade, and there was
even the suggestion of deposing him in favour of his brother
Robert. But Louis paid no heed to his kingdom. He was
wholly occupied with personal cares. He lingered on in
Palestine to visit the Holy Places ; he was meditating revenge
on the Emperor Manuel ; above all, he was worried by the
behaviour of Eleanor, who had gone with him on crusade,
and the practical certainty that she was being unfaithful to
him. He had begun to talk of consanguinity and the annulment of the marriage. When he did decide to return, he
came by way of Italy, and stayed first with Roger II, whose
scheme against Manuel he welcomed with enthusiasm, and
then at Rome with the Pope. Eugenius III did him a great
service by bringing about a reconciliation between him
and Eleanor, and refused to hear the word consanguinity
mentioned. At last in November 1149 he arrived back in
France.

Relieved for the time from his personal worries, Louis
seemed to have recovered his sense of kingship. He suffered
an irreparable loss when Suger fell ill in 1150 and died in
January 1151. Yet for the moment he did better without
Suger to advise him. For he had at last perceived the danger
of Geoffrey's progress in the north, and Suger, consistently
pacific, had tried to deter him from taking steps to check it.

Louis forces
Geoffrey of
Anjou to
make peace After Suger's death he acted with resolution. Geoffrey had
handed over the duchy of Normandy to his son Henry ; Louis
put forward Eustace, the son of king Stephen of England, as
his rival, and so allied himself with the house of Blois once
more. He made a bold and successful attack on Normandy,
and though prevented by illness from pushing it to completion, he had the satisfaction of seeing his enemies sue for
peace. Geoffrey and Henry came to Paris in August 1151
and signed a treaty, by which they handed over the whole of
the Norman Vexin, including Gisors, to Louis.

His marriage
with Eleanor
annulled It is possible that, if Suger had been alive and able to
prevent hostilities, this useful advantage might not have
been gained. On the other hand, it is almost certain that he
would have managed to prevent Louis from the crowning

folly that ensued.   The reconciliation with Eleanor was short-lived.   She had recently borne Louis a second child, a daughter as the first had been, not the son for whom he had been hoping.   Probably he saw in this the hand of God, for he began to talk again of consanguinity.   Then, in August 1151, when the young Henry of Anjou was in Paris, Eleanor was so obviously attracted by him that Louis' jealousy flared up again.   He was determined now to make an end.   Taking her with him to Aquitaine, he dismantled fortresses and withdrew his garrisons ; in a word, he evacuated the territory which went with the marriage.   Back in his own domain, he summoned an ecclesiastical council at Beaugency in March 1152, which declared the marriage annulled.   Eleanor escaped to Aquitaine and was there joined, doubtless by pre-arrangement, by Henry, who had succeeded his father as count of Anjou the previous September.   In May 1152 Henry and Eleanor were married ; Aquitaine passed out of the hands of the French king to be united with the territories of his powerful rival.

Marriage of Eleanor with Henry (II)

Then Louis realised what he had done.   Renewing his policy of the previous year, he invaded Normandy with a large army.   Allied with England he had a splendid opportunity.   But the energy he had displayed before seemed to have vanished now.   Content with the trifling success of capturing a frontier fortress, he consented in August to a truce of eight months, and when that expired continued to waste his time in unimportant sieges.   Henry had taken advantage of the truce to land in England and press his claims there, and the sudden death of Louis' protégé Eustace improved his chances enormously.   Stephen was induced to accept Henry as his heir, and Henry could then return to Normandy to confront Louis, who immediately gave up the struggle.   He made peace in August, consenting to evacuate Normandy in return for an indemnity and to cease to style himself duke of Aquitaine.   In October, Stephen died and Henry II, duke of Normandy and Aquitaine, count of Anjou, Maine, and Touraine, French territories far more extensive than those over which the king of France ruled, became king of England as well.

Henry becomes king of England

CHAPTER XV

EAST AND WEST, 1100–1155. THE SECOND
CRUSADE

THE First Crusade in its inception had been a religious The after- war for the recovery of the Holy Places of Jerusalem. math of the This it had achieved and, moreover, the road to the First Crusade Holy Land was now in Christian occupation. The offensive of the Western Christians against the Eastern Moslems had been successful ; the task they had before them was to defend what they had won. So far it seems a normal part of the ordinary story of Christianity versus Islam, of conquest and reconquest. But there is an important difference. What the Latins had recovered was territory that had formerly been Greek. The Eastern Empire was not concerned with Palestine, which had been lost to it for centuries. But Syria had only recently been lost, and in this, especially in Antioch, it was deeply interested. When the crusaders were at Constantinople, it had been agreed that Palestine should be theirs, while Syria should be restored to Greek suzerainty. Alexius, though he failed in his promise to assist in the capture of Antioch, regarded the creation of Bohemond's principality as a shameless breach of the bargain. Therefore it was not Moslems alone, but Eastern Christians as well, who were trying to recover what the Western Christians had won. The Latin States were the bone of contention. The Greeks wanted to recover Syria, the Fatimites to recover Palestine, the Seljuks to recover both Syria and Palestine. Naturally there was no co-operation between them ; and the lack of unity among their foes was still one of the chief assets of the Westerners. On the other hand, their own lack of unity was their most serious cause of weakness. And where they were at one, in their aggressive Westernism, which was evinced both ecclesiastically and politically, they only widened the breach with their Eastern co-religionists. Instead of the simple issue of Christianity versus Islam, the story of the crusades becomes rather one of West versus East.

The kingdom of Jerusalem The Latin kingdom suffered from the fact that it was the child of the First Crusade, and in it were reflected all the characteristics of its parent. The Crusade was a Holy War, so the Church claimed a leading place in the occupied territory ; it was led by feudal barons, so a government based on feudal customs was instituted ; its ultimate victory had been due to the assistance of the naval powers, so their commercial ambitions had to be fully satisfied ; and its success had been limited in the main to the coastal area, so that owing to their geographical situation the Latin States could not easily be governed as a single unit, while on the whole of their elongated eastern flank they were bounded by hostile Moslems. From the beginning, then, there were numerous factors militating against unity, which prevented the creation of a solid and centralised State.

The king The Western barons were strangers in a strange land, ruling over territories accustomed to an autocratic régime and inhabited by a mixed population, partly Moslem, partly Greek Christian in religion. Such had been the situation of Roger I when he conquered Sicily, and he had shown his genius by the skill with which he had utilised the various elements to serve the common purpose of his own authority and his country's prosperity. Roger, however, had the advantage, denied to Godfrey of Bouillon, of having been the single leader of a conquest designed and executed by himself. Godfrey was only one of a number of leaders, three of whom before his elevation had been endowed with separate States of their own. He was elected as *primus inter pares*, not as sovereign lord, and he had not the power, even if he had had the necessary imagination to realise the advantages of imitating the wise policy of Roger. Nor had he the time, for he died in 1100 and was succeeded by his brother Baldwin, who handed over his county of Edessa to another Baldwin, a near kinsman. Baldwin I took the title of king which Godfrey had refused. This added to his dignity, but made little difference to his authority. The kingdom of Jerusalem was the largest and the most important of the four Latin States, but its ruler was only the nominal overlord of the other three. They owed him fealty, he owed them protection in case of attack ; sometimes he intervened to settle disputes, but in all main respects they were independent principalities. The geographical position of the four States, so awkwardly situated for the purpose of a single government, may have deterred him from an attempt to assert his authority as king over them ; his former environment was probably a stronger influence in the same direction. In his native Lorraine the central authority was little regarded, and his barons, mainly French, were equally unaccustomed to its exercise.

Even in the kingdom of Jerusalem he had not the real authority of a monarch, for it was organised as a feudal State with great baronial fiefs on the French model. There was a High Court, similar in appearance to the *Curia Regis* but in fact rather a parliament of vassals, and there were great officers of State—Seneschal, Marshal, Chamberlain, Chancellor ; the local government was in the hands of the barons, who had their seignorial courts ; in the towns a royal official (viscount) presided over the courts of the burgesses and was responsible for the royal revenues. Besides this, there were commercial and maritime courts, an outcome of the important interests of the Italian naval powers ; while the only concession to the customs of the non-Latin inhabitants were the courts for native Syrians. It was a more elaborate organisation than in France, but it was essentially French in character.[1] The baronial side of the feudal contract was given particular weight, while the barons also claimed the right of electing the king. In practice, however, the king was always able to ensure the election of his heir, so that hereditary right in fact prevailed. Baldwin I was succeeded by his nephew Baldwin II of Edessa, who like his predecessor had no son. His daughter Melisande he had married to Fulk V of Anjou, who after resigning his country to his son Geoffrey (the father of Henry II of England) had gone on pilgrimage to Palestine. In 1131 Fulk succeeded his father-in-law, and reigned until

The feudal organisation

---

[1] The " customs," deliberately imitated from Western models, were worked up into a definite constitution by the lawyers of Cyprus in the thirteenth century (when the rulers of Cyprus were titular kings of Jerusalem), and were published as the " Assizes of Jerusalem." These provide the most complete statement of feudal law known to us, but probably not a very faithful picture of the practice in the kingdom of Jerusalem in the twelfth century.

1144 ; his two sons, Baldwin III and Amaury I, succeeded
him in turn. After the death of Amaury in 1174 the line
degenerated, and there were frequent contests for the throne.
But up to that time the kingdom had been fortunate in a
succession of rulers who, within the limits imposed upon
them, proved to be both capable and energetic. The king
had to live of his own, without an adequate domain ; much,
therefore, depended on his personality and resource.

The power
of the
ChurchThe barons, importing their Western ideas, imposed a
limitation upon royal authority. The Church, imported too
from the West, constituted almost a rival authority. In land
conquered under its auspices it was natural that it should
assume a leading position. A powerful hierarchy was established—two patriarchs (of Jerusalem and Antioch), eight
archbishops, and sixteen bishops ; and numerous abbeys and
priories were also founded. It was richly endowed with
lands, and was able constantly to exercise a controlling influence on the direction of affairs. Nor was the Papacy disinterested in the kingdom which it regarded as under its
special protection and guidance. It was anxious, too, to
keep the crusading spirit alive and to assist the settlers by
reinforcements from the West. There was throughout the
twelfth century a regular flow of crusaders to the Holy Land.
Sometimes this diminished to a mere trickle, occasionally it
reached the dimensions of a flood, to which the title of a
particular Crusade has been given. Grave causes led to
these greater expeditions. For the lesser there were diverse
motives, the pilgrim spirit perhaps the commonest of all,
though this was not infrequently prompted by the spiritual
indulgences which were still the reward of the journey.
There were, however, as before, the landless adventurers,
and there were criminals seeking an escape from justice
and a fresh field for their talents. These new crusaders,
if they avoided the perils of the journey and reached their
goal, were sometimes a welcome addition to the military
strength of the kingdom, and like Fulk of Anjou were enrolled
among its subjects. More often they were a nuisance. The
original crusaders were settling down, imbibing something
of the spirit and culture of the East ; the rank and file,
especially in the towns, were intermarrying with the native
population. The new-comers were a disturbing element,

aggressively Western, not amenable to order or obedient to the government.

While the secular government had to recognise the independent position of the Church in the Holy Land, it also had to admit the existence of another independent authority —that of the maritime powers of Italy. Pisa and Genoa had not only assured the victory of the crusade; their assistance had also made possible the conquest of the seaports, without which the position of the crusaders would have been extremely hazardous. They were not concerned with the religious side of the crusade; their interests were entirely commercial, and as they had made themselves essential to success by their dominance of the Eastern Mediterranean, they could dictate their own terms. They were granted exemption from tolls throughout the kingdom; a definite quarter was allotted to them in each of the seaports; and the supreme authority of their own magistrates in these areas made them extra-territorial. But if they were not under the orders of the government, they often swayed its counsels and they constantly disturbed its peace. Pisa and Genoa no longer co-operated as they had done in the Western Mediterranean; they were fierce rivals for the Levantine trade. Moreover, a third competitor soon appeared in Venice, which had taken no part in the First Crusade but after the capture of Jerusalem realised the opportunity it had missed. An expedition was immediately equipped, and arrived opportunely to assist in the capture of Haifa and to receive a trading quarter in that town. This was only a small beginning. The Genoese and Pisans had played a much larger part. They had assisted Godfrey to capture Jaffa, and in Baldwin I's reign were instrumental in reducing Beyrout, Sidon, Acre, Caesarea, and Arsuf. Of the chief ports there only remained Tyre and Ascalon to conquer. Venice had to bestir herself if she was to have any share in the Levantine trade. In 1122 an expedition on a grand scale was launched, and it arrived off Jaffa in 1123 in time to make itself indispensable. First of all it decisively defeated the Fatimite fleet from Egypt, and then in 1124 played a large part in the capture of Tyre.[1] It had already

The privileges of the Italian sea-powers

---

[1] It was debated whether the attack should be made on Tyre or Ascalon, and the question was decided by casting lots. Ascalon was only taken in 1152 by Baldwin III.

dictated its terms : in every town of the kingdom the Venetians were given a quarter of their own and all the other privileges possessed by their rivals. So the conflict for trade became more intense. These Italian city-states added materially to the strength and resources of the kingdom and by their naval victories secured the whole of its western flank. On the other hand, by their bitter rivalries they seriously impaired its unity, and by the selfishness of their commercial interests they contaminated the pure sources of the crusading movement, using it to serve their own particular ends.

Yet all the rival interests had one thing in common : the desire to defend what they had won and to add to their gains. The line of the Jordan formed a natural boundary for Palestine, and it was rarely passed. But Syria was only partially occupied by the Christians. Such important towns as Damascus and Aleppo remained in Moslem hands, and the county of Tripolis, awarded to Raymond of Toulouse, was not conquered until 1109. The northern State, Edessa, was in the most precarious position of all, stretching with ill-defined frontiers eastward beyond the Euphrates. Forming a salient into Moslem territory it was strategically important, though difficult to defend. Unfortunately there was no proper co-ordination even in the military sphere. But to all the States alike military strength was of the first importance, and in the kingdom of Jerusalem this was recognised by the fact that the military service of the tenants-in-chief was not confined to the conventional forty days. Church lands were not liable to military service, but the Church made its own contribution to the fighting forces by the creation of the two great Military Orders, the members of which combined obedience to the monastic vows with the duty of fighting the infidel. The Knights Templars, so-called from the contiguity of their house to the site of Solomon's temple, were formed with this purpose in 1108. The community of the hospital of St. John of Jerusalem imitated their example six years later, and became the Knights of St. John of Jerusalem (Knights Hospitallers). In the early years they were a valuable addition to the defence of the country. Famous castles, such as Krak des Chevaliers, attest their skill in military architecture. Their wealth and military efficiency attracted recruits from the West, and they were able together

The Military Orders

to put more knights into the field than the king himself.   As their numbers increased, so did their pride and independence, and they too became a disturbing element, especially owing to the rivalry between the two Orders.   Nor did they long maintain the high ideals with which they had been formed. They learnt to take an interest in commerce, especially the Templars, who even in the Holy Land embarked upon the financial career which later was to lead them to disaster in France.

From various directions, therefore, the rulers of the Holy Land acquired allies, who rendered valuable aid at first, but whose self-interest made them later most dangerous to the harmony and unity of the kingdom.   The country was distracted by the rivalries of these independent elements, each in its way indispensable, but each subordinating the common good to its own interest.   It is surprising indeed that the kingdom lasted so long.   That it did was due to the ability of the kings, the divisions among the Moslems, and to the crusading spirit which only slowly yielded to material influences.   Baldwin I (1100–18) undertook a vigorous offensive, and besides capturing seaports advanced into Transjordania, where the district east and south of the Dead Sea was defended by the castles of Karak and Montreal.   Baldwin II was defeated in 1123 and was in captivity for a year, but he avenged his defeat by a great victory in 1125.   It was during his captivity that the important capture of Tyre by the Venetians occurred.   The first quarter of the twelfth century was the great period of crusading success; for shortly afterwards the Moslem power began to revive.   On the whole the position of the Christian States remained unaltered during the reign of Fulk.   It was with his death in 1144 that the decline began.

Even in the earlier period, however, the kings had been unable to make any sensible conquest of the mainland of Syria; this in part was due to the handicap imposed on them by the conditions that existed in the kingdom, in part to the weakness of the two northern States, to whom they had frequently to render assistance.   In Edessa Joscelin I, the successor of Baldwin II, was an able soldier, but he was exposed on three sides to attacks from the Moslems.   The

Early successes

The Eastern Empire and its policy

principality of Antioch had to suffer the hostility of the Eastern Emperors as well.

The First Crusade had come as an interruption to the working out of Alexius' policy of recovery. It had helped him to regain a part of Asia Minor, and had diverted the attention and hostility of many of the Moslem leaders. At the same time it had introduced other complications, and an additional objective—the recovery of Antioch from the Latins. Imperial policy under Alexius, under his son John, and (for a short time) under his grandson Manuel was directed primarily to the double aim of driving back the Moslems in Asia Minor and subjugating the Christians in Syria. Occasionally their attention was directed to the north by raids of Cumans or Patzinaks or by conflicts with Hungary, where both John and Manuel intervened on the occasion of disputes for the throne. Their western territories caused them frequent anxiety, owing to the danger of Norman invasion, particularly after the acquisition of South Italy by Roger II. But the main preoccupation, at any rate of Alexius and John, was with Asia Minor. John followed in his father's footsteps, equally determined but more straightforward in his methods. He was not in the desperate position of his father, and he had no need of cunning schemes ill-suited to his character, the nobility of which is attested even by a Latin writer. Manuel continued the policy, but with him it was only part of a greater scheme. In many ways more brilliant, or at any rate more versatile, than his father, his qualities were of much less solid worth. He neglected the substance and grasped at the shadow. He could not master the situation in the East, and yet he indulged in rash ventures in the West, seeking to restore the authority of the Eastern Empire in Italy. Withal he added immensely to the financial burdens of his subjects, overweighted already by the measures adopted by Alexius in his task of restoration. Manuel was keenly interested in letters and in astrological speculation, and, like his grandfather, in theology ; he claimed to dictate even in matters of doctrine. In these various ways his reign recalls that of Justinian ; though he never attained to the greatness of that Emperor, his similarly grandiose policy had equally disastrous results.

The two parts of the Eastern policy of the Emperors were closely linked together. No advance could be made against

Antioch while the Moslem rulers in Asia Minor—especially the Sultan of Rūm (Iconium) and the Danishmandite emirs farther east—were strong enough to threaten them in flank or rear. The road to Cilicia via Attalia had to be maintained and guarded. And then Cilicia itself, where was the principality of Lesser Armenia, had to be subdued in order to open the path to Syria. The new Armenian dynasty owed much of its security to the crusaders, but it was anxious to preserve its independence even of them. It was often forced to ally with the Latin ruler of Antioch, owing to the attempt of the Byzantines to conquer its territory. Alexius himself owed much to the crusaders. They had carved out the way to Cilicia and Syria, and had defeated the Sultan of Iconium so severely that for a time he was scarcely a danger. Therefore Alexius was able easily to follow in their footsteps. He was further assisted by the difficulties of Bohemond, who from the time that he became prince of Antioch seemed to have been deserted by fortune and to have lost also his former skill in battle.

Already in 1100 Bohemond had been taken prisoner by the Turks and remained for over two years in captivity. Again, in 1104, he suffered a disastrous defeat at Harran. Alexius seized the opportunity for which he had long been waiting and overran Cilicia ; while his fleet captured Laodicea and the other seaports of the principality of Antioch, thereby cutting off Bohemond from all direct contact with the West. Hemmed in on both sides, by Turks and Greeks, Bohemond was in despair. At last, in 1105, he handed over the care of his principality to his nephew Tancred and himself departed for the West, to organise an expedition against Alexius. It took him two years, but in the meantime the stories that he spread helped to establish in the West a firm tradition of the perfidy of the Eastern Emperor, which was not without its effect on the future. In 1107 he landed in Greece, only to find that the Byzantine army was a very different one from that which he and his father had defeated so easily. Alexius refused battle and skilfully outmanœuvred his enemy until he had completely encircled him. Bohemond was forced to capitulate and to submit to a humiliating peace by which he became the subject of Alexius ; he was allowed to retain Antioch (where the patriarch was to be of the Greek faith) and a few outlying districts as a fief from the Emperor, but he had to relinquish all claims to Cilicia and to leave the seaports of his principality in Alexius' hands. The treaty was not carried out, as Bohemond was broken by his misfortunes and retired to Italy ; Tancred refused to be bound by it. The Eastern Emperors, however, regarded it as valid, and in their attempts to obtain its enforcement persisted, in spite of Bohemond's overthrow, in their hostility to the ruler of the principality. So long as they held the seaports and Cilicia they were in a strong position.

For the rest of his reign Alexius was too much engaged with the Moslems in Asia Minor to be able to pursue his advantage in Cilicia and Antioch. The Seljuks resumed the offensive in 1109. Alexius was for some time on the defensive, and his attention was diverted by a troublesome raid of the Cumans ; at last in 1114 he won a victory which enabled him to stabilise his eastern frontier on a line passing through Gangra, Ancyra, Amorium, and Philomelium (he already held the coast line of the Black Sea as far as Trebizond). But south of Smyrna only the coastal area was securely his, so that the road through Pamphylia to Cilicia was dangerously exposed to attack. This he did nothing to rectify, as his victory in 1114 was his final achievement. His last years were embittered by another plot, engineered in his domestic circle by his wife Irene and his daughter Anna (his future biographer), to supplant John and to gain the succession for Anna's husband Nicephorus Bryennius. On his death-bed in 1118 Alexius displayed his last feat of cunning to checkmate them and ensure the crown for his son.

The first year of John's reign was also disturbed by the ambition of his sister ; but her plot was unmasked, and she spent the rest of her life in retirement, the fruit of which was her famous *Alexiad*. After this John was hardly troubled by the court intrigues which had been so serious an embarrassment to the government in previous reigns ; indeed it was only after the death of Manuel in 1180 that they resumed their former activity. The Emperor was able to continue the work left unfinished by his father ; in 1119 he was successful in the south of Asia Minor in capturing a number of places in the region of Attalia, and so restoring direct communication by land with Cilicia. He was not able to follow up his success, however, for during a number of years the European portion of his Empire engaged his attention. There was a raid of Patzinaks in 1121 which was not finally repelled until the following year ; and in 1128 there was a troublesome war with Hungary. In between these two conflicts in the north came a long period of discord with Venice. The Emperors were not averse to ending their dependence on this dictatorial ally ; it had become less essential to them, owing to the temporary weakness of the Normans in South Italy and to the revival of the Byzantine fleet, which had proved its worth in the operations against Antioch. Alexius had interfered with the Venetian monopoly by granting the Pisans trading privileges in Constantinople ; John not only renewed these, but even attempted to cancel the privileges of the Venetians. So, when they fitted out an expedition in 1122 to establish themselves in the Holy Land, they retaliated on the Emperor by attacking Corfù on the way out, and by raiding various of the Aegean islands on the return journey. In 1126 John decided to make peace with them on the old terms. Clearly they were too dangerous as enemies, and the incident provided a warning which his successors were not wise enough to heed.

In 1130 the Emperor was able to resume his eastern policy. **John conquers Cilicia** Civil war among the Moslems had prevented them from taking advantage of his absence ; but though he attempted to profit by their dissensions, this only had the effect of closing their ranks against him. At last in 1135 he was able to make headway by the capture of Gangra and other towns in its vicinity. He then felt himself sufficiently secure to undertake the second half of his programme, in which Antioch was the objective. Since the victory of Alexius, the Armenians under Thoros I and Leo I had recovered the chief towns in Cilicia, and had successfully defended them against the princes of Antioch. John invaded Cilicia in 1137 with complete success ; the towns were recaptured, and Leo was taken prisoner. For eight years the Armenians were without a prince, and Cilicia was a Greek province.

This brought John face to face with the principality of **Asserts his authority over Antioch** Antioch, which had changed hands several times since Bohemond had left it to its fate. Tancred had died in 1112, and his nephew and successor, Roger, was killed in battle in 1119.

Then Bohemond II, the young son of Bohemond I, was chosen. During the seven years of his minority, which he spent in Italy, the king of Jerusalem, Baldwin II, took charge of the principality, and both it and the kingdom were benefited by their temporary union under a single ruler. Bohemond II arrived in 1126 but only survived for four years, to be succeeded by his daughter Constance. In 1136 she married Raymond of Poitiers, uncle of Eleanor of Aquitaine who married Louis VII of France in the following year. So, when John Comnenus began the siege of Antioch, Raymond was prince. He was forced to agree to the fulfilment of the treaty of 1107, and took an oath of fealty to the Emperor. They agreed to unite their forces against the Moslems, but the mutual distrust and dislike was too strong, and John soon abandoned the expedition. In 1142 he came again to Syria, and faced by Raymond's refusal to abide by the conditions of the treaty determined to take Antioch by force. However, the season was late and he had to postpone operations; in the spring of 1143, before they could be resumed, he died in Cilicia, where he had taken up his winter quarters. Raymond was emboldened to invade Cilicia, but the success of the Greek troops against him forced him to go to Constantinople to throw himself on the mercy of the new Emperor. Manuel seemed to have victory in his hands, but once again the course of events was interrupted by the initiation of a Crusade in the West.

Growing hostility between Eastern and Western Christians

This continued conflict between the Eastern Emperors and one of the Latin States was an important factor in the embitterment of relations between Eastern and Western Christians. Already in the First Crusade suspicion of the Eastern Emperor had been aroused, and Bohemond had been effective in fostering its growth. It seemed an obvious confirmation of Bohemond's stories when the Emperors were seen to be putting forth all their strength against a Christian State, instead of uniting with the Latin Christians against the infidel. To this extent the West was certainly justified: the Emperors were only intent on the recovery of their territories, from Moslem and Christian alike, and were not concerned with the Holy War. On the other hand, the Emperor could justly complain of the perfidy of the princes of Antioch, who had broken the original compact and also refused to abide by the treaty of 1107. Nor were the Latins in Palestine and Syria less selfish in their aims than the Greeks; they were mainly occupied in a struggle for territory, and did not scruple to attack their fellow Christians, Greek and Armenian. Each side was equally concerned with its own interests, equally unjust to the other. The Latins as much as the Greeks were responsible for the disunion of Christendom. The mutual hostility was disastrous to both in turn; during the second half of the twelfth century it was the Latins that suffered most, but in the Fourth Crusade they took an ample revenge.

The disunion among the Christians had been matched by the disunion among their Moslem opponents. The chief Moslem towns in Syria were held by independent emirs, who only acted in common to prevent a Christian advance. The change began when Zangi became emir of Mosul on the Tigris, the ancient Nineveh. His ambition was to unite all Moslem Syria under his single authority. His immediate success was considerable, for within three years he had captured both Aleppo and Hamah, and confronted the principality of Antioch along its eastern frontier. It was partly the pressure from this quarter that caused Raymond to submit to John Comnenus, and Aleppo was one of the objectives of their alliance. Though this came to nought, Zangi reverted to his original plan and marched south against Damascus, the only important Moslem town not in his possession. Its emir, however, with some help from the Latins, successfully defended himself. Zangi once more changed direction; he turned north against the Latin State of Edessa, which, after the death of Joscelin I, had declined rapidly under the indolent rule of his son Joscelin II. In 1144 Edessa fell, and the whole line of the Euphrates was in Moslem hands. Two years later Zangi was murdered, but his son Nuraddin proved a capable successor and eventually completed his father's original purpose. *The fall of Edessa*

The news of the capture of Edessa came as a great shock to Western Europe, and in the horror of it awoke again the old crusading zeal. The Pope once more took the initiative, but Eugenius III entrusted St. Bernard with the mission of preaching the crusade, and his strong will and evangelistic fervour won instant success. Louis VII and his wife Eleanor immediately responded, and Bernard was able to persuade *Organisation of the Second Crusade*

Conrad III also to take the cross. Yet, though on this occasion the rulers of Germany and France participated, they did not make common cause ; and the contingents that came from England and South Italy, though they joined the French, retained their independence of command. If Conrad had been crowned Emperor, he might have had more authority ; but he was only king in fact of part of Germany, and could only leave Germany because the Welf party engaged in a crusade against the heathen Slavs. Moreover, there was a strong feeling of enmity between French and German crusaders, breaking out often in insults and opprobrious nicknames ; it was something that they usually kept from blows, and they had in common their hatred of the Greeks. Naturally they acted separately. Though both took the same route—the old pilgrim road via Hungary to Constantinople—the Germans left Ratisbon in May 1147, the French over a month later.

Manuel I and the Crusaders

For Manuel the Second Crusade was even more of an embarrassment than the First had been for Alexius. He had not asked for aid from the West, and he could not employ it as Alexius had done in conquering part of Asia Minor ; nor could he expect kings to take the oath of fealty to which the baronial leaders had consented. The best he could hope was to shepherd them through his dominions with all possible speed. He made the same dispositions as his grandfather— envoys to greet them, arrangements for supplying them with food, troops to guard against their rapacity—and he was more fortunate in that he had only one route to guard. But all his care could not prevent friction or keep the Germans from plundering when their greed was excited. He did his best to persuade them not to come to Constantinople, but to cross the Hellespont at Sestos and follow the coast road. It was excellent advice, though he was only considering his own interest when he gave it. But Conrad was determined to follow in the track of the first crusaders to Nicaea and thence through Asia Minor. Afflicted by famine and disease, harassed by the Turks, and finally deserted by their Greek guides, the Germans suffered a severe disaster on October 26 near Dorylaeum, the place where the first crusaders had inflicted a decisive defeat on the enemy. Conrad retraced his steps with great difficulty to Nicaea, where the French had

The defeat of the Germans

already arrived ; he himself with a few of his troops joined forces with Louis VII, but the majority of the survivors returned at once to Germany.

The French, following the track of the Germans into Greece, had suffered from the hostility created by the German excesses. So indignant were the French barons with their reception that many of them counselled an immediate attack upon Constantinople. Manuel had to do his best to counteract this by giving as warm a welcome as possible to Louis VII, and indeed he hoped to divide the crusaders by playing off the French against the Germans. Later, when Conrad had been defeated and he had nothing more to fear from him, he transferred his favour to the Germans. This shifty policy, dictated by the instinct for self-preservation, only added in the West to the growing hatred of the Byzantines. At any rate, Louis took his advice and followed the coast road to Smyrna. From there he marched by the most direct route to Attalia, encountering severe losses on the way from the Moslems who hung on his flanks. To avoid further mishaps he decided to go from there by sea to Antioch. This put the French at the mercy of the Greeks, whom they already suspected of being in league with the Turks against them. However, they had no alternative ; they had to take what ships they could get at the price the Greeks demanded, and this made it possible for only the leading barons and knights to accompany the king. The mass of the army, for whose security Louis, as he believed, had obtained guarantees from the Greeks, found itself in a desperate position after his departure ; some perished of hunger and disease, others trying to struggle on by road were cut to pieces by the Turks. So the second crusading army, like the first, was decimated in Asia Minor.

The failure of the French expedition

In April 1148 Louis with Eleanor and his barons arrived at Antioch, where Eleanor's uncle gave them a warm welcome. Conrad, who had left the French before they reached Smyrna and returned to Constantinople, was readily provided with ships by Manuel and landed at Acre shortly before Louis reached Antioch. After collecting together such German contingents as had managed to complete the journey, he made his way to Jerusalem where he was given a royal reception. Louis, too, started to come south, and the three kings—of Jerusalem, Germany, and France—met in con-

Louis VII in the Holy Land

ference at Acre. The prince of Antioch in his own interest wished the crusaders to take the field against Nuraddin, and this was undoubtedly the right course. However, the interests of the kingdom of Jerusalem prevailed, and the safer and more attractive scheme of attacking Damascus was adopted. But the defences of the city were strong, the difficulties of supply were great, and there was little unity among the allies ; the Moslems were even able to bribe some of the barons of Jerusalem to desist from the undertaking. So the siege was

The end of the Second Crusade abandoned, and with this last fiasco the Second Crusade came to an end. Conrad immediately took ship for Constantinople. Louis stayed on for some time, as a pilgrim rather than as a crusader, visiting the Holy Places and quarrelling with his wife ; her behaviour at Antioch justified his suspicions of her infidelity and led him to make his most fatal mistake, of obtaining a divorce.

The effect on the Latin kingdom This was one of the minor ill-consequences of the expedition. The Crusade was a grievous failure, but it was more than that ; the general situation after it was worse than before. Western Europe was both ashamed and disgusted ; even St. Bernard's reputation was temporarily affected ; and it needed a lapse of forty years and the violent shock of the fall of Jerusalem to galvanise the crusading spirit into life again. So the Latins in the East were left to themselves at a time when their enemies were gathering strength against them. Nuraddin was able quietly to complete his conquest of Edessa by the capture of Tell-Bashir in 1150, and Damascus, which the Latins had first helped to defend against him and had then tried to take for themselves, fell an easy prey in 1154. The whole of Moslem Syria was in his hands, and he now confronted the kingdom of Jerusalem and the county of Tripolis as well as the principality of Antioch. One victory King Baldwin III achieved—the capture of Ascalon in 1152 —but this was won over the Egyptian Fatimites. They were declining rapidly to their extinction ; the arena was being cleared for the final contest between the Seljuks and the Latins.

The widening of the breach between Eastern and Western Christendom The Second Crusade widened the breach between Eastern and Western Christendom. It was natural that the unsuccessful crusaders should seek to cast the blame on the Eastern Emperor, and it was certain that with his co-operation they could have escaped the disasters they met with in Asia Minor.

He had left them to their own devices, being only too thankful
to get rid of them, and he was strongly suspected of having
betrayed first Conrad and then Louis to the Turks. Conrad,
indeed, with schemes against the Normans in South Italy,
resumed friendly relations with Manuel; but Louis openly
denounced the Eastern Emperor as responsible for the disaster, and provided useful propaganda for Roger II whom
he met on his return. This was the danger-point for Manuel,
as he well knew. Roger II, like Robert Guiscard and Bohemond, was greedy for conquest in Greece, and had even taken
advantage of the crusade to attack the Eastern Empire.
The Eastern Emperors had tried to join forces with the
Western against the common enemy. As John Comnenus
had entered into negotiations with Lothar, so had Manuel
with Conrad, and in 1146 had married Conrad's sister-in-law
Bertha of Sulzbach. He reopened negotiations with Conrad
on his return from Syria, and got into touch with the Pope as
well. A counter-offensive against the Norman king was the
surest way of protecting his western territories, but his
ambition overtopped the mark. He made the grave mistake
of aiming at conquest, in spite of the counter-claims of
Western Emperor and Pope, in order to re-establish Greek
dominion in South Italy. Naturally this was not to the taste
of his Western colleagues. Frederick Barbarossa refused to
renew the alliance made with Conrad, and in his treaty of
Constance with the Pope in 1153 it was expressly stipulated
that no territory in Italy was to be ceded to " the king of
the Greeks." The phrase was a marked insult to the older
Emperor, who was beginning to dream of the union of the
two Empires under his sceptre. His occupation of Ancona
in 1155 raised his hopes, which were not extinguished by his
subsequent defeat in South Italy. Yet the Normans were
as strong as ever, and he had created a new enemy in the
Venetians.[1] Though he had lost all his friends in the West,
he still clung to his dream of a single Empire.

SUGGESTIONS FOR READING ON CHAPTER XV (AND XXII)

Cambridge Medieval History, Vol. IV, new edn. (see p. xx); Vol. V, chapters
8,9. Also the works of Bréhier, Grousset, Runciman and Setton suggested on
Chap. XI, above.

---

[1] These events, which needed brief recapitulation here, have been more
fully told in Chapter XIII, above.

CHAPTER XVI

THE SPANISH PENINSULA IN THE TWELFTH CENTURY

Moslem
recovery
under the
Almoravides

BY the end of the eleventh century the conflict between Christianity and Islam in the West was practically confined to the Spanish peninsula. During the twelfth century there is little change to be recorded there ; the first victorious period of the Reconquest was concluded, and it was not until the beginning of the thirteenth century that the forward movement was to be resumed. In the first place, the Christian advance had been brought to a halt by the new wave of Moslem invaders from North Africa. The impulse was religion as well as conquest, for the Almoravides (as their name signifies) were religious zealots. For this very reason they were as hostile to the unorthodox and free-thinking Moslems in southern Spain as they were to their Christian antagonists ; and so, while they came in response to the appeals of the rulers of the *taifas*, they ended by reducing them to submission. The restoration of Moslem unity seemed to presage a reconquest by the Moslems ; they did indeed recover Valencia in 1102, three years after the death of the Cid, and in 1108 Alfonso VI of Castile was again defeated and his son Sancho slain. But otherwise the Christian territories remained intact. The Almoravides were mainly intent on the task, which occupied all their powers, of consolidating their empire in Morocco and over their co-religionists in Spain. Soon, too, they were themselves threatened by the rise of another body of zealots in Morocco, the Almohades (Unitarians). A long and bitter conflict ensued, which resulted in the overthrow of the Almoravides after they had lost their leader, the son of Yusuf, in 1143. During this period of conflict the kingdoms of the *taifas* were restored and Moslem unity in Spain was again shattered. That the Christians failed to seize the opportunity of resuming the

The
Almohades
replace the
Almoravides

offensive was due to the simultaneous outburst of civil war in Castile, which resulted in the birth of a new kingdom, Portugal. The kingdom of Aragon, indeed, made some advance, and was strengthened by its union with Catalonia, but it was as much concerned with winning profit for itself from the civil strife in Castile as with the prospect of gaining territory from the Moslems.

So Christian disunion ruined the opportunity, which Moslem disunion had presented, of conquering the whole peninsula and dominating the narrow sea so as to cut the link which bound Moslem Africa with Moslem Spain. In 1146 the Almohades, victorious in Morocco, advanced in their turn into Spain. Once more the kingdoms of the *taifas* were subjected and a single power ruled southern Spain and Morocco. The Almohades, however, did not pursue a vigorous offensive against the Christians. They, like their predecessors, were more concerned with dominating their fellow-Moslems, and they extended their empire in North Africa eastward as far as Tunis and Tripoli. But during the second half of the century the Christians in Spain were forced on to the defensive ; for a long time, still distracted by their own dissensions, they were content, apart from isolated exploits which brought little permanent gain, to keep their frontiers intact. It was only a severe defeat at the end of the century that aroused them to the need for unity and a resumption of a determined offensive.

The conflict of Christianity and Islam in the West was The kings of not entirely confined to Spain, for they came into contact Sicily and at one other point, where again the contiguity of North Africa North Africa with Europe brought them closely together. But here the positions were entirely reversed. The Norman conquerors of Sicily invaded the adjacent shores of North Africa in the twelfth century. Commerce was one motive, Norman lust for territory was another ; it was definitely not a religious war. Roger II was defeated in his attack on Mahdiyah in 1123, but thanks to his great admiral, George of Antioch, he was able to retrieve this disaster, and at the time of his death the whole coast-line from Tripoli to Bona, as well as some portions of the interior, was held by his garrisons. Already, however, the Almohades, successful in Morocco, had begun to push eastwards ; **they won over their co-religionists to**

12

revolt against the Normans, and reaped the fruits of victory
themselves. William I was too much engrossed with the
dangers that assailed his kingdom in Italy to be able to pay
any heed to Africa ; and when Mahdiyah was captured by
the Almohades in 1160, the Normans lost their last foothold
on the African continent. William II, apart from an isolated
raid in 1163, made no effort to recover his grandfather's
conquests. There was at any rate no danger to the Christians
from this quarter. The Norman fleet commanded the sea,
and a Moslem invasion of Sicily was therefore impossible.
The Moslems had regained the whole of North Africa, but
only at its western end was any contact with Western Europe
maintained.

The Christian States

The history of the Spanish peninsula in the twelfth century
is largely conditioned by the position of affairs in North
Africa. Yet, for the reasons that have already been indicated,
the work of Reconquest was practically at a standstill ; the
chief events of the history are concerned with the domestic
affairs of the Christian States. At the beginning of the
century these States were three in number. Of prime importance was the kingdom of Castile and Leon, which occupied
the west and centre of the northern half of the peninsula.
The line of the Tagus had had to be abandoned, and in the
west Castile's southern boundary was now the river Mondego,
with Coimbra as the principal town in that region. Adjacent
to Castile on the north-east was Navarre, but on most of its
eastern as well as its southern frontiers the kingdom was
bounded by the Moslems, who after their conquest of Valencia
occupied the eastern portion of the peninsula to a line north
of the Ebro and almost reaching to Barcelona on the coast.
So the remaining Christian States were confined to the north-
east, and together occupied an area much smaller than either
the Castilian or the Moslem territories. Navarre, lying astride
the Pyrenees, had temporarily ceased to be a kingdom and
was subject to its eastern neighbour Aragon. Hitherto of
little account, the kingdom of Aragon began rapidly to expand
under Alfonso I the Warrior, who became king in 1104. His
prime achievement was the capture of Saragossa in 1118,
a conquest comparable with that of Toledo by Castile in the
previous century. After this first success he made daring

raids through Valencia to the south, from one of which he
returned with some thousands of Mozarabs whom he settled
upon the territory he had conquered, imitating the earlier
policy of Castile to overcome the difficulty of peopling his
new lands.   At the time of his death in 1134 he was successfully engaged on the task of pushing his frontiers to the line
of the Ebro.   His neighbour on the east, the count of Barcelona, was no less enterprising.   Count Raymond-Berengar
III, master already of the greater part of Catalonia, also won
castles from the Moslems in the region of the Ebro, so that
his frontier began to advance side by side with that of Aragon ;
a more daring exploit was his attack, in alliance with Pisa,
on the island of Majorca, which was made tributary.   His
advance on the other side of the Pyrenees was equally remarkable.   Though the counts of Barcelona had ceased to recognise
the suzerainty of the kings of France, they were continually
adding to their possessions in France ; and the most important
acquisition of all was made by Raymond-Berengar III, who
obtained Provence in 1112 by his second marriage with
Douce, the heiress to the county.

While the Christian States in the north-east were thus Queen
expanding their frontiers at the expense of the Moslems, Urraca
Castile was in the throes of civil war.   Alfonso VI had of Castile
frequently experienced the bitterness of defeat after the
coming of the Almoravides, and on the last occasion, at Ucles
in 1108, he lost his only son Sancho.   So when he died in
1109, there was only a daughter, Urraca, a widow with an
infant son (Alfonso), to succeed him.   Her husband Raymond, son of count William of Burgundy (Franche-Comté),
had fought with Alfonso VI against the Moslems and been
rewarded with the hand of Urraca and the governorship of
Galicia, which included also the territory to the south as far
as Coimbra.   He was joined by his kinsman Henry from The county
French Burgundy, a member of the ducal house ; on him of Portugal
Alfonso VI bestowed the hand of his illegitimate daughter
Theresa and an appanage on the west coast under Raymond's
overlordship.   This stretched from the Douro to the Mondego,
and as Oporto and the territory adjacent to it was known as
the *terra Portucalensis*, the whole sphere of Henry's authority
came to be called the county of Portucale or Portugal ; later
it was extended northwards by Alfonso as far as the river

Minho and conferred on Henry as a hereditary fief. The death of Raymond in 1107, followed by that of Sancho in 1108, raised in Henry the hope that he might be given a share in the kingdom. But Alfonso VI left everything to Urraca, and Henry, in lieu of the greater position of which he had been disappointed, determined to create from his county of Portugal an independent principality for himself.

Civil war
in Castile The situation in Castile favoured the scheme. The Castilian nobles, wanting a man at the head of the State to conduct the war against the Moslems, found him in the warrior-king of Aragon, Alfonso I, and forced Urraca to marry him. The marriage was a failure from both points of view, for Urraca hated the match and was soon at open enmity with her husband, while Alfonso, ambitious to be political master as well as military leader, at once estranged the Castilian magnates. Even the annulment of the marriage by an ecclesiastical council on the ground of consanguinity made no difference, for Alfonso did not relax his efforts for political control. Henry of Portugal was able to make capital out of this conjugal strife. By giving his help first to one and then to the other, he obtained promises from them both of additional territory and an independent government; and when he died in 1114, his widow Theresa, left with an infant son Afonso Henriques, carried on his policy with success. In this she was helped by the attitude of Galicia, where the bishop of Compostela, Diego Gelmirez, was the dominant figure; wealthy and ambitious, he typified the particularist spirit which was becoming noticeable in the western part of the Castilian kingdom. Diego not only took the lead in checkmating the ambition of Alfonso of Aragon, he put forward the claims of Urraca's son Alfonso to be king both of Galicia, as his grandfather had designed, and also of Leon. In 1121 Diego achieved his personal ambition when Pope Calixtus II raised his see to the rank of an archbishopric; he now began, in concert with Theresa, to promote the plan of replacing Urraca on the throne by her son. Urraca tried to wreak her vengeance on Theresa, but had to be content with a compromise, by which Theresa obtained a large stretch of territory in Leon, formerly promised to her husband, on condition of recognising herself as Urraca's vassal. Such was the unhappy state of Castile during Urraca's reign. She was engaged in a constant struggle with Alfonso I of Aragon, and at the same time had to face the attempts of her step-sister to form an independent principality as well as those of Diego and the Galician nobles to dethrone her in favour of her son. Fortunately, owing to the divisions among the Moslems, she was not exposed to attack from the south; but equally it was impossible to take this golden opportunity of an offensive against the Moslems.

The death of Urraca in 1126 somewhat relieved the situation, as there was no opposition to the succession of her son Alfonso VII.[1] But he had to face the continued hostility of his stepfather Alfonso of Aragon, and also the particularist spirit in Galicia and Portugal. Theresa attempted to throw off his suzerainty, but in a short campaign in 1127 Alfonso forced her to submit. Then she experienced the fate she had plotted for her sister. Her son Afonso Henriques claimed the government for himself, and in 1128 was able to make good his claim; his mother went into exile and died there two years later. This in itself was a defiance of Alfonso VII, Theresa's overlord; but for some years the king of Castile was too much occupied to be able to enforce his authority over the young count. However, in 1137, when Afonso Henriques was hampered by a Moslem invasion, Alfonso led an expedition against him and forced him to take an oath of feudal allegiance. In accordance with this he summoned him to a joint expedition against the Moslems, in which considerable success was obtained; Afonso Henriques especially distinguished himself by crossing the Tagus and winning a brilliant victory at Ourique in 1139. Inspired by this success, he once more asserted his independence; he assumed the royal title and had himself proclaimed as king Afonso I of Portugal. Alfonso VII, while he vehemently denounced this audacity of his vassal, was disinclined to proceed to action, and was more interested in his campaigns against the Moslems; and in 1143, at the intervention of a papal legate, a definitive peace was made and Afonso's title was recognised by the king of Castile. Afonso also obtained papal recognition[2]

Alfonso VII of Castile

Afonso I, first king of Portugal

---

[1] He is termed Alfonso VIII by some writers, since Alfonso I of Aragon claimed to be king Alfonso VII of Castile.

[2] At first as a duchy. Alexander III in 1179 was the first Pope to concede the title of kingdom.

by placing his kingdom under papal overlordship and paying an annual tribute. So came into being the kingdom of Portugal.

Aragon, after the death of Alfonso I

Meanwhile a very different development was in process in the north-eastern States, where Navarre snapped the link that bound it to Aragon, while Aragon was joined in a much more satisfactory, and an enduring, union with its eastern neighbour Catalonia. The death of Alfonso I of Aragon seemed likely to be the prelude to disorder and disintegration such as had followed the death of Alfonso VI of Castile in 1109 ; the more so, as Alfonso I had no child and bequeathed his territories in equal shares to the Knights Templars and Knights Hospitallers. Needless to say, the eccentric bequest was not carried out, but for the moment there was grave confusion and perplexity, of which Navarre and Castile were prompt to take advantage. The Navarrese broke off the hated connection with Aragon ; the kingdom of Navarre was revived, and Garcia V, a member of the old royal family, was placed on the throne. Alfonso VII of Castile, for his part, claimed to be king of Aragon by virtue of his mother's marriage with Alfonso I—a fitting retaliation for his step-father's claims on Castile—and he actually took possession of the new capital, Saragossa. The Aragonese nobles repudiated his claim and chose as their king Alfonso I's brother, Ramiro, a monk, who was released from his vows by papal dispensation ; to secure the succession a marriage was hastily arranged for him, and in 1135 he became the father of a daughter, Petronilla. To obtain the evacuation of his territories by the king of Castile, he had to recognise the feudal overlordship of Alfonso, whose suzerainty was also acknowledged for a time by Navarre and Barcelona. There was,

Alfonso VII of Castile, " Emperor of Spain "

therefore, some justification for Alfonso's assumption in 1135 of the title of " Emperor of Spain," a title formerly held by his ancestor Ferdinand I and denoting both the dominant position held by Castile in the peninsula and also the exclusion of Spain from the Empire of the German kings. The title survived for Alfonso's lifetime only, and had little meaning even then ; the separatist feeling in Spain was too strong to admit of unity under a single ruler, even against the Moslems. Apart from the loss of Portugal, the rest of Alfonso VII's reign was not unsuccessful. He made a notable advance against the Moslems, penetrating through Andalusia and capturing Cordova in 1144 and Almeria on the south coast in 1147. But these were isolated points that could not permanently be held, and the Castilian frontier was not actually advanced. For in 1146 the Almohades entered Spain, and though at first they contented themselves mainly with subjecting the rulers of the *taifas*, a task which was not complete until 1172, they were able to prevent any permanent occupation of Moslem territory in South Spain by the Christians.

Union of Aragon and Catalonia under Alfonso II

Ramiro II of Aragon, having played his part both of preserving the separate kingdom of Aragon and providing an heir to it, was anxious to retire again into a monastery, which he did after betrothing the infant Petronilla to Raymond-Berengar IV, who had succeeded his father as count of Barcelona in 1131, and leaving him to govern as her guardian. Ramiro's abdication took place in 1137, so from that year dates the real union of Aragon and Catalonia in a single government. Raymond-Berengar married Petronilla in 1150, and himself died in 1162. Their son Raymond succeeded to Barcelona and Catalonia, and, when his mother abdicated in 1164, to Aragon as well, taking as king the name of Alfonso II. This marks the formal union of the two principalities, known henceforward as the kingdom of Aragon, though it was Catalonia rather than Aragon that was the more important, and in some ways the dominant half. It had this compensation for the hiding of its identity, which was not completely merged in that of Aragon; the Catalans jealously preserved their Usages, which had been drawn up as a code of law in the eleventh century. In most respects, however, the union was complete, and harmony, thanks to common advantages and common interest, was maintained. The common sense of the Aragonese in consenting to the government of the count of Barcelona, and the wisdom and tact of Raymond-Berengar during the years of regency, tided over the difficult twenty-five years that followed the abdication of Ramiro. Alfonso II, heir to both principalities, was therefore troubled by no internal difficulties on his accession. Moreover, his father had consolidated the southern advance made by the two States when separate; he had conquered the whole of the territory north of the Ebro, the navigation of which was secured by the capture of Tortosa in 1148.

While the newly-constituted kingdom of Aragon was thus settling down, Castile was passing through another period of internal discord. Unlike Alfonso VI, who had no son, Alfonso VII had two, and when he died in 1157 the family tradition of division of the inheritance was allowed, as usual, to override the interests of the kingdom. He left Castile to his elder son, Sancho III, Leon to the younger, Ferdinand II. Leon remained a separate kingdom for seventy-three years ; and moreover, from the beginning it was almost continually at enmity with Castile. A further calamity befell Castile when Sancho, after a year spent in resisting the attacks of Ferdinand, died in 1158 leaving a son, Alfonso VIII, only three years of age, to succeed him. Civil war was added to foreign invasion to distress the country. The two most powerful noble houses, the Lara and the Castro, contested the government, the advantage resting with the former, who had obtained possession of the person of the young king. It was not until 1166 that Alfonso escaped from their custody, and managed to win support from the rest of the nobility and from the towns, until at last he established himself in control at Toledo and the two great families had to renounce their ambition. At the early age of eleven Alfonso had already proved himself to be a worthy successor to the two Alfonsos who had preceded him ; his achievements were eventually to surpass theirs. But several years were still to elapse before Castile was freed from the dangers which threatened it from its neighbours. Aragon and Navarre were eager to have their revenge for the subordination to which Alfonso VII had reduced them. Ferdinand II of Leon was ambitious to unite the Castilian crown with his own. His attention, however, was to a large extent occupied by the invasion of his territories by Afonso I of Portugal, who made several attempts, from 1161 onwards, to acquire the lands in Galicia and Leon which had been held by, or promised to, his mother. At last in 1169 at the siege of Badajoz he was defeated and taken prisoner, and he was only released after he had surrendered both his acquisitions and his claims on Leonese territory. Humbled in spirit, and crippled in body as the result of the wounds he had received at Badajoz, Afonso made no further attempt to renew those old pretensions, and he left the effective direction of affairs more and more to his son Sancho I.

It was fortunate for the king of Castile that during these Support given by Aragon to Alfonso VIII of Castile years the attention of the king of Leon was distracted else- where, but this was only a temporary relief ; it was by coming to terms with the king of Aragon shortly afterwards that he finally overcame his difficulties. The co-operation hence- forward between the two kings was an intimate one, and most fortunate for Castile and indeed for Christian Spain. It was first manifested when Alfonso II assisted in the capture of Cuenca from the Moslems in 1177. In return for this, the king of Castile formally renounced his claim to suzerainty over Aragon, and in 1179 an important treaty was made which not only settled all questions in dispute as to frontiers, but also decided the respective spheres of each kingdom in the Moslem territories they hoped to conquer. Valencia was allotted to Aragon, Andalusia and Murcia to Castile ; and common action for the future was greatly facilitated by this agreement. Unusual as such co-operation was in the Spain of this age, it was not limited to united action against the Moslem ; the help of Aragon was forthcoming also against Navarre and Leon, who were continually seeking to advantage themselves at the expense of Castile. Thanks to this help, Navarre was eventually brought to book at the end of the century, and itself had to cede territory to Castile. Leon made peace in 1180, but was soon at war again. Once more the combined strength of Aragon and Castile compelled Ferdinand's successor, Alfonso IX,[1] to make peace. This was cemented by his marriage with Berenguela, Alfonso VIII's daughter, in 1197, and though this marriage did not bring about harmony it did result in the reunion of the crowns of Castile and Leon thirty-three years later.

Portugal, meanwhile, was pursuing a path of its own. Portugal The capture of Lisbon Though, like most of the Spanish rulers of his time, Afonso I's principal aim was to widen the borders of his State, at the expense of his Christian neighbours as well as of the Moslems, his essay against the king of Leon had proved so disastrous that afterwards, as before, he directed his efforts southwards. The situation of his country provided him with

[1] Notice that both Alfonso IX and his father Ferdinand II are numbered as in the succession of kings of Castile (or Castile and Leon united). So after the reunion of Castile and Leon, the first king is known as Ferdinand III, his successor as Alfonso X.

an initial advantage in his warfare with the Moslems, for it lay on the sea-route from Northern Europe to the Mediterranean. Commercially this was of considerable value to it, but what mattered most at the time was that it was by this route that fleets of crusaders from England, Flanders, and Scandinavia passed on their way to the Holy Land, and that they were often willing to expend their crusading zeal against the Moslems who were attacking or being attacked by Portugal. The first and most famous instance of this occurred in 1147, when a fleet of English accompanied by Flemish and German crusaders, on the way to Palestine to participate in the Second Crusade, put in at Oporto. Afonso was engaged in a successful campaign which had brought his arms beyond the Tagus, but to achieve the final triumph of the capture of Lisbon a fleet was necessary. Here was one ready to hand, and for the crusaders there was the obvious duty of fighting Moslems and the prospect of booty as well. So came about the capture of Lisbon, and the definitive occupation by the Portuguese of the territory from the Mondego to the Tagus. Most of the English continued on their journey or returned home, but some of the crusaders stayed as settlers of the newly-conquered lands. The chief part in its colonisation, however, was taken by monastic corporations (especially by the monastery of Alcobaça founded for the purpose in the district), which with the aid of settlers from the north built towns and villages and put the land into cultivation.

Sancho I and the Moslems

After his defeat by the king of Leon at Badajoz in 1169, Afonso's activity diminished. He associated his son Sancho with himself in the government and made a truce for ten years with the Moslems. However, Sancho had not the same reasons as his father for remaining quiescent, and in 1178 he made a daring raid into Andalusia which reached to the suburbs of Seville. This bold stroke nearly brought disaster. For the Almohad Emperor of Morocco, Yusuf, after the failure of a preliminary attempt by sea, prepared a great military expedition for the recovery of Lisbon and the invasion of Portugal. In 1184 Afonso was in great straits, from which he was only rescued by the timely intervention of the king of Leon and the archbishop of Compostela; finally Yusuf's death brought the invasion to an end. Afonso I died in 1185, and Sancho I's early years were mainly spent in warfare with the Moslems. Having repelled an attack from the new Emperor of Morocco, Yakub, he himself took the offensive, and began an attack by land and sea in 1189. This was the first naval enterprise to be undertaken by the Portuguese, and they were again fortunate in obtaining the co-operation of a crusading fleet—mainly Scandinavian, on its way to join in the Third Crusade—which enabled him to invade the Algarve for the first time and to capture the important town of Silves. The crusaders proceeded on their way to Palestine, and Sancho left to himself had to face a strong counter-attack from Morocco in 1190. Yakub crossed the Tagus and advanced almost to Coimbra ; once more the timely arrival of a crusading fleet came to reinforce Sancho and caused Yakub to retire. So the line of the Tagus was held, but the conquests in the Algarve had to be abandoned, and it was not until half a century later that they were recovered.

The co-operation of crusaders in the conflict of Portugal with the Moslems gave to that conflict itself the character of a crusade. And it seems to be true of Spain as a whole that, during the second half of the twelfth century, the Reconquest had become much more than it was before, of the nature of a Holy War. Apart from the particular instance of Portugal, it was natural that in the great age of the Crusades any conflict between Christian and Moslem, especially for the recovery of territory once Christian, should be regarded as a Holy War. This was intensified by the fervour and religious zeal of the enemy, the Almohades, so unlike the easy-going rulers of the *taifas*. Moreover, the presence of the Military Orders (of the Hospital and the Temple) in Spain emphasised the religious character of the Reconquest, since their task was essentially to defend Christian territory from the infidel. Their importance can be seen already in 1134 from the proposal of Alfonso I of Aragon to divide his kingdom between them. But still more emphasis was given to the conception of Spain as a land where a continual crusade was in progress by the creation of new Military Orders within the peninsula itself. By an analogous development to that of the Knights Hospitallers, Cistercian monks who had undertaken the defence of Calatrava were in 1164 formed into a community of Knights of Calatrava. A similar foundation, also from

The crusading character of the Reconquest

Cistercian monks, produced the Knights of Alcántara shortly afterwards. A third Castilian Order, the Knights of Santiago (of Compostela in Galicia) was founded in 1171 ; they adopted the rule of Augustinian canons. In Portugal, the Knights of Avis were founded in 1181, again under Cistercian patronage. We find, too, that these new Orders began to be very active soon after their foundation, and, in Castile especially, they were instrumental not only in defence but also in vigorous offensives against the Moslems. They carried on the success won by Alfonso VIII at Cuenca in 1177, and pushed their advance as far as the region of Cordova.

Defeat of Alfonso VIII in 1196
It was the steady progress, especially of these Military Orders, that roused the Emperor of Morocco, Yakub, who had already made a successful attack on Portugal in 1189–90, to organise an expedition on a large scale against Castile. Alfonso VIII made his counter-preparations, and tried to unite all the Spanish kingdoms to resist the challenge. He was too impetuous, however ; without waiting for the complete levying of all his resources, he accepted battle in spite of his numerical inferiority at Alarcos in July 1196. The result was his complete defeat, in which the greater part of his army was destroyed ; he himself only escaped with difficulty from the pursuit of the victors. The Castilian frontiers were passed, and Toledo had to stand a siege. Leon and Navarre, as usual, took the opportunity to invade Castile from the north, but Peter II of Aragon, who had just succeeded Alfonso II on the throne, came to the rescue of Castile as his father had done in the past. The king of Castile was able to arrange a truce with Yakub, and after the marriage alliance with Leon in 1197 and the final humiliation of Navarre in 1200, to give his mind once more to an offensive against the Moslems. Then in good earnest a crusade was preached, with the special sanction of the Pope himself, but the story of this and of the great victory which crowned it belongs to the thirteenth century.

Changes in Spain during the twelfth century
The net result of the Reconquest during the twelfth century was not very striking. The Portuguese regained the line of the Tagus, the Aragonese and Catalonians attained to the line of the Ebro. In both cases permanent occupation was assured by the colonisation of the newly-won territory.

In the centre, however, the Christian frontier was not advanced. There were striking feats of arms, bold expeditions which penetrated miles of enemy country and captured towns even in the extreme south. But these distant gains could not be held in the middle of hostile territory and in face of a foe as resolute as the Almohades, who were able continually to draw on Morocco for reinforcements. As between Moslem and Christian, then, the map shows little change. Within Christian Spain, on the other hand, the century witnessed changes of considerable magnitude, destined, except for the separation of Leon from Castile, to be of a permanent character. Navarre renewed its independence as a separate kingdom, Aragon and Catalonia were merged into one state, and a new kingdom—Portugal—was created. *The creation of the kingdom of Portugal* This was the most surprising change of all, for there was no geographical reason for the separate existence of Portugal, and no racial reason either, especially as Galicia was not a part of it. It came into being because of the ambition of its French count and his Spanish wife to achieve the objective at which so many feudal nobles aimed—an independent principality. Yet it not only preserved its independence, but also acquired peculiar traits of its own. Racially it became distinctive, it had a language of its own (for it preserved the old Galician dialect when Castilian prevailed elsewhere), and its long seaboard on the Atlantic was to have a marked effect on its future history.

Castile, forced to recognise the independence of Portugal, *Castile and Aragon compared* was thus, except for Galicia, excluded from the western coast ; by the bargain it made with Aragon as to the partition of Moslem territory it allowed itself to be excluded from the eastern coast as well. And so it developed as an internal State, its interests were confined to the peninsula, it had few relations with external powers. The only direction in which it could expand was to the south, at the expense of the Moslems. Naturally, then, it concentrated on the Reconquest, in which, as before, it was to play the leading part. The case of Aragon was entirely different, for by its union with Catalonia it immediately became entangled in external relations. The count of Barcelona already had a fleet and was in touch with the Italian maritime states. The advance along the west coast made naval power a necessity, and

increased external contacts and commercial relations. But
there was also the connection with the South of France, where
considerable territory was held by the count of Barcelona,
directly or under his suzerainty. This, from the Spanish
point of view, was a hindrance rather than an advantage,
and it was all to the good that the counts, like the kings of
Castile, held to the principle of division of the inheritance.
Provence, acquired by Raymond-Berengar III, passed at his
death not to Raymond-Berengar IV but to his younger
brother. However, it came back by inheritance to Alfonso
II of Aragon, who in the same way acquired Roussillon and
was overlord of the greater part of Languedoc. He in his
lifetime began the division of his French territories among his
sons, but Peter II had enough left to him to be fatally impli-
cated in the Albigensian crusade. Aragon, therefore, was
as much concerned with foreign politics as with the domestic
affairs of the peninsula.

Their
different
constitu-
tional
development
So the future destinies of Castile and Aragon were already
indicated. And there was evidence, too, of the way in which
their constitutions were to shape. In both kingdoms there
were powerful noble houses with almost autocratic authority
over the numerous serfs on their estates ; their local independence was an obstacle to the power of the central government. In Castile, during the troubled years of Urraca's
reign and again during the minority of Alfonso VIII, they
had directly attempted to control the government in their
own interests. In Aragon they were never so troublesome to
royal authority, and there was no tradition of their lawless
control ; while the union with Catalonia brought to the
crown the widespread authority exercised by the count
of Barcelona. In both kingdoms the general characteristics
of feudal government were present : the nobles rendered
military service to the crown, and attended his Council when
summoned. To this Council, in which both lay and ecclesiastical magnates participated, was given, already in the first
half of the twelfth century, the name of Cortes. Another
element was rapidly developing during the century—the
middle-class burghers of the towns. Among these Barcelona
held a unique position, as it was commercially important and
was possessed of a civic government, with " consuls " at
the head, like an Italian city. The towns as a whole were

important to the king, both because of the taxes they paid and also because they could usually be relied upon to support him against the nobles. For both reasons, he was not averse to admitting them to a share in his councils, and it is a feature of Spanish history that this took place much sooner than in any other country in Europe. The first instance of representatives of the towns sitting in the Cortes with the other two estates of nobles and clergy was at the Cortes of Leon, which met in 1188.

But twelfth-century Spain was not only unique in this respect. The Moslems had made it remarkable for culture and learning during the time that Cordova was the seat of a Caliph, and some of the fruits of this accrued to the Christians as the prize of victory, especially when towns like Toledo and Saragossa came into their possession. In the population that passed under their control there were three elements : Jews, Mozarabs, who had adhered to Christianity while under Moslem rule, and Mudejares, Moslems who now became dependent on Christians. These were all to be found, in varying numbers, in every kingdom in the peninsula ; the Mudejares were especially numerous in Castile and Portugal, the Mozarabs in Aragon, to which large numbers of them had been brought as settlers by Alfonso I. It is a feature of this period of Spanish history that the rulers of all the kingdoms allowed free exercise of their religion and local autonomy both to Jews and Moslems ; in spite of the influence of the Crusades on the character of the Reconquest, there was no religious persecution. It was the zealous Almoravides and Almohades who persecuted Jews and Mozarabs, and thus drove them to seek protection within the Christian kingdoms. Therefore these kingdoms profited by the financial and commercial experience of the Jews, the artistic instincts of the Mudejares, the learning of Jews and Mozarabs. Their greatest contribution was in science (especially mathematics and medicine) and philosophy, and in the translations they made from Aristotle and other Greek writers ; and this new knowledge, as it passed through the peninsula to be eagerly absorbed in northern Europe, was the greatest contribution of Spain to European civilisation in the Middle Ages.

The three cultural elements in the population

Their contributions to learning

In literature and art there were northern as well as southern influences. The Romanesque architecture of the eleventh

Literature and art

and twelfth centuries derived, as its name implies, from older
Roman models, but it was modified in Aragon and Navarre
by French influences, and in Catalonia by Italian influences
as well. In Castile, Moorish influence was predominant, and
the Mudejares eventually developed a mixed style of their
own in architecture, and especially in sculpture, which is one
of the abiding glories of twelfth-century Spain. In the realm
of letters, Latin became the normal medium, but the Castilians
already had some poetry in their native tongue, patriotic lays
and epics of the heroic past. This again was modified by
northern influences, especially in the subject-matter ; Frenchmen who came to fight in Spain as adventurers or crusaders
brought with them their *Chansons de geste*, and into Catalonia
came the chivalrous poetry and the troubadours of southern
France. For the most part, then, art and learning in Spain
were derivative, mainly from Moslem civilisation (itself largely
derived from Byzantine), with some native and some northern
elements. The progress that was made in culture was as
extensive as the territorial advance. The Reconquest in
Spain was not merely a recovery of territory ; it was a
renaissance as well.

SUGGESTIONS FOR READING ON CHAPTER XVI

Cambridge Medieval History, Vol. VI, chapter 12 ; Vol. VIII, chapter 16.
Altamira, R. : *A History of Spanish Civilisation*. (Eng. trans.) London,
   1930.
Chaytor, H. J. : *A History of Aragon and Catalonia*. London, 1933.
Lane-Poole, S. : *The Moors in Spain*. London, 1889.
Lévi-Provençal, É. : *Histoire de l'Espagne musulmane*. 3 vols. Paris,
   1944–53.
Menéndez Pidal, R. : *The Cid and his Spain* (Eng. trans.). London, 1934.
Merriman, R. B. : *The Rise of the Spanish Empire*, Vol. I. New York, 1918.

CHAPTER XVII

THE NORTHERN AND EASTERN NEIGHBOURS OF GERMANY

T HE main current of history has frequently shifted its
course. During the eleventh and twelfth centuries,
at any rate as far as Western Christendom was concerned, it ran through Germany and Italy. France was more
or less in a backwater, and the Spanish peninsula had its
own quite separate stream ; England, more directly important, lies outside our ken. There were, however, several minor
streams which were tributary to the main current. From
their association with Germany, the Scandinavian kingdoms
(especially Denmark), the Slav principalities of Bohemia and
Poland, the Magyar kingdom of Hungary, all derived their
chief historical importance in these centuries ; without it,
they would have played little part and, moreover, there would
have been hardly any record of their doings. To such an
extent were they for some time tributary streams that it has
hitherto been more convenient to include them in the general
story of the German kingdom. As German missionaries and
German colonists made their way into these little-known
lands, so they became more and more exposed to view, and
they soon came to participate in the general trend of Western
civilisation. They lose the character of tributary streams,
as they react against the yoke that the German rulers for
a time had imposed upon them ; they begin to plan out a
course of their own and each of them to play a distinctive
part in European history. Bohemia is exceptional, in that
it remained a tributary and was to become an integral and
a most important part of the German kingdom. The others
vindicated their independence, but still in the twelfth century
their association with Germany is a close one. Differing as
they did in race, in customs, in national characteristics, they
had much in common owing to this association, and though

The neighbours of Germany

their stories need to be told separately, they can usefully be combined in one chapter.

Links in their history

There is a general thread of similarity. Christianity had been introduced into Scandinavia mainly by English missionaries, into the Slav countries by Greeks, but in both cases its real establishment, as in Hungary also, was due to German monks and clergy. In each country one family had the right to rule, but there was no law of succession, and constant civil wars were the result. This gave the opportunity of political interference to the German rulers, and for shorter or longer periods every one of these principalities (except Norway and Sweden) acknowledged German overlordship. The civil wars in Germany, which began in the reign of Henry IV and lasted with hardly a break until the accession of Frederick Barbarossa, weakened the imperial power and made it impossible in many cases for it to maintain its yoke, except in Bohemia and also in Denmark, where a long period of civil conflict gave the opportunity for it to be reimposed. But while the political influence of Germany declined, its cultural influence increased. The rulers of these outlying States used German clergy and German colonists to civilise and to develop their territories. As far as Bohemia, Poland, and Hungary were concerned, the immigration came at first from South Germany, but North Germans soon participated; and the largest immigrations of all were from the Netherlands and the lower Rhine into Silesia, and from Saxony into Transylvania in south-eastern Hungary.

The three Scandinavian kingdoms

Of the three Scandinavian kingdoms, the largest in area was Norway, while Denmark was the smallest. On the other hand, Norway was a country of mountains, moorlands, and forests, and was therefore sparsely populated; the same was true for the most part of Sweden; but Denmark with its fertile plains had considerably the largest population of the three. And so, despite its small area, it was much the most important. Its geographical position added to its importance. Sweden had at this time no access to the North Sea; its outlet was by the Baltic eastwards, though at present it was too backward to make much use of this. Norway was debarred from the Baltic, but had access to the North Sea. Denmark faced both ways, and by its control of the Sound was in a

position to profit from the trade which flowed from the one
sea to the other. That this was mainly in German ships was
one cause of the association of Denmark with Germany;
another was the fact that on its western side it was bound by
a ligament with the mainland, which gave an opportunity for
the Danes to seek expansion into Holstein and Schleswig, and
for the Germans to retaliate by the invasion of Denmark.

In spite of the differences, there were essential similarities *Constitu-*
other than racial between the three kingdoms. In all of *tional*
them the original organisation into provinces, before these *organisation*
were grouped in kingdoms, was preserved in law and justice.
There was not one law, but various law-districts, in each
kingdom. These had been reduced to three in Denmark,
and to five in Norway, but in the more backward Sweden
there were as many as sixteen. In each law-district the
freemen met in the *thing*, where justice was administered and
the law proclaimed; but this duty was becoming a formality,
since the landed aristocracy, acting as leaders of the people,
exercised a predominating influence, and the popular voice
was only expressed in the local courts, which corresponded
roughly to the English courts of the shire and the hundred.
Yet though the power of the landed aristocracy helped to
keep alive provincial distinctions, the over-riding authority
of the king was a unifying factor. He had the duty of seeing
that justice was enforced, and therefore received a portion
of the fines paid in every law-district. Besides this source
of revenue he also had the right of imposing general taxation,
which was for some time paid in kind. It was his prerogative,
too, to order the assembling of the whole people for war.

In addition to the monarchy the Church acted as a strong *The Church*
unifying force within each kingdom. At first, indeed, it
seemed to be an anti-national influence, attaching Scandinavia
to Germany, for it all came within the province of Bremen,
and archbishop Adalbert had exercised metropolitan authority
in all three kingdoms. But in each kingdom the bishops
acted as royal servants, and the hostility to German interference prevented Adalbert's successors from maintaining his
position. In 1104 the German connexion was broken when
the Pope, at the request of the king of Denmark, created the
archbishopric of Lund, thereby making Scandinavia into
a separate province. However, the authority of a Danish

archbishop was not welcomed in the other two kingdoms,
and in 1152, when Nicholas Breakspear came as papal legate
to organise the Norwegian Church, a Norwegian province was
created with an archbishop at Nidaros.   In 1164 the Swedish
Church was similarly given a province of its own under an
archbishop at Upsala.   Thus in Scandinavia, as elsewhere,
the Papacy recognised the separation into national Churches,
and each of these kingdoms had its saint round whom national
sentiment crystallised.   In the case of Denmark, St. Canute
had been killed in 1086 in a riot against his taxation, especially
his imposition of ecclesiastical tithes ;   and, as his murder
took place in a church, he may be regarded as an ecclesiastical
martyr.   St. Olaf of Norway, who had died fighting against
Canute in 1028, was a purely national hero.   So was St. Eric
of Sweden, who was murdered in 1160 by a Dane, though
the fact that he was on his way back from church gave a
certain flavour of martyrdom to his end.

Papal
authority

But the successful division of the Scandinavian Church
into three national Churches had another aspect.   Papal
authority which had been invoked to create the division could
not be disregarded in the future, and the Churches though
national were made definitely subordinate to Rome.   The
English cardinal Nicholas Breakspear (later Pope Hadrian
IV), besides creating an archbishopric for Norway and increasing the number of bishops, had introduced the payment of
Peter's Pence on the English model, and he seems to have
introduced it into Sweden at the same time.   The association
with Rome had the effect of making the Scandinavian
Churches normal members of Western Christendom in rules
and organisation.   Ecclesiastical reform was promulgated,
especially clerical celibacy, which it was found difficult to
enforce ;   cathedral chapters were formed for the canonical
election of bishops ;   monasticism was encouraged, the Cistercians especially, on the initiative of St. Bernard, founding
several monasteries ;   and, to provide for the upkeep of this
expanding ecclesiastical organisation, the kings made grants
of lands and forced the payment of tithes on the people.
This last measure was naturally unpopular and took some
time to establish ;   it had been the chief reason for the murder
of St. Canute.   On the whole, the system was not unlike that
introduced into England by the Conqueror.   The kings took

a large share in bringing their Churches into line with the rest of Western Christendom ; at the same time they were not prepared to yield authority over them. In Denmark, in the latter part of the twelfth century, archbishop Absalon played the part of a Lanfranc, working in complete harmony with his royal master ; in the civil wars in Sweden, the different factions took different sides on the issue between royal or ecclesiastical control ; while in Norway, towards the end of the century, King Sverre actually adopted a violently anti-clerical policy.

After the heroic age of the Vikings, Scandinavia had passed out of the main current of European history, into which it was only temporarily drawn again by the exploits of Canute the Great. Norway and Sweden remained in the backwater for some time ; Denmark, in contact with the mainland, was affected by the ebb and flow of German politics. After the death of Canute's son Hardicanute in 1042 it had to submit for five years to the rule of king Magnus the Good of Norway.[1] On Magnus's death in 1047, the link with Norway was broken ; Canute's nephew, Svein Estrithson, became king, and was succeeded by five of his sons in turn,[2] the last of whom died in 1134. This was a period of ecclesiastical organisation, begun by Svein, who was in friendly correspondence with Pope Gregory VII, and completed when the archbishopric of Lund was created in 1104 ; of social reform, to which the abolition of slavery in the reign of St. Canute especially contributed, and which was furthered by the peaceful reign of Eric the Ever-Good ; and finally of constitutional change, especially in the curtailment of popular liberties and the imposition of taxation for monarchical and ecclesiastical purposes by St. Canute. His consequent murder was followed by a period of famine during the reign of his brother Olaf (nicknamed, accordingly, Hunger), and the Church pointing the moral exalted Canute to the rank of saint, and was the more easily able to enforce the payment of tithes. One social result was the formation of gilds [3] of a religious char-

Denmark
The reign of Svein and his five sons

---

[1] By the terms of the treaty made between Hardicanute and Magnus in 1038 it was agreed that if either died without male heir, the other should succeed to his kingdom.

[2] Harold, Canute (St.), Olaf Hunger, Eric the Ever-Good, and Niel.

[3] Similar gilds were already in existence in Norway (where they were especially dedicated to St. Olaf) and Sweden.

acter, dedicated to St. Canute; these were of the nature of friendly societies, affording to the middle classes economic and legal protection which the State could not as yet adequately provide.

The period of civil wars The period of Svein and his five sons was on the whole one of tranquillity, in which the revolt culminating in the murder of St. Canute was the most violent episode. There was the danger, to which Denmark was constantly exposed, from the attacks of Wendish pirates, who made it suffer what other countries had experienced from it in the past. But there were no serious disputes over the succession, and the German king was too much occupied with civil war to attempt to reimpose his suzerainty. At the end of the period, however, the internal harmony was completely broken. In the reign of Niel, the king's son Magnus murdered his cousin Canute Lavard, who as duke of Schleswig had been successful against the Wends and was therefore a likely candidate for the throne. There was now a strong German king, Lothar, who being a Saxon was especially interested in the Danish march and in authority over the Wends. He had an excuse for intervention, as Canute had received Wagria and the territory of the Obotrites as a fief from him, and therefore was his vassal. The king of Denmark found it prudent to pay compensation for the murder, and Magnus did homage to Lothar. Niel and his son continued, however, to make war on the family of Canute Lavard, but they were both killed in 1134, and Canute's brother Eric became king. He, too, found it wise to seek recognition from Lothar, whose protection he needed, and so the link of subordination to Germany continued. Eric's abdication in 1147 was followed by ten more years of internal strife, three cousins disputing the succession. The survivor, Waldemar I, the son of Canute Lavard, ascended the throne in 1157, and his accession brought the period of civil war to an end.

Waldemar I But the tie with Germany was not yet broken. One of Waldemar's rivals, Svein, had sought the protection of Frederick Barbarossa and done homage to him in 1152, and Saxon troops had fought on his side. Waldemar himself was as yet too insecure to stand alone, and he too recognised the overlordship of the German king. Further, Denmark, exhausted by civil war, was unable to cope with the raids of the Wendish pirates. Henry the Lion, who was practically viceroy of North Germany, came to Waldemar's aid and established a semi-protectorate over the Danish king; in Henry's final victory over the Wends Waldemar took an active part. But the bond was irksome, and Waldemar was anxious to escape from it, and even dared to risk the hazard of open conflict. In 1171, however, he had to come to terms, and the association was made closer by the marriage of his son Canute with Henry's daughter Gertrude. Ten years later the fall of Henry the Lion gave Waldemar his opportunity. He joined forces with the Emperor, and it was the Danish fleet that dealt the *coup de grâce* by the capture of Lübeck. He had allied with his official against his unofficial suzerain, but the days of Danish dependency were over. He died in 1182, the year of Henry's exile, and his son Canute VI refused the demand of Frederick Barbarossa that he should do him homage, and was able to make good his defiance of the Emperor.

The end of German suzerainty

There now began a period of prosperity for the Danish kingdom, marked by the consolidation of the dynasty, strong government, and external expansion. Though the kingship had remained in one family, in theory it was still elective; there was no rule of primogeniture, and hence the frequent disputes over the succession. Waldemar, imitating continental practice, had obtained the election of his son during his own lifetime, and Canute had no difficulty in acquiring general recognition after his father's death. The Church, led by the warrior-statesman Absalon, gave great assistance to Waldemar and Canute in the preservation of internal order. The archbishops of Lund had from the beginning taken a leading part in affairs; archbishop Eskil was prominent during the civil wars that preceded Waldemar's accession. Waldemar himself had been supported by Absalon, who succeeded Eskil as archbishop in 1177. With Waldemar, and afterwards with Canute, his co-operation was complete. His warlike enterprises helped to crush the Wendish pirates; the kings lent him their aid to enforce clerical celibacy and the payment of tithes. Absalon was the spokesman when the claim of Barbarossa to overlordship was repudiated, and it was he that led the expedition against the Pomeranian Slavs which brought them into subjection to Denmark in

Canute VI and archbishop Absalon

1184. The result of this success was a hostile coalition of German nobles, jealous of Danish interference, but once more Canute triumphed; Adolf of Holstein was taken prisoner, and Lübeck and Hamburg came temporarily under Danish control. Denmark was on the way to becoming a European power. Even Philip Augustus looked to it for aid in his projected attack upon England, and though his marriage with Canute's sister Ingeborg turned out so disastrously, it was a sign of the position which the king of Denmark had now attained that his alliance should be courted by the king of France.

Sweden
Civil wars

The other two Scandinavian kingdoms were connected ecclesiastically with the continent, though not politically as Denmark was, and their aloofness retarded their development. They, too, had been passing through a long period of civil war and struggles for the succession, but, unlike Denmark, they had not emerged from it by the end of the twelfth century. Of Sweden there is little to be said; it is historically unimportant until the middle of the thirteenth century, and its records are exceedingly meagre. The house of Stenkil held the throne in the eleventh century, but from the middle of the twelfth century until the middle of the thirteenth two families, both connected with this house, fought for the mastery. The first began with Sverker, who was king from 1130 to 1155, when he was murdered; the second with Eric in 1155 who was also murdered (in 1160) and was subsequently canonised. The descendants of Sverker and Eric fought for possession of the throne for a century, and each family held it in alternate succession.[1] Only during the reign of Eric's son Canute was there a period of comparative

The rival houses of Sverker and Eric

---

[1] The houses of Sverker and Eric from 1130 to 1250, the numbers denoting the order of the kings:

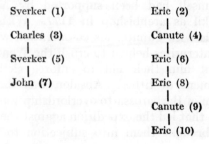

Sverker (1)   Eric (2)
   | |
Charles (3)   Canute (4)
   | |
Sverker (5)   Eric (6)
   | |
John (7)   Eric (8)
                         |
                       Canute (9)
                         |
                       Eric (10)

peace and of internal development; one notable undertaking was the protection of the country against the raids of Esthonian pirates, which resulted in the building of Stockholm. But the general state of civil war kept Sweden in a backward condition. It was only loosely united; the chief power had passed to the southern provinces, which had been Christianised much earlier than the rest. In Upsala the heathen temple was not destroyed until the end of the eleventh century, but when this was done Upsala became the chief ecclesiastical centre as well as the place of royal residence. In the national development, indeed, the Church was playing a more prominent part than the monarchy. The mission of Nicholas Breakspear in 1152, resulting in the foundation of bishoprics and monasteries, the creation of a national saint in St. Eric, the establishment of a Swedish archbishopric at Upsala in 1164, were all stages in this development, which enhanced the power of the Church. But until the long dynastic struggle was over, it was unable fully to exert its influence or to carry into effect its own programme of ecclesiastical reform and obedience to canon law.

In Norway, though there was a long and disastrous period of civil war in the twelfth century, the monarchical authority both before and after this period was stronger than in Sweden, and the development of the kingdom was less retarded. The son of St. Olaf, Magnus, was for five years king of Denmark as well as of Norway, and though on his death in 1047 the two kingdoms were again divided, his successors were men of energy and determination. Harold Hardrada, half-brother of St. Olaf, was a restless warrior, aiming continually at the recovery of Denmark until his mind was diverted by the scheme of conquest of England, in which he met his death at Stamford Bridge in 1066. His son Olaf Kyrre was a man of peace, who fostered the internal development of his kingdom, and especially the organisation of the Church as a civilising factor and as the ally and subordinate of the monarchy. In 1093 he was succeeded by his son Magnus Bareleg, who reversed his father's policy and displayed the martial and Viking spirit of his grandfather. The principal achievement of his reign of twenty years was his reconquest of the Norwegian colonies—especially the Orkneys, Man, and the

Norway

Magnus and his successors

Hebrides—which he made directly subordinate to the Nor-wegian crown. Two of his sons, Eystein and Sigurd, ruled jointly after his death in 1103, and though the difference in their temperaments led to conflict the harmony was little disturbed, since Sigurd expended his martial energy on crusade in the Holy Land, and Eystein was left to resume the peaceful policy of Olaf Kyrre.

The period of civil war

But the death of Sigurd, who outlived his brother by two years, in 1130 was followed by a long period of civil war and disorder. There was no definite rule of succession, save for the rights of members of the royal house, and there were now frequent claimants, both genuine and pretenders ; at one time there were as many as four kings, each with his adherents.

The power of the Church

In this period of confusion there was one event which intro-duced both a new order and an additional competitor for power—the mission of Nicholas Breakspear as papal legate in 1152. The archbishopric of Nidaros was created, and so the Norwegian kingdom now formed a separate ecclesiastical province, within which were included the Norwegian colonies as well. Moreover, the new province was brought definitely within the sphere of the Roman Church, and all the rules of canon law were introduced ; bishops were to be canonically elected by their chapters, and the payment of Peter's Pence was regarded at any rate by the Papacy as a sign of the subordination of the Norwegian Church to Rome. This new organisation meant freedom from lay control, which had been dominant before ; in fact, the position was reversed, for in the weakness and division of the monarchy the Church, allied with the aristocracy, was able to play the leading part. Archbishop Eystein, who received his pallium from Alexander III in 1161, was for some years the power behind the throne. He consented to the coronation as king in 1164 of Magnus, the seven-year-old son of Earl Erling ; in return, the king had to recognise himself as the servant of the Church, and to promise that the kingship should in future be elective, the decisive say in the election being given to the clergy.

King Sverre and the Church

This hierarchical authority lasted for nearly twenty years, but it produced an inevitable reaction. A new pretender appeared, Sverre, claiming to be the son of a former king ; after a long struggle he was able to overthrow both Eystein and Magnus and to establish himself on the throne. He set

himself to restore the old régime and to make both Church
and aristocracy subordinate to monarchy again. This produced revolts, against which he was uniformly successful;
it brought him also into conflict with the Papacy, and in
1194 a papal bull of excommunication was issued against
him. But he was able to defy that too, and when the twelfth
century closed the king of Norway could boast himself
powerful enough even to resist the spiritual weapons of
Pope Innocent III.

Norway has one feature which marks it out from the other Iceland
Scandinavian countries. They had all shared in the Viking
raids which had established settlements of Northmen especially round the British Isles and in France. But the Norwegian colonies, unlike those of Denmark and Sweden, had
remained for the most part in association with the mother-
country, and many of them had been forced by king Magnus
Bareleg to submit to her political authority; ecclesiastical
subordination had followed in 1152. There was one colony,
the most important of all, which cherished its association
with the mother-country and yet refused political obedience
to it—Iceland. Leading aristocratic families had migrated
thither from the ninth century onwards, and the island was
ruled by the chieftains of these families, with whom were
associated the bishops, after the introduction of Christianity.
The Icelanders, clergy as well as laity, were proudly national
and until the thirteenth century vindicated their political
independence. At the same time they were proud of their
Norwegian origin, and the aristocratic families, themselves
literate, kept alive memories of the past by encouraging the
professional story-tellers. These stories were both plain and
embroidered, and from the one came a school of historical
writers, from the other the *saga*, which had its origin in
twelfth-century Iceland. An outstanding figure in both
respects was Snorri Sturluson (1179–1241), a leading noble,
who in his *Younger Edda*, a manual for poets, gives a key to
the legendary poetry of Scandinavia, and in his *Heimskringla*
tells the history of the Norwegian kings down to the accession
of Sverre. Iceland, and through Iceland Norway, played
a unique part in literary development. It was a home production, whereas Denmark and the eastern neighbours of
Germany owed the preservation of their records largely to

German writers. It was the work of the laity, not of ecclesiastics ; and so the native tongue, not Latin, was the medium.

Bohemia
Its dependence on Germany

The closeness of the association of Bohemia with the German Crown has already been noted. The duke was invested with his duchy by the German king and did homage to him ; the bishops of the two Bohemian sees—Prague and Olmütz—received investiture from the king of Germany and consecration from the archbishop of Mayence, their metropolitan ; German culture and civilisation had been diffused by the clergy and monks who had been introduced to further the spread of Christianity. Their constant feud with Poland had been an incentive to the dukes to maintain this association ; but even when they felt strong enough to stand alone, the kings of Germany had soon been able to suppress their attempts at independence. The last of these had occurred in 1041, and henceforward the dukes of Bohemia were loyal in their attachment to the German Crown and frequently gave practical demonstration of their loyalty. Vratislav II, in return for his participation in Henry IV's Italian campaigns, was rewarded with the title of king ; and though this lapsed on his death in 1092, a further sign of royal favour was shown when early in the twelfth century the duke of Bohemia was acting as " cupbearer " of the German kingdom,[1] and so held one of the formal offices of State.

Power of the duke

But Bohemia did not become merely one of the German duchies. It was a separate, if a vassal, State. The Bohemians elected their own duke, and he was the absolute master of the duchy. Justice, with all its perquisites, was in his hands ; he had the power of raising direct taxation, as well as the other sovereign rights of coinage, tolls, and the like. The army assembled at his summons, and he was not hampered by the limitations of the feudal levy. Local government was under his control, and was maintained by a system of ducal castles, in each of which a castellan on behalf of the duke administered the adjacent territory. These officials were the leading nobles of the land, with the numerous class of knights forming a second grade. The nobles owed their importance to their position in the duke's service, and

---

[1] This was afterwards claimed as a hereditary title by the rulers of Bohemia ; but the dukes of Bavaria disputed the right with them.

they had not the landed status of a feudal nobility to give them a basis of independence.

Within this semi-patriarchal State the feudal ideas of Western Europe were slow to take root. At present it was little affected by their decentralising tendency, and the powers of the ruler were therefore considerable. On the other hand, the central authority was enfeebled and the exercise of its powers limited by the constant state of civil war arising out of disputes over the succession. The ducal office was confined to one family—the Premyslids ; there was, however, no custom of primogeniture and the eldest male member was considered to have the best right to succeed. But there was no actual rule to this effect, so that the death of a duke was usually followed by a disputed election, in which the decision lay ultimately with the nobles, and especially with the castellans ; moreover, the rule of the successful candidate was usually disturbed by the revolts of his disappointed rivals. There was a particularly troubled period at the beginning of the twelfth century, when the deposition of duke Borizoi in 1107 was followed by the murder of his successor Svatopluk two years later. Vladislav I, the brother of Borizoi, then held the duchy for sixteen years, but on his death in 1125 the succession was disputed between his brother Sobieslav and Svatopluk's brother Otto of Moravia. The new king of Germany, Lothar, intervened on behalf of Otto, but his army was defeated and Otto slain at the battle of Kulm in 1126. Lothar had to recognise the victor as duke, and Sobieslav did homage and remained a faithful vassal of the German king, assisting first Lothar against the Hohenstaufen and later Conrad against the Welfs. Apart from an abortive conspiracy in 1131 he was untroubled by revolt, and in the usual conflict with the duke of Poland he was able to gain a distinct advantage. They took opposite sides in the disputed succession to the Hungarian throne, but Sobieslav supported the victorious candidate Béla II and thereby gained a valuable ally ; while after its disruption in 1138 Poland was no longer a serious rival.

Sobieslav's death in 1140 provoked another civil war. He had done homage to Conrad and rendered him military assistance in return for a promise that his son Vladislav would be recognised as king after his death. However, the

Bohemian nobles elected another Vladislav, the nephew of Sobieslav, as duke and Conrad, whose half-sister he had married, not only enfeoffed him with the duchy but also intervened to restore him when he was expelled by his rival. The new duke, Vladislav II, adhered to his obligations as

Vladislav II receives the title of king

vassal, and reaped his reward. For in 1157 Frederick Barbarossa, in return for the help he had received from Vladislav against the Poles, conferred on him the title of king, and thereby assured his whole-hearted co-operation in the Italian expedition of 1158. The title was intended, not as in Vratislav II's case for one lifetime only, but as a permanent grant to Vladislav II and his successors. However, the schism between Emperor and Pope brought about a rift with Bohemia. Vladislav's young son Adalbert was elected archbishop of Salzburg in 1168, and persisted like his two predecessors in his allegiance to Alexander III. Frederick accordingly refused his assent to the election and eventually in 1174 was able to effect Adalbert's expulsion from his see, and only consented to his return when there was a fresh

The title lost by his immediate successors

vacancy in 1183 and Pope and Emperor were at peace. The fault of the son was visited on the father also, and when Vladislav II abdicated in favour of his son Frederick, the Emperor refused his consent and appointed in his place Sobieslav II (the son of Sobieslav I) in 1174. He was unable to maintain his nominee and had eventually to enfeoff Frederick, but only as duke; the title of king again lapsed. Moreover, the Emperor was determined to reduce the authority of his vassal. In 1182 when a rival to Frederick arose in Conrad Otto, he created him margrave of Moravia, separating Moravia from Bohemia and making it a direct dependency of the Empire. Again in 1187 he took advantage of a conflict between duke Frederick and the bishop of Prague to declare the bishopric also to be immediately dependent on the Empire. As the twelfth century drew to its close, it appeared that Bohemia was gradually being partitioned, and that its complete absorption into the Empire was only a matter of time.

Poland
Its constitution

The Polish State bore a superficial resemblance to that of Bohemia. The ruler [1] was supreme in government and

---

[1] Boleslav the Mighty had assumed the title of king, and Boleslav II also had himself crowned in 1076. The usual title of the Polish ruler was henceforward "prince."

justice, and the army was under his command; and the
Piast dynasty, which had consolidated a number of Slav
tribes under its rule, maintained its sole right to the throne.
But Poland was in a more primitive condition than Bohemia.
The survival of the clan system handicapped the authority
of the princes; to counteract it they attached a number of
local magnates to themselves as officials or as knights,
creating, on the Bohemian model, a new nobility, both
official and military. But as the reward for military
service was land, a semi-feudal system was created; while
the new landed magnates in each of the provinces comprising the Polish State tended to keep alive the old tribal
distinctions, and thus ultimately exercised a decentralising
influence.

Another cause of division lay in the practice of partitioning
the inheritance among all the sons. Civil war was the usual
result until one of them was able to establish his supremacy.
Such a period of disorder had followed the great reign of
Boleslav the Mighty, and had enabled the German kings to
establish their suzerainty. Poland, unlike Bohemia, was
hostile to association with Germany; its Church was independent, and the Poles were not prepared to acquiesce in
political subordination. The civil wars of Henry IV's reign *End of*
gave Boleslav II the opportunity to throw off the yoke. *German
suzerainty*
Under him Poland bade fair to recover its former greatness,
but his violent character and the weakness of his successor
Vladyslav I alike impeded its orderly development. At the *Expansion*
beginning of the twelfth century, however, Boleslav III *under
Boleslav III*
(1102–38) revived the glories of his namesake of a century
before, though the first seven years of his reign were disturbed
by the constant intrigues of his half-brother Zbigniev. He
refused to be drawn into the entanglements of Russian
politics, which had lured Boleslav I in his later years away
from his Western conquests; Boleslav II, too, had been
drawn thither and had captured Kiev and held it for a year.
Boleslav III's outlook was Western. He had the double
purpose of expanding the area of his dominions and spreading
Christianity among the heathen, and he found in Pomerania
a suitable objective for both his ambitions. He first of all
achieved the conquest and then, with the aid of bishop Otto
of Bamberg, the Christianisation of his new province. His

latest enterprise was less fortunate. He took part, in opposition to the duke of Bohemia, in the disputed succession to
Hungary in 1131 ; not only was the candidate he supported
unsuccessful, but the king of Germany Lothar, intervened
decisively to bring about peace and to force the recognition
of his suzerainty. Boleslav, who had ignored all previous
summonses, felt obliged to appear before the royal diet at
Merseburg in 1135. There he had to do homage, and to
pay the arrears of tribute from the beginning of Lothar's
reign.

The
partition
of Poland
(1138)

Boleslav III had not only enlarged his kingdom. By the
strength of his personality he had kept his heterogeneous
dominions together, and as a means of overcoming their
primitive and local outlook he encouraged the introduction
of Western institutions and culture, which might be hoped
to create unity of ideas and so further political unity. But
the principle of the division of the inheritance remained, and
Boleslav tried to design a scheme which would preserve this
principle, while at the same time maintaining unity without
the evil of civil war. His scheme came into being on his
death in 1138. It resembled the division of the Empire of
Charlemagne among the sons of Louis the Pious. For four
of his sons Boleslav created a principality ; the fifth, Casimir,
was considered too young, but he obtained one later owing
to the early death of the fourth brother, Henry. There were
thus four princes, but the eldest with the title of Grand Prince
was to have the suzerainty over his brothers ; to provide him
with the necessary resources as well as to enhance his authority, he was given a large additional domain with the capital
Cracow as its centre, and also the suzerainty over Pomerania.
The analogy with the ninth-century Empire is very close, and
the consequences were similar. The younger brothers were
not prepared to accept the authority of the eldest, and combined against him ; each aimed at the title of Grand Prince
for himself. Secondly, the landed aristocracy, especially in
the region of Cracow, proved a formidable obstacle to the
authority of the monarch. Finally, there was an external
danger as well. The steady advance of German arms among
the northern Slavs, especially the expansion of the mark of
Brandenburg, robbed the Polish ruler of a large part of
Boleslav III's acquisitions ; the Danes were encroaching too ;

and by the end of the century only eastern Pomerania remained under Polish suzerainty.

The eldest of Boleslav's sons, Vladyslav II, was the first The struggles for the office of Grand Prince Grand Prince. His attempt to reunite the country into a single kingdom resulted in a coalition of his brothers against him, and after eight years he was dethroned in favour of the second brother, Boleslav IV. Vladyslav sought the protection of Conrad III of Germany, who invaded Poland without success ; in fact, the intervention of the German king resulted in increased support for Boleslav in Poland. But in 1157 Frederick Barbarossa took up the cause of Vladyslav, and invaded Poland at the head of a large force, which included the Bohemian army with the duke at its head. The Emperor was successful in his campaign, and Boleslav was forced to render submission. Against the restoration of Vladyslav he remained firm, but he assented to all the other conditions—the rendering of homage to the Emperor, the payment of tribute, the promise to send a contingent to Frederick's Italian expedition—and on these terms he received Frederick's recognition of his title. Actually he failed to keep his promises, and Frederick had not the leisure to raise another expedition to enforce his suzerainty. Virtually it came to an end, and Boleslav IV was the last Grand Prince of Poland who was forced to do homage to the king of Germany. There was, however, one result of the imperial intervention in Polish affairs, for Vladyslav's sons recovered his province of Silesia (which had received a large colony of German settlers), and unlike the other Polish princes their sentiments were pro-German.

On Boleslav IV's death in 1173, the third brother, Mesco, succeeded him as Grand Prince. Though he did not make the mistake of trying like Vladyslav to upset the partition, he tried at any rate to centralise his power in his own dominions and thereby roused the landed aristocracy against him. In 1177 he was deposed in favour of his youngest brother, Casimir II, who had earlier succeeded to the principality of his brother Henry and soon by the premature death of Boleslav IV's son acquired a second principality, as well as the special domain accruing to the Grand Prince. He reigned for seventeen years, conciliating the magnates, lay and ecclesiastical, by concessions, and refraining from any

13

attempt to check the German advance in Pomerania. He therefore avoided the misfortunes that had befallen his brothers, at the price of a diminished authority, and was able to hand on his title to his son, who, however, had to experience eight years of civil war with his uncle Mesco before he was able to assume the title of Grand Prince in 1202. Poland was free from German suzerainty when the twelfth century closed, but its partition was an established fact.

Hungary

The kingdom and its constitution

Since the coronation of St. Stephen in the year 1000, Hungary had been a kingdom. The crown remained for three centuries in the same family—the descendants of duke Arpád, who had led the Magyars into Hungary in the ninth century. The king ruled in semi-patriarchal fashion, like the duke in Bohemia; his power was supreme in administration and jurisdiction, and the assembling of the army was his prerogative. Furthermore, he was the owner of a great part of the land; and when German immigrants had helped to develop the mineral resources of Upper Hungary and the salt-mines of Transylvania, the riches that accrued to him from these sources, added to the revenues of his vast domain, made him one of the wealthiest sovereigns of Europe. Again, there was a small class of great nobles, royal officials, and a large class of lesser nobles, knights. The country was divided into counties, with a royal *foïspan* (not unlike the English sheriff) in charge of each, so that in local as well as central government the king was supreme. Later, the granting of lands to officials and knights tended to impoverish the king and to create a feudal, decentralising class; but until the thirteenth century this was hardly evident.

The Church was a strong supporter of monarchy. Hungary had its own archbishop at Gran, the ancient capital, and so formed a separate province, linked not with Germany but directly with Rome. The Papacy in the eleventh century showed special favour to the Hungarian kings, two of whom, Stephen I and Ladislas I, were canonised. Partly this favour was due to the papal claim of overlordship, deriving from the supposed gift of a crown to Stephen I by Pope Sylvester II; partly it arose out of the contest of the Papacy with the Empire, since the Popes could count on the support of Hungary, which was anxious to sever completely its link with Germany. For the same situation had arisen in Hungary as in Poland. There was no rule of primogeniture; every member of the royal family might be a claimant for the throne, though the eldest was regarded as having the best right. The struggles for the succession that began in 1039 had enabled the king of Germany to establish his suzerainty, but civil war in Germany made it impossible to maintain it; and though the German kings intervened afterwards in Hungarian affairs,[1] they could not exact homage, and Hungary ceased to be a vassal-state.

Hungary, too, was more fortunate than Poland in that, after it had shaken off the German yoke, the capable rule of Ladislas I (1077–95) and Koloman (1095–1114) built up a powerful State. It was first of all strongly defended by castles, especially on its western frontiers, where the marshy nature of the ground provided an additional protection against a German invader. To develop its natural resources, German immigration was encouraged, and Slavs and Patzinaks were also settled as cultivators. Finally, the boundaries of the kingdom were extended in the south-west by the conquest of Croatia, begun by Ladislas and completed by Koloman, who reached the Adriatic and acquired part of the Dalmatian coast. This involved war with Venice, which jealously regarded the northern Adriatic as its own preserve; the Dalmatian towns were destined to change hands several times in the succeeding centuries. Its expansion under Ladislas I and Koloman

At the beginning of his reign Koloman had to cope with the passage of the crusaders through his territories on their way to Constantinople to participate in the First Crusade. At the end he had the much more formidable danger of civil war. His brother Álmos repeatedly revolted against him, and at last Koloman took him prisoner and blinded both him and his son Béla. This did not end the civil strife, which recurred again and again during the twelfth century, and was one of the causes of the weakness of the monarchy in the thirteenth. Álmos once more revolted during the reign of Koloman's son Stephen II (1114–31), but was defeated and Disputes over the succession

---

[1] For instance, Lothar III in the disputed succession between Béla II and Boris; Conrad III and the duke of Bavaria on behalf of Boris again in 1146; and in 1158 Géza II found it wise to promise a contingent to Frederick Barbarossa's Italian expedition.

had to take refuge in Constantinople, where he died. However, he had a posthumous triumph, for his son Béla II the Blind, after a long contest with Stephen's half-brother Boris, was able to assume the crown, and his son Géza II succeeded him without opposition in 1141. But again on Géza's death in 1161 there was civil war. His eldest son Stephen III was opposed by two of Géza's brothers, who asserted their right by seniority ; they sought the help of the Eastern Emperor, and the ambitious Manuel was thus given the opportunity to intervene. Though he was not able to dethrone Stephen III, he obtained a valuable hostage in the king's younger brother Béla, who was recognised as heir to the Hungarian throne and received Dalmatia as an appanage.[1] Manuel planned to marry Béla to his daughter and thus to unite Hungary to the Eastern Empire, but the birth of his son Alexius changed his plans and Béla was married instead to a princess of Antioch, Manuel's sister-in-law. In 1173 Béla returned to Hungary as king, and though he remained on friendly terms with Manuel the association of Hungary with the Eastern Empire virtually came to an end.

The reign of Béla III

It had never been popular in Hungary, and Béla III was for some time regarded with suspicion as a protégé of the Eastern Emperor. Though Hungary had secured its independence of the Western Emperor, its kings had encouraged German immigration and its cultural contacts were all Western. The official language was Latin ; its Church acknowledged papal headship ; and education and learning came to it firstly from Germany and secondly from France. Béla III's second wife was the daughter of Louis VII, and in her train came French clerics and monks, while a number of Hungarian students found their way to Paris to sit under the famous teachers at its cathedral school. Béla's long reign (1173-96) was distinguished by the skill with which he utilised Western civilisation to advance that of his own country and to promote its material prosperity. This was the more possible since it was for the most part a period of peace. Unfortunately his régime was not to be maintained ; after his death there was once more the disturbance of civil

---

[1] Manuel practically had control of Dalmatia while Béla was under his charge, and afterwards Béla had to contest the possession of it with the Venetians.

war, followed by a rapid decline in the authority of the Hungarian monarch.

In Poland and Hungary, though not in Bohemia, the final German conquest of the northern Slavs separation from Germany is a significant feature of their political development. On the other hand, the rulers of these two countries, once they were relieved of the tie of subordination, deliberately encouraged the immigration of Germans into their lands. This peaceful penetration eastwards was some compensation to Germany for the loss of its political authority. But it had a more direct compensation elsewhere, for the twelfth century saw the fulfilment at last of the work begun by Henry I and Otto I—the conquest and conversion of the northern, or Wendish, Slavs. Most of this work had been undone by the revolt of the Wends at the end of Otto II's reign, and until the twelfth century little progress towards recovery was effected. The work of conversion was frequently attempted, notably by archbishop Adalbert of Bremen, but his endeavours were frustrated by the jealous hostility of the Billung dukes of Saxony. With the reign of Lothar began again the successful advance of German arms and German civilisation. It was preluded by successful missionary work. First of all, bishop Otto of Bamberg, under the auspices of Boleslav III of Poland, conducted a mission in Pomerania in 1124 ; and he consolidated his work in a second mission in 1127, when he had the support of Lothar III. In 1134 the Premonstratensians, under the direction of archbishop Norbert of Magdeburg, their founder, were responsible for the revival of Christianity in Brandenburg. At the same time a priest, Vicelin, later to become bishop of Oldenburg, was working with untiring zeal in Holstein. The effect was cumulative. The numerous Wendish tribes had little in common save hostility to Christianity and to German rule ; as Christianity spread, resistance to the invader weakened.

The Wendish Slavs may conveniently be classified in two The leaders of the German advance groups, the one to the north, the other to the east and north-east of the ancient duchy of Saxony. The first group comprised the Obotrites and Wagrians in Holstein and Mecklenburg, the latter the Liutizii and others in the old North Mark of Saxony, east of which lay Brandenburg, and north-east of that Pomerania. Roughly these groups represented the spheres of influence of the two families descended from the marriages of the two daughters of Magnus, the last Billung duke of Saxony.[1] In the middle of the twelfth century the heads of these two families, Henry the Lion and Albert the Bear, were the leading protagonists in the advance against the Slavs. Henry had the advantage, especially in the north, of being the duke of Saxony; Albert, besides being margrave of the North Mark, acquired Brandenburg by inheritance from its last Wendish ruler, Pribislav, in 1150. A third competitor was Adolf, count of Holstein, whose possessions brought him into close contact with the Wends, but exposed him also to the keen rivalry of his overlord, Henry the Lion.

The work of colonisation and development   There was only occasionally concerted action among the German leaders, for Henry the Lion was not content to see his subordinates reaping the harvest that he wished to make exclusively his own. His method was conquest by force of arms, theirs the peaceful and the more permanent way by means of conversion and colonisation. Adolf of Holstein supported the missionary work of Vicelin among the Obotrites, with whose prince, Niclot, he was on friendly terms; and he encouraged settlers to come in large numbers from Westphalia, Frisia, and Holland—lowlanders, accustomed to drain swampy areas and put them under cultivation. Albert the Bear, who had given active support to the missionary work of the Premonstratensians, imitated Adolf in encouraging Dutch and Flemish settlers.[2] They introduced everywhere their own place-names, so that their settlements can be distinguished at the present day; they were allowed by charter to retain their own customs and judicial institutions; on the other hand, they were rid of some of their old liabilities, for they were freeholders, exempt from the burdens of manorial tenants, and except for a nominal rent to their immediate overlord they owed services only to the margrave. Among the peasants of Germany they held a unique position.

The policy of peaceful penetration was interrupted in

---

[1] See above, pp. 255-6.

[2] Wichmann, who was archbishop of Magdeburg from 1152 to 1192, shared in this work of colonisation, as well as continuing the missionary work of his predecessor Norbert.

1147, when the launching of the Second Crusade inspired in The Slav crusade (1147) the Saxon nobles the idea of a crusade against the pagan Wends. One army, under Albert the Bear, advanced from the Elbe to the Oder, and threatened Stettin in Pomerania ; but it returned without any achievement to its credit. The other, under Henry the Lion, was successful in capturing Niclot's fortress of Dobin, but otherwise effected nothing. The crusade was disastrous from every point of view. The vast preparations had produced feeble results ; the Wendish leaders, such as Niclot, who had co-operated with Adolf of Holstein, were alienated ; the new colonists saw their lands ravaged by the devastations of both sides. The policy of Leading position of Henry the Lion peaceful penetration was for the time abandoned ; Adolf of Holstein, its inspirer, was forced to play second fiddle to Henry the Lion, to whom he had to surrender his town of Lübeck in 1158. Henry, when he was not engaged in the Emperor's Italian expeditions, was eager to press on with the work of conquest, eastward, in rivalry with Albert the Bear, as well as northward. At last, in a campaign conducted in alliance with king Waldemar of Denmark in 1160-2, Niclot was killed and the resistance of the Wends in Holstein and Mecklenburg finally overcome. Adolf of Holstein was killed in battle in the latter part of this campaign, but his policy was now able to triumph. Peace having been restored and the raids of the Wends at an end, the colonists could resume their task of reclaiming the marsh and putting it under cultivation. And Henry, having succeeded in his conquest, was anxious to reap the fruits. Besides the important charter which he gave to Lübeck in 1163, he encouraged settlers as Adolf had done, and missionaries to complete the work of conversion. The increasing prosperity of his newly-won territories added materially to his resources.

The fall of Henry the Lion caused a temporary set-back, Situation after the fall of Henry the Lion owing to the confusion and disorder that prevailed in Saxony when his strong hand was withdrawn. There was no loss of territory, however, though there was a change in personnel. Adolf the younger of Holstein was able to recover the position his father had formerly held. Albert the Bear had died in 1170, but his son Otto, margrave of Brandenburg, continued the extension of the margravate, and German influence began to penetrate into Pomerania. A new competitor now

CHAPTER XVIII

ECCLESIASTICAL LIFE AND LEARNING

FROM the middle of the eleventh century onwards the most important fact in Church history is the independence of the Papacy and its development of the monarchical organisation of the Church. Recognition was tardy, conflict with the lay power frequent, but progress was constant. The result was a considerable absorption in the details of administration, governmental and judicial, in which the Popes found their time fully engaged; thus, the appeals that came to the papal court for decision, though they betokened its importance, bade fair to embarrass it by their numbers. St. Bernard protested that the Pope was giving all his time to hearing suits, and that the spiritual duties of his high office were being neglected. Papal councils were still held, though no longer at regular intervals. Reform of the secular clergy was still insisted upon, and indeed was more widely promoted. But administrative work almost inevitably took first place, and much valuable co-ordination was effected, in conformity with Roman custom. The chief advance, therefore, seemed to be in the constitution of the Church as a body politic. *The Church in the eleventh–twelfth centuries*

Yet, as before, monastic reform provided a vitalising factor in the spiritual life of the Church. The impulse did not come, as in former times, from lay rulers and bishops; nor was the Head of the Church responsible for the new movements, though his sanction was necessary for their establishment on a permanent basis; it was unimportant individuals who inaugurated them. The new monastic revival which began in the latter part of the eleventh century recalls the early days of monasticism, when the worldliness of the clergy caused men to seek salvation out of the world by rigorous asceticism as hermits or in the common life of monasteries. Material conditions had greatly improved in *Monastic reform* the eleventh century, and the increase of wealth had had its effect in producing laxity in monastic life ; while if Cluny was still at its zenith, its pomp and magnificence and the princely position of its abbot were a cause of offence to many. Already early in the eleventh century there had been a revival of hermit life in Italy, where various congregations of ascetics were formed, especially by Romuald (the friend of Otto III) at Calmaldoli, and by John Gualbert at Vallombrosa ; in the second half of the century the most notable figure in this movement was Peter Damian, whom Stephen IX made cardinal. These hermit communities were only of local importance, and it was not found possible to maintain the severity of discipline which the first enthusiasm demanded. But there was one such Order which was to spread far and wide and to retain its original characteristics. Its founder Bruno, a native of Cologne, was a canon of Rheims when he went with some companions into the wilderness in 1084 and found in the rocky and desolate Chartreux (Cartusia) near Grenoble the environment he desired. This was the beginning of the Carthusian Order, and in the twelfth century Charterhouses were founded in several parts of Europe. Bruno's plan was a community of hermits living each in his own cell though within the walls of the monastery. He gained the isolation he coveted, for the spot was so wild and rugged that few cared to approach it ; complete poverty was the rule, and the character of the soil was such that only the barest livelihood could be extracted from it. But strict as the Order was, it preserved its primitive zeal intact.

Hermit monks

The Carthusian Order

The Cistercian Order

The hermit sought in isolation and asceticism a refuge from the materialism of the world, both lay and ecclesiastic. It was a reaction against laxity in monastic life that led to the beginnings of the Cistercian Order. In 1098 Robert, abbot of Molesme, with some of his monks, sought in the desolation of Cîteaux in French Burgundy a place where they could live more truly in accordance with the Rule of St. Benedict. The Englishman Stephen Harding, who became abbot in 1110, compiled the constitution of the Order, the *Charter of Charity*, and may be regarded as its real founder. But the third, and the most important, stage in its development was the accession to the Order in 1113 of St. Bernard, who two years later went as abbot to found the daughter-house of Clairvaux. His fame led to the universal popularity of the Order, and by his death in 1153 it had spread to most parts of Western Europe and over 300 houses had been founded. In its constitution it retained the essential idea of abbot Robert, a rigid conformity to the principles of the Benedictine Rule, and it especially reacted against the pride and pomp of Cluny. It avoided contact with the world and discouraged the visits of the great ; gold and silver ornaments were forbidden, its crosses were of wood, its vestments of the simplest material. But the Cistercians departed from the Rule and approximated to Cluny in one important respect. A Benedictine monastery was an independent, self-governing community. Every Cistercian house, however, was subject to visitation by the house from which it had been colonised ; the mother of them all, Cîteaux, held pride of place in the organisation, and at Cîteaux a yearly chapter was held, so that provision could be made for uniform working and a general supervision. But the abbot of Cîteaux, though the official head, was not an autocrat like the abbot of Cluny. He was a ruler whose authority was limited by constitutional safeguards, and he was himself liable to visitation. Moreover, the Cistercian abbeys were originally subject to their diocesan bishops ; it was only later that they too obtained exemption, and direct dependence upon Rome. A special feature of the Cistercians was the admission of *conversi* or lay brethren in considerable numbers. In this way those whose lack of learning made them unfitted for the services in the choir or at the altar were given a share in the life of the monastery, sometimes being engaged as labourers within its walls, more often on the cultivation of the abbey lands. Thanks to them the Cistercians played an important part in the draining of swamps and putting them under cultivation, as in the lands conquered by the Germans from the Slavs, in sheep farming especially in England, and in the colonisation, for instance, of the territory won from the Moslems by the Portuguese.

A third and a more peculiar type of new foundation was that of canons regular (i.e. canons living under a Rule). Besides the bodies of secular canons that served cathedrals, communities of clerks were not uncommon, the service of a

Canons regular

church or churches being their main function. Various attempts had been made to impose a rule upon these secular canons, without much permanent effect; in England many cathedrals had been put in charge of monks. Canons regular were in effect monks performing the duties of secular canons. Leading a common life with no individual possessions, they differed from secular canons, who normally had their own prebends and houses and when residing allowances from the common fund as well. They differed from monks, on the other hand, in that their work lay frequently outside the monastery, in the service of cathedral or parish churches; moreover, their Rule was an easier one than the monastic. The original and the most important Order of regular canons, **Augustinian** the Augustinian, first appears in the eleventh century. Its beginnings are shrouded in obscurity, since the Augustinians themselves traced them back to St. Augustine, and based their Rule on the instructions he had given to a community of religious women. In the twelfth century they spread throughout Western Europe, and they played an important part in revivifying ecclesiastical life; but after this century the right to serve parish churches was denied to them by canon law, and it then becomes difficult to distinguish them **Premonstra-** from ordinary monks. Another Order of regular canons, **tensian** more strict in its Rule, was able to preserve more definitely its individuality. This was the Premonstratensian, founded by St. Norbert at Prémontré in the diocese of Laon in 1120. With the advice and assistance of his friend St. Bernard, he made the Rule of St. Augustine more severe by the addition of customs derived from the Cistercian Rule. In 1126 Norbert became archbishop of Magdeburg, and under his guidance Premonstratensian canons were responsible for the spread of Christianity in Brandenburg. Perhaps in consequence of their missionary work, the service of parish churches remained a feature of this Order. Connected with the Orders of canons **Military** regular were the Military Orders founded at Jerusalem as a **Orders** result of the crusades. Their Rule was largely based on the Augustinian, because they too were principally concerned with work outside their monasteries, in their case military service against the Moslems. Military Orders were founded also in the Spanish peninsula, in Castile and Portugal,[1] partly

---

[1] Cf. above, pp. 343–4.

on Augustinian lines, partly on Cistercian, for the Cistercians, especially in Portugal, played a considerable part in the settlement of the newly-won territory.

There were, besides, a number of smaller foundations, some of which preserved their individuality, such as the Trinitarian Order for the redemption of captives, while others were incorporated into other Orders, such as that of Savigny into the Cistercian. But they all approximated to one of three types—congregations of hermits living in isolation severely ascetic lives, monasteries grouped with a central organisation seeking to maintain the essential principles of the Benedictine Rule, or communities of canons living under a rule but with their work lying rather outside the monastic walls than within. The purpose of these new foundations was for the heightening of the spiritual life, whether by individual asceticism, common effort, or the general service of the Church. Though new, there was little truly novel ; rather they represented a reaction against the departures from former strictness, and a conservatism in adhering to the principles of older tradition.

In these aspects St. Bernard may fitly be taken as the St. Bernard ideal representative of the monastic spirit of his day, and his career shows how profound an influence this spirit was able to exercise. In the first place, the spiritual ideal was obviously the noblest that man could pursue, and the monastic life was regarded as the best means of attaining it, even though with many the monastic profession was a career rather than a vocation. The truly spiritually-minded man, especially a spiritual mystic like St. Bernard (and in the next century St. Francis and St. Louis) won universal veneration, and whatever his station could, if he willed, exercise unbounded influence. St. Bernard, too, had the gift of eloquence with which he disturbed the consciences of his hearers and a compelling personality which enabled him to get his way with them. He was unique in the arts of conversion, especially in winning recruits for the monastic life ; we read that mothers, fearful of losing their sons, hid them when his presence was expected. So it was that he became the dominant figure in the Cistercian Order, though not its official head, and that it became for a short time the most popular Order in the West. Nor was his influence confined to his own

Order. He was instrumental in bringing Benedictine monasteries back to stricter observance, both directly and
indirectly ; for Cluny, after a lapse under abbot Pons,
revived again under the control of Peter the Venerable, who
was often stung by the lash of Bernard's criticism. The
Premonstratensian Order owed much to his friendly co-
operation with St. Norbert ; and he encouraged the formation
of the Military Orders, giving practical assistance to the
Knights Templars in the making of their Rule.

This unofficial supremacy in the monastic world was not
all, for his influence extended far beyond that. He was
doubtless sincere in his expressed desire to be left in peace
to his life as a monk, but it was not possible for him. Partly
this was due to his own temperament, partly to the appeals
that came to him from others. A cause that had him as
champion was sure of success, for few dared to resist him,
and once he had persuaded himself of its justice he would
relax no effort until he had brought it to victory. Some of
the most important instances of this have already been described—the championing of Innocent II against Anacletus II
in the papal schism (the constitutional issue did not trouble
him ; it was enough for him to feel that Anacletus was
spiritually unfit for the office) ; the change of mind that he
brought about in Louis VII of France ; the successful preaching of the Second Crusade. To these must be added his
prosecution of Abelard, which has yet to be mentioned. He
became almost a spiritual dictator, lecturing bishops and
clergy as well as monks on their duties, and often the papal
Curia itself ; the cardinals grew restive, but they were not
able to stop his criticisms, though they did administer one
check when Gilbert de la Porrée was acquitted of the charge
of heresy in spite of Bernard's vigorous prosecution of him.
Often he wrote friendly admonitions to the Pope, especially
to his former pupil, the Cistercian Eugenius III, and it was
to him that he addressed his treatise on the character of the
papal office, the *De Consideratione*. He complains that the
Pope's time is engrossed day and night with judicial appeals ;
let him rid himself of all this and keep his mind on things
spiritual. The papal office was supreme, Bernard recognises,
for he anticipates Innocent III's doctrine of the *plenitudo
potestatis*, and Boniface VIII's utterance about the two swords.

But this power is in things spiritual not in things material. Here, as always, it is the spiritual ideal that he champions, regardless of practical considerations. He was no statesman, and in the matters in which he interfered his judgment was often wrong, for he was a man of one idea and absolutely conservative. But because his idea was on behalf of the spiritual he stands out as the leading personality in Western Christendom in the first half of the twelfth century. He was revered as a saint in his lifetime, and after his death his writings were quoted with the veneration that was usually reserved for the Early Fathers or Pope Gregory the Great.

In the history of the Church in the eleventh and twelfth **Intellectual** centuries, besides the administrative and constitutional **development** development, and the considerable quickening of spiritual life in the great monastic expansion, there was also an intellectual development so remarkable as to justify its designation as the Renaissance of the twelfth century. This falls within the Church's sphere, for the centres from which it arose were for the most part north of the Alps and in France, while it was only south of the Alps, in Italy, that the tradition of lay education had been maintained. There was, indeed, a **Italy** considerable revival in Italy too, but there it took a definitely practical form : in the south the school of Salerno was famous for medical science ; in the north, especially at Bologna, the chief study was law. The class of notaries, a hereditary profession of long standing, became more important as their services were required in the cities, many of them self-governing communities with considerable trading and commercial interests. Bologna was also the centre of the revived study of canon law, and in this way was associated with the life of the Church, at any rate on its practical side.

North of the Alps there were no lay schools. Education **North of** was entirely in the hands of the Church, and designed for the **the Alps** training of ecclesiastics ; to be a scholar, one must be a clerk **Monastic** and receive the tonsure. Furthermore, it was mainly a **schools** matter for the secular clergy. The monasteries were only indirectly concerned. Just as a number of Cluniac monks took part in the reform of the secular clergy, though the Cluniac movement was concerned with monastic reform and organisation, so many monks shared in the renaissance of learning from which the monasteries as a whole stood aloof. They did play a certain part in the diffusion of knowledge. They often provided the materials for study, for some of them had well-stocked libraries, where the work of copying still went on. Occasionally a monastery attracted students owing to the fame of one of its monks as a teacher. The school at Bec was started to raise money for the monastery, and became famous because of the reputation of Lanfranc, and then of Anselm. But this was accidental and temporary. The monasteries were places of prayer and contemplation, and so far as monks engaged in study and learning they did so mainly from a purely practical and religious standpoint. Their attitude was strictly conservative, so that they were hostile, as St. Bernard was, to the new spirit that was becoming so manifest. This new spirit was one of enquiry, curious, eager to know and to know why and wherefore; it was not indeed emancipated from the past, but it was not too closely tied to the apron-strings of authority.

Cathedral schools

For the demand thus created it was the cathedral schools that catered. Every bishop was supposed to provide instruction for his clergy, and though several failed to do so, there were a number of cathedrals which had schools, and which welcomed scholars from outside. Monastic schools remained private, cathedral schools became public schools. The education of the clergy was supposed to be given free of charge, but it was the custom for pupils to give presents to their masters, and the masters thus made a fair livelihood and the schools at first were not burdened with the payment of stipends. It was a competitive business, and schools waxed and waned with the fame of their masters. Scholars would come from long distances to sit at the feet of a famous master, for education, like the Church itself, was international in character; nor was language a bar, since Latin was the universal language of the Church, and therefore of education. It was all rather fortuitous for a time. Students would move from one school to another, as John of Salisbury describes himself as doing, to listen to different masters. For some schools acquired particular fame in one branch of learning, Montpellier in medicine, Chartres in letters, Paris in philosophy, Laon in theology. Some of them, Laon and Tours for instance, had only a brief existence; Chartres, despite its fame from the days of bishop Fulbert in the first half of the eleventh century, and its lustre in the first half of the twelfth, was afterwards to fade into unimportance.

Gradually, however, a more regular state of affairs came into being, owing to the working of various causes. Paris, the most famous of all medieval universities, on which so many others modelled themselves, may be taken as the example. Students were attracted to it by unofficial as well as by official teachers, for Paris owed much to the popularity of Abelard. Secondly, they were attracted by the fact that they could qualify there for a licence to teach, which was given by the chancellor of the cathedral on behalf of the bishop.[1] Also, the particular subject for which Paris was famous was most generally required by students. As the numbers of students increased, so inevitably did the numbers of masters, and the masters of the faculty of Arts (in which philosophy was included) were soon sufficiently numerous at Paris to be able to form themselves into a gild (*universitas*). Acting thus in concert they were able to obtain some corporate rights, and they began to claim an essential part for themselves in the granting to their pupils the licence to teach. The development is a gradual one, and though 1170 is usually given as the date when to the cathedral school of Paris may be assigned the title of University,[2] it was not until the thirteenth century that the change is really clear. For it was only at the beginning of that century that the gild of masters was able first of all to free itself from the over-riding authority of the chancellor of the cathedral, and secondly to gain a charter making it a corporation independent of the city, within which both masters and students were aliens.

Circumstances thus led to the schools of Paris becoming a university under the control of the masters of arts. This was the organisation consequently adopted by many later universities, while others chose to adopt that which came into being at Bologna. There the Church had little influence at first, while the main control was in the hands of the muni-

Side notes: The beginnings of universities. Paris. Bologna.

---

[1] Alexander III in the Third Lateran Council (1179) prescribed that in each diocese a *scholasticus* (master) should be appointed to teach poor scholars *gratis*, and that no charge should be made for the licence to teach.

[2] The original name for a university was *studium* (place of study). It was eventually called a university, because as at Paris the gild or university of masters of arts had control of it.

cipality. It created a close corporation for teaching purposes, and the masters had to be citizens of Bologna. In this case the students alone were the aliens, and it was they that had to organise in self-protection. Their presence was a necessity for the masters and a source of revenue to the city, so that they were able to claim privileges for themselves and eventually to gain effective control. As law was the principal faculty, it was the students of law whose corporation became eventually the university of Bologna. So two types of university came into being—the one controlled by the masters as at Paris, the other by the students as at Bologna.[1] The twelfth century, however, saw only the development towards, and not the perfection of, these two types of organisation.

The courses of study
The courses of study were similarly only in process of organisation. The main subjects of study were still the Seven Liberal Arts of the *trivium* and *quadrivium*, for which Boethius and Cassiodorus in the fifth century and Isidore in the sixth had written text-books which were still used. The dependence on the past is very noticeable. The authors used all belong to the classical or early Christian periods ; " author " and " authority " have become synonymous terms. But some of the subjects received much greater attention than others, and in Northern Europe concentration was almost wholly on the *trivium* (the arts) to the neglect of the *quadrivium* (the sciences). First of all came *Grammar*, the rules of which were still studied by boys in Donatus and by older students in Priscian. Examples were taken from classical authors, and the students had to do pieces of composition with Cicero as the principal model in prose, Vergil and Ovid in verse, though a number of other authors were used as well. Sometimes these were only known in anthologies, but many scholars, for instance John of Salisbury, were widely read and show considerable acquaintance with the originals. *Rhetoric* came next, with Cicero and Quintilian as the principal authorities. It was studied no longer for the purpose of oratory but of writing, especially official correspondence, and it was little more than an adjunct of

---

[1] Thus Oxford and Cambridge both followed the Paris model ; the Scottish universities, where the Rector is still chosen by the students, followed that of Bologna.

grammar. Literary style was thus cultivated; it was the form rather than the content of the Latin writers on which they concentrated. *Dialectic* was ultimately far the most important of the three parts of the *trivium*. Here Aristotle was the principal authority, though at first they only knew his *Categories* and *De Interpretatione*, translated by Boethius. These were known as the Old Logic, but about the middle of the twelfth century the New Logic, Aristotle's remaining works on the subject, reached them in Latin translations and gave a renewed impetus to the study. It was not until the last years of the century that the more important works of Aristotle began to arrive. He was known to the twelfth century as the great master of logic, and as " the philosopher " he replaced Plato in their esteem. Plato might more naturally have been their model in dialectic, but though, through Neoplatonic channels, his influence on Christian thought was pronounced, the only work of his that most of them knew was the *Timaeus*.

In the cathedral schools the *quadrivium* (geometry, arithmetic, astronomy, music) was relatively unimportant. The old text-books afforded very slight information on the subjects, and they were only studied for practical purposes. Mathematical knowledge was used to work out the tables for Easter, and had a very practical value for those clerks who entered the royal service and assisted, as in England, at the Exchequer. Astronomy had its practical side in astrology, which soon became a popular and a paying pursuit. Music was principally important for the offices of the Church. But mathematical and medical science, though little regarded in the schools, did in fact receive a great impetus during this period owing to the translations that were made from Greek and Arabic. Something has already been said of the court of Roger II of Sicily, where Greeks and Moslems were encouraged by royal patronage of literary pursuits and scientific knowledge. Spain had received its full measure of Arab culture; much of it the Arabs had taken second-hand from the Greeks, though their own contributions to mathematics [1] and medicine were not unimportant. Numerous translators,

Mathematics and medical science in Spain and South Italy

---

[1] Already in the tenth century Gerbert (Pope Sylvester II) had acquired in Spain from the Arabs the mathematical knowledge which had excited the wonder of his contemporaries.

most famous of whom were Adelard of Bath in the first half of the twelfth century and Gerard of Cremona in the second half, helped to convey this learning to the rest of Europe. Arab numerals, algebra, the *Elements* of Euclid are among the acquisitions of the Western world during this period. At the same time translations direct from the Greek were being made in the Sicilian kingdom. Medical science was considerably advanced by translations of Hippocrates and Galen. The translation of Ptolemy's *Almagest* made accessible the astronomic knowledge of the ancient world, though the popularity of astrology, revived from Arab sources, tended to pervert its true character and also to taint the pure stream of medical science. The study of alchemy, again largely derived from the Arabs, started men after a will-of-the-wisp, the hopeless attempt to convert the baser metals into gold and silver; on the other hand, it did impart a certain amount of chemical knowledge which would otherwise not have been available. The sum total of the scientific knowledge acquired is impressive, but the major part of it did not enter into the curriculum of the schools, which, content with the material they possessed, were sharpening their wits upon it by the aid of the fascinating study of dialectic.

Theology   Moreover, the schools, being Church schools intended for the education of the clergy, were in their origin designed for the practical ends of the ecclesiastical life. The sum of knowledge, as represented in the Seven Arts, was known as *philosophia* or *sapientia*, but it was intended to be the handmaid to, and only the preparation for, the highest of all studies, that of the " sacred page," the Bible. Out of this study a system of theology was evolved; the term " theology " only came into currency in the twelfth century, perhaps first with Abelard. The interpretation of Scripture was by tradition threefold—literal, allegorical, tropological (figurative)—and since the Bible was the inspired Word of God, only the interpretations of inspired authorities (of whom St. Augustine was the chief) could be recognised. The accepted text was the Vulgate, but this had undergone considerable revision since the days of St. Jerome. Verbal exactitude was of less importance than the real meaning, and alterations were made to accord with Christian ethics, while allegorical interpretations of names or words given by St. Augustine and others were admitted into the text. By the end of the twelfth century most of the work had been done, and a standard text of the Bible produced ; the final part in this work was probably played by Peter Lombard.[1]

It can be seen, then, that the teacher was not supposed to be original (he was not himself an authority), but he could and did play an important part in the development of knowledge as well as in its diffusion. The ordinary method of instruction was for the teacher in any subject to start with a reading (*lectio*) of the text of the prescribed authority, which, owing to the scarcity of books, had often to be committed to memory by the students. He then would expound the text and dictate his commentary upon it. In the case of a particularly famous teacher this commentary became attached to the text in the form of a " gloss," partly written between the lines to explain the meaning of particular words, partly in the margin in the form of a general commentary. The original *Gloss* on the Bible, the work of Walafrid Strabo in the ninth century, was considerably supplemented in the twelfth century, and like the Vulgate text it reached a standardised form. Differences of interpretation gave rise to various problems (*quaestiones*), which were posed and answered by the teacher with the aid of the views (*sententiae*) of the authorities. Various compilations (*summae*) were made of these answers, the most famous of which was the *Summa Sententiarum* of Peter Lombard. It retained its popularity throughout the Middle Ages, and was a regular accompaniment of Biblical study. It has been described as a collection of the *quaestiones* posed by him in his lectures and arranged as a corpus of theological doctrine.

The methods of teaching

If the subjects taught and the manner of teaching were alike traditional, the importance of the renaissance of learning in the twelfth century does not lie merely in the great increase in the number of students and the general diffusion of knowledge, but rather in the quickening of mental activity and the quality of some of the leading minds of the period. There was both the desire for knowledge and a keen spirit of enquiry ; men were eager to discuss and to argue with their

Nominalism and Realism

[1] Any reader interested in the rather intricate story of the transmission of the text of the Vulgate should consult Dr. H. H. Glunz's *History of the Vulgate in England* (Cambridge, 1933).

fellows, and in argument dialectic was a sure weapon. It was this that gave rise to the protracted though rather academic discussion as to whether the abstract ideas of things have a more real existence than the things themselves, or, as they put it, whether universals precede particulars (*universalia ante res*). Those who held this view have been termed Realists [1]; the opposite view, known as the Nominalist, was that, as our own senses reveal the individual to us, universals are only generalisations from observed facts, names not realities (*universalia post res*). The former was the more orthodox view, the latter was dangerous in that it might and sometimes did lead to heresy; though there were few who were, except in the opinion of their opponents, complete Nominalists. Dialectic was a dangerous instrument; it sharpened the wits, but it often blunted the perception of truth; victory in argument became to many all-important.

Berengar of Tours and Lanfranc Already in the eleventh century the controversy had been joined. Berengar of Tours was led by sincere doubts as to the doctrine of the material change of the elements in the Eucharist to adopt a nominalist position, and to defend himself by rationalist arguments; Lanfranc, his opponent, reluctantly adopting the dialectic method to refute him, won a victory for orthodoxy, though his arguments were often sophistical. **Roscelin** Roscelin, towards the close of the century, was first and foremost a dialectician of the nominalist school; not by conscientious doubts but by the force of honest logic he came to dispute the doctrine of the Trinity. He indeed **St. Anselm** recanted his heresy, but not before it had been answered by St. Anselm, who, while he adopted a definitely anti-nominalist position, at the same time exposed the nonsense of denying a reality either to universals or particulars. But Anselm was not a dialectician. He was a fervent believer whose serene faith accepted unquestioningly the tenets of Christianity, and at the same time a profound thinker who anticipated some of the conceptions of modern philosophers. His famous principle, " I believe in order that I may understand," expresses the order in which he puts faith and reason; though faith is first and all-important, understanding can follow it and have a rightful place of its own. He was a

---

[1] A somewhat misleading title, since Realism in this medieval sense is exactly the opposite of Realism in the modern sense of the word.

teacher, too, among his monks at Bec, for whom in the *Mono-logion* and the *Proslogion* he constructed his argument for the existence of God, arriving in the latter at the well-known conclusion that the existence of God is proved by our thought of Him. His other famous work, the *Cur Deus Homo*, on the Atonement, was written shortly after his treatise on the Trinity during his exile from England. With Anselm may Hugh of be mentioned another notable figure of the twelfth century, St. Victor Hugh of St. Victor, who also avoided the snare of dialectic. He was a mystic rather than a philosopher, and his chief work was theological, on the study of the Bible.

But dialectic was after all to win the day, and for this Peter the person chiefly responsible was its most brilliant practi- Abelard tioner, Peter Abelard. From his own *History of his mis-fortunes* we are able to form quite an intimate picture of him. He was one who loved the *ars disputandi*, and though genuine in his assertion of his orthodoxy, his standpoint, " By doubt-ing we are led to enquire ; by enquiry we perceive the truth," must have seemed to many of his contemporaries to be dan-gerously unorthodox; it is the antithesis of the *credo ut intelligam* of Anselm. A brilliant thinker, he was only too well aware of his brilliance. He displayed it in his lectures, which were immensely popular, so that students followed him wherever he went ; and his popularity and his self-confidence proved to be his undoing. He had sat under the leading teachers of his day—the nominalist Roscelin, the realist William of Champeaux, the theologian Anselm of Laon, and he quarrelled with each of his teachers in turn and derided his teaching. William of Champeaux eventually left Paris, where Abelard's lectures proved so much more attractive to students. Anselm of Laon was roused to great indignation by the criticisms of his pupil, who described him as a windbag whose language was wonderful but its sense void of reason. Having attacked both the extremes of nominalism and realism, Abelard now proceeded to apply his dialectic to theology ; but his book on the Trinity resulted in his first set-back. He had made many enemies by his criticisms, and they procured his condemnation at Soissons in 1121.[1] There

---

[1] Roscelin, anxious to prove his own orthodoxy as well as to be revenged on his former pupil, was the first to accuse Abelard of the very errors for which he himself had previously been condemned. Abelard, like Roscelin, arrived at his unorthodox position by pure force of logic.

followed a long interval during which he first went into retirement, whither crowds of students followed him, and then after some unhappy years as abbot of a Breton monastery returned to teach in Paris. Once more his enemies were on his trail, and this time they sought the aid of St. Bernard. To the religious mystic Abelard's insistence on reason was abominable, a direct flouting of authority, and St. Bernard did not rest until he had obtained Abelard's second and more complete condemnation at Sens in 1140. Abelard was now a broken man; he found a refuge at Cluny, but he was silenced for good and he died there in 1142. Yet his work lived on, and his standpoint was to be victorious over his victor's. In his most famous book, *Sic et Non*, he had set side by side the divergent opinions of various Fathers on topics of theology and ethics, without attempting to reconcile or to solve contradictions. For him it was a wholesome exercise designed to stimulate enquiry, and in his preface he lays down the principles by which this enquiry should be conducted. To such as St. Bernard this appeared to be the attitude of a cynic intent on the destruction of authority. Yet even in the twelfth century, as in the *Sentences* of Peter Lombard and the *Decretum* of Gratian, two standard works of unimpeachable orthodoxy, it was to become the accepted way of arriving at the truth. And, in spite of St. Bernard, the memory of Abelard that remained was not of a heretic but of an inspiring teacher and a great thinker.

John of
Salisbury
Among those who admired Abelard, though not in full agreement with him, was a former pupil of his in dialectic, John of Salisbury. In his *Metalogicon*, John has given an account of his studies and teachers, which is especially valuable for the picture it gives of the scholastic life of the period. In particular, he makes known to us the school at Chartres, where the emphasis was on grammar and rhetoric rather than on logic, and grammar meant a wide reading in classical authors. John of Salisbury had studied dialectic at Paris, he was later to be infused with religious mysticism by reading the works of Hugh of St. Victor; but the humanism he had learnt at Chartres was a constant factor in his life. Not only did it flavour all his writings, treatises and letters alike, in which quotations from classical authors are of frequent occurrence; it tempered his judgment too, so that he could

see the value of dialectic and yet deplore the use that was being made of it.   With the aid of the New Logic of Aristotle he gives in his *Metalogicon* the reasoned view of a sane and shrewd thinker ; if not as brilliant as Abelard, he had the sounder judgment.   He also had considerable experience in practical affairs.   He was for a time in the papal chancery, and afterwards was secretary first to archbishop Theobald of Canterbury and then to Becket, before becoming finally bishop of Chartres.   Of all the supporters of Becket he shows the most temperate judgment, though he was never a trimmer. He turns his practical experience to good account in his *Polycraticus*, where he displays himself as a holder of strong hierarchical views.   The secular power should, he considers, be subject to the spiritual, and he is careful to make the distinction between a legitimate ruler and a tyrant ; what is surprising in one so little inclined to fanaticism, is to find him actually advocating tyrannicide, but in this respect his views were largely coloured by his classical reading.

John of Salisbury had shown the right direction, and it would have been well if his contemporaries could have followed in his footsteps.   But his temperance of judgment found few imitators.   Dialectic was winning the victory over humanist culture, and was tending to become an end in itself, and not merely a means to an end.   The school of Chartres was losing its lustre.   Then in the last years of the century the greater works of Aristotle began to come to the schools. Plato was now completely effaced, and Aristotle was the one ancient philosopher to be esteemed.   But, at the same time, the *trivium* continued to hold pride of place in the schools, and the *quadrivium*, a proper study of which would have helped to the understanding of the real Aristotle, was still ignored.   Further, there was a general standardisation in progress, as of the text and interpretation of the Bible. These were some of the factors that, acting and reacting upon one another, brought about the change from the vigorous but experimental thought of the twelfth century to the scholasticism of the thirteenth.

The victory of dialectic

We are in a different atmosphere when we turn to the legal studies which were being so actively pursued at Bologna.

The study of Civil Law

The study of Roman Law was not for practical purposes only ; it had become an academic science, the first task of which was to recover the exact text of the Justinianean law-books, and to disentangle from them the later accretions which from time to time had been necessitated by the social needs of the day. The completed Corpus of Roman Law (*Jus Civile*) was composed of five volumes, which contained the whole of Justinian's work. The *Digest,* curiously divided into three parts,[1] occupied the first three volumes ; volume **IV** contained the first nine books of the *Code* ; while the last three books of the *Code,* as well as the *Institutes* and *Novellae* (under the medieval name of *Authenticum*) comprised the fifth volume, which also included some Lombard and imperial law to bring it up to date for practical purposes. The text thus established, the work of interpretation began. The initiator in this was Irnerius, and to him is to be attributed the fame of the school at Bologna [2] ; he had been employed first by countess Matilda and later by the Emperor Henry V, so that he had practical as well as academic experience. The method of interpretation was, as with the schoolmen in France, the gloss, both interlinear and marginal. Irnerius was followed by the " Four Doctors," who were employed by Frederick Barbarossa at the diet of Roncaglia.[3] A succession of glossators ended in the thirteenth century with Accursius, whose *Glossa ordinaria* was accepted as definitive. The study of Roman Law at Bologna was both scientific and practical, for its chief interpreters were also employed, especially in the imperial service, as practitioners, though the law they had to administer was often feudal law. Already in the twelfth century the influence of Roman Law north of the Alps is noticeable, and there too is beginning to have its effect upon those whose normal practice was in feudal law. But at this date its chief importance was in the training it gave to ecclesiastics engaged in the newly revived study of the law of the Church ; young clerics, especially archdeacons, were sent to Bologna to study Roman Law

---

[1] For an account and explanation of this, see *Camb. Med. Hist.,* Vol. V, p. 735.

[2] There was a school at Bologna before Irnerius, and other places in Italy, especially Pavia, had law schools. The great revival of the study is, however, always associated with the name of Irnerius.

[3] See below, p. 437.

as a necessary prelude to the study and practice of Canon Law.

The task with regard to Canon Law was not the recovery, but the creation, of an authoritative code of law.[1]   The subject was a living one, and there was constantly new material to be taken into consideration.   The lack of centralisation in the Church had prevented the creation of a code of law of universal acceptance, though there were two or three older collections, especially the *False Decretals*, which had a fairly wide currency in the ninth and tenth centuries.   But in fact it was open to anyone to make a collection of his own, and the particular collection in use in any district depended on what book or books were in the local monastic or cathedral library.   It was a haphazard business, and so it long remained. The movement for Church reform revived interest in the law of the Church.   In its first stages this movement was independent of the Papacy, as yet unreformed, and so collections of law were still mainly local in their use.   In the first half of the eleventh century, bishop Burchard of Worms compiled a book which had quite a wide vogue ; it mirrors the conditions of the time, for papal authority plays a very small part in it.

Canon Law
The collections up to the time of Gratian

When the Papacy was itself reformed and seeking to make real its headship of the Church, it naturally was interested in the legal basis of its authority.   So a collection was made, probably during the Papacy of Leo IX, of decretals (mainly from the *False Decretals*) which had a bearing on papal authority, and numerous dicta of Gregory the Great on the same subject were added.   This was obviously not a code of Church law, but it became the core of all the law of the Church in the future.   Other, and much more complete, collections were made in Rome or its neighbourhood, some of which had only local currency, but some were carried by papal legates to France and elsewhere and helped to establish the new tradition.   Independently of these, there were other collections being made in France, but they all start from the same premiss.   The papal authority holds the first place in the Church, and other churches are regarded as dependent upon it ; the papal headship is thus provided with its legal basis.   The chief part in France in this work of com-

---

[1] Cf. above, pp. 123–4.

pilation [1] was played by bishop Ivo of Chartres; of his various collections, the last, known as the *Pannormia*, was the book most widely used north of the Alps during the first half of the twelfth century. But this was to yield in its turn to the work of a monk at Bologna, Gratian by name, who making use of the collections of his predecessors, Ivo and others, compiled his *Decretum* about the year 1140. It was so successful that it superseded all earlier collections everywhere, and it forms the first portion of the later Corpus of Canon Law. The influence of Roman Law is noticeable, especially on the judicial procedure which was based on that of the Roman State; so too is the influence of the French theologians, for Gratian made considerable use of the books of *Sentences*, for instance those of Alger of Liége and Anselm of Laon. His work, in fact, bears somewhat the character of a textbook of the schools, especially in the second of the three parts into which it is divided; this consists of a number of selected cases (*causae*), on each of which *quaestiones* are posed. Gratian follows the method of Abelard's *Sic et Non*, giving the views, often divergent, of different authorities; but he does attempt to reconcile them, and to explain away the differences. Of his work various *Summae* were made, and soon interpreters began to add glosses, though it was not until the thirteenth century that the Gloss on the *Decretum* took final shape.

The first official collection

As has been said, the law of the Church was a living law, and all the time the Popes were adding new material in the shape of decrees of papal councils or of decretals, their own judgments on particular points; for, like the common law of England, Canon Law was to a considerable extent judge-made law. In the second half of the twelfth century, collections were being made of this new, post-Gratian material, especially of the decretals of Alexander III; and eventually various "Compilations" of new law were made, which were utilised by Gregory IX in the formation of his book of *Decretals*, the first truly official book of Canon Law. This again belongs to the thirteenth century, but it is the direct

---

[1] A feature of it, as of most of the collections from Burchard onwards, was the arrangement by subject-matter. This was a great improvement on the older collections, which had been arranged chronologically and were therefore not handy for practical purposes.

result of the work of the twelfth. The *Decretals* of Gregory IX formed the second portion of the Corpus of Canon Law ; they did not supersede, but were supplementary to, the *Decretum* of Gratian.

The writing of Latin was the beginning of all ecclesiastical education, whether for monks or secular clergy. This was turned to good use outside the scholastic curriculum, and there was a very considerable outflow of literature both in prose and verse. In prose this sometimes took a practical turn, in the writing of political pamphlets, for which the contest of Empire and Papacy provided the occasion ; dialectical training bred eager disputants, though the arguments were often sophistical. The art of letter-writing, too, was encouraged for practical purposes. The instruction in this was known as the *ars dictaminis*, which was especially cultivated along with legal studies at Bologna. A branch of rhetoric, it prescribed both the structure of the letter (often a diplomatic document) and the form of the language to be used. The most important of such letters were naturally the bulls emanating from the papal chancery, and a distinctive type of rhythmical prose was devised for them, known as the papal *cursus*, which came to be imitated in other chanceries.[1]

Prose writings in Latin

Letter-writing

Of a different nature was the very considerable output of historical literature. In this the monks played a larger part than the secular clergy. For historical writing had its origin in monastic chronicles and annals, which were begun originally in the form of entries to the tables of Easter.[2] At first one entry a year, or less, sufficed, but gradually this was expanded into a regular chronicle or into annals, and some of those responsible were ambitious enough to develop them into proper histories. Usually these took the form of world histories, starting with the Creation or at least with the birth of Our Lord, the earlier part being copied usually from Bede and then from more recent writers, until the author's own

Historical literature

[1] For an account of the papal *cursus*, see R. L. Poole, *The Papal Chancery*, chapter 4 (Cambridge, 1915).

[2] This development is described by Dr. R. L. Poole in *Chronicles and Annals* (Oxford, 1926). Dr. Poole deals especially with England, where the development is most noticeable ; the works of William of Malmesbury, Geoffrey of Monmouth, and finally Mathew Paris testify to the results achieved.

lifetime was reached ; they did not acknowledge their borrowings, for plagiarism was not considered an offence. A writer
like Lambert of Hersfeld, in the second half of the eleventh
century, had ample opportunities for acquiring knowledge of
events, since Hersfeld was a royal abbey and was frequently
visited by the king and other personages. He had access
to a good library, and shows it in his use of classical writers
such as Livy, Sallust, and Lucan. His writing is tedious
because of the rhetoric in which he delights, and untrust-
worthy because of his violent bias against the king, Henry
IV. But he has some excellent passages, such as his account
of Henry's journey over the Alps to Canossa, which is not
imitated from Livy and can only have been derived from the
stories of eyewitnesses. A good instance of a monastic
historian in the early twelfth century is Orderic, a monk of
St. Évreul in Normandy, whose history of the abbey and of
contemporary events gives us an excellent picture of the life
of the period. Later in the twelfth century an outstanding
writer was bishop Otto of Freising, uncle of Frederick Barbarossa. His *Chronicon* contains a philosophy of history based
on St. Augustine's City of God ; he sees little but gloom in
the past, which is depicted as leading naturally to the age
of Anti-Christ and the approaching end of the world. Of
more historic interest is his *Gesta Frederici I*, which contains
some descriptive writing of high quality ; after 1156 his
work was continued by Rahewin, a more pedestrian scribe,
though his wealth of documentary material makes him even
more useful as a historian.

Biographies   Much of the historical writing took the form of biographies,
of which Suger's life of Louis VI is the most distinguished
example. The Lives of the Saints sometimes afforded a
model for the type of pure panegyric, but often biographies
were little more than a form of annals, the annalist telling
the tale of his monastery by recording the doings (*gesta*) of
its abbots. Of the same type was the *Liber Pontificalis*, the
official series of lives of Popes, which were enlarged and
brought up to date by cardinal Boso in the second half of
the twelfth century. The most notable work of this kind
was the *Gesta* of the archbishops of Hamburg (Bremen) by
Adam of Bremen in the second half of the twelfth century,
which gives an interesting account of missionary work among

Scandinavians and Slavs, and tells also of the distant islands
to which Viking explorers made their way. Of somewhat
similar interest, though not written in the biographical form,
is the *Chronica Slavorum* of Helmold, continued from 1172
by Arnold.   Finally, it is of interest that there was already
a Bohemian able to write the history of his native country—
Cosmas of Prague, who had studied grammar and dialectic
at Liége, and who continued his *Chronica Boemorum* up to
his death in 1125.

The difference in character and in quality of these numer- Latin poetry
ous historical works makes it possible to attempt only a
rough classification of them.   There is the same diversity
and inequality of merit in the considerable volume of Latin
poetry that has survived from the eleventh and twelfth
centuries.   Much of it was in metre, hexameter or penta-
meter, Ovid being the natural model for the latter, while
Lucan, whose formal exactness and rhetorical expression
made him dear to the schoolmen, was as much as Vergil the
model for hexameters.   The subject-matter was very diverse,
ranging from historical writings such as the *Carmen de bello
Saxonico* (*c.* 1075) or the *Gesta* of Frederick I in Italy to
philosophic treatises such as John of Salisbury's *Entheticus*.
The best example of poetry on the classical model is provided
by Hildebert of Lavardin, bishop of Le Mans and later archbishop of Tours, in the first half of the twelfth century, who
wrote on a variety of subjects, largely religious, though perhaps
his noblest poem is a secular one, in praise of ancient Rome.

The other group of poetical writings owed little to classical Hymns
authors.   It was based on rhythm, and perhaps had its
source in folk-song ; at any rate in form and sentiment it
conveys so much of the medieval spirit that it deserves more
emphasis than the poetry which was directly imitative of
the classical metres.   It was especially used for hymn-writing,
which had been a common method of expressing religious
emotion in a poetical form from early Christian times.   Not
a few of the well-known ecclesiastics of this period wrote
hymns, for instance, Peter Damian, Abelard,[1] Peter the

---

[1] A well-known hymn of Abelard is :

O quanta qualia
Sunt illa Sabbata,

translated by J. M. Neale, " Oh, what their joy and their glory must be."

Venerable of Cluny. The greatest and most prolific of them all was Adam of St. Victor, who employed various rhythms ; a favourite one with him and others, which has many variants, can be seen in a hymn on the Nativity :

> Nato nobis Salvatore
> Celebremus cum honore
> Diem natalicium.
> Nobis natus, nobis datur
> Et nobiscum conversatur
> Lux et salus gentium.

Finally, the most remarkable religious poem of the period was the *De Contemptu Mundi* of Bernard of Cluny, written in rhyming dactylic hexameters, each line having an internal rhyme as well. In spite of its artificial structure, the author has managed to create a stirring and most impressive effect, and he maintains his effort for nearly three thousand lines. The opening couplet is well-known :

> Hora novissima, tempora pessima sunt, vigilemus.
> Ecce minaciter, imminet arbiter ille supremus.

And though not itself a hymn, it has been the source of several.[1]

Goliardic poetry

There was, besides, another group of versifiers, who used much the same rhythms as the hymn-writers ; they, too, were ecclesiastics, and they show even more clearly their debt to popular folk-songs. Otherwise they were quite dissimilar ; they were not concerned with edification or with expressing spiritual emotion, but with giving vent to their enjoyment of life and with carnal emotions. This was a fraternity of wandering clerks, students and such like, who proclaimed themselves as followers of Golias,[2] and were consequently called Goliards. Current among them, and composed by some of their number, were various drinking songs and love-songs, songs in ridicule of the official hierarchy, and even songs that parodied the religious hymns or the offices of the Church. Many of these songs have a catching refrain and a

---

[1] Four English hymns, in J. M. Neale's translation, have been carved out of it : " The world is very evil," " Brief life is here our portion," " For thee O dear, dear country," " Jerusalem the golden."

[2] It seems likely that by Golias they meant Goliath, whom they must, like their contemporaries, have identified with the devil or anti-Christ.

lilt that would make them a success in any jovial gathering.
It is not hard to visualise such a gathering roaring out:

> Meum est propositum in taberna mori,
> Ut sint vina proxima morientis ori.
> Tunc cantabunt letius angelorum chori :
> " Sit Deus propitius huic potatori." [1]

This is said to be the work of the man who was styled by his
associates the Archpoet, of whom we know nothing save
that he was in the entourage of Rainald of Dassel, Frederick
Barbarossa's chancellor.   Another of their leaders, Hugh, a
canon of Orleans, was known as the Primate.   Probably this
jovial and loose-living fraternity was largely composed of the
less respectable students, to many of whom the tavern was
the natural place of relaxation at the end of the day.   But
it is clear that among their associates were ecclesiastics of
some position, men of considerable gifts and with facility in
literary expression.   So, even among the clergy, there was
a strong free-thinking element.   They must be distinguished,
of course, from heretics, who were often laymen and were
at any rate men of sincere beliefs.   The numbers of the
heretics were already beginning to be a cause for alarm in
official quarters, as can be seen by Alexander III's decree
against them in 1179.   But the history of the Church's attack
on heresy belongs to the thirteenth century.   The Church
pronounced its ban on the Goliards also, but it did not take
them too seriously ;   they were not very serious themselves,
and were not a real menace to the accepted beliefs or to the
position of the hierarchy.

In all the literature, prose and verse, there is evidence of *Ecclesiastical architecture*
the creative, rather than the purely imitative, spirit.   It is
still more evident in the art of the period, especially in its
most important manifestation, ecclesiastical architecture.
This is a subject too technical and too varied in character to
admit of description in a limited space ;   it is necessary,
however, to call attention to the creative achievement of
these centuries.   Ecclesiastical architecture had begun in
direct imitation of the Roman and Byzantine, both in

[1] This and a number of other Goliardic songs have been translated by
J. A. Symonds in *Wine, Women, and Song.*

14

structure and form. In the eleventh and twelfth centuries
what is known on the Continent as Romanesque, in England as Norman, was still the prevailing style. Building is
essentially a practical business ; especially when wooden
ceilings (dangerous because of their liability to catch fire)
began to be replaced by stone vaults, Romanesque cathedrals
had to be held up by massive walls and supported by towers
and buttresses to counteract the outward thrust of the weight
from above. As the builders experimented to devise still
better means to match thrust with counter-thrust, they discovered new principles. Ribbed vaulting (already used at
Durham Cathedral in 1093), the flying buttress, the structural
use of the pointed arch (in itself no novelty)—these taken
together changed the whole character of the building and
caused the gradual evolution from Romanesque to Gothic.[1]
They made it possible to reduce the massiveness of walls and
columns, to do away, in fact, with much of the wall space and
enlarge the windows accordingly ; so that the gloomy barrelled
Romanesque buildings with narrow windows gave way to the
lofty well-lighted Gothic with large windows, on the tracery
of which the artist could display his skill. Science and Art
went hand in hand to the making of the Gothic cathedrals.
The full religious significance of them has often been pointed
out, but it must be remembered that the great discoveries of
the builders preceded the artistic or the religious conception ;
what the builders did for practical reasons was given an
allegorical significance later on. So it was with the form of
the church. The building of transepts was a response to the
need for space ; the result was to give to the church the
shape of a Latin cross, which befitted its religious character,
though again the building of aisles might, unless the transepts
were enlarged, deprive it of its cruciform appearance.

Sculpture
and painting
Sculpture and painting were subordinate to the great
business of building, but were fostered by it. They were
affected by all its changes. The vast wall-spaces of the
Romanesque cathedral afforded a field for decoration in
colour, the capitals of the columns for devices in carving, the

---

[1] The name " Gothic " derives from the fifteenth century, when the
Italian Renaissance was cultivating the passion for the classical ; the rounded
arch became fashionable again, the pointed arch was labelled barbaric,
Gothic.

tympana (the panels of the arches over the doors) an opportunity for more ambitious sculpture. The Gothic cathedral,
with its skeleton walls and vast windows, reduced the field
for the painter of walls but gave magnificent opportunities for
the worker in stained or painted glass; the tracery of the
windows gave scope to the carver, and the great façades were
admirably fitted for figure sculpture. This development first
took shape in North France, and the building of the abbey
church of St. Denis by its abbot, the famous Suger, may be
taken as the prelude; it was completed in 1145 and with it
the Gothic style may be said to have come to birth. Not
only in architecture, but also in monumental sculpture and
in glass-painting Suger may be said to be an initiator; the
fashion he set was soon followed in other churches in North
France and England. The most notable work in sculpture,
both in the round and in relief, that was executed in the
twelfth century is in the cathedral of Chartres; this was
modelled on the sculpture at St. Denis, so for this too Suger
may be said to have given the inspiration.

Painting had a sphere apart from buildings—in books. Manuscripts
Here again in North France and England the creative talent
surpasses that in Italy, where as also in the case of sculpture
the artist was still to a large extent imitative. It is mainly
to be found in the beauty of colouring of the initial letters
and the decorative designs in the margins, though there are,
especially in England, some notable paintings of figures and
scenes. Apart from their decoration, the manuscripts by
themselves are works of art. The rounded hands of the
eleventh and twelfth centuries are clearly descended from
the Carolingian, though the course of time has produced many
changes. Much labour and skill must have gone to the
writing of these manuscripts. The letters are usually large
and are beautifully formed; in England especially, the
twelfth-century handwriting is unsurpassed. Then at the
end of the century came the change that had come earlier in
architecture. The rounded hand gave place, almost as
naturally, to the pointed (Gothic) hand, which was to be
universal throughout Europe until the Renaissance. The
letters become much smaller, the contractions more numerous,
as the demand for books becomes greater. The delicacy of
some of this small lettering is quite remarkable, but book-

making is now an industry, and commercial considerations are often inimical to the tardiness of artistic production.

The part played by France in the Twelfth Century Renaissance

When we review the cultural side of this period, and consider the strivings after spiritual development, the mental and intellectual activity, the literary and artistic output, there is one fact which forces itself on our notice—again and again it is Frenchmen that play the chief part. It is natural to associate the idea of a renaissance in thought and art with Italy; moreover there is no doubt that this cultural revival was associated with the revival of material prosperity, which was most marked in Italy. For both were made possible by the same conditions, the restoration of order which began in the reign of Otto I. Italy certainly had its part both in the spiritual and, especially in the south, in the intellectual progress. But on the whole it was more remarkable for economic and political development than for cultural. France was politically still in a backwater, but it was the source of most of the reforming movements in monasticism, the chief centre of scholastic learning and speculation, the pioneer in architecture, sculpture, and painting and in the devising of new forms of literature.[1] In these respects Germany (at any rate Germany east of the Rhine), though in the van of political history, follows humbly in the rear; it owed most of its culture to France and Italy, inaugurating little of its own. The reform movement had always been strong in France, and this doubtless accounts for the monastic revivals that took place there. But neither in them nor in cultural progress were the great achievements of Frenchmen due to authority, ecclesiastical or lay; here again the Twelfth Century Renaissance differs from the greater Italian Renaissance, which owed so much to the patronage of the great. Whatever the reason for this phenomenon, the position of France was entirely different as a result of it; she was a centre of attraction for students, a source of inspiration for artists and writers. Politically she was only beginning to struggle for a place in European affairs; culturally she was almost a dictator.

---

[1] Not only in Latin but also in the vernacular. As this concerns the laity rather than the clergy, it will be mentioned in the next chapter.

SUGGESTIONS FOR READING ON CHAPTER XVIII

In general :
  Haskins, C. H. : *The Renaissance of the Twelfth Century.* Cambridge, Mass., 1927.
  Artz, F. B. : *The Mind of the Middle Ages.* New York, 1953.
  Southern, R. W. : *The Making of the Middle Ages.* London, 1953.
Monasticism, etc. :
  Vacandard, E. : *Vie de Saint Bernard.* 2 vols. Paris, 1910.
  Schmitz, P. : *Histoire de l'Ordre de S. Benoît.* 5 vols. Maredsous, 1942–49.
  Knowles, D. : *The Monastic Order in England, 943–1216.* Cambridge, 1940.
  Knowles, D. : *The Historian and Character and other Essays.* Cambridge, 1963.
  Wilmart, A. : *Auteurs spirituels et textes dévots du moyen âge latin.* Paris, 1932.
Education, Learning, etc. :
  Gilson, É. : *History of Christian Philosophy in the Middle Ages* (Eng. trans.). London, 1955.
  Haskins, C. H. : *Studies in the History of Medieval Science.* Cambridge, Mass., 1924.
  Paré, G., Brunet, A., and Tremblay, B. : *La renaissance du xii siècle. Les écoles et l'enseignement.* Ottawa, 1933.
  Poole, R. L. : *Illustrations of the History of Medieval Thought and Learning,* 2nd ed. London, 1920.
  Rashdall, H. : *The Universities of Europe in the Middle Ages,* new ed. by F. M. Powicke and A. B. Emden. 3 vols. Oxford, 1936.
  Sikes, J. G. : *Peter Abailard.* Cambridge, 1932.
  Wulf, M. de : *History of Medieval Philosophy* (Eng. trans.). Vol. I (revised ed.). London, 1952.
  Seidlmayer, M. : *Currents of Medieval Thought* (Eng. trans.). Oxford, 1959.
Literature :
  Raby, F. J. E. : *History of Christian Latin Poetry,* 2nd ed. Oxford, 1953.
  Raby, F. J. E. : *History of Secular Latin Poetry in the Middle Ages,* 2nd ed. 2 vols. Oxford, 1957.
  Waddell, H. : *The Wandering Scholars.* London, 1927.
  Waddell, H. : *Medieval Latin Lyrics.* London, 1929.
  Gilson, É. : *Héloïse and Abélard* (Eng. trans. by Shook, L. K.). London, 1953.
  Ghellinck, J. de : *L'essor de la littérature latine au XIIième siècle.* Brussels, 1946.
Civil and Canon Law :
  Fournier, P. and Le Bras, G. : *Histoire des collections canoniques en Occident.* 2 vols. Paris, 1931–2.
  Vinogradoff, P. : *Roman Law in Medieval Europe,* 2nd ed. Oxford, 1929.
  Le Bras, G. (ed.) : *Institutions ecclésiastiques de la Chrétienté médiévale,* Vols. I– , Paris, 1959– .
Art and Architecture :
  Clapham, A. W.: *Romanesque Architecture in Western Europe.* Oxford, 1936.
  Panofsky, E. : *Abbot Suger on the Abbey Church of Saint-Denis.* Princeton, 1946.
  Von Simson, O. : *The Gothic Cathedral.* New York, 1956.
  Grabar, A., and Nordenfalk, C. : *Romanesque Painting.* Geneva, 1958.
  Grivot, D., and Zarnecki, G. : *Gislebertus, sculptor of Autun.* London, 1961.
  Evans, J. : *Art in Medieval France.* Oxford, 1948.
  Mâle, E. : *L'art religieux du douzième siècle en France,* 6th ed. Paris, 1953.

CHAPTER XIX

THE LIFE OF THE LAITY

The three classes in feudal society

THE feudal society of the Middle Ages was based on the ownership of land, which determined both social status and the principles of government. Primarily there were two main classes—the noble or semi-noble owners, comprehensively known as *milites*, the fighting class, and the base-born peasants who subsisted on the soil, fed their masters, and were liable to be exploited by them at will. Between these two classes there was a great gulf fixed, which was hardly to be bridged. There was, however, a third class, of those who dwelt in towns, alien indeed to the feudal environment but fitted artificially into it. Though composed of different grades, they may fitly be regarded together as a middle class, which linked together the other two. They were recruited largely from the peasant class, and they were dependent on the peasants for their subsistence, though unlike the nobles they had to pay for it. They were the creators of wealth, and attracted to their ranks members of the lesser nobility, while for the upper class as a whole they provided the luxuries of life and many of its necessities; the nobles might despise the ignoble trader, but they were forced to have recourse to him, and they could not exploit him at will.

The peasants

It is obvious to begin with the peasants, for on them everybody ultimately depended. They were, moreover, far the most numerous class, and even in the twelfth century, when the townsmen began to approximate in numbers to the peasants in North Italy and the Low Countries, the rural population of Western Europe was probably nine times as large as that of the towns. At the beginning of our period the disparity must have been much greater, for the invasions of Northmen, Moslems, and finally Magyars had interfered with the development of civilised life, and commerce and trade had dwindled to a minimum. The occupation, and often the status, of the peasants was determined by the geographical characteristics of their environment. In mountainous country and on moorlands their principal task was the care of sheep ; living secluded lives, they were not subject to the oppressive propinquity of the lord or his bailiff and had greater personal freedom. Another more favoured class were the dwellers in districts devoted to vineyards or olive growing ; usually they were wage labourers of free status. For the most part, those not employed on arable land were dependent for their food on purchase ; they could obtain a market for their own produce, and in this way there was always some circulation of goods and, even at the beginning of our period, some local trading.

But ultimately everyone had to depend on the cultivators *Agricultural* of the soil, who produced the staple food for man and beast. *life* The mass of the peasantry was settled on the plainlands where arable farming was possible. Agricultural science was still in a primitive state, and custom dies hard in the countryside. Moreover, for a long time farming was conducted mainly for subsistence rather than for profit, and the crushed condition of the peasantry made change impossible until their masters realised that it would be to their own advantage. In the northern lands a heavy wheeled plough was normally employed, and as this was cumbrous for turning, long and narrow rectangular fields were the fashion. In the Mediterranean lands the Roman *aratrum* was still used ; as it was easy to turn the fields were squarer in shape, but as it was light they needed to be ploughed in both directions. In the south the two-field system was usual, half the fields being cultivated while the other half were left fallow to recuperate. In the north the three-field system was the more common, one-third being sown in the winter with wheat (for the better classes) or rye (for the peasant), one-third in the spring with oats, barley, and peas, while the remaining third lay fallow.[1] Such an arrangement implied a communal method of farming, and in other ways too this was manifest : a peasant's holding

---

[1] Here and elsewhere, it must be borne in mind that, owing to limitations of space, it is only the more usual methods that are being described, and that thereby an unreal appearance of uniformity is created. Certain localities had their own peculiar customs, which affected both the status and the work of the peasant, and there are numerous exceptions to most of the generalisations in these paragraphs.

was usually composed of a number of strips in different fields,
so that all had a share in good and in bad land alike ; and
most of them had to co-operate with others in the use of a
plough and the care of livestock. The woodlands, too, and
the open fields after harvest, were common land which provided food for the animals, an important element in the life
of the peasant. These were necessary to him for draught
purposes (oxen in particular, though horses were beginning
to be used) ; they were useful for food, and indeed most of
the cattle, owing to the difficulty of feeding them, were
slaughtered in the winter and their carcases salted ; and
finally the skins of the cattle provided leather, while the wool
of the sheep was utilised for clothing. A large estate was
often a self-sufficient community.

The
peasant's
relation to
his lord

　　　　There was a long tradition of the communism of village
life. But upon it had been imposed the dominance of the
owner of the land, the lord of the manor. He did not co-operate ; he only enjoyed the fruits of co-operation. The peasants
were left to arrange as they thought fit for the cultivation of
their own strips, provided that each took his share in the
cultivation of the lord's. A regular amount of labour was
required from them each week, and on special occasions such
as harvest exceptional services were exacted ; in every case
work on the lord's land took precedence. The primary
requirement of the lords was subsistence : nobles, and kings
too, travelled from manor to manor with their households
to live on the stored produce ; sometimes it was sent to them,
and this was regularly the case with monasteries which
possessed manors at some distance from their house ; in these
circumstances, either a bailiff looked after the lord's interests,
or the tenants rendered services in kind instead of in labour.
Whatever the local arrangement, the result was the same.
The owner of the land and his household subsisted on the
labour of the peasants. But this was not all. The lord
expected still further advantages from the possession of land,
and it was only the workers on the soil who could provide
them. He had a monopoly of mill, bakery, winepress ; the
peasants had to resort to them and to pay a percentage of the
proceeds to the lord. Further, in any event that resulted
in the loss of services to the lord, such as the marriage of a
peasant's daughter, a fine was exacted ; especially on the

death of a tenant, for then his heir had to pay a succession
duty, which usually meant the surrender of his best beast.
In France, where this succession duty was not usually the
custom, an annual impost (*taille*) was exacted ; elsewhere
there were aids, often annual, due to the lord. Finally, the
parish church was as a rule built upon the property of the
lord, who therefore was the patron of the living ; the tenants
had to contribute by tithes (which frequently went into the
lord's pocket) to the upkeep of the church and its priest,
while the priest also claimed a burial fee—the second-best
beast—on the death of a tenant.

   Not all the agricultural peasants were subject to these
burdens. Status and custom differed from place to place,
and there were a number of free tenants who were not bound
to the soil and whose dues were much less oppressive. But
the large majority were, like the villeins in England, attached
to the soil on which they worked and unable to leave it.
They were, as a rule, completely subject to the lord's jurisdiction, so that they lay at his mercy. He was supposed to
give them protection against other lords, but in time of war
that might mean very little. The one thing that did protect
them was custom. This gave security of tenure to them
and their sons after them ; in such times as harvest, it ensured
them good meals at the lord's expense. He could invoke it
to multiply their burdens, but it could also be invoked against
him. And the fact remained that they were a necessity,
and therefore, like the animals, must be kept alive. The size
of their holdings, which was often considerable, enabled them
to subsist, and no more was considered necessary. Even the
Church, though it recognised that they had souls to be saved,
rarely evinced any compunction for their treatment ; it was
rather concerned with teaching them to be content with the
way of life to which God had called them. If we are to
believe contemporary accounts, which derive, of course, from
those who were responsible for their treatment, the condition
of the mass of the peasants was wretched indeed ; they were
little better, morally and intellectually, than brute beasts,
and they often received less consideration than those animals
which shared in the pursuits of the nobles—the horse, the
dog, and the falcon. We are told of their cunning knavery,
which indeed is a natural outcome of oppression, and we

can believe that it often stood them in good stead, but the patient endurance of the countryman was probably their greatest asset. By the twelfth century, at any rate, their patience was to have its reward. There was no change of heart among their masters, but there was a change of mind when at last they realised that the better treatment of the peasants was in their own best interests.

The effect of better political order

In the absence of detailed information, and naturally contemporary writers were rarely interested in describing the condition of the lower classes, it is impossible to trace with precision the process of the change. But the prospect of better times opened in the middle of the tenth century, when the worst raids of Northmen and Moslems were over, and when the devastating invasions of the Magyars had been brought to an end by the victory of Otto the Great at the Lechfeld in 955. A revival of civilised life began, evinced on its material side by the expansion of industry and commerce and the development of town life. The rural population was doubly affected : it benefited directly from the cessation of the invasions and the renewal of a more orderly state of affairs, and indirectly too, since the requirements of a growing industrial population could not be met by a system of purely subsistence agriculture ; there was a ready market for surplus produce. The improvement at first was local rather than general, and the private wars in which the nobles delighted were a frequent cause of disorder and devastation. In Germany the kings were usually strong enough to suppress local turbulence, except during the civil wars in the eleventh and twelfth centuries, but in France the monarchy was at first too weak to preserve order. The Church did what it could by its promulgation of the Truce and Peace of God, which may have eased the situation somewhat. In the eleventh century, however, the territorial princes in North France—in Normandy, Flanders, Anjou, Blois—set the example of good government and the enforcement of justice in their dominions, while at the beginning of the twelfth century Louis VI by suppressing the robber-barons established order in the royal domain. In North Italy it was the towns that overcame the feudal nobility and enfranchised the peasants, but they proved to be as hard taskmasters as the nobles they supplanted. A large agricultural population was essential for the food supply of these city-states ; they tried to bind it to the soil, and they forced the peasants to sell their produce to them alone, and themselves fixed the price. At the same time they made the task of the peasants harder by the continual warfare that they waged, whether separately with one another or united against the Emperor.

An important result of the more orderly state of affairs was the decline in the risks to life and the consequent increase in the population throughout the period. It was evident in all ranks of society. Young men of noble family had to seek homes elsewhere : the Norman conquest of South Italy was one result of this ; it brought recruits to the Christian armies in Spain, and it swelled the numbers of the crusaders. The rapid growth of the towns is a clear evidence of the rise in population, especially among the peasantry. For while some of the surplus peasants enrolled in military adventures, and others joined the caravans of travelling merchants or the crews of seafarers, the majority sought employment in the towns. To the lords, increased numbers on their lands meant increased services, and they did what they could to prevent this drift to the towns, usually without success. Economic conditions, of which they were ignorant, were too powerful for them ; for one thing, the peasant holdings could not support more than a certain number, so that the surplus had to find employment elsewhere. To the need for employment was soon added the desire for better conditions, which attracted further immigrants ; for the towns gave protection and free status ("town air is free" ran the saying), and if the newcomer could settle for a year and a day custom gave him his freedom and deprived the lord of all rights over him. In the twelfth century the ruling classes in France saw that this movement could be turned to their advantage, by increasing the number of their vassals and therefore of their rents. The king himself, and some of the nobles, founded new towns (*villes neuves*) on their domains, and attracted settlers to them by the grant of freedom of status and a measure of self-government ; these were agricultural and not industrial centres in origin, and remained dependent upon the lord.

As time went on, too, it became evident there was an increasing demand for agricultural labour, which could only be met by the granting of better conditions. The existing

Marginal notes: Increase in the population, and its results

The reclamation of waste lands

arable land was insufficient to supply food for the increased
population, and it was necessary, and profitable, to put further
areas under cultivation. So there began in the eleventh
century a movement, which was accelerated in the twelfth,
to reclaim lands from the sea, from swamps, and from forests.
In France and in South Germany it was the cutting down of
the forest that enlarged the arable area ; in the Low Countries
swamps were drained and dykes built to keep back the sea ;
while in Italy, too, marshy lands were brought under cultivation. Sometimes it was adventurous peasants themselves
who encroached upon the forest and settled there as squatters,
until by lapse of time they acquired a right to their holdings.
More commonly the initiative came from above, especially
from the counts in Flanders and Holland, and in Italy from
the city-states. Labourers had to be attracted to the work
and to be rewarded by freedom of status ; while in place of
the customary burdens they were either employed for wages
or were given holdings in return for the payment of rent.
The Cistercians were among the pioneers in this work of
reclamation. They chose isolated spots in which to dwell,
away from human habitations, and they had to gain their
subsistence from the soil by hard labour ; soon they had
numerous peasants as lay brothers to assist them, and became
prosperous by putting waste land under cultivation or by
sheep farming as in England. They, and also the Premonstratensians, shared in the greatest work of reclamation
in the twelfth century, when, as has already been described,[1]
the territory newly conquered from the Slavs was colonised,
especially with peasants from the Low Countries. The
emigration of German peasants into Bohemia, Poland, and
Hungary has also already been mentioned. This eastward
trend, and the advantages enjoyed by the settlers, had a
considerable effect on the betterment of rural conditions
generally.

General
improve-
ment in
rural life

Elsewhere, too, economic change brought about a new
outlook and a revision of the older conditions. Both lords
and peasants were encouraged to produce a surplus by the
demand from the towns, the more so as this demand was
producing a considerable rise in prices. There was thus a
circulation of money in the countryside ; peasants began to

[1] See above, chapter XVII.

save, and were able sometimes to purchase their freedom, sometimes to convert their services into money rents. Many lords, too, were anxious for money rather than for service. They needed it for their wars and for the purchase of the luxuries which commerce was providing; and the more prudent realised that they could gain more from their land by hired labour than by forced services. In France, with the diminution of services the lord's domain tended to disappear; he got adequate compensation, however, by an increase of *taille*. So, in these various ways in different countries, the character of rural life was altered and the condition of the peasants considerably ameliorated. Theirs was still a hard life. Nobles and towns, dependent on them for food, were alike interested in keeping them in subjection. And, as always, they were the chief victims in times of political disturbance. But by the end of the twelfth century they were in far happier circumstances than they had previously experienced; far better, too, than they were to experience later.

What was true of the change in rural conditions was equally true of the renewal of town life and the development of industry and commerce. The beginnings may be dated from the cessation of invasions in the tenth century; the twelfth century witnessed the efflorescence of the movement. The earliest manifestations are naturally to be observed in those localities where town life had not entirely disappeared, and which were in contact with the routes along which some trade still continued to pass. In the Eastern Empire there had been no cessation of town life. Constantinople was the centre which attracted traders from east and north, and even when the sea route to the West was closed owing to the dominance of Moslem sea power, there continued a steady trickle of trade by the overland route, especially into North Italy. In this Jewish merchants played a notable part, and their enterprise and wealth made them a valuable addition to the towns in which many of them settled.[1] The Italian towns, decayed but not dead, were stimulated by the peace which the Ottonian régime assured. Venice, which had *The revival of commerce*

The part played by the Italian cities

---

[1] In eleventh-century charters to German towns, the Jewish colony is often referred to as an important element and given special privileges.

maintained its link with the Eastern Empire, was already helping to distribute north by the Alpine passes into Germany and France, and south by sea to Moslem Africa, the wares which its geographical situation and political affinities enabled it to acquire. To the south it sent mainly necessities, such as metals and timber; the north was given the taste for luxury articles, such as furs from Russia, silks and spices (especially pepper) from the East. Then came the second stage. Venice made herself the mistress of the Adriatic, Pisa and Genoa followed suit in the Tyrrhenian Sea and effected the conquest of the Western Mediterranean, in which the Normans of Sicily also played a part. The sea route to the East was opened again. Commercial supremacy began to pass from the Greeks to the Latins; the victorious Seljuks having no fleet did not compete; and finally the maritime powers of the West were assisted by the Crusades to obtain the complete control of the trade from the Levant.

And by the Northmen

In the North it was the Scandinavians who were the pioneers. The Northmen always displayed a two-fold characteristic, a ruthlessness in destruction followed by a genius for construction. They came as pirates in the first place, seeking for plunder; eventually they turned into traders, for they had goods to sell. From Russia, where commerce had been initiated by the Swedes, the products of the East, exchanged for furs and honey and slaves at Constantinople, came to Scandinavia and were carried thence to the ports of the North Sea. In the work of re-export the Danes and Norwegians played the chief part, making trading settlements in the basins of the Scheldt, the Meuse, and the Rhine to replace those they had previously destroyed, and when Canute was king of England in London also. Thus they helped to initiate a movement from which they were soon to be dissociated. Civil war broke their cohesion and engrossed their main attention; they lost much of their trading enterprise, which was assumed by the peoples whom they had previously plundered.

Sea and river routes

Piracy and trade were indeed kindred pursuits in the Middle Ages. A merchant fleet had to be equipped for fighting, and while it was prepared to defend itself from attack it was also on the alert to plunder its weaker rivals. The sea was the main highway for commerce, since it provided the

easiest and the least expensive form of transport. Navigable
rivers were equally important, for they enabled goods to be
brought direct to the interior without transhipment ; depots
were naturally established on the coast, where there were
safe harbours, and also inland, especially at the point where
a river (such as the Thames at London) could first be bridged
or forded. The early commercial development of the Low
Countries was due to the long coast-line and internal waterways ; and numerous towns grew up to monopolise the trade
which had been inaugurated by the Northmen. The development continued up the Rhine, and spread to the German
towns, old Roman camps for the most part and now reconstituted as urban centres. Cologne, which could be reached by
large sea-going vessels, and where the Rhine could be forded,
early rose to eminence in the commercial world. It eventually, in co-operation with other German towns, engrossed
much of the carrying-trade in the North Sea, having a depot
at London and also in some of the Flemish towns, which soon
neglected commerce in order to devote themselves wholly
to industry.

Land transport was a more difficult matter, for the roads Land
were rarely in a fit state of repair for the accommodation of transport
heavy traffic. It was less profitable, because a much smaller
volume of merchandise could be borne by wagons and pack-
horses. And it was equally dangerous, since highwaymen
lurked on the roads, and many nobles were addicted to
brigandage ; even a king, as Gregory VII accused Philip I
of France, was sometimes not above utilising this means of
adding to his resources. Civil war, as in Germany, added to
the danger of the roads. Gradually, however, an improvement came about in the twelfth century. Louis VI suppressed the robber-nobles of the domain and made the roads
safe for merchants and travellers ; Frederick Barbarossa kept
order with a strong hand, and in the north of Germany Henry
the Lion maintained a similar security until his downfall ; in
the South, the Sicilian kings were active in ensuring the
uninterrupted movement of trade. Merchants usually travelled in caravans, making their way to centres where markets
or fairs had been established, and where the advantages the
lords derived from tolls assured protection for the trader.
The greatest meeting-place of all was the county of Cham-

pagne, through which passed the high road from north to
south, and which was in close contact with central France
and western Germany. Here, by the second half of the
twelfth century, fairs were held almost continuously throughout the year, and at them a regular code of international law
was instituted, to which the merchants of all countries
adhered ; a credit system was also instituted, the debts at
one fair being carried forward to the next. Thus commercial
development was materially enhanced, fostered by the interested solicitude of the count.

Commerce
and the
revival of
town life

Commerce then, both by water and by land, was one of
the principal causes of the revival of town life and also of
the creation of new towns. Access to the sea was responsible
for the early development of the towns in the Low Countries
and in the Rhine district of Germany. It was responsible
for the foundation of Lübeck by count Adolf of Holstein,
and again for its forcible acquisition by Henry the Lion, since
he realised its commercial possibilities. Barcelona was a
thriving port in the twelfth century, in commercial contact
with Italy, and, under its counts and later the kings of Aragon,
linked up with the towns of South France. Bordeaux, in
the midst of a vine-growing country and situated on a navigable river, was a natural centre of the wine trade. Paris
owed both its political and its economic importance to its
geographical situation. The Northmen had sailed up the
Seine, and the counts of Paris had been able to defend themselves on the island on which the town of Paris had its beginnings. The fact that the counts of Paris became kings of
France made it the capital of the kingdom, but the use of
its river as a highway would have assured its commercial
position in any case ; the most important of its corporations
was that of the *Marchands de l'Eau*, which in the twelfth
century was endowed with a royal charter. Towns also
tended to spring up at the junction of routes, where rivers
met (as at Lyons and Mayence), or where they could be
bridged or forded, or again where high roads intersected. At
these natural meeting-places merchants established depots
and men came together to exchange their goods, so that a
regular settlement was eventually created.

Other causes
for the rise
of towns

There were towns, of course, especially in Italy and the
South of France, which even in the darkest age never lost

their urban character. There were many others, in France and Germany, which were the seat of bishops, and therefore still contained a number of residents; here was a nucleus for town life, and the walls, even if needing repair, afforded shelter. The necessity for protection was naturally a consideration uppermost in the minds of the traders, who frequently established their depots under the shadow of a monastery or a lord's castle. From this they derived the further advantage that there were on the spot consumers for their wares, and a market was soon established. Other and more permanent settlers, whose main concern was with the production of food, would be attracted to the spot, but there would also be a number of small craftsmen and tradesmen to supply local needs; occupations in a growing community necessarily became differentiated. The site and its juxtaposition to the main course of trade determined whether the settlement would develop into a town or remain little more than a village. But in most cases the burg was a necessary feature, and those who dwelt under its protection were known as burgesses; [1] they lived outside the burg in the *foris burgus* (*faubourg*, suburbs), and this they protected with a wall of their own. As their numbers grew, the *faubourg* became the real town and took to itself the name of the burg.

Thus commerce, geographical situation, past history, and the need for protection were all factors determining the position and the rise of towns. They were factors, too, in determining the size of towns and the scale on which business was transacted in them. Where commerce on a large scale, especially on shipboard, was concerned, we can see the beginnings of " big business "; crews and workmen were the hired servants of their employers, the modern conditions of capital and labour were already in evidence. Merchants travelling by land were usually little more than pedlars; when they settled in a burg they may best be described as small tradesmen. Much the same is true of industry. In places where industries had never wholly disappeared, as in Italy, the revival was soon on a large scale; artisans and craftsmen worked for wages under employers who were concerned not only with local but also with distant markets, and who

The same causes affect the scale on which commerce and industry were conducted

---

[1] In Germany, the term *burgenses* first appears in a privilege for Huy in 1066.

required considerable capital for their enterprises. This is true also of the Low Countries, where the cloth-making and metal-working industries, ruined by the invasions of the Northmen, revived again directly the invasions were over. Weaving, fulling, and the like were at first rural crafts, but the workers were attracted into the towns and became the wage-earning employees of the great merchants. They were soon organised in gilds, which in their case were trade unions to protect the interests of the workers. It was very different in those smaller towns which had newly sprung into existence, where the crafts were designed primarily to satisfy local needs. There everything was on a small scale. A master craftsman might have apprentices training under him in his house; he might be assisted also by trained journeymen. But he was a worker himself and not a middleman, and the gilds that were formed were composed of all the workers, masters and employees alike; they were designed for the furtherance and protection of the craft as a whole, for the material and spiritual advantages of its members. The familiar conditions of early gild life in England were to be found in the twelfth century in most of Germany and in northern France.

The place of towns in the feudal system   It is evident that merchants and town-dwellers, except in so far as they were concerned with the production of food and the necessities of life, had no normal place in the structure of feudal society. Their wealth and position did not depend on the possession of land but on the acquisition of money. Since they were a non-feudal element, they had originally no status and no rights. But as they served a useful purpose, they were allowed to pursue their vocations, and eventually to acquire rights; they were assimilated into the feudal régime, but the process was often an uncomfortable one. The land on which they founded their settlement was the property of some lord, so that they became his tenants and had to pay heavily for the privilege; they were under his jurisdiction, and if they obtained his protection they were also at his mercy. Trade was hampered by the tolls that were levied on all waterways, on bridges and highways, at the entrance into a country and often into each town in a country. Here again the trader by land had far more obstacles in his way than the seafaring merchant. The lords recognised the usefulness of townsmen as sources of profit, but they were often slow to recognise that it was to their own interest to encourage rather than to victimise those whose task was the production of money.   There were notable exceptions, such as the counts of Flanders, who already in the eleventh century assisted the development of the great industrial towns of the Low Countries, and kept in check the pillaging instincts of the feudal nobility.   Soon there came a change of mind in others, when they realised how much it was to their own interest.   The circulation of money was beginning to be a matter of importance to lay society.   The lay lords required money for crusades and other military expeditions, and also for the purchase of luxuries which commerce was bringing to their doors.   They were often forced to borrow, and money-lending became a thriving business, at first mainly in the hands of the Jews.   By the twelfth century many lords had come to recognise the profits they could acquire from fostering the work of the townspeople, and allowing them rights which were necessary for their economic development.   Besides the personal freedom which was assured to every inhabitant of a town, they might obtain the right of acting together as a corporation to regulate their economic life and sometimes their political life as well.   The privileges they acquired varied considerably from place to place, ranging from almost complete self-government to the bare right of exemption from tolls in certain districts.   But none of them, north of the Alps, escaped from the feudal environment; they were all, even the most highly privileged, under an overlord.

While towns that were under a lay lord could take advantage of the pecuniary needs of their masters, those that were under a bishop or a monastery were much less fortunately placed.   The lay nobles usually did not live in the towns, except in South France and Italy.   The bishops' palaces were in the towns, and it was natural that the formation of a commune should appear to them as a subversive element dangerous to their authority.   And so it often was.   Risings against a bishop,[1] and the temporary formation of an independent commune, begin in the second half of the eleventh century to be a regular phenomenon.   When the local clergy

<table>
<tr><td>Hostility to episcopal lords</td></tr>
</table>

[1] In South France these risings were as often directed against a lay lord as against an ecclesiastical.

were notoriously defiant of the decrees for Church reform, the burgesses used this as a lever against them, as at Milan in 1056 and again at Cambrai in 1077 ; but it was a pro-papal bishop whom the citizens of Worms expelled in 1074, and a reforming archbishop against whom the people of Cologne rose in 1075. The same movement became common a little later in France, where the outbreak at Laon in 1112, culminating in the murder of the bishop, was perhaps the most striking example of many. This hostility to the bishops was due almost entirely to their refusal to grant corporate rights to the townsmen. Certainly the bishop was less in need of ready money than the lay noble, and therefore less likely to make concessions ; the Church also officially set its face against the business of loans and usury, and the acquisition and use of capital. But many bishops were not averse to making their profit out of the labours of the townsmen. Royal charters to German towns were almost always in the form of grants [1] to the bishops as lords of the towns ; in 1086 the bishop of Spires planted a colony of Jews in his town for the furtherance of its trade, and obtained confirmation of this from the king four years later.

The towns on the side of monarchy

The towns had no idea of escaping from the feudal environment. But they did aspire to the rank of corporate tenants-in-chief, so that they could hold direct from the central authority. It was only the king who could grant them the rights they coveted—of self-government, local justice, the collection of their own taxes, freedom from tolls in other towns. These were all royal rights, *regalia*, which could only be conferred by a king, or by a noble who had received them from the king or had usurped them. There was another asset in kingship, that its authority was not local but, in theory at least, universal throughout the kingdom. It was all to the interest of merchants and towns that this theory should be put into practice, for it ensured the maintenance of peace and order ; the towns are therefore a pro-monarchical element.

In France

We have seen already that when Louis VI restored order within the domain, his protection was invoked from outside. He was too conservative to pay much heed to burgesses, though in a few cases he raised money by granting

[1] Generally of freedom from tolls in royal towns. There was naturally no question of self-government.

charters. Louis VII was more open-handed in his grants
to towns outside the royal domain ; his sense of duty caused
him to respond to appeals for his protection, and he was
ready to increase his authority by giving charters to towns
not previously under his control. Philip Augustus had a more
real sense of the financial and political advantages of attaching
the towns directly to the crown, and within as well as outside
the domain was lavish in granting charters. Rarely was a full
measure of self-government allowed ; a provost maintained
close royal control ; but the towns, though varying widely
in the extent of their privileges, gained the freedom from
local tyranny to develop their resources, and the king
acquired loyal subjects and a considerable addition to his
revenues.

 The situation was different in Germany, where the towns In Germany
were almost all episcopal. The king depended so much on
episcopal support that he could not take the towns directly
under his control. Only when the bishop was opposed to the
king could they expect royal favour, as in the revolt of
Worms in 1074, of Cologne in 1075, and of Mayence which
expelled its archbishop and the anti-king Rudolf in 1077.
In the case of Worms, Henry IV rewarded it with a charter
(conferring freedom from tolls in certain royal towns), which
was the first granted to the " citizens " of a German town and
not to the bishop. Henry IV indeed was constantly alive
to the potentialities of the trading element in his kingdom.
When the preaching of the First Crusade led to an outbreak
of anti-Semitic violence in the Rhine towns, in which some
bishops had a share, he was absent in Italy and helpless. But
on his return in 1097, he saw to it that the Jews were restored
to their rights and the exercise of their religion. His re-estab-
lishment of order was of great value to the Rhine towns, and
they showed their gratitude in the intense loyalty with which
they supported him in his last days, when nobles and Church
allied with his son against him ; even to his banned corpse
Liége and Spires paid their tribute of affection. In consequence they never overcame their dislike of Henry V, in spite
of the charters with which he tried to win their support.
Later, Frederick Barbarossa, who restored peace and order to
Germany, could rely on the loyalty of the towns. Their
support might have made all the difference to the monarchy

in the thirteenth century, had not Frederick II, after yielding
to the Pope his control over the bishops, yielded also to the
nobles his control over the towns.

The Italian
cities
So far we have been dealing with town life on quite a
small scale. The only exceptions were in the Low Countries
and the Rhine district, but even there the population of very
few towns can have reached five figures before the thirteenth
century. Elsewhere we have to visualise for the most part
small market towns inhabited by craftsmen producing and
selling their own wares and small tradesmen selling the goods
imported by travelling merchants. It is an entirely different
picture when we turn to Italy, which in economic development
was a century ahead of the rest of Western Europe, since
town life was there traditional, and the peace given by Otto I
made a rapid recovery possible. The political authority of
the bishop was also traditional, but there were besides numerous noble families, some of them living inside the town, others
in the adjacent countryside, who were accustomed to share
in the life of the town. For urban life was not a novelty but
a familiar and a normal condition in Italy, and we hear of all
classes meeting together in the assembly ; usually, however,
it was an assembly of notables, only the more wealthy
merchants being allowed to act with the nobles as advisers
to the bishop. City patriotism was very marked ; an early
instance of this was the solidarity of the Milanese under
archbishop Aribert in opposition to Conrad II. The city-state
was already in embryo.

Venice,
and its
peculiar
position
In Venice it was actually in being, but Venice was a law
unto itself. Protected by its lagoons, it had escaped the
worst evils of both periods of invasion, and had preserved
something of the older system of government ; its doge (duke)
was the natural successor of the Roman imperial governor of
the district, and it continued to acknowledge the Emperor at
Constantinople as its sovereign. It was never subject to the
Western Emperor, to the political authority of a bishop, to
the conditions of feudal government. It had a long lead in
the field of commerce, and was a real republic in the tenth
century, when it began to assert its sovereignty over the
Adriatic. There was quite a possibility, especially during
the years (991–1009) when Peter Orseolo II was doge, that
a tyranny might be created if the dynastic ambitions of the

doge could be realised.   There were various factors, however,
which combined to prevent this : the rivalry of other families,
the electoral nature of the doge's office, and the ultimate
authority of the popular assembly.   All interests in Venice
were concentrated on trade, so that the richer merchants soon
came to have a large share in the direction of policy.   Elsewhere [1] is described the part played by Venice in the Crusades,
its gradual estrangement from the Eastern Emperor, and the
unsuccessful expedition against Constantinople in 1171 which
led to a reform in the constitution.   The popular assembly
had proved too unstable in times of crisis, and 480 leading
citizens were elected to form a Great Council, which ultimately
became a hereditary body.   The government of Venice was
already, and was to remain, oligarchic.

Venice was alone in being outside the feudal régime, and
the other cities had to obtain a similar freedom before they
too could become self-governing States.   Milan led the way,
when the *popolani* overcame archbishop and nobles and set
up a commune.[2]   Other towns followed suit, helped by the
struggle of Empire and Papacy.   In many cases there was
the excuse, as at Milan, that they were allying with the Pope
against the unreformed clergy ; but at Lucca the rising was
against a reforming bishop, Anselm.   Self-government was the
real aim, and they were helped on their way by charters from
Henry IV and Henry V, who were anxious for their support.
But they went far beyond the grants made to them by charter.
They elected their own magistrates—consuls for the most
part, since the tradition of republican Rome was continually
being invoked in the formation of these new Italian republics.
They fixed their own tolls and kept the revenues from them ;
they had their own judges and notaries, and adhered to the
proceeds of justice.   They had thus usurped sovereign rights,
and during the long period in which the king of Germany was
unable to assert his authority they so accustomed themselves
to freedom that it had become in their eyes a traditional right.
In the next chapter it will be seen how they vindicated this
right against Frederick Barbarossa.   At the Peace of Constance in 1183 they recognised the Emperor again as their
suzerain, but in all essentials they remained free and they
preserved their non-feudal character.   This is true at any

*The cities
assume
rights of
self-
government*

<hr>

[1] Chapters XV and XXII.   [2] See above, chapter IX.

rate of the Lombard cities.   In Tuscany the development was
generally slower ; Pisa of course was a notable exception, and
Lucca had already begun its keen rivalry with Pisa ; Florence,
which owed its rise to the favour of countess Matilda, was
not to take a leading place until the thirteenth century.
In the South the beginnings of city autonomy had been
crushed by the Normans.   It revived again under the weak
rule of Robert Guiscard's son, and Roger II was lavish
with charters before his succession was assured.   Afterwards he revoked them, and while he encouraged trade he
kept the towns in submission to the will of a centralised
monarchy.

The position of the nobles in the cities   Though the popular classes had mastered the feudal
nobility, they did not exclude them from participation in the
life of the town.   They allowed those already residing to
remain there, encouraged those in the countryside (*contado*)
to settle in the town, and forced others to come in so that
they could keep them under surveillance.   In this way they
were able to extend their hold over the *contado*, which was
essential for the food-supply of the city.   They gained also
an important accession of trained soldiers for their militia.
An army was necessary to them, since each city-state was
anxious to extend its borders at the expense of its neighbours,
and economic rivalry was so keen that inter-city wars were
from the twelfth century onwards a regular feature of North
Italian history.   The nobles were not even excluded from
political rights.   Many of them were able to obtain election
as magistrates ; it was the lower classes who were gradually
excluded, and in place of a popular assembly a council of
notables—nobles and merchants—shared with the consuls the
direction of affairs.   But the presence of so many noble
families within the city was a cause of confusion and disorder.
They introduced into it their old factions and feuds and
disturbed its harmony.   What had once been done had to
be done over again ; the nobles were once more mastered
and this time were excluded from political power ; but
this was a development that took place after the twelfth
century.

Trade rivalries   Whatever the government, its purpose was always to
enhance the economic prosperity of the city, and whether
industrial or commercial in its interests, to gain control of

all the possible outlets for its trade and push aside neighbours
that blocked its path or were rivals for the same markets.
Milan, for instance, which had an early start both as a commune and as a great manufacturing centre, was soon thrusting
its way along the highways which converged from different
sides upon the city, trying to elbow aside or to make subject
to itself those towns that interfered with its expansion. So,
though peace might be considered the first necessity for a
commercial State, there was instead constant warfare ; it
hampered trade as a whole, but it advanced the prosperity
of the successful competitor. Many of the towns were situated on the great Roman roads, which were still in good
repair ; Parma, Modena, Bologna and others were along the
Via Emilia, which traversed Lombardy and joined the sea
at Rimini, whence the Via Flaminia led to Rome ; some were
at the meeting-place of several roads, such as Milan, Bologna,
and Florence. Then there were the great waterways, especially the Po in Lombardy and the Arno in Tuscany. Pisa
controlling the outlet of the Arno was at constant strife with
Lucca which commanded an important highway across the
river, and farther upstream was Florence, soon to be a second
rival. Pisa had its outlet to the sea, but here it had to face
fierce competition from Genoa and Venice. Venice and the
Lombard towns were all concerned with the land routes to
Northern Europe, which could only be reached through the
Alpine passes. Asti, Ivrea, Como, Verona, Brescia were all
strategic points on these routes. Everywhere the struggle
went on, and as all were organised for trade, the modern
accompaniments of trade soon came into being—loans, letters
of credit, exchange, and a complete banking system. These
were especially fostered by the Transalpine trade. Dealing
with several countries with their different currencies, the
Lombard cities organised a regular system of exchange. The
inflow of money from all parts of Europe, often in quite small
sums, to the Papacy was dealt with by the Lombard moneychangers, who acted as papal bankers, keeping accounts on
deposit, sending drafts, and making loans. They were soon
able to take the place of the Jews as moneylenders in Northern
Europe ; canon law did not deter them from the practice of
usury. So, in this part of the Western world, trade and not
land created wealth, rights, and status ; a new nobility,

non-feudal, arose to political eminence ; and ideas in conflict with the medieval came into being.

The training of the nobles for war

If the merchant's was a proud calling in North Italy, it was a humble calling elsewhere. Pride of place went with the possession of land, and this was the perquisite of the Church and the nobility. They must be kept by the toil of others, for they had the higher functions, the priest of praying, the noble of fighting. The profession of arms was for a layman essentially the noble profession ; soldier (*miles*) and knight were synonymous terms. The young noble was trained in a rough school, in which he was taught to develop his physique and his powers of endurance, to give hard knocks and to receive them, to perfect himself in horsemanship and in the use of arms (the lance in particular) and armour. Such mental training as he received was largely directed to the same end : recitations of the deeds of great fighters and legendary heroes inspired him to emulation of their exploits. Little wonder, then, that, when he grew to manhood and was dubbed knight, his main interest and his chief pleasure were in fighting. If no important campaign was in progress, there was always a feud with a neighbour to be pursued or an ecclesiastic's lands to be harried.

Their castles

As war was the chief interest of the noble, he was as liable to be attacked as to attack, and therefore he had to take measures for defending himself ; his dwelling place was a fortress. Originally the house was surrounded by a wooden stockade and an earthwork, as was the early burg. Then the castle developed, of wood at first, with a tower-shaped house perched on an artificial mound (*motte*) and surrounded by a ditch ; a second ditch starting from the first enclosed a courtyard (*bailey*) defended by a stockade. Later a rectangular stone tower or keep replaced the wooden, and the mount was dispensed with. This was the earliest and simplest form, which soon received improvements, until a much more elaborate fortress was constructed. Military, like ecclesiastical, architecture displayed the inventiveness and skill of twelfth-century builders. But the building of castles was not only designed to secure a noble's home from attack. It was also part of the general scheme employed by a prince for the controlling or the defence of a district or a kingdom.

This is the case with the burgs erected by Henry the Fowler in Saxony, the castles built by William the Conqueror to maintain his hold over England, by Henry IV to protect the royal domain in Saxony, by the first Hohenstaufen dukes to establish their authority in Suabia, and by French and English alike in the territory disputed between them in Northern France. The character of warfare was directly affected thereby. Pitched battles were, on the whole, of rare occurrence. A campaign consisted mainly of a series of sieges and counter-sieges, so that the chief efforts had to be directed on the one hand to perfecting the defences of the castles, on the other hand to improving the devices for attack and creating still more formidable machines for destruction. In both respects Richard I of England was pre-eminent among his contemporaries, and his great fortress of Château-Gaillard marks the acme of achievement in castle building in the twelfth century.

In other respects there was no development of military science. A battle, like a tournament, was a direct encounter of heavily-armoured knights, and was a matter of personal skill and prowess. There was rarely any suggestion of tactics, still less of strategy. To conceal one's dispositions from the enemy was unusual; it was much more customary to advertise directly one's intention to attack. When a distant campaign was adventured—and this is particularly true of the Crusades—lack of information about the country and of forethought in the matter of supplies, insufficient use of scouts to explore the enemy's dispositions (which had proved fatal to Otto II against the Moslems in South Italy), and a general ignorance of the methods employed by the enemy were all causes of disaster. Against the light cavalry of the Moslems the use of infantry was developed, and a great soldier like Richard I was alive to its tactical importance. But this had no result on warfare in Europe, where foot soldiers, often present in large numbers, were mainly used for attacking castles, and in a direct encounter were hopelessly at the mercy of the opposing knights. They were the chief victims of a battle, since knights, helpless when unhorsed, were not usually butchered; they were more valuable as prisoners, for the sake of their ransom. North Italy provides an exception in this as in other ways. The battle of Legnano was won

Lack of military science

by the sturdy resistance of the citizen infantry, after their cavalry had been broken.

Tournaments and hunting

When the nobles were forced to keep the peace time hung heavily on their hands, for they had little with which to occupy their leisure. They could indulge in the mimic war of tournaments, a sport which in the twelfth century flourished particularly in France and was believed to be of French origin—*conflictus Gallici* an English writer called them. They were regular battles on a small scale, in which severe and sometimes mortal wounds were received, and the victor, as in real warfare, held the vanquished to ransom. They were a training ground for the more serious pursuit of war, and Richard I is said to have introduced them into England for this purpose. Hunting took second place in the pursuits of peace. It, too, was a mimicry of war since there was something to be killed, and if a wild boar was the quarry there was the added excitement of danger. The hunting of the stag was also a means of filling the larder with their favourite meat—venison. The preservation of the deer forests was therefore doubly important, and it was a serious crime for a peasant to kill deer, even though his crops were being ruined by them. Falconry was a less energetic pursuit, and one in which the ladies joined and were often highly proficient.

Lay education

This absorption in martial or semi-martial pursuits was typical of the majority of members of the noble class; but there were some who had wider interests. As we have seen, there were lords who were giving their attention to the management of their estates, developing waste lands, and encouraging settlers. The need for money stimulated them to these undertakings, and they required it not only for military expeditions but also for the purchase of luxuries, silks and tapestries, jewels, spices, and so on. Luxury might undermine their vigour, but it certainly tended to soften their natural savagery. Lay education, confined to Italy for the most part, was not unknown in noble houses in other countries. The greater nobles, like the king, employed learned clerks to teach their sons, some of whom were destined for the Church and so needed Latinity. This was the fate of younger sons and daughters in a large family; it has been shown that in Germany in the twelfth century the leading monasteries and nunneries were exclusively recruited from noble families. Some who had begun their training might be recalled to the world by the death of an elder brother, and perhaps would not altogether lose their taste for learning. Moreover, the ordinary training of those destined for a secular career was beginning to widen; they learnt more of the world, and some of them became extremely proficient in speaking foreign languages.

The quickening of the human spirit, which has been described in the last chapter, was noticeable even in the unreceptive atmosphere of the noble's castle. It gave an opportunity for the development of vernacular literature, especially in France, and the result was a softening of the mood and manners of these violent warriors and their women-folk. They were accustomed in their moments of relaxation to be entertained by clowns and jesters, but also as an accompaniment of a feast they listened with pleasure to a minstrel who sang tales of the past, mostly of a stirring and martial nature. Charlemagne on such occasions had more gravely listened to the reading of Augustine's *City of God*. They preferred instead to hear about Charlemagne himself and other heroes, historical and legendary. In an environment like that in which the poems of Homer had been composed were written the *Chansons de geste* in the eleventh and twelfth centuries, about Charlemagne and his paladins; the most famous and the most popular was the *Chanson de Roland*. This had a natural appeal to the feudal noble; it was full of violent acts, but it also inculcated the duties of courage and endurance, of loyalty to lord and friend, of Christian warfare against the paynim. These *chansons*, too, had a wider appeal than the baronial circle. They were told and sung by companies of pilgrims on their way to the shrines of saints, by merchants travelling the highways in their caravans, by crusaders on the long journey to the Holy Land. Of a similar character, but with a less popular appeal, were the " stories " of Rome (Troy and Aeneas) and of Alexander the Great, which deviated into extraordinary fantasies such as the journey of Alexander to Paradise.

It was a sign of the times that the rougher *Chansons de geste* began to lose their flavour, and that the much more romantic Arthurian cycle eventually won greater popularity

Vernacular literature

The Chansons de geste

The Arthurian cycle

among the upper classes. This first found literary expression
in England in Geoffrey of Monmouth's prose work, the
Historia Regum Britanniae, which appeared about 1135. But
it was mainly from the popular lays of Brittany that the
stories spread in verse form through Northern France in the
second half of the twelfth century. In them the historical
element is slight; we find ourselves in a world of fairies and
magicians, in which knights fight giants and demons, and into
which is woven the mystic story of the Grail. There is much
more conscious literary form in these romances than in the
martial *chansons*, especially in the works of Chrestien de
Troyes, author of *Erec*, *Yvain*, and *Perceval*. These romances
were definitely intended for recital in royal or seignorial halls.
They depict the knightly environment, its manners and customs, the pride of station and the contempt for those beneath
it. But there is another and a newer element, of chivalry
and courtly love, which is already becoming typical of the
period.

The troubadours   The *trouvères*, as the writers of these epics and romances
were called, wrote in the dialect of Northern France, the
langue d'oïl. The *langue d'oc* was the dialect of the South,
the land of minstrels or *troubadours*, who composed lyrics
rather than epics, treating of various subjects, and were
singers as well as poets, for the music was often as important
as the words. Bertrand de Born is the most famous name,
because of the part he played in the strife of Henry II with
his sons and later in association with Richard I; but Giraud
de Borneil had perhaps the greatest reputation. Bertrand's
themes are martial; Giraud's treat of love. He is a moralist
and a psychologist in his analysis of feelings, and so is the
more typical troubadour. Courtly love is depicted and
praised, and respect for women is inculcated. The troubadour is always a lover, usually of a married woman, but his
theme is generally platonic love. He is a knight who wishes
to merit the love of his lady by adventure in war or on
crusade, and will ask little in return save to be the acknowledged lover, and to receive the occasional favour of a ring
or a kiss. It was a pleasant game of make-believe, which
wiled away many hours of idleness at royal and seignorial
courts. William IX of Aquitaine was himself a composer of
songs and has been styled the first of the troubadours. His

granddaughter Eleanor inherited his tastes, and at her court, both as queen of France and later as queen of England, trouvères and troubadours alike were welcomed. The daughters of her first marriage, the countesses of Blois and Champagne, followed her example; Marie of Champagne was the patroness of the famous Chrestien de Troyes.

It had naturally taken some time for vernacular French to evolve from Latin, so that the rapid development of the literature is remarkable. The Teutonic peoples who had retained their old tongues had always had their epic songs in the vernacular, but these were slow to take literary form. It is only as the twelfth century is closing that the *Sagas* appear in Iceland and the first form of the *Niebelungenlied* in Germany. In this history and myth are inextricably mixed. On the one hand there are historical figures such as Etzel (Attila) and Dietrich (Theodoric the Ostrogoth), on the other mythical, Siegfried and Brünnhilde. It is not the age of chivalry that is depicted, but the period of the blood feud and of clan loyalty; the stories are still the primitive folk stories. But at the same time one great noble, Herman, landgrave of Thuringia, was holding a court in the halls of his castle at Wartburg which was to rival the seignorial courts in France. Minstrels (*minnesingers*) competed in festivals with one another, Walter von der Vogelweide composed his courtly poems, Wolfram of Eschenbach his *Parzival*. This has its beginning in the twelfth century, but as a whole perhaps belongs more properly to the thirteenth. German vernacular literature

French influence would therefore seem to have spread already to Germany, and at any rate it is clearly evidenced in the introduction of Arthurian romances by Wolfram. We have already seen that it had spread to Spain.[1] As in the intellectual and artistic development described in the last chapter, so in the cultural life of the laity it is once more France that takes the lead and sets the fashion.[2] In military as in ecclesiastical architecture this is largely true, but especially in vernacular literature, both epic poems which depicted Chivalry

[1] See above, chapter XVI, *ad fin.*
[2] The words " romance," " chivalry " and the like are indications of this French influence.

the manners of the day and love lyrics which set a new standard for life. For out of it was born the new idea of Chivalry, of courtliness in place of boorishness, of the constancy and devotion of a knight to his lady; it becomes the fashion to show respect to a lady, and the effect on the position of women is remarkable. If at first it was highly artificial, it had a softening and a civilising influence, so that out of it something real and permanent was evolved.

SUGGESTIONS FOR READING ON CHAPTER XIX

In general :
> Cambridge Economic History of Europe. Vol. I–. Cambridge, 1941–.
> Boissonade, P. : Life and Work in Medieval Europe (Eng. trans.). London, 1927.
> Crump, C. G. and Jacob, E. F. (editors) : The Legacy of the Middle Ages. Oxford, 1926.
> Heaton, H. : Economic History of Europe. New York, 1936.
> Inama-Sternegg, K. T. von : Deutsche Wirtschaftsgeschichte. 3 vols. Leipzig, 1879–1901.
> Luchaire, A. : Social France at the Time of Philip Augustus (Eng. trans.). London, 1912.
> Pirenne, H. : Economic and Social History of Medieval Europe (Eng. trans.). London, 1936.
> Ganshof, F.-L. : Feudalism (Eng. trans. by Grierson, P.). London, 1952.
> Stephenson, C. : Mediaeval Feudalism. Cornell U.P., 1942.
> Bloch, M. : Feudal Society (Eng. trans. by L. A. Manyon). London, 1961.
> Painter, S. : French Chivalry. Baltimore, 1940.
> Mitteis, H. : Der Staat des hohen Mittelalters. Weimar, 1948.

Rural Life :
> Bloch, M. : French Rural History (Eng. trans. by J. Sondheimer). London, 1966.
> Duby, G. : Rural Economy and Country Life in the Medieval West (Eng. trans. by C. Postan). London, 1968.
> Sée, H. : Les classes rurales et le régime domanial en France au moyen âge. Paris, 1901.

Town Life, Commerce, Industry :
> Cambridge Economic History of Europe, Vol. III. Cambridge, 1963.
> Lopez, R. S., and Raymond, I. W. : Medieval Trade in the Mediterranean World. New York, 1955.
> Mundy, J. H., and Riesenberg, P. : The Medieval Town. Princeton, 1958.
> Pirenne, H. : Early Belgian Democracy (Eng. trans.). Manchester, 1915.

Italian Cities :
> Cambridge Medieval History, Vol. V, chapter 5.
> Butler, W. F. : The Lombard Communes. London, 1906.
> Renouard, Y. : Les hommes d'affaires italiens du moyen âge. Paris, 1949.

The Jews :
  Cambridge Medieval History, Vol. VII, chapter 22.

Warfare :
  Cambridge Medieval History, Vol. VI, chapters 22, 23.
  ffoulkes, C. : *Armour and Weapons*. Oxford, 1909.
  Oman, C. W. C. : *History of the Art of War in the Middle Ages*, 2nd ed. 2 vols. London, 1924.
  Viollet-le-Duc, E. : *Military Architecture* (Eng. trans.), 3rd ed. Oxford, 1907.
  Lot, F. : *L'art militaire et les armées au Moyen Age en Europe et dans le Proche Orient*. 2 vols. Paris, 1946.
  Smail, R. C. : *Crusading Warfare*. Cambridge, 1956.

Vernacular Literature :
  Cambridge Medieval History, Vol. VI, chapters 24, 25.
  Bédier, J. : *Les légendes épiques*, 2nd ed. 4 vols. Paris, 1914–21.
  Menéndez Pidal, R. : *La Chanson de Roland et la tradition épique des Francs*. Paris, 1960.
  Chaytor, H. J. : *The Troubadours*. Cambridge, 1912.
  Gautier, L. : *La chevalerie*. Paris, 1890.
  Ker, W. P. : *Epic and Romance*. London, 1908.
  Saintsbury, G. : *The Flourishing of Romance and the Rise of Allegory*. Edinburgh, 1897.

15

CHAPTER XX

THE SECOND CONTEST OF EMPIRE AND PAPACY, 1157–1177

The issues
between the
Empire and
the Papacy

THE treaty of Constance between Emperor and Pope had been of short duration. Its terms satisfied the immediate requirements of both parties, but neither was able to fulfil them, and the consequent breach of the treaty by both sides gave rise to considerable ill feeling. In the background there were other issues of more fundamental importance, since they involved the relations between the *regnum* and the *sacerdotium* ; for the sake of peace they had been tacitly ignored in the treaty of Constance, but with its breach they emerged to exaggerate the state of tension which had already been created. The situation was not unlike that in England, where Henry II, regarding the reign of Stephen as a period of anarchy, was trying to return to the practice of Henry I's reign. Frederick was similarly returning to the practice of Henry V's reign, ignoring the precedents that had been created in the papal favour by the complaisance of Lothar and the weakness of Conrad. He kept a close watch on episcopal elections, a vital matter to the German king, and constantly saw to it that his nominee was elected. In the case of disputed elections he revived the concession of the Concordat of Worms, with the added interpretation that the right of appointment devolved upon him,[1] so that he could dispose of both candidates and nominate a third person as bishop. Already in 1152 this had happened when the archbishopric of Magdeburg was vacant. It was of equal importance to him to keep a control over episcopal territory and he exercised the right of *regalia*, by which the episcopal lands reverted to the crown during a vacancy, and even of

---

[1] Known as *Devolutionsrecht*. This was claimed afterwards by the Papacy. A notable instance of its exercise was the appointment of Stephen Langton to Canterbury by Innocent III.

spolia, which gave him control of the movable property of a dead bishop. To make the parallel with England more complete, article 6 in Frederick's edict enforcing peace (*Landfriede*) in 1152 laid down that a cleric committing a breach of the peace was to be punished in the lay court of the local count as well as in the bishop's court.

Here was material, and to spare, for discord. The Papacy, which during the last two reigns had been peacefully advancing its programme of ecclesiastical freedom, was both startled and embarrassed by the reaction that had set in. The change was more striking since in a measure Lothar III had recognised the subordination of the temporal power, and this had been impressed on Barbarossa at the time of his coronation as Emperor. Besides the particular question of imperial control over the Church in Germany, the issue of the relations between Pope and Emperor had once again to be decided. The Papacy had now the more immediate precedents, but the Emperor still had the long range of tradition behind him. To Frederick, keen lover of justice in accordance with the principles of feudal custom, precedent was law. He had submitted at Rome to the precedent set by Lothar, though it offended his dignity ; but it was novel, and he wished to get behind it to the established tradition of the past. There was the consciousness, too, that his German subjects were of one mind with him, which gave him the backing that Henry IV had so conspicuously lacked. With the exception of archbishop Eberhard of Salzburg, he could rely on the episcopate, and many of the lay nobility were as ardently imperialistic as himself. Those whose counsel he took in these early years, such as Otto of Wittelsbach, were emphatic in their defiance of papal claims. The most outspoken of all was Rainald of Dassel, who became chancellor in 1156. Well-read and of wide interests, he used all his gifts wholeheartedly in the imperial cause ; he was violent in his exaltation of it especially against ecclesiastical pretensions, and it was his forceful influence that principally swayed the policy of Frederick Barbarossa and increased the bitterness of the ensuing conflict. The mediating influence of abbot Wibald of Stablo, friend of both Pope and Emperor, was henceforward disregarded.

For Frederick the task of recovery was not limited to the

ecclesiastical sphere. It had to be undertaken also in his Italian kingdom, where his predecessors had been equally neglectful of their rights. Here the change was much more complete, and the old system could not be restored. Frederick could no longer govern through the bishops, since they had lost most of their political power and ecclesiastically had become subject to the Papacy. The ecclesiastical issue entered in here as in Germany, since control over the bishops was still important to the king, because of the lands they held from the king and the services due from those lands. But for the restoration of his political authority he had to deal not with bishops or Pope but with communal governments, which, following the example of Milan, had been established in most cities. In some cases the commune had received a royal charter, which recognised its existence and granted it certain rights in the matter of tolls ; but in every case much more had been usurped than had been granted. The communes had arrogated to themselves all those sovereign rights (*regalia*) which could only legally be granted by a king ; under this heading were included the governmental and judicial functions (normally exercised by bishop, marquis, or count), the right of the overlord to maintenance, rights of mint, tolls, control over roads and waterways, all of them valuable sources of revenue. So the Lombard towns had become almost sovereign States. They were the authors of their own independence, having obtained by their own efforts the mastery over the feudal nobles, against whom in other countries the towns were wont to seek royal assistance ; this independence, which they valued for its own sake as well as for the material prosperity it enabled them to achieve, they were prepared to defend at all costs. In such a situation a ruler like Frederick Barbarossa could not be expected to acquiesce. Not only was his prestige and his authority as ruler of Italy at stake ; his treasury was being defrauded of its lawful income, and a natural source of men and supplies for his army when he came into Italy was denied to him.

The old order could not be restored, especially since Milan, which under its archbishop, the nominee of the Emperor, had been the pivot of the old system, was now the champion of anti-imperialism. There were, however, certain elements in Frederick's favour. For each of these self-governing communes was eager to add to its territory and to extend its trade at the expense of its neighbours, and there were rival groups bitterly hostile to one another. So Frederick could hope to obtain allies, especially against Milan, whose domineering methods gave rise to jealousy and alarm. Hatred of Milan brought Pavia and Lodi to his side when he made his first entry into Italy. On that occasion his objective was Rome and his imperial coronation, and after that the expedition he had planned with the Pope against the king of Sicily. He ignored for the time the usurpations of the cities, satisfied with a general recognition of his authority; he could not engage in a campaign in the south, if a hostile north cut his communications with Germany. So he displayed his sovereignty only by enforcing peace, dictating terms to settle disputes between cities, especially between Milan and Pavia. But the Milanese would take no orders from him, and when he passed through their territory their deliberate acts of hostility led him to reprisals, culminating in the siege and destruction of one of Milan's smaller allies, Tortona. This fulfilled its purpose of overawing the communes, but it was hardly satisfactory that the capture of a little town should occupy the imperial army for over two months. This long delay, moreover, upset Frederick's programme: after his coronation it was too late to undertake the Sicilian campaign, and anyhow with unrest in the north he could not risk his army in the south. His return from Rome, though he avoided the dangerous vicinity of Milan and took the east-coast route, was not achieved without fighting.

He knew now the problem with which he was faced, and he gave much time and careful preparation to its solution. Meanwhile there was one preliminary undertaking that first engaged his attention. It was natural for a king of Germany who was concerned to make himself master of North Italy to pay some heed to his Burgundian kingdom, since with Burgundy in his possession he controlled all the passes into Italy. This had been the main purpose of Otto I's control of its ruler, and of its actual acquisition by Conrad II. Since Conrad's day the power of the German kings had steadily declined, as their interest had grown less; it was manifestly difficult for an absentee ruler to have any authority over a kingdom that had neither geographical nor political unity.

Frederick's assertion of sovereignty in Burgundy

Lothar III had tried the expedient of an imperial rector, and had appointed duke Conrad of Zähringen; neither he nor his son Berthold who succeeded him as rector was capable of mastering the independent nobility. Frederick had held his court at Besançon in 1153, but had then contented himself with receiving the homage of the Burgundian nobles and enforcing peace. In 1155 he decided on a new policy. First of all, he made himself acceptable to the powerful episcopate and won their support by his favours; secondly, he took the opportunity of dissensions among the lay nobles to intervene in person. The heiress to the county of Burgundy, Beatrice, was in the custody of her uncle, William of Mâcon, who had seized her inheritance when his brother Rainald died. The way was cleared by the death of William of Mâcon, and Frederick, who had already divorced his first wife, married Beatrice in 1156, and thus acquired a considerable domain and a direct control within the kingdom. The rectorate was abandoned, and the house of Zähringen compensated by the extension of its jurisdiction in Switzerland. In October 1157 Frederick came again to Burgundy to impress on its inhabitants the reality of his sovereignty. He was then at the height of his power, which was acknowledged by all his neighbours. The king of Denmark was his vassal. The duke of Poland had just been compelled, after a brief expedition by Frederick, to do homage and to promise a contingent to the forthcoming Italian expedition. The king of Hungary had come in person to Germany and made the same promise.[1] The duke of Bohemia, Vladislav II, had proved his loyalty in the campaign against the Poles; he was to be rewarded a few months later by his duchy being raised to the rank of **The diet at** a kingdom. The famous diet which the Emperor now held **Besançon** at Besançon was attended by all the magnates of the Burgundian kingdom, and Germans and Italians were also present in large numbers; finally, there were ambassadors from France, from England, and from Spain. It was one of the rare moments when the medieval Empire seemed to have a real significance.

The letter It was into this august assembly that was thrown the **from the** apple of discord which was to inaugurate twenty years of **Pope, and its effects**

---

[1] Poland did not fulfil its obligation, but a detachment of Hungarian archers took part in the expedition under the command of the duke of Austria.

strife. Two cardinals, the chancellor Roland and Bernard, arrived with a letter from the Pope, referring to the treatment of the Danish archbishop, Eskil of Lund, who had been set upon by bandits on his return from a visit to Rome, and complaining especially that Frederick had taken no steps to punish this outrage though it had been perpetrated in his dominions. This was a delicate matter, for Eskil was a stout champion of papal authority and had offended Frederick by his utterances. But in the wording of the letter lay the particular sting. Framed in a tone that would perhaps have been natural if addressed to Lothar III, it was exactly calculated to provoke the temper of Frederick I. The Pope bade him remember that the Roman Church had most willingly *conferred* upon him the distinction of the imperial crown ; he himself, so far from regretting that he had fallen in with Frederick's wishes in all respects, would gladly confer even greater *beneficia* upon him. These were the phrases that gave particular offence, with the seeming implication that the Emperor was the vassal of the Pope and held the Empire as a fief (*beneficium*) from him. Rainald of Dassel translated the letter aloud for the benefit of the German nobles, and gave this technical interpretation to the Pope's words. Immediately there was a violent uproar. Cardinal Roland, who had doubtless had a hand in the wording, added fuel to the flames by exclaiming : " From whom then does he have the Empire, if not from the Pope ? " At this evident justification of all their suspicions, the assembly was still further exasperated, and Otto of Wittelsbach rushed at the legate with his sword drawn ; murder might have been done, had not Frederick himself intervened. He dismissed the legates with a safe conduct, on condition that they returned directly to Rome.

Back in Germany, the Emperor issued a strongly-worded manifesto [1] to the bishops, in which he recalled the picture of Lothar III he had seen at Rome and the inscription beneath it, and described the Pope's recent letter as the last in a series of steps by which he had advanced to his ultimate claim of authority ; moreover, in the legates' baggage had been found documents which revealed that they had been given a free

---

[1] Like Henry IV in similar circumstances he is careful to state that he holds his office from God alone, stressing the divine right of the ruler.

hand to make any dispositions they thought fit in any of the churches in Germany. The Pope also issued a manifesto, complaining of the attitude of Frederick and especially of the treatment his legates had received. This failed in its effect, for the German bishops were of the same mind as the Emperor, and replied to the Pope in Frederick's own words. Even in the papal Curia there was not complete unanimity, for one or two cardinals had been won over by the favour shown to them by Frederick. The Pope had further cause for alarm. Early in 1158, Rainald of Dassel and Otto of Wittelsbach, the very men whose conduct to his legates he had most strongly reprobated, came to North Italy to prepare the way for the Emperor's forthcoming expedition, and by the success of their mission threatened even the papal security. So Hadrian decided that his position was untenable and that he must retire from it with as much dignity as possible. Two other cardinals were sent to the Emperor with a letter explaining away the phrases that had given so much offence. The Pope insisted that he had been misunderstood. The literal meaning of *beneficium* was " kindness," and this was the sense in which he had used it ; by *conferring* the imperial crown he had meant nothing more than *placing it on the head* of the Emperor. Frederick gracefully accepted the explanation ; but, though the incident was allowed to drop, the irritation remained.

Temporary reconciliation

Frederick's second Italian expedition

Having thus vindicated the imperial authority against the encroachments of the papal power, he concentrated upon the recovery of imperial dominion in North Italy. The way had already been prepared by the skilful diplomacy of Rainald and Otto in the north-east, and in July 1158 Frederick himself appeared at the head of the largest army that any Emperor had ever led over the Alps ; he was accompanied by the king of Bohemia and all the leading nobles of central and southern Germany. Pavia, Cremona, and other enemies of Milan joined him at once ; the first sign of resistance, at Brescia, was quickly overcome, and other towns were awed into submission. Frederick's aim, as he announced, was to reconstitute on the basis of peace and justice the rule of law and order in Italy. But first rebellion must be crushed, and it was the insolent defiance of his authority by Milan which necessitated the assembling of so large an army ; nothing would satisfy him but its complete surrender, and he proclaimed against it the ban of the Empire, summarily rejecting the appeals of its ambassadors for milder terms. Milan, almost isolated, fought heroically to preserve its independence; but it was not provisioned for a long siege, and was compelled by famine to surrender at the end of a month. The terms imposed were not crushing, but were calculated to rob it of all that it most prized. Its walls were left intact, and it retained its separate entity, with some measure of local self-government. But its magistrates (consuls) were to be subject to imperial confirmation ; all its citizens had to swear fealty to the Emperor ; Como and Lodi, whose walls it had destroyed, were to be rebuilt and to remain exempt from its authority ; and, besides paying a large indemnity, it had to sacrifice all the *regalia* it had usurped. It was, in fact, to enter into the feudal régime again, to become a vassal city.

Surrender of Milan

With the surrender of Milan the purpose of the military expedition was achieved and most of the troops were allowed to return home. The Emperor himself proceeded to Roncaglia, where he held a diet in November to settle the future government of the Italian kingdom and the relations of the cities with their sovereign. This being a matter to be decided by law and custom, he summoned to assist him in his deliberations the bishops of North Italy, formerly the masters of the cities, and doctors of law, especially the four famous experts in Roman Law at Bologna.[1] With these great jurists as his leading advisers, it might have been expected that the principles of Roman Law would have triumphed over feudal custom ; and, indeed, utterance was given to them, especially by the archbishop of Milan, who in a rhetorical pro-imperial declamation quoted the famous sentence from the *Institutes* beginning : " What has pleased the prince has the force of law." But Frederick was nothing if not traditional in his outlook, and he missed this great opportunity of creating a truly imperial administration and inaugurating a system of imperial law. He was the feudal monarch *par excellence*, without a vision of any other possibility. Yet he was wise

The diet of Roncaglia (1158)

---

[1] The " Four Doctors "—Bulgarus, Martinus, Jacobus, and Hugo—whose commentaries (glosses) on the Roman Law played such an important part in the development of its study.

to employ the experts in Roman Law, for men trained in the greatest system of law ever known would be the most capable of exactly interpreting the rules of law, whatever the system. And this was his purpose. He wanted the old customs to be interpreted in accordance with the strictest rules of justice, which would guarantee to all his subjects as well as to himself their customary rights. He was trying to revive a system that was out of date in Italy; but to his own mind he was wiping out a period of anarchy and usurpation and restoring the old order to its rightful place. In this spirit were issued the decrees of the diet of Roncaglia. The *regalia* were carefully defined, and an exact inventory made of those royal rights, whether governmental or financial, which were being exercised by each city. Those which had been conferred on a city by charter from a previous ruler were re-granted to it by Frederick, but all the rest had to be resigned, as had already been done at Milan. The financial effect of this recovery of the *regalia* was to add a large sum to the annual income of the imperial treasury. To ensure the permanence of this, and that the cities remained in feudal subordination to himself, he appointed in each an official known as *podestà* (from the Latin *potestas*), who, like the royal provost in French towns, controlled on behalf of the king the government of the city. The relations of the cities with one another were restricted by the prohibition of private wars, which emphasised both the dependence of all upon him and his duty of enforcing peace; while a long edict against alienation or partition of fiefs without the consent of the overlord made it clear that property was to be held on a strictly feudal basis. Two other acts of this diet, both provocative of trouble, may also be mentioned. Monza was declared to be the traditional place of coronation of the Italian kings and was therefore transferred from Milan to the Emperor; and Welf VI, who had already been created marquis of Tuscany, was invested by the Emperor with the lands of countess Matilda, regardless of the papal claims of overlordship.

Milan and other cities again in revolt

Frederick had dismissed the greater part of his army before the diet at Roncaglia, and the decrees of that diet seemed to him so obviously just and reasonable that apparently he anticipated no trouble in their execution. He decided to winter in Italy, and early in 1159 dispatched the most important members of his entourage as commissioners to the various cities to arrange the appointments of podestàs, accompanied by clerks to assess the *regalia*. He was soon disillusioned. Only those cities, such as Pavia and Cremona, which counted on his alliance against Milan gave a welcome to his nominees. Elsewhere, there was a sullen submission as at Piacenza, or a definite outbreak as at Brescia and above all at Milan. Chafing at its recent humiliation, which the loss of Monza had exaggerated, the arrival of Frederick's two favourite councillors, Rainald of Dassel and Otto of Wittelsbach, to make secure the imperial yoke provoked a violent explosion. The royal commissioners were set upon by the populace and were forced to escape from the city. Such a defiance of the imperial authority could only have one result. Once more the ban was proclaimed against Milan, and after the usual formalities a state of war declared. This meant the raising of a fresh army, and Frederick wrote to Germany for levies, entrusting to the Empress and to Henry the Lion, who had not accompanied him in 1158, the task of raising them. Both of them made a ready response, and in July they appeared together in Italy at the head of a considerable army. After a preliminary campaign, in which he laid waste the country round Milan, and then by a stratagem induced the Milanese to leave the shelter of their walls and inflicted on them a severe defeat, he laid siege to Crema. To this he *The siege* was induced by the Cremonese, anxious for their revenge on *of Crema* this town which they claimed to be subject to themselves and which preferred alliance with their enemy. It was an insignificant objective for the whole might of the German army, but the little town held out for six months, conducting an epic defence against overwhelming odds. It was only in January 1160 that it at last surrendered, and long before that greater issues had emerged to engross the attention of the Emperor.

In the earlier relations of Frederick Barbarossa with *Papal* Hadrian IV, the Emperor was defending the *regnum* against *grievances against the* the *sacerdotium*. He had vigorously repudiated the sugges- *Emperor* tion that he held his crown from the Pope, and Hadrian, whatever his actual opinion, had been obliged to render a formal assent. But by the end of 1158 the positions had become entirely reversed. Frederick not only controlled ecclesiastical appointments in Germany, but when he became master of North Italy he expected and obtained the obedience of the Italian bishops, who did homage to him, attended his court when summoned, and submitted to his claims for maintenance. This extension of Frederick's influence in the ecclesiastical sphere was naturally obnoxious to the Pope, who was still further alarmed by Frederick's encroachment on papal territory, especially his arbitrary disposal of the lands of countess Matilda. In both its ecclesiastical and its temporal jurisdictions the *sacerdotium* was now being threatened by the advance of the *regnum*. There were various incidents provocative of friction early in 1159, for instance when Frederick nominated Guido, the son of the loyal count of Biandrate, as archbishop of Ravenna, and the Pope refused to release from his duties this subdeacon of the Roman Church. At last in the summer the Pope formulated his grievances in an embassy in which four cardinals participated, two of whom [1] were members of the small party in the Curia which favoured the Emperor. Though this seemed to show a conciliatory spirit on the part of the Pope, the effect of it was lost by the character of the papal demands. These were four in number, and to two of them—that the Emperor should exercise no rights of maintenance in the Papal States except on the occasion of his coronation, and that various territories, including the whole of the lands of countess Matilda, should be at once restored to the Pope—Frederick vouchsafed no answer. To the demand that the Italian bishops should only take an oath of fealty and not do homage to the Emperor, and that they should not be obliged to entertain imperial messengers in their palaces, Frederick replied that if the bishops would surrender all the land they held from him he would not ask for homage, and that episcopal palaces built on royal lands were in fact royal palaces. Finally, the Pope asserted his absolute authority over the city of Rome, and denied the right of the Emperor to send ambassadors to the Roman people save with his permission. To this Frederick replied with a direct negative. What

---

[1] Octavian, later Victor IV, and Guido of Crema. This party especially favoured a renewal of the treaty of Constance and a breach with Sicily ; the majority so thoroughly distrusted the aims of Frederick that they preferred an alliance with the king of Sicily.

meaning was there, he asked, in his title of Roman Emperor (which he held by the appointment of God), if in Rome itself he was denied authority. Actually an embassy from the Roman Senate, asking for his recognition and promising obedience to him in return, arrived at this moment ; by the favour he showed it he underlined his reply to the Pope, in which he put forward also his own grievances, especially the breach of the treaty of Constance, the passing hither and thither of cardinal-legates without his leave and their active interference with local churches, and the abuse of appeals to Rome. In this verbal conflict fundamental issues were being raised, and the Pope might well feel that the imperialism of Frederick constituted a grave menace to his own authority and to ecclesiastical independence. He began to take steps to defend himself. He went to Anagni, and there met representatives of the king of Sicily, and also of Milan, Brescia, and Piacenza, with whom he made a compact of mutual assistance ; it was even asserted that he promised to issue the ban of excommunication against the Emperor. However, these negotiations were interrupted by the sudden death of the Pope, which took place on September 1, 1159.

The Pope's body was brought back to Rome for burial on September 4, and three days later the cardinals assembled in St. Peter's for the new election. Almost all of them were in favour of the chancellor Roland, a man of wide practical experience and profound legal knowledge, the foremost among the advisers of the late Pope. But the small group that favoured the Emperor and opposed the Sicilian alliance insisted on putting forward their leader, Octavian, and they were encouraged by the presence in Rome of an embassy from Frederick to the Roman Senate, headed by Otto of Wittelsbach. The result of this division among the cardinals was, as in 1130, the creation of a papal schism. Roland was proclaimed as Pope Alexander III, Octavian as Pope Victor IV ; and an unseemly scrimmage took place in the basilica, each candidate striving to be the first to be clothed in the papal mantle. It was especially important for Octavian to be able, by this formal act, to claim priority. His cause was obviously very difficult to defend, since he had only a handful of supporters among the cardinals. It was later argued on his behalf that in the schism of 1130 Innocent II

The Papal schism of 1159

had only had a minority of the votes and yet had been recognised as the true Pope ; and Victor's supporters among the cardinals issued a statement asserting that there were 9 of them against 14 on the other side. If this had been true, the parallel with 1130, when the voting was 16 to 27, would have been a close one. Actually, however, only 5 cardinals signed the statement, while a similar statement issued by Alexander's supporters was signed by 23. With such an overwhelming majority Alexander III could justly claim to be the rightful Pope. But it was not merely a question of numbers, and the personal ambition of his rival cloaked a deeper issue. The situation was, in fact, not unlike that in 1061, when the imperial court, allied with the Lombard bishops and the Roman nobles, had tried to set up a subservient Pope, Honorius II, and the cardinals, with Norman support, had enthroned their choice, Alexander II. So, too, in 1159, Victor IV had the support of the Emperor, the German and most of the Lombard bishops, and republican Rome ; Alexander III, the true choice of the cardinals, was able to maintain himself thanks to the aid of the Normans. The chief difference was that in 1061 the supporters of Honorius were challenging the Election Decree ; in 1159 this had to be accepted and the pretence made that Victor was elected in accordance with its rules.

Frederick's attempts to gain recognition for Victor IV

How far Frederick was responsible for the schism, it is impossible to say ; perhaps, in previously creating a party favourable to himself in the Curia, he had contemplated the election of a Pope amenable to his views. But there is no question that he welcomed the situation when it arose. It gave him the opportunity to assert that, when the Church was in peril through schism or other disorder, it was the function of the Emperor to intervene, as had been done in the past by Constantine and others, and more recently by Charlemagne and Otto the Great. Accordingly he summoned a general council of the Church to meet at Pavia, and ordered the two rival Popes to appear in person before it. The holding of the council, originally fixed for Epiphany, was deferred in order that the Emperor might concentrate on the capture of Crema, which was now imminent. Crema surrendered on January 26, 1160, and the council of Pavia met on February 5. But it was not a council representative of the Western Church 'as Frederick had intended. The higher clergy of Germany, Burgundy, and North Italy were well represented, and a large number of abbots and lesser clergy from Rome and its neighbourhood were present; but no Church outside the Empire was represented, though some kings sent their representatives to watch the proceedings. Alexander III naturally refused to recognise the jurisdiction of such a council, or indeed the legality of the imperial summons; Victor IV, as naturally, appeared before it and stated his case. In these circumstances its deliberations were merely formal, and anyhow the result had been pre-determined by the will of the Emperor. Political rather than ecclesiastical considerations guided the decision of the assembly, and it was apparently only the reluctance of many Italian bishops to acquiesce that caused a delay of seven days before Victor IV was declared the rightful Pope. All the German and Burgundian archbishops signed the resolution, in person or by deputy, except Eberhard of Salzburg,[1] but only a few Italian bishops. On the whole, however, the Emperor could be satisfied that in his dominions Victor was recognised. But though he made strenuous efforts to obtain this recognition elsewhere in Europe, he was almost uniformly unsuccessful. The kings of England and France, each of whom in his enmity to the other had courted the alliance of Frederick, agreed nevertheless to unite in supporting Alexander III. The case for Alexander was so obviously the better, and neither of them wished to see the Papacy subject to the dictation of the Emperor. The council of Pavia had, therefore, only made the schism more definite. Its Pope had issued a sentence of excommunication against Alexander III and his supporters; he in his turn excommunicated the Emperor and all who adhered to Victor IV, and openly allied himself with Milan and the other cities which resisted imperial authority. The Emperor had thus united his two adversaries against himself, and had also put himself in the wrong in the eyes of the rest of Europe. The lawful Pope was bound to triumph. The

Alexander III recognised outside the Empire

---

[1] He was not present at the council. His reputation for piety and theological learning was so great that every effort was made to obtain his signature. Not even the pleading of his friend, bishop Eberhard of Bamberg, who sent him the carefully prepared version of Victor's case, could shake his adherence to Alexander.

"general council" of Pavia must rank as Frederick's greatest political blunder.[1]

Capture and demolition of Milan

This was not evident at first, for in spite of the alliance of the Pope with Milan, Piacenza, and Brescia, Frederick clearly held the upper hand in Lombardy. But while his mind was engrossed with the aim of establishing Victor IV as Pope, his original purpose of a campaign against Milan was interrupted; he did little in 1160 beyond devastating the surrounding territory and beginning the encirclement of the city. In the spring of 1161, when reinforcements reached him from Germany, he was able to move closer and submit the city to a rigorous investment. The Milanese had profited by the long pause to strengthen their fortifications and provision themselves for a long siege, so that for a whole year they withstood the attacks of the powerful imperial army. At last, in March 1162, complete exhaustion compelled their unconditional surrender. Frederick would not listen to any appeals for clemency. He was determined to prevent any recrudescence of rebellion by the destruction of its chief fomentor; its walls were demolished and its buildings destroyed by fire. Yet with a singular lack of prescience the surviving inhabitants were given four localities in the neighbourhood in which to settle, and no garrison was maintained to prevent them from returning to the ruins. From Milan Frederick went to Piacenza and Brescia, which were forced to demolish their walls and give hostages for their future behaviour. His victory in Lombardy was complete, and Rome and Sicily anticipated his coming attack. Alexander III felt that his position was untenable; a month after the fall of Milan he set sail for France on a Sicilian galley; there he remained for three years, eventually establishing his court at Sens, with his authority as Head of the Church in no way impaired by his enforced exile.

Alexander III takes refuge in France

Frederick in Germany

Frederick had certainly intended to march on Rome, but the escape of the Pope frustrated his purpose. He therefore retraced his steps and crossed the Alps into Burgundy, hoping by diplomatic means to decoy Alexander from his shelter in

[1] The ill-considered violence of Frederick's proceedings seems out of tune with his earlier disposition and his love of justice, and a complete contrast to the cool diplomacy of his later years. Probably this may be attributed to the influence of Rainald of Dassel, who had become archbishop of Cologne in 1159 and was, by virtue of that office, arch-chancellor of Italy.

France. His tortuous negotiations with Louis, however, ended in failure.[1] So he returned to Germany, where indeed his presence was required to settle the local feuds which were always so liable to break out during the absence of the king in Italy. The most serious disturbance had occurred at Mayence, starting in 1158 when archbishop Arnold imposed a tax to pay the expenses of the contingent which Frederick had demanded for his Italian expedition. The Emperor was not unaware of the value to himself of the growing wealth of the towns, especially in the Rhine district, but he was content to leave them under episcopal control and thus indirectly to reap his profit from them. The citizens of Mayence rose against the tax imposed upon them by Arnold, and the revolt reached its climax in the murder of the archbishop in 1160. For this Frederick now exacted a stern revenge, not only punishing the chief offenders but also depriving the city of its privileges and demolishing its walls.

Meanwhile the cities in North Italy were being controlled, under the direction of Rainald of Dassel, by the imperial podestàs, and here, too, the financial advantage of the crown was the prime consideration. The cities were not only galled by the loss of their independence, but also oppressed by the burden of taxation. Frederick was curiously blind to the dangers of this policy. He came himself to Italy again in October 1163, to hold his court and hear disputes, accompanied only by an ordinary retinue ; haughtily he rejected the appeals against the oppression of his agents. He soon had occasion to repent that he had not come at the head of an army, for there was disaffection on all sides, and he could count on the allegiance only of Pavia, Como, and Lodi. Within a year he had to retire once more to Germany, leaving the position much worse than he had found it, and imperial prestige gravely tarnished. Meanwhile in 1164, before he left Italy, the death of Victor IV deprived him of his principal excuse for combating the title of Alexander III. There were hopes, even in Frederick's entourage, of an end of the schism, and it was obvious wisdom for the Emperor to make his peace with the Church when all his energy was needed to maintain his hold over Lombardy. But Frederick was still obsessed with the idea of impressing his will, and he had

His third expedition to Italy

The death of Victor IV

[1] For an account of these, see below, pp. 464-5.

Rainald of Dassel at his right hand to urge him to persist; his personal animosity against Alexander was another factor. So it was decided to find a successor to Victor IV, and there was an obvious choice in Guido of Crema, who had been Octavian's constant ally in the Curia during Hadrian IV's Papacy; he took the name of Paschal III. This time there was not even the semblance of a general council to justify the election, and Frederick could not obtain the recognition even of his own subjects for the new anti-Pope. Except for Rainald all the archbishops of Germany were opposed to the continuance of the schism, and the archbishop-elect of Mayence, Conrad of Wittelsbach, fled to France to avoid compliance. Frederick promptly replaced him by Christian of Buch, a prelate of the temper of Rainald, so that at Mayence and Cologne he had at least two martial and capable archbishops, who were willing to place the dignity of the Empire before all ecclesiastical considerations. But the German Church as a whole was opposed to the election of Paschal, so that Frederick could no longer boast a united Empire behind him. The situation seemed so much more promising

Return of Alexander III to Rome

to Alexander III that he decided to risk his return; in 1165, with an escort of Sicilian vessels, he made a triumphant re-entry into Rome.

Frederick's fourth Italian expedition

Frederick would have come to Italy in any case. He was preparing an expedition to quell the growing disaffection in Lombardy; but the magnet of the Pope's presence drew him irresistibly to Rome, to aim for the prize of which he had been foiled by Alexander's flight in 1162. His preparations took time, and there were local feuds in Germany with which he had to deal. So it was not until November 1166 that he arrived in Italy at the head of a large army. The situation in Lombardy was so threatening that he was delayed by the necessity of overawing the rebels and taking hostages from the more dangerous, such as Bologna. He chose the eastern route to the south and stopped to invest Ancona, which had once more given its allegiance to the Eastern Emperor; its capture delayed him for several weeks. Meanwhile the archbishops of Mayence and Cologne had been sent in advance with a portion of the army to prepare the way, and succeeded in inflicting a severe defeat on the papal forces outside Rome. When Frederick himself arrived at

the end of July 1167 he was able speedily to capture the Entry into Rome
Leonine City, and with his wife was crowned by the anti-
Pope in St. Peter's. Negotiations passed between him and
Alexander III, but Frederick's proposal that both Popes should
resign and a new election be held was naturally unacceptable
to the Curia. It found favour with the Romans, however,
who, anxious for peace, were eager for its adoption. Alexander, therefore, found his position in Rome untenable ; he
made good his escape, and placed himself under Norman
protection at Benevento.

Frederick was now master of Rome, and with the prospect His prospects in South Italy
of a fleet [1] he planned an advance into South Italy, to reduce
the kingdom of Sicily as well as to gain possession of the
person of the Pope. The moment seemed propitious, for
William I had died in the preceding May, and the tender age
of his son William II necessitated a regency under the queen-
mother Margaret. This was the opportunity of the nobles,
who engineered a conspiracy against the queen's favourite,
Stephen of Perche—appointed by her to be both chancellor
and archbishop of Palermo—and they were eventually successful in driving him from power. Until William II attained
his majority, the feudal nobility held the upper hand, so that
the royal power was ill equipped to encounter the might of
Germany. But Frederick had reached Rome too late, and
the summer was now at its height. This had been his reason
for refusing a campaign in the south and returning home
after his coronation in 1155, but on this occasion he lingered
too long. The deadly malaria of the Roman Campagna, His army decimated by malaria
which had so often proved fatal to the German kings, now
dealt its most crushing blow. Frederick's great army was
literally decimated, among the victims being many of the
leading nobles and bishops in the entourage of the Emperor,
including the chief of them all, the archbishop of Cologne,
Rainald of Dassel. Hastily the Emperor retraced his steps His flight to Savoy
over the Apennines into Tuscany with such as had remained
unstricken, to find the roads to the north blocked against
him, so that only by devious routes was he able to make his

---

[1] Some vessels had already arrived from Pisa, and more were expected
both from Pisa and Genoa. These two cities had both remained loyal to
the Emperor, but owing to their bitter rivalry he was frequently disappointed
of their assistance.

way to the shelter of Pavia in September.   For the Lombard
cities had begun to arm directly he had left their territory ;
it was indeed surprising that he had taken so little care to
guard his communications with Germany.   Under the lead of
Verona, Padua, and Vicenza a Lombard League had sprung
into existence, and was almost daily receiving fresh adherents.
In April the forces of the League had gone to Milan, and
while they stood on guard to prevent any attack from Pavia,
the Milanese raised their city from its ashes and fortified it
anew, so that it was able to resume its natural place at the
head of opposition to the Emperor.   Only nobles like William
of Montferrat and Guido of Biandrate remained loyal, and
gave him shelter in their castles during the winter of 1167–8.
In the early spring the approach of a Lombard army made his
position desperate.   In this crisis he made terms with count
Humbert III of Savoy, at the price of a large sum of money
and the restoration of lands which he had previously taken
from him ; this opened to him the Mont Cenis pass.   Even
so, when he came to Susa, the citizens rose and virtually held
him prisoner.   In disguise and under cover of night he made
his escape, and rode over the dangerous snow-bound pass
safely into Burgundy.   Such was the humiliating conclusion
of the Emperor's fourth expedition into Italy.

Failure of negotiations with the Pope   During the next six years Frederick remained in Germany.
Though he had lost an army and had to leave Italy as a
fugitive, he was still as determined as ever on mastering the
Lombard communes.   With regard to the Pope, too, his
attitude was at first unaltered.   For when Paschal III died
in 1168, and a successor to him (Calixtus III) was elected,
though the election had even less legal justification than that
of Paschal, Frederick adhered to him and expected the compliance of the German Church.   This was the easier to obtain,
since he had been careful to fill vacant bishoprics with men
on whom he could rely, and the disaster in Italy had created
numerous vacancies ; moreover, bishops created during a
schism could expect little mercy from the Pope whom they
had rejected, and therefore their interests were bound up
with those of the Emperor.   But Frederick soon realised the
wisdom of making his peace with Alexander.   Firstly, it
would give him a free hand to deal with the rebels in Lombardy.   And, secondly, he was concerned with establishing

his dynasty on the German and imperial thrones. In 1169 his son Henry was elected king and crowned by the new archbishop of Cologne, Philip; possibly his coronation as Emperor was also in Frederick's mind. At any rate, an embassy was straightway dispatched to Alexander, headed by Bishop Eberhard of Bamberg, who though a loyal subject of the Emperor was known to be a constant advocate of peace. The end of the schism was a possibility, since Frederick was prepared to recognise Alexander. But the Lombards proved an embarrassment, since Frederick refused to admit them to the negotiations, and they insisted that the Pope was pledged not to enter into negotiations without them. And there was the difficulty of the German bishops appointed during the schism, whom the Pope would not recognise and whom Frederick refused to sacrifice. So the negotiations broke down. There was nothing left for the Emperor but to resume his old policy and to make preparations for another expedition to Italy, equipped to face the renewed alliance of the Pope, the Lombard League, and the king of Sicily.

The element of time was an important one, since the longer the Emperor delayed the more formidable would be the opposition he would have to overcome. But after the loss of one large army there was bound to be delay in the raising of another, and his preparations were hampered by the situation which had arisen in Saxony. The duke, Henry the Lion, had not been satisfied like his predecessors with authority in East Saxony only. His ambition extended to the central and western portions as well, and throughout the duchy he claimed a well-nigh sovereign authority over bishops as well as over lay nobles. This brought him into conflict, in the western half, with the archbishop of Bremen in Mecklenburg and with the archbishop of Cologne in Westphalia. On the other side, he was in constant rivalry with his cousin Albert the Bear east of the Elbe, and there was friction also with the archbishop of Magdeburg and the landgrave of Thuringia. Nor was it only the greater nobles to whom he gave offence. The counts resented his treatment of them as his officials, and his claim that if they left no direct male heirs their lands escheated to him. Only by the middle classes was his rule welcomed; he was quick to realise that

Henry the Lion and his enemies

commercial development furthered the prosperity of his duchy and was also to his own financial advantage. The town of Lübeck owed to him its future greatness, though its foundation was due to count Adolf of Holstein, from whom Henry forcibly wrested it.[1] Throughout he had had the constant support of the Emperor. They were united by ties of kinship and personal friendship, and also by common interests. Since Frederick was preoccupied with Italy, he was content to leave Henry the Lion with almost viceregal authority. He was thus saved from any difficulties with the troublesome duchy of Saxony, and also from any anxiety with regard to his eastern frontiers ; while he could rely on Henry to provide the necessary quotas for the Italian expeditions, and even to appear himself when summoned, as he had done in 1155 and 1158. Henry was the more ready to fulfil his obligations in this respect, since in return he could count on the king's support in his conflicts with his rivals and subordinates.

The beginning of friction between Henry and Frederick

This was still the situation when Frederick returned to Germany in 1168. In that year Henry the Lion married Matilda, the daughter of Henry II of England, but, though this was to have important consequences in the future, Frederick does not seem to have been concerned at the time. Henry's position, too, was rendered the more secure by the deaths of some of his most formidable opponents—the archbishop of Cologne in Italy in 1167, the archbishop of Magdeburg in 1169, and Albert the Bear in 1170. He felt sufficiently secure to leave his duchy in Matilda's care while he went on pilgrimage to the Holy Land in 1172. But his relations with the Emperor were no longer as satisfactory as before. He had one grievance in 1169, when his uncle Welf VI, whose son Welf VII had been one of the victims of the Italian disaster, offered to sell him his inheritance (which included the territories of countess Matilda), and then when he was slow to produce the money sold it to Frederick. Again, when he returned from the Holy Land, he complained that Frederick had been encroaching on his domains during his absence. Besides his grievances, he was now less anxious for Frederick's

[1] So, too, in his other duchy, Bavaria, he was responsible for the commercial development of Munich, by diverting to it trade which had formerly passed through a town belonging to the Emperor's uncle, bishop Otto of Freising.

support, since he believed that he no longer needed it ; and he did not wish to pay for this support by assisting in another Italian expedition in which he had no personal interest. Frederick tried to placate him, for he needed Henry's assistance ; but he refused to pay the price which Henry eventually demanded—the cession of Goslar, the chief town in the old Saxon domain of the German kings.

When the Emperor started on his fifth Italian expedition in the autumn of 1174, the disagreement with Henry the Lion had not reached its final stage. But it had gone so far that Henry sent no detachments to the imperial army, which was accordingly not so formidable an array as that which Frederick had led into Italy on three former occasions. On the other hand, the enemy he had to meet was much more formidable. During these six years the alliance between the Pope, the Lombards, and the king of Sicily had been more closely cemented, and the Eastern Emperor had assisted it with large sums of money. All the cities of Northern Italy were enrolled, voluntarily or perforce, in the Lombard League, which, in order to preserve its federal unity and to prevent the dominance of any single member, took in hand the building of a new city. The site selected was to the east of Asti at the junction of two rivers, the Tanaro and the Bormida, so that besides forming a federal centre for the League it was also designed to command the roads that led into the plains of Lombardy. It was very strongly fortified on all sides and soon had a population of 15,000 citizens ; as a compliment to the Pope it was given the name of Alessandria. Besides this, the Lombards could now enrol an army considerably larger than that which Frederick commanded, though in weight of armour the latter still had an advantage. *The formation of the Lombard League*

Marching over the Mont Cenis pass through Piedmont, the Emperor's first action was to take his revenge for his former humiliation by the destruction of Susa. Continuing on the eastward road he obtained the submission of Turin and forced Asti to surrender ; and these early successes brought over to his side Pavia, Como, and other adherents such as the marquis of Montferrat. He then took in hand the siege of Alessandria. But the confederates had done their work well, and the city defied all his efforts. At last after six months, when a sally of the defenders had resulted in the destruction of his siege *Frederick's fifth expedition to Italy*

machinery, Frederick decided to raise the siege and marched
to meet the main Lombard army. Neither side, however,
wished to risk a direct encounter, and a truce was arranged
at Montebello in April 1175. But they could not come to
terms, and Frederick then tried negotiations with the Pope,
which failed once more over the question of the recognition
of the German bishops appointed during the schism. So
hostilities were resumed, but of a very desultory character.
The Lombards, in spite of their superiority of numbers,
remained on the defensive, and Frederick dared not venture
an attack until the reinforcements, which he had urgently
summoned, arrived from Germany. It was now all-important
to him to obtain the co-operation of Henry the Lion, and it is
said that he went to Chiavenna to a personal meeting with
Henry in which he humbled himself to appeal for his vassal's
aid ; but the sacrifice of Goslar was too much for the imperial
pride, and so he received from Henry a direct refusal, a refusal
which decided the fate of the expedition. For the reinforcements when at last they arrived, in April 1176, were not

The battle of Legnano (1176)

adequate for Frederick's needs. He hurried with a small
detachment to Como to meet them, but as he led them to
join the remainder of his army he was intercepted by the
Lombards and forced to battle at Legnano on May 29. The
heavy German horse broke through the opposing ranks and
pressed their charge almost to the *carroccio*, the ox-drawn
waggon carrying the standard, the emblem of civic liberty ;
round this the Lombards rallied, and in close fight their
preponderance of numbers gradually gave them the upper
hand. The slaughter was immense and the result quite
decisive. The Emperor, thrown from his horse, was believed
to have perished, but he managed to escape from the field ;
for some time he had to lie hidden to evade capture, until at
last he reached the refuge of faithful Pavia.

Negotiations with the Pope

He could not hope to continue the struggle. Even for a
purely defensive campaign the troops that remained to him
were insufficient, and there was little to be got from Germany
in the way of reinforcements. In this period Frederick's
mind seems to have been passing through a stage of transition ;
he was abandoning the earlier mood in which he had been
determined to impose his mastery by force, but had not yet
become endowed with the diplomatic temperament which was

later to win for him what force had failed to achieve. He recognised that a cessation of warfare was necessary, but, while willing to make a definitive peace with the Pope, he could not bring himself to more than a truce with the rebels. He was not yet prepared to accept the full consequences of his defeat, and this is one of the reasons why negotiations, that at first promised to be quickly concluded, dragged on so long before a final settlement was reached. The Pope, for his part, was anxious for peace ; he wanted the end of the schism and the opportunity of reuniting the Church under his government ; he was weary of the long strain of nearly twenty years of conflict ; and his resources were almost exhausted, since the income of the Papacy, adequate in time of peace, was not equal to the burden of prolonged warfare. He had had to borrow, and to repay by further borrowings ; and while the allied cities charged no interest on the sums which they lent him, he complained bitterly of the usury of his Roman creditors. The Papacy needed a rest to recover from its exhaustion, and he was willing to make the great concession of confirming in their sees the German bishops who had been appointed during the schism, even though this bore hardly on the faithful few who had been dispossessed for their adherence to him. So, on terms of mutual recognition a settlement between Pope and Emperor was made at Anagni in October 1176. Alexander was mindful of his allies ; he insisted that peace should also be made with them, and this was promised by Frederick's representatives. It was not easy, however, to arrange the terms, since Frederick was not prepared to surrender the sovereign rights he had assumed at Roncaglia, and the Lombards naturally would not yield as victors that for which they had fought. Papal mediation was of no avail, for the Lombards felt themselves betrayed, and bitterly complained of the Pope's breach of faith in entering into negotiations to which they were not a party. Their co-operation was necessary for the completion of peace, but it was difficult to obtain it. It was difficult, too, to find a place of meeting acceptable to both sides, until at last Venice offered itself ; though a member of the League it had not taken a leading part, and it was itself anxious for peace. Finally, then, the settlement at Anagni was confirmed by the Treaty of Venice in July 1177, and Pope and Emperor were

The Treaty of Venice (1177)

at peace. It was still impossible to arrange peace between the Emperor and the Lombards, so a truce for six years was agreed upon ; and the Emperor also entered into a truce for fifteen years with the king of Sicily.

So the second [1] great contest between Empire and Papacy in which the issue of the relations between the *regnum* and the *sacerdotium* was involved had come to an end. Again the result was indecisive, and the tremendous effort put forward by the Emperor to impose his will and establish a Pope subservient to himself had failed. The imperial defeat is the most obvious result of the struggle. But it must be remembered that Frederick had only adopted his policy as a counterattack after his own position had been challenged by the papal claims, and in this way he had at any rate successfully defended himself. Alexander III did not put forward the assertions that he had championed as Hadrian's legate. In fact, the effect of the Treaty of Venice was a return to the situation that preceded the conflict. It did not restore to the Papacy the position it had gained under Lothar and Conrad ; Frederick maintained the authority over the German Church that he had assumed immediately after his accession, continuing to control appointments, to interfere in disputed elections, and to exercise the rights of *regalia* and *spolia*. He had been defeated in his attack on papal independence, but his own position had remained unassailed.

Yet out of this struggle the Papacy not only emerged unscathed ; in defeating the attack on its independence it made itself the more secure against such attacks for the future. Never again was an Emperor to attempt to impose upon the Church a Pope of his own creation.[2] The Church was indeed fortunate that it had as its Head a Pope of the calibre of Alexander III, and also that he outlived the schism, since a vacancy during its course might have been disastrous. Alexander's practical experience and common sense were of great value especially in the early years of his Papacy. At the most difficult moment of his conflict with the Emperor, when he was in exile in France, he was faced with the risk

---

[1] I prefer to say " second " rather than " third," for the contest of Henry V with the Papacy was concerned with the question of lay investiture, and not really with the major issue.

[2] The feeble attempt made by Lewis the Bavarian in the fourteenth century can hardly be counted as an exception to this statement.

of another conflict, owing to the quarrel between Henry II and Becket. There was the danger that, if Henry were alienated, the two most powerful sovereigns of the West would join hands against him, with very grave consequences for the Church. To avert this, he did his best to bring about a reconciliation between king and archbishop, and had to face the reproaches of his own supporters for his lukewarmness in the cause of Becket; Becket himself complained that he was fighting the Pope's battle with no support from the Pope. But Alexander saw more clearly than his critics how best to act in the interests of the Church, and his diplomatic patience was ultimately rewarded. When Henry was disgraced by the murder of Becket, he had to make concessions which restored to the Papacy much of the authority which it had exercised before his accession. The results of the papal victory were more marked in England than in Germany. In consolidating the advance that had been made, Alexander's expert legal knowledge was of great service. His definition of the law and his judgment on doubtful points, especially in his correspondence with the English Church,[1] the instruction he gave as to the rules and procedure of the ecclesiastical courts to introduce conformity with Roman custom, brought him, both as the source and the authoritative interpreter of the law of the Church and as supreme judge, into close contact with the various churches; they, deferring to his opinion and accepting his direction, became accustomed to his monarchical government. His legislative work was as important for the future of Canon Law as for the necessities of his own day; in the first official collection—the *Decretales* of Gregory IX—nearly 500 of Alexander III's decretals were included. Certainly his Papacy was of unusual length, but he was engaged, during eighteen of the twenty-two years that he was Pope, in a conflict with the Emperor which might well have absorbed all his energies; in spite of this his achievement was such that he is entitled to rank among those Popes who have contributed most to the internal government and jurisdiction of the Church.

Legal greatness of Alexander III

His greatest moment as a law-giver was at the Third Lateran Council in March 1179. This, like its two prede-

The Third Lateran Council (1179)

[1] Cf. my article on this subject in the *Cambridge Historical Journal*, Vol. II, n. 3.

cessors, was summoned to celebrate the end of a schism; the large attendance from various countries made it even more representative of Western Christendom. The most important of its canons was that dealing with papal elections. It provided that, in the event of a disputed election, the candidate who received two-thirds of the votes of the cardinals present should be declared Pope. This remedied a defect in the Election Decree of Nicholas II, and had it been in existence already Alexander's own election could not have been contested.[1] The principle of a two-thirds majority was to apply to the election of the bishop of Rome only; it was expressly stated that in other churches the old canonical rule [2] was to maintain, since doubtful cases could be decided by the judgment of a superior, whereas in the case of Rome there was no superior. This was the first canon. It was followed by a large number of others directed at contemporary evils within the Church, many of them enforcing older regulations: as usual, measures were taken to check simony, clerical incontinence, and the holding of pluralities; monks were forbidden to leave their monasteries or to be in charge of parishes, clergy in possession of ecclesiastical stipends were not to act as advocates in lay courts; the minimum age for ecclesiastical offices was prescribed, and a strict limit set on the expenses that could be charged by officials holding visitations. Others, some of them new, particularly affected the laity, who were as usual forbidden to dispose of churches or tithes, to impose taxes on ecclesiastical property, or to summon clerics before their courts. The Church's ban was placed upon "those detestable festivals, commonly called tournaments," in which men fought just for the sake of fighting and often came to their death unshriven. Alexander's own

---

[1] The canon also enacted that no one who received less than two-thirds of the votes could become Pope. A novel situation arose in the thirteenth century. Without any interference from outside, the Curia was divided within, and sufficient agreement for any one candidate to obtain the necessary quota was difficult to obtain and caused serious delay. This was met by the canon of Gregory X at the Second Council of Lyons in 1274, which established the conclave system, and thus finally completed the law of the Church for the election of a Pope.

[2] That "the opinion of the *major vel sanior pars* was to prevail." This vague phrase did not imply that a mere majority was sufficient; the views of the more important electors were to have special weight (cf. the part given to the cardinal bishops in Nicholas II's Election Decree).

bitter experience was doubtless responsible for the decree that manifest usurers were not to be admitted to communion or to receive Christian burial. An interesting canon is the one which prescribed that every cathedral church was to assign an adequate stipend for a master to teach clerks and poor scholars *gratis*, and that no charge was to be made for the licence to teach. Finally, a strong decree against the Cathari, Patarines, and other heretics shows how much the growth of heresy, especially in the South of France, was at last beginning to disturb the rulers of the Church.

Though he lived for another two years, this Council was the last important act of Alexander III's Papacy, and it constitutes, as it were, a summary of his work as Pope. It celebrates the triumphal end of the schism, and it displays him busily legislating for the Church. It repeats many provisions that were needful for existing conditions and it breaks new ground; since Nicholas II's Council in 1059 no Church Council had passed so many acts of importance. The representative attendance ensured a general diffusion of the canons; in England especially they had a wide circulation. Innocent III in his more famous Fourth Lateran Council in 1215 incorporated several canons from the Third Lateran Council; and, if Alexander's fame has been somewhat dimmed by the greatness of Innocent, it must be remembered that he was the originator of much of the legislative work of his successor.

SUGGESTIONS FOR READING ON CHAPTER XX (AND XXIII)

Cambridge Medieval History, Vol. V, chapters 12, 13, 14.
Hampe, K.: *Deutsche Kaisergeschichte* (as in Chapter III).
Poole, A. L.: *Henry the Lion.* Oxford, 1912.
Cf. also, relevant documents in Laffan and Pullan (see Bibliographical Note).
Barraclough, G.: *Origins of Modern Germany.* 2nd ed. Oxford, 1947.
Jordan, E.: *L'Allemagne et l'Italie au XIIième et XIIIième siècles,* Paris, 1939.

CHAPTER XXI

FRANCE AND ENGLAND IN THE SECOND HALF OF THE TWELFTH CENTURY

The Angevin
Empire

THE accession of Henry II to the throne of England opened a new chapter in French history which was to cover half a century. The Angevin Empire, occupying practically the western half of France, divided the kingdom into two : an unequal division, for of only part of the eastern half was the French king the actual ruler. Henry's ambition was not limited by the extensive territories of which he was master in 1154. He wished to add to them and round them off on various sides. Brittany, with its Channel coast, was one objective. His brother Geoffrey acquired the lordship of Nantes in 1156, and when he died childless in 1158, Henry claimed the succession and with it the suzerainty over Brittany ; and, surprisingly enough, Louis readily gave his sanction. In the south, the second husband of Eleanor, like the first, was covetous of Toulouse ; here Louis frustrated him for a time, but in 1173 count Raymond did homage to Henry's son Richard. Aquitaine was further extended by the acquisition of Auvergne in spite of Louis' protests, and Henry gained a controlling position in Berry also ; in 1177 he acquired by purchase the county of La Marche. Moreover, he increased his importance and influence by the external marriages he contracted for his daughters. In 1168 the eldest, Matilda, married Henry the Lion, duke of Saxony and Bavaria ; in 1169 the second, Eleanor, married king Alfonso VIII of Castile ; and in 1177 the youngest, Joan, married king William II of Sicily. The betrothal of Henry's youngest son John to the heiress of Humbert III of Savoy opened up possibilities of a further extension of Angevin influence, but as she died in the next year the marriage did not eventualise.

Henry II
and
Louis VII

Both in France and in Europe, Henry occupied a much larger place than the king of France. Yet he must not be

458

credited with any vast plan of European domination, and it is probable that he was not at any time looking far beyond his immediate achievements. There is no indication that he coveted the crown of France for himself; on the contrary, he was perfectly ready to recognise the king of France as his suzerain, and felt no humiliation in what seems to us an anomaly. The danger to Louis VII was not that he would lose his kingdom, but rather that he would be reduced to insignificance within it, just as his ancestors had reduced the Carolingians to insignificance. And this seemed the more likely since Louis had completely discarded the energy and passion of his early years, and was now clothed in the attributes by which he is known to posterity: devout, almost it seemed a saint, so gentle and unworldly was he, eminently pacific and timorous. But he was deeply conscious of his royal position, especially of the duties it imposed upon him. He could be roused to action, even to martial energy, by appeals for royal protection. He was much less vigorous in defence of his rights; for, though he keenly resented any injury to the royal dignity, such as he often experienced from Henry II, he usually confined himself to vehement protests. But, if he was reluctant to draw the sword, he was not without the wit to perceive and the will to make use of the opportunities that not infrequently presented themselves.

For there were distinct weaknesses in the apparently overpowering position of Henry. The " Angevin Empire " was an agglomeration of several principalities differing widely from one another in customs, modes of government, and racial characteristics. The differences between them might temporarily be obscured by the strong central control introduced into each by its very capable master and his subordinates; even the loosely-knit territories of the duchy of Aquitaine were eventually linked together. That the unity was merely superficial, however, depending on the genius of the ruler to maintain it, was to be shown when it was dissipated at the beginning of the next century. Henry as his sons grew up, designed to employ them as his lieutenants in the government of the separate principalities. This was similar to the policy of Otto I, and it had a similar result. The sons quarrelled with one another and, impatient of the parental authority which allowed them so little initiative,

Weaknesses in Henry's position

they rebelled against their father. Here was an opportunity for the French king, and he was not slow to avail himself of it. Another such was the quarrel of Henry II with Becket and the Pope.

Potentialities of the monarchy in France So the difficulties of the English king, both ecclesiastical and domestic, gave opportunities to Louis of which he took advantage; and in this way he was saved from being completely overshadowed by his powerful vassal. Apart from this, too, Louis was not so helpless as might appear. To be king of France was now, thanks to his father, a great asset. The sovereignty claimed by the earlier Capetians, and formally acknowledged, had been meaningless since it could not be asserted; but in Louis VI's reign it had received a real recognition, even though in a limited area. What had thus been gained was not lost; in spite of the long reign of a successor so much feebler than himself, this recognition did not become less, but rather continued to expand. There was a considerable increase in the appeals from outside the royal domain for the royal protection, which had begun in Louis VI's time; and it was the chief service that Louis VII rendered to the monarchy that he never failed to respond to these appeals. They came, as before, from churches whose territory was exposed to lay violence. They came also from lay vassals, even in the south. Thus count Raymond of Toulouse sought his protection against Henry II, and Louis' presence at Toulouse was sufficient to cause the English king to depart. Though Toulouse eventually recognised Henry's overlordship, there was compensation for Louis in the recognition he received in Languedoc, especially from the viscountess of Narbonne; she even reminded him of his royal rights and sought his help. Finally, many towns also sought his protection, and though he had no clear idea, as his son had, of the value of an alliance with them, he went much further than his father in that direction. His policy was fluctuating, but on the whole he was ready to grant charters to towns outside the royal domain and to protect them against their lay or ecclesiastical overlords. His point of view was different from his father's. For a commune as such he, too, had little sympathy; he granted charters, however, not as a means of making money, but rather as a means of increasing his authority outside the royal domain

or of giving protection to the oppressed.   He gave no charter
to a town within the royal domain, but he created new towns
within it, to which he attracted refugees from the domains
of other lords.

The practice of appealing to the royal protection showed
how much the royal prestige had increased, and with this
went a general interest in the royal house and its fortunes.
This was strikingly evinced in 1165 when at last a male heir,
the future king Philip II, was born to Louis by his third wife
(by each of his former wives he had had two daughters).
Not only in Paris and the domain, but in the kingdom generally there was widespread rejoicing, and a deep sense of
relief that the uncertainty about the succession had been
dispelled.   For the hereditary right of the eldest son had
now become an accepted tradition, thanks to the fact that
the Capetian line had never failed of a male heir ; and so
divine hereditary right became the rule in France.   Witness
the letter written by bishop Arnulf of Lisieux, a Norman
bishop and so an immediate vassal of Henry II, whom he
stoutly supported against Becket.   " God," he wrote to the
king of France, " has visited his people, and has displayed his
mercy to the whole kingdom of France, in that he has given
you a sure heir and has ordained a righteous lord for all the
princes of the French kingdom."   Arnulf was a time-server,
who knew which way the wind was blowing, and his letter
very accurately expresses the general feeling in France.

This general feeling indicated what were the possibilities The
of the royal office ; but at present these lay dormant, for government
Louis VII was not the man to exploit them.   He continued of Louis VII
the régime that had prevailed in the later years of his father's
reign.   He was the actual ruler of the royal domain and of
certain ecclesiastical territories outside it.   On these he
depended for his financial resources and for soldiers, though
he also began the practice of hiring mercenaries as well.   The
local officials who governed the different parts of the domain
were known as provosts ; very sensibly he guarded against
their natural desire to make their posts hereditary, for, had
they done so, an official nobility would have arisen and might
have attained to the dangerous independence of the old
feudal nobility.   The central government—administrative,
financial, judicial—was conducted in the king's court, the

16

Curia Regis. Here the tradition of Suger rather than that
of the Garlandes prevailed. The office of seneschal was
relatively unimportant, especially under so pacific a king;
he even left it vacant for two years after the death of Ralph
of Vermandois, and then for the rest of the reign it was held
by his brother-in-law, count Theobald of Blois, whose main
interest was in his own county. The real ministers of the
king were the clerks of his household, men like the chancellor
Cadurc, of non-noble birth, who depended for their career
on the king and whose interests were bound up in his service.
This created a tradition of immense value for the future, but
at present the range of government was as confined as in the
previous reign; the king was only ruler of the territories of
which he was the actual lord. In one respect, however, there
was a very decided advance. The growing practice of appealing to the king increased very considerably both the number
and the importance of the cases which came before the king's
court from districts lying outside the king's domain, and
from the southern as well as the northern half of the kingdom.
Bishops brought suits against nobles and against towns, towns
and sub-tenants against their lords, and so on; it was significant that personages such as the duke of Burgundy and
the count of Nevers appeared at the king's court to answer
accusations brought against them. Certain members of the
Curia regularly attended to assist the king in deciding these
cases, and in his absence they were empowered to give
decisions; thus a class of specialist lawyers came into existence. As the king usually resided at Paris, it was there in
the majority of cases that the suits were heard. So, though
there is yet no actual differentiation of the various functions
of the Curia, the germs of the future Parlement, with its
fixed personnel and its meeting-place at Paris, are already to
be seen. On its judicial side, then, the king's court had a
comprehensive authority which on the administrative side
was at present lacking; and this was largely due to Louis'
keen sense of his duty to render justice to those who appealed
to the royal protection.

1154–60
Henry in
the
ascendancy
Louis, then, had decided assets in his favour, due to his
royal office, and his position sensibly improved as the difficulties of Henry increased. But in 1154 and for some years
afterwards he seemed likely to be completely eclipsed; the

contrast between the masterful nature of Henry and the
docility of Louis was most noticeable. Louis had made a
show of opposition to the accumulation of territories by the
Angevin house; he was temporarily aroused by the danger
of Henry's marriage with Eleanor, and still more by Henry's
accession to the English throne; but, as usual, he allowed
himself to be dominated by a stronger will and soon lapsed
into acquiescence. He contented himself with the homage
of Henry, and, so far from any attempt to retaliate, he was
prepared to give the *status quo* his solemn recognition. In
1158 he met Henry at Gisors and concluded with him a treaty
and a marriage alliance. His daughter Margaret [1] was
betrothed to Henry, the eldest son of Henry II, and pending
the marriage (they were still infants) she passed under the
guardianship of the English king; Louis assigned as her
dowry the Norman Vexin with the all-important fortress of
Gisors. It is difficult to understand his readiness to acquiesce
in a settlement so completely to his disadvantage. Henry,
naturally elated by this easy success, went off to seek further
triumphs in the south, prosecuting the old ambitions of the
dukes of Aquitaine against Toulouse. His advance was
rapid, and Toulouse itself seemed likely to fall. The count,
Raymond V, appealed for help to his overlord, the king of
France—a novel appeal from the south and fruitful in results.
For Louis went at once to his aid, and failing to deter Henry
by his protests threw himself into Toulouse. His courage
(he had no army with which to resist Henry) was successful.
Henry was not prepared for the breach with feudal principle
that a direct attack on his overlord would have entailed;
and he withdrew from the siege. Louis was thus able to
vindicate his kingship where previously it had been completely
ignored.

The next year, 1160, was an important one. The queen,
Constance of Castile, died, and Louis, anxious above all for a
male heir, immediately contracted a third marriage, with
Adela, daughter of the late count of Blois and Champagne,
Theobald IV. This brought him into permanent friendly
relationship with that powerful family which, flanking the

Louis' third marriage and its results

---

[1] In 1154 he had married Constance of Castile, who, like Eleanor, bore
him two daughters. Margaret was the elder of Constance's daughters;
Alice, the younger, was later betrothed to Richard.

domain on both sides, had been so dangerous to his father.
The alliance was further cemented when Louis' two daughters
by Eleanor married Adela's brothers, Henry count of Champagne and Theobald V count of Blois. Louis had other ties
in Champagne, for his own brother Henry became archbishop
of Rheims in 1162 and the bishop of Châlons sur Marne was
also immediately subject to him. The royal domain, therefore, with Blois and Champagne to the left and right of it
formed a compact little family group. Unfortunately Louis
was as usual easily dominated, and his two brothers-in-law
were rather overpowering neighbours.[1] At the time, at any
rate, it was a successful marriage, and it created a counterpoise to the power of Henry II. So he regarded it, and he
retaliated by causing the marriage of his son with Margaret to
be celebrated, and immediately took her dowry, the Norman
Vexin, into his control. This was an unworthy trick, at
which Louis was justly incensed, and he made a show of
force ; but as usual he resigned himself to the *fait accompli*,
and in 1162 consented to a renewal of the treaty with the
king of England.

**1160–70
The
ecclesiastical
situation**
So far Henry had been having things all his own way.
But in the next phase Louis was to play a larger role, and
Henry to find difficulties beginning to gather in his path.
The main events of the decade from 1160 to 1170 were ecclesi-
astical, and in ecclesiastical politics Louis had definite assets.
The prelude to them was the great papal schism in 1159.
Frederick Barbarossa vainly attempted to gain recognition
for Victor IV outside the Empire ; in 1160 both Henry II
**Pope
Alexander
III in France**
and Louis VII gave their adhesion to Alexander III. Yet
in North Italy, as well as in Germany, Frederick had the
upper hand, and when he wreaked his vengeance on Milan
in 1162, Alexander was fearful of his own security and,
following precedent, took refuge in France. But he made
the natural mistake of thinking that Henry's protection was
all-important while Louis could be ignored ; accordingly he
gave his sanction to the marriage of the young Henry with
Margaret, and so set in motion a train of bewildering negotiations and intrigues. Louis was deeply offended, and lent
an ear to the blandishments of the Emperor. His brother-

[1] Their influence was further increased when archbishop Henry died and
another of Adela's brothers, William, became archbishop of Rheims in 1176.

in-law, count Henry of Champagne, was the go-between, and he had already shown his goodwill to the Emperor when, with other French nobles whose territories were adjacent to the imperial, he had been present at the famous diet of Besançon in 1157. With the Emperor he devised a cunning scheme, designed doubtless to entrap Alexander. Louis was to bring Alexander, Frederick to bring Victor to a meeting on the frontier-bridge over the Saone at Saint-Jean-de-Losne ; and the count of Champagne pledged himself to transfer his allegiance to the Emperor, if Louis failed to appear with Alexander. He himself was only a pawn in the imperial game, for his allegiance was of little account to Frederick, who was wholly set on the much greater issue of establishing Victor IV as the sole Pope. Louis, unaware of the count's treachery, was eager for the meeting ; he had no intention of disowning Alexander, but he was simple-minded enough to believe that he could reconcile him with Frederick, and thus win a diplomatic success over the English king. Alexander knew better ; he refused to fall into the trap, and remained safely under the protection of Henry II. As the Pope did not appear, Frederick withdrew from the meeting-place and the scheme was abandoned.

This curious episode had fortunate consequences for the French king. Alexander III had learnt that Louis could not be ignored in his own kingdom, and realised too that his own freedom of action was more secure under Louis' protection than under Henry's. So he left the domains of Henry and took up his residence at Sens. There for two years he reigned with no less authority than he could have wielded at Rome. Louis appears almost as the humble servant of the Pope. Yet his wishes had to be respected, for his goodwill was necessary to the Pope ; in 1163 Alexander sent a " golden rose " to him as the secular ruler who had done most to deserve the favour of the Head of the Church. It was, indeed, almost a privileged position in the Church that the French king was obtaining.

This was an asset rather for the future. Louis was himself too devout a son of the Church to take advantage of the papal difficulties. But another ecclesiastical crisis—the quarrel of Henry and Becket—provided him with an opportunity which he was only too ready to use. His piety, too, was shocked by

The quarrel of Henry with Becket

the treatment of the archbishop, and both from instinct and
interest he gave Becket a warm welcome when the archbishop
took refuge on French soil in 1164. He even took up arms in
his defence, emboldened by the embarrassment of Henry,
who wished for a settlement in his favour but saw that it
could not be won by force of arms. The war was, therefore,
a half-hearted affair of frontier raids, and was frequently
interrupted by conferences between the kings. Louis' bold-
ness was in striking contrast to the timidity of the Pope.
Alexander dared not alienate the king of England, who
threatened to ally himself with the Emperor. But when
Frederick was forced to retreat from Italy in 1167 Alexander
was secure once more, and the murder of Becket in December
1170 enabled him to take a strong line and to extract
important concessions from Henry. Louis, who had consistently championed the martyred archbishop, gained
nothing but credit from an episode so damaging to the prestige
of the English king. For six years he held a decided advantage over the vassal who had inflicted such humiliations on
him in the past.

Henry's domestic difficulties
The chief cause of the events which led to the murder of
Becket was the coronation of the young Henry as king of
England ; Becket's retaliation on the bishops who had vio-
lated his rights by performing the ceremony brought about
Henry's fatal outburst. This coronation was also the prelude
to the domestic difficulties of Henry's later years ; and, as
before, the domestic difficulties of the king of England were
the opportunity of the king of France. It was Henry's
policy, now that his sons were growing up, to use them as his
lieutenants ; to give to each of his French provinces, so
different from one another in racial characteristics and traditions, its own governor, so that its internal independence
would be formally recognised, while his overriding authority
would in fact direct and control the whole. In 1169, at a
conference with Louis at Montmirail, the young Henry did
homage to the French king for Anjou and Brittany ; Geoffrey
received Brittany as a fief from his elder brother ; and finally
Richard did homage to Louis for Aquitaine. The coronation
of the young Henry completed the scheme, which was designed
also to provide for the succession and the division of government after Henry II's death. He had, indeed, no intention

of abdicating any of his powers in his lifetime. He gave his
sons no personal domain or revenue which would have enabled
them to act independently of him; the young Henry had a
royal seal of his own, but his counsellors were chosen for him
from among his father's trusted servants. Moreover, the
sons were still too young to be given responsibility; in 1170
the eldest, Henry, was only fifteen years of age.

But, young as they were, they chafed at the leading The revolt
strings; and when, in 1173, Henry II gave an appanage in of 1173
Anjou to his youngest son, John, on the occasion of his
betrothal to the daughter of the count of Savoy, the jealousy
and indignation of the other three brothers knew no bounds,
and a formidable conspiracy was hatched. The young Henry
fled to the court of Louis, who took up his cause with enthusiasm; Geoffrey and Richard joined them; and they gained
numerous other adherents, who had cause to dislike Henry
or to wish for his downfall—many of the leading barons in
England, the king of Scotland, the count of Flanders. As
events proved, Henry was too strong in England to be successfully countered there; but in France he might have been
defeated. It all depended on the king of France, who had
most to gain. However, as usual, Louis, when it came to
the point, dared not face Henry in the field. In 1173 he ran
away from the siege of Verneuil when Henry appeared to
defend it, and the same thing happened at Rouen in 1174.
His panic on this occasion was so great that he decided to
give up the struggle, and counselled his allies to do the same.
Henry's sons made their submission, Richard last of all and
most reluctantly, and peace was signed at Montlouis in
September. Henry pacified his sons by granting them a
revenue of their own, and so made his position once more
secure. Louis had had the greatest chance of his life, and
by his timidity and lack of resolution had thrown it away.

The harmony in the English royal family was only temporary, but it lasted for the rest of Louis' reign. Richard proved
himself a most efficient lieutenant in Aquitaine, reducing it
to an order unknown before; thus early he displayed his
military genius by the speed with which he crushed the unruly
vassals of his province and destroyed their castles. Henry II
seemed to have Louis at his mercy and to be contemplating
his overthrow. In 1177 he even acquired more domain in

the south by the purchase of the county of La Marche, and he then commenced an armed attack upon the French king. But the Pope intervened to rescue his former protector, and a papal legate forced Henry, under threat of an interdict, to make a definitive peace. Thus Louis was saved, and his only interest now was to secure the peaceful succession of his son. In 1179 there was the unusual spectacle of a general assembly of lay and ecclesiastical barons at Paris, at which unanimous assent was given to Louis' proposal that Philip should be crowned king. The coronation took place at Rheims on November 1, again in the presence of a notable assembly, including two of the English princes, Henry and Geoffrey. But Louis himself was absent. A sudden chill had been followed by a stroke, and though he lingered on until the following September, his reign was virtually at an end ; he took no further part in the direction of the government of his kingdom.

The election of Philip II as king (1179)

Death of Louis VII

Philip Augustus

This was now in the hands of his son, Philip II, known to posterity as Philip Augustus.[1] A greater change could hardly be imagined, for the son was the antithesis of the father. Louis had been scrupulous about his duties, less careful of his rights ; Philip was most careful of his rights, less scrupulous about his duties. The advancement of the monarchy was his object, and to this everything was subordinated. Calculating though he was, his nature was not cold. He was hotheaded and passionate, and this sometimes led him astray, especially in his violent antipathy to his second wife, Ingeborg of Denmark. As a rule, however, he made his will the master of his passions, and he was able to do this because his vision of his objective was so clear. In milder sentiments, such as gratitude, he rarely indulged. In fact, in each stage of his advancement he relied on the assistance of those who were to be the objects of his attack in the next stage. Thus against the house of Blois he was assisted by the count of Flanders ; against Flanders he obtained the backing of Henry II ; against Henry II he allied himself with the young Henry and

---

[1] For, said the contemporary who gave him this name, the Romans called their Emperors Augustus (from *augere* " to increase ") because they increased the imperial domain ; so the name was fitting for Philip who increased so greatly the royal domain.

then with Richard; and against Richard he gained the support of John, who was to be his ultimate victim. He had, therefore, nothing of the chivalric temper of his grandfather, whom indeed he resembled only in his energy. But with him energy found expression in mental rather than in physical achievement. He had no delight in military exploits or daring adventures; in fact, he was very careful of his life, as of everything that mattered to the monarchy. Nor did he share Louis VI's partiality for the noble classes. On the contrary, he saw in them the natural foes of monarchy, and on them his hand pressed most hardly. To the poor he seems to have been instinctively generous; his favour to the middle class was more calculated. Here was a section of the community which not only earned, but saved, money, and was ready to pay the price of royal support; he was the first French king properly to realise this and to encourage wholeheartedly a development so much to the financial advantage of the ruler. Free from the prejudices which hampered his father and grandfather, he could turn to the fullest account the advantages they had already gained, and especially could exploit the potentialities that lay in kingship.

At the time of his coronation he was only fourteen years of age. Yet he was mature beyond his years, and exhibited thus early his ability and his determination to be the effective ruler of France. What immediately stood in his way was the hold that his mother's family had acquired over the government. Adela naturally expected to guide the counsels of her young son, though not by herself alone; there were her two brothers, of Blois and Champagne, on both sides of her; a third brother was archbishop of Rheims, and therefore a natural adviser of the king; while the fourth, Stephen count of Sancerre, though territorially unimportant, was a martial adventurer with wide experience in Palestine and elsewhere, and was perhaps the most vigorous and daring of the four. From this domestic encirclement Philip determined to extricate himself, and he found a ready ally in the ambitious count of Flanders, Philip of Alsace, who also anticipated that over so young and inexperienced a king he would easily be able to obtain a dominating influence; yet, experienced intriguer as he was, he proved to be no match for the king. It was arranged that Philip II should marry Isabella, the

His emancipation from the control of the house of Blois

And the count of Flanders

daughter of count Baldwin of Hainault, brother-in-law and vassal of the count of Flanders, who had no children of his own. Philip of Alsace gave his niece as her dowry a group of fiefs in western Flanders, including the important towns of Arras and Saint-Omer, which later became known as Artois. At present he kept them in his own hands, for he purposed to direct everything in the king's name; Philip II had other intentions, and their ultimate addition to the royal domain was one of the fruitful results of his early policy. The marriage took place in April 1180, and the young queen was crowned by the archbishop of Sens instead of by the archbishop of Rheims, whose right it was. This was the final insult to the house of Blois. Adela and her brothers appealed to Henry II for help, and the king of England and his eldest son came to France with an army. But the unexpected happened; Henry and Philip met at Gisors in June and there renewed the treaty of amity concluded in 1177. Philip could now rely on Henry's protection, at any rate on his benevolent neutrality. Henry looked on, in the attitude of the old stager seeing that the plucky youngster has fair play; and certainly he had no cause for liking Blois or Flanders. But, as everyone else, he was misled by the immediate prospect. Philip had the longer vision and he turned to account the foibles of his elders, who became the steps on the ladder by which he mounted to his ultimate triumph.

League against him

His victory with English help

All these events happened while Louis VII was still alive. Philip had emancipated himself from the control of his mother and her family, had used and discarded the count of Flanders, and was making decisions and signing charters as if he were the sole king. When his father died in September 1180, the powers that he had provoked came together against him. The moving spirit was Philip of Alsace, who realised that the treaty of Gisors had frustrated his expectations; and the wound thus inflicted by the boy king on his self-esteem could only be healed by a satisfactory revenge. The house of Blois was deeply offended, too, and was persuaded into a meeting in May 1181, where a powerful league was formed; besides the counts of Flanders and Hainault and the three surviving brothers of the house of Blois,[1] the duke of Burgundy and

---

[1] Count Henry of Champagne had just died, and his son Henry seems to have played no part in the conspiracy.

the count of Nevers joined in the coalition. The king was
thus encompassed with enemies on every side, and a combined attack might have been fatal. But concerted strategy
was not in accordance with the practice of the time, nor with
the mind of the confederates. The count of Flanders could
only rely on one supporter as whole-hearted as himself,
Stephen of Sancerre ; he had nothing to lose and everything
to gain by the military adventure in which he delighted.
Theobald of Blois and the archbishop were both men of
peace, and neither had any desire for the aggrandisement of
Flanders ; while there was always Henry II in the background, with a tolerant eye on the prowess of the young king
and unlikely to let him be overwhelmed ; indeed, he allowed
his sons, Henry and Geoffrey, to fight on Philip II's side. So
things took a normal course : sieges and counter-sieges,
negotiations and truces. Then in 1184 Philip caused further
disunion in the coalition by threatening to divorce his wife
as reprisal for her father's disloyalty ; to save his daughter,
Baldwin of Hainault made his peace with the king. This
diverted the fury of Philip of Alsace to Hainault, which he
invaded and ravaged. But he was now almost isolated.
Philip II in great force marched to the siege of Boves near
Amiens in 1185 ; for three weeks the two armies faced one
another, but no pitched battle resulted. The count of
Flanders vainly endeavoured to get the assistance of Henry
II, who refused even to mediate ; and in July 1185 he was
forced to conclude with his suzerain the treaty of Boves.
Of the confederates, only the duke of Burgundy remained ;
Philip II invaded Burgundy in 1186, and the duke, after
vainly appealing to the Emperor, was forced to submit.

In 1182 another question had arisen to complicate the **The**
relations between the king and the count of Flanders. The **succession to**
countess of Flanders, Isabella, died leaving no children, and **Vermandois**
the future of her inheritance, Vermandois and Valois, was at
issue. Philip of Alsace tried to retain it, against the claims
of her sister Eleanor, wife of the count of Beaumont, the
king's chamberlain. Philip II naturally supported Eleanor
against the count ; but he also put forward his own claim,
since Isabella was the heiress of Ralph of Vermandois, who
was the grandson of a French king, Henry I. By the treaty
of Boves, Eleanor retained Valois ; the Vermandois was

divided, the western half, including Amiens and several
castles, passing to the king, the eastern half being retained
by Philip of Alsace for his lifetime only.[1] The count had
realised his defeat and accepted it ; for the rest of his life he
remained loyal.   So the first period of the reign ended with the
victory of the king over the great feudatories adjacent to the
royal domain.   The result was a most important extension of
the domain, immediate and in prospect ; moreover, there was
the ultimate addition of Artois to be anticipated also.   Philip,
before he had reached the age of twenty-one, had achieved
two things : the greatest addition to the domain and the most
decisive victory over the great vassals that had been achieved
since the Capetian house came to the throne.

His intrigues against Henry II   But this was all preliminary to the ultimate issue which
was never far from his mind, the trial of strength with the
English king.   He could not be sovereign in his kingdom
while the Angevin house occupied so large a part of it.   The
domestic difficulties of the English king were his opportunity,
and, whereas Louis VII had made but feeble use of them,
Philip II exploited them to the full.   Moreover, he was careful
to foment them, and we find him intriguing in turn with the
young Henry, with Geoffrey, with Richard, and with John.
Henry and Geoffrey had been at his coronation and had
supported him against the count of Flanders ; it was natural
that he should send help to them when they were at feud with
Richard in 1183.   Henry II settled this conflict by siding
with Richard, and the sudden death of the young Henry
brought it to an end and left Richard as his father's heir.
This episode had not affected the relations between the two
kings, for Philip's action had preceded Henry's intervention ;
and Henry persisted in his policy of neutrality during Philip's
struggle with his barons.   But when his victory had been
won, Philip could begin to plot the greater undertaking.   In
1186 he had Geoffrey at his court, and subtly worked on his
jealousy of his elder brother ; but the sudden death of Geoffrey
brought this scheme to an end.   Philip now came more into
the open with personal grievances against Henry.   First of
all there was the Norman Vexin, the dowry of his stepsister

---

[1] When Philip of Alsace died at the siege of Acre in 1191, the whole of
the Vermandois became royal domain ; and when Eleanor died in 1213,
Valois was added too.

Margaret, which had not been returned when her husband died. It was arranged that it should be the dowry of her sister Alice who was betrothed to Richard. This created a further grievance, because Henry retained the Vexin and would not arrange the marriage ; there was an ugly rumour that he was too fond himself of Alice to give her to his son. Philip demanded the return both of his sister and of the Vexin, and to support his demand made a sudden attack upon Berry and took possession of various towns. Henry and Richard came to defend it, and a truce for two years was agreed, Philip remaining in possession of his conquests. Now he began to court the goodwill of Richard, who visited him at Paris ; and, since Henry II, whose daughter was married to Henry the Lion, took the side of the Welfs against the Emperor, Philip was able to conclude an alliance with the Emperor against the English king.

The prospect, therefore, was not unfavourable when in 1187 the news of the capture of Jerusalem caused an interruption in the development of this policy. For Richard immediately took the cross ; and early in 1188 the archbishop of Tyre persuaded both kings to do the same. Preparations for the crusade were on foot when a dispute between Richard and Raymond of Toulouse turned into war, and to avert the threatened fall of Toulouse Philip intervened. Once more he had to face the combined forces of Henry and Richard. But his intrigues with Richard had sown the seeds of distrust between father and son, and Richard was irritated by his father's delay in recognising him as heir to the throne and giving Alice to him in marriage, and his jealousy was aroused by Henry's partiality for John. There was a dramatic moment when, at an interview between the two kings, Richard suddenly left Henry and did homage to Philip. Together they were more than a match for the ageing Henry. In 1189 they invaded Maine and seized Le Mans. Henry capitulated to their terms : he recognised Richard as his successor, and yielded to Philip the suzerainty over Auvergne as well as his conquests in Berry. He was a broken man. The last and worst news for him was that his favourite, John, had conspired against him, and he died almost immediately afterwards.

Defeat and death of Henry II

So Henry II was brought low, and a further addition made

to the domain of the French king. Now he had to deal with Richard, a young man in place of an old man, active and vigorous, the greatest soldier of his age, yet unstable, too prone to adventure and reckless enterprise. Outwardly they were still friends ; and they went together, as arranged, on crusade in 1190, Richard full of excitement and enthusiasm. But Philip was deeply regretting that he had been moment-arily led astray by his emotions into taking the crusading vow ; it was galling to him to be diverted thus from the main purpose of his life ; and he had the further mortification of seeing his own vassal preferred to himself as the obvious leader of the crusaders. So there was constant friction. It began at Messina, where Richard married Berengaria of Navarre, and Philip had to receive back Alice and at the same time leave the Vexin in Richard's hands. In Palestine, Philip, irritable and neurotic, was only a hindrance to the progress of the crusade. He escaped from it on the first pretext and by the end of 1190 was back in France, and in his accustomed environment he began to recover his mental balance. His mind became busy with schemes for the ruin of Richard, for whom he had conceived a violent hatred ; but as Richard was still on crusade he could not outrage opinion by attacking his possessions. For the moment, too, he was occupied in entering upon his inheritance in eastern Vermandois, since Philip of Alsace died in 1191 ; and as the new count of Flanders, Baldwin of Hainault, proved most complaisant, he was able to prepare the way for the acquisition of Artois also.

His opportunity came with the capture of Richard in December 1192, and then he took action at once. He easily won over John against his brother, he allied himself with the king of Denmark in order to have naval assistance for an invasion of England, he tried to bribe the Emperor Henry VI to keep Richard a prisoner, and he seized the Norman Vexin. But his scheming was to little purpose, and it seemed that with all his mental qualities he could not prevail with his contemporaries against the dazzling personality of Richard. John's influence in Normandy and England proved to be insignificant, and Henry VI preferred his captive enemy to his French ally. Most unfortunate of all was the Danish alliance, which brought him no material advantage but only

a disastrous marriage in 1193 with Ingeborg, the sister of the His marriage
Danish king. His first marriage, with Isabella of Hainault Ingeborg
(who died in 1190), had been one of policy, and he showed no of Denmark
affection for her or for his son and heir, Louis. His second
marriage was equally one of policy, but he allowed his feelings
to overcome him. Beautiful though she was, he immediately
conceived for her an aversion so extreme that it could not
be controlled by the dictates of policy. Possibly the diseased
mentality of his crusading year may account for this ; yet,
if this was so, the effect considerably outlived the cause. At
any rate, he who had used to such purpose the domestic
difficulties of the English king, was now allowing himself to
be handicapped by his own domestic difficulties, so as even
to estrange the Pope against him. In 1195 he actually
repudiated Ingeborg, and a council of French bishops dissolved the marriage. This was immediately annulled by a
papal bull, but in spite of this he persisted and contracted a
third marriage, with Agnes of Meran, in 1196. Papal threats
became sharper and culminated at last in an interdict. It
was only towards the end of his reign that Philip allowed
policy to prevail, and this was when he once more was
contemplating the invasion of England.

So he gained nothing by Richard's captivity except his Richard's
conquest of the Vexin, and when Richard returned in 1194 of his
he was unable to retain that. Richard began at once to territories
recapture the lost castles, and though, as usual, the war was
interrupted by truces, the complete reconquest was achieved
by 1198. Richard showed himself as masterly in building
fortresses as he was in capturing them, and one of the greatest
feats of medieval military architecture, the construction of
the Château Gaillard, belongs to these years. Philip had to
bide his time. But he had not long to wait. For, a year
later, Richard dashing off to Aquitaine on a foolish adventure,
received a mortal wound. Of the English royal family only
John survived and Arthur, Geoffrey's son. At last Philip's
chance had come.

The story of his eventual triumph lies outside the scope The advance
of this volume. Yet even in the first and less notable half of monarchical
his reign he had made great progress towards his goal of a authority
real sovereignty in the French kingdom. Within the royal by 1198
domain his authority was of course complete, thanks to the

work of Louis VI; and already he had considerably enlarged its extent and so increased the area of direct government. Beyond its limits, he had begun to press his rights as suzerain even over the greater vassals, stressing their obligation to render him the feudal aids, and to seek his leave for the marriage of their children and his confirmation of their grants by charter. The development of royal sovereignty, begun in the reign of Louis VI, continued apace as the desire, especially of towns, for royal protection increased. He was lavish in his grants of charters to towns, from whom he exacted an annual payment and military service in return. He did not refuse them, as Louis VII had done, to towns within the domain. He granted them in the newly-added territories, such as the Vermandois, with the politic aim of conciliating the inhabitants to his rule. In the old domain he gave them especially, for military reasons, to towns near the frontiers, which were thus provided with a series of defences. But above all, particularly outside the domain, his object, besides the extension of his authority, was a financial one. He needed money and here was a money-making class, willing to pay for the economic advantages it gained and demanding little in the way of self-government. Of this he was chary, and the political government even of Paris was largely under the control of the royal provosts. It was increased facilities for commerce and industry that the towns wanted and that he bestowed; the more their wealth increased, the greater was the annual contribution that he could demand from them.

Of all the towns Paris held pride of place, as the capital city of the kingdom, the seat of the principal organs of government, and the king's most usual place of residence. It was gaining in international importance. The fame of its Schools attracted students from all countries. Its river made it an *entrepôt* for commerce, and the *hansa* (gild) of " Marchands de l'eau " was given special privileges by Philip, including a monopoly of carrying rights; at the same time he encouraged the craft gilds, many of which derived their earliest charters from him. He even employed leading burgesses to assist him in the work of government, mainly, where their genius lay, in finance; it was to six of them that were entrusted the revenues collected by the local officials,

The towns — marginal note

Paris — marginal note

so that they became as it were a body of royal treasurers.

This use of the trained man of business is analogous to The
the use of trained clerks in the general administration, and administration of the
of trained lawyers to hear cases in the royal court.   The great domain
offices of State became less and less important.   Theobald of
Blois continued to have the name of seneschal, but after his
death in 1191 the office ceased to exist, as that of chancellor
had ceased in 1185.   The others remained, but only with
formal and ceremonial functions.   For the administration of
the domain Philip II created a new official—the *bailli*—on
the model of the *baillis* instituted in Normandy by Henry II.
When Philip departed on crusade in 1190, leaving his mother
and the archbishop of Rheims as regents during his absence,
he drew up a *Testament*, which contained careful instructions
for the government, especially of the domain.   The duties of
the *baillis* were minutely detailed : they were to hold monthly
assizes, to collect the royal revenues, of which they had to
render account three times a year, and in general to supervise
the work of the provosts.   In fact their duties were very
similar to those of the sheriffs in England.

The domain was still the principal sphere of royal govern- Justice and
ment.   But the king's Curia was not solely preoccupied with revenue
the domain, since the king was now definitely exercising his
sovereignty beyond it.   The suits that came to the king's
court from different parts of the country were steadily increasing in number, and once again, though at present infrequently,
assemblies of the great vassals, lay and ecclesiastical, were
being held.   Nor was the king entirely dependent on the
domain for his resources.   Military service was frequently
commuted for a money payment, and the king was relying
more and more on paid soldiers.   The domain was still the
principal source of the king's revenue, derived from feudal
dues and the profits of justice, but there were now other
sources as well, besides the Church.   The towns have already
been mentioned.   There were also the Jews, whom Philip
ruthlessly exploited : he began by expelling them, then
allowed them to return on payment of a huge sum of money,
and finally levied an annual tax from them.   There was even
one occasion when he raised a general tax, the " Saladin
tithe " in 1188 for the purpose of the crusade.   This was
exceptional, and the Church was strong enough to prevent

its repetition in the following year, but it created a precedent which was to be followed.

Royal government mainly confined to the domain

However, it must still be emphasised that the principal work of royal administration lay in the domain. In the past the nobles had ignored the central government and jealously guarded their local independence. The king was able now to ignore them, as far as the central government was concerned (hence the infrequency of general assemblies), but he could not interfere with their local government. His officials administered for him only the domain. Every extension of it was therefore an extension of royal government, and so if Philip was to achieve his idea of monarchy this must be the means. In 1198 he was on the brink of his greatest triumph, when he was to be Philip " Augustus " indeed. By the victory which ended the English domination in France and more than doubled the royal domain, Philip's idea of monarchy was in great measure fulfilled.

SUGGESTIONS FOR READING ON CHAPTER XXI

Cambridge Medieval History, Vol. V, chapter 18 ; Vol. VI, chapter 9.
Lavisse, E. : *Histoire de France*, Vol. III, 1.
Also the works of Luchaire, Petit-Dutaillis, Fawtier, and Lot and Fawtier suggested on p. 109, above.

CHAPTER XXII

EAST AND WEST, 1155–1198. THE THIRD CRUSADE

BETWEEN the Second and Third Crusades there was The Latin
an interval of forty years, during which the Latin West States
had little contact with the Latin East. The danger Second after the
to the Latin States was grave, since the Moslems in Syria Crusade
were now united under the single rule of Nuraddin, but it
was impossible to raise an expedition in the West ; the Pope,
who might have urged it, was for many years engaged in
conflict with the Emperor, and anyhow the disillusionment
created by the disaster of the Second Crusade made it impossible to arouse the necessary enthusiasm. Left to themselves,
the Latin States naturally turned to the Eastern Emperor for
aid, and Manuel was quite ready to grant it. Indeed, he had
a great opportunity, if he could have confined his attention to
the East and concentrated on a campaign against the Moslems.
The first necessity was to secure his communications with
Cilicia and Syria by driving back the Moslems in Asia Minor.
Then he might reasonably hope, in alliance with the Latin
Christians, for the successful issue of an offensive against
Nuraddin. It is only too probable that the alliance would
not have survived victory, since neither Greeks nor Latins
showed any disposition to subordinate their selfish interests
to the common advantage of Christendom. But Manuel
might at least have anticipated securing Syria for the Empire,
if he were content to leave Palestine to the Latins. An
extended Empire and more secure frontiers would have been
the fruits of this policy.

However, it was not in Manuel's nature to concentrate Manuel's
methodically on a single objective, and he was already deeply persistence
committed to his Western plan. There was the same excuse Western in his
—the recovery of territory that had been Byzantine ; for it ambition
had been conquered by the Normans actually at the same
time that Syria had been conquered by the Seljuks. Also,

in view of the aggressive policy of the Normans, the Eastern
Emperor had to be continually alert on his western frontiers ;
an offensive against them was perhaps his best method of
defence. But he had already advanced beyond that. In
spite of the hopeless failure of his first attempt, he was still
wedded to his idea of reuniting the two Empires by the
acquisition of Italy, and the conflict of Empire and Papacy
seemed to give him his opportunity. His efforts in this
direction were worse than useless. Frederick Barbarossa
was as hostile as were the Normans ; the Papacy, again allied
with the Normans, would never consent to the loss of its
suzerainty over South Italy ; and the Venetians were alarmed
for their dominance of the Adriatic by the Byzantine occupation of Ancona and then of Dalmatia on the opposite coast.
Yet Manuel persisted in his hopeless attempt in the West,
and thereby wasted time and resources that would have been
better employed in the East. His attention alternated first
to this side and then to that, as opportunities presented
themselves to his sanguine mind. Engaging on both fronts
with tortuous negotiations and sometimes with armed expeditions, he actually formed almost the sole point of contact
between East and West ; and the story of their relations
during these years is the main part of the history of the
Eastern Empire.

The Second Crusade had interrupted the Eastern policy
of Manuel, at a moment when his hold on Cilicia and Antioch
was becoming established. Thanks to Roger II of Sicily he
was prevented for some years from taking it in hand again.
He had first of all to deal with Roger's invasion of Greece,
then with a revolt of the Serbs engineered by Roger's agents,
and finally with a Hungarian war also probably due to the
diplomatic intrigues of the Norman. When at last he made
peace with the Hungarian king Géza II in 1155, he had
embarked on his counter-offensive against Roger's successor,
William I, so that until 1157 his interest was almost wholly
confined to the West. This was the more unfortunate, since
during these years the principality of Antioch, hard pressed
by Nuraddin and attacked also from the north by the sultan
of Iconium, was anxious for his assistance and willing to pay
his price. At the same time the Armenians in Cilicia
reasserted their independence. Thoros II, the son of Leo I

whom the Emperor John had overthrown, escaped from captivity and, assuming the title of prince, was able to recover a large part of his father's dominions. Manuel, engrossed in Western affairs, entrusted his cousin Andronicus with the task of reducing Thoros to submission. It was an unfortunate choice, for Andronicus was reckless in self-indulgence and quite irresponsible ; and both now and afterwards, when he became Emperor, proved himself the evil genius of the dynasty. Thoros had no difficulty in defeating him, and Manuel, who could spare few troops, had to resort to other expedients. He first of all allied with Masud, the sultan of Iconium, who invaded Cilicia twice without success. Then he sought the help of Reginald of Châtillon, temporarily prince of Antioch,[1] but Reginald chose instead to ally with Thoros and together they attacked and plundered Cyprus. This occurred just at the time that Manuel was launching his expedition to Italy, and when that ended in disaster he at last turned his mind from his Western dreams to the more practical problems in the East.

If the prince of Antioch had foolishly taken sides against the Emperor, the king of Jerusalem, Baldwin III, was wiser and saw that the assistance of Manuel was necessary if the Christians were to make headway against Nuraddin. Accord- ingly he sought his alliance and in 1157 married Manuel's niece Theodora. The prospects were bright for Manuel when he set out in 1158 at the head of a considerable army, with the object of restoring imperial authority in Cilicia and Antioch and then of leading the Christian forces against the Moslems in Syria. The first objective was quickly achieved. Thoros and Reginald of Châtillon were both forced to submit, and were only allowed to retain their principalities as vassals of the Emperor. In April 1159 Manuel, with Baldwin III in his train, entered Antioch, and in the festal scenes which marked the recognition of his sovereignty he reached the zenith of his career. In May at the head of a united Christian army he started on the road for Edessa. But he was satisfied with negotiations, and after obtaining from Nuraddin the

---

[1] Raymond of Antioch had been killed in battle in 1149, and his son Bohemond III, until he came of age in 1163, was under the guardianship first of his mother Constance, and then of her second husband Reginald of Châtillon, who took the title of prince of Antioch.

release of thousands of Christian captives he abandoned the campaign. The suggestion that he was reluctant to destroy the power of Nuraddin, since it guaranteed the dependence of the Latins on himself, is only too likely; the victory of Christianity was made impossible because both Greeks and Latins were concerned primarily with their own interests. It was a short-sighted policy on Manuel's part; he lost a splendid opportunity of recovering the former possessions of the Empire, and by his departure threw away most of the actual fruits of the expedition.

The Armenians re-assert their independence

His authority was still recognised in Antioch after his return to Constantinople—the replacing of the Latin by a Greek patriarch is a sign of this—and he made his connexion with the principality more intimate by taking as his second wife Constance's daughter Mary. But his hold on Cilicia did not long survive his departure. Thoros soon began to recover the towns which had been taken from him, and defeated the Greeks in 1163. Once again Manuel made the mistake of sending Andronicus to Cilicia. This time he was not only unsuccessful in battle. He actually deserted his post in order to run off first with Philippa of Antioch, Manuel's sister-in-law, and then with Manuel's niece Theodora, the widow of Baldwin III of Jerusalem, who died in 1163. The result was the overthrow of Greek authority in Cilicia; the Armenian prince became independent, and his successor Leo II at the end of the century took the title of king, with the full approval of the Western powers. So the land route to Syria was no longer available to the Byzantines. Moreover, Manuel had neglected to take the necessary steps to secure his line of communications. He suffered from Moslem attacks on his return from Syria in 1159, and though he was able to come to terms with them (they were for some time divided by internal strife), he was only able to ensure peace on his frontiers by paying an annual subsidy to the new sultan of Iconium, Kilij Arslan II.

Manuel's relations with Hungary

The reason for this was that he was once more concerned with Western problems, and particularly with Hungary, where the death of Géza II in 1161 was followed by civil war in which Manuel was able successfully to intervene. His reward was the acquisition of an important hostage in Béla, the heir to the throne, whose appanage of Dalmatia fell into

Manuel's hands in 1166.[1]   The next year the Latin East again demanded his attention, for the new king of Jerusalem, Amaury I, sought his alliance and married a Byzantine princess.   Manuel sent the Greek fleet to assist him in his invasion of Egypt in 1169, but the plans of the allies were badly concerted, and the siege of Damietta, the first objective of the expedition, had to be abandoned.   The alliance was resumed in 1171, but nothing came of it; and the Eastern Empire ceased to play a part in the affairs of the Latin East. This was mainly due to the Emperor's preoccupation with his Western schemes, and by 1171 these had involved him in a situation of extreme gravity.

Manuel's return from Syria in 1159 had coincided with the papal schism which followed the death of Hadrian IV.   He grasped eagerly at the chance this seemed to offer of realising his ambition and being recognised as Emperor, at any rate in Italy and at Rome.   He opened up a correspondence with Pope Alexander III, friendly in tone on both sides, which lasted for some years; there were two obstacles to their alliance—the schism between the Eastern and Western Churches, and the hostility of the Norman allies of Alexander to the Eastern Emperor—and nothing practical resulted from these negotiations.   Later, when the Lombard League was founded, Manuel redoubled his efforts to form a coalition that would isolate Barbarossa and confine him to his German kingdom.   The advance he had been making in Hungary seems to have been part of the same policy; he had already renewed friendly relations with Louis VII of France; and he now even proposed an alliance with William II of Sicily, and offered him the hand of his daughter Mary.   Above all, he entered into negotiations with the leading Italian cities and supplied them with money to assist their revolt against the Western Emperor.   The maritime towns were of especial importance to him.   Both Genoa and Pisa nibbled at the bait of trading advantages, but neither would commit itself to an actual breach with Barbarossa.   There remained Venice, whose alliance with the Eastern Empire was traditional.   But Venice was seriously alarmed by the Byzantine occupation of the Dalmatian coast and re-entry into Ancona.   She

---

[1] Béla became king in 1173 and remained loyal to Manuel.   It was only after the Emperor's death that he recovered Dalmatia for Hungary.

refused to entertain Manuel's proposals for an offensive
alliance against Barbarossa. His patience, which had withstood the disappointments of so many years of fruitless

Breach with
Venice

negotiation, was exhausted by this final rebuff. In his anger
with the Venetians he determined on revenge, and at last in
1171 he caused all the Venetians in Constantinople to be
arrested and their property confiscated. The result of twelve
years of scheming was that he had gained no ally and had
made a dangerous enemy.

The Venetians hastily raised a fleet of 120 ships, which,
under the command of the doge, captured Ragusa and
plundered the shores of Greece and the Aegean islands. But
the doge then allowed himself to be drawn into negotiations
which dragged on for months ; finally, plague attacked the
expedition and only a feeble remnant straggled back to Venice
in 1172.[1] Manuel, however, was foolish enough to throw

And with
the king
of Sicily

away all the advantages of this good fortune. He had sought
the alliance of the Norman king against Venice, and had
renewed the marriage proposal ; everything was arranged,
and William II made all preparations to receive his bride.
Suddenly, in 1172, Manuel changed his mind ; Frederick
Barbarossa had made an offer for Mary's hand for his own
son, and though the offer was probably not serious, Manuel
was deluded by it into breaking his agreement with the king
of Sicily. William suffered the indignity of waiting in vain
to meet his bride, and was naturally furious at the insult.
The result of Manuel's diplomacy was his own isolation. In
1173 Venice gained the support of Barbarossa in an attack
on Ancona, and though this was not successful the republic
in 1175 made a political and commercial treaty with the king
of Sicily, which was especially designed against the Eastern
Emperor. To pacify Venice, Manuel had to accept its terms
and to restore all its old privileges at Constantinople. But he
could not pacify William II, who was planning his revenge,
nor Frederick Barbarossa, who in his turn began to negotiate
alliances to encircle the Eastern Emperor, and was successful
in coming to terms with the sultan of Iconium. The tables

---

[1] Popular indignation was vented on the doge, who was murdered. The
chief result of the expedition was a reform of the Venetian constitution :
the oligarchic control was strengthened, and increased limitations were placed
on the authority and power of initiative of the doge.

were now completely turned ; surprisingly enough, the diplomatic victory had been won by the Westerner.

While he had thus been pursuing the mirage of Empire in the West, Manuel had let slip the chance of conquest in Asia Minor. During these years Kilij Arslan II was constantly engaged in civil war with his co-religionists, his own brother being his principal enemy. Manuel not only failed to take advantage of the splendid opportunities offered him by the dissensions among the Moslems ; he even paid regular subsidies to Kilij Arslan in order to be free from any aggression from that quarter. By 1175 the sultan of Iconium had mastered his rivals, and was leagued with Barbarossa against Manuel. The latter now at last summoned all his resources in the effort to eradicate the danger that was so near at hand. In 1176 he himself led his principal army against the main objective, his enemy's capital, while a subsidiary force under Andronicus Vatatzes was directed to capture Neo-Caesarea. Vatatzes' army was routed and himself slain ; Manuel, neglecting the obvious precaution of discovering the disposition of the enemy's forces, was caught in an ambush at Myriocephalum, and his army was almost annihilated. Manuel's military incompetence had precipitated the disaster to which his political blunders had been slowly preparing the way.

The disaster of Myriocephalum (1176)

This fatal year, 1176, saw the defeat of the Western Emperor at Legnano as well as of the Eastern Emperor at Myriocephalum. For Barbarossa it was only a momentary set-back, and he was able to recover his position in Italy ; but there was no recovery for Manuel or for the Eastern Empire. Myriocephalum was, as Manuel himself declared, a second Manzikert. The immediate consequences were not so obvious, for Kilij Arslan did not pursue his victory and granted peace on very lenient terms. But the imperial army had been destroyed, and Alexius' great work of reconstruction ruined ; and if there was less danger than his grandfather had had to fear from the East, Manuel had thoroughly embittered the West. Those old enemies, the Normans and Venetians, had allied against him, and the Western Emperor was a determined enemy and in league with the Moslems. Barbarossa had too much to occupy him in Italy to meditate an attack on Constantinople, and Manuel did what he could

Dangerous situation of the Eastern Emperor

to make Frederick's position more difficult by subsidising his enemies in Italy. Not that he could look any longer for recognition there himself; his only hope was to ensure himself against attack. With one Western sovereign he managed to maintain friendly relations—Louis VII of France—and in March 1180 his son Alexius married Louis' daughter Agnes. There was no political importance in this alliance, though it revived Manuel's optimism and self-esteem; and it was only effective for a few months. In September both Louis and Manuel were dead.

Alexius II Comnenus

The dynasty of the Comneni, like the Macedonian dynasty which it superseded, rendered great services to the Empire and then collapsed amid scenes of disorder and misgovernment, leaving the Empire almost in ruins. The end of the Macedonians had been a lingering one. In the case of the Comneni it came very rapidly: two Emperors, the one a boy the other a life-long libertine, succeeded Manuel in turn, and five years after his death they had both been murdered and the dynasty was extinct. Alexius II, the heir of Manuel, was only twelve years old when his father died, and remained under the guardianship of his mother, Mary of Antioch. It was to be expected, in accordance with precedent, that she would choose a husband to assist her in government, and there were numerous candidates for the position. But she preferred a lover to a husband, and a worthless one to boot, Alexius, a nephew of Manuel; his vainglorious assertion of power created ill feeling against her, and she herself contributed to her unpopularity by showering favours on the Latins in Constantinople, and preferring them to Greeks in the highest offices of State. She was faced, too, with plots within the imperial family, led by her stepdaughter Mary,[1] who till Alexius' birth had been sole heiress to the imperial throne, and hoped to gain it for herself and her husband Renier; though he too was a Latin, she utilised the anti-Latin feeling in the capital to gain support against her stepmother.

Andronicus Comnenus seizes the throne

In these conditions of misgovernment, of domestic plotting and of popular unrest, there was the opportunity for an

---

[1] After Manuel's various negotiations with William II of Sicily and Frederick of Barbarossa, he had married his daughter to Renier, son of William marquis of Montferrat, who was at the time in revolt against Barbarossa in Italy.

ambitious man to seize the power. And such a one was at hand in Andronicus Comnenus, whose dashing qualities seem to have made him a popular favourite in Constantinople, in spite of his disservices to the Empire. A born intriguer, in politics as well as in love, it was partly to get rid of his dangerous presence that Manuel had employed him on two occasions so disastrously in Cilicia. Now he saw his chance and took it. Making himself the champion of the Greeks versus the Latins, he won over not only the people of Constantinople but also the army to his cause, had no difficulty in ousting Mary of Antioch from the government, and was himself proclaimed joint Emperor with Alexius in 1183. He instituted a regular holocaust in the imperial family, to get rid of all possible rivals. His principal victims were the Empress-mother, Alexius himself, whose widow Agnes he married, and Alexius' half-sister and her husband. The methods of the "enlightened tyrant" seem to have been the guiding principle of his reign. He was savagely brutal to the aristocracy, a friend to the lower classes, especially in the provinces where some measure of prosperity began to reappear, and a patron of learning and the arts.

But he had not time to establish his régime. His policy of murder not only ranged the aristocracy against him; it provoked foreign invasion as well. For, as a preliminary to obtaining power in 1183, acting as champion of the anti-Latin party, he had won popular favour by instituting a massacre of the Latins in Constantinople. Venice had reacted violently against Manuel's milder method of expulsion in 1171; it had now a still more grievous injury to avenge, and took more determined measures to assure success. It appealed to its ally, William II of Sicily, to join it in a direct attack on Constantinople, and William (who had already had the vision of an imperial crown when his marriage with Manuel's daughter had been mooted) threw himself whole-heartedly into the enterprise.[1] It was the easier because the Byzantine government was distracted by civil discord and threatened by other invasions as well. The sultan of Iconium was advancing on

League of Venice and the king of Sicily against Andronicus

---

[1] He justified his expedition by declaring that he came to restore the rightful ruler to the throne. An impostor, pretending to be Alexius II, appeared in Italy, and was supported by William II, just as Robert Guiscard had championed the cause of a pseudo-Michael in his first invasion of Greece.

Attalia in the south-east, and Béla III of Hungary, to whom
Mary of Antioch had appealed for help, was invading the
Empire from the north-west. William took time over his
preparations, and it was not until 1185 that the Normans
started. Crossing to the coast of Greece they captured
Durazzo and then marched overland to Thessalonica, which
was also captured ; from there a concerted advance was made
by land and sea against Constantinople. Andronicus was
supine in face of the danger to the capital, but it gave him
the excuse for further executions of nobles said to be in league
with the Normans. Defeat and disgrace brought the inevitable reaction against the tyrant. The people turned against
him, the army deserted him, and in a sudden revolt he was
seized and brutally tortured to death. With him the line of
the Comneni came to an end. Isaac Angelus, a personage of
little note whose release from arrest had been the immediate
cause of the popular revolt, was acclaimed as the inspirer of
the overthrow of the tyrant and raised to the imperial throne.

The murder of Andronicus

It was an unlucky chance that brought Isaac Angelus
into prominence. He was quite incompetent as a ruler, and
it needed a man of exceptional ability to cope with the
internal anarchy and the external dangers. Yet he was able
to deal with the immediate crisis. The Byzantine army,
taking the Normans by surprise under cover of negotiations,
routed them and drove them back in headlong flight to
Thessalonica, where they hastily re-embarked for Sicily ;
the Norman and Venetian fleets, finding themselves unsup-
ported, also abandoned the siege of Constantinople ; and
William II, after an unsuccessful expedition against Cyprus
which had proclaimed its independence under a certain Isaac
Comnenus, abandoned his attempt against the Eastern
Empire. Venice, for its part, was appeased by a restoration
of its privileges at Constantinople. But Isaac was quite
unable to cope with the anarchy which still prevailed in the
government, and then came a new moment of peril with the
launching of the Third Crusade.

Isaac Angelus Emperor

The struggle for Egypt

During these years the kingdom of Jerusalem was experi-
encing similar scenes of anarchy and civil discord, as it also
declined to its fall. Already in the reign of Amaury I (1163–
74) it had become evident that the kingdom, left to itself,

was unequal to the task of resisting the Moslem advance.
A new situation had been created, since Egypt was now the
battlefield on which Amaury engaged Nuraddin. The Fatimite Caliphate at Cairo had long been in decline : for more
than a century the Caliphs themselves had been as helpless
as their Abbasid rivals ; they had had to submit to the
dictation of mercenaries, usually of Turkish race ; and the
government was conducted in their name by a grand vizier,
who in fact had complete control. The Fatimites, too, had
suffered more from the crusaders than had the Seljuks. The
latter, never a naval power, were not vitally affected by the
loss of the coast towns ; the Fatimites, on the other hand,
besides being driven out of Palestine, had had their fleets
destroyed by the Italian maritime powers, and by losing
control of the sea lost all chance of resuming the offensive.
In the year of Amaury's accession, a contest for the government began between two rival viziers, and the ensuing civil
war gave both Nuraddin and Amaury an excuse for intervention. The opportunity of acquiring Egypt was naturally
attractive to Amaury, but it was still more to his interest to
prevent Nuraddin from acquiring it and thus gaining both a
fleet and a base of operations from which to attack Palestine
from the south. The possession of Egypt, therefore, became
the chief objective in the struggle between Moslems and
Christians.

It seemed at first that victory would rest with the Latins ;
in 1167 Amaury was so successful that the Seljuks had to
withdraw from Egypt. But by an ill-timed invasion in 1168
he alienated his Egyptian allies, so that they once again
turned to the Seljuks for aid. Nuraddin's general Shirkuh
was able to compel the Latins to retire, and then forced the
Caliph to name him vizier. He died a few months later, and Saladin
was succeeded, both as general of the Seljuk forces and as master of
vizier, by his son, the famous Saladin. In 1169 Saladin won Egypt
his first victory over the Christians when he defeated the joint
expedition of Amaury and the Byzantines at Damietta. In
1171 the Caliph died, and Saladin refused to allow the appointment of a successor ; so the Fatimite Caliphate came to an
end. Saladin's action was a dangerous one, for it provoked
a formidable conspiracy among his Egyptian subjects, who
in 1173 turned again to Amaury for help. Amaury himself

had been canvassing the West for aid, and at this juncture
he received a response to his appeal from William II of Sicily.
The Norman king assembled a large fleet, which was intended
to act in concert with Amaury and the Egyptian conspirators.
But when it arrived in 1174, the conspiracy had been discovered and crushed and Amaury had just died, so that it
had to act on its own.   Its appearance before Alexandria
caused great alarm, but though the Normans effected a land-
ing they failed to capture the city, and the arrival of Saladin
in person caused them hastily to re-embark, with considerable
loss of men and material.   During the next four years,
William II sent two other expeditions to the coasts of Egypt,
but these were only on a small scale and achieved nothing
save plunder.   Once again the kingdom of Jerusalem was
left without any help from the West, and Saladin was completely master of Egypt.   He soon became more than this.
For Nuraddin died in 1174, leaving a boy, Salih, as his heir.
In normal circumstances this would have led to a weakening

Saladin
becomes
Sultan of
Damascus
and probably a division of the Moslem power.   But Saladin,
as general of the Seljuk army and as ruler of Egypt, was so
strong that he was able to dispose of Salih and supersede him
as Sultan of Damascus.   Master now of Moslem Syria as well
as of Egypt, he threatened the kingdom of Jerusalem both
from the south and the east.   And, being a devout Moslem,
his natural objective was Jerusalem.

The last
days of
the kingdom
of Jerusalem
Like Nuraddin, Amaury I, who died the same year, left
a boy as his heir, Baldwin IV, who had the additional mis-
fortune of having contracted leprosy, which eventually
deprived him of his sight.   In the Christian kingdom there
was no single man strong enough to discipline the conflicting
elements.   The struggle for power began at once, though for
a time the worst consequences were delayed by the appointment of count Raymond III of Tripolis as Baldwin's guardian.
Until 1185, when Baldwin died, Raymond was able to maintain some kind of unity, but afterwards faction had its way
and the collapse of the kingdom soon followed.   There were
two main parties—the " natives," led by Raymond, who had
settled down and were not averse to living at peace with
their Moslem neighbours ; and the " foreigners," led by Guy
of Lusignan (the second husband of Baldwin's sister Sibylla),
who wanted to make a place for themselves and who in their

ignorance of the situation demanded an immediate offensive against the Moslems.   They might have been negligible but that they received the powerful support of the Military Orders.   Raymond continued as regent for Baldwin V, the young son of Sibylla's first marriage.   But he died in 1186, and then the " foreigners " obtained the election of Guy of Lusignan as king.

Raymond had given the kingdom a further breathing space by making a truce in 1185 with Saladin.   It was one of the foreign adventurers, Reginald of Châtillon, who brought about a renewal of war.   Forced to leave Antioch on the death of Constance, he had acquired by a second marriage the county of Montreal in Transjordania.   In 1182 he performed a daring exploit when he advanced to the Red Sea and managed to establish there a small fleet, which for a year was a danger to Moslem pilgrims to Mecca, until at last he was driven off by Saladin.   He took his revenge in 1187, when he plundered a caravan containing a sister of Saladin, but this flagrant breach of the truce provoked Saladin to immediate action.   He proclaimed a Holy War, and crossing the Jordan in May fell upon the combined forces of the Military Orders at Nazareth and completely routed them. In face of the common peril the Christians united at last under the banner of the king of Jerusalem, and Guy, impatient of the prudent caution of Raymond, determined to give battle at once.   Outmanœuvred and forced to fight under the hot midday sun, the Christian army, exhausted by heat and thirst, was cut to pieces at Hittin on July 4.   The king himself and many of his leading followers were taken prisoners ; among them Reginald of Châtillon, on whom Saladin took his revenge by executing him with his own hand.   After this disastrous defeat the Christians could put up little resistance. Jerusalem fell at the first assault on October 4, and by the end of the year Tyre was the only important place in the kingdom that the Moslems had not captured.   The principality of Antioch remained intact, and Tripolis was saved by the timely appearance of a Norman fleet in 1188.   These were all that were salved out of the wreckage of the Latin States.

Saladin's victory at Hittin

The capture of Jerusalem (1187)

The disaster did, however, galvanise the West into action again.   The recapture of Jerusalem appeared as a more

Prepara-
tions for the
Third
Crusade

terrible calamity even than its first capture by the Seljuks; for it had now been taken from the Christians. The general conscience was shocked by the disgrace and horror of the event. The Papacy took the initiative in the new crusade, but it had little to do, for in all countries there was an immediate rush to take the Cross, and for the time even the greater enmities were laid aside. Emperor and Pope united in the cause, and so did the kings of England and France; William II of Sicily made peace with the Eastern Emperor, the maritime cities of Italy for once acted in concert; and Danes, Norwegians, and Swedes joined in a common expedition. The Scandinavian fleet was soon afloat, but had a long way to travel; the Sicilians, near at hand, were first on the scene, and were instrumental, as has already been mentioned, in saving Tripolis from capture by Saladin. However, William II died in 1189, and the struggle for the succession in Sicily prevented the Normans from taking any further part in the Crusade.

The
expedition
of Frederick
Barbarossa

It was fitly the Emperor who really inaugurated the Third Crusade, and under him the largest and best-equipped force that any crusading leader had commanded started from Ratisbon in May 1189. He chose the old land-route, and was careful to make arrangements with the Hungarians, so that he had an easy passage through their territory. But it was very different when he came to Greek soil. Instead of providing the crusaders with an escort and provisions as his predecessors had done, Isaac Angelus put every possible obstacle in the way; he had even formed an alliance with Saladin against Barbarossa's ally, the sultan of Iconium. Barbarossa had set the example of allying with Moslems against Christians, but Isaac's treaty with the conqueror of Jerusalem was to the Westerners the unforgivable treachery which justified the overthrow of the Eastern Empire. Frederick took his toll of plunder but was not to be diverted from his objective. He was content to frighten Isaac into acquiescence, and supplied with provisions and ships he crossed the straits of Gallipoli into Asia Minor. There he experienced further treachery, for the Seljuks from Iconium harassed his troops on the march; he had to turn aside to capture Iconium before his route was secure, thus overcoming the obstacle which the Eastern Emperors had failed to surmount. From the Armenians in Cilicia he received a warm welcome, and he was preparing the last stage of his journey when suddenly in the river Salif he came to his death by drowning. Some of the German crusaders went home forthwith, though the majority continued under the command of Barbarossa's son Frederick to Antioch ; but here they were attacked by pestilence, and only a remnant of the splendid army which Barbarossa had led from Ratisbon eventually arrived at Acre.

The second great expedition—led by the kings of England Philip II and France—had not yet arrived. The final conflict of $\frac{\text{and Richard}}{\text{I in Sicily}}$ Henry II with Philip Augustus, followed by Henry's death and Richard's accession, caused a long delay. It was not until July 1190 that Richard and Philip at last made a start. They chose the sea route, Richard sailing from Marseilles, Philip from Genoa, and met at Messina in Sicily. Here there was another six months' delay, in which seeds of discord were sown which were to have a fatal effect on the Crusade. First of all, Richard repudiated his French bride and was betrothed to Berengaria of Navarre ; secondly, the friendliness with king Tancred was a natural source of offence to the Germans, since Henry VI claimed the throne of Sicily ; and finally, even this friendship was broken when Richard claimed from Tancred the dowry of his sister Joan, William II's widow. He even hoisted his banner over Messina, and it was with difficulty that Philip brought about peace. At last, in March 1191, the expedition set sail again, but while Philip went direct to Acre, Richard turned aside to Cyprus to rescue his fiancée Berengaria, whose vessel had been driven ashore in a storm. He stayed to conquer the island from Isaac Comnenus, and it was not until June that he reached Acre.

With the arrival of Richard the concentration of the The crusaders was completed. They had been assembling for $\frac{\text{concentra-}}{\text{tion at Acre}}$ two years at Acre, and the whole of that time had been spent on the siege of the city. The king of Jerusalem, Guy of Lusignan, had been released from captivity in 1188, and had managed to collect a sufficient force to commence the siege in June 1189. The Scandinavian fleet, which on its way round Spain had rendered valuable assistance to the Portuguese against the Moslems, arrived in September, accompanied

17

by English and Flemish ships with archbishop Baldwin of Canterbury on board. Then, after various smaller detachments from Italy and elsewhere, the remnant of the German expedition under Frederick of Suabia arrived in September 1190, Philip II of France came in April 1191, and finally Richard in June. Acre was certainly a key point, the chief port in the former kingdom of Jerusalem. But it was typical of the crusading movement that so much effort should have been expended for so long with so little result. There was, as usual, no unity of command ; the various contingents acted for the most part independently. Besides this, the old internal discords had revived, and when Guy's wife Sibylla died childless in 1190, the " native " party set up a rival to Guy in Conrad of Montferrat, who married Sibylla's sister Isabella. Saladin had come to the rescue of the beleaguered city, and though not able to relieve it managed to supply it with provisions and even to invest the besiegers. But by 1191 the condition of the city's garrison was becoming desperate, and the arrival of Richard decided its fate. The first success of the Third Crusade was won with the fall of Acre on July 12, 1191.

Friction
among the
crusaders

Richard brought a great asset to the crusade. His fame as a soldier made him the natural leader, and provided a certain unity of command. But the European enmities that had been temporarily laid aside were quickly resumed when the various nations met at Acre. Richard and Philip were constantly antagonistic, and Philip, whose heart was not in the crusade and who was mortified by the recognition of Richard as the natural leader of the Christian army, re-embarked for France after the capture of Acre ; he left most of the French troops behind him, but their leaders were instructed not to act under the orders of Richard. The Germans, too, were naturally hostile to the king of England, the ally of the Welfs against the Hohenstaufen. Richard was thus unfavourably placed, and his domineering and headstrong nature created further enmities of a personal nature. Thus he made a bitter foe of duke Leopold of Austria by tearing down his banner from one of the towers of Acre and replacing it with his own. When he supported the claims of Guy of Lusignan to the kingdom of Jerusalem, the Germans and French gave their support to Conrad of Montferrat, and

Richard had to yield; he indemnified Guy by selling him the island of Cyprus, which was made into a kingdom. Conrad was actually murdered on the day of his coronation, and Henry of Champagne succeeded him both as king of Jerusalem and husband of Isabella; as he was the nephew both of Philip and Richard, his election gave rise to no further friction. But still Richard could not count on the co-operation of the French and German contingents, and there were other old rivalries to hinder united action; thus the Genoese and Pisans, once restored to their former position in Acre, were soon at deadly enmity as before.

With all his faults and in face of all his difficulties, Richard certainly proved himself to be a great soldier. In the autumn of 1191 he captured Caesarea, defeated Saladin at Arsuf, took Jaffa, and came within twelve miles of Jerusalem. The campaign was then interrupted by the dissensions over the kingship of Jerusalem, which were not ended until April 1192. Hostilities were resumed in the summer; Saladin was driven off from Jaffa in August, and once again the crusaders were within easy reach of Jerusalem. A bold stroke, such as was to be expected from Richard, might have won the city, but his health had broken down, and as the French refused to co-operate timid counsels were allowed to prevail. Richard made a truce with Saladin in September, by which the Christians obtained access to the Holy Places and were confirmed in their possession of the coast line from Ascalon to Acre. He was a sick man and had lost his zest for the crusade, and he straightway embarked on the disastrous voyage in which he was to be driven onto the northern coast of the Adriatic, and as a result to fall into the hands of his enemy Leopold of Austria and to pass a year in captivity in Germany. It was a disastrous end to a thrilling story, for the period of his leadership is the most romantic in the history of the Crusades, owing to the glamour of his prowess and the fame of his great antagonist. The contest between Christianity and Islam seems no longer a Holy War but rather a duel between two champions, a duel of chivalry, determined and bloody, but engaged in without hatred, indeed with mutual respect and admiration. So Richard could set the precedent of negotiating with the infidel, and even bestow the honour of knighthood on Saladin's nephew when he came as ambassador.

Exploits of Richard I

His departure

Death of Saladin

It was in the fitness of things that they should disappear from the scene at the same time; Saladin died a few months after Richard's departure. Here was a chance for the Christians, as there was immediate division of his territories, his brother seizing Egypt and his numerous sons contesting Syria between them. But the great expedition was over, ruined by the enmities in the Christian camp, and the forces that remained were neither united nor powerful enough to make use of the opportunity. Moreover the native lords were content with their possessions and not anxious for a resumption of hostilities.

The expedition of Henry VI

However, the Third Crusade was not at an end, for the new Emperor, Henry VI, saw in it an opportunity for his ambition. Having at last secured himself in possession of Sicily, he was free to turn to wider schemes. In March 1195 he took the cross, and during the next year made careful preparations for the equipment of a German expedition. The start was delayed by revolt in his Sicilian kingdom, and it was not until September 1197 that the main German army, led by archbishop Conrad of Mayence, set sail for the East. On the way, the archbishop crowned Amaury of Lusignan (brother and successor of Guy) as king of Cyprus,[1] and Leo II as king of Cilicia; thus they recognised the Western Emperor as the source of their authority. Henry himself was intending to follow shortly, though it is possible that he was meditating first an attack upon Constantinople. His diplomacy was certainly aimed at the Eastern throne. He had obtained the hand of Irene, Isaac Angelus's daughter, for his brother, Philip of Suabia. In 1195 Isaac was deposed and blinded by his brother, who assumed the throne as Alexius III, and Henry had an excuse for intervention against the usurper. But his sudden death, shortly after the German crusaders had departed, brought all these schemes to an end. In the few months before the news reached Palestine, the Germans had obtained some successes, especially the capture of Beyrout, which linked up the kingdom of Jerusalem

---

[1] In the same year, 1197, Henry of Champagne died and Amaury (II) became king of Jerusalem as well as of Cyprus. He in his turn also married Isabella. It is noticeable that the barons, who by their election decide upon the king, seem to feel the necessity of a hereditary sanction as well. When the direct male line failed, this is provided by marrying the kings to the daughters of Amaury I, Sibylla and Isabella.

again with the county of Tripolis. But when they learnt of
Henry's death they made a truce with the Sultan of Egypt,
Saladin's brother, who was anxious for peace in order to win
Syria from his nephews, and then immediately returned home.
The only abiding result of the expedition was the founding of
a new Military Order—the Teutonic Knights—which was soon
to be transferred to north-eastern Germany, to carry on there
much more effectively the work of conquering the unbeliever
and advancing the imperial frontiers.

With the departure of the Germans the Third Crusade *Character
reached its conclusion. It had been hampered by grave *and results
misfortunes—the death of one Emperor at the beginning *Crusade*
and of another at the end had ruined what seemed on each
occasion a splendid prospect ; but it was the enmities among
the crusaders themselves that wrecked the glorious promise
of the middle period. And so, for all the enthusiasm in its
inception and for all the man-power expended by so many
kingdoms, there was very little to show. Two of the Latin
States, Antioch and Tripolis (the prince of Antioch was soon
to be master of them both), remained intact. The kingdom
of Jerusalem was in part recovered, but, lacking Jerusalem,
it was only a shadow of its former self. Yet, if religious zeal
had been disappointed of its objective, the trading interests
were satisfied. The ports had been recovered, and in them
the Venetians, the Genoese, and the Pisans had settled again
in their quarters and reopened their warehouses. They were
the real gainers from the Crusade, and with the kingdom
restricted to the coastal area their importance was enhanced
and their influence increased. Peace was more to them
than Jerusalem, and so it was to the " native " lords, who
were satisfied with their possessions and disliked the disturbance of the peace caused by the crusade of Henry VI.
The religious purpose—the impulse which had called the
Crusade into being—was already becoming secondary to
material interests ; in other respects, too, it can be seen to
be waning. There was little of the crusader in Henry VI,
less still in Philip Augustus ; indeed it would have been
better for the success of the expedition if he had never participated in it. Even in Richard the change is manifest.
Though, as a good general, he never lost sight of the objective,
yet his ardour is rather for the adventure, the delight of

matching his sword and his wits against a worthy antagonist.
It was not the hated infidel, the enemy of the Cross, that he
was fighting, but a fellow knight; and he was not alone in
this novel conception of the enemy. That the tolerance
thereby engendered tended to a freedom of thought dangerous
to Christianity is not unlikely; but on the whole the mental
attitude of the Westerners was little affected. They could
only appreciate the qualities of the Moslems by making them
like to themselves; they could not appreciate what was
unlike themselves, and therefore failed to gain a knowledge
that might have broadened their whole outlook.

Effects of the crusading movement The crusading movement had been in progress for just a
century, and during that time very large numbers of West-
erners had come into contact with Eastern civilisation. It
might be expected, and it has often been assumed, that the
effect of this on the West must have been considerable. But
it is difficult to find evidence to justify the assumption.
Western civilisation was little altered; it continued to profit
by contact with Constantinople, but what it got of culture
and learning from the Moslems came to it mainly from
Spain. The Crusades did have a profound effect on the
West, but it was rather by accelerating developments already
in progress than by introducing novelties. Firstly, there
was the enhancement of the papal power. The papal headship of the Church was already becoming a reality; but the
fuller recognition of it, the stabilisation, as it were, of the
papal position was due to the part played by Urban II and
his successors as the natural leaders of Western Christendom
in the Holy War, which they proclaimed and inspired.
Secondly, the intensification of the feeling against the Eastern
Empire; what had been a passive dislike before was converted into a violent hatred, which was soon to find expression
in action.

In the economic and social spheres the same thing is true.
Genoa, Pisa, and Venice did not owe their wealth and importance to the Crusades, but they became wealthier and more
important because of them. They had already been supplying the West with the spices and other luxuries of the East,
but they were now able to do so on a larger scale. There
was also a larger demand, partly because so many people
had acquired the taste for them while on crusade, but partly

also because the increase of material prosperity in the West created more purchasing power. We have seen that towns could afford to pay for charters from kings and nobles, and could meet heavy subsidies imposed upon them. It was not always, or even usually the desire to go on crusade that created the need for money in their lords. War was the favourite occupation of the upper classes, and a crusade was only the most expensive of these wars because of the lengthy journey to be undertaken. The crusades, too, were much more costly in human lives than were wars in Europe ; while the fact that so many remained as settlers further diminished the numbers of those that returned home. This, it has been inferred, must have made things easier in Europe by reducing the competition for territory, and especially must have alleviated the task of the rulers by ridding them of so many turbulent vassals. But again it is difficult to find much evidence for this. The Norman duke was in a much happier position in South Italy when Bohemond and Tancred had established themselves in Antioch ; William II and Henry I of England in turn profited by the absence of their brother Robert on crusade. The counts of Toulouse, as we have seen, allowed their crusading zeal to interrupt the process of consolidation of their fiefs, to the great advantage of the duke of Aquitaine and ultimately of the kings of England and France. But no social changes can be attributed to the crusades of the magnitude of that which took place in Germany, especially in the civil wars of the eleventh and twelfth centuries, when noble houses died out, and men rose, as it were, from the ranks (sometimes from servile status) to found new houses to replace the old.

It is impossible, therefore, to be precise in estimating the effects of the first century of the crusading movement ; it cannot be isolated as a distinct episode with particular results of its own ; it was one of many causes, though certainly an important one, tending to produce changes in the life of the West. Probably the most obvious feature of it is the terrible waste, the vast outlay yielding so little return. Against this must be set the value of a high ideal inspiring so many thousands to unselfish ends, and giving a feeling of unity to Western Christendom, which, however temporary, had a permanent effect upon the Church and its government. If

CHAPTER XXIII

GERMANY AND ITALY, 1177–1197

EVER since the acquisition of the Italian crown by Otto I, Italy had engaged a considerable share of the attention of the German kings. After the death of Otto III, however, and until the accession of Frederick Barbarossa, it had played a subordinate part ; the interests of the German kingdom had been the first consideration. In the second half of the twelfth century, there was a complete reversal of imperial policy. Italy became the chief preoccupation of the Emperor, and his conduct of German affairs was guided largely by his trans-Alpine interests. This had been true of the first twenty-five years of Frederick's reign, when he had concentrated all his efforts and used all the resources of Germany with the object of recovering authority in Lombardy and obtaining mastery over the Pope. And, in spite of his failure to achieve these ends, it was equally true of the last years of his reign, and still more so of the reign of his son Henry VI. But after the Treaty of Venice in 1177 there were six years at any rate when the centre of interest shifted to Germany, fateful years which saw the downfall of Henry the Lion and momentous changes in the map of Germany.

1177-83 German affairs divert the Emperor's attention from Italy

Henry the Lion was almost sovereign ruler in the north, and as he pushed German colonisation eastward the range of his authority extended. He had vision beyond that of his fellow-countrymen, and the dominion he achieved in the Baltic prepared the way for the future greatness of the Hanseatic League. Lübeck owed to him its commercial importance, and for it he obtained special privileges in Scandinavian markets ; he made the sea safe by ridding it of Wendish pirates ; and he took advantage of disputes for the throne of Denmark to obtain a quasi-protectorate over its king. But he had numerous enemies, and it was the backing

Breach with Henry the Lion

of the Emperor, not his own strength alone, that had made them impotent against him. He had become blinded by the sense of his own power, until in 1176, as has been said, he felt himself able to stand alone, and dared to refuse the help the Emperor so urgently needed in Italy. It might have been expected that Frederick's first impulse on his return would have been to take direct action against his disobedient vassal, but the Emperor was wise enough to let opportunity come to him rather than to strive to create it. Before Frederick returned, indeed, Henry the Lion's enemies were already in arms against him : in East Saxony Bernard of Anhalt, the younger son of Albert the Bear, inflicted a defeat upon him, and in Westphalia the archbishop of Cologne and the bishop of Halberstadt organised a powerful coalition. The Emperor, again in Germany in October 1178, took measures to restore peace, enforcing it on Henry as well as on his enemies. He had withdrawn his support from Henry, and for the first time the charges against Henry were allowed

Feudal process against him a hearing. There followed the normal procedure of customary and feudal law. Henry, since the original home of the Welfs was in Suabia, was summoned to answer before a court of Suabian nobles at Worms on January 13, 1179. He disdained to appear, and a second and a third summons were equally fruitless. He now had to answer to his sovereign for contumacy, and the ban was pronounced against him. Finally, when a year and a day had elapsed since the first summons, on January 13, 1180 a diet at Würzburg sentenced him to the loss of his duchy and all his northern fiefs.

Partition of Saxony and Bavaria Effect was given to this sentence three months later at Gelnhausen, when the duchy of Saxony was partitioned. Westphalia was made into a separate duchy and bestowed upon the archbishop of Cologne ; and the title of duke of Saxony was conferred upon Bernard of Anhalt. On June 24, a year and a day after the second summons, sentence of complete outlawry was proclaimed, and the duchy of Bavaria declared forfeit. Three months later it too was partitioned. Styria was made into a separate duchy under its former margrave Ottocar, and the remainder of Bavaria was bestowed, with the title of duke, upon Otto of Wittelsbach, so long the leading lay counsellor of the Emperor. Thus for a year and a half the slow customary process was followed out to its ultimate conclusion. Henry did not submit without a struggle. Indeed for some time he seemed to be gaining the upper hand over his enemies, until at last in July 1181 the Emperor himself took the field to enforce the final judgment. His intervention was effective, and Henry found himself deserted by most of his vassals. Moreover he had counted on aid from his father-in-law, Henry II of England, who failed to supply it, and also from king Waldemar of Denmark, who seized the chance to escape from his dependence and sided with the Emperor against him. Only the burghers of Lübeck remained staunch, until the co-operation of the Danish fleet with Frederick forced their surrender. So Henry had to yield. He was left in possession of much of the allodial [1] territory which had come to the Welfs by inheritance from the Billung, Nordheim, and Brunswick families, especially the towns of Lüneburg and Brunswick. But he was banished from Germany for three years, and in the summer of 1182 he went into exile in England.

As a result of his downfall the map of Germany was radic- *Changes in the map of Germany* ally altered, especially in the north. The old duchy of Saxony virtually disappeared, and in its place a congeries of small States came into being. Westphalia was a separate duchy, and over the remainder Bernard's title of duke was almost meaningless. The great ecclesiastics, especially the archbishops of Bremen and Magdeburg, controlled extensive territories, and the ecclesiastical fiefs of which Henry the Lion had obtained possession were restored to the bishops ; the new duke had no control over the allodial lands of the Welfs, and farther north the count of Holstein [2] regained the position his father had formerly held ; there was also the rich imperial domain in eastern Saxony. In the Baltic, Lübeck, restored at first to Holstein but subsequently a free city under imperial charter, renewed its prosperity ; while the king of Denmark, at last able to renounce German suzerainty, gained a footing in Holstein and Mecklenburg. Bernard's authority, therefore, was mainly confined to his own small possessions in the south-eastern corner of the old duchy, and a small area north of the Welf domains round the fortress he built at Lauenburg. These two portions

---

[1] i.e., lands held in full possession and not as fiefs from a feudal overlord.
[2] Adolf, who had succeeded his father Adolf in 1162.

were separated in the thirteenth century, and the name of duchy of Saxony came to be applied only to the former. This little State was to expand in later centuries into the kingdom of Saxony, just as the Welf domains were to expand into the kingdom of Hanover. To the fall of Henry the Lion was due the great transformation which completely altered the position of Saxony in the map of Germany. Compared with this the change in Bavaria was of small significance. Yet there had been a radical change since the old days when Bavaria, second in importance to Saxony, had acted as the bulwark of Germany against the Magyars. Three duchies—Carinthia, Austria, and Styria—had been carved out of it, and it was now cut off from all contact with Hungary. Though truncated, it was still second in importance of the German duchies, but the pride of place had now passed to Suabia.

Constitutional changes

These great alterations in the map of Germany mirror the sweeping changes that were taking place in the constitution of the body politic. The old tribal duchies had disappeared with the break-up of the largest and the most exclusive of them all. There were more numerous duchies, but, except for Suabia, they were not comparable with the former ones in size, in importance, or in cohesion. The title of duke had not the same significance as before, and other powers had arisen, of lesser rank but equal authority, such as the landgrave of Thuringia (now freed from its semi-dependence on Saxony) and the margrave of Brandenburg; Otto of Brandenburg, elder brother of the new duke of Saxony, was able to expand rapidly towards the Weser now that the formidable rivalry of Henry the Lion was removed. By this distribution of authority among a number of lesser, instead of a few greater, princes, the monarchy was rid of the chief menace to its power and thereby was in a position of much greater security. Frederick, with his family duchy of Suabia intact, the royal domains elsewhere at his disposal, and his authority over the Church unimpaired, seemed so much to overtop his greatest subjects that only a general coalition against him, of which there was not the least likelihood, could give him cause for uneasiness. Had he been of like mind with his contemporaries, Roger of Sicily and Henry II of England, he would have seized the opportunity to consolidate his authority, and by creating a proper system of central administration to place the monarchy on a firm basis of permanent stability.

But Frederick was not a statesman, and all his instincts were conservative ; as his imperial aim in Italy had really been only the restoration of the old order, so its maintenance was his sole consideration in Germany. He could not see beyond customary and feudal law, though he did something to develop the latter. For Germany was not as yet feudalised to the extent that France had been already for two centuries. In France the great nobles held as tenants-in-chief from the king ; and when, at the beginning of the thirteenth century, the greatest of them, the king of England, was adjudged a traitor to his overlord, his French territories escheated to the king of France, who was immensely enriched by the overthrow of his over-mighty vassal. Very different was it in Germany, where dukes and counts were still nominally royal officials, and did homage to the king for the offices they held, as his subjects not his tenants. When Henry the Lion was adjudged a traitor, his offices were declared forfeit and apportioned among his enemies ; his family retained the allodial lands, for which they owed no service to the king. Frederick got none of the spoil himself ; only indirectly, by the disappearance of his over-mighty vassal, was he the gainer. Yet all the time a change was coming about, which might have made all the difference if it had already been completed. He was introducing feudal conditions by which the greater nobles held directly from him, while the lesser nobility remained as their subordinates. Only the greater nobles now ranked as " princes of Germany " ; to them alone belonged the task of electing the king, and there was a grading in their ranks too. So also with the ecclesiastical nobility, who all held directly from the king, though the customary rights of the three Rhenish archbishops gave them priority. The process of narrowing down the number of electors to a chosen few had already begun ; they were jealous of their privileges, and, though they followed custom in electing Henry VI in his father's lifetime, they would not countenance Frederick's ambition to institute hereditary succession.

These changes were the result of a gradual process. During the civil wars, which had agitated Germany for nearly a century before the accession of Frederick Barbarossa, the

The growth
of particu-
larism
in the
German
kingdom
kings had more and more been forced to depend on the goodwill of the nobles, and to make concessions to them in order
to win their co-operation, especially their military support.
This meant the recognition of their particularist aspirations,
the grants to them of sovereign rights in their dominions,
including authority over the lesser nobility and also hereditary
succession ; dukes as well as counts could pass on their titles
and lands to their sons. The idea of official status grew
fainter as the idea of feudal status, involving military obligations to the king, became more pronounced. In Frederick's
case it was his obsession with Italy which caused him to
favour this process. He wished both to leave a peaceful and
contented Germany, and also to obtain military contingents
for his Italian expeditions. To these ends he was willing to
make large concessions (the first instance of which was at the
creation of the new duchy of Austria) and to give away
sovereign rights with a lavish hand—jurisdiction, exemptions,
tolls, mints, and the like ; thus it was only in the royal
domains and the royal towns that his own coinage remained
current. He went even farther than that to ensure goodwill, for he was content with the limited military service that
became customary in a feudal régime. For longer service it
was necessary to provide pay, involving an additional strain
on the royal resources. The claims of the Italian kingdom
thus reduced the efficacy of monarchy in Germany. Particularism, which might seem to have suffered a set-back
with the downfall of Henry the Lion, was in fact becoming a
definite feature of the German system, which was beginning
to have the appearance of a federated rather than a unitary
State. At present this was disguised owing to the personality
of the ruler and the great family possessions of the Hohenstaufen. When the one was lost and the other dissipated, the
truth was revealed. In the thirteenth century the selfish
interests of particularism were able to obtain the upper hand,
and Frederick II, even more than his father and grandfather,
was content that this should happen.

The position
of the
Papacy
Affairs in Germany having been settled to his satisfaction,
Frederick could turn his attention again to his Italian kingdom. During these years a complete transformation had
taken place in Italian politics. The anti-imperial confeder-

ation had dissolved. The king of Sicily was at peace with the Emperor and was prepared for even closer relations. The Lombards were estranged from the Pope, whom they regarded as having broken faith with them when he made a separate peace with the Emperor. The Papacy was therefore isolated, and rendered the more insecure by renewed discord with the Romans. Alexander III, soon after his triumph at the Third Lateran Council, had to leave the city, and he died at Città Castellana in 1181. His successor, Lucius III, was also unable to maintain himself in Rome; both he and Urban III lived almost continuously at Verona. The Papacy was in financial difficulties, too, for the long struggle, during which it had often been deprived of its normal revenues, had taxed its resources to the utmost. Alexander III had frequently been forced to borrow, and complained bitterly of the usury of some of his creditors. So, though the Papacy had emerged triumphant from its contest with the Emperor, it was now in a position of considerable embarrassment. Impoverished, exiled from Rome, and without allies, it had to adopt a cautious policy. The Curia as a whole was united in this course, and the cardinals, having the control of papal elections, had the means to carry it into practice. They determined to wait upon events. The Popes they elected were all old men, so that their reigns were bound to be short [1]; the cardinals could reckon that if opportunity arose they would soon have the chance to make use of it. They could not bind the Pope during his lifetime, but if his views were too pronounced for their liking they could soon redress the balance. Thus Alexander's successor Lucius III proved to be too complaisant to the Emperor. On his death in 1185 they chose the anti-imperial Urban III, who, however, went too far in the opposite direction. So in 1187 the peace-loving Gregory VIII was elected, and, as he only survived two months, Clement III, also pro-imperial, succeeded him. He was followed in 1191 by Celestine III, who showed great resource in resisting, so far as he was able, the autocratic policy of Henry VI. The oldest of all these Popes, his reign was the longest, and he was ninety-two years of age when he died in January 1198.

The policy of the papal Curia

[1] There were five Popes in the seventeen years between the death of Alexander III and the accession of Innocent III.

Frederick
and the
Lombard
cities

    This then was the political situation of which Frederick
Barbarossa was to take advantage to win the most striking
success of his reign.   It would not have been achieved, however, but for a complete reversal of his policy.   He had
previously tried to gain his ends by force, and had failed ;
he now adopted the method of diplomacy, cultivating the
friendship of his former enemies, and founding his authority
in the Italian kingdom on a basis of consent as in Germany.
During his last campaign he had tried to separate his enemies,
and this at last he did achieve in the treaty of Venice ; each
of them was now seeking his friendship, and he made his
terms with them one by one.   First of all the Lombards.
The truce with them was running out, and both sides wanted
a definitive peace, which was arranged to mutual satisfaction

The treaty
of Constance
(1183)

at Constance in June 1183.   The cities were left in possession
of the regalia, and allowed to elect their own magistrates
(consuls or podestàs) and even to raise taxes themselves.
Thus they got the complete self-government for which they
had fought.   On the other hand, the Emperor's sovereignty
was admitted ; the magistrates took an oath of fealty to him
on behalf of their city, and he or his representative conferred
the regalia by investiture.   So his overlordship was restored
and a semi-feudal régime reintroduced.   To celebrate the
happy state of affairs in both his kingdoms Frederick held a
great festival at Mayence in the summer of 1184, long celebrated in German song and legend, at which his son Henry,
already elected king in 1169 and now nineteen years of age,
was dubbed knight and associated with his father in the
government.   When Frederick went to Italy in the following
September, he left Henry as regent in Germany.

Frederick's
new Italian
policy

    The treaty of Constance was the beginning of Frederick's
new policy in Italy.   To the terms he had made he intended
faithfully to adhere, but he had done more than merely to
sever the Lombard connexion with the Papacy.   The Lombard cities having no longer cause for acting in common
broke up again into their old factions, and these Frederick
encouraged in his own interests.   But this time he threw his
weight on to the stronger side and gave his favour to Milan
and its adherents, so that he turned his most dangerous
enemy into his best friend.   Thus, on the same principle as
previously in Germany, he ruled by co-operating with his

leading vassal, and in return he was able to piece together
the royal lands and build up a powerful imperial domain
from Savoy eastwards. In Central Italy, to which the provisions of the treaty of Constance did not apply, he could
continue the feudal régime. There too the imperial domain
was consolidated ; but it was the feudal powers that were
favoured there, and he was able to institute a system of direct
rule. The key to the situation was the territory of countess
Matilda ; to maintain his hold on this was all-important.
In this he was risking another encounter with the Papacy, His relations
and it was not the only cause of disagreement between them. with the
Papacy
The general issue of royal control over the Church in Germany
was raised by a disputed election at Trèves in 1183 ; the
Emperor claimed the right of decision, by virtue of the
Worms Concordat, and the disappointed candidate, Folmar,
appealed to the Pope. In September 1184 Frederick came
to Italy to negotiate with the Pope in person at Verona. On
minor points he was prepared to be extremely conciliatory,
promising his help against heretics and at the Pope's inter-
cession granting leave to Henry the Lion to return from
exile. The Pope, for his part, was inclined to yield in the
matter of the Trèves archbishopric, though he refused all
the compromises which Frederick proposed with regard
to Matilda's inheritance. Frederick raised another equally
delicate question when he requested that his son might be
crowned co-Emperor, as had been done by previous Popes
for Louis the Pious and Otto I. Lucius was willing enough
to satisfy the Emperor, but in view of the obvious hostility
of the cardinals to the proposal he could do no more than
temporise. So, though the discussion was friendly, on none
of the major issues had any decision been reached when
Frederick left Verona.

Having established cordial relations with the Lombards, Marriage
and discussed amicably with the Pope the points at issue alliance
with the
between them, the Emperor then turned to the third of his Norman king
former enemies—the king of Sicily. William II was of quite
different mould from his predecessors. Though famous for
his exploits against the Eastern Emperor and the Seljuk
Turks, he did all his fighting by deputy and took part in no
campaign himself. His easy-going disposition endeared him
to his subjects, who named him " William the Good," and his

reign was undisturbed by civil war. He had continued his father's policy of supporting Alexander III (though mainly by subsidies) against Frederick Barbarossa, but his envoys had played a considerable part in the conclusion of peace at Venice. He had no inclination to continue his support of the Papacy. His mind was set on revenge against the Eastern Emperor ; for this he wanted the alliance of the Western Emperor and welcomed his overtures, which was a complete reversal of Norman policy. A month after Frederick's conference with the Pope, in October 1184, the betrothal was announced of Frederick's son Henry with Constance, the aunt of the king of Sicily. In January 1186 the marriage was solemnised at Milan, and as it was at the special request of the Milanese themselves that their city was chosen, it can be seen how successful Frederick's diplomacy had been in the north of Italy. Constance was next in succession to the Sicilian throne, and at the time of her marriage was publicly recognised by William II as his heir. The daughter of Roger II, though born after his death, she was actually a year younger than her nephew. But her prospects of succession were not bright ; they depended both on her outliving William and on William dying without issue. William indeed had been married for over six years and was still childless. But his wife Joan, daughter of Henry II of England, was a child at the time of her marriage, and was barely nineteen when Constance's betrothal was announced ; William himself was only thirty-one. However, the unlikely happened, and so the marriage was to prove of the first importance since it united the imperial and the Sicilian crowns. At the time it was only the alliance of the Empire with the king of Sicily that was achieved, though this was itself of great moment. It marked the culmination of Frederick's diplomatic success in Italy. It would have been far better for the Empire if his success had stopped short at this point ; the acquisition of Sicily by Henry VI fatally antagonised the Papacy and led to the downfall of the imperial power in Italy.

Hostility
of Pope
Urban III

Pope Lucius III did not visualise these consequences ; in his anxiety to ensure the peace of Italy and placate the Emperor he seems to have welcomed the betrothal. But the cardinals were not of his mind, for when he died in November 1185 they elected Urban III, a Milanese and

archbishop of Milan; and Urban was notorious for the
hatred which he, unlike his fellow-citizens, still cherished
against the Emperor. He could not prevent the marriage,
nor its celebration at Milan, galling though this must have
been. But he made his attitude quite clear on all the issues
that Frederick had negotiated so amicably with Lucius III.
He supported the anti-imperial candidate at Trèves, and
made a special attack on the royal exercise of *spolia* and
regalia during the vacancy of a bishopric. It was obviously
impossible in these circumstances to hope that he would
consent to crown Henry VI as co-Emperor. But during the
wedding festivities Frederick had crowned his son as king
of Italy, and when he departed for Germany he left him in
charge of the Italian kingdom. Henry was Emperor in all but
name; he was even given the significant title of Caesar. This
association of his son with himself in the government made
for the greater security of Frederick's authority in both kingdoms, since there was always a king in each, and so Frederick's
own absence from either was not attended by the usual risks.

Urban's hostility was not confined to thwarting the aims
of the Emperor. He openly fomented revolts against him
both in Italy and Germany. In Italy they were soon
quelled and Henry VI took his revenge by occupying and
devastating the Papal States, so that Urban was forced to
abandon his aggressive attitude; nor did he have any
further opportunity of resuming the offensive before his
death in October 1187. His intrigues in Germany met with
more success, for under the lead of archbishop Philip of
Cologne a regular coalition was formed against Frederick
in North Germany. This had two aspects, ecclesiastical and
secular. The archbishop championed the papal point of
view by attacking the royal control of the Church, and his
revolt had Urban's blessing; while in his capacity as duke
of Westphalia, he had become a champion of the particularist
views of the nobles, which won him the adhesion of the
landgrave of Thuringia and count Adolf of Holstein. He
anticipated that the king of Denmark would join him, and
he looked for aid also from England,[1] the ally of the Welfs,

Intrigues in Germany

___

[1] He had obtained personal contact with England on a recent mission
as imperial envoy. Moreover, he recognised the importance of commercial
prosperity, and friendship with England was essential to the trading interests
of Cologne.

though Henry the Lion, now back in Brunswick, remained quiescent. But the return of the Emperor to Germany in 1186 was sufficient to put an end to all these schemes, and without recourse to arms. Frederick summoned a diet, at which he was assured of the support of the German Church against papal interference, and of the mass of the nobles against the separatist ambitions of a few. To avert danger from England he made an alliance with the king of France. When Urban III died, the archbishop of Cologne was practically isolated ; threatened with the imperial ban he hastened

Peace restored with the Papacy

early in 1188 to tender his submission to the king. So peace was restored in Germany, and simultaneously it was being effected in Italy too, since Urban's successors, Gregory VIII and Clement III, were disposed to friendship with the Emperor. In Gregory's brief Papacy of two months nothing could be done, but Clement, who was not over-scrupulous in his promises, effected a complete reconciliation. He had first of all made his peace with the Romans and restored the Papacy to Rome, by promising to destroy Tusculum [1] ; and early in 1189 he came to terms with Frederick The two candidates for Trèves were set aside, and the imperial chancellor John became archbishop ; Clement promised the imperial crown to Henry VI [2] ; while Frederick for his part agreed to evacuate the Papal States.

The Third Crusade

There was an additional reason for both sides desiring a peaceful settlement. In October 1187 Jerusalem was captured by Saladin, and immediately the news reached the West plans for a crusade were set in hand. Gregory VIII began, and Clement III continued, the task of organisation, for which the co-operation of the leading sovereigns of Europe was essential, particularly that of the Emperor. Frederick needed no persuading. It seemed to him natural that he should lead the forces of Western Christendom to rescue the Holy Places from the infidel ; apart from his religious convictions it was his imperial duty and privilege. He could visualise, too, a further extension of his Empire by the establishment of his authority over the Latin States

---

[1] During his lifetime this promise remained unfulfilled.

[2] It was not possible, owing to circumstances, for this promise to be fulfilled in Frederick's lifetime. So the Emperor failed to establish what would have been a most important precedent.

and Cilicia, and an exaltation of the Western as opposed to
the Eastern Empire, against which he had already entered
into friendly negotiations with the Seljuks of Iconium.   So
he began his preparations at once.   He could leave the
government in his son's hands without apprehension, since
Henry was king both of Germany and Italy, and had already
had experience as regent in both kingdoms.   The only danger
to be feared was from the ambition of Henry the Lion, and
he provided for this by obliging him to retire again to England
for another three years.   When the agreement with Clement
III had been completed, Frederick was ready to start.   In Death of
May 1189 the expedition set forth from Ratisbon.   Frederick Frederick
left Germany never to return ; in June 1190 he was drowned Barbarossa
in Cilicia.

Henry's reign may be said to begin with the departure Henry VI
of Frederick from Germany, for from that date he was sole
ruler.   There was no obvious change, as he carried on the
same policy in Germany and in Italy ; his objectives were
the same, as was his high conception of his office.   But, even
superficially, there was a marked contrast between the robust
figure of the father, with his genial appearance and his famous
beard, and the spare figure and pallid and almost beardless
countenance of the son ; and this external contrast mirrored
the essential difference between them.   Frederick had been
trained as a knightly warrior, and though he had proved
himself fully equal to the exalted rank he had attained, he
was instinct with the ideas of contemporary chivalry ; his
personality inspired devotion besides commanding respect.
Henry, born in the purple and educated to be a ruler of men,
was a scholar who was widely admired for his learning, and
a statesman rather than a warrior ; his qualities were not
knightly but intellectual, and of the purely cold and unhuman
type that wins respect and fear but not affection.   He was
as unattractive as his predecessor Henry V, whom he much
resembled ; and as unchivalrous a figure as Philip Augustus,
like whom he subordinated all human feelings to the supreme
purpose of exalting the monarchy.   Calculating in all his
actions, he dealt with men as a chess master with his pieces ;
in the excessive cruelty with which he punished revolt in
Sicily there was not even the excuse of passion.

**Trouble
with Henry
the Lion**

The chief difficulty in Germany lay in the disturbed condition of the north. Since the break up of the old duchy
of Saxony there had been no one man capable of preserving
order. Duke Bernard was feeble and lethargic; a contemporary chronicler, Arnold of Lübeck, looking back regretfully to the peace that the strong hand of Henry the Lion
was able to enforce, laments the state of anarchy that followed, when every man did what was right in his own sight,
and force was the only law. Frederick had done nothing to
cure these evils, but he had hoped to make his son's task the
easier by removing the most likely source of disturbance.
However, no sooner had he departed on crusade than Henry
the Lion appeared again. He was able to rally many of
his old vassals round him; in the absence of count Adolf on
crusade he overran Holstein, and he captured duke Bernard's
stronghold of Lauenburg. But when the young king came
in person to deal with the situation, the tide began to turn
against the Welfs, and by the summer of 1190 they were
forced to come to terms. There was the opportunity of a
proper settlement, but the king's mind was elsewhere; he
was impatient to be off to Italy and only anxious to come to
some accommodation. Henry the Lion promised to surrender
the Holstein lands (though he was allowed a share in Lübeck),
to dismantle the walls of Brunswick and destroy the fortifications of Lauenburg. The king hurried off, taking two of
Henry the Lion's sons as hostages, but the conditions remained
unfulfilled; as the king was absent in Italy, Henry the Lion
retained all that he had seized and kept his fortresses intact.

**Death of
William II
of Sicily**

**The reign
of Tancred**

The king's urgency was quite comprehensible. In November 1189 William II of Sicily had died without issue, so
that Constance was the lawful queen. But there was strong
nationalist feeling in the island of Sicily, which would not
have objected to Constance as queen, but did strongly object
to her husband, a foreigner, as king. Its leaders determined
to prevent this by electing a native king, and the choice
finally fell on Tancred, a grandson, though illegitimate, of
Roger II.[1] Capable and cultured, he was a worthy descendant of the great king, though he lacked kingly presence; his
enemies made mock of his ungainly appearance and dwarfish
stature. He won papal support, at any rate; the Papacy

[1] He was the natural son of Roger duke of Apulia, Roger II's eldest son.

had doubtless not anticipated the early death of William II without issue, and even a Pope as friendly to the king of Germany as Clement III had shown himself to be could not but foresee the danger to the Papacy, if the Sicilian crown was united with the German, as well as the loss of its suzerainty. So the old alliance with the Normans was once more resumed. Tancred had a hard struggle to maintain himself. In the island of Sicily the Moslems revolted, and it took him the best part of a year to reduce them to submission. In South Italy, the Norman barons refused to recognise him, and he had to depend on the support of the towns, which he won by grants of privileges ; he did succeed, at any rate, in defeating the German troops that were dispatched against him in the summer of 1190. Then in September he was embarrassed by the arrival of the kings of England and France on their way to participate in the Third Crusade. Richard, the brother-in-law of Henry the Lion, was a natural ally against Henry VI ; but unfortunately for Tancred, he had imprisoned Richard's sister Joan, William II's widow, and retained her jointure. Richard therefore arrived full of fury, and extorted large sums from Tancred before he could be pacified ; there were constant broils between the people of Messina and the English, and this unwelcome visit lasted altogether for six months. It was small compensation to Tancred that he concluded an alliance with Richard against Henry VI, for Richard's help could not be immediately forthcoming, and it was immediately needed.

Hardly was Tancred rid of the crusaders when news came of the arrival in Italy of Henry VI himself. Just as Henry reached Rome occurred the death of Clement III, followed by the election of the aged Celestine III. The new Pope agreed to carry out his predecessor's promise and crown Henry as Emperor, but a condition was made that Tusculum should be surrendered to the mercy of the Romans. This sacrifice of a town that had been faithful to the Empire Henry did not scruple to make ; but it was the Pope that was the gainer, for this tardy fulfilment of Clement's promise secured Celestine's position in Rome. Henry then hastened south, and his advance progressed with great ease until he encountered a stubborn resistance from the town of Naples. The delay was fatal : the heat of summer had its usual effect on

Henry VI's failure to conquer the kingdom

the German army; there were numerous casualties, and
when Henry himself was stricken with illness, he had to
abandon the expedition and return to Germany. He left
German garrisons behind him, some of which were expelled
by Tancred, though he did not live long enough to complete
his task. His success, however, decided the Pope to come
into the open. In June 1192 he invested Tancred with the
kingdom of Sicily, in return for the surrender of the concessions made to William I in the treaty of Benevento. Tancred
had proved himself, against great odds; but his reign was
brief, and his early death two years later was fatal to the
national cause.

Renewed discord in the north of Germany   During these years Henry was fully occupied in Germany.
Disorder and civil war were raging in the north once more.
Adolf of Holstein had returned from crusade at the end of
1190, and with the aid of duke Bernard of Saxony and his
brother Otto of Brandenburg he recovered his territory from
Henry the Lion, and forced Lübeck to submit to his authority
again. For their part the Welfs began to build up a coalition,
which had the support of the king of England and of Tancred
of Sicily. An ecclesiastical crisis brought them additional
allies. It arose out of a disputed election for the bishopric
of Liége, when Henry, like Frederick in the case of Trèves,
asserted his right to appoint. One of the rejected candidates,
Albert, brother of the duke of Brabant, appealed to Rome,
and by papal orders was consecrated bishop by the archbishop of Rheims in September 1192; two months later he
was murdered by German knights. There seemed in this
something analogous to the murder of Becket, and the odium
of the crime fell largely on the king; as a result the nobles
of the lower Rhine, headed by Albert's brother, made common
The capture of Richard I and its consequences   cause with the Welfs. Finally, in February 1193, Richard I
returning from crusade was shipwrecked in the northern
Adriatic and was taken prisoner by his enemy duke Leopold
of Austria, who handed him over to the Emperor. This
outrage on the person of a crusader at first had the effect
of increasing the unpopularity of Henry, and several princes,
including the archbishop of Mayence, joined the coalition
against him. But in such a position Henry was more than
a match for the combination of his opponents; he could
make his moves to ensure checkmate, since he had captured

their chief piece. He was able to work on their and Richard's fears, by threatening to hand him over to Philip Augustus, who was willing to pay highly for the prize. To avoid this, Richard agreed to surrender his kingdom and receive it back as a fief from the Emperor ; to abandon Tancred ; and to pay an enormous ransom, which provided Henry with the means of financing his forthcoming expedition into Italy. Through Richard's mediation, too, the Welfs were reconciled with the Emperor, and Henry the Lion's eldest son, Henry, married Agnes daughter of Frederick Barbarossa's brother Conrad, count palatine of the Rhine. So the Welf coalition was dissolved. Henry the Lion was no longer a source of danger. He spent the last year of his life peacefully at Brunswick as a patron of art and letters ; in August 1195 he died.

The trouble in the north was over, but again Henry took no steps to establish an orderly régime, for once more he was in a hurry to be off to Italy. In the same month that Richard was released from captivity (February 1194), king Tancred of Sicily died. He left a young son, William III, under the guardianship of his mother Sibylla, but Tancred's ablest councillor, his chancellor Matthew of Ajello, who had largely engineered his elevation to the throne, was also dead, and Sibylla had no one on whom to depend. In these circumstances Henry had an easy task : his right-hand man, Markward of Anweiler, by skilful diplomacy persuaded those old enemies, Pisa and Genoa, to co-operate in the expedition ; the German princes willingly lent their aid ; and on Christmas Day 1194 Henry was crowned king of Sicily at Palermo. On the following day, at Jesi in the march of Ancona, Constance gave birth to a son, who was named after his two grandfathers Frederick Roger. Henry had now overcome all his difficulties. With diplomatic tact he had reconciled his new subjects to him by the leniency he displayed in victory ; but when a sudden revolt broke out he showed that he must be feared as well. Sibylla and all her family were sent off into exile in Germany, and disappear from history. Henry's path was clear.

He now began to formulate a plan of government. As far as Germany was concerned, he was content to continue his father's régime, though the recent disturbances must have shown him how unsatisfactory this was ; however, he

Henry achieves the conquest of the Sicilian kingdom

His government of Germany and Italy

had no desire to risk a conflict with German particularism, for his real interest was in Italy. The acquisition of the Sicilian kingdom gave him a field where his autocratic ideas could have full scope, and he began to apply them to the Italian kingdom as a whole. The first stage in this was the partitioning of Italy into provinces ruled over by officials directly dependent on himself, the inauguration of a true system of imperial government. He began with the south and centre. Conrad of Urslingen, who had been duke of Spoleto since 1183, was made vicar of the kingdom of Sicily. Henry's brother Philip was made duke of Tuscany. Markward of Anweiler,[1] who had proved his worth in the recent expedition, was given the title of duke of Ravenna and the government also of the march of Ancona and the Romagna. At present Lombardy was not included in the scheme, though the control of it was essential. There was a change, indeed, but of a less definite character. It was not in Henry's mind to continue the diplomatic friendship which Frederick had so successfully cultivated ; he preferred the iron hand, and the Lombards, divided by their inter-city feuds, were cowed and temporarily in a state of political paralysis, hemmed in on both sides by the imperial power.

Failure of his plans for hereditary succession   Thus Henry's government of his two kingdoms was entirely different. In Germany he was only feudal overlord, in Italy he was developing a truly imperial constitution. His inheritance of Sicily gave him the inspiration and the opportunity ; it inspired in him a further design as well. The Sicilian crown was hereditary. If it was to be permanently attached to the German crown, the latter must be hereditary also, and he did his best to effect this. But it could only be done with the assent of the electors, the princes of Germany, and to induce them to abrogate their rights he had little to offer—to the lay princes unchallenged hereditary succession, even in the collateral line if direct descent failed ; to the ecclesiastical princes the renunciation of his claims to *regalia* and *spolia* during a vacancy. But some of the lay princes (for instance, the duke of Austria) had already

---

[1] Markward was a royal *ministerialis* (cf. above, p. 79), and his career is a notable instance of the reliance placed by German kings on those unfree tenants of their domain, and of the heights to which the *ministeriales* could rise. Markward was now given his freedom and raised to the rank of a prince of the Empire.

obtained the promised concession, and all hoped to acquire it,[1] while it was no concession to the bishops to renounce what the Church regarded as a usurpation. The princes temporised; Henry tried coercion at a diet which he summoned, and extracted a promise from the majority. But some of the more important princes were absent, including the archbishop of Cologne, whose prerogative of crowning the king would become valueless if the crown were hereditary, and who again formed a coalition of Saxon and Rhenish nobles in order to resist the proposal. Henry then adopted an alternative policy to secure the same end. He tried to make the imperial crown hereditary; but this needed the Pope's consent, which Celestine stubbornly refused. So he had to fall back on the traditional policy. He was able at any rate to induce the princes of Germany to elect his infant son Frederick as king. This, it seemed, ensured the union of the two crowns under his son, and for a generation at least the continuance of the dynasty.

But it was a distinct set-back, and it revealed his limit- *Papal* ations. He was dependent on the consent of the princes in *resistance* Germany, and in Italy the Pope, feeble as he was, still had the power to foil him. Celestine III was in one of the most difficult situations that any Pope had had to face. It had naturally been his policy to keep Sicily as a separate kingdom, and while Tancred was alive he had someone to defend him against the Emperor. Now Tancred was dead, and Henry was king of Sicily and dominated all Italy, even the Papal States, which fell mainly in the sphere of government of the low-born Markward; only Rome was inaccessible to the Emperor. But Rome was isolated, and Celestine could look nowhere for help. Yet, old as he was, he never gave in, and his dogged Fabian policy was the greatest impediment to Henry's ambition. The Emperor did not make the mistake of his predecessor Henry V and resort to violence against the Pope. He put forth all his diplomatic skill to win the Pope's favour. In 1195 he took the cross and began

---

[1] In 1191, when the landgrave of Thuringia died without direct heirs, Henry tried to ignore his brother and make an appointment of his own, but was prevented by the general opposition of the princes. In 1195, however, after his successful pacification of the north, he was able, without any protest being raised, to leave vacant the march of Meissen (where again a brother was the next heir) beyond the traditional period of a year and a day.

preparations in Germany for a crusade. The Pope had to yield to this, though reluctantly, and order a crusade to be preached in Germany. But this enforced co-operation did not last long. When in 1196 Henry made his proposals for the hereditary succession of the Empire, Celestine would not entertain the proposal, in spite of all that Henry offered in return.[1] This was not mere obstinacy ; it was sound political sense, for, if Henry had obtained his end, the independence of the Papacy would have been in jeopardy.

Henry, therefore, had to abandon all hope of accommodation with the Pope. He did not, however, abandon the idea of a crusade, for he had not entertained it merely as a diplomatic move to win papal favour. To him, as to his father, the leadership of a crusade was an imperial function ; and furthermore it was part of the grandiose conception of Empire which he had formed in his mind. Already in the West he was more truly an Emperor than any of his predecessors since Charlemagne. The king of England, next to himself the greatest of Western rulers, was his vassal, and as such could be encouraged in his conflict with the former ally of the Hohenstaufen, the king of France. The foundation of an imperial organisation had been laid in the kingdom of Italy, and Sicily already was not unaccustomed to an autocratic régime. But he was not content with a Western Empire. Heir to the Norman kings, he had inherited a Mediterranean outlook and ambition extending to the further shores of the Mediterranean. It was not with him, as it had been with Robert Guiscard and his successors, merely the lust for conquest or for revenge. He visualised a Mediterranean Empire such as Rome had once dominated. Syria, Palestine, and Egypt were to be part of this, but a still more important part was Constantinople. He was working his way towards this by diplomatic means. His brother Philip was married to Irene, daughter of the Emperor Isaac Angelus. In 1195 Isaac was deposed by his brother Alexius III and there was a pretext for intervention ; Isaac to gain Henry's support had recognised Philip and Irene as his heirs. Doubtless, had he lived, Henry would have anticipated the Fourth Crusade.

Henry's eastern schemes

---

[1] According to Innocent III, Henry even offered to hold the Empire as a fief from the Pope.

In 1196, then, he directed all his energies to the prepara- The organisation tion of a great expedition to the East, in which the first of a crusade objective was to be Palestine.   He was delayed by nationalist revolts in Sicily, the most serious of which, in February 1197, was engineered with the cognisance of the Pope and, it was said, even of Constance herself.   It was suppressed with a pitiless ferocity exceeding that of the original Norman con- querors, and Henry's cold-blooded cruelty was extended to those who had been political prisoners since 1194.   He was then free to resume his undertaking, and early in September 1197 a great expedition set sail for the Holy Land.   He did Sudden not accompany it, but was intending to follow very shortly, death of when suddenly he fell ill.   The Italian climate claimed its (1197) greatest victim, and was responsible for a catastrophe such as the Empire since its re-foundation by Otto I had never experienced.   There was not only an end to all the schemes that Henry had been planning ; the solid edifice that he had actually raised was blown sky-high when on September 28, 1197 he died.

SUGGESTIONS FOR READING ON CHAPTER XXIII

See books suggested on Chapter XX above.

EPILOGUE

THE period with which this volume is concerned opens
with the gradual recovery of Western Christendom
after a century of collapse and disaster. It closes
with an event that resembles the " catastrophe " in a Greek
tragedy, producing not general disaster but a complete
reversal of fortunes. And it was followed by other " catas-
trophes "—in France, at Constantinople, in Spain—which
produced their reversals of fortune too, so that a new Europe
came into being in the thirteenth century, politically quite
unlike the Europe of the twelfth century. The major part
of the change occurred within the space of three years, and
was brought about by the deaths of two men ; it would be
difficult to find a parallel in history for a change of this
magnitude arising from such comparatively trivial causes.

The death of Henry VI marks the end of an epoch. All
the elements that he had bottled up so successfully were
released by his death ; by their explosive force they shattered
his handiwork and cracked the foundations on which it had
been built. The Italian cities awoke from their torpor and
threw off their chains ; the Lombard League was re-formed,
and the Tuscan cities soon followed suit with a league of their
own. North and Central Italy were free, and so was the
Pope, who was now able to emerge from his enforced isolation.
Only in the Sicilian kingdom did the semblance of the former
government remain, for Constance could command the allegiance of her father's subjects, acting as regent for her son,
and there was still the faithful Markward in arms to salve
what he could out of the wreckage. Even this was of short
duration, for Constance died in 1198, Markward in 1202,
and the Pope was suzerain once more of South Italy and
Sicily and guardian of its young ruler, Frederick. The
recovery of the Papacy was as startling in its suddenness as
the collapse of the Empire. Only a few months after Henry

his aged antagonist Pope Celestine III died, and now the hesitation of the cardinals was at an end. They need no longer wait upon the event and pursue a cautious policy. For the event had come, and so in January 1198 they chose the youngest and the most vigorous of their number, cardinal Lothar of Segni, to be Pope as Innocent III. The transformation was complete. From the mightiest of all the Emperors we pass at once to the mightiest of all the Popes. Yet it seems hardly surprising, if we remember, on the one hand, the essential weaknesses of the Empire, and the gambler's risks that had been taken, when everything depended on one man's life; on the other, the undying Papacy, always able to rise to the opportunity, and with a universal authority to which the Emperor could never aspire. It is true that Frederick II raised again the imperial authority to great heights in Italy. But this was merely a brilliant episode, and his real power lay only in his Sicilian kingdom. After his death, the Italian crown was, in effect, lost to the ruler of Germany; Italy and Germany became definitely separated.

The result in Germany of Henry VI's death was in its way *(b) in Germany* almost equally decisive. Philip of Suabia, Henry's brother, had started south to fetch the infant Frederick, already elected king, from Sicily so that he might be crowned and consecrated in Germany. He had to flee back hastily to Germany immediately his brother died, for the explosion in North Italy cut a chasm between Germany and Sicily which could not be bridged. It made all the difference that at the fatal moment Frederick was in Sicily and not in Germany; it determined the place and character of his education and the whole of his future development. It made all the difference, too, that he was still uncrowned, for it gave the German princes the opportunity to disown him. And for the first time they failed to arrive peaceably at an election. The result was civil war between the rival factions of Welf and Hohenstaufen. Particularism now came into its own, and the electors took sides according to their own interests and with little regard for the interests of the kingdom. And when the strife was over and Frederick II was universally recognised as king, it was to a monarchy shorn of its old strength that he succeeded. It had lost the bases of its power: authority over the bishops had been surrendered, and the royal domain had been dissipated by alienations and usurpations. Another great change consisted in the shifting of political interest from west to east. Not only were the frontiers of Germany advanced, when the Teutonic Knights began their forcible colonisation of Prussia. The centre of political importance moved eastwards too. There the vassal-State of Bohemia had become a semi-independent kingdom ; its ruler had recovered his control over Moravia and the bishopric of Prague, and governed the most powerful principality in the German kingdom. When the Hohenstaufen line came to an end, there was no great house in Western Germany to take its place.

Effects of the death of Richard I

The death that produced the second catastrophe was that of Richard I in 1199. John was no match for Philip Augustus, who was able to reap the fruit of his patient scheming and to acquire for himself the greater part of the English king's possessions in France. Here, too, was a complete reversal. The conquered territory fell by escheat to the French crown, which also ultimately reaped much of the fruits of the Albigensian Crusade. As a result, the royal domain, so limited in extent before, comprised nearly half the French kingdom, so that the monarchy was as powerful as formerly it had been weak. Moreover, its position was enhanced by the course of events in Germany. France in the thirteenth century became the leading power in Europe ; the French king is the champion of the *regnum* in the next great contest with the *sacerdotium*.

The capture of Constantinople by the Latins

The accident of death was not responsible for the other great changes in the political constitution of Europe. The death of Henry VI indeed brought the Third Crusade to an end, and with it the prospect of success against the Eastern Moslems. But the other side of Henry's Eastern policy, which in a sense he had assumed as part of his Sicilian inheritance, did not die with him ; it may be said to have come to fruition when the Fourth Crusade was diverted to Constantinople in 1204. Constantinople was captured and a Latin Empire instituted. Shocking as was this act of brigandage, it can hardly be described as startling, for it was but the culmination of the hostility between Western and Eastern Christendom which had been growing in intensity during the twelfth century. It was none the less an epoch-making event. The Eastern Empire recovered its capital in 1261, but it had lost most of its Western provinces and was only the shadow of its former self; its decline and fall, directly attributable to the Latins, can justly be dated from 1204. One other reversal of fortune remains to be chronicled. The condition of stalemate between Christians and Moslems which had persisted throughout the greater part of the twelfth century in the Spanish peninsula came to a sudden end in 1212. Alfonso VIII of Castile, who in 1196 had been severely defeated, won a decisive victory at Las Navas de Tolosa. The Empire of the Almohades was soon in disruption, and the Christian kingdoms—Portugal in the west, Castile (now re-united with Leon) in the centre, Aragon in the east—advanced rapidly southwards until only the kingdom of Granada was left to the Moslems in Spain. *The decisive victory of the Christians in Spain*

Thus within the space of fifteen years events occurred which produced a complete reversal of the political situation throughout the greater part of Europe. But the general order was not affected thereby; a new régime replaced the old. So the normal pursuits of the mass of the population went on undisturbed. The developments in rural conditions, in town life, industry, and commerce, in learning, art, and letters, both Latin and vernacular, which have already been observed, continued unchecked. In these respects it is often impossible to distinguish the thirteenth century from the twelfth, except in the fuller growth and greater maturity that were attained. There was to be no further threat to Western civilisation. On the contrary, Constantinople was losing its pride of place, and under the lead of France and the Italian city-states the civilisation of Europe as a whole was acquiring its predominantly Western characteristics. *Continued development, without sudden change, in departments other than political*

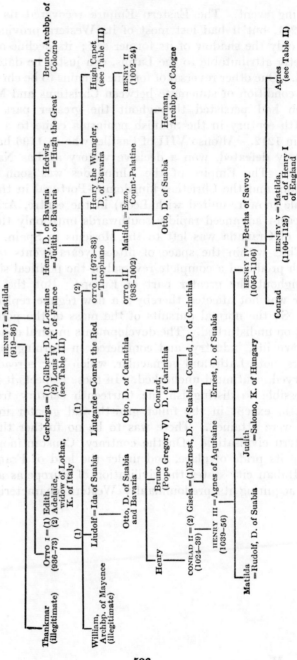

I.—GERMANY—THE SAXON AND SALIAN KINGS

HENRY I = Matilda
(919–36)

Thankmar (illegitimate) | OTTO I = (1) Edith
(936–73) (2) Adelaide, widow of Lothar, K. of Italy | Gerberga = (1) Gilbert, D. of Lorraine
(2) Louis IV, K. of France
(see Table III) | Hedwig
= Hugh the Great | Henry, D. of Bavaria
= Judith of Bavaria | Bruno, Archbp. of Cologne

Hugh Capet
(see Table III)

William, Archbp. of Mayence (illegitimate)

(1)

Liudolf = Ida of Suabia | Liutgarde = Conrad the Red | Otto, D. of Carinthia | Henry the Wrangler,
D. of Bavaria | HENRY II
(1002–24)

Otto, D. of Suabia and Bavaria | Bruno
(Pope Gregory V) | Conrad,
D. of Carinthia | OTTO II (973–83)
= Theophano | Matilda = Ezzo,
Count-Palatine | Herman,
Archbp. of Cologne

Henry | Otto, D. of Carinthia | OTTO III
(983–1002) | Otto, D. of Suabia

Conrad, D. of Carinthia | Ernest, D. of Suabia | HENRY IV
(1056–1106) = Bertha of Savoy

CONRAD II = (2) Gisela = (1) Ernest, D. of Suabia
(1024–39)

HENRY III = Agnes of Aquitaine
(1039–56)

Conrad | HENRY V = Matilda,
(1106–1125) d. of Henry I
of England

Agnes
(see Table II)

Matilda
= Rudolf, D. of Suabia | Judith
= Salomo, K. of Hungary

526

II.—GERMANY—THE WELFS AND THE HOHENSTAUFEN

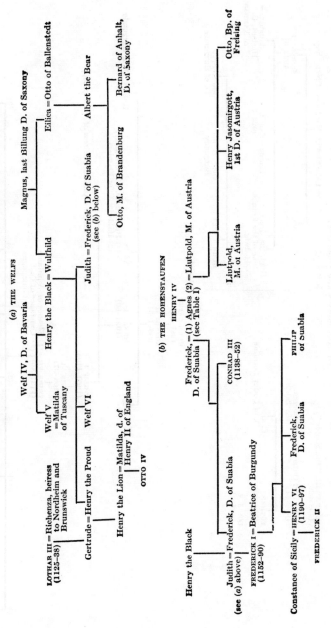

(a) THE WELFS

Welf IV, D. of Bavaria

LOTHAR III = Richenza, heiress to Nordheim and Brunswick
(1125–88)

Welf V = Matilda of Tuscany

Henry the Black = Wulfhild

Magnus, last Billing D. of Saxony

Eilica = Otto of Ballenstedt

Albert the Bear

Gertrude = Henry the Proud

Welf VI

Judith = Frederick, D. of Suabia (see (b) below)

Bernard of Anhalt, D. of Saxony

Henry the Lion = Matilda, d. of Henry II of England

OTTO IV

Otto, M. of Brandenburg

(b) THE HOHENSTAUFEN

HENRY IV

Frederick, = (1) Agnes (2) = Liutpold, M. of Austria
D. of Suabia   (see Table I)

CONRAD III
(1138–52)

Liutpold, M. of Austria

Henry Jasomirgott, 1st D. of Austria

Otto, Bp. of Freising

Henry the Black

Judith = Frederick, D. of Suabia
(see (a) above)

FREDERICK I = Beatrice of Burgundy
(1152–90)

Frederick, D. of Suabia

PHILIP of Suabia

Constance of Sicily = HENRY VI
(1190–97)

FREDERICK II

527

III.—THE KINGS OF FRANCE

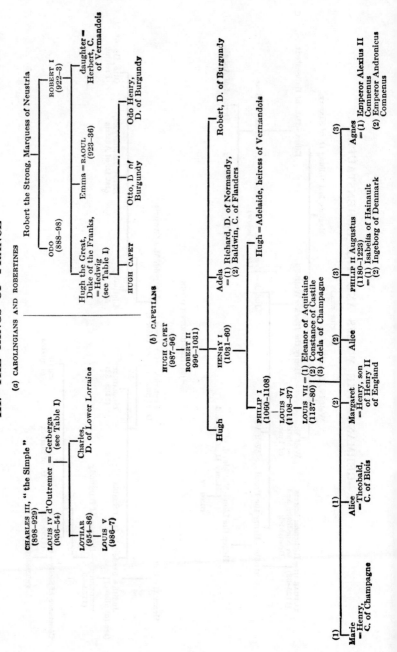

(a) CAROLINGIANS AND ROBERTINES

Robert the Strong, Marquess of Neustria

ODO (888–98)

ROBERT I (922–8)

CHARLES III, "the Simple" (898–929)

LOUIS IV d'Outremer (936–54) = Gerberga (see Table I)

LOTHAR (954–86)

LOUIS V (986–7)

Charles, D. of Lower Lorraine

Hugh the Great, Duke of the Franks, = Hedwig (see Table I)

Emma = RAOUL (923–36)

daughter = Herbert, C. of Vermandois

HUGH CAPET

Otto, D. of Burgundy

Odo Henry, D. of Burgundy

(b) CAPETIANS

HUGH CAPET (987–96)

ROBERT II 996–1031

HENRY I (1031–60)

Hugh

Adela = (1) Richard, D. of Normandy, (2) Baldwin, C. of Flanders

Robert, D. of Burgundy

PHILIP I (1060–1108)

Hugh = Adelaide, heiress of Vermandois

LOUIS VI (1108–37)

LOUIS VII = (1) Eleanor of Aquitaine (1137–80) (2) Constance of Castile (3) Adela of Champagne

Alice = Theobald, C. of Blois

Margaret = Henry, son of Henry II of England

Alice

PHILIP II Augustus (1180–1223) = (1) Isabella of Hainault (2) Ingeborg of Denmark

Agnes = (1) Emperor Alexius II Comnenus (2) Emperor Andronicus Comnenus

Marie = Henry, C. of Champagne

(1)   (2)   (2)   (3)   (3)

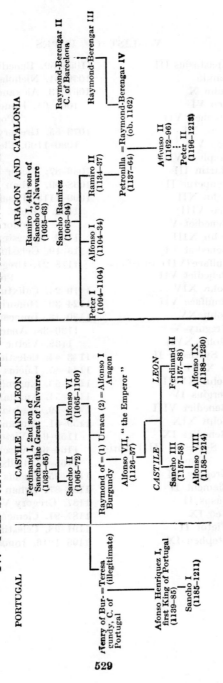

IV.—THE SPANISH KINGDOMS IN ELEVENTH AND TWELFTH CENTURIES

PORTUGAL

Henry of Burgundy, C. of Portugal = Teresa (illegitimate)

Afonso Henriquez I, first King of Portugal (1139–85)

Sancho I (1185–1211)

CASTILE AND LEON

Ferdinand I, 2nd son of Sancho the Great of Navarre (1033–65)

Sancho II (1065–72)

Alfonso VI (1065–1109)

Raymond of Burgundy = (1) Urraca (2) = Alfonso I Aragon

Alfonso VII, "the Emperor" (1126–57)

CASTILE

Sancho III (1157–58)

Alfonso VIII (1158–1214)

LEON

Ferdinand II (1157–88)

Alfonso IX (1188–1230)

ARAGON AND CATALONIA

Ramiro I, 4th son of Sancho of Navarre (1035–63)

Sancho Ramirez (1063–94)

Peter I (1094–1104)

Alfonso I (1104–34)

Ramiro II (1134–37)

Petronilla = Raymond-Berengar IV (1137–64)   (ob. 1162)

Raymond-Berengar II C. of Barcelona

Raymond-Berengar III

Affonso II (1162–96)

Peter II (1196–1213)

529

V.—LIST OF POPES

911–13. Anastasius III
913–14. Lando
914–28. John X
928–29. Leo VI
929–31. Stephen VII
931–36. John XI
936–39. Leo VII
939–42. Stephen VIII
942–46. Martin III
946–55. Agapetus II
955–63. John XII
963–64. Leo VIII
964–65. Benedict V
965–72. John XIII
972–74. Benedict VI
   974. Boniface (VII) Anti-Pope
974–83. Benedict VII
983–84. John XIV
984–85. Boniface VII
985–96. John XV
996–99. Gregory V
(997–98. John XVI)
999–1003. Sylvester II
1003. John XVII
1003–09. John XVIII
1009–12. Sergius IV
1012–24. Benedict VIII
1024–33. John XIX
1033–45. Benedict IX
   1044–46. Sylvester (III) Anti-Pope
1045–46. Gregory VI
1046–47. Clement II
1048. Damasus II
1048–54. Leo IX
1055–57. Victor Il
1057–58. Stephen IX

(1058–59. Benedict X)
1059–61. Nicholas II
1061–73. Alexander II
   1061–64. Honorius (II) Anti-Pope
1073–85. Gregory VII
   1080–1100. Clement (III) Anti-Pope
1086–87. Victor III
1088–99. Urban II
1099–1118. Paschal II
   1102. Albert
       Theodoric } Anti-Popes
   1106. Sylvester (IV)
1118–19. Gelasius II
1118–21. Gregory (VIII), Anti-Pope
1119–24. Calixtus II
1124–30. Honorius II
1130–43. Innocent II
   1130–38. Anacletus (II) } Anti-Popes
   1138. Victor
1143–44. Celestine II
1144–45. Lucius II
1145–53. Eugenius III
1153–54. Anastasius IV
1154–59. Hadrian IV
1159–81. Alexander III
   1159–64. Victor (IV)
   1164–68. Paschal (III) } Anti-Popes
   1168–78. Calixtus (III)
1181–85. Lucius III
1185–87. Urban III
1187. Gregory VIII
1187–91. Clement III
1191–98. Celestine III
1198–1216. Innocent III

VI.—LIST OF THE EASTERN EMPERORS

The Macedonian Dynasty—
867–86. Basil I
886–912. Leo VI
912–59. Constantine VII Porphyrogenitus
 919–44. Romanus I Lecapenus
959–63. Romanus II
963–1025. Basil II (and Constantine VIII)
 963–69. Nicephorus II Phocas
 969–76. John I Tzimisces
1025–28. Constantine VIII
1028–42. Zoe
 1028–34. Romanus III Argyrus
 1034–41. Michael IV, the Paphlagonian
 1041–42. Michael V Calaphates
1042–56. Zoe (ob. 1050) and Theodora
 1042–55. Constantine IX Monomachus

1056–57. Michael VI Stratioticus
1057–59. Isaac I Comnenus
1059–67. Constantine X Ducas
1067–78. Michael VII Ducas
 1067–71. Romanus IV Diogenes
1078–81. Nicephorus III Botoniates

The Comneni—
1081–1118. Alexius I
1118–43. John II
1143–80. Manuel I
1180–83. Alexius II
1183–85. Andronicus

The Angeli—
1185–95. Isaac II
1195–1203. Alexius III
1203–04. Isaac II and Alexius IV

1204. Alexius V Ducas

INDEX

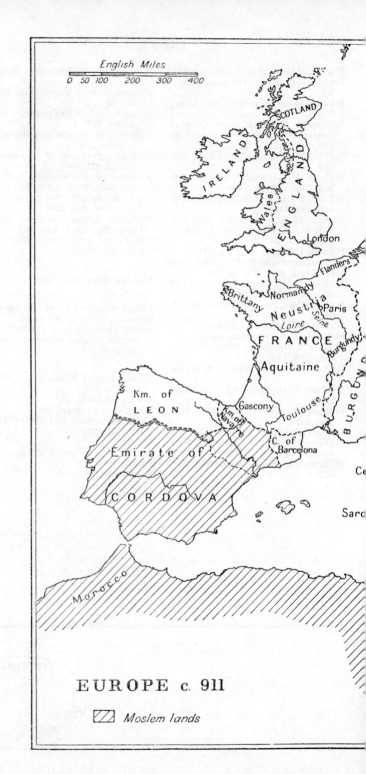

EUROPE c. 911

Moslem lands